THE OPERAS OF VI

The Operas of Verdi, Volume 1

Oberto Conte di San Bonifacio
Nabucco
Ernani
Giovanna d'Arco
Attila
I Masnadieri
Il Corsaro
Luisa Miller
Rigoletto

Un Giorno di Regno
I Lombardi alla Prima Crociata
I Due Foscari
Alzira
Macbeth
Jérusalem
La Battaglia di Legnano
Stiffelio

The Operas of Verdi, Volume 2

Il Trovatore
Les Vêpres Siciliennes
Aroldo
La Forza del destino

La Traviata
Simon Boccanegra
Un Ballo in maschera

JULIAN BUDDEN

The Operas of Verdi

3

From *Don Carlos* to *Falstaff*

Revised edition

CLARENDON PRESS · OXFORD
1992

Oxford University Press, Walton Street, Oxford OX2 6DP
Oxford New York Toronto
Delhi Bombay Calcutta Madras Karachi
Petaling Jaya Singapore Hong Kong Tokyo
Nairobi Dar es Salaam Cape Town
Melbourne Auckland
and associated companies in
Berlin Ibadan

Oxford is a trade mark of Oxford University Press

First published in 1981 in Great Britain by
Cassell & Company Ltd., London. First published in the
United States in 1981 by Oxford University Press, Inc.

First issued in paperback in 1984

This revised edition published in 1992 by
Oxford University Press, Oxford,
and by Oxford University Press, New York

ISBN 0-19-816263-4

Printed in Great Britain by
St Edmundsbury Press Ltd., Bury St Edmunds, Suffolk

CONTENTS

I DON C.

DON CARLOS

Grand Opera in five acts
by
JOSEPH MÉRY and CAMILLE DU LOCLE
(after the dramatic poem *Don Carlos, Infant von Spanien* by Friedrich Schiller)

first performed at the Académie Impériale de Musique, Paris, 11 March 1867

PHILIPPE II, King of Spain	PREMIER BASSE	Louis-Henri Obin
DON CARLOS, Infante of Spain	PREMIER TÉNOR	A. Morère
RODRIGUE, Marquis of Posa	PREMIER BARYTON	Jean-Baptiste Faure
THE GRAND INQUISITOR	PREMIER BASSE	David
A monk	PREMIER BASSE	Armand Castelmary
ELISABETH DE VALOIS	PREMIER SOPRANO	Marie-Constance Sass
THE PRINCESS EBOLI	PREMIER MEZZO-SOPRANO	Pauline Gueymard-Lauters
THIBAULT, page to Elisabeth de Valois	PREMIER SOPRANO	Leonia Levielly
THE COUNTESS OF AREMBERG	MIME	Dominique
THE COUNT OF LERMA	TÉNOR	Gaspard.
A royal herald	TÉNOR	Mermant
Flemish deputies	BASSES	Cléophas, Mechelaere, Freret, Delahaye, Jolivet, Varnier
Inquisitors	BASSES	Thuillart, Mouret, Hano, Schmitt, Boussagol, Leger, Hourdin
(Students of the Imperial Conservatoire)		Christophe, Solon, Bacquier, Derrey, Maurel, Gailhard, Lassalle

Lords and ladies of the courts of France and Spain – woodcutters – people – pages – guards of Henri II and Philippe II – monks – officers of the inquisitions – soldiers.

The first act takes place in France; the other four in Spain
Epoch: about 1560

REVISED VERSION IN FOUR ACTS

French text revised by CAMILLE DU LOCLE: Italian translation by ANGELO ZANARDINI, based on that of the original version by ACHILLE DE LAUZIÈRES

First performed at the Teatro alla Scala, Milan, 10 January 1884

FILIPPO II	Alessandro Silvestri	EBOLI	Giuseppina Pasqua
DON CARLO	Francesco Tamagno	TEBALDO	Amelia Garten
RODRIGO	Paolo Lhérie	AREMBERG	Angelina Pirola
GRAND INQUISITOR	Francesco Navarini	LERMA	Angelo Fiorentini
MONK	Leopoldo Cromberg	ROYAL HERALD	Angelo Fiorentini
ELISABETTA	Abigaille Bruschi-Chiatti		

The action takes place in Spain

'. . . We considered suggesting to you Schiller's *Don Carlos*. Of course it would merely serve as a point of departure, and we should modify it so as to provide you with a scenario that would satisfy you in every respect. You have already drawn on Schiller for the plots of *I Masnadieri* and *Luisa Miller*. *Don Carlos* I would say offers you a much larger and more poetic frame. It has all the emotional power you need. . . . *Fiesco* is also a fine subject, but love plays a smaller part in it than in *Don Carlos*.'* When the authors of *Jérusalem*, acting on behalf of Roqueplan, tried to lure Verdi back to the opera in 1850, the year of *Stiffelio*, they could hardly have guessed that they had named the subject which would one day furnish the most ambitious and wide-ranging of all his operas. Anyway, for the moment he was not to be tempted. *Don Carlos* was not mentioned for another fifteen years, though a comment of Verdi's on the Escurial made during his stay in Madrid for the Spanish première of *La Forza del destino* becomes significant in the light of later events. 'It is severe and terrible,' he said, 'like the savage monarch who built it.'† Within four years the savage monarch was to become a musical reality.

Meanwhile Verdi returned to Paris for a revival of *Les Vêpres Siciliennes*, then to S. Agata and his occupation as a gentleman farmer. There was now little to tempt him outside his own front gate. Since Cavour's death he had virtually ceased to take his seat as deputy for Borgo San Donnino in the new Italian parliament in Turin. The cultural life of north Italy was now dominated by the 'scapigliati'. Through the columns of the *Perseveranza* and his own *Figaro* Boito was preaching the regeneration not only of instrumental music but of the spoken drama; and he and his fellow editor, the poet Emilio Praga, set the example with their comedy *Le Madri galanti*. But the goal to which his activity was directed was the New Opera. With the première of Franco Faccio's *I Profughi fiamminghi*, to a libretto by Praga, Boito believed it to have come within sight. Hence his unfortunate Sapphic ode hailing Faccio as the young man destined to cleanse the altar of Italian opera 'now defiled like the walls of a brothel'.‡ Two years before, Verdi had been prepared to give the author a pat of encouragement for the sake of Clarina Maffei, who had taken both him and Faccio under her wing. He had even collaborated with Boito on the *Inno delle Nazioni* and rewarded him with the gift of a watch. But now his benevolence dried up at once. 'If I too, amongst others, have soiled the altar, as Boito says,' he wrote to Tito Ricordi, 'let him clean it and I will be the first to come and light a candle.'§ Friends of both parties tried their best to minimize the implied offence. One who certainly did not was Piave, an inmate of the Maffei salon ever since, through Verdi's help, he had obtained the post of resident stage director at La Scala, Milan. In 1865, the year of Faccio's *Amleto*, his application for the chair of dramatic literature at the Milan

---

* Letter from A. Royer and G. Vaez, 7.8.1850. *Copialettere*, pp. 104–5. The second play is of course Schiller's *Die Verschwörung des Fiesco zu Genua*.

† Letter to Arrivabene, 22.3.1863. A. Alberti, *Verdi intimo* (Verona, 1931), p. 24.

‡ P. Nardi, *Vita di Arrigo Boito* (Verona, 1944), p. 128.

§ Letter to T. Ricordi, undated (1863). Abbiati, II, p. 764.

Conservatory was turned down in favour of Emilio Praga. It was a bad choice, since Praga was an unstable character who soon destroyed himself through drink and drugs; but it was predictable. For despite their mature years Lauro Rossi, the director, and most of his staff, including Alberto Mazzucato, who was also conductor at La Scala, were firmly on the side of youth. As well as this, Piave had proved himself notoriously incompetent as stage director. It was understandable that he should be embittered; sad, however, that he should vent his feelings on the entire Maffei salon, not sparing even his hostess. Verdi would not hear a word against Clarina Maffei, and Piave was duly penitent ('She is truly adorable; but what a pity one has to adore her through a thicket of old sticks and young sprigs!').* But the composer was only too ready to lend an ear to gibes about the pretensions of the 'futurists', the reformers, the 'sferici', not to mention hints that Tito Ricordi's son Giulio had espoused their cause to Verdi's own prejudice.

> Don't lose heart [*he wrote back*], send the Conservatory to the devil. Your dream could never have come true. Things are best as they are. You would have found yourself quite out of your element. . . . I like things to have some character. The Conservatory will start to have it when someone gives the Director a good kick – and that will soon happen. Don't let yourself be scared by that Babylon, as you call it, of the music of the future. Even all this is as it should be. . . . These so-called apostles of the future are the initiators of something grand and sublime. It was essential to cleanse the altar befouled by the pigs of the past. What is needed is a pure, virginal, holy, *spherical* music!. . . .†

The atmosphere was no more congenial nearer home. In 1864 the citizens of Busseto had at long last realized their cherished project of building an opera house. Twenty years before, when the idea was first mooted, Verdi had shown an interest in it and had even promised to try to engage Erminia Frezzolini and her husband Poggi for the opening night. Now that the Bussetani had fulfilled their side of the bargain it was up to Verdi to fulfil his – especially as the theatre had been built in honour of himself, the local boy who had made good. So argued the mayor and the local dignitaries. Meantime, however, Verdi had changed his mind about the enterprise. He deplored that it should have been undertaken at a time of national emergency, in 1859, and refused to have anything to do with it. His brother-in-law, Giovanni Barezzi, tried to bring moral pressure upon him to support their cause; the result was the final shattering of a friendship of more than thirty years' standing. No one was more active in the feud than Giuseppina (she had always detested both Verdi's brothers-in-law).‡ Naturally when offers of contracts arrived from abroad she was the last to discourage them. She wrote to Léon Escudier:

> For a very long time now I have heard him singing in every key, 'I don't want to write,' and frankly I'm keen that he should write because though I love the country very much, three hundred and sixty-five days in it are too many – far too

---

* Letter from Piave, July 1865. Abbiati, III, p. 28.

† Letter to Piave, 21.5.1865. *Carteggi Verdiani*, II, pp. 354–5.

‡ For a detailed account of the affair and the eventual settlement, whereby Verdi handed over 10,000 francs for a box while refusing to set foot in the theatre, see Walker, pp. 251–9.

many! We have never stayed so long in the midst of these idiots. I feel myself sticking out my claws like a wild beast and a wild longing comes over me to go on the rampage so as to get my own back on this everlasting immobility. True, I am no longer young, but intellectual life is ageless and here it is non-existent. . . . I know him. Once he is caught up the picture will change. He will leave his trees, his building, his hydraulic engines, his guns, etcetera. As always he will give himself up to the fever of creation; he will devote himself wholly to his poem and his music and I hope the whole world will benefit from it.*

In fact, Verdi's retirement was more apparent than real. Much of the year 1864 was spent on the revision of *Macbeth*, of which nearly a third was newly composed. He was also taking an interest in Ricordi's publication of some of the instrumental classics, whose influence will be discernible in his own mature masterpieces, notably the string quartet. 'Among other pieces,' he wrote to Tito Ricordi, 'there's one I liked, the study in F sharp minor by Clementi in 3/2. I don't know whether it counts as classical or romantic, of the past or of the future; but it's very beautiful and far superior to that famous prelude by Bach on which Gounod built his "Ave Maria". . . . Why didn't they include amongst Scarlatti's works the so-called Cat Fugue? It's a fine piece and perfect for demonstrating the clarity of the old Neapolitan school. With so odd a subject a German would have made something chaotic; whereas an Italian has made something as limpid as sunlight.'† Another Italian, Giuseppe Verdi, would do likewise with the 'Scala enigmatica' in the first of his *Quattro Pezzi Sacri*.

It was in the summer of that same year that Emile Perrin, director of the Paris Opéra, found among the papers of the recently deceased Meyerbeer a libretto by Scribe entitled *Judith*, which he sent to Verdi. The composer's reply was negative but not unduly discouraging since he added, 'If I should one day write for the Opéra I shall do so only to a poem written to my entire satisfaction, and above all one which I find really striking.'‡ At all events, Perrin kept up the pressure through Léon Escudier, with whom Verdi was in constant touch over the revision of *Macbeth*. Various subjects were suggested including *King Lear* and *Cleopatra*. Verdi replied:

Are you joking? Write for the Opéra!!! Do you really think I would be in no danger of having my eyes scratched out after what happened two years ago at the rehearsals of *Vêpres*?§ Write for the Opéra with that trifling matter of priorities arranged by Madame Meyerbeer, who flaunts brooches, snuffboxes, medallions, batons, etc. What a business! Even Art has turned banker and one has to be a millionaire, otherwise there's no chance of success! But let's leave aside all these petty intrigues and jokes, since I'd be ready to stand up to all the rage and the cursing once I had on my side a director of intelligence and firmness as M. Perrin

* Letter from Giuseppina Verdi to Léon Escudier, June 1865. *Carteggi Verdiani*, II, pp. 21–2; quoted more extensively in Walker, p. 251.

† Letter to T. Ricordi, 2.11.1864. *Carteggi Verdiani*, IV, p. 241.

‡ Letter to Perrin, 12.9.1864. Archives Nationales, Paris, AJ XIII 409. See U. Günther, 'La Genèse de *Don Carlos*, Opéra en 5 Actes de Giuseppe Verdi, représenté pour la première fois à Paris le 11 mars 1867', in *Revue de Musicologie*, LVIII (1972), p. 22; A. Porter, 'The Making of *Don Carlos*', in *Proceedings of the Royal Musical Association*, Vol. 98 (1971–2), p. 75.

§ See Vol. II, p. 240.

undoubtedly is! Nothing could be easier than to come to an understanding about writing an opera; and we should agree in a couple of words once there were a libretto or at least a subject ready to hand. *King Lear* is magnificent, sublime and full of pathos but it hasn't sufficient visual splendour for the Opéra. *Cleopatra* is better from that point of view but the loves of the chief characters, their personalities and even their misfortunes arouse little sympathy. . . . In short everything depends on the libretto. A libretto, a libretto and the opera is made!!*
. . . [*A fortnight later:*] Have another word with Perrin about *King Lear* and get him to explain to you briefly the kind of spectacle he has in mind. Make it clear that if by any chance we did choose *King Lear* we should have to stick closely to Shakespeare. He's the kind of poet with whom you can't tamper without taking away all his immensely powerful character and originality.†

In July 1865 Escudier arrived at S. Agata bringing with him the libretto of *Cleopatra*, written by the poet Joseph Méry in collaboration with Perrin's son-in-law, Camille du Locle, and also their scenario for a *Don Carlos* after Schiller. During the consultation Verdi wrote to Perrin:

Cleopatra is not a subject for me. *Don Carlos*, a magnificent drama, possibly a little lacking in spectacle. Otherwise it's an excellent idea to make Charles V appear; likewise the scene at Fontainebleau. I should like as in Schiller a little scene between Philip and the Inquisitor, the latter blind and very old. (Escudier will tell you why by word of mouth.) I should also like a scene between Philip and Posa. For *King Lear* there are casting difficulties, and it's almost impossible to find a Cordelia. This play too is lacking in spectacle; apart from that it is a sublime subject and one which I adore. St Georges has sent me the scenario of a *Phaedra*. I have no liking for Venus and Diana; despite that it seems worth serious consideration. I suggest trying another subject, *El Zapatero y el rey*, a Spanish play by Zorilla. In my view it's powerful and original in the highest degree.‡

Verdi's interest in Zorilla's play survived at least until 1870, when he asked Ricordi to send him a copy of it along with Gutiérrez's *Catalan Vengeance*.§ Nevertheless, it was fairly clear from his letter to Perrin that *Don Carlos* was the most likely candidate for Paris; and we shall return to his remarks on it when we come to consider the scenario in detail. Certainly Escudier was in no doubt where the choice would fall. He wrote back to Perrin:

Don Carlos has really thrilled him. I think that this drama, instinct as it is with real passion, is just what he needs. He has found it perfectly framed [*charpenté*]. What worries him most is the lack of one or two scenes which will really take hold of the public. He would like something unexpected, like for instance the skaters' ballet in *Le Prophète* or the scene in the church – a point of culmination. . . . To

---

* Letter to Escudier, 19.6.1865. Prod'homme, 'Lettres inédites de G. Verdi à Léon Escudier' in *Rivista Musicale Italiana* XXXV (Rome, 1928), pp. 190–1.
† Letter to Escudier, 30.6.1865, *Ibid.*, p. 191.
‡ Letter to Perrin, 21.7.1865. Günther, *op. cit.*, p. 30.
§ Letter to Giulio Ricordi, 13.2.1870. Abbiati, III, pp. 331–2.

sum up, Verdi accepts, subject to the conditions agreed upon, to write a work for the winter of 1866–7. It will be either *Don Carlos* or *King Lear*.*

Even at the last moment it seems that Verdi was reluctant to close the door on his beloved Shakespearian project.

The upshot was that Escudier left Busseto with a firm commitment on Verdi's part to write a grand opera for production in about eighteen months' time, linked contractually with a *Forza del destino* revised for the Paris Opéra. About the same time Blach, absolute ruler at S. Agata, put the matter in blunt dog-to-dog terms to his colleague Ron-Ron in the Arrivabene household. 'My male and female secretaries send you their greetings. As regards the first. I read in some paper or other that he's getting ready to make some more little hooks. I shall have him certified and send him to the big cities.'† That same month Verdi approved the draft of a contract which mentioned *Don Carlos* but did not exclude the possibility of a different subject should the composer so decide. In November he left for Paris and appended his signature. A second draft of what appears to be the definitive contract makes no mention of an alternative subject; the commission is for 'an opera in four or five acts based on Schiller's *Don Carlos* to a libretto by Méry and Du Locle'.‡ The only change that followed was the adjournment *sine die* of the French *La Forza del destino*.§

Verdi's affinity with Schiller, as with Hugo and Shakespeare, has been remarked upon often enough. But it seems to have been slower to develop than in the other two cases. Of the four so-called Schiller operas, the first, *Giovanna d'Arco*, has no closer link with the poet's work than Donizetti's *Maria Stuarda* or Rossini's *Guillaume Tell*. All three plays had furnished libretto fodder to Italian composers; and in view of Solera's claims to originality one may even doubt how far at the time Verdi was aware of his librettist's debt to the German playwright. *Die Räuber* too he accepted without comment through the medium of a librettist, though admittedly one who had made the standard Italian translation of the original play. Not until *Luisa Miller* is there any indication that Verdi had read the drama before considering the subject for operatic treatment; and even there, though he regretted Cammarano's dilution of Schiller's content, he ended by bowing to the 'convenienze' in a way that he would never have done in a Shakespearian opera. But with *Don Carlos* the situation is quite different. He knew the play; and it caught his imagination as Hugo's *Hernani* and *Le Roi s'amuse* had done in years before. It was the first time that he had confronted a Schiller play in all its vast complexity; and this is something which he could never have contemplated before the 1860s with the experience of *La Forza del destino* behind him. For the truth is that *Don Carlos*, infinitely richer in ideas and variety of passions than either of the Hugo plays, is very shapeless. This is a rare fault in Schiller, and mainly to be accounted for by the fact that it was written over four years, having begun as a prose sketch published in a German periodical in 1783. Its composition was interrupted by that of *Kabale und Liebe*; and by the time it emerged in 1787 as a

* Letter from Escudier to Perrin, 17.7. 1865. Günther, *op. cit.*, p. 24.

† Letter to Arrivabene, 28.8.1865. Alberti, p. 58. 'Little hooks' (*rampini*) is a reference to a conversation that Verdi overheard between two of his farm-hands, one of whom was marvelling at the way in which their master could accumulate possessions merely by making little hooks on ruled paper.

‡ Günther, *op. cit.*, p. 33.

§ See *L'Art Musical*, 28.12.1865. Quoted in Günther, *op. cit.*, p. 35.

monster piece in over six thousand lines of blank verse its dramatic purpose had become curiously diffused; moreover what happens at certain points and why is not always immediately clear – faults which are less vital to an opera than to a spoken drama.

Schiller takes as his starting-point the tendentious, pseudo-historical *Don Carlos, Nouvelle historique* by César Vischard Saint-Réal, which first appeared in 1672. Since the same work had already inspired several tragedies, including Thomas Otway's *Don Carlos, Prince of Spain* (1676) and Alfieri's *Filippo II* (1776), there is nothing surprising about this unless it be that Schiller was shortly to occupy a chair of history at the university of Jena; for Saint-Réal's account is not borne out by the known facts. Don Carlos, only legitimate son of King Philip II of Spain, was a violent, uncontrolled young man who at an early age developed an unreasoning hatred of his father and was soon declared by him unfit to succeed to the throne. His attempts to raise support for his rights abroad led to his being placed under house arrest; long fasts alternating with bouts of overeating together with copious draughts of ice-cold water resulted in his death at the age of twenty-three. Saint-Réal's hero, on the other hand, dies because the King has discovered his secret passion for his stepmother, Elisabeth de Valois, to whom he was once affianced. Various other characters, some historical, some invented, are woven into the intrigue: the Infante's uncle Don Juan, future hero of Lepanto, who also falls in love with Elisabeth; the Marquis of Posa, whom he suspects along with Carlos as a possible rival; and the Princess Eboli, who works for Carlos's downfall after being repulsed by him. A strange farrago to have interested a serious historian! But then Schiller was never too scrupulous about sacrificing the facts of history on the altar of poetic drama; what is more, the story of Don Carlos as presented by Saint-Réal has the making of an archetypal myth, rather like that of Marie Duplessis at the hands of Dumas *fils*. Freudians might see in it the classic Oedipal situation. Schiller enriched it with a number of complex personal relationships. Notable here is the Saul–David–Jonathan syndrome that emerges in the King, Don Carlos, and his bosom friend the Marquis of Posa. A further thread in the tapestry is the philosophy of liberalism for which Posa is the chief mouthpiece. This is, of course, the greatest anachronism of all, and far grosser than the antedating by twenty years of the destruction of the Armada in order to allow Philip to show magnanimity to the defeated Duke of Medina Sidonia. In later years Verdi himself was particularly aware of this, and at one point even thought of removing Posa from the opera.* On the other hand it was not difficult to see the attraction for him of Posa's fearless appeal to the King to allow his subjects freedom of thought:

> Cast your eye about you in
> The splendour of His nature! It is founded
> On freedom – and how rich it is by virtue
> Of freedom! He, the great Creator, casts
> The worm into a drop of dew and lets
> Free will take its delight amid the very
> Death spaces of corruption. Your creation,
> How cramped and poor! The rustling of a leaf

---

* See letter to Faccio, undated (but probably from January 1879). R. De Rensis, *Franco Faccio e Verdi* (Milan, 1934), pp. 182–5.

Strikes terror in the lord of Christendom –
You must fear every virtue. *He* – lest Freedom's
Delightful presence be disturbed – He sooner
Allows the entire ghastly host of Evil
To rage throughout His universe – of Him,
The Maker, one is not aware; discreetly
He veils himself in His eternal laws.
The freethinker sees *these* but not *Him*. Why have
A God? says he; the world is self-sufficient.
No Christian's piety has ever praised
Him more than that freethinker's blasphemy.*

Needless to say, such a defence of agnosticism would have placed Posa in the charge of the Holy Office before he had finished uttering it. Yet it is vital to the development of his relationship with both King Philip and his son, and to the catastrophe which overtakes all three. For it is characteristic of Schiller's richness of invention that *Don Carlos* is a tragedy of more than one hero.

As might be expected from one who had grown up in an oppressive petty state, Schiller was much preoccupied in his early plays with the nature of absolutism; but not until *Don Carlos* does he explore all facets of the despotic mentality in the person of King Philip II. It is not an unsympathetic portrait. The King is a man of iron, entirely alien to the sensibilities of his son, fair to those who, like the Admiral, have failed through no fault of their own, utterly inflexible in matters regarding, as he thinks, the safety of his kingdom. But even he cannot escape a human vulnerability. The completeness of his power has thrown him into isolation; there is no one among his courtiers to whom he can open his heart, least of all regarding his suspicions of his young wife's fidelity. Hence the dramatic necessity of Posa, and the consequent paradox. Just because the Marquis, a man of courage and honour, not only has shown himself independent of Philip but dares to speak out in front of him, he is the one person in whom the King can confide, however little he may share his views.

But this new intimacy is doomed from the start. The lesson that Schiller is concerned to drive home is that *between liberalism and absolutism no compromise is possible.* Posa uses his newly granted permission to visit the Queen at all hours unannounced in order to further the cause he has so deeply at heart – that of having Carlos sent to the Netherlands to protect the people against the Duke of Alva. Meanwhile, the Count of Lerma, one of the Infante's few friends at Court, mistakes Posa's activity for treachery towards the Prince, whom he warns accordingly. Posa himself is forced to put Carlos under arrest to protect him from his own rashness, and at the same time (and this is the most obscure part of the plot) write letters which incriminate himself with the monarch. As a result the King has him shot while he is visiting Carlos in prison. But the monarch's disillusionment – the courtiers find him weeping when the deed has been done – is only the first step in his humiliation. Learning the real reason for Posa's self-sacrifice he bursts out:

Would he were still alive! I'd give the Indies for it.
Oh woe-begone omnipotence that can

* Schiller, *Don Carlos*, trs. Charles E. Passage (New York, 1959), III, iii, 3217–35. Reprinted by permission of F. Unger Publishing Co. Inc., New York.

> Not even stretch its arm forth into graves
> To right a little hastiness with human
> Life. Dead men resurrect no more. Who can
> Tell me that I am happy? In the grave
> Dwells one man who withheld respect from me.
> What do I care about those still alive?
> A spirit, *one* free man rose up in all
> This century – just one – and he despised me
> And died.*

Finally he has to endure the accusing figure of the Grand Inquisitor (Samuel to Philip's Saul), in what must be one of the most chilling dialogues in all dramatic literature.

INQUISITOR Who authorized you to
Deprive the Holy Office of this victim?
Is this the way to trifle with us? If
The crown stoops to concealment – reaches understandings
Behind our backs with our worst enemies, –
Where will we be? If one man is shown mercy
By what right can a hundred thousand then
Be sacrificed?

KING He has been sacrificed.

INQUISITOR No! He was murdered – wantonly! Ingloriously!
The blood that should have flowed for us in glory
Was shed by an assassin's hand. The man
Was ours – Who authorized *you* to lay hands
Upon the Order's sacred property?
To die for us was his excuse for living.
God granted him unto this Epoch's need
To make of swaggering reason an example
By formal degradation of his mind.
That was my well-considered plan. And now
It lies wiped out, my work of many years!
We have been cheated, robbed, and you have nothing
But bloody hands.†

Their agreement to sacrifice Don Carlos is casual to the point of anti-climax:

KING Can you create a new religion which
Supports the bloody murder of a son?

INQUISITOR To expiate eternal righteousness
God's own son died upon the cross.

KING   Do you
Agree to sow this notion throughout all Europe?

INQUISITOR As far as they adore the cross.

* Schiller, V, ii, 5036–46.
† *Ibid.*, V, ii, 5167–87.

KING   I outrage
            Nature too. Will you put silence on
            That mighty voice as well?
INQUISITOR   Before the Faith
            No voice of Nature has validity.*

But the struggle is a mild one. The voice of nature has long been silent in Philip regarding his own son. When he traps Carlos in the Queen's apartments where he is taking a chaste leave of his stepmother before setting forth to Flanders it costs him little to say stoically to the Inquisitor:

                    Cardinal! I have
        Done what my part required. Do your part now.

So Carlos is handed over to the Inquisitor as the curtain falls. In fact the character of King Philip seems to have fascinated Verdi from the beginning. It is not surprising that among his first requirements when the synopsis by Méry and du Locle was presented to him was that the two dialogues with Posa and the Inquisitor respectively should be included.

The eponymous hero of the play has been compared to Hamlet, who was indeed for such as Schiller the archetype of all lonely and brooding young men. But there is a vital difference. Hamlet's nature remains fundamentally close; he is inclined to keep his own counsel to the end. Even to Horatio he confides his anger but not his suffering. Carlos, like Major Ferdinand in *Kabale und Liebe*, is by nature frank and impulsive and only too ready to confide in anyone who gives him a kind word. Only with the Duke of Alva and the wily Jesuit Domingo does he maintain a Hamlet-like aloofness. For an age which cultivated sensibility he had the same kind of appeal as Goethe's Werther. Beethoven, it would seem, was among his admirers, if one can judge from two quotations scribbled in the personal albums of his friends. (He too hated his father, it will be remembered.) Credulity is somewhat taxed by his dog-like devotion to Posa, whom he has every reason to believe is betraying him, and especially by the passive, self-accusing way in which it is expressed. But to Verdi the soft side of Carlos's nature is of the utmost importance; it enabled him to create what is, apart from certain anticipations, notably in Henri in *Les Vêpres Siciliennes*, a new type of tenor in which the simple ardour of the Italian high male voice is tempered by half-lights and subtleties of emotion and mood which will yield a new wealth of musical invention.

Of Schiller's two women, Elisabeth is little more than a plaster saint; the traditional image of wifely and womanly virtue, who springs to life only when defending herself against King Philip's false accusations. The Princess Eboli on the other hand exists in all three dimensions – proud, wilful, passionate, capable of great charm in the pursuit of her own ends. The long scene between her and Carlos where each misunderstands the other has the same importance as that between Major Ferdinand and Lady Milford in *Kabale und Liebe*. A frequent attendant at meetings between Carlos and the Queen, Eboli has assumed that she herself is the cause of Carlos's often agitated manner; she therefore summons him to a rendezvous by

* Schiller, V, ii, 5267–75.

means of an anonymous note, which he assumes to have been written by the Queen. In the course of their conversation she shows Carlos a love letter from King Philip. Carlos, exultant, makes off with it, not in order to ruin the Princess whom he believes to be innocent, but hoping to show it to Elisabeth as proof of her husband's unfaithful intentions. Posa, after making him tear up the letter, opens Carlos's eyes to what he has done with a neat vignette of the Princess:

> POSA   The Princess Eboli
> Saw through you. Not a doubt of it, she pierced
> Down to the inmost secrets of your love.
> You have hurt her severely. She controls
> The King.
> CARLOS (*confidently*)   But she is virtuous.
> POSA   She is so,
> From the self-interest of love. This virtue –
> I gravely fear I know its kind – how little
> It measures up to that ideal which
> From the maternal seed-ground of the soul,
> Wherein it was conceived in lovely grace,
> Grows up of its free will and without tending
> By gardeners, bears abundant bloom! This is
> An alien bough which in harsh latitudes
> Has flowered with a counterfeited south.
> Or call it rearing, rule of conduct, what
> You will, this is an *innocence acquired*,
> From hot blood wrested by craft and hard struggle
> And conscientiously and carefully
> Ascribed to Heaven which requires it and
> Rewards it. Think it over. Will she ever
> Be able to forgive the queen when some
> Man has passed over her own hard-won virtue
> Just so that he in turn may be consumed
> With hopeless passion for Don Philip's wife?*

Posa's analysis of her character proves perfectly correct. Stung by Carlos's indifference to herself and rightly guessing its cause, she at last yields to Philip's importunities with the whole-hearted encouragement of Father Domingo, burgles the Queen's jewel casket and shows Philip a medallion of the Infante as evidence that she has committed adultery with him. Too late she tries to undo the consequences of her action; and after making full confession to the Queen she is dismissed the court. Here was the kind of ambivalent character that since *Il Trovatore* Verdi had learnt to embody in the mezzo-soprano voice, the female equivalent of the baritone. After Philip, he told Faccio, the most important part in the opera was that of Eboli.†

The immediate problem confronting his librettists was how to impose a convinc-

---

* Schiller, II, v, 2325–47.
† Letter to Faccio, undated (*c.* January 1879). De Rensis, pp. 182–5.

ing operatic shape on Schiller's sprawling drama. Their first thoughts are set out in the prose synopsis brought by Escudier to S. Agata, where it is fortunately preserved. The additions, omissions and alterations are many; and it would be natural to ascribe them in the first place to Joseph Méry, who was a prose dramatist in his own right and therefore capable of sound invention. In fact for their first scene and for several other significant details in the course of the action both writers drew upon Eugène Cormon's play *Philippe II Roi d'Espagne*, produced unsuccessfully at the Théâtre de la Gaîté, Paris on 14 May 1846.* The Prologue, entitled *L'Etudiant D'Alcalá*, is played in the royal palace of St-Germain, where a number of gardeners are trimming the bushes in preparation for a royal visit. One of them, Maître Jean, has been given a bunch of flowers to hand to the Princess from an unknown Spanish student, whom he is lodging in his house. The nosegay contains a note inviting her to a rendezvous. The Princess Elisabeth accepts the invitation, but proves somewhat constrained in her manner towards the student, since she is officially betrothed to the Infante of Spain. The student then produces a medallion of her destined bridegroom. Recognition and a mutual declaration of love. The student /Carlos then retires as King Henry II arrives with his court. He tells his daughter that after his recent defeats in battle all his hopes of peace with Spain rest in her marriage with the Spanish royal house. Enter the Duke of Alva, who solicits the hand of Elisabeth for his master, Philip of Spain. To content her father Elisabeth consents with despair in her heart. From all this to the first act of *Don Carlos* was a short step. St-Germain was turned into Fontainebleau, the gardeners into woodcutters, the Duke of Alva into the Count of Lerma. Elisabeth submits to her fate for humanitarian rather than for filial motives, and her encounter with Carlos is made accidental – a far more sensible arrangement than Cormon's. As if a royal princess, her hand already bespoken, would be likely to make secret assignations with unknown young men!

Anyway, in his letter to Perrin, Verdi approved this preliminary scene wholeheartedly; it makes the subsequent action much clearer and at the same time provides a fund of musical reminiscence to be drawn upon in later acts. Act II of the synopsis follows the order of events in Schiller's Act I, with a scene for Carlos and Posa, who has just returned from Flanders, then a tense and unhappy dialogue between Carlos and Elisabeth for which Posa has prepared the way. Economy, however, dictated the abolition of Domingo and the Duke of Alva, whose quarrel with Carlos, resulting in a near-rapprochement between father and son, has no place in the operatic scheme. Likewise the final scene of Schiller's first act, in which Posa and Carlos swear eternal friendship, is in the opera spatchcocked into their previous dialogue.

Act III of the synopsis contains two scenes. In the first, Carlos keeps his tryst with Eboli in the mistaken belief that it was Elisabeth who summoned him. Eboli soon discovers the truth and storms out vowing vengeance. (No mention here of the letters she has received from Philip.) Posa arrives and persuades Carlos to hand over to him a miniature portrait of Elisabeth. The second scene is pure grand opera owing nothing to Schiller, but a little to Cormon. It is set in the gardens of Aranjuez where Philip and Elisabeth are receiving the homage of their subjects from Italy to the

---

* See Marc Clémeur, 'Eine neu entdeckte Quelle für das Libretto von Verdis *Don Carlos*', in *Melos: Neue Zeitschrift für Musik*, Vol. III (1977), pp. 496–9. Cormon is remembered chiefly as the librettist of Bizet's *Les Pêcheurs de perles*.

Americas. What better excuse than this for a ballet of the nations? Then Philip notices that Flanders is not represented. Enter the Flemish deputies dressed in mourning. They plead with Philip to spare their fellow-Protestants. Philip rejects their plea with contumely; Carlos springs to their defence and draws his sword on his father, who at once orders his arrest. None of the guard dares lift a finger against the Infante. It is left to Posa to induce Carlos to give up his sword; and the curtain falls as the prince is led away into custody.*

In the first scene of Act IV, loosely derived from Schiller's Act V, scene ii, Philip, surrounded by his grandees, including the Grand Inquisitor, deliberates on his son's punishment. The Inquisitor demands that he be surrendered to the Holy Office and accuses Philip of failing in his duty towards the Church. The Count of Lerma pleads for mercy. But the King adjourns the meeting without declaring his intention. The Queen enters in great agitation complaining of the theft of her jewel box. An angry scene between her and Philip is followed, as in the play, by Eboli's confession and dismissal.

The rest of the synopsis deals with the death of Posa as he visits Carlos in prison (Act IV, scene ii) and the lovers' final meeting (Act V). In contrast to the play, Carlos is saved by the apparition of his grandfather in the guise of a monk. As we have noted, this curious expedient was approved by Verdi at the time, though he was to find fault with it later. In asking for the Philip—Inquisitor and Posa—Philip scenes to be reinstated he showed not only that he had read the original play, but that he shared with the 'scapigliati' a desire to come to grips with material traditionally regarded as unoperatic. Both scenes were to be inserted, though not at the points where they occur in the original drama. The first takes place before Posa's death, not after, as in Schiller. The second precedes the Carlos—Eboli débâcle where originally it had followed it – an alteration which confused Verdi himself at one stage in the opera's evolution. His demands for a spectacular scene like the coronation in *Le Prophète* (how that *coup de théâtre* haunted him!) were eventually met by setting Philip's confrontation of the Flemish deputies against the background of an impending *auto da fé* – another idea borrowed shamelessly from Cormon. †

Verdi remained in Paris until mid-March 1866 working with his poets. Progress was slow and laborious. By the middle of February Méry was confined to his room with the illness which was to kill him a few months later; and du Locle was obliged to continue alone. When Verdi returned to Busseto the libretto was virtually complete. Only the final act needed some modification, and for this he was in no hurry. 'Take your time,' he wrote to du Locle in April, '. . . since it will be a good while before I get to that point.'‡

Despite the throat trouble which so often afflicted him while composing, Verdi had managed to complete Act I before leaving Paris; and if the paucity of correspondence between him and du Locle prevents us from knowing precisely how it and the next three acts reached their final form from the prose synopsis, useful clues

* In Cormon's Act IV Carlos is surprised by Philip and the Spanish nobles as he attempts to escape to Flanders. When Philip orders his son's arrest, the guard hesitate; only when he himself is about to lay hands on Carlos do the grandees interpose themselves.

† Cormon, *Philippe II*, II, i–vii. Ursula Günther (*loc. cit.*) suggests further sources for this scene in the contemporary description of an *auto da fé* in Valladolid in May 1559, as well as the sixteenth-century engraving 'Hispanisches Inquisition' by Franz Hogenberg.

‡ Letter to du Locle, 17.4.1866. Günther, *op. cit.*, pp. 32–3.

are provided by three draft libretti (the so-called brown, blue and pink copybooks), each representing a successive stage in the formation of the final text, and each heavily annotated and sometimes altered by Verdi himself. Not every act exists in all three versions; presumably Verdi either lost or threw away those of the originals which needed too much reworking. At all events the 'pink' libretto – or as much of it as exists – is clearly the latest of the three. The progress of Act I from the prose synopsis through the brown, blue and pink libretti and the singers' rehearsal books to the definitive text has been minutely charted by Ursula Günther.* Several points which emerge from her essay will be referred to in the analysis of the opera. For the present, let us merely note the general shortening which the text underwent at Verdi's hands and the fact that the shape of the final scene, in which Elisabeth takes her irrevocable decision, was his work entirely and differs considerably from the original intentions of the librettists.

During the late spring and summer months of 1866 Verdi ploughed his way slowly through the four remaining acts, all of which had been reshaped more or less according to his requirements. The duet for Posa and Philip had been tacked on to the end of Act II, making it, as everyone knows, extremely long. ('It isn't an act, it's half an opera!' Verdi wrote to Escudier. 'Then the genre is extremely difficult. The scene between the King and Posa has made me spit out my lungs, and there are other scenes like this.')† Indeed the scene in question was to cost the composer three versions and fifteen years before finding a form that truly satisfied him. In Act III the ballet had been brought forward into the first scene, preceding the duo between Carlos and Eboli which was now developed into a trio with the arrival of Posa. This was followed by the coronation of Philip and the scene with the Flemish deputies, now moved to the main square by the cathedral of Valladolid and embellished with contrasting choruses; but only in the pink libretto is there any mention of an *auto da fé* and a voice from on high which promises the martyrs a heavenly crown. Then, following the example of *Les Vêpres Siciliennes*, the first scene of Act IV abandons spectacle to centre on a drama of individuals, laid out in a scheme of perfect symmetry: Aria (Philip), Duo (Philip–Inquisitor), Quatuor (Philip–Elisabeth–Eboli–Posa), Duo (Elisabeth–Eboli), Aria (Eboli). This point Verdi seems to have reached at the beginning of June, and he was now working at full speed. 'Eight days ago,' he wrote to du Locle, 'I wrote to you asking you to re-do for me the quatuor, but now I've set it to music just as it stands, and this quatuor too is finished. I just need a few tiny little changes, amounting to a few words, and a few accentuations, not just for the sake of the music but to give more vitality to the scene.'‡ He then drafted out the tense dialogue between Philip and Elisabeth where the Queen, complaining of theft, finds herself accused of adultery. It was Verdi's idea to include from Schiller the Queen's lofty rebuke that causes Philip to lose control of himself:

ELISABETH How I pity
Your Majesty!
PHILIP You pity me! The pity
Of an adulteress!§

* See Günther, 'Le Livret français de Don Carlos; le premier acte et sa revision par Verdi', in *Atti del II° Congresso dell' I.S.V.* (Parma, 1971), pp. 90–140.
† Letter to Escudier, 20.5.1866. Günther, 'La Genèse de *Don Carlos*', p. 40.
‡ Letter to du Locle, 16.6.1866. *Carteggi Verdiani*, IV, pp. 163–4.
§ Schiller, *Don Carlos*, IV, iii, 3791–3.

Thereupon the Queen faints. Changes of metre were specified for the ensemble, in which Verdi was particularly concerned that Eboli should not anticipate the confession of her guilt that forms the burden of her duo with Elisabeth. Five days later he was asking for an extension of this same duo – 'it will be necessary to add a calmer strophe so as to make room for a little more cantabile';* and once again he drafted out the text, this time in Italian. Unfortunately, it was a duo that the Parisian public was never to hear. In the same letter he insisted that the first line of Eboli's aria should be 'O don fatal et détesté' in place of the librettist's 'Que de pleurs brûle ma paupière'. The result is a change in the rhyme scheme from *abab* to *baab* for the first verse only, and the insertion of the somewhat otiose line 'Présent du ciel en sa colère'; but the gain in force and clarity is ample compensation.

The revised Act V had reached S. Agata by the middle of June accompanied by an enthusiastic note from Perrin. It was a valiant attempt to resolve the drama on a note of grand spectacle and high emotional tension far removed from the low-key ending of the play. Schiller's Carlos is still in the palace at this point and at liberty (his sword had been restored to him after Posa's death). He gains access to the Queen's apartments by disguising himself as the ghost of the Emperor Charles V that is supposed to haunt that wing of the palace – but only to bid her a chaste farewell. Since the murder of his friend his feelings for Elisabeth have been transformed; all traces of passion have vanished. From now on he will devote himself to the cause for which Posa has laid down his life: the freedom of mankind.

```
CARLOS                         . . . I shall erect
        A monument to him such as no king
        Has ever known – a Paradise shall bloom
        Above his ashes.†
```

Surprised by the King and handed over to the Inquisition he behaves with stoical fortitude.

In the opera, however, events had already taken a different turning after Posa's death. The King had duly arrived at the prison and proclaimed his son a free man. Then both had joined in a lament over Posa's corpse accompanied by a sympathetic murmuring of grandees. Suddenly there were sounds of tumult. An angry crowd burst into the prison demanding Carlos's freedom. The instigator was Eboli in the guise of a young man, who in the general turmoil that followed spirited Carlos away – a somewhat unnecessary act, since by this time Carlos was no longer a prisoner, but then Eboli could not be expected to know that. In fact this was another episode adapted from Cormon's *Philippe II*, where the mob leader is even more improbably Elisabeth herself. In both play and opera the tumult is quelled by the appearance of the Grand Inquisitor.

Act V of the opera is therefore set no longer in the Royal Palace but outside the Monastery of St-Just, the scene of Act II. Carlos is on his way to the Netherlands; and it is Elisabeth who has taken what for the Queen of Spain was the monstrous risk of meeting him there to wish him God-speed. The original draft began with a long solo for Carlos as he waited for her to arrive. Du Locle now followed it with a duet of

---

* Letter to du Locle, 21.4.1866. *Carteggi Verdiani*, IV, pp. 164–5.
† Schiller, *Don Carlos*, V, x, 5295–8.

Tristanesque fervour in which the Prince, having declared that his love for her is dead, suddenly takes her in his arms crying out, 'Je t'aime, je t'aime' while she succumbs, calling on heaven to take pity on her. Then:

> En vain le foudre gronde
> Sur nos fronts éperdus;
> Nos deux coeurs confondus
> Ont oublié le monde.
> O Dieu! Juge éternel,
> Que ta sainte justice
> A jamais nous unisse
> Pour l'Enfer ou le Ciel!

'. . . this explosion of a passion held so forcibly in check up to that point seems to me necessary to conclude the drama,' Perrin wrote. 'I hope you will be of my opinion.'*

Verdi was not. In his reply, drafted by Giuseppina in her habitually tactful style, he stated his objections, beginning with Carlos's opening solo – 'an hors d'oeuvre which is not happily placed in a fifth act. The duo which follows has gained nothing throughout its first part; and the ending has become, if I may say so, just a little commonplace. By bringing back the love you *depoeticise* (or whatever the word should be) the situation which is so lofty and sublime in Schiller's conception. At a moment like this "Je t'aime, je t'aime" – je ne l'aime pas du tout.' He went on to criticize the sequel as too protracted and would-be spectacular. 'I don't like Carlos's outburst, calling on the Emperor; I don't like the Seigneurs de la Cour, and still less the apparition of Charles V robed as Emperor and surrounded by monks. The imagination will always be gripped by the sight of the Emperor alone and isolated; after that Philip must not be allowed too much time to consider whether this is a ghost or a living person. In my view if you want something of a spectacle there's only one way of achieving it; a chorus of the Inquisition, a kind of judgement, but rapid and violent.'† Once again, Verdi drafted out the scheme, which belongs to that line of ritual trials that reaches from Act III of *Jérusalem* to the last act of *Falstaff*. Carlos is accused by the King of alienating his wife's affections, by the Grand Inquisitor of heresy, by the King again of raising rebellion in the land. After each accusation the chorus of inquisitors pronounce their anathema. There is a general outcry and Carlos's arrest is ordered. As he retreats towards the church the doors open, the Emperor appears, recognized with awe by all present, and draws him inside. This plan would serve unaltered for the first version of the opera.

The unwanted tenor aria appears to have been the long apostrophe beginning 'O portiques muets' that occurs in the first of two alternative texts given in the 'pink' libretto.‡ The lines indicate a full ternary aria *à la française* with a freely organized central episode, like that of Elisabeth's 'Toi qui sus le néant' which was ultimately to replace it. For the present Verdi set as a free 'scena' the newer and briefer alternative

---

* Letter from Perrin, 14.6.1866, *R. de M.*, LX, p. 90. In the event part of this text found its way into Carlos's final outburst in his Act II duet with Elisabeth.

† Letter to Perrin, 21.6.1866. Abbiati, III, pp. 91–2; sketched also in *Carteggi Verdiani*, II, p. 25.

‡ See A. Porter, 'A sketch for *Don Carlos*', in the *Musical Times* (Sept. 1970), p. 883, for a fuller quotation.

provided by du Locle ('Proscrit, abandonné de tous'). The text is concerned mainly with Fontainebleau and memories of blighted hopes, accompanied by appropriate musical reminiscences. All this would also be taken over in the aria assigned to Elisabeth.

Verdi arrived in Paris by the end of July with all but the last act ready to be put into the singers' rehearsal books. The journey had not been undertaken without some heart-searchings. Ever since April the likelihood of a war between Italy and Austria had loomed. By May troops were massing along the Po; there were even rumours that the Crown Prince Umberto was to take up his lodgings at S. Agata, as a patriotic gesture. Verdi's first idea was to go at once to Paris if Busseto should find itself in the front line.* But he soon thought better of deserting his country in her hour of trial and even considered asking permission of Perrin to stay in Italy longer than his contract stipulated. To this end he consulted his fellow deputy Giuseppe Piroli as to whether he would be justified in violating the relevant clause for reasons of patriotism;† but Piroli's reply was categorical. It would do no good to Italy's name abroad if her foremost composer were to break his word; moreover there was a strong possibility that Napoleon III would once again intervene on Italy's behalf, and might even defer the year of the Universal Exhibition until European hostilities had ceased, and therefore Verdi's request would be pointless.‡ However, by the beginning of July the situation had resolved itself with the Italian defeat at Custozza, aggravated by the naval disaster at Lissa. Only Garibaldi with his march into the Trentino at the head of a troop of volunteers that included Faccio and Boito remained to mitigate the Italian sense of humiliation. Fortunately, the Prussian victory at Königgrätz turned Austria into the loser. Peace was made by ceding the Veneto to the Emperor of the French, who in turn handed it over to Italy after a plebiscite. This was not the way that Venice had hoped to regain her freedom. Verdi was furious at the outcome. From Genoa he wrote to Escudier, 'You can see that the general picture is not a pretty one, and that prospects for the future are black. Given this state of affairs how could you want me to have the heart to come to Paris? In small matters as in great ones, and certainly in this case, there can only be one solution: to dissolve my contract with the Opéra. Ask this of M. Perrin, and if he allows it I shall reckon it a favour for which I will be very grateful.'§ At the same time he wrote again to Piroli asking what he should do if his request were refused. The deputy's reply has not survived; but evidently Verdi did not see fit to press the matter. After receiving Perrin's refusal (presumably by telegram) he wrote to Escudier announcing his departure for Paris and begging him to instruct the owner of the house in the Champs-Elysées whose lease he still held to make sure and beat the carpets before his arrival since dust would have a disastrous effect upon his throat.¶

Having delivered the first four acts to the management of the Opéra, he went away for a few weeks to the Pyrenean spa of Cauterets, partly for his health and partly to finish the opera in peace and quiet. During his absence a typical comedy was played out at the Opéra. Belval, the bass assigned to the part of the Grand In-

* Letter to T. Ricordi, 10.5.1866. Abbiati, III, p. 80.
† Letter to Piroli, 9.6.1866. Carteggi Verdiani, III, pp. 39–40.
‡ Letter from Piroli, 17.6.1866. Ibid., p. 40.
§ Letter to Escudier, 14.7.1866. R.M.I. (1928), pp. 521–2.
¶ See Walker, p. 264.

quisitor, was dismayed to find that his role was smaller than that of Obin (Philip II) and accused Perrin of breaking their contract, which had stipulated a leading part. Perrin replied caustically that if Verdi had decided to write an opera with two leading basses in it that had nothing to do with Belval's contract. But that did not satisfy the singer, who not only refused to come to rehearsals but instituted proceedings against the management. The tribunal decided to invite the composer Ambroise Thomas to look at the score and judge whether the Grand Inquisitor qualified as a leading role. Verdi was furious when the matter was reported to him, and wrote to Escudier that the score of *Don Carlos* was still his property and if anyone were allowed to examine it without his permission he would withdraw it.* In these circumstances Thomas tactfully retired. The tribunal then approached the critic and composer Ernest Reyer, but he also declined. Finally, a certain Duprez accepted the assignment which, however, remained a dead letter since Verdi continued to with-hold his consent to the examination of his music. Belval meanwhile was replaced with David, who had originally been given the role of the Monk/Charles V.

Two letters to du Locle in early and middle September† tell us of further changes and adjustments, the most notable of which regards the terzetto between Posa, Elisabeth and Eboli in the second scene of Act II. This Verdi promised to arrange on his return to Paris, not having the complete score with him at Cauterets. The original version of the terzetto has been reconstructed in outline from the rehearsal books and can be consulted in articles by Andrew Porter and Ursula Günther.‡ Much shorter than the definitive version, its only point of interest is that it shows Eboli en-couraging the Queen to receive her stepson – which would certainly be in the spirit of Schiller but only if Eboli herself were to be present during their conversation (she always imagines that Carlos's audiences with the Queen are merely an excuse to be in her own company). The graceful theme that later accompanies the small-talk between Posa and Eboli is here only touched upon; while Posa's romance 'L'Infant Carlos, notre espérance' is absent altogether. Its insertion later was doubtless due less to dramatic considerations than to regard for Faure's prowess as a lyric baritone; but it turned out a fortunate concession since on the first night the piece was encored.

The other modifications concern the final act. The ending was to be tightened and the accusations against Carlos made more explicit. Early doubts about Morère's ability to sustain the title role had by no means been allayed; and though for the present he retained his solo, the duet with Elisabeth which followed it was to be centred chiefly on the soprano from the outset; but that idea too underwent a change once the tenor solo had been discarded.

Indeed problems of casting had been more than usually acute. The singer originally proposed for Eboli had been the young contralto Rosine Bloch. In order to conserve her resources for the occasion Perrin removed her from the part of Fidès in current revivals of *Le Prophète*, and replaced her with Pauline Gueymard-Lauters, a soprano of wide extension who had created Leonora in *Le Trouvère* in 1857. She ac-quitted herself so well at rehearsals that Perrin suggested to Verdi that, 'If she commits herself firmly to undertake deep mezzo-soprano roles you might perhaps entrust her with the part of Eboli without changing a note of the tessitura, and we

* See letter to Escudier, 1.9.1866. *R. de M.*, LX, p. 105.
† 4 and 11.9.1866. *Carteggi Verdiani*, IV, pp. 166–7.
‡ Porter, 'The Making of *Don Carlos*', pp. 76–7; and Günther, 'La Genèse de *Don Carlos*', pp. 56–60.

should gain by having two proven artists and an incomparable female cast.'* Verdi's reply was cautious. 'If you are not afraid of embarrassment resulting from rivalry between Mme Sass and Mme Gueymard, nothing could be better than Mme Gueymard for Eboli. It's true that the pieces written for the second and third acts are a little low; but if the role of Fidès . . . suits her, she can perfectly well sing Eboli. For the moment I would think it advisable not to say anything to her about it.'† Perrin wrote again suggesting that Verdi should hear Mme Gueymard-Lauters in *Le Prophète* when he came to Paris before making up his mind irrevocably. In due course Verdi did so and agreed to the proposed change; but it was not until rehearsals began that he realized that certain transpositions and adjustments would after all be necessary for the new Eboli. In this way he created a problem for all Ebolis which has remained to this day. Those who can sing the Song of the Veil (Act II) transposed up a tone for Mme Gueymard-Lauters are usually ineffective in 'O don fatal', and vice versa. The original of the first, in G major, can be found in Mme Gueymard-Lauters's rehearsal book, but there are no orchestral parts to go with it. From the same source we can see how much labour it cost Verdi to adapt both solos to the means of his new Eboli. The Veil Song contains no less than five alternative cadenzas and a new final phrase, still in G major, but better suited to Mme Gueymard's higher range. 'O don fatal' underwent three transformations before reaching its final form, as though the composer were torn between the desire to parade the full extension of the singer's voice and a determination to keep the drama moving. In the second of the discarded versions there are lingering traces of 'cabalettism' which vanish entirely from the final product.‡ It was clearly a painful and embarrassing business for all concerned. Indeed on 18 October Verdi missed a rehearsal altogether, 'mainly,' so du Locle told Perrin, 'because he was annoyed by Mme Sass's grimacing at the alterations made for Mme Gueymard.'§ Doubtless this was one of the factors that led to the eventual dropping of their one duet.

'We progress,' Verdi wrote to Arrivabene, 'but, as always at the Opéra, at a snail's pace.'¶ Giuseppina too grumbled about the 'Tortoises of the Opéra' and the fact that 'they argue for twenty-four hours before deciding whether Faure or La Sass is to raise a finger or a whole hand'.‖ This was hardly an exaggeration. In that deeply conservative institution the authority of the conductor made its way even more slowly than in Italy. Until his dismissal in 1863 Dietsch used to conduct from a first violin part. His successor, Hainl, may have used a score; but he was no Costa or Mariani. Ensemble was secured by endless rehearsal; and as music became more elaborate over the years and stage machinery more ingenious (by 1867 a primitive form of electric light without filament was available for special effects) so operas took increasingly long to mount.** Consequently by the time the first night arrived all spontaneity had been lost. This was a favourite theme of Verdi's complaint, as was

---

* Letter from Perrin, 10.5.1866. Günther, *op. cit.*, p. 39; Porter, *op. cit.*, p. 76.

† Letter to Perrin, 24.5.1866. Günther, *op. cit.* See also letter to Escudier, 20.5.1866. *Ibid.*, p. 40.

‡ Günther, *op. cit.*, pp. 61–4.

§ Memo from du Locle to Perrin, 18.10.1866. Günther, *op. cit.*, pp. 51ff; Porter, *op. cit.*, p. 78.

¶ Letter to Arrivabene, 28.9.1866. Alberti, p. 72.

‖ Letter from Giuseppina Verdi to M. Corticelli, 7.12.1866. Walker, p. 267.

** Statistics quoted by Ursula Günther in *R. de M.*, LX, pp. 109–13, show a rising graph of rehearsal time expended successively on *Les Vêpres Siciliennes*, *L'Africaine* and *Don Carlos*, for which the number of sessions excluding the coaching of individual singers exceeds two hundred.

the continual criticism to which a new work was subjected when still in the preparatory stage.

> In your musical theatres [*he wrote to du Locle three years later*] . . . there are too many Savants. Each one wants to air an opinion, express a doubt; and after living for a long time in this atmosphere of doubts, the author can't help being eventually rather shaken in his convictions and he ends by correcting, adjusting, and, I would even say, spoiling his own work. Thus you finish up not with an opera cast at a single throw, but a *mosaic* – a fine one, if you like, but still a mosaic. To this you'll reply that at the Opéra you have a string of masterpieces all composed in that way. All right, I'll grant you, they're masterpieces; but allow me to say that they would be still more perfect if one wasn't aware from time to time of the chipping and tinkering. Certainly no one will deny Rossini's genius; and yet for all that genius, you can discern in *Guillaume Tell* the fatal atmosphere of the Opéra, and sometimes – though more rarely than in other composers – you feel that there's a bit too much here and not quite enough there, and that the piece doesn't move as freely and surely as *Il Barbiere*.*

That for *Don Carlos* the chorus masters were Léo Delibes and Victor Massé cannot have added to Verdi's comfort.

A little more here, a little less there – in this way *Don Carlos* slowly took shape during the last months of 1866, with the ballet yet to be composed. Posa's romanza had been added and the preceding terzetto expanded. Carlos's short scena at the start of Act V had become a grand aria for Elisabeth. Something would clearly have to go. The first item to be discarded was the duet between Elisabeth and Eboli in Act IV. Why this was so we can only guess. But quite apart from any possible bad blood between the two prima donnas, this piece dwells upon what for a bourgeois nineteenth-century audience was one of the most problematical aspects of the plot – Eboli's adultery with the King. In the romantic age, a man who eats his heart out in an aria such as 'Elle ne m'aime pas' will lose sympathy if it is made too clear that he is carrying on with another woman at the same time. Yet their liaison can hardly remain unmentioned, since Eboli's confession of it is the reason for her dismissal from court. Therefore its date of occurrence was left tactfully vague in the opera; and to this day there are those who believe that it was over by the time of Philip's marriage, and wonder why Elisabeth should punish her lady-in-waiting for so ancient a lapse. In the original version of their scene Eboli first confessed that she loved Carlos and Carlos had repulsed her; whereupon the Queen was all sisterly compassion, and joined her in an extended cantabile. But when Eboli mentioned her relations with the King, Elisabeth left the room without a word; it was the Count of Lerma who arrived to offer Eboli the choice between exile and a convent. By cutting the formal duet du Locle played safer still. As a result the Elisabeth of 1867 never hears the full confession; the news that Eboli loves Carlos is sufficient to induce the Queen to dismiss her; but at least she does it in person by taking over the text previously assigned to Lerma. By this time there is nothing to show that Eboli and Philip were more to each other than subject and sovereign; and Eboli's cursing of her own beauty becomes singularly pointless.

* Letter to du Locle, 7.12.1869. *Copialettere*, pp. 219–22.

Next to go was the duet for Carlos and Philip following Posa's death. Again no reason is given, though doubtless Faure's objection to prolonged recumbence as a corpse had something to do with it. Finally an exchange between Elisabeth and Eboli during the 'sommossa' (riot) was cut, again perhaps with a view to lessening Faure's discomfort, since he had to remain on the ground until the curtain fell.

By mid-December Verdi ventured to tell Arrivabene that the opera was complete and in full score except for the ballet and would probably be performed in mid-January. But he was over-optimistic to the extent of two months. The ballet had been entrusted to Arthur St-Léon, husband of the dancer Fanny Cerrito and future choreographer of *Coppélia*. The idea of a ballet of the nations had long since been discarded in favour of an allegorical dance-drama worthy of the baroque age – and one which allows full scope for the use of electric light. It begins as the old story of the fisherman who happens upon some deep unfathomed cave of ocean, bearing, as in Gray's poem, full many a gem of purest ray serene. Furious at his audacity, the God of the Waves, Korail, condemns him to be hurled into some remote abyss. But the sentence is never carried out; for the fisherman is really a genie, who straightway transforms himself into a page from the court of King Philip II. He has come, he says, to seek the finest pearl of the universe to offer to his royal master. The god orders that all the treasures of the sea be poured into one shell. The shell then turns into a magnificent chariot upon which Elisabeth de Valois appears in all her beauty and finery – the most precious gem of all. In the event it will not be Elisabeth; but that is to anticipate.

Unfortunately, in the autumn of 1866 St-Léon was under contract to the Imperial Theatre of St Petersburg. He was expected to return to Paris in December. But despite a number of urgent telegrams from Perrin he could not leave Russia before the middle of January. So for the third time the choreography of a Verdi ballet was entrusted to Lucien Petipa. In his hands the scenario seems to have undergone a slight modification. The fisherman is no longer a genie, and Philip's page is played by a different dancer altogether, whose timely entrance saves the fisherman from his fate. Korail changes his sex, to become the Queen of the Waters; and the ballet itself acquires the title of *La Peregrina*, a neat allusion to a famous gem once owned by the historical Philip II and at the time of the opera in the possession of Napoleon III himself.* The brief annotations in Verdi's autograph, however, seem to have been based on the original plan as submitted to the censor on 11 February, rather than that of the printed libretto; and in one or two places it is a matter of conjecture what happens during which passage of music.

Detailed sketches in the Bibliothèque Nationale† bear witness to the care which Verdi brought to this, the least known of all his ballet scores. The first rehearsal took place on 17 February, followed a week later by the first Generalprobe of the whole opera. The musical duration was found to be three hours forty-seven minutes – seventeen minutes longer than *L'Africaine*. An anonymous correspondent of Ricordi's *Gazzetta Musicale di Milano* was either present on the occasion or else in the composer's confidence. In the issue of 3 March he reported as follows:

Having started at seven o'clock in the evening the show finished around mid-

* See Porter, 'Verdi's Ballet Music and *La Peregrina*', in *Atti del II° Congresso del I.S.V.*, pp. 355–67.
† A. 619, suppléments 1 and 2.

night.* It is true that the intervals had lasted longer than usual; but even if they had been made as short as possible, the opera would have lasted a quarter of an hour longer than it should have done. In Paris the duration of operas is fixed and the rule cannot be broken. The show cannot go on beyond midnight because the last train for the suburbs and the outlying districts leaves at 12.35. For the convenience of those who live in the suburbs or the environs of Paris the show must be shortened so as not to go beyond midnight. Nor can the curtain go up any earlier since no one wants to make opera-goers hurry their dinner! All these considerations of rather menial, not to say downright slavish factors have induced, nay forced [Verdi] to shorten the duration of the music by a quarter of an hour.†

A fine duet for Elisabeth and Eboli had already gone, the writer continued, and he added that this kind of butchery was a thankless task for a composer who justly prided himself on rapidity of action and the avoidance of otiose repetition.

The problem was mostly solved by the omission of the introduction to Act I, involving a chorus of woodcutters and their wives and the first appearance of Elisabeth. The rest of the time was made up by cutting a short solo for Posa in Act II, scene i ('J'étais en Flandre') and part of the duet between Philip and Posa – as maladroit a piece of surgery, this, as the cutting of the Elisabeth–Eboli duet, since it presents Philip about to confide in Posa then failing to do so. It was the discovery of this last-mentioned passage by David Rosen, not in the autograph but in the manuscript score of the Bibliothèque Nationale, that was to lead to the recovery of all the discarded music (eight items in all if we include a couple of repetitions) whose existence had been totally unknown to Verdi scholars until then.‡

One more hurdle remained: the Imperial Censorship, who issued their report on 28 February. They demurred at parts of Posa's appeal to his sovereign; and they shook their heads over the treatment of the Grand Inquisitor ('Taken as a satire on religious absolutism this scene might find complete favour in the classic land of reform; but will it be the same for us, who have not the same reasons for applauding it?')§ Meanwhile the archivist of the Opéra, Charles Nuitter, had prepared a defence by copying out certain passages hardly less daring from Prince Poniatowski's *Piero de Médicis* which had been performed intact at the Opéra in 1860. Presumably his arguments carried weight, since in the event no attempt was made to tamper with the text of Méry and du Locle.

'Yesterday *Don Carlos*,' Verdi wrote to Arrivabene on 12 March; 'it wasn't a success!! I don't know what will happen after this, but I shouldn't be surprised if matters were to change. Tonight I leave for Genoa.'¶ Before going he authorized a further cut which allowed the second scene of Act IV to end with Posa's death. A flow of letters and telegrams from Paris gave him reassurance; and the box-office takings remained gratifyingly high. On the other hand the number of performances given that year was no more than forty-three – only three more than the number

* 00.23 a.m., to be precise; see *R. de M.*, LX, p. 143.
† See Günther in *Atti del II° Congresso del I.S.V.*, pp. 102–3.
‡ See D. Rosen, 'Le quattro stesure del duetto Filippo–Posa', in *Atti del II° Congresso del I.S.V.*, pp. 368–88.
§ *R. de M.*, LX, p. 152.
¶ Letter to Arrivabene, 12.3.1867. Alberti, p. 75.

stipulated in the contract for *Les Vêpres Siciliennes*.* Reports on some of the later ones, both in *The Musical World* and the *Journal de la régie*, speak of heavy cuts, the inadequacy of Morère's voice and the bored, listless playing of Mme Sass. A witty flautist had found time to scribble on his part:

> Verdi d'une nouvelle pièce
> A l'opéra vient de faire abandon
> C'est un bien triste DON
> CAR L'OS ne vient guère à la caisse.†

After 1869 *Don Carlos* vanished from the Opéra *affiche* until modern times.

The critical reception had been mixed. Théophile Gautier in *Le Moniteur* had approved; Ernest Reyer of the *Journal des débats* was enthusiastic. But there were others who felt that the composer of *Rigoletto* had taken a wrong turning. Typical is the remark quoted by the critic Filippo Filippi: 'Verdi est trop sorti de lui et il n'est pas assez entré dans les autres.'‡ The young Bizet, a wholehearted admirer of *Trovatore* and *Rigoletto*, enlarged upon this same theme. 'I've just come from *Don Carlos*. It is very bad. . . . No melody, no *accent*. It aims at a style – but only aims.'§ Elsewhere, 'Verdi is no longer Italian. He wants to write like Wagner. He no longer has any of his own faults; but he also lacks a single one of his own virtues.'¶ 'In other words,' Verdi remarked with scorn, 'I am an almost perfect Wagnerian. But if the critics had paid a bit more attention they would have noticed that the same kind of ideas are present in the terzetto from *Ernani*, in the sleepwalking scene from *Macbeth* and in so many other pieces. . . . But the point is not whether *Don Carlos* belongs to this or that system but whether the music is good or bad.'‖ On this score at least one eminent musician had no doubts. 'Tell [Verdi] from me,' Rossini wrote to Tito Ricordi, 'that if he returns to Paris he must get himself very well paid for it, since – may my other colleagues forgive me for saying so – he is the only composer capable of writing grand opera.'**

Meanwhile the Italian version, by Achille De Lauzières, had been prepared the previous autumn. In offering it together with the Italian rights to Tito Ricordi, Verdi tried yet again to insist that it should not be made generally available without certain safeguards, such as the rival firm of Lucca had succeeded in imposing for the many foreign operas whose rights they held and which were now flooding the peninsula. 'But then Lucca,' Verdi had said, 'is a bourgeois publisher who even demeans himself so far as to look after the goods he has acquired – for shame! How prosaic! An aristocratic publisher allows them to be murdered, murmuring grandly the while, "Let us not talk of them; look and pass on."'†† This, after a particularly bad perform-

---

* The contract for *Don Carlos* contains no stipulation regarding the number of performances; see *R. de M.*, LVIII, pp. 33–5.

† *R. de M.*, LX, pp. 156–7.

‡ See M. Conati, 'Verdi, il Grand Opéra et *Don Carlos*', in *Atti del II° Congresso del I.S.V.*, p. 271.

§ Letter from Bizet to E. Galabert, March 1867. E. Galabert (ed.), *Lettres à un ami* (Paris, 1909), pp. 40–1.

¶ Letter from Bizet to Paul Lacombe, 12.3.1867. H. Imbert, *Portraits et études: lettres inédites de G. Bizet* (Paris, 1894), p. 168.

‖ Letter to Escudier, 1.4.1867. *R.M.I.* (1928), pp. 425–5.

** Letter to T. Ricordi, 21.4.1868. L. Rognoni, *Rossini* (Parma, 1956), pp. 264–5.

†† Letter to T. Ricordi, 18.4.1866. Abbiati, III, p. 75. The quotation is from Dante's *Inferno*, III, 51.

ance of *La Forza del destino* in Genoa. *Don Carlos* must be assured of very different treatment. In the first place 'it must be performed in its entirety as it will be performed for the first time at the Paris Opéra. *Don Carlos* is an opera in five acts with ballet; if nevertheless the managements of the Italian theatres would like to pair it with a different ballet, this must be placed either before or after the uncut opera, never in the middle, following the barbarous custom of our day.' The casting requirements were two 'prime donne di gran cartello' (Elisabeth and Eboli), a 'gran tenore' (Carlos), 'gran baritono' (Posa), two primi bassi (Filippo and the Inquisitor) and a good comprimario bass (Monk/Carlo V). An augmented orchestra (i.e. with four bassoons and cornets as well as trumpets) was essential.[*]

However, the first performance in Italian was given not in Italy but at the Royal Italian Opera House, Covent Garden on 4 June 1867 under Sir Michele Costa. Up to that time, Costa is said (on no very certain authority) to have been hostile to Verdi and his music, and is even credited with having prevented the *Inno delle Nazioni* from being performed at the Exhibition of 1862. As he himself had composed a *Don Carlo* in 1844, if ever there was an occasion on which he might have been expected to vent his spite this was surely it. In the event he excelled himself. Verdi wrote gleefully to his French publisher:

So it was a success in London? And if that is so what will the gentlemen of the Opéra say when they realize that in London a score can be rehearsed in forty days, when *they* need four months? For the rest you're not telling me anything new when you declare that Costa is a great conductor and that their military band is better than that of Saxe. All stage bands are better than Saxe's – I'm not surprised that some of the numbers were encored. That may seem odd in Paris, but I can well imagine the effect the terzetto could produce when sung by three singers who have *rhythm*. Rhythm is just a dead letter at the Opéra. Two things are always lacking at the Opéra – rhythm and enthusiasm. . . .[†]

and he continued to tilt at French *bon goût*, *comme il faut*, and so on. He also wrote to Costa expressing his gratitude – which might have been cooler, however, if he had known the form in which Costa had presented the work. The first act he removed completely, likewise the ballet, though he retained the scene in which Elisabeth and Eboli exchange masks. He shortened the duet between Philip and the Inquisitor by four lines; of Elisabeth's great aria in Act V he gave only part of the central episode and the reprise; while the tenor's solo aria ('Io la vidi') he removed from Act I to just before the terzetto in Act III where Carlos receives a note of assignation from Eboli.[‡] None of this implied any disrespect on Costa's part. Cutting and rearranging were standard practices at Covent Garden, as at most European opera houses, and remained so even during the relatively enlightened regime of Sir Augustus Harris during the 1890s. What is more remarkable is the extent to which Costa's scheme anticipates that of Verdi's own revision of 1883. None the less when he learned of the displacement of Carlos's aria, Verdi was irritated. 'This is a cantabile which is all

[*] Letter to T. Ricordi, 18.11.1866. Abbiati, III, pp. 109–11.

[†] Letter to Escudier, 11.6.1867. *R.M.I.* (1928), p. 525.

[‡] For details of Costa's version, see H. Beard, '*Don Carlos* 1676–1969 on the London stage', in *Atti del II° Congresso del I.S.V.*, p. 67.

right at the start of the action,' he wrote to Camille du Locle, 'but not when the action is already under way.'* His own subsequent solution was subtler and more apt.

By contrast the Italian première, given at the Teatro Comunale, Bologna, on 27 October, under the baton of Angelo Mariani in Verdi's absence made no concessions to singers or public. This too was an instant success and won the conductor golden opinions; indeed the critic Filippi went so far as to declare that through sheer artistic bravura Mariani had created a *Don Carlos* of his own within Verdi's†– a fact that was soon to be chalked up with the conductor's other misdeeds on Verdi's reckoning board.‡ The Roman première of February 1868 serves to remind us that the new Italy was still without its true capital; for the Papal authority reigned supreme, together with a Papal censor who changed the Inquisitor into a Gran Cancelliere and the Monk/Emperor into a 'Solitario'. The Milan performance of the following month is chiefly important for a series of letters written by Verdi to the conductor Alberto Mazzucato about the musical interpretation§ (these will be referred to in their context). But despite these and other prestigious performances throughout the peninsula the Italians were slow to take *Don Carlos* to their hearts. Soon the ballet was dropped and then the Fontainebleau act.¶ Inevitably *Don Carlos* failed to compete with *Aida*, which has all its grandeur without its length and difficulty.

The first Neapolitan performance in 1871 was clearly a failure despite all De Sanctis's loyal attempts to pretend to the contrary. Verdi's explanation was simple. 'You have not one, *not one*, of the elements necessary for grand opera. . . . Go back to cavatinas.'‖ After such a categorical pronouncement it was naturally left to Giuseppina to hint delicately that her husband might be disposed to come to Naples and supervise a production there the following year provided that he could be assured of a suitable cast.** Accordingly a production was set up for the carnival season of 1872–3 with what was to become a familiar pairing of Teresa Stolz and Maria Waldmann in the leading female roles.

Verdi took the opportunity of repairing some of the damage done to the Philip–Posa duet by the enforced cut. To Giulio Ricordi he wrote, 'I shall redo a substantial part of the duet between the two basses at the end of Act II and this must be put in all the scores and arrangements since it is shorter and more vivid from the theatrical point of view.'†† For the new verses he turned to Antonio Ghislanzoni.‡‡ He also

* Letter to du Locle, 5.12.1867. Günther, 'La Genèse de *Don Carlos*', p. 18.

† See Alberti, p. 76.

‡ In fact there is some evidence that Mariani took it upon himself to 'improve' Verdi's scoring. See F. Schlitzer, *Mondo teatrale dell'ottocènto*, p. 143. The finale to Act II is mentioned; but as this had been rewritten at the time Mariani's presumption was supposed to have been remarked (see below), the report is hardly reliable. Monaldi (*Verdi, la vita, le opere*, 4th ed., p. 219) talks of a beneficial improvement given to one of the ballet movements; but he fails to indicate its nature despite a music quotation.

§ See F. V. de Bellis and F. Ghisi, 'Alcune lettere inedite sul *Don Carlos* dal Carteggio Verdi–Mazzucato', in *Atti del II° Congresso del I.S.V.*, pp. 538–41.

¶ See A. Porter, 'Don Carlos and the Monk/Emperor', in *Musical Newsletter* (New York, October 1972), p. 11.

‖ Letter to De Sanctis, 22.3.1871. *Carteggi Verdiani*, I, pp. 137–8.

** Letter from Giuseppina Verdi to De Sanctis, 21.1.1872. *Ibid.*, pp. 140–1.

†† Letter to Giulio Ricordi, 10.10.1872. Abbiati, III, pp. 606–7. As so often Verdi here relapses into the habit of regarding a baritone as a 'primo basso'.

‡‡ This fact, first stated without information as to source by Ulderico Rolandi in his monograph,

removed two movements from the Carlos–Elisabeth duet of Act V. He was to regret both modifications; but they were to remain in all vocal scores of the opera printed over the next twelve years.

But still the fortunes of *Don Carlos* disappointed the composer's hopes. When given at all it was liable to the kind of disfiguration against which he had been campaigning for years. A letter to Ricordi's agent Tornaghi tells us that in Reggio Emilia in 1874 Antonia Fricci had replaced some of her part with music from *Les Huguenots* and *Macbeth*.* Small wonder if when Faccio reported a successful revival at La Scala in the carnival season of 1878–9 Verdi replied in sarcastic vein:

> Since you say so I believe in the success despite my suspicious nature and my constant opinion that the thermometer of success is indicated only by the prosaic matter of the takings at the fifth or sixth showing. I had my doubts, knowing as I did that the theatre was not full the first evening; that it was empty the second; and that at the third they lowered the prices. I was even more doubtful when I knew that the part which stood out was that of Posa – a marginal and purely singing role. . . . Neither the quartet nor Posa's aria nor Eboli's have prime importance. These too are essentially episodic which can awake momentary interest but not lasting impressions. Applause is one thing, impression is another, and it is impression which fills a theatre. I know that the pieces I've mentioned are the ones which most easily bring out the rowdies in the front rows, who enjoy the sound of their own voices, the din of their own clapping and love to be able to say to the artist, 'Ah, what a success last night, I've no voice left . . . I've split a pair of gloves . . . it was I who prompted the fourth curtain call. . . .'

From the audience Verdi's diatribe passed to the present state of the Italian theatre.

> It is sick to the point of death and it must be kept alive at all costs. . . . Find operas – good or bad, it doesn't matter for the moment so long as they attract the public. You will say that this is unworthy, inartistic and 'soils the altar' [*after fifteen years he had still not forgotten*]; never mind, clean it afterwards. Once theatres are closed they will never open again. And if *Don Carlos* doesn't make money, put it aside and ask for *Le Roi de Lahore*, an opera of many virtues, an opera of our own day, not a human drama, eminently suited to this age of *Verismo* in which there is not a scrap of verity; an opera which is practically safe, especially if you have the composer there, who is a gentle creature and not too exacting and will make himself liked by the performers, the chorus and orchestra and, for this reason and that, the public. Then he's a foreigner!! . . . Hospitality!! . . . The usual artistic banquet. . . .†

Yet within a year of this comprehensive swipe at Boito, Massenet, the Italian public and the spirit of the age there began that long upward haul that was to lead from the

---

Libretti e librettisti verdiani dal punto di vista storico-bibliografico (Rome, 1941), has been confirmed by a letter to Ghislanzoni now in the possession of Mr Ralph Ferrandino of America; see Günther, Preface to *L'edizione integrale del Don Carlos di Giuseppe Verdi* (Milan, 1974), p. 23.

* Letter to Tornaghi, 8.9.1874. *Copialettere*, pp. 294–5.

† Letter to Faccio, ? January 1879. De Rensis, pp. 182–5.

revision of *Simon Boccanegra* to the final summits of *Otello* and *Falstaff*. The revised *Don Carlos* of 1882–4 was an important stage in the ascent.

The idea of reducing the opera to more manageable proportions first emerges in a letter of 1875 to the singing teacher Salvatore Marchesi, who was acting as intermediary between Verdi and the Viennese impresario Jauner over a proposed performance at the Kärntnerthor Theatre. 'I haven't yet replied to the House of Ricordi,' Verdi wrote, 'on the subject of *Don Carlos*; nevertheless I've been seriously thinking about it. I find it very difficult to make any cuts without doing as so many *maestri concertatori* do – whom I would rather call master butchers' [*lit. 'flayers'*]: as you will gather, I must not and will not do likewise. To cut this opera down to a more limited scale I need time to study it all and do what I did over *La Forza del destino*.'* But seven years were to pass before the subject was mentioned again, this time by Muzio in a letter to Giulio Ricordi. Verdi was about to come to Paris to help in straightening out the confusion in his French rights caused by the bankruptcy and death of Léon Escudier, under whose management the Théâtre des Italiens had failed, its building had been pulled down and its conductor, Muzio himself, deprived of a job. 'As to my inquiry about *Don Carlos*,' wrote Muzio, '[Verdi] writes back to me, "I would need a poet at my elbow and he would naturally have to be the original author. That is impossible." You know what du Locle, author of the words, did to him.'†

The story of what Camille du Locle had done to Verdi is set out in all its sad and unedifying detail by Ursula Günther in *Analecta Musicologica*, Vol. XIV.‡ In 1870 Verdi had been paid an instalment of 50,000 francs for the composition of *Aida*. Of these he donated 2,000 for the benefit of the French wounded at Sedan. The remainder he entrusted to du Locle to be invested in Italian government bonds ('cartelle di rendita italiana'), allowing du Locle possession of the certificates to serve as additional security for his newly undertaken direction of the Opéra-Comique. Five years later, Verdi needed the capital and certain arrears of interest for purposes of his own; but du Locle was not in a position to make restitution. Under his management the Opéra-Comique had fared badly, and in 1875 the total failure of Bizet's *Carmen*, on which he had set all his hopes, gave it the coup de grâce. Du Locle suffered a complete breakdown for which the only treatment, it seems, was a pleasure cruise to Egypt. But for the present Verdi did not despair of coming to a satisfactory arrangement. Du Locle's father-in-law was Emile Perrin, now director of the Comédie française. He was to assume financial liability for the affairs of the Opéra-Comique and might be expected to settle his son-in-law's more outstanding debts. As well as that du Locle had a very aged and wealthy aunt, the Comtesse Mollien, to whom he had more than once turned for help in difficulty. Meantime, however, a letter from Giuseppina Verdi to Marie du Locle, written in early April 1876, shows that a new element had entered the situation. 'To have stayed with your husband after the misfortunes which have befallen him and which perhaps were the cause of his illness was

* Letter to S. Marchesi, autumn 1875. Abbiati, III, pp. 777–8. See also Giuseppina's draft of 17.9.1875. *Carteggi Verdiani*, II, p. 45. Porter is surely correct in maintaining that Luzio's attribution of a similar suggestion to De Sanctis in 1872 is due to a mistranscription – see *R.M.A. Proceedings*, Vol. 98, p. 83 – 'ridurre' for 'ridare'.

† Letter from Muzio to Giulio Ricordi, Feb. 1882. Abbiati, IV, pp. 198–9.

‡ 'Der Briefwechsel Verdi–Nuitter–du Locle zur Revision des *Don Carlos*', Teil I, *Analecta Musicologica*, XIV (Cologne, 1974), pp. 1–31.

the duty of any woman of feeling, and that you have always been. To say that if he hadn't married you he wouldn't be in such a disastrous situation is to judge matters from an excess of grief which doesn't permit you to judge aright. Anyway, you have shown such courage in the past, try to be calm and not despair for the future . . . above all think of the future of your children. . . . Pay no attention to the world and its "on dits". . . .'* In other words Marie du Locle was about to leave her husband, and not all Giuseppina's tactful hints about her own worries and the need to bear them with fortitude could dissuade her. Du Locle was to spend the rest of his life in Rome and Capri; Marie remained in Paris with the children, where she obstructed all Verdi's attempts to recover his money on the grounds that it would leave her family unprovided for. All his lawyer's letters to her husband's relative were intercepted. Verdi tried to enlist the support of Escudier and even Perrin but without result. Eventually he had no alternative but to go to law. From notices in Escudier's journal *L'Art musical* it seems that the case was to be heard in August; but whether it ever came to court is doubtful, since there are no records of the proceedings. However, by October Verdi had clearly been indemnified to his satisfaction,† and at Giuseppina's suggestion considered devoting part of the sum to charitable purposes.‡ A further appeal from Marie du Locle in 1879 resulted in a remittance in her favour.§ One's heart bleeds, of course, for the poor absent du Locle; yet a man who can take refuge from his creditors on a Mediterranean cruise cannot be in a state of abject destitution.

Alas, this was not the only friendship in Verdi's life to founder during this period on the rocks of finance. In the spring of that same year, 1876, a storm blew up between him and Escudier over their respective rights in the French translation of *Aida*. Amongst the composer's other complaints was the fact that the text prepared by du Locle and Charles Nuitter was theatrically and musically false to the original, however correct it might be in the matter of rhyme and metre. These faults Verdi set out to remedy, together with Nuitter himself. After an exchange of letters, severely accusing on Verdi's part, woundedly innocent on Escudier's, a fresh contract was drawn up between them in the presence of witnesses,¶ and for a while correspondence between composer and publisher resumed its old cordiality, helped no doubt by the sustained success of *Aida* at the Théâtre Italien as well as Escudier's solicitude over the du Locle affair. But by the end of the year Escudier was no longer in a position to honour the terms of the new contract, and once more found himself the recipient of bitter, stinging reproaches ('In the midst of your many and complicated affairs you have certainly forgotten one which is quite tiny, indeed a real bagatelle . . . a residuum of 4,000 francs due from 15 November.')‖ But the debt remained unpaid, as did the much larger sum of 15,000 francs due in the New Year. Meanwhile, accounts came pouring in from Muzio of *Aidas* miserably cast and a general falling off of box-office receipts. A letter from Verdi written in late summer

---

* Letter from Giuseppina Verdi to Marie du Locle, undated (but drafted 4.4.1876). *Ibid.*, XIV, p. 14.

† See draft of letter to Cartier, 6.11.1876, entered in Giuseppina's *Copialettere. Ibid.*, p. 22.

‡ See Walker, p. 435.

§ See Günther, 'Der Briefwechsel Verdi–Nuitter–du Locle', Teil II. *An. Mus.*, XV (Cologne, 1975), pp. 398–401.

¶ See letter from Escudier, 18.5.1876. *An. Mus.*, XIV, p. 25. Letter to Escudier, 19.5.1876. Abbiati, III, pp. 801–2. Letter to T. Ricordi, 20.5.1876. *Ibid.*, p. 799.

‖ Letter to Escudier, undated (December 1876). Abbiati, IV, p. 29.

finally closed the accounts of their long friendship,* though not of their business dealings. When *Aida* in French at last reached the stage of the Paris Opéra, Escudier remained the proprietor. 'After long-standing ties of more than thirty years between publisher and composer, it's hard to break off,' Verdi wrote to Muzio. 'All those who now say he's a *fripon* would cry out against me were I to change my publisher. That's the way the world goes!'† When he came to Paris to direct the performances he avoided all contact with his old friend. A year later Escudier was dead. Characteristically Verdi contributed to a fund in aid of the distressed widow.

One person who throughout the various imbroglios had managed to remain on excellent terms with all parties was Charles-Louis-Etienne Truinet, *alias* Nuitter, archivist of the Paris Opéra and himself a librettist and translator of no mean skill. An amiable, respected yet curiously faceless figure, whose private life remained a sealed mystery, he enters the Verdian gallery almost unnoticed as part-translator of *Macbeth* in 1864–5. Next he appears as collaborator with du Locle on translations of *La Forza del destino* and *Aida*. He remained in correspondence with du Locle during the latter's voluntary exile. So, from Muzio to Ricordi, once more: 'I shall talk about *Don Carlos* to Nuitter, and when Verdi comes to Paris which I hope will be not later than 1 April I will have him assailed from all sides to get him to shorten it, and make it into an opera that will circulate throughout the world.'‡

Verdi was persuaded. He had already been in touch with Nuitter over certain adjustments made for the French *La Forza del destino*; he left Paris with Nuitter's scheme for a shortened *Don Carlos* without the Fontainebleau act. Meantime the Vienna project had evidently been revived. 'When I was in Paris,' he wrote to Maria Waldmann, 'I was approached by someone representing the management of the Vienna Opera about giving *Simon* and *Don Carlos*. No obstacle about *Simon*, but for *Don Carlos* I should like first to shorten it, naturally redoing a few passages here and there.'§ Later, to Piroli, in more jocular vein: 'In that city as you know the porters close the main gates of the houses at ten o'clock in the evening, by which time everyone is eating gâteaux and drinking beer. . . . Operas that are too long are savagely amputated. . . . Since my legs have to be cut off I prefer to sharpen and apply the knife myself.'¶ In fact Vienna was not to see *Don Carlos* until 1933 in a German translation by Franz Werfel and Lothar Wallerstein.

The revision proved a long and laborious business, lasting nearly nine months, that is twice the length of time taken over the far more radical reworking of *Simon Boccanegra*. Considering that the first and indeed practically all subsequent performances were to be in Italian it may seem odd that Verdi chose to collaborate indirectly with one of the original librettists instead of turning to a Boito or a Ghislanzoni, with whom he was on much friendlier terms. The reason is twofold. Firstly, he counted upon a circulation in France, which du Locle would have been in a position to obstruct if the new version had been made without his sanction. More important, *Don Carlos* was conceived from the start as a French opera, conditioned by French prosody and traditional French verse metres. In revising it to a French text for an

---

* Letter to Escudier, 9.8.1877. *R.M.I.*, XXXV (1928), p. 552.
† Letter to Muzio, 7.10.1879. *Copialettere*, pp. 312–13.
‡ Letter from Muzio to Giulio Ricordi, Feb.–March 1882. Abbiati, IV, p. 199.
§ Letter to M. Waldmann, 25.6.1882. *Carteggi Verdiani*, II, p. 255.
¶ Letter to Piroli, 3.12.1882. *Carteggi Verdiani*, III, pp. 158–9.

Italian première Verdi was doing in reverse what he had already done for *Macbeth* and for the same reason. His first Shakespearian opera was conceived in Italian and had to be remade to an Italian text before a French translation could be applied.

The three-cornered correspondence, scrupulously preserved by Nuitter in autograph or copy and now held in the Archives Nationales in Paris, has been published in *Analecta Musicologica*.* It is long and complicated by delays and crossed letters, with Nuitter content to act as a post office, never proffering suggestions of his own to either party once he had handed to Verdi a rough scheme for the opera's abridgement. Next he despatched to S. Agata a copy of the original libretto. Verdi studied it in conjuction with the scheme and wrote back with his immediate objections. '. . . It isn't enough to cut here and there; there's something more to say and to explain. I must tell you again that the duo between Posa and Philippe is always a *black spot*. I would say the same about the Monk/Charles V. . . .'† A few days later: 'Charles V alive has always shocked me. If he's alive how can it be that Carlos doesn't know? Besides, if he's alive, how could Philip be an old man, as he says he is? This is an imbroglio which will certainly have to be unravelled.'‡ Rather than leave him half-man, half-ghost, could they not make the monk an old confrère of Charles V who has come to pray at his tomb? As for the Philip–Posa duet, that would have to be redone completely and given a different form. In a long memorandum§ du Locle addressed himself to both problems. He defended the appearance of Charles V on a number of counts. Although he died in 1558 there would be nothing inconsistent in prolonging the Emperor's life for another ten years, considering the number of liberties Schiller himself had taken with history throughout the play. What is more Charles V did in fact make a mystery of his last years by ordering his own funeral and, like Puccini's Edgar, attending it in the guise of a monk. It would be quite natural for both Philip and Carlos to be in some doubt as to whether he were alive or no. More important, dramatically, was that the final appearance of the Emperor in propria persona was prepared by what in the revision would become the opening scene. If there were to be no such appearance and if the monk were to be a monk like any other that opening scene would lose all its grandeur and significance. He (du Locle) was all for making Charles V intervene at the end like a deus ex machina in a classical tragedy, preferably in full imperial regalia.

For the Philip–Posa duet no radical change of sentiment was possible; but they might be able to change it from a string of short cantabili into a dramatic dialogue like that between Philip and the Grand Inquisitor.

These and various other suggestions Verdi mulled over for several weeks before replying. He agreed to leave in the appearance of Charles V 'despite the small liking I have for this half-fantastic character' (du Locle had still not made it clear whether he was alive or a ghost);¶ also that the Posa–Philip relationship could retain its original content under a different form. With these two preliminary hurdles cleared away the

---

* *An. Mus.*, XV (Cologne, 1975), 'Der Briefwechsel Verdi–Nuitter–du Locle zur Revision des *Don Carlos*', Teil II. 'Die Dokumente herausgegeben von Gabriella Carrara Verdi und Ursula Günther. Einleitung und Anmerkungen von Ursula Günther', pp. 334–401.

† Letter to Nuitter, 9.6.1882. *An. Mus.*, XV, p. 349.

‡ Letter to Nuitter, 14.6.1882. *Ibid.*, pp. 349–50.

§ 'Note sur des projets de modification au libretto de *Don Carlos*'. *Ibid.*, pp. 350–2.

¶ Letter to Nuitter, 21.9.1882. *Ibid.*, p. 353.

revision could now begin to take shape. In summarizing it we will for the sake of clarity take the affected passages in the order in which they occur in the score rather than in the correspondence.

Nuitter's scheme began with a combination of contrasted choruses à la Meyerbeer, the monks chanting in the cathedral, the people acclaiming the King and Queen as in the Fontainebleau act ('O chants de fêtes et d'allégresse').* But after a while Verdi decided against this, even though it had been his own idea. 'Now I realize that the contrast is too violent and the effect overdone to no purpose. Besides it destroys the solemnity of the scene.'† So the opening of the original Act II (now Act I) would stand as it was and the departure of the monks would be followed by the entrance of Carlos. In the second of his letters, Verdi had insisted that at this point Carlos should explain his feelings of love for Elisabeth to whom he was betrothed. . . . 'Souvenir de Fontainebleau, and perhaps, I say perhaps I will have him sing (to other words) the romance that was in the first act, "Je l'ai vue, etc." But even this has its disadvantages.'‡ Later: 'If the poet wants to colour the last two lines more strongly I would change the final bars.'§ In the event he was to change a good deal more. The following duet between Carlos and Posa was to be drastically reduced. 'From the first movement I would cut out everything that is purely musical and keep in only what is strictly necessary for the dramatic situation up to the words "Ton sécret par le Roi s'est-il laissé surprendre".'¶ In effect this meant turning the movement into a mere scena, as he made clear in a subsequent letter.‖ For the start of the second scene du Locle had suggested removing Thibaud, since with the Fontainebleau act cut he had no function in the dramatic scheme. Verdi, however, preferred to keep him in for musical reasons – to take part in Eboli's Veil Song as well as the concertato of Act II (formerly III).

Less easily solved was the problem of the Posa–Philip duet. 'On rereading Schiller,' Verdi wrote, 'I find one or two phrases which make a most powerful impression and a huge theatrical effect.' He then subjoined various lines from the dialogue in Maffei's translation with the comment that there was no question here of writing 'cantabili' and 'tunes' for which any lines would do.** But when the new text arrived Verdi found it dull and diffuse. It would do well enough in a spoken play, he said, 'But as we're dealing with musical work, we've got to make as much of this blessed music as we can, and I can't find anything to get hold of to make at least a few musical sentences.'†† If only operas could be written to unrhymed verse! To illustrate his point he drafted out a part of the scene in a macaronic blend of French and Italian with indications of where he wanted the accent placed and where he would like a further shortening. Before du Locle could reply he proposed another cut earlier in the duet in which he felt, reasonably enough, that Posa had talked too boldly to his King too soon.‡‡ This was a simple matter of surgery, which gave no problem. For

---

* See Nuitter's draft. *Ibid.*, pp. 347–8.
† Letter to Nuitter, 13.10.1882. *Ibid.*, p. 363.
‡ Letter to Nuitter, 14.6.1882. *Ibid.*, pp. 349–50.
§ Letter to Nuitter, 21.9.1882. *Ibid.*, p. 353.
¶ *Ibid.*
‖ Letter to Nuitter, 23.9.1882. *Ibid.*, pp. 353–4.
** Letter to Nuitter, 28.9.1882. *Ibid.*, pp. 355–7.
†† Letter to Nuitter, 28.10.1882. *Ibid.*, pp. 364–6.
‡‡ Letter to Nuitter, 1.11.1882. *Ibid.*, pp. 367–8.

the rest of the duet du Locle sent a new draft in which certain words were underlined in red, which meant that though printed in the libretto they could be omitted in the score – a practice often adopted by Scribe, he said, in the operas written for Meyerbeer.* With this solution Verdi professed himself entirely satisfied and announced, 'The most difficult part is over and done with.'†

For the start of Act II (formerly III) no alterations were at first envisaged. It would merely be a matter of removing the ballet for the Italian stages and joining together in a single tableau the scene where Elisabeth and Eboli exchange masks and that in which Carlos reads the letter summoning him to a tryst in the gardens.‡ Later it occurred to Verdi that if the ballet were cut the exchanging of the masks would be unnecessary. 'So where should we begin? Has the poet nothing to add? Will a few bars of prelude be enough?'§ Du Locle, however, was in favour of keeping the Elisabeth–Eboli duo but of cutting Carlos's reading of the letter; and he pointed out that if the meeting between him and Eboli could appear to be fortuitous this would be a way of softening Eboli's character and making her more sympathetic to the audience.¶ But Verdi held obstinately to his opinion. He did not like the music of that opening scene particularly and he felt it added nothing to the dramatic situation. 'As to making Eboli appear less odious, I'm always of the opinion that even the most odious characters must be shown to the public for what they are. Eboli is not and cannot be anything but a coquine! Indeed if she's presented as such it becomes more exciting when she reveals her crimes to the Queen.'‖ If du Locle thought it necessary for Eboli to be disguised as the Queen (and he himself had never been in favour of this idea) then the matter could be explained in the course of the duet. But he would prefer to begin with a new prelude followed by the entrance of Carlos reading the letter.** To this du Locle made no objection.†† But it is worth noting that in a subsequent letter to Giulio Ricordi, Verdi insisted that when the ballet was performed the new prelude should be replaced by the changing of the masks.‡‡ 'In the fourth act (now the third) I shall alter a few musical passages in the quartet, but the poet will have nothing to do.'§§ Six weeks later he had changed his mind. 'In the . . . scene between the King and Queen I find the verses of the Queen's solo feeble, and the music more feeble still. We should change both lines and music. I would like the Queen to speak out with more boldness. . . . "You well know that I was betrothed to Don Carlos. . . . And can you doubt me . . . a daughter of France and the Queen of Spain!"' This would of course bring her nearer to Schiller's Elisabeth who, when accused by Philip of adultery in the presence of her own small daughter, reacts with dignity and a veiled threat to seek redress abroad. Nor was that all. 'In the aria afterwards for Eboli there's a point in Schiller that we've passed over and which I

---

* See note from du Locle and letter from Nuitter, 12.11.1882. *Ibid.*, pp. 369–72.
† Letter to Nuitter, 16.11.1882. *Ibid.*, pp. 372–3.
‡ See note from du Locle. *Ibid.*, p. 352.
§ Letter to Nuitter, 16.11.1882. *Ibid.*, pp. 372–3.
¶ Note from du Locle, undated. *Ibid.*, p. 375.
‖ Letter to Nuitter, 1.12.1882. *Ibid.*, pp. 375–6.
** Letters to Nuitter, 15.12.1882 and 8.1.1883. *Ibid.*, pp. 384–5.
†† Letter from Nuitter, 19.1.1883. *Ibid.*, pp. 387–8.
‡‡ Letter to Giulio Ricordi, 22.3.1883. Abbiati, IV, pp. 213–14.
§§ Letter to Nuitter, 14.10.1882. *Ibid.*, p. 364.

find fine and very important.'* He meant of course Eboli's confession of her adultery with Philip which had been cut before the première of 1867; and he copied out part of the original libretto, interspersing the lines with others taken from Maffei's translation of the play. The first variants sent by du Locle failed to satisfy him. 'The fault is certainly due to the rhyme, to the masculine endings and feminine endings which have obliged du Locle to write four lines merely to say, "I was the fiancée of Don Carlos". One might just as well leave in the eight lines of the old libretto. But I suggested that change because I wanted to remove that stupid cantabile in the old score and write instead something declamatory and energetic; first because Elisabeth's role is throughout an inward one, and here she could be given a phrase in which to show her teeth. Secondly, because after having found her jewel-case broken into and the letters from Don Carlos stolen Elisabeth should be upset and very angry and I find the words "Et que Dieu fit" which give a feeling of resignation quite out of place. To conclude: a mere four long alexandrine verses will do for me. Proud and forceful; the last of which should run: "Moi! fille de Valois! Moi la Reine de France [sic]!" The actress would have the chance of a good yell, which would not be beautiful poetically or musically, but it would be theatrical. And as you know only too well, my dear Nuitter, when you write for the theatre you have to make theatre.'† In reply du Locle supplied three variants of which Verdi, somewhat inconsistently, set the longest. Eboli's confession took longer to shape ('Oh, composers, composers! What a scourge for poor poets!').‡ And it was Verdi himself who worked out the definitive text, which du Locle accepted.§

The next problem was where to end the second scene of the new Act III. At first sight it seemed sensible to ring down the curtain with the death of Posa, as had been common practice since the first night, until Verdi noticed that in that case the last words of Eboli's aria ('Un jour me reste! Je le sauverai!') would make no sense. So should they remake the 'sommossa' in a very abbreviated form? 'I am completely undecided. Let me know your view together with du Locle's.'¶ But before Nuitter could reply it seems that Verdi had made up his mind more or less. 'If du Locle thinks the sommossa is necessary it could be done but it must go presto, prestissimo, prestississimo, vite, vite, vite, vite, vite, vite up to the end for many reasons.

'First: because it can't have much musical interest.

'Second: because it would be impossible to leave Posa lying on the ground for any length of time after he has sung a very tiring aria.'‖ And in two successive drafts he indicated the lines he would like to use, once more drawing on Maffei/Schiller for those which did not exist in the original libretto. A fortnight later he raised the question again: should they or should they not redo the 'sommossa'? But this was in a letter which he forgot to post for a month** and in the meantime du Locle sent the necessary verses.†† Verdi decided that with the addition or suppression of a word

---

* Letter to Nuitter, 30.11.1882. *Ibid.*, pp. 373–4.
† Letter to Nuitter, 15.12.1882. *Ibid.*, p. 384.
‡ Letter to Nuitter, 26.1.1883. *Ibid.*, p. 389.
§ Note from du Locle. *Ibid.*, p. 390.
¶ Letter to Nuitter, 30.11.1882. *Ibid.*, pp. 373–4.
‖ Letter to Nuitter, 2–3.12.1882. *Ibid.*, pp. 376–8.
** See letters to Nuitter, 15.12.1882. *Ibid.*, p. 384.
†† Note from du Locle, undated. *Ibid.*, pp. 382–3.

here and there they would do.* But it was not until February that du Locle was able to send him a version that he found satisfactory.†

In the last act it had been agreed from the start that the opening of the scena between Carlos and Elisabeth should be shortened in conformity with the version of 1872.‡ Next Verdi decided that the final scene with the inquisitors should also be reduced,§ then that it would have to go altogether since 'it prolongs the action and slackens the interest'.¶ He drafted out the lines he needed with the usual help from Maffei's translation. 'I realize,' he added, 'there's a disadvantage here. There are no choruses in the last two acts.' (Evidently he had forgotten about the 'sommossa'.) 'So much the better as far as I'm concerned! You can breathe a little when you haven't these everlasting *masses* on your stomach! All the same it is a disadvantage! What do you think?' Neither du Locle nor Nuitter had any fault to find with this arrangement provided the composer himself was happy with it. ‖ Lastly, Verdi decided at some point to reinstate in modified form the Allegro marziale, which is the second of the two movements that he had removed in 1872; but there is no mention of this in the correspondence. In dispatching this final act to Ricordi he quashed in advance any doubts his publisher might entertain about the propriety of the changes.

Don't be too surprised to see the Chorus of Inquisitors removed. It was mere note-spinning. The drama didn't need either those notes or those words. On the contrary – once events had reached this pass the curtain should have fallen quickly.

Philip has nothing further to say.

Elisabeth can only die and as quickly as possible.

The Inquisitors have only to lay hands on Don Carlos. Charles V appears robed as Emperor!! It isn't very likely. The Emperor had been dead a number of years. But in this drama, so splendid in form and in its highminded concepts, everything is false.

Don Carlos was a fool, a madman, an unpleasant fellow.

Elisabeth was never in love with Don Carlos.

Posa is an imaginary being who could never have existed under Philip's reign.

Philip, who amongst other things says:

> Garde-toi de mon Inquisiteur . . .
> Qui me rendra ce mort!

Philip wasn't as soft-hearted as that.

In other words in this drama there is nothing historical, nor is there any Shakespearian truth or profundity . . . so one thing more or less won't do any harm; and I myself don't mind this appearance of the old Emperor. What do you think?'**

* Letter to Nuitter, 26.1.1883. *Ibid.*, p. 389.
† See letter to Nuitter, 23.2.1883. *Ibid.*, pp. 394–5.
‡ See Nuitter's scheme. *Ibid.*, p. 348.
§ Letter to Nuitter, 14.10.1882. *Ibid.*, p. 364.
¶ Letter to Nuitter, 6.12.1882. *Ibid.*, pp. 378–80.
‖ Letter from Nuitter, 19.1.1883. *Ibid.*, pp. 387–8.
** Letter to Giulio Ricordi, 19.2.1883. *Ibid.*, p. 340.

Meanwhile all that remained to be done was to settle with du Locle via Nuitter the ownership of the libretto outside France, and here it is pleasant to record that Verdi offered to bury the hatchet and shake his old collaborator by the hand if ever they should meet in Rome or Paris. The two men remained in cordial correspondence as late as 1894.

The new score was complete in March, but had to wait for January the following year for its first performance at La Scala. The new lines had been Italianized by Angelo Zanardini, who also revised the original translation by De Lauzières.* Apart from insisting that the three basses, Philip, the Inquisitor and the Monk, should all be of the highest quality since all had the same importance both musically and theatrically,† and that especial attention should be paid to enunciation and correct tempo – 'qualities that are more essential in *Don Carlos* than in any of my other operas'‡ – Verdi concerned himself not at all with the casting and only minimally with the rehearsals. Of the principals only Tamagno was in any way outstanding, though the new Eboli, Giuseppina Pasqua, would nine years later score a notable success as Mistress Quickly. But Verdi himself was satisfied. On completing the revision he had already told Arrivabene that he believed that the cuts, far from damaging the original, had improved it – had given it 'more concision, more muscle'.§ After the first performance, Arrivabene, echoing more than one critic, asked the composer whether he did not feel 'remorse or at least regret at having sacrificed so much of what was there before'.¶ Verdi, however, held stoutly to his opinion, adding with perhaps a touch of irritation, 'Of course, those who are dissatisfied on principle, that is to say the subscription holders, are complaining that the first act, whose music they say is so beautiful, is no longer there. It is "very beautiful" now; then they quite probably didn't notice its existence.'‖ Yet by implication Verdi was to change his mind yet again; for nearly three years later Ricordi's *Gazzetta Musicale di Milano* reported on a performance given in Modena on 29 December 1886 in which the four-act version was given together with the Fontainebleau act and the tenor romance restored to its original position and form. This new edition was described as being 'allowed and approved by the illustrious author'. The following year it appeared in print. That this version should have been published without Verdi's express wish is unthinkable, though how the decision was arrived at we shall never know until the relevant correspondence comes to light. Meanwhile, it must be taken as representing the composer's last thoughts on the matter; and with it the twenty-year Odyssey of *Don Carlos* comes to an end, leaving several loose ends and several problems unsolved.

No other opera of Verdi's contains such a wealth of alternative and superseded material, so little of which can be dismissed out of hand. It has already provided a treasure trove for researchers and Verdi students and will doubtless continue to do so for years to come. Allowing for various permutations and combinations we may for the purpose of this analysis recognize five basic versions: (1) the original full-length

* Both translators prefer Isabella, the Spanish equivalent of Elisabeth, to the five-syllabled Italian Elisabetta.

† Letter to Giulio Ricordi, 30.6.1883. Abbiati, IV, pp. 217–18.

‡ Letter to Giulio Ricordi, 15.12.1883. *Ibid.*, pp. 224–5.

§ Letter to Arrivabene, 15.3.1883. Alberti, p. 300.

¶ Letter from Arrivabene, 25.1.1884. *Ibid.*, pp. 304–5.

‖ Letter to Arrivabene, 29.1.1884. *Ibid.*, pp. 305–6.

conception of 1866 preceding the cuts made before the first performance; (2) *Don Carlos* as published in 1867 with five acts and ballet; (3) the Naples version of 1872, identical with (2) except for the alterations in the Posa–Philip and final Carlos–Elisabeth duets; (4) the new four-act version without ballet of 1884; and (5) the Modena amalgam of 1886, published by Ricordi as 'new edition in five acts without ballet'. All five will be referred to by their respective dates. Finally there are two 'disposizioni sceniche' in existence – one for the 1867 version 'compilata e regolata secondo la mise-en-scène del Teatro Imperiale dell'Opera di Parigi', and a so-called 'terza edizione' published about twenty years later in grand format and corresponding to the Modena score.* No second edition, presumably belonging to the 1884 version, has yet come to light.

ACT I

Scene: The Forest of Fontainebleau. Winter. On the right a huge rock forms a kind of cave. Backstage in the distance, the royal palace. It is snowing.†

Prelude and Introduction (1866): Woodcutters, their wives and children. Some are engaged in chopping felled oaks. Others cross the stage carrying bundles, pieces of wood and work tools.

This is the longest and arguably the most valuable of the passages struck out before the first performance – a magnificent evocation of winter and hardship. There is nothing problematic about its reinstatement since the original material is complete; and above all it gives the foresters and their wives a reason for being present since they have something to sing. The action is of the simplest. First there is a long chorus in which all complain of the misery caused by winter and the war with Spain. Sounds of the royal hunt are heard in the distance; the Princess Elisabeth approaches with her suite. The women decide to appeal to her well-known kindness ('Elle est aussi bonne que belle'); they present to her an old widow who has lost two sons in the war (at the battle of St-Quentin, so one of the draft libretti informs us). The Princess gives her a golden chain and promises a speedy end to hostilities; even now, she says, the Spanish envoy is on his way to Paris to ask for her hand in marriage to the Infante of Spain. The woodcutters and their wives call down blessings on her head, as the royal fanfares fade away in the distance.

Had they been able to hear this scene the Parisian critics would doubtless have invoked the name of Wagner again; and Verdi himself would once more have been able to point to his earlier operas for instances of the same 'intenzioni' – not, however, to *Ernani* or *Macbeth* but rather to *Giovanna d'Arco*, which opens with just such an introduction; a richly woven orchestral prelude, a minor-key chorus, fragmented and in dialogue, that gathers itself up into a long choral period in the major. Needless to say its counterpart in *Don Carlos* is on a far grander scale and its components are correspondingly more various. Both pieces begin with two parallel statements; but in *Don Carlos* they no longer need the strict symmetry of the earlier work. The second statement is here an expansion of the first.

---

* A copy of the first can be found in the Brera Library, Milan, and of the second in the Library of the Milan Conservatory.

† *The floor should be spread with a cloth depicting snow, with footprints, paths, etc. etc.* (*Disp. scen.* (1867), p. 3; (1886), p. 5.)

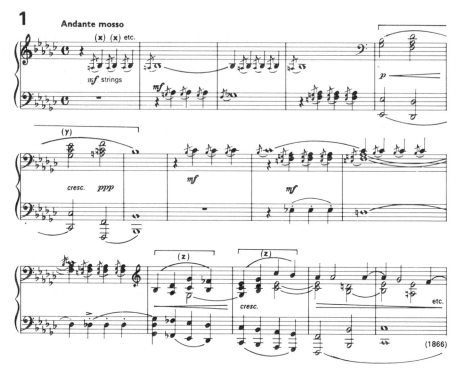

(1866)

The generating motif (x) is the acciaccatura figure used in its most basic musical sense as a lament, and building up with a weary insistence into a succession of chords. Throughout we are given the feeling of men moving slowly and laboriously about their work, occasionally pausing to draw a moment's breath. But the branches must be hewn and the cold kept at bay. So, to a new idea, the axes are swung and the forest echoes to their blows.

(1866)

Throughout the prelude the dramatic associations of each motif reach far beyond the immediate scene. The 'laments' of Ex. 1 will dominate the opera's centrepiece, King Philip's soliloquy. The minim chords (y) anticipate the sepulchral atmosphere of the preludes to Acts II and V outside the Monastery of St-Just; while the four-note pattern of (z) will recur in many of the opera's principal themes almost in the manner of an Urgestalt. The brutality of the Inquisition sounds in Ex. 2 with its sudden bursts of unison brass. In other words, Verdi was establishing the opera's 'tinta' at the outset, aided thereto by the special resources afforded by the Paris Opéra: two cornets to reinforce the trumpets, and four bassoons to lend extra resonance to lower regions – an effect of which the composer was to avail himself again in the Requiem and *Otello*.

The opening choral exchanges ('L'hiver est long. . . . La vie est dure') are bleakly unmelodic; all the musical interest lies in the orchestra, which weaves patterns of grief beneath the chanting of the sopranos ('Hélas, quand finira la guerre?'); only when the contraltos take over ('Et nos fils dans notre chaumière') does the line take on a lyrical expressiveness. But there is work to be done; back therefore to Ex. 2 wrought into a pattern of rising sequences each crowned by the women's cry of 'Hélas', until a figure of *Giovanna*-like triplets in the orchestra ushers in the main theme of the introduction, corresponding to 'Maledetti cui spinge rea voglia' in the earlier opera.

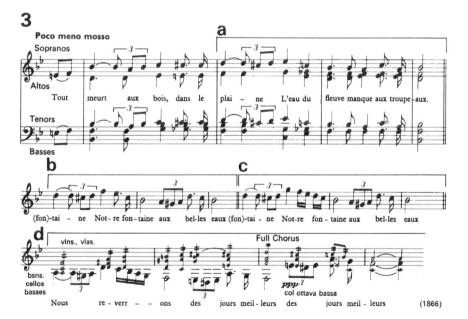

Characteristically, what has been a bold, somewhat inflexible eight-bar phrase of generalized emotional content in *Giovanna d'Arco* is in *Don Carlos* a mere four bars more restrained in mood and sensitively harmonized. Yet one result of the improvement is that a split opens up between the verbal and musical sense. For while the verse continues to speak of misery and hardship, as well as giving us a lesson in etymology ('Et l'hiver glace la fontaine, *notre fontaine aux belles eaux*' – i.e., Fontainebleau), the music indicates the beginning of a long ascent towards courage and hope, to be built on recurrences of Ex. 3 progressively varied by wider melodic contours, a more active bass line, a more rapid harmonic rhythm, and finally – and most subtly of all – by its repositioning in the musical paragraph. It accounts for the first, second and fourth lines in the present strophe in the form of (a), (b) and (c) respectively. Only the third phrase returns briefly to the stress of Ex. 2; after which a two-bar extension both recovers the sense of optimism and at the same time saves the paragraph itself from squareness. There is a brief episode in which four basses in unison urge the men to work hard for their families' sake and to hope for peace and better days. This too ends with Ex. 3, now in the dominant, and harmonized from above by tremolando strings with a curiously poignant veering towards D minor, corrected by the full chorus as they echo the last 'des jours meilleurs' in a dream-like murmur (Ex. 3d).

Suddenly distant fanfares are heard with a theme that will be familiar to all who know the opera as performed today.

The stage band score does not specify the instruments employed, but the men of the chorus make it clear enough. (Basses: 'Entendez-vous? Les trompes sonnent!' Tenors: 'Entendez-vous? Les cors resonnent!') Trumpets, then, to the left, horns and a brass bass to the right – an antiphony foreshadowing the 'Hunt' scherzo in Bruckner's Fourth Symphony. Each group is matched by an offstage chorus of huntsmen. 'Que le sort des rois est heureux!' cry the woodmen and their wives in unison. A galloping figure on an expectant G major chord announces that the hunt is coming their way. At Elisabeth's entrance, accompanied by the page Thibault, several lords of the court and the ever mute Countess Aremberg,* it is the contraltos of the main chorus who present to her the widow in one of those short but telling solos into which Verdi crams a wealth of sorrow through a skilful deployment of the most traditional figures. The lower voices presumably represent the older women, the sopranos their daughters.

---

* See U. Günther, *Atti del II° Congresso del I.S.V.*, p. 99.

5

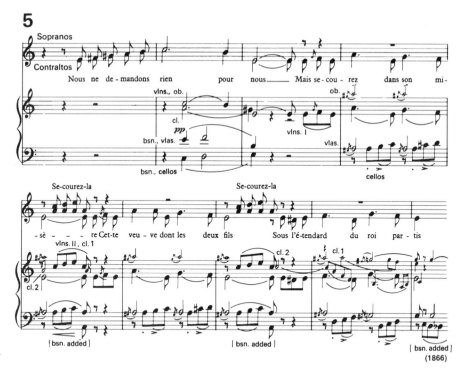

The princess's gift and her words of hope are conveyed in arioso recitative studded with a few gracious triplets and enhanced by a melting key-change from C to A flat ('. . . de beaux jours pour nous luiront encore') and a long, swooping conclusion ('. . . renaîtront, renaîtront les bienfaits'). The vast choral paragraph which follows begins with an entirely new idea ('Noble dame, que Dieu vous donne') which, with its prominence of plangent wind tone and G minor tonality, suggests that the chorus have tears in their eyes; and of course there is a fine irony in their wish that the

6 Allegro moderato

princess may be granted a 'young bridegroom, a crown', as though the two were inseparable.

By a stroke of unexpected logic the answer to Ex. 6 is given by Ex. 3c to which a striding bass line, not to mention the inevitable shifting of the anacrusis to the fourth beat, imparts a new air of confidence: there is a brief restatement of Ex. 4 by way of parenthesis; then Ex. 3d makes as if to conclude the period. But the final cadence is interrupted to prolong itself in a sequence of revolving dominant sevenths (an effect repeated less happily in the *auto da fé* scene) while the fanfares of Ex. 4 blast in from the *coulisses*. As they fade away in the distance the music moves into a codetta of swaggering triplets ending in one of those cadential phrases which to an audience of today always connotes *Tannhäuser* or *Lohengrin* but which is in fact nothing more than mid-century French grand-opera cliché. Unusually for 1866 the scoring is unashamedly 'banda-like'.

(1866)

The scene now winds down to a *piano* as the woodmen and their womenfolk disperse. Faraway fanfares are answered by a last statement on the strings of Ex. 3, epitomized in two bars with caressing harmonies on each note. A clutch of applause-soliciting tutti chords bring the introduction to a close.

As a piece of musical architecture it is quite remarkable. All the more surprising therefore to notice that it is founded on the unorthodox tonal plan of E flat minor–B flat major, the same as that of the tenor romanza from *Oberto* ('Ciel che feci') —a useful lesson, this, for any writer who may have been tempted to ascribe it to the composer's immaturity. Here, at least, there is no question that the progress from the original minor key to dominant rather than tonic major emphasizes that sense of proceeding from darkness to light which Verdi achieved independently of his librettists; for the draft libretto ended with a reprise of the opening line ('L'hiver est long', etc. . . . .) which he wisely suppressed.*

* Günther, *op. cit.*, p. 101.

ACT I (1867, 1872, 1886)

Scene: Some foresters are cutting wood; their wives are seated round a large fire. Elisabeth de Valois enters L. on horseback escorted by Thibault, her page. A numerous following of huntsmen. Elisabeth crosses the stage to the sound of fanfares and throws money to the foresters. Don Carlos appears L. hidden among the trees. The foresters gaze at the retreating princess, and, taking up their tools, set forth on their way and disperse along the paths at the back. *

Here the events of the omitted prelude are compressed into a brief mime of fifty-four bars, *allegro brillante*. Musically, it is a miniature rondo with Ex. 4 as its main theme, played first by two sets of offstage horns in alternating phrases; then reinforced by the double male chorus; and finally by both vocal and instrumental groups together.† The episodes are formed from the galloping triplets which heralded Elisabeth's approach in the introduction. Dramatically and musically it is no more than a blackboard demonstration of what Verdi had been forced to suppress. Elisabeth is shown as a lady bountiful, but no kind words accompany her actions and no gratitude is expressed by the woodmen, who might well be forgiven for resenting such offhand patronage. The only advantage offered by the new opening is that building up from casual beginnings to mighty ends which is a feature of many a French grand opera – notably *Le Prophète*.

(*All five-act versions.*) To a clarinet figure coiling up from the chalumeau register Carlos steps out of hiding. His opening utterance ('Fontainebleau, forêt immense et solitaire') establishes him at once as a tenor of sensibility, of a dreamy inwardness quite foreign to the Rodolfos and Manricos of Verdi's Italian operas. Only the Henri of 'O jour de peine' in *Les Vêpres Siciliennes* approaches him in vocal character, as he addresses the vast and lonely forest whose frozen aspect is worth all the summer gardens in the world since it has seen the smiling Elisabeth pass by. It is all pure declamation without any trace of a formed melody; but there is no reliance here on recitative cliché. Every phrase reflects the prince's mood, half rapt, half melancholy. But as soon as Carlos tells us that he has left the court of Madrid, risking his father's anger, an abrupt figure quietly raises its head in the orchestra as if to warn us from which quarter the tragedy will arrive. The lower register of the clarinet is enough to suggest that faint chilling of the spine that puts the listener on his guard. (Ex. 8) It is, of course, the 'terrible colère' of Philip on the horizon; yet it cannot be called a leitmotif. It will recur only once, but at a highly significant moment.

The recitative concluded, the solo clarinet proceeds to furnish the bass of Carlos's cavatine 'Je l'ai vue et dans son sourire', his only solo in the opera. The text is no more than an avowal of love at first sight and of faith in a happy future. But evidently the 'first sight' was important to Verdi since he rejected the original strophe beginning

---

* The production books specify Elisabeth's escort as follows: *Enter from the wings: 4 valets on foot, Thibault, Elisabeth (mounted), 2 valets (mounted), 4 valets on foot. Disp. scen.* (1867), p. 5. Curiously the foresters' wives are not mentioned as being present, but only an old peasant woman who is the recipient of Elisabeth's bounty.

† Once again the instruments of the band are unspecified; but the printed material supplied for the Modena edition is for five horns. In 1867 the first two would surely have been trumpets, as in the omitted introduction. At what point this was changed, and whether the change was made with Verdi's knowledge or consent, is still a matter of conjecture.

with the vaguer 'Mon âme est pleine d'espérance' for one which opens with the present words.*

* Günther, *op. cit.*, p. 104.

The rhythmic cut of the melody is characteristic of Meyerbeerian grand opera with its smooth, marching rhythm, its lifting of the second semi-phrase in the manner of *Les Vêpres Siciliennes*. But the form, far from being the expected French ternary, is an old-fashioned a^1-a^2-b-a^2 complete with coda and a rest for the voice at the start of the third phrase. The effect of such apparent reversions (compare Alvaro's 'No, d'un imene il vincolo') is to suggest an essentially simple nature beneath sophisticated trappings. As in the play, Carlos, for all his scheming, is a guileless boy at heart. Yet the antiquated form does not preclude a very precise definition of his present mood – witness the *schwärmerisch* upward-reaching gestures combined with moving chromatic inner parts, the perfect expression of a young man in love with love.

10

As usual, an enrichment of the harmonic palette engenders a new subtlety of scoring; so that where once we should have expected a string accompaniment with sustaining wind at the points of harmonic emphasis, here it is the wind instruments that provide the scaffolding and the strings that underline the important contours with varieties of arco and pizzicato. Tradition, however, prevails in the coda with its valedictory phrases played first by oboe and clarinet, then repeated with added flute and tremolando strings throughout.

The fanfares of Ex. 4, fragmented by distance, prompt Carlos to further recitative. The hunt is now far away. Night is falling, and the first stars shimmer (violins tremolando); how will Carlos find his way to the palace in the evening mist? Just then the voice of Thibault the page is heard calling to the woodmen for help. A steady throbbing starts up in the strings, soon reinforced by galloping triplets. But the two figures who enter – Thibault and Elisabeth – are on foot. A viola shudder on each crotchet indicates that both are cold and frightened, having lost their way. Thibault wishes to press on, but Elisabeth is desperately tired. All at once the page sees with alarm Don Carlos standing by. Carlos explains that he is a Spaniard. 'One of the Count of Lerma's suite?' Elisabeth hazards. His answer is interrupted by Thibault who has just seen the lights of the palace in the distance and now proposes to run there at once and fetch an escort. Elisabeth agrees to this; the noble Spaniard will protect her meanwhile. Exit, therefore, Thibault. In all this scena he is given the nearest approximation to a formed melody ('O bonheur sous la nuit claire') since he alone has a definite plan of action. The other two are merely improvising.

It is in this feeling for the natural that Verdi's break with the Parisian grand opera can be most clearly sensed. He had already thrown out Méry's original idea of presenting the encounter as a formal duet between Elisabeth and Thibault which turns into a trio at the intervention of Carlos. Here Elisabeth was enjoying her strange predicament, lost in a forest at night – just the time to meet a fairy prince! That this solution should have been thought appropriate is a measure of the extent to which Meyerbeer's encyclopedic methods, designed as they were to grab the audience's attention at all costs, blurred the distinction between the serious and the comic. 'What delight to be lost in a wood!' might do for the heroine of *L'Etoile du Nord* or *Le Pardon de Ploërmel*, still more for the lady in Offenbach's *Robinson Crusoe* who, about to be eaten by cannibals, thinks nothing of breaking into a waltz song at the footlights. It would lower Elisabeth's stature at once.

The same naturalness marks the following duet ('Que faites-vous donc?'). Its opening is in the manner of polite conversation, with a bow and a curtsey in every gesture of the string introduction.

The music proceeds on the two levels of 'Malerei' and 'Ausdruck der Empfindung' – to use Beethoven's terms. Carlos is making a fire of dead brushwood (Ex. 12a) from which in due course the flames begin to flicker (Ex. 12b).*

* It is tempting on the basis of Ex. 12a, in whose sound there is no trace of flint, to claim Carlos as the first Boy Scout who kindles a fire by rubbing two twigs together. Alas, the production books make it clear that he is merely gathering twigs off the ground, breaking them, throwing them on the brazier left by the foresters and finally fanning them into flame with his breath. See *Disp. scen.* (1867), p. 7; (1886), p. 8.

But there is also a note of mild alarm in Ex. 12a which is at once soothed by the caressing phrases of Ex. 11, while the access of warmth in Ex. 12b is spiritual no less than physical, emphasized by the delicately glowing colours of sustaining wind. If Carlos's talk of camp fires as symbols of victory or love is a mere piece of French frippery, it is acceptable in its context since at this point the conversation must appear quite uninvolved. Only when to a variant of Ex. 12b Carlos steers it towards Elisabeth's marriage and the key of E flat major is there an obvious quickening of interest. Elisabeth begs to know more about her bridegroom; and the duet enters a new

phase as she finds herself opening her heart to this sympathetic stranger. Twice, in a period of gradually soaring phrases poised on a typical axis of F minor–A♭–F major, she voices feelings that hover between apprehension and hope; twice, with increasing ardour, Carlos gives her reassurance. His tone of voice she finds strangely moving. There is an *allegro agitato* transition full of string tremoli shifting chromatically in a tonal limbo, during which Carlos, acting the prince's envoy, gives Elisabeth a sealed portrait of himself which she opens with trembling fingers. With a cry of 'O Dieu puissant' she recognizes in it the man who kneels before her. The music emerges briefly into a blazing E major, then immediately reverts with a sense of courtly restraint to the D flat major of the opening for what is in effect the cabaletta of the duet ('De quels transports poignants et doux'). (Ex. 13)

This is the theme by which the blighted idyll of Fontainebleau will be recalled throughout the opera; and its absence in extended and definitive form is the one serious defect of the 1884 revision. Here, even more than in the preceding movement, are precipitated all the traits of Verdi's 1867 French style; the smooth 4/4 gait, the long phrases articulated variously in crotchets, simple quavers and quaver triplets, that cosmopolitan flavour of melody which at the time many of his admirers regretted (note the doubtless coincidental echo of Weber's *Euryanthe* overture at (*x*)). If the emotion is apparently more restrained than usual, the reason lies in the text with its constant reference to 'chastes amours' that God has blessed. But the electric charge is there, to be felt partly in the propulsive three-bar structure of the opening,* partly in the rapturous climb of the final phrase, partly too in the har-

* The unusual verse metre was almost certainly imposed by Verdi himself since it represents his third attempt; it would seem too that he thought of it first in connection not with Elisabeth's but with Carlos's subsequent 'Ne tremble pas, reviens à toi, ma belle fiancée'. Günther, *op. cit.*, pp. 115–116.

monies which have the sensuousness of Gounod's without any of his lapses into square-cut banality. Carlos takes up the strain in a gentle rejoinder which suggests a pendant, or codetta, rather than a 'dissimilar' reply. (Ex. 14)

It is left to Elisabeth to guide the music into the ceremonial key of C major. At this point the firing of a cannon is heard, a signal that peace has been concluded. To Carlos and Elisabeth it is like a sign from heaven approving their union. An orchestral crescendo culminates in another modulation to E major, as though confirming the previous one where Elisabeth had recognized the portrait. As in *Un Ballo in maschera*, the climax of the love duet is reached between statements of the cabaletta theme. Here the string tremolando, the intense, short-breathed phrases overlapping from singer to singer, the prolonged high notes, all bring to mind the incandescent climax to the love duet of *Les Huguenots*.

Once again Ex. 13 returns in D flat major sung, almost with an air of surprise, by both parties in unison; this time the coda (Ex. 14) is allowed to wind its way sweetly and with the utmost tenderness, enhanced by some magical writing for high woodwind, to a close in the home key.*

* It is sad that this scène et duo with its masterly portrayal of young love ripening is usually subjected to a vile cut, according to which the moment Thibault has left the stage, Carlos produces his portrait and without more ado the lovers plunge into 'De quels transports'. The reason for this butchery is not far to

But for Carlos and Elisabeth D flat major is the key of unreality, as they become speedily aware. For Thibault now returns with more than a touch of self-importance (note the regal brass cadences and swaggering string triplets). To a brisk A major march theme ('A celui qui vous vient, madame') he asks Elisabeth's permission to remain permanently in her service. This she grants; whereupon he hails her as 'Reine, épouse de Philippe deux'. The brass chords are this time in C major. Hastily Elisabeth

16

seek. The omitted section requires a tenor who is in every sense an actor; one who can not only dissimulate but also perform certain physical actions by which most star tenors would feel themselves demeaned even if they were capable of performing them convincingly. One cannot altogether blame conductors and producers for deciding that what is bound to be done badly is best not done at all.

protests that she is destined for the Infante. 'No,' announces Thibault in triumph, 'Henry II has given you to Philip; you are Queen.'

The lovers' frozen horror finds expression in a typically murky orchestral gesture, based in a diminished seventh with prominent use of a low clarinet; it is repeated three times, leading to the first of the two themes from which the main structure of the finale is built ('L'heure fatale est sonnée'). (Ex. 16) In the march-like tramp of the rhythm we seem to hear the remorseless approach of the 'cruelle destinée' of which the lines speak; yet like so many Verdian melodies of this period which present a plain square-cut appearance at the outset, it develops complexities both rhythmic and harmonic after the first eight bars; the last limb not only extends a predicted four bars to ten, but shifts the main attack from the first to the third beat of the bar and finally annihilates the triplet rhythm with a despairing quaver descent. To this the sung march ('O chants de fête et d'allégresse') supervenes as the traditional major key complement – destiny made palpable in the cheers of a happy crowd.

17

Chorus unaccompanied

It is one of the most ingenious uses to which the stock Italian device has ever been put. Both themes complement each other vertically as well as horizontally to the extent that their rhythmic patterns can be combined if made to begin on the same beat of the bar. This is virtually what happens; but not before the orchestra have allowed eight bars of implied C minor based on Ex. 17 rising to a poignant minor ninth during which the lovers can vent their feeling does the theme itself return in full panoply and private grief is swallowed up in public rejoicing. The triplet figure of Ex. 16 to which they now cling is rendered all the more ineffectual as a protest for being doubled by the cellos in the form of a persistent accompaniment to the sung march, now fortified by wind chords. A codetta plunging into A flat, then returning to C in one of those downward spiralling sequences of dominant sevenths beloved of the Parisian Opéra, of which the original introduction has already furnished an example, brings the full chorus of courtiers and people on to the stage. At their head is the Count of Lerma.* In a recitative he announces that Philip's price for ending the war is the hand of Elisabeth in marriage; but he does not wish to force her to accept against her will. While she hesitates a unison chorus of women, the counterpart of Ex. 5 (and all the more effective if Ex. 5 has already been heard), beseeches Elisabeth not to refuse. Lerma presses her for an answer; and in 'a dying voice' she replies, 'Yes.' Then in the same E major that had marked the lovers' embrace at the

---

* The production books specify the following order: *4 valets with torches; the Count of Lerma holding by the hand the Countess of Aremberg; 2 ladies of the court; 4 French lords; 4 Spanish lords; a palanquin borne by 8 valets; 7 French royal bodyguards. (Disp. scen.* (1867), p. 8; (1886), p. 9.)

centre of the duet the gratitude of the people wells up in a heartfelt sequence that reminds us of Verdi's enthusiasm for the opening scene of *Norma*.

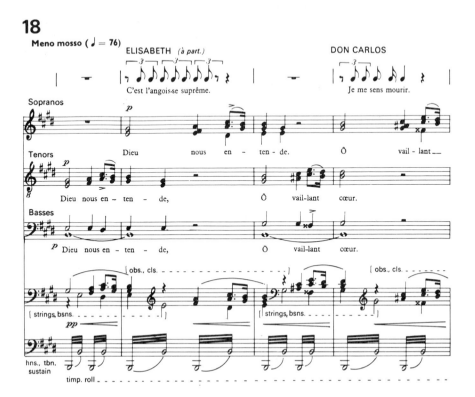

Four bars of agony for the lovers and then the C major chorus returns doubled by full orchestral chords and a busy bass of semiquavers. But in the strenuous tonal shifts that mark the beginning of the coda we can again hear Carlos and Elisabeth tugging desperately against their fate, moving the music chromatically up to F sharp minor then being pulled back through A minor to the inexorable C major. A further chain of modulations in 'pseudo-polonaise' rhythm hammers home the tonic more firmly still. Elisabeth steps into the litter that is to carry her to the palace; then follows Ex. 17 as an orchestral march with vocal interjections ('Gloire, gloire à vous') retreating in a long diminuendo. Over it can be heard Carlos's despairing cries of 'Hélas'; for he alone has remained on stage.

Altogether this is one of Verdi's longest and most complex 'play-outs', since its character is partly determined by the subjective feelings of the man who remains behind. Hence the minor inflections, the chromatic sighs which make their way into the texture, the 'fatal' drum rolls that accompany the theme's last statement as a sung march, the restless shifts of orchestral colouring and above all the grim bass sonorities that obtrude in the final bars. But there is nothing factitious about these effects; they are all implicit in the contours of Ex. 17.

Reviewing the first performance at Modena of the *Don Carlos* 'nuovissimo', Virgilio Tardi referred to the reinstatement of Act I 'which the composer by general consent had been wrong to sacrifice in 1884'.* 'Far be it from me to deny the public what it wants,' Verdi had said on another occasion; and it may well be that the 'consent and approval' of which the same writer speaks might have been wrung from him unwillingly. But there is much to be said for living through Carlos's desolating experience on which the plot of the opera hinges, rather than merely having to assume it, especially since it has been portrayed so movingly. The method remains one of dialectic applied on a grander scale than usual and enriched by a sense of transition as well as a rough tonal scheme: C major (cavatina, reality and hope) – D flat major (duo, illusion and happiness) – C minor–major (finale, reality and despair). The high points of duet and finale are in E major, each time seen in a different perspective. And surely it is a pity to lose the first of the three love duets, partly because without it the musical reminiscences of Ex. 13 are not reminiscences at all; and partly because its essentially uncomplicated nature makes such an effective contrast with the more tortuous encounters between the two lovers later on.

ACT II

Scene 1 (all versions): *The cloisters at St-Just.*† *On the right a lighted chapel in which can be seen the tomb of Charles V behind a gilded grille. On the left a door leading to the exterior. At the back the inside door of the cloisters. A garden with tall cypresses. It is dawn.*

Like the prelude of Act I and unlike the start of Act I as actually performed, the introduction to this scene establishes the opera's 'tinta' in a most uncompromising way: a lugubrious melody for four horns starting with the all-important pattern of four notes revolving round a rising minor sixth observed in Ex. 1.‡

19

Andante sostenuto assai (♩ = 72)

The design is that of a sixteen-bar period expanded at various points and prolonged to form twenty-five bars, the final cadences underlined by the bassoons, trombones and a soft roll of drums. From this emerges, like some mysterious reverberation, the sound of monks praying for the soul of the departed Emperor ('Charles Quint l'auguste empereur').§ The rise of curtain discovers a solitary monk kneeling in prayer before the tomb. Throughout this so-called 'Choeur, Prière et Scène' he comments on the words of the chorus, eventually adding his own prayer to theirs.

* *Gazzetta Musicale di Milano*, XLII, No. 2 (9.1.1886).
† Clearly a contraction of San Jeronimo de Yuste, the monastery to which the Emperor retired after abdicating in 1556. See Hughes, p. 301.
‡ Such was Verdi's hatred of the valve-horn – in regular use at the Opéra for the preceding thirty years – that in order to ensure evenness of execution he chose to employ four natural horns each crooked in a different key (D, B (basso), E, A (basso)). Whether he also intended a mysterious shifting of colour as each instrument resorts to its stopped notes we shall never know until the passage is played as presented, using crooks and a manual technique.
§ This is one of the very few places in which the Italian version 'Carlo, il sommo imperatore' may be preferred to the French, since it avoids disturbing the smooth flow of the music with semiquavers.

The scheme of this number is characteristic – a tonal axis based on keys a third apart, and already epitomized in Ex. 20.

Its extremes are, approximately, the chord of D major (x)* and that of B flat major (y) seen as the dominant of E flat minor. Twice the monk insists on this outer limit of B flat as he proclaims the Emperor's pride and folly and declares that God alone is great; and each time the force of gravity draws him back to the middle of the axis, a symbol of the humbling of human presumption. But at the point where monk and chorus combine a note of austere tenderness (to borrow a phrase from Gustav Holst) steals in.† (Ex. 21)

The key, the mood, the pentatonic contours of (x), the chanting of the male chorus, above all the postlude which seems to be generated by the intensity of the preceding melody, all bring to mind Fiesco ('Il lacerato spirito'); nor is this inappropriate. Alive or dead, the Emperor himself or, in Verdi's infelicitous suggestion, a surviving friend of his, the monk represents the superhuman force of conscience, a remorse that persists beyond the grave. Such, we may be sure, would be Fiesco's remorse, the logical consequence of his inexorable character, if *Simon Boccanegra* were to have a sequel. Both characters share the granite-like quality typical of that long line of bassi profondi which will end with Ramfis in *Aida*. Here there was no need to insist on a particular timbre, since by the deployment of chorus and an orchestra whose internal weight is tilted towards brass, lower strings and lower woodwind, Verdi has created

---

* P. P. Varnai observes that this gives the chant a vertical kinship with Ex. 19. 'Unità musicale e drammaturgica nel *Don Carlo*', *Atti del II° Congresso del I.S.V.*, p. 403.

† At this point the monk *retires slowly backstage left. At the same time 10 monks enter backstage centre, forming three groups: the first of 4, the second of 2, the third of 4. The first group comes forward and exits left; the others cross the back of the stage.* (Disp. scen. (1867), pp. 10–11; (1886), p. 10.)

a sonorous ambience in which the singer cannot fail so long as he has the required compass. The two flutes, oboe and piccolo are reserved for the mysterious, bell-like chord spanning four octaves with a horn pedal note as its bass and no clarinets which punctuates the return of Ex. 20 and will accompany all its future appearances;

typically the climax of the period which evolves from Ex. 21 is marked not by a high note but by a brief modulation outside the tonal orbit of the movement, the return being managed by a smooth enharmonic change (A flat to G sharp). As the monk descends, like Fiesco again, to a low F sharp a bell sounds; and to the strains of a postlude based on the preceding melody the monks file out of the chapel, pass across the stage and disperse through the cloisters. The scoring, with its abundance of tremolando strings, is solemn, rich and entirely personal (who else would have embellished a final cadence with an internal figure played by cornet, bassoon and second violins throughout?). The sense of sadness is maintained partly through the lamenting patterns on bassoon and cello, partly by the oboe which adds its keening edge to the main melody of first violins and clarinet.

Carlos has meanwhile entered 'pale and terrified' beneath the vaults of the cloister. At the sound of singing he has bared his head; at which point there is a divergence between the five- and four-act versions.

Entrance of Carlos (all versions except 1884)

The Infante's first words ('Au couvent de St-Just') show little sign of terror; they are a bleak reflection on the memory of his grandfather who renounced the world to find peace of mind in this very convent. Just so Carlos himself hopes here for a respite from the love that is tormenting him. The orchestral melody (Ex. 22) prompted by this reference takes up Carlos's mood at the end of Act I, and prepares for the form and manner in which he will address his stepmother in the second of the great soprano and tenor duets – two identical phrases followed by a new idea reaching out as though to break free from the formal implication of the theme, then falling back exhausted.

The E flat minor tonality is important, less for its position relative to the other keys employed than for the strangely desolate quality with which it invests the tenor voice in the register chosen. A harsh bass replied, 'Mon fils, les douleurs de la terre nous suivent encore en ces lieux.' It is the monk who has now risen from prayer; his utterance is in Verdi's most uncompromising 'hermit' style, Jorg rather than Fiesco; sharp dotted phrases of religious overlapping fourths to an accompaniment of bassoons, trombones, ophicleide and final timpani roll. Carlos shrinks back; was it not the Emperor's voice? The monk passes slowly in front of him and as he vanishes into the cloisters repeats his warning that earthly sorrows will end only in heaven, his measured utterance contrasting with Carlos's terrified exclamations ('Cette voix . . . je frissonne . . . O terreur!'). The scene ends on a half-close like a question mark for a question that he dare not ask.

Entrance of Carlos (1884)

The Infante's agitation is made palpable in a burst of scurrying strings leading to a tutti outburst and the words – eminently scenic – 'Je l'ai perdue'. In an impassioned melodic declamation (C minor) he cries out that another, his own father, has stolen the bride that was promised to him. The orchestra gives out a reminiscence of Ex. 13;

only of course in its present context it is not a reminiscence at all, and for most critics can never compensate for the loss of the original duet. Yet there is one gain which is all too easily overlooked. Only in the 1884 version does Verdi make it clear that Carlos and Elisabeth remember the idyll of Fontainebleau in quite different ways. To Elisabeth it is an ethereal dream to be recalled sadly but in tranquillity and in all its pristine sweetness; and as such it will recur in her final grand aria. To Carlos it appears through a veil of spiritual torment. His first reminiscence is harmonically akin to that which occurs to him later in the prison cell; it is in C major beginning with an A minor bias. But here there is a more restless movement in the bass; anguish has not yet subsided into leaden *accidie*.

23

There is a brief kindling of remembered happiness as the melody opens into four bars of hushed E major with tremolando strings; but with a diminished seventh on D the flame is extinguished, the vocal line freezes into monotony, while a pattern of shifting chords pivoting on the tenor's D prepares for B flat major, the key of the revised cavatine (Ex. 9). Like all Verdi's revisions it is longer breathed and less repetitive than the original, though it occupies the same number of bars. There is no reprise of the opening phrase and no separate coda; while, by incorporating the last orchestral phrase of the preceding recitative into that of the cavatine itself Verdi re-inforces the continuity between scena and formal number. Most of the changes, however, are clearly designed to reflect the altered mood of the singer, and a hundred deft touches transform joyful anticipation into nostalgic memory. Not only is the key lowered by a tone from C to B flat; it is approached through G minor, so affording that yearning for lost happiness which the Italian romantics never failed to draw from the relative major used in such a context. In general the cavatine is simpler and plainer than before. The opening phrase is shorn of its gruppetto. No glinting upper woodwind colours relieve the gloom of the low clarinet; G minor is again touched upon in the third limb of the melody, whose phrases now have a downward droop; and instead of the caressing chromaticisms of Ex. 10 there is a viola fidget to give a sense of nagging restlessness. The final sentence prolongs itself in cadence after cadence of heartfelt grief without ever exceeding the bounds of the purest Leopardian poetry. It is one of the few disadvantages of the Modena version of 1886 that by restoring the cavatine to its original form and position it prevents us from hearing the piece as Verdi finally wrote it.

The mysterious monk comments as before, leaving Carlos to react with a terror that transforms itself into joy as he recognizes the approaching figure of Rodrigue, Marquis of Posa. But as the scores have meantime converged, if only briefly, with the monk's intervention, it will be useful to return to the original scheme and note how the scene which follows becomes progressively shorter with each revision, as though the idea of a great friendship duet like that between tenor and baritone in Halévy's *La Reine de Chypre* were steadily receding.

1866, 1867, 1872

As the previous half-close dies away Posa is heard indicating Carlos to a silent monk who has conducted him in. With an impetuous 'O mon Rodrigue!' Carlos is about to throw himself into his friend's arms when Posa stops him with a gesture and formally craves an audience. Taking the hint Carlos gives him a gracious but cool welcome. Both wait until the monk has retired before giving full rein to their feelings in a typical 'joyful reunion' theme with pounding accompaniment over a dominant pedal, here embellished with a counter-theme for cello and bassoon which, if it contributes little to the emotional impact, doubtless won the approval of the Parisian savants.

Theatrically this encounter is effectively contrived, though it belongs less to the opera than to the original play where Carlos is, like Hamlet, surrounded by spies and false friends. Schiller opens his first act with a scene in which Father Domingo tries to worm his way into the Prince's confidence. As neither Domingo nor any other treacherous monk figures in the opera, Verdi doubtless was content to shorten and simplify the scene in 1884.

1866

The cadence reached after nine bars, Posa straightaway launches into an account of the terrible state of Flanders, from which he has just returned ('J'étais en Flandre'). Carlos must come to their aid. But what is this? Why is the prince so pale? Why does a tear glisten in his eye? Let him unburden himself to his childhood friend.

All this to a rapid 6/8 movement of forty bars originally designed as the first paragraph of a highly developed two-movement duet whose plan may be described roughly as: *scena—a¹—a²* (with episode and reprise) – *b* (cabaletta with episode and instrumental reprise). The melodic line ranges widely with many an expressive appoggiatura over an eventful accompaniment evolved from the semitonal lament in the first bar.

(1866)

The section has considerable structural importance, providing as it does the minor key statement of which the following moderato is the 'maggiore' complement; but whether because Faure found it too tiring, whether it was felt that the text was somewhat superfluous since we shall hear plenty about the misery of Flanders later on, whether because he himself sensed an anti-climax at the harmonic stasis that supervenes at Posa's change of subject, Verdi agreed to cut it out except for the last twelve bars, reducing the rest to nine bars of declaimed recitative ('L'heure a sonné. La voix des Flamands vous appelle. Soyez leur Dieu sauveur!') and turning ('Mais qu'ai-je vu? Quelle pâleur mortelle', etc.) into a genuinely propulsive sequence. But if the interest is chiefly historical, it is worth noting that the heart-easing phrase with which in all versions of the opera Posa persuades Carlos to confide in him is a variant of one occurring at the mid-point of his solo where he urges him to come to the aid of the Flemings – yet another instance of the composer's growing mastery of musical transition. (Ex. 26)

26a Allegro giusto

RODRIGUE

se - cou - rez __ la Flan - dre, se - cou -

[cls., bsns., hns.] f strings dim.

- rez __ la Flan-dre oppri - mé - e!

p pp

(1866)

26b Allegretto

RODRIGUE dim. très doux

Mon Car-los, don - ne - moi, mon Car-los, don-ne - moi ma part, ma part de tes ___ dou (leurs)

strings etc. pp

1866, 1867, 1872

With the changes mentioned above the duet now assumes the form: *scena – a* (with episode and reprise) – *b* (etc.) with Carlos's 'Mon compagnon, mon ami, mon frère' (Ex. 27) as the first formed melody, to which Posa supplies a 'dissimilar' answer in the dominant and a slightly faster tempo ('Au nom d'une amitié chère') which takes the form of Ex. 24.

The pace quickens still further for the episode, a long transitional passage during which Carlos manages to bring out the fatal words, 'J'aime d'un amour insensé Elisabeth.' 'Ta mère!' exclaims Posa. Certain now that he has lost Rodrigue's friendship Carlos vents his despair in another desolate E flat minor passage whose bass-heavy instrumentation suggests a universe falling ('Malheureux! mon Rodrigue lui-même'). (Ex. 28)

But Posa quickly restores D flat major ('Non, Carlos, ton Rodrigue t'aime'), so leading to a reprise of the two principal ideas, now shared between the two voices and the second (Ex. 24) by an unusual homage to the principles of sonata form transposed into the home key. An emphatic coda of eight bars winds up the movement. In the following recitative Posa takes charge of the situation. Has the King the least suspicion of Carlos's secret? No? Well, then, he must obtain the royal permission to set out for Flanders at once and by sinking his private grief in that of a whole people learn his trade as a future king. As Carlos humbly promises to obey, a bell sounds and a group of monks cross the stage. 'Listen!' Posa cries. 'The doors of the monastery are about to open. Undoubtedly Philip and the Queen.' Carlos starts;

while his friend urges him to pray to God for a hero's strength, so preparing the way for the final cabaletta.

1884, 1886

In his correspondence with du Locle via Nuitter, Verdi had declared his intention of removing from the early part of this duet 'everything purely musical' – by which, of course, he meant anything in the nature of an independent musical structure. Accordingly all that has been described so far is epitomized in a long and varied scena whose musical interest is if anything greater than before. The revision takes up after the departure of the ghostly monk, which no longer leaves a half-close hanging in the air. Instead, Carlos's alarm is further embodied in a new figure whose rhythmic, though not melodic, outline is derived from Ex. 24 (which in fact we shall never hear) with a suggestion of throbbing heartbeats in the bass.

29

(1884)

As Posa's voice is heard outside the figure transforms itself through a broad crescendo into another and simpler expression of 'joyous reunion' in B major as before but of no particular thematic interest. Posa's intervention remains approximately as in 1867 but more expressively inflected and variously harmonized. His concluding Ex. 26b is now entirely in sharps since it leads into C sharp minor for a new, briefer and more poignant setting of 'Mon compagnon, mon ami, mon frère' ('Mio salvator, mio fratel, mio fedele'). Like its predecessor it is an allegro in 6/8; and though no longer a large ternary structure of lyrically expansive ideas it is far from formless. Behind the continuously evolving dialogue can be sensed the framework of an extended thirty-two-bar period with Carlos's confession, eked out by a hesitant oboe and bassoon, falling on the last limb. Posa reacts even more violently than before; while Carlos rejoins with a more elaborate version of Ex. 28, still in E flat minor, without timpani or brass but with a telling combination of high double basses and cellos in expressive chromatic patterns. Again Posa leads the music to D flat and a firm cadence. The linking recitative ('Ton secret par le roi s'est-il laissé surprendre', etc.) is as before up till Carlos's involuntary cry of 'Elisabeth!'; after which Posa's exhortations take on an almost ecclesiastical solemnity. Brass, bassoons and pizzicato strings underpin the final 'Demande à Dieu la force d'un héros' (or in its rather feebler if better known Italian translation, 'Domanda al ciel dei forti la virtù!').

All versions

For the cabaletta 'Dieu tu semas dans nos âmes' the two voices are yoked indissolubly in thirds and sixths as they vow to live and die together in brotherly love for the cause of freedom.

30

Except for Duncan's entrance march in *Macbeth* none of Verdi's themes has come in for more criticism or lamer apology from the older generation of English writers than this.* Doubtless if pressed to give a reason they would have pointed to the progression in the second bar which sounds all too like the kind of improvised harmony to be heard in any Welsh public house shortly before closing time. But it has a decent enough French pedigree. Similar roughnesses can be found throughout Auber's scores and are one reason why his music tends to make a poor impression from the printed page. In fact, given a French text and French accentuation, Ex. 30 will be found to make a genuinely strong effect; whereas the flaccid 'Dio che nell'alma infondere', with its verbal inversions that run counter to the musical phrasing, merely stresses the harmonic gaucherie. No other point in the score gives more support to the case for performing the opera in the original language.

For the basic simplicity of the design, a symmetrical scheme of thirty bars (11 + 8 + 11), no apologies are needed. It represents the world of straightforward loyalties in which Carlos seeks relief from the torments of conflict in which his love for Elisabeth has plunged him. Ex. 30 will recur to him throughout the opera at moments of crisis – a reminder that in a world of falsehood and oppression sterling values still exist. In the versions of 1884 and 1886 the movement has a special importance as the formal coping stone of what has become a rather freely organized duet.

The scene now proceeds to an impressive coda which gathers up the main threads of what has gone before, after the manner of the inn scene in *La Forza del destino*. First, there is a massive processional which takes up the triplet rhythm of Ex. 30 with striding bass and brass fanfares as Philip and Elisabeth, preceded by monks, enter the monastery and do homage before the tomb of Charles V. As they do so the almost fierce brilliance of the music darkens, the sonority thins out and the melody turns towards the key of F sharp minor to end in the soft chanting of Ex. 20 by the monks, complete with sustaining wind, to which are added Carlos's broken cries ('Elle est à lui . . . je l'ai perdue . . .'). It is as though the chill atmosphere of the cloister has descended on the royal cortège, blotting out all suggestions of earthly grandeur – a paradigm of the relations of Church and State as set forth in both operas and play. So it comes as no surprise to hear the voice of the monk rising above the chorus as he proclaims God's greatness and his infinite mercy. But this time Carlos, obsessed with

* See Toye, p. 387; Hussey, p. 163; Hughes, p. 333.

thoughts of Elisabeth, pays him no heed. It is Posa's, the third voice in the ensemble, that rouses him from despair. As Philip rises to his feet and prepares to leave, the two men repeat their vow ('Soyons unis . . . pour la vie et la mort . . .') whereupon Ex. 30 surfaces again on oboes, clarinets, bassoons and violas over a dominant pedal and beneath high violin triplets. The passage is prolonged for eight bars, so effectively obliterating the previous F sharp minor with a firm assertion of Beethoven-like C major. After the final cadence parades in all its glory on violins, violas and woodwind, the rest of the orchestra beats out the supporting harmonies. For the moment friendship and idealism have won the day.*

> *Scene 2: A pleasant spot by the gates of the cloisters of St-Just. A fountain, banks of turf, groups of orange, pine and gum trees. The blue mountains of Extremadura on the horizon. In the background on the right the monastery approached by some steps. Princess Eboli, Thibault, the Countess of Aremberg, ladies-in-waiting seated on the turf round the fountain. The pages stand in the background. A page is tuning a mandoline.†*

No French grand opera could afford to dispense with purely decorative elements; and it is to Verdi's credit that he scouted the librettists' original idea for this scene as set forth in the prose synopsis. Debarred by their sex from entering the monastery (apart from the two accompanying the Queen of Spain) the ladies were to while away the time by teasing the page Thibault. Surely, at his age, he must already be 'amoureux'. Will he not oblige them with a song in praise of his lady-love? Thibault consents; but the loved one turns out to be his native land of France whose praises he sings in a romance. Clearly there were limits of irrelevance to which Verdi was not prepared to go, however flattering the result to a Parisian audience. There will indeed be a *romance* but it will be sung by Princess Eboli and it will have a subtle relevance to the central dramatic theme.

The opening chorus of women, however ('Sous ces bois au feuillage immense'), is no more than an episode designed to provide light relief from a drama that threatens to become oppressive; and like all the decorative elements in *Don Carlos* it is very

---

* The production books set out the final scene as follows: *After the ensemble* [i.e., the duet] *Carlos and Rodrigue retire and make as if to leave; but Rodrigue, seeing the cortège, says, 'Les voilà'; and Carlos comes down hurriedly to the left saying, 'Je frémis.' Rodrigue puts a hand on his shoulder and says to him, 'Courage!'*

Philip enters backstage left giving his hand to Elisabeth. 2 pages follow each carrying a prayer-book on a velvet cushion; after them the Count of Lerma, 2 of the Queen's ladies, 4 Spanish lords and 4 monks.

Philip comes forward and, having arrived at the tomb, releases Elisabeth's hand, uncovers his head and kneels down; Elisabeth remains standing; the 2 pages follow and remain standing behind the Queen; the Count of Lerma behind the pages, the 2 ladies behind the Count. The 4 monks and the 4 Spanish lords remain at the entrance within view of the audience; these last together with the Count uncover their heads.

At Carlos's words, 'Je l'ai perdue', Philip rises and gives his hand to Elisabeth; the cortège leaves R.

When all have left Carlos and Rodrigue come downstage and, clasping hands, cry, 'Soyons unis'; then, loosening the clasp, 'Pour la vie et la mort.' At the end of the piece they clasp hands once more and exeunt backstage L. Disp. scen. (1867), pp. 12–13; (1886), pp. 11–12. Needless to say the duet cabaletta is delivered from the footlights.

† The production books direct that the women should enter in two groups from opposite wings and that 10 peasant girls should likewise enter R. and throughout the scene group themselves behind the women. Next 4 pages appear and place cushions for the ladies to sit on. See *Disp. scen.* (1867), pp. 14–15.

richly inlaid. The opening minor-key ritornello (Ex. 31a) with its abundance of triangle and piccolo suggests the harem manner of *I Lombardi* and *Il Corsaro* enhanced by Gallic sophistication (though one may be sure that no derogatory inference was thereby intended). A similar Parisian fragrance marks the chorus itself (Ex. 31b), which Verdi recalled with pride during his collaboration with Ghislanzoni on *Aida*,* and which owes part of its charm to a characteristic irregularity. Beginning with two eight-bar sentences it reaches what seems to be a half-way point with a strong tilt to the dominant; after which a mere four-bar phrase of great sweetness is sufficient to bring the stanza to a close.

* See letter to Ghislanzoni, 16.8.1870. *Copialettere*, pp. 639–40.

Over an interlude in the style of the opening prelude Thibault enters with Princess Eboli, to whom he points out the beauties of the garden. Then the chorus is resumed to a second stanza ('Qu'il fait bon assis sous les arbres') with Thibault joining the top line. The four-fold repetitions of the opening idea offer several possibilities for varied embellishment – (a) sustaining wind and a pattern of viola semiquavers, (b) alternating octaves on first and second violins, arco and pizzicato respectively, with chromatic scales in the violas, (c) trilling figures on violins, flute and piccolo, (d) 'snaps' for first and second violins with leaping octaves for flute and piccolo. To all this the smooth march of the voices and the quaver bass line supply a constant background. A short scene follows based on material from both the introduction and the chorus. Princess Eboli suggests that they find a game to occupy their time while waiting for the Queen. 'We shall all follow your whim, charming Princess Eboli', say the chorus with an attractive modulation into C major. Eboli calls for a mandoline and suggests that they sing together the old Saracen 'Song of the Veil'. It would need a subtle perception to tell that the turn into A minor in her recitative was originally a turn into G major, the key in which Rosine Bloch would have sung the piece in question.

The Chanson du Voile ('Au palais des fées') is a pleasant little mock-Moorish folly of no great pretensions. It is the story of King Achmed of Granada who made advances to a veiled lady in the palace gardens only to discover that she was his own wife. The introduction makes use of one of those folk-dance rhythms with which nineteenth-century composers from Offenbach to Chabrier liked to signalize a Spanish ambience – allegro 6/8 with implications of 3/4. The verse (Ex. 32a) has the same kind of stylized exoticism as Carmen's Seguidilla, witness the flattened leading note in the third bar (x), the decoration on the eleventh and the flamboyant pseudo-flamenco cadenza at the end. The refrain (Ex. 32b), in which Thibault takes over the tune, happily throws off the Spanish disguise for a sprightly 4/4 full of sparkling piccolo trills; and though it forms the most regular of eight-bar sentences, Verdi creates an impression of both irregularity and rightness by altering the stresses in the last three bars.

The chorus dutifully takes up the refrain in three-part harmony, Eboli comes forward with a second verse ('J'entrevois à peine') and the procedure is repeated. Verdi's first idea, it would seem, was for Elisabeth's entrance to take them all by surprise so that the final cadence should die on their lips; but for a singer of Pauline Gueymard-Lauters's eminence to be deprived of her applause was clearly unthinkable. A full close was therefore added with crashing orchestral chords and doubtless an appropriate burst of laughter. Alas, Eboli will soon discover that disguises and mistaken identities are not always a laughing matter.* The chorus exclaim 'La Reine'; the Queen makes no reply, but a short oboe solo depicts the sad thoughts which, in Eboli's subsequent words, 'keep her soul in thrall'. As she murmurs to herself about the happiness of all those around her, Posa appears at the back of the stage. Thibault goes to meet him, exchanges with him a few words, then comes

---

* Immediately after the song the peasant girls move backstage and group themselves by the steps of the church to greet the Queen. Thibault retires and hands the mandoline to a page who carries it away into the wings. Elisabeth comes out of the monastery. She is accompanied by the Countess of Aremberg and two ladies-in-waiting. All bow. . . . The peasant girls exeunt. . . . The page who took away the mandoline re-enters to announce to Thibault the arrival of Posa. See Disp. scen. (1867), p. 16.

32a

32b

forward and announces, 'The Marquis of Posa, Grandee of Spain.' In the next four bars for strings we can hear Posa advancing with a proud yet respectful gait, then bowing low before his sovereign. He hands the Queen a letter which he claims to have brought from her mother in Paris, and with it he slips a note which he begs her to read for 'her soul's salvation'. He then proceeds to converse nonchalantly with Eboli, who is all agog to hear about the latest fashions in Paris. Posa contrives to load every reply with a compliment to Eboli herself so extravagant that only the most outrageous vanity could be taken in by it. But this is perfectly in character. Eboli is quite sincere when in the fourth act she curses that 'fatal gift of beauty', of whose workings the audience has been given so little evidence. The theme which serves as background to the conversation belongs to the same family as Ex. 11 in which Carlos was making similar small talk to Elisabeth; but it is that much the more consciously graceful, not to say coquettish.

Like many of the mature conversational themes it has the ability to prolong itself indefinitely, as Elisabeth hesitates to open the secret note and Eboli passes from a royal tournament and the feasts at the Louvre to the wearing of silk embroidered with gold. Not until Ex. 33 is resumed with a typical embellishment of cello pizzicato quavers does Elisabeth at last manage to read aloud Carlos's cryptic message: 'By the memory which binds us both, in the name of your peace of mind and of my life, trust this man. CARLOS.' With a plea so devious and indirect it hardly matters if the words remain inaudible amid Eboli's bright chatter. However, it has its effect. Elisabeth bids Posa ask for any favour he chooses; Eboli, drawn by his flattery, supports her mistress's offer ('Qui plus digne que vous peut voir ses voeux comblés par la reine?'). Ex. 33 has by this time worked its way out in a series of rhythmic diminutions and swiftly changing harmonies; and a half-close prepares the way for Posa's romance, or 'ballade' as it is called in the published vocal score ('L'Infant Carlos, notre espérance'). This too, like the Song of the Veil, is very much a set piece for a star singer – here the lyric baritone, Faure. As such it conforms in its rhythmic cut to the Grand Opera baritone or bass cantabile of which Brogni's 'Si la rigueur et la vengeance' (La Juive) is an early model and Wolfram's 'Oh Du, mein holder Abendstern' a near relation. Musically it is an expression of plain baritonic idealism executed with all the melodic craftsmanship of which Verdi now disposed. As so often in the past, sustaining wind is used at the point of modulation.

34

In the course of two verses – the second decorated by a figure derived from Ex. 33 in diminution – Posa begs Elisabeth to receive Carlos, who is pining in misery, and to give him the sympathy his father denies him; while in a ritornello Eboli recalls with satisfaction having seen the Infante tremble and grow pale in her presence. There is little here to interest the music dramatist; and one can well understand Verdi's original wish to dispatch the entire scene in a brisk allegro movement, and also his subsequent irritation when the 'episodic' part of Posa attracted all the attention.*

Elisabeth is convinced; she tells Thibault 'with dignity' that she is ready to receive her son. In a joyous aside Eboli hopes that Carlos may at last declare his passion for her. Posa, his mission accomplished, takes her hand and they depart, talking in low voices; a reprise of Ex. 33 with a viola accompaniment in rhythmic diminution allows us to speculate on the light badinage that passes between them.

Carlos now appears, escorted by Thibault. Posa has just time to whisper a word to the page, who then enters the monastery, presumably to keep watch for the King's approach. The second of the soprano and tenor duets takes us straight into the heart of this vast music drama. The plaintive woodwind phrase with which Carlos approaches the Queen and bows without raising his eyes resumes the mood and tonality of Ex. 22; but how infinitely more desolate it sounds striking in immediately after the bright D major chord which ended the previous scene!

Carlos's opening gambit (Ex. 35) furnishes the structural paradigm for one of the most original duets in the Verdi canon. With its great predecessors it shares a dialectical basis and little else. Nor do its successive stages fall into separate movements. True the speed varies either side of the 'mean' allegro moderato, but otherwise the music proceeds in the steady, dignified 4/4 which characterizes the opera as a whole. The rest is made up of sentences, phrases, short periods, mostly irregular, but showing a recurring pattern of structure strictly determined by the emotional current of the dialogue, which, be it noted, is not that of the equivalent scene in Schiller.†

* For a more detailed analysis of this romance see my 'L'influènza della tradizione del Grand' Opera francese sulla struttura ritmica di *Don Carlos*', in *Atti del II° Congresso del I.S.V.*, pp. 316–18. Once again one is struck by the ineptitude of the Italian translation. 'Carlo ch'è sol il nostro amore' is, to say the least, a tactless way of referring to the Infante in present company. Yet producers have been known to turn it to a kind of advantage by making Posa address those words to Eboli rather than the Queen.

† Most of the following observations are prompted by the essay by Karl Dietrich Gräwe in *Atti del II° Congresso del I.S.V.* (Parma, 1971), pp. 193–203, to which the reader has already been referred.

35

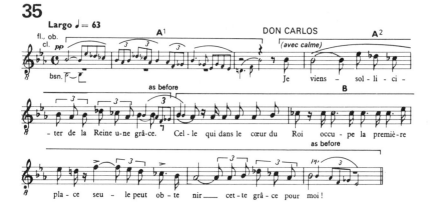

In the play Carlos's entrance takes Elisabeth by surprise and his bitter, aggressive arguments find her at first unprepared. Gradually her calm dignity takes control of the situation. Ironically, she challenges him to take on the mantle of Oedipus: to murder his father and then drag his mother to the altar. Carlos is sobered immediately; and it is at her exhortation that he decides to sublimate his love by devoting himself to the cause of Flanders and freedom.

In the opera the progress is all the other way, from calm self-control to an unleashing of personal emotion which will end with Carlos's running away in despair, and, not for the first time, Verdi couches the various stages of the dialogue in a form which mirrors the duet as a whole – two parallel phrases, mostly but not always identical (a^1 and a^2) followed by a much longer third phrase (b) in which strong emotion breaks through the surface. (Ex. 36a)

Throughout the duet b will vary in character and function according to the mood of the singer. In the early part it will follow the model of Ex. 35, falling back from its highest note in a kind of uncertainty, as though abashed at its own daring. Nor will the answering voice press hard on its heels in the early Verdian manner. In a passage of free declamation Carlos begs his stepmother to intercede with the King to have him sent to Flanders, since the air of the court is stifling him. No parallel phrases here; but a series of orchestral gasps, illustrative of suffocation, obtrude on Carlos's apparently composed line. 'Mon fils!' Elisabeth exclaims tenderly. But the words cause Carlos to cry out as if stung. As Elisabeth turns away his voice rises in a cry of despair. ('Le ciel avare ne m'a donné qu'un jour, et si vite il a fui.') Summoning all her self-control Elisabeth replies that if the King will listen to her Carlos can set out for Flanders the next day (Ex. 36a). The doubling of the melody in the bass à la Puccini indicates the strength of her submerged feelings; and even if the effect of b is here to restore the regularity of an 8-bar phrase upset by two units of two and a half bars each (a^1 and a^2) the restless shifting harmonies on the last pair of triplets betray the effort of will.

Again she turns to go; but Carlos is deeply wounded by her seeming indifference. Not a word of regret for his leaving? Truly she must have a heart of stone. In his long period, half lyrical, half declamatory, of seventeen bars (G major – minor) the pattern of Ex. 35 is repeated with a^1 and a^2 forming a sequence at the words 'Hélas, mon âme se déchire! Hélas, je me sens mourir.' b is accounted for in the lines:

> Insensé! J'ai supplié dans mon délire
> Un marbre insensible et glacé.

Now it is Elisabeth's turn to be hurt. She is far from indifferent, but she has pride and a sense of duty. Here the pattern emerges twice: first in a forlorn reproach in G minor of only 5 bars; then in more expansive form in B flat major as Elisabeth dwells on the forces that keep them apart (Ex. 36b). In the concluding modulation from B flat to F she seems to be directing the emotional charge latent in *b* into a new, nobler channel.

36a

Carlos, however, seems not to hear her, being lost in nostalgic dreams of the past. Although his next entry (Ex. 36c) for once follows Elisabeth's last words without a break it is in no sense an answer to them, but rather suggests one of those soliloquies that so often typify the cantabile or second movement of a grand duet.

Note too that *b* has changed character yet again. The tide of energy inherent in it is now on the ebb; its irregularity is no longer disruptive now that the singer's thoughts

36b

36c

have turned from present feelings to fond memories. But it is a plane on which Carlos and Elisabeth can safely meet – or so they think; hence her repetition note for note of the entire period of Ex. 36c, its delicate scoring now enhanced by a sustaining cor anglais, oboe punctuations and intermittent triplets from muted first violins.

Its effect is to send Carlos into a strange visionary trance (Ex. 36d) in which he can only murmur brokenly that heaven has taken pity on him at last. These fourteen bars form the centrepiece of the duet and also its furthest point from reality (note the 'illusory' D flat major). Here too the pattern a^1–a^2–b appears, but in a very different guise. Formerly the elements a and b were in opposition, a with its regularity standing for outward control, b for the repressed feeling that continually threatens to upset it. Now a form of osmosis, already discernible in Ex. 36c, has transformed b into the smooth, regular extension of a from which all tension has vanished.

36d

The fashion for cutting this remarkable passage can only be explained by a determination to shorten the opera at all costs, and how unfortunate that the woodwind cadence underlying the words 'c'était le Paradis' should recur twenty-two bars later in the same key, making the excision all too painless. Verdi himself took infinite trouble with both the scoring and the distribution between voice and orchestra. According to Morère's rehearsal book Carlos was originally to have sung the triplets later given to the woodwind soloists; the muttered declamation was an afterthought and a very apt one. Then too Verdi wished the violins and violas to sustain harmonics throughout, thus anticipating an effect to be found in the last act of *Aida*; eventually he settled for high sustained notes at the limit of the compass, leaving at the point a gap of more than three octaves between violas and cellos. The soft chords on trombones and ophicleide which distinguish the 1884 and 1886 versions from their predecessors were part of the original conception, but they were differently spaced. Again one can only guess why the composer should have removed them in the course of rehearsals only to reinstate them seventeen years later.

Carlos concludes with the words, 'Je meurs . . . je meurs,' whereupon he appears to lose consciousness, so causing Elisabeth to fear that he really has died ('Dieu puissant, la vie s'est éteinte'). To Ex. 36e, starting in E flat but returning to the original key, she prays that heaven may restore life and peace of mind to 'him who was my fiancé'. Her words do indeed seem to revive Carlos but not in the way that she had intended ('Par quelle douce voix mon âme est ranimée'). In his delirium he seems to see Elisabeth as she had appeared to him at Fontainebleau, turning the bare forest to green by her presence.

36e

Again the familiar pattern appears; and again the barriers are down between its two constituents, as present emotion floods back into the vocal line. Ex. 36e is extended to form a seventeen-bar paragraph of extraordinary intensity, comparable to the moment when Amelia confesses her love for Riccardo in *Un Ballo in maschera*. Nor is this as inapt as it might seem; for though the tenor's ardour is feverish and the soprano merely compassionate their real feelings for one another can no longer be in doubt. Carlos's final phrase ('ma bien aimée, ma bien aimée, c'est toi') subsides on to an

36f

interrupted cadence. There is a four-bar transition, with typically sepulchral scoring – trombone chords, death-raps on the timpani, strange low trills on the flute – as he comes to himself, muttering brokenly ('A ma tombe fermée . . . au sommeil éternel . . . pourquoi m'arracher, Dieu cruel?'). 'Carlos!' Elisabeth cries softly. The tempo quickens to an allegro and Carlos with a sudden access of strength breaks into the concluding cabaletta. (Ex. 36f)

Here the basic design has become finally transformed so that a^1 and a^2 *prepare* for the explosion of b. Emotion has apparently won the day – or would have done if Carlos's outburst had not evoked in Elisabeth an equally fierce determination to resist. She hurls at him the taunt with which Schiller's Elisabeth had brought her stepson to reason, uttered not in a tone of dignified reproof but with real anger ('Eh bien, frappez donc votre père!', etc.). Her music, though 'dissimilar' to that of Carlos and in a different key, follows the same pattern except for a longer, more emphatic b section (eleven bars as against Carlos's six) which she needs in order to gain the necessary ascendancy; and indeed it is Carlos himself who provides the cadential bars with his 'Ah fils maudit! fils maudit!' He rushes from her presence; a glorious sweeping phrase in E flat major ('Sur nous le Seigneur a veillé') (Ex. 36g) brings the duet to a close, as Elisabeth falls on her knees, thankful that the crisis has been surmounted. The modern listener may be reminded here of another Elisabeth beset by a similar mental anguish at the close of Act I of Britten's *Gloriana*.

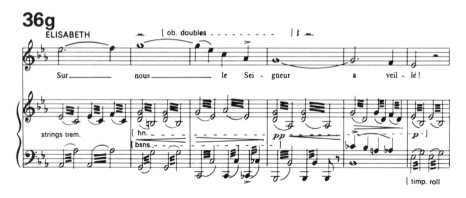

The duet ends at the middle of the equivalent scene in Schiller, having reached it by a very different route. The fainting is an invention of the librettists, possibly designed to show they knew that, according to one report, Carlos was an epileptic. The effect is to make the hero even more a creature of sensibility than his counterpart in the play – a Werther rather than an Infante von Spanien, whose main weakness had been his tendency to act on impulse. Accordingly the scoring frequently shows that morbid transparency associated with the last act of *La Traviata*, though achieved by rather more sophisticated means in which the three flutes have an important part to play. With these new données, therefore, the duet is formed independently of Schiller; yet it remains not only satisfying as musical structure but one of the most impressive fusions of music and drama to be found in all opera. It could also be called the perfect illustration of the famous American definition of Platonic love – 'the gun you didn't know was loaded'.

True to his instructions Thibault comes hurriedly out of the monastery to announce, 'Le Roi!'* Obin's rehearsal book shows that the King's entrance was first conceived as a series of gestures in dotted rhythm and nothing else, and that his first words ('Pourquoi seule, Madame?') were pitched in the upper, emphatic part of his voice. Later Verdi decided, as so often, to transfer the weight of utterance to the orchestra, adding powerful plagal cadences for full orchestra, and a pattern of syncopated crotchets for strings and higher wind to strive against the upward-thrusting bass line. Without any correspondence of notes the passage is reminiscent of that in Act I where Thibault returns from the palace of Fontainebleau with Philip's proposal of marriage. But there the page had only Philip's reflected glory; here we are brought face to face with the monarch himself in all his formidable strength. The King demands to know why the Queen has been left unattended contrary to court etiquette. Whose duty was it to wait upon Elisabeth that day? The Comtesse d'Aremberg, a silent role, steps forward and bows low before the King. 'Countess, tomorrow you will leave for France!' A brutal tutti gesture and a rolling drum give force to the King's words. As the countess retires in tears the bystanders murmur indignantly at this affront to the Queen, so furnishing the cue for Elisabeth's romance, 'Oh ma chère compagne, ne pleurez pas.' Theme-spotters will have no difficulty in identifying the opening bar of the cor anglais melody in the ritornello with the start of Amelia's 'Orfanella, il tetto umile' from *Simon Boccanegra*, even down to the melodic–harmonic semitonal clash on the fourth beat; but a glance at the continuation should be enough to dispel any suspicions of self-plagiarism (Ex. 37). Like Posa's

* Enter Philip deep in thought. He goes slowly towards the Queen, looking around him for signs of other people. He is followed by Lerma and two lords. Ladies-in-waiting, Rodrigue and peasant girls all re-enter and with them the men of the chorus (though in what capacity – nobles, people, guards – is not specified). See Disp. scen. (1867), p. 19.

'L'Infant Carlos, notre espérance' this is a set piece in two verses to which the final two lines, being the same in each case, give the character of 'couplets'. But as always, when Verdi employs this form, all sectionalism, in Meyerbeer's manner, is avoided since the melody floats from beginning to end on a single breath. Unlike the Posa romance, this has a dramatic function; it enables Elisabeth to give full rein to those feelings of compassion which she has forcibly held in check during the preceding duet. The countess, she says, has been expelled from Spain but not from her heart. She gives her a ring in token of their friendship and bids her salute the fair land of France where she herself had spent the happy days of her youth. Apart from its plangent cor anglais obbligato, a notable feature of this romanza is the modal touch in the third bar (x) which will be amplified in the seventh and eighth – a typically mid-century Gallicism perfectly assimilated into Verdi's melodic style. Note too the compression of the traditional minor–major formula into a single melody of four sentences of which only the last is extended beyond the four-bar unit; and finally the way in which the climax ('Tu vas le revoir') is thrown into extra relief by a 'non functional' 6/4 (A major) and an increased rate of harmonic change which only slows up at the final cadence. Rarely has so much lyrical craftsmanship been deployed on so small a scale – so small in fact that most Elisabeths fail to win the applause they deserve at this point; the melody is just too short and too gentle to stimulate an audience. The courtiers, however, Posa and Philip, are duly moved, as they attest in one of those multi-textual codas in which not a word can be distinguished but the general mood is clear enough.* A short postlude for cor anglais and bassoon based on the final limb of the melody brings the piece to a close. Elisabeth, her ladies and the grandees retire; Posa is about to follow them but the King detains him.

So begins a duet which gave Verdi more trouble than any other single piece in the opera, even though he himself had asked for its inclusion over and above the original scheme. He was to write it – or part of it – no less than three times, yet it may be wondered whether even at the end it fulfilled his expectations. Unlike Wagner's, Verdi's characters do not find it easy to philosophize in music; they cannot argue with each other effectively without a basis of contrasted emotional attitudes. This is because to the end his art remains vocally orientated; he could never contrive the kind of orchestral discourse that for instance makes the debates of the Mastersingers musically interesting. In the duet which follows Posa is indeed emotionally committed, if only to a principle; Philip on the other hand is quite uninvolved. He does not believe a word of what Posa is telling him; he is merely impressed enough by the young man's boldness first to counter argument with argument, then to confide to him his own domestic troubles. And no one is more surprised at this confession than Posa himself, so little does it appear a logical consequence of what has gone before. Whether any of the solutions attains the perfection of the duets between Carlos and Elisabeth or Philip and the Inquisitor, whose form was reached at the first attempt, may be doubted. None, however, are without musical distinction; and they are all

---

* According to the production books Philip must make his exit at the start of the first strophe after having exchanged a few words with the Count of Lerma. He returns in time to take part in the choral codetta. (See *Disp. scen.* (1867), p. 20.) If this is a slightly clumsy expedient for allowing the full limelight to the Queen it is preferable to the device adopted by the late Visconti, whereby Philip remained on stage throughout the romanza, making much of two enormous staghounds, so ensuring that not the slightest attention should be paid to the unfortunate singer.

the more interesting to the Verdi student as the attempts of a genius to come to grips with a task with which his art was hardly equipped to deal.

All versions start in the same way. Posa approaches the King, bows, then calmly covers his head – a somewhat bold gesture in the presence of a sovereign and reflected in the austere, half military flourishes in the strings. Philip wants to know why alone among the grandees of Spain Posa has never asked for admission to the royal presence. He has served his sovereign nobly in the field, yet never asked for any reward. Posa replies that he is quite happy to live by his country's laws. 'I love pride,' Philip observes; 'I pardon boldness – sometimes.' But why has Posa resigned his officer's post? So far all has been conventional recitative stiffened at the outset by an orchestral motif; but with Posa's reply the duet begins to take on a novel shape. Here the divergences begin.

1866, 1867, 1872

The melody is almost a parody of a French march – a defiant protestation of the singer's simple, soldierly virtues. But when he declares that he will wield the sword but will leave others to wield the headsman's axe, the melodic trajectory carries him outside the tonal orbit into D minor without, however, disturbing the regularity of the phrase-structure. Philip reacts, as well he might, with an angry 'Marquis!'; but Posa presses home his advantage of surprise. 'God guided me into your presence, sire,' he says in a quick, almost breathless climbing declamation which opens out into one of those lyrical expansive phrases in which the first version of the duet abounds ('Les desseins de la providence'). This in turn is extended according to the pattern noted in the second Carlos–Elisabeth duet, ending on the emphatic words 'La vérité'.

Philip bids him continue. The narration that follows ('O Roi, j'arrive de Flandre') is sufficiently powerful for Verdi to include it intact in all versions of the duet. It is built on a melodic idea dissolved into a series of syncopations over a restless bass line such as might have been suggested by the opening of Mozart's D minor piano concerto.

Posa paints a far more vivid picture of the sufferings of Flanders than he did to Carlos (a further reason why that earlier passage could be regarded as expendable). This land, once so fair, has become a desert, an abomination of desolation; everywhere rivers running with blood, orphans begging in the streets, widows mourning over the bodies of their slaughtered husbands. The music evolves through an accretion of string figures, lamenting acciaccature, clashing chromatic scales in contrary motion, death figures on timpani and trumpet, successive diminished sevenths, harmonic side-slips and the like. It has the bludgeoning force of Telramund's fierce diatribe against his wife (of which, however, Verdi had not heard a note), but is more successful in masking the heavy, insistent rhythm which was both his and Wagner's legacy from French grand opera. Having finished his recital on a succession of syncopated diminished seventh chords Posa breaks off with another lyrical phrase ('Ah, la main de Dieu soit bénie', Ex. 40) giving thanks to God for having allowed him to make these things known to the King. Repeated in G flat major it gradually brings the long solo back to its starting-point of E flat major.

Philip's reply is simple. Only by getting rid of the reformers can he ensure peace and prosperity to the world ('J'ai de ce prix sanglant pàyé la paix du monde'). The reader may find it useful to see the three successive settings of this statement side by side, even if at the moment we are concerned only with the first of them. (See Ex. 41a, b, c)

In 1867 Philip's language recalls that of Federico Barbarossa in *La Battaglia di Legnano*, but with an appropriately larger scale of phrase. Here too the bass line is doubled and the assertion of power is conveyed by the upward-reaching line (*x*) which covers more than an octave. But unlike Barbarossa, Philip is calm, almost smiling – a rare occurrence for him; and it may perhaps be the reason why Verdi recalls this theme in the orchestra in a later context where the monarch is again benign. But despite the suave harmonies the mailed fist appears all too clearly at the words 'La mort entre mes mains peut devenir féconde', with heavy rappings from brass and drums. Posa proceeds undeterred. 'Nothing,' he says, 'can stop humanity's progress.' 'Mine!' cries Philip, and a violent, Donner-like roll on the timpani indicates the force behind his words.

What follows has the formality of a 'dissimilar' duet cantabile in which the voices, beginning separately, end by uniting in lyrical extended phrases. Posa, however, retains the initiative throughout. 'A breath of fire has passed over the earth; all Europe is rocked by it. . . . God is telling His will. . . . Give your children freedom.'

41a

41b

(1872)

(1884)

The marching crotchets (Ex. 42a) are humanity's march towards the new dawn; the cello semiquavers, the steadily blowing wind of liberty. To Posa's impassioned plea ('Donnez, donnez la liberté') Philip's reaction (Ex. 42b) is curiously ineffectual, almost, as one writer has put it, in the style of opera buffa.* Not one, he says, has

* For this and other valuable observations on the duet finale of Act II see G. Pestelli, 'Il personaggio di Filippo dalla versione parigina a quella del 1884', in *Atti del II° Congresso del I.S.V.*, pp. 449–54.

42a

Meno mosso ♩ = 104

RODRIGUE *sotto voce* *avec chaleur*

cresc.

Un souf – fle ar – dent a pas-sé sur la ter – re! il a fait tressail-

– lir ___ l'Eu-ro-pe tou-te en-tiè ___ re!

(1867)

42b

PHILIPPE

pp (à part)

Quel lan-ga-ge nou – veau! Ja-mais, au-près du trô – ne, per-son-ne n'é-le-

– va la voix si haut.... per – son-ne,

(1867)

ever spoken to him so freely before. The purpose of these short phrases is clearly to contrast with Posa's cantilena; but the basic weakness of the duet is already becoming apparent. A baritone of Posa's type and a bass of Philip's do not provide the ingredients for Verdian vocal dialectic in the present context. Only at the words 'Jamais, jamais, non, non jamais' twelve bars before the end of the movement does Philip's utterance resume a majestic note. In reply Posa throws himself at Philip's feet. In a few lines of string-accompanied recitative the King bids him rise. He will forgive Posa much because of his youth: 'Votre tête est bien blonde pourque vous invoquiez le fantôme imposteur devant un vieillard, Roi de la moitié du monde.' But he must beware of the Inquisitor; and never has the Verdian six-four appeared in more sinister guise than beneath the words 'gardez-vous de mon Inquisiteur'. For the second time Posa is about to leave when the King calls him back. So much does he approve Posa's courage and pride that he wants to confide to him his own troubles. At this point there occurs another passage that was removed before the first night and which may briefly be considered here.

1866 only

Posa, says Philip, has only seen him in his regal state. His domestic life is beset by treason and falsehood. He suspects his wife and his son. Posa, courageous as ever, will not hear a word against Carlos ('Son âme est noble et pure'). Philip, whose line has been mostly a brooding 'parlante', bursts out with tortured vehemence ('Rien ne vaut le bien qu'il m'a ravi!'). To Posa's astonished reaction ('Qu'osez vous dire?') the King replies that from now on he will confide entirely in Posa's judgement where his private relations are concerned. It is interesting to hear in his phrase 'Toi qui seul es un homme au milieu des humains' those religious overlapping fourths which in the mouth of the minister Jorg set the tone of *Stiffelio*; almost as though the monarch had undergone a religious conversion.

43

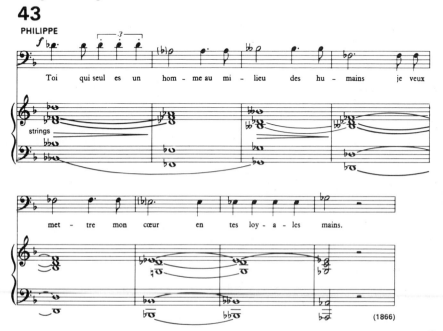

Posa's 'C'est un rêve' uttered to high ethereal string chords is hardly surprising.

1867

Again, considerations of length made this a possible excision and, it seems, a fairly late one. The dialogue is a somewhat crude reproduction of what happens in Schiller, with Philip embarrassingly explicit in the presence of someone he hardly knows. In the musical realization he appears vulnerable to the point of losing his dignity; and Verdi may well have thought it wise to cut short his self-revelation after the couplet:

> Non, reste, enfant, j'aime ton âme fière,
> La mienne à toi va s'ouvrir toute entière.

Set to a less expansive gesture than formerly this promise was judged sufficient to induce the sense of release, not to say euphoria, of the final cabaletta ('Enfant! à mon coeur éperdu'), a smooth, grateful cantilena eminently suited to the creator of Procida in *Les Vêpres Siciliennes* (Ex. 44a).

1866, 1867

Posa's 'dissimilar' reply (Ex. 44b, 'Quel rayon du ciel descendu') balances this neatly, moving up where Philip's line moves down and vice versa. Yet it was evidently an inspired afterthought, since the baritone rehearsal books contain the passed-over traces of a different idea (Ex. 44c) which has in it the making of a tolerable Strauss waltz, but is quite out of place here. As if at a signal the Count of Lerma enters with several grandees. Philip gives him orders to admit Posa to the palace at any hour of the day or night. As to why the grandees should have been present the autograph tells us that they, together with Lerma, were originally intended to sing during the internal ritornello of the cabaletta to the words 'Ah, c'est un astre nouveau'. In the end Verdi decided to finish the duet as a strict tête-à-tête, with the two voices singing Ex. 44a in unison.

Despite the smooth expertise of the writing, and the attractiveness of the melody, this remains in the context of the opera as a whole a weak cabaletta, in which the character of Philip is fatally compromised. In the earlier part of the duet, so long as he stands his ground against Posa he becomes just another 'cavalier-bariton' with a range lower than Posa's but no real difference in vocal expression. Contrast, the

(1867)

essence of Verdian dialogue, is lacking; and the duet which began so impressively ends becalmed.

For the Naples performance of 1872, the first in Italy of which he took personal charge, Verdi set himself to remedy this glaring defect.

1872 only

The point of revision begins with Philip's reply to Posa's appeal (see Ex. 41b). Although the new version saves only two bars, already one can discern the beginnings of the process that was to turn the duet into a 'dramatic dialogue'. Much that smacks of traditional French grand opera has been eliminated – the pompous, march-like tramp, the richly spiced harmonies redolent of Liszt and Meyerbeer. There is even a recollection of Amonasro at the words 'che illudono le genti con sogni mentitor'. Curiously, 'la mort' is replaced by 'il ferro' (only to become once more 'la mort' in the final revision); but the death 'rat-a-tat' remains as before. Throughout, Philip's tone is coolly, almost brusquely dismissive, and in general truer than before to his real character. The change involves one drawback, however; the recurrence of

Ex. 40a in Act IV no longer has any retrospective significance. However, as we have had occasion to note before, back references were less important in Verdi's scheme of things than is often supposed. Posa's reply ('No! rugge invan la folgore') is both shorter and stronger than before; Philip's 'Il mio' is reduced to a short sharp rap from the full orchestra.

The cantabile ('Un soffio ardente') is shorn of its twelve final bars where the voices join and in consequence – fortunately – of that anticipation of the triumphal scene in *Aida* which a Neapolitan audience would certainly have spotted and remarked on, since both operas were being produced there in the same season. Instead Philip decides after Posa's second 'Date la libertà' that his subject has been given enough licence for one day; and he cuts him short with 'Taci omai, ne invocare il fantasma impostor' in which trumpets, trombones and ophicleide play their usual minatory role. Philip's dignity is thus restored and the music prevented from running aground in the shallows of a conventional coda. From here to the end of the act everything is rewritten entirely. Verdi and Ghislanzoni decided to recover the King's confession which had been suppressed in 1867 but to express it in a manner more worthy of an

45

absolutist monarch. After his warning to Posa he subtly changes the subject. The marquis has been bold enough to gaze upon the throne. Why will he not cast a glance around him in the palace? What is there to see, Posa asks, except a son and an 'angelica donna'? Has no rumour reached him, Philip asks, which accuses them of guilt? 'I have the proof in my possession.' 'Who would dare?' Posa exclaims, which is certainly more suitable than 'What do you dare to say?' as in 1867. 'Eboli . . . the Duke of Alva . . . the priest. They are their enemies.' This is less happy – a maladroit compression of Schiller, Act III, lines 3320–30. It is surely expecting too much of an operatic audience to imagine that it would identify the 'sacerdote' as Father Domingo or to understand what the Duke of Alva had to do with the matter. Besides, Eboli was hostile neither to Carlos nor to Elisabeth at this stage. Evidently both Verdi and Ghislanzoni had forgotten that this dialogue had been brought forward from its position in the play. 'My heart is torn,' Philip continues, 'by a fearful doubt which only a man of proven loyalty can dispel. I need such a man; and I choose you.' So Philip gains a favour by appearing to grant one; and this too is in character. It is why men of his stamp rule vast empires.

Musically the revision is a vast improvement. Its basis is a sinuous orchestral theme mounting by semitones, not in the triple formula associated with ritual scenes but in diminishing repeated fragments, like ever-tightening coils, through which Posa would do well to step warily. It is the work of a composer who has already written the Radames–Amneris duet in Act IV of *Aida*. (Ex. 45)

The cabaletta ('Di lei, di Carlo in core lo sguardo tuo discenda') is far better than its predecessor, avoiding the latter's four-square design and at the same time giving the right touch of imperiousness to Philip's words (he is, after all, issuing an order). (Ex. 46)

Posa's reply ('Oh Carlo, Carlo mio! Se a te vicino sarò') is in slightly faster tempo and has one of those fleet bass lines characteristic of the later Verdi. There is no entrance for Lerma with or without grandees; instead the King dismisses Posa with a warning to be careful of the old Inquisitor. No trombones, trumpets and ophicleide this time, but a spine-chilling succession of soft chords for strings alone, including a shift from E flat major (I) to D major (I) worthy of Beethoven at his boldest. Ex. 46 is heard high on the violins like the perfect love that casteth out fear, then answered by both voices forte over a huge orchestral climax which brings the movement to a close.

Strong as it is, this solution still failed to satisfy Verdi from the standpoint of 1883. It was too long, too lyrical and in a word too conventionally 'grand operatic'. The text, although taking Schiller as its starting-point, missed the highlights of the original dialogue which it diluted in a rather vague sentimental manifesto for the cause of freedom, such as offered no basis for a real confrontation between the two singers. Not for the first time the composer had recourse to the work of his friend Andrea Maffei whose translation of Schiller's play had been published in 1858.* Indeed several of Maffei's lines, thinly camouflaged in the French text, reappear almost unaltered in the Italian version. Above all, the 'dialectic' of their duet is conveyed in an entirely new manner, and one which will reappear in the love duet of *Otello*. Its characteristics are: a succession of sentences, basically regular but freely

* For a correlation of the two texts of this duet with Schiller's play see M. Chusid, 'Schiller revisited: some observations on the revision of *Don Carlos*', in *Atti del II° Congresso del I.S.V.*, pp. 156–69.

46

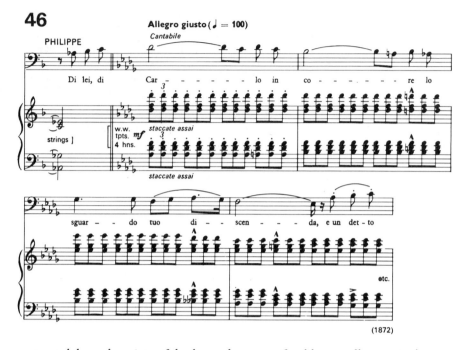

(1872)

protracted through variety of rhythm and accent, a flexible rate of harmonic change; a continual colouring of the vocal line by progressions which though often unpredictable yet remain within the main tonal orbit (here mostly F major and B flat); and the whole so constructed as to form an organic unit crowned, as usual, by a movement of pure symmetry. The underlying tramp of the grand opera ceremonial march has faded away. Indeed this is one reason why this definitive version of the duet so often disappoints the unprepared listener. Not only does it come at the end of an act which is just too long for comfort; its subtleties of harmony and form do not appear to best advantage in the context of an opera which mostly operates through more obvious means.

1884, 1886

The revision begins at the point where we expect Posa's 'Pour mon pays' (Ex. 38). The sentiments are the same, so too the martial rhythm; but all suggestions of a closed movement with a tempo to itself have gone. 'Si mon pays a besoin' takes on the quality of a comment on Philip's previous phrase, a single sentence, modulating where the first had kept strictly to E flat and extended by small sequences to finish on a cadence in C minor. Happily, too, the charge of Posa's audacity is not detonated too near the outset as in previous versions. He no longer mentions the executioner's axe. Indeed in the following parlando bars with their continuously subsiding bass line, the Marquis, impeccably respectful to his sovereign ('Je parlerai, Sire, si vous le voulez'), descends to a submissive low A, a rare enough occurrence for a Verdian baritone. The Flanders speech, beginning from Ex. 39, with its rhetorical insistence, fitted well enough into the revision to be retained as it stood, but its sequel (Ex. 40) is treated quite differently. In 1867 it had been stated then repeated, Bruckner fashion, a major third below, from which point the music found its way to a concluding cadence in E flat. Now Posa's appeal is all the stronger for remaining in the key of B flat throughout. Ex. 40 is repeated at pitch with modifications and a woodwind state-ment of the same theme spliced into the gap; the line is then extended through a climactic high F to a B flat major cadence, so compressing into seven bars what had previously taken nine to say. In many ways it is a simpler solution than the original; but it is a simplicity born of extreme concentration as a glance at the harmonic rhythm will show. Once more, too, Verdi has avoided falling into those quasi-mechanical triplets that so often figure in his first thoughts for this opera.

With Philip's reply (Ex. 41c) the *Otello* manner develops still further. His words are the same as before but they are couched in a musical language more appropriate to a thought strongly expressed rather than to a general attitude of mind. Moreover, the vocal line is sufficiently pliant rhythmically and harmonically to be able to reflect the sense of the passing word. (In 1867 the 'crushing of the reformers' pride' was accom-panied by the suavest of progressions.) The 'deluding dreams' are emphasized with an unexpected off-beat plunge into E flat minor followed by a bar of sighing chromatics; after which 'La mort' with a fortissimo blow from full orchestra no longer needs the conventional death-figure to make its meaning clear. Now comes an entirely new section based on Schiller's lines, ingeniously reshuffled.

POSA	You want to plant for all eternity,	
	And you sow death	(II, 3181–2)
KING	Look	
	About you in this Spain of mine. The welfare	
	Of citizens blooms here in cloudless peace;	
	And this peace I grant to the Flemish people.	
POSA	The peace of cemeteries!	(II, 3158–62)

Philip's praise of his own peaceful government is blown to atoms by Posa's 'La paix du cimitière' with one of those orchestral thunderbolts with which the late Verdi seems to anticipate the 'Veristi' but with far greater force; an almost atonal tremolo on the strings with sustaining clarinets, bassoons, horns, trombones and ophicleide (all in their lowest register) and rolling timpani; the initial major second gradually widens to a bare fifth in E minor fading away on the two clarinets as Posa warns the King not to go down to history as a second Nero (this also from Schiller). The long solo that follows ('Est-ce la paix que vous donnez au monde?') clothes Posa's plea for freedom with a new and far more compelling eloquence. The text of both this and the original derives from Schiller, but the shift of emphasis is interesting. In the first version with its insistence on the irresistible progress of humanity we can find an echo of the famous letter sent to Piave in 1848, 'Be sure, the hour of [Italy's] liberty has struck; the people wills it and when the people wills there is no absolute power that can resist them.'* In 1867 it was still possible to think in this way; but 'tempora mutantur, nos et mutamur in illis'. By 1884 there was little reason to trust in the automatic triumph of progress. The new Posa therefore appeals merely to the King's sense of what is right. Everywhere in Flanders, he says, Philip's name is spoken with curses; let him give new life to the entire world by granting freedom. Posa begins in dialogue with the cellos and bassoons.

* Letter to Piave, 21.4.1848. Walker, pp. 187–8; Abbiati, I, p. 745.

47

(1884)

This is again a cumulative discourse on the analogy of 'O Roi, j'arrive de Flandre', but more symphonically treated. Whereas the earlier example had depended for its effect on the accretion of ever new accompanimental material, here everything derives from Ex. 47 mounting in ever-tightening progressions to the powerful dominant pedal at '. . . immense, où le nom de Philippe est maudit'. For Posa's earnest plea ('Répandez comme un dieu') the music by a familiar process smooths out into broad regular phrases, until by a final expansion it is brought to rest in the key of E major at the words 'Donnez la liberté'. Like a stone cast into the dark pool of Philip's mind Posa's eloquence seems to create a succession of ripples that spread round the central point of E. We are in the harmonic world of Liszt (though the figuration is rather less Lisztian than appears from the piano reduction).

48

(1884)

'Strange visionary,' murmurs Philip; and gradually the gloom of F sharp minor seeps in as he reflects that Posa would change his opinion if he knew human nature as well as Philip himself. This too is directly from Schiller; but like so much else it suffers a sea-change in its transference from play to opera. Schiller's monarch is speaking 'mit gemildertem Ernst', i.e. with 'lightened seriousness'. His tone is both good-humoured and dismissive, as he produces the platitude with which age always counters the idealism of youth. Verdi's Philip speaks from the depths of a brooding pessimism, as one who would gladly have entertained Posa's sentiments had experience not taught him otherwise. Rousing himself, Philip then tells Posa in the kind of elliptical style which Verdi always tried to coax from his librettists that the King in him has understood nothing; but Posa must beware of the Grand Inquisitor. It is a solemn speech, delivered over soft string chords; but there is a spine-chilling non-sequitur (F sharp major to A minor), fortified by sustaining wind at the all-important 'mais'. The words 'Grand Inquisiteur' form a C major cadence – a muffled tutti explosion which rumbles away into silence beneath Posa's astonished 'Quoi! Sire?' Still with C major hanging in the air the King commands Posa to remain close to his person; Posa refuses and Philip growls at his subject's excess of pride. Why this should all be dispatched in the most perfunctory and monotonous recitative becomes clear when we consider the design as a whole. The previous section, as far as Posa's 'donnez la liberté', concerned as it is with public and political issues, had revolved round an A minor–E major axis, touching on the related keys of both. To this Philip's reply forms a transition to an entirely new subject, namely his own domestic affairs. As in *Rigoletto* and elsewhere the new sphere is reached by a shift of tonal area – in this instance to F minor–major. The C major, to which Philip had conjured up the spectre of the Inquisition, forms the link between two regions. Having silenced Posa with this threat it only remains for the King to pass on with all haste to the matter which is on *his* mind, and which Posa's fearless outspokenness has encouraged him to broach. The text of what follows reverts mostly to the lines of 1866, but their musical setting is entirely different. The opening motif makes its dramatic points subtly and without the slightest exaggeration, while remaining true to the natural inflexions of human speech; nor is Verdi afraid by this time to exploit the lower register of a principal bass in a conversational context – an effect which the great bassi cantanti of his youth would not have tolerated for a moment. Although Philip does not voice his jealous suspicions at once, it is surely significant that his opening phrase anticipates Iago's about the green-eyed monster.

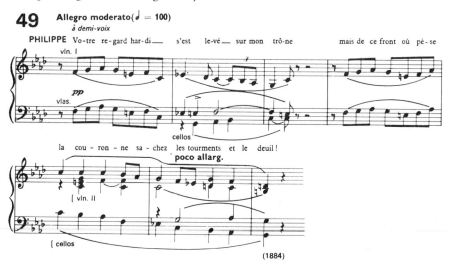

Throughout Philip's long, flexibly articulated solo the King allows us to enter into his agony of soul without ever losing his dignity. There is a wealth of unspoken grief in 'Oui, père malheureux! plus malheureux époux' where a single harmonic idea is varied by changes in scoring as well as in the contour and rhythm of the melody.

50

After his outburst ('Rien me vaut, sous le ciel, le bien qu'il m'a ravi'), set far more movingly than in 1866, Ex. 49 is taken over in diminution by the orchestral strings to form an accompanimental pattern, so anticipating a device to be found more than once in *Falstaff*.* The solo culminates in a noble, expansive phrase in F major ('Toi qui seul es un homme au milieu des humains, je veux mettre mon coeur en tes loyales mains'), in which variously sustaining wind colour the basic tone of tremolando strings. The climax is reached on the word 'humains' supported by oboes, clarinets, horns, bassoons, cornets, trumpets and rolling timpani; after which the strings are left on their own. The phrase carries a charge sufficient to launch what is in effect the final movement, though there is no change of tempo. ('Ah, quelle aurore au ciel se lève'.) (See Ex. 51a.) Although the text bears no relation to that of 1872, the music recalls Ex. 46 clearly enough; this time, however, it is entrusted to Posa in his 'transport of joy' instead of Philip. Indeed it is interesting to observe how the three different endings to the duet move Philip and Posa ever further apart. The cabaletta of 1867 finished with them singing the same melody in unison; in 1872 they had remained in the same key and joined in the final phrase. In the present version, which can hardly be called a cabaletta at all, not only do they never sing each other's music; they establish themselves in different keys (F major for Posa, A minor for Philip), so that even where the laws of musical structure compel them to join, there is no danger of our confounding Posa's extravagant joy with Philip's only half-lightened gloom. True, Verdi had achieved this kind of distinction as early as *Ernani*; but here it is managed with something of the subtlety by which Mozart separates Donna Anna and Ottavio in the duet from the first act of *Don Giovanni*. Thus, when Ex. 51a returns the time-signature changes to 2/4, so that Rodrigue's enthusiasm receives a fresh boost from the consequent doubling of main beats. It is left to Philip twelve bars later to restore the more sober 4/4 – again without any alteration of the metronome marking. (Ex. 51b)

Observe too what the mature Verdi is able to do with the three note figure (x). Not only is it echoed over and over again throughout the orchestral texture; it emerges as a natural consequent of Ex. 49, which in turn originates with the version of 1872.

There is a final surprise before the curtain falls. The music is arrested in its swift

* See Rosen, *op. cit.* Instances include 'Te lo cornifico', 'Dalla due alle tre', 'Riempirvi la pancia'.

progress towards the final cadence as Philip once more warns Posa to beware of the Grand Inquisitor. It is a typical harmonic ellipsis; the orchestra breaks off on a chord of D minor; Philip utters his caution on an unaccompanied F; the full orchestra replies with a chord of D flat pianissimo. The effect is startlingly novel; yet Verdi had used the full orchestra in this way in the last act of *Il Trovatore*; while the same harmonic device can be found in all essentials in Giselda's prayer in *I Lombardi*. As if to indicate how deeply Philip is in earnest the final 'Garde-toi' is rapped out to a peremptory fortissimo chord. He holds out his hand to Posa who kneels and kisses it as the orchestra reasserts F major in all its glory.*

---

* The production book of 1886 carries the typical exhortation:

The artists should be recommended to pay great attention to this piece [i.e., the whole duet] *which is very*

In his correspondence with Nuitter over the revision of this duet Verdi had more than once inveighed against the exigencies of metre and rhyme. 'I believe that for an opera in modern music one should adopt unrhymed verse; and moreover that the effective word, the word which both strikes and sculpts [*colpisce e scolpisce*] is often weakened when it is anticipated by a rhyme.'* In fact the third version of the duet is entirely liberated from the tyranny of regular verse. This is its strength – and also its weakness. The listener is required to make a mental adjustment for the last, densely packed ten minutes of a very long act. As in *La Forza del destino*, Verdi strains the musical digestion of his audience.

ACT III

Scene 1 (1866, 1867, 1872): The Queen's Gardens in Madrid. An enclosed grove. At the back beneath a leafy arch are a statue and a fountain.

Nowhere in the opera does Verdi make a more conscious display of skill and sophistication than in the third act of *Don Carlos*. It begins with another of those essays in local colour which at this time a Spanish setting would be thought to require. As usual, the exoticism is of the boulevardier variety. Cornets, trumpets and trombones rap out a figure in that characteristic 3/8 rhythm heard at the beginning of the Veil Song, and are answered by full orchestra in the same vein. A Chopinesque theme (Ex. 52a) follows to which alternating flute and piccolo give an attractive sheen.

This leads through unaccustomed paths, boldly trodden (Ex. 52b), to the nub of the scene, a long, offstage chorus ('Que de fleurs et que d'étoiles'), unaccompanied except by tambours basques and castanets.† Sometimes for men only, sometimes for mixed chorus, its chain of melodies shows a wide variety of texture yet the result is always limpid. Verdi's Spain may not be particularly authentic but it has something of the charm of Tchaikovsky's China or Grieg's Arabia (Ex. 52c).

To a resumption of Ex. 52a Elisabeth enters with Eboli. The Queen was supposed to take part in the evening's *divertissement*; but she is tired, and, since the next day will

---

difficult not only musically but also theatrically. *The actors should thoroughly identify themselves with the two characters who stand face to face and who represent two great principles in the history of mankind. (Disp. scen.* (1886), p. 19.)

* Letter to Nuitter, 28.10.1882. *An. Mus.*, XV, pp. 364–6.

† During the offstage chorus the production book of 1867 prescribes the following mime for members of the corps de ballet: *Seven ladies and 6 gentlemen enter backstage R. and exeunt backstage L. – 2 ladies enter front of stage R. each holding a mask in her hand. A gentleman enters backstage L. and approaches the two ladies offering an arm to each; the latter will have donned their masks and refuse the gentleman's offer since they are unacquainted with him; then they move away L. At that moment, enter backstage L. a lady and a gentleman whom they do know, and they unmask. The two gentlemen shake hands, and the first begs his friend to introduce him to the two ladies; after which both ladies accept his arm and all five exeunt backstage L.*

At the same time two other gentlemen enter backstage L. One of them believes he knows one of the ladies who are leaving; and after having exchanged a few words together they hastily follow the people who have just left. . . .

Towards the end of the chorus Elisabeth enters with Eboli backstage R; they are followed by Thibault, 2 other pages and 4 ladies of the court; of the first two ladies one carries the Queen's cloak, the other her mask. See Disp. scen. (1867), pp. 23–4.

52a

52b

52c

see Philip's official coronation, she wishes to spend the night in prayer. Eboli must take her mask, mantilla and necklace therefore and stand in for her; nobody will notice the difference. To a broad sweeping phrase over tremolando strings ('Va! Je me sens dans l'âme') she declares her 'thirst' for communion with God – who presumably will not regard the deception as unethical; whereupon she leaves.*

Again the chorus are heard offstage hymning the beauties of the night. Eboli enjoys a short, coolly seductive solo ('Me voilà reine pour une nuit') of which appropriately the central section is the refrain of the Veil Song in all its orchestral finery as Eboli compares herself to the queen in the legend. By recalling this melody in G major within the prevailing tonality of A minor Verdi adds a piquantly modal touch to what is otherwise a conventional diatonic design.

Eboli then writes hurriedly on a piece of paper and gives it to one of the pages. As

* *Followed by Thibault and 2 of the ladies-in-waiting. Disp. scen.* (1867), p. 24.

Ex. 52c dies away on distant voices she declares that this night she will 'intoxicate Carlos with love'. This scene has nothing to do with Schiller; but it entered the minds of the librettists at quite an early stage. Doubtless they felt that the audience had to be shown a more obvious reason why Carlos should keep a tryst with Eboli in mistake for Elisabeth than the one supplied by the playwright. The original prose synopsis, it is true, keeps strictly to Schiller at this point (rather more in fact than the final result), but already in the 'pink' libretto there is a scene in which Eboli, veiled throughout, always playing the character of the queen, continually appears before Carlos and flees from him, making him drunk with love and desire'. This clumsy anticipation of *The Sleeping Beauty*, Act III (as if Don Carlos even at the height of his illusion could ever have credited such behaviour to the Elisabeth who had rejected him with such dignity in the previous act!) was happily dropped; but the exchanging of the masks had two advantages to offer: a link with the Veil Song just noted; and a means – to be noted later – whereby the ballet could be linked with the main drama instead of remaining a purely irrelevant *divertissement*. Indeed, versions which include the ballet retain it; but Verdi himself was most insistent that once the ballet is removed the scene has no raison d'être, and if, as in one or two recent productions, it is restored without the ballet there is a risk that Eboli's last lines will be misunderstood since they will imply that she is not only aware of Carlos's passion for the Queen but content to be made love to in mistake for her royal mistress. The role of Strauss's Zdenka is certainly not for Eboli. Her vanity, it should be remembered, is boundless. She is convinced that when she appears in her borrowed finery in the ballet's crowning 'set piece' Carlos will penetrate her disguise, and that seeing her attired in a manner befitting her charms he will become more besotted with her than ever.

Ballet: La Peregrina (1866, 1867, 1872; 1884 if required)

Sustained chords of G major and B major decorated by sweeping string arpeggios, joined after a while by flute and piccolo, introduce us to 'a magic grotto formed of mother of pearl and coral, where the most marvellous pearls of ocean are hidden in their shells and guarded by jealous waves . . .' (so run the jottings in the manuscript score). The Black Pearl is admiring herself in a mirror which the waves hand to her . . . the Pink Pearl is trying on garlands of marine flowers. . . .* The operations would seem to be consecutive rather than simultaneous; but in fact it is not easy to match music and incident in this first piece, in which Verdi seems to have done little more than establish a pictorial ambiance. (Ex. 53a)

The musical ideas in general are less striking than their treatment. The scoring of Ex. 53a, with its tightly packed figuration, results in a soft yet shallow sound like the lapping of waves on shingle. Its companion theme (Ex. 53b) beats out a well worn Franco-Italian track. But at its reappearance after a short episode in the minor it is scored with a magnificent opulence, trumpets and trombones adding to the warmth without ever suggesting a conventional tutti. Here, according to the later scenario, 'A fisherman descends. . . . Dazzled by so many splendours he believes himself to be dreaming; the pearls coquettishly delight in parading all their seductive charms before him.' The genie, so the autograph tells us, was apparently meant to drift down

---

* The 1867 production book prescribes a bluish electric light, three large shells for the three pearls and three trapdoors through which various characters will appear. *Disp. scen.* (1867), p. 25.

a ray of light about ten bars earlier; and the curve of the music does indeed suggest a descent of some sort. The pearls in this version take fright and hide; the waves do their best to hold back the intruder. A long decrescendo, based on Ex. 53a embellished with ingenious chromatic harmonies denotes the weakening power of the would-be guardians. The fisherman/genie finds himself alone in the cave. He then notices the White Pearl sleeping in her still-open shell; he approaches her, and plants a kiss on her forehead.* Here for the first time since *I Lombardi* Verdi employs a concertante violin† – and how differently! Then its style had been homespun Paganini; here it moves in the world of Chopin and Delibes. Its entry is made in one of those passages of instrumental recitative that had come down from C. P. E. Bach via Beethoven to Chopin but are quite foreign to the Italian tradition (Ex. 54a). This develops into some skilful action music: a pattern of ascending chords for three horns answered by rapid arpeggio flourishes on the violin; then a pleading melody of real eloquence (Ex. 54b). The pearl awakes in terror causing the violinist to skip nimbly about in the lower register (Ex. 54c) but the fisherman/genie coaxes her (Ex. 54b again) and lulls her fears with further cadenzas and some rather sugary double-stopping.

* So the scenario of the autograph; in the printed score the waves try to hide the sleeping pearl – but the music tells us that this is a solo passage; and anyway the waves have withdrawn for the present.

† Originally it was to have been a viola d'amore, as the sketches in the Bibliothèque de l'Opéra (A 619, supp. 1) make clear. Nor was it until he had written twenty-two bars of full score that Verdi changed his mind. Mostly the sketches are continuity drafts like that of *Rigoletto* with bars and melody line only. But there are fuller workings-out for the first movement of the waltz.

The fisherman takes the White Pearl in his arms and they start to waltz in a dance-like movement which Verdi sketched three times before it fully satisfied him. Again it is the texture and treatment that command attention rather than the melody itself, whose first phrase ends rather lamely for so graceful a piece of music.

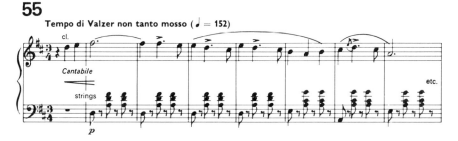

There is a D minor episode (replacing a different idea in the sketch) with a popping bassoon accompaniment, an attractive dialogue of overlapping phrases between clarinet and cello, and a transition to the reprise that uses the flute and piccolo to good effect. Ex. 55 returns more richly scored and embellished by a busy bass line. Sixteen bars of coda wind up the movement.

The next dance begins with an allegro agitato which was evidently a late interpolation to judge from the evidence of sketches and autograph score. 'The White Pearl, who had been terrified at the fisherman's approach, gradually takes heart,' says the printed copy; but as she has been already dancing quite happily with the fisherman, this is presumably a delayed reaction. It is over in a matter of eighteen bars, to be followed by the 'variation' of the White Pearl, ushered in by a tripping theme with a choreographic vividness about it that reminds us that between the time of *Les Vêpres Siciliennes* and that of *Don Carlos* romantic ballet had entered its era of virtuosity. As its vocabulary of steps expanded so ballet music took on a new toughness, a new piquancy of rhythm and scoring. The dances in the earlier opera belong to the relatively uncomplicated tradition of Adam, Hérold and Pugni; those of *Don Carlos* look forward to the greatest of all composers to serve the romantic ballet, Tchaikovsky, whose Danse des Mirlitons is foreshadowed in a B minor episode (Ex. 56b).

56a

56b

The waltz is resumed with further intricacies which include a cello counter melody so that Ex. 55 is all but engulfed. Wisely did Verdi warn Mazzucato after attending a rehearsal, 'When the clarinet takes up the waltz for the second time all the strings should play pianissimo and produce a distant murmur. . . . Here too it could be said that there are too many instruments; but no — even if there were a thousand strings they will never drown the clarinet if they use the bow properly.'*

Meantime the other pearls and the waves have been observing their sister's scandalous behaviour, half shocked, half jealous. Gradually all join in the dance which develops into a 6/8 romp, shot through with brilliant and variegated tone-colours (Ex. 57a). Daunting feats are required of flutes and piccolo, of which the piano reduction gives very little idea (Ex. 57b).

Like an angry headmistress the Queen of the Waters bursts in upon the scene to crashing A minor chords on brass and bassoons. Busy figuration on cellos and basses conveys her wrathful sentence; the pearls implore her in a plangent melody for

* Letter to A. Mazzucato, 20.3.1868. Ghisi and De Bellis, *Atti del II° Congresso del I.S.V.*, pp. 540–1.

57a

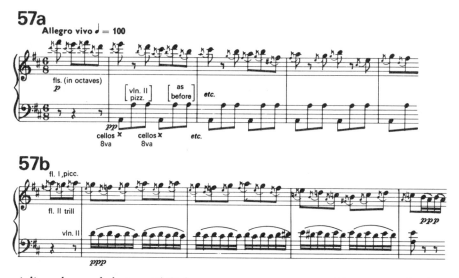

57b

violins, oboe and clarinet. Philip's page enters to a ceremonial hymn – resplendent on brass.*

58

The finale – a 'maritime striptease', in Andrew Porter's phrase† – is a gallop, as in all Verdi's grand opera ballets written to date. Like that of *Les Vêpres Siciliennes* it is based on a theme that sweeps vigorously up and down (in this case, down and up) but the touch is lighter, the scoring more brilliant and a wealth of swift modulation gives an effect of wit that the earlier piece lacks. The skaters' gallop from *Le Prophète* has provided a model here, and as usual Verdi has improved upon it with his greater fluency and sense of large-scale structure. In form it is a rondo with episodes which sometimes develop the main theme, and sometimes contrast with it. Offenbach, Rossini and even Mendelssohn have left their mark on this attractive *jeu d'esprit*; but of these only the author of 'Péchés de vieillesse' would have risked a string of epigrams such as make up Ex. 59.

Full orchestra intone Ex. 58 with brass and bassoons taking over bars 9–12 as Eboli, representing La Peregrina, appears through a trapdoor, and all bow to her in homage.‡

* Although it is referred to in the scenario as the 'Spanish Hymn' (*Disp. scen.*, p. 26), no musical source for this melody has yet been found.

† 'Verdi's ballet music and *La Peregrina*', in *Atti del II° Congresso del I.S.V.*, p. 563.

‡ At one point it was thought necessary to halve the melody by removing the middle eight bars, presumably in order to save time. Having crossed these out on the autograph Verdi then added the words, 'C'est bon', as he was to do later at the end of Act III, i.

59

Like the ballet in *Macbeth*, *La Peregrina* takes the new age of virtuoso conducting into account; it is designed to 'make the orchestra dance' (to use a phrase of Verdi's)* no less than the ballet dancers. But the taste of audiences and the purses of managements soon found it expendable, and not unreasonably. Not even Eboli's role in it can prevent it from remaining a composition on its own, cut off from the dramatic artery of the opera. As well as this – perhaps even because of it – one senses a certain split between the musical ideas and their treatment, the first rather commonplace, the second sophisticated and highly wrought. Not until his next opera did Verdi succeed in writing a ballet that belonged. No one would dream of removing the dances from *Aida*.

Prelude (1884, 1886)

This begins with the first six bars of 'Je l'ai vue' ('Io la vidi') in its revised form, harmonized as before but differently scored (horn, clarinets and bassoon on the melody, cellos accompanying) and re-transposed to C. Thence it wanders away in a series of climbing sequences all based on the first phrase. It is impossible to miss the influence of the prelude to *Lohengrin*, one of the few parts of that opera to meet with

* Letter to Arrivabene, 10.6.1884. Alberti, pp. 311–15.

Verdi's unqualified approval; only here the general direction is inverted. Wagner's piece starts in the upper atmosphere, moves to the middle regions then returns aloft. Verdi's prelude ascends from a warm sonority in the middle register to a high central cadence in F sharp major on tremolando divisi violins. Then, while these continue, the sequential figure recommences at an immense distance below, alternating cellos with solo bassoon; the lower line rises to join the tremolando chords now sustained by upper woodwind, after which the music floats downward on a chain of slow chords played by strings only with cellos reduced to two for the first two bars. An eight-bar coda based on the same rising sequence concludes the piece. Never was Verdi's ear more finely attuned than in the scoring of this prelude whose chain of sequences gives the effect of a continuous flowering. Yet the utmost economy is used: strings are muted throughout; there are no trumpets, trombones, ophicleide or bassoons; and horns are reduced to one apiece. It is the selective instrumentation of the early operas used with a far greater imagination, combined with a sense of proportion and logic which can make a satisfying finite statement of thirty-five bars proceeding from C major to F sharp major and back again.

All versions

To a sustained chord of C major Carlos enters reading a letter: 'At midnight in the Queen's Gardens under the laurel by the fountain . . .'.* The scene which follows is one of the most successful of the 1867 score and therefore passed without modification into all subsequent versions. Like the Posa–Philip duet it reshuffles Schiller's original scheme which would have proved highly resistant to operatic treatment. The playwright spins out the tragi-comedy of Carlos's tryst with Eboli in 350 lines of mutual misunderstanding during which Eboli provides the prince with the damning evidence of King Philip's love letter. Only when he has left brandishing the letter in triumph does she put two and two together. Her first thought is to destroy the queenly hypocrite, whose air of being above all mortal passions she has always envied. She decides to yield to Philip's importunities and to arouse his suspicions about his wife's virtue. In the end her trickery is exposed by Posa in his new role as Philip's counsellor; but unfortunately he has by this time ceased to take Carlos into his confidence. The well-meaning Lerma starts to hint to the prince that Posa is playing a double game. It is with some difficulty that Carlos can bring himself to hand over his private papers at Posa's request. Finally, he decides that his only friend at court is the Princess Eboli; their interview is interrupted by a furious Posa crying out that Carlos is raving and Eboli should pay no attention to him. He puts Carlos under arrest; and as the prince is led away, Posa threatens to kill Eboli.

The prose project for the opera kept closer to Schiller's scheme than does the finished result, if only because the writers confined themselves at this point to Schiller's Act II, scenes viii and xv. They envisaged first of all a long duet of misunderstanding in which Eboli should reveal Philip's intentions towards her and warn Carlos against Posa. When she had left in a rage after discovering the true state of affairs, Posa would enter and reassure Carlos of his loyalty and obtain from him his private papers. Verdi, however, preferred a direct confrontation between the

* Originally it was thought necessary to repeat the offstage chorus, presumably to make it clear that we are back at the spot where the act opened. But time pressed, and the reprise survives only in the chorus rehearsal books.

characters concerned; the duet was therefore turned into a trio by the intervention of Posa, using lines from later on in the play. Instead of the thrust and parry of argument the scene is resolved into a succession of clearly defined emotional stances realized in an anticipation of what might be called the *Aida* manner: a profusion of basically symmetrical melodic ideas so closely packed as to seem separate articulations of a single cantilena. It is a new classicism distilled from the crumbling remains of the post-Rossinian tradition. By 1867 there was no longer a common stock of phrases to be drawn upon, no pre-determined methods of construction, no standardized accompaniments and harmonic procedures. In such an atmosphere, as we have noted, the lesser composers wilted; only Verdi was able to achieve self-renewal. In the *Aida* style you cannot safely predict the direction a phrase will take nor by what harmonies it will be accompanied, nor whether a melody will be repeated or replaced by a new one. All you can be sure of is that the sense of proportion will be unerring and that not a single note can be removed from the whole. A favourite pattern is *a–b–c* or *a–a–b–b–c*, *c* arriving where you might be led to expect *a* in a modified form. Thus in catching sight of Eboli coming to meet him, dressed as Elisabeth, Carlos is overwhelmed by a flood of emotion which he tries to control; but the effort is plain from the displaced stresses of the melody.

60

His solo begins with two pairs of parallel phrases of which one is based on Ex. 60. Eboli, still veiled, contributes a fresh idea ('Un tel amour, c'est le bien suprème. Il est doux d'être aimée ainsi') after which a return to Ex. 60 might be expected; instead of which Carlos, all heroic tenor, explodes in a phrase Radames might envy. (Ex. 61)

Both these examples are in D flat major, as always for Carlos the key of illusory happiness. Eboli responds meltingly, and Ex. 61 is heard once more before the princess unmasks. As in the play she misconstrues his reaction (she is not supposed to have heard his 'Ah, ce n'est pas la reine!'), ascribing it to an excess of caution. She knows the traps that have been set for him and will be his protector — so she says to an insinuating theme, horn moving in sixths with the voice. (Ex. 62) This will form the basis of the next movement.

61

62

During the musical discourse, sometimes singing with Ex. 62 and its variants, sometimes declaiming against it, Eboli tells the prince that Philip and Posa have been discussing him in secret. Carlos praises her angelic goodness of heart. Then in the coda again, romantically coloured by solo horn with cello counter-theme and lamenting woodwind acciaccature, he lets fall the expression which causes Eboli to realize the true situation: 'Nous avons fait tous deux un rêve étrange . . . .'. Her accusation 'Vous aimez la reine' is a wonderful instance of the parola scenica – an emphatic declamation of no musical interest since it keeps to one note, unsupported by orchestra, with a leap to the octave above for the first syllable of 'reine'. How infinitely feebler is the Italian 'Voi la regina amate', with its verbal inversion and its accent placed on the wrong word. Carlos's cry of 'Pitié' brings in Posa for a furious exchange with Eboli ('Que dit-il? . . . Il est en délire . . .') in which we hear for the first time since Act II the four-note pattern that plays so important a part in the opera's 'tinta'. The allegro agitato, strictly transitional, is balanced on an F minor–E major axis effectively exploited at Eboli's triumphant 'Je sais votre pouvoir, vous ignorez le mien' with its successive cadences in A major and A flat.

The confrontation expands lyrically in the andante ('Redoutez tout de ma furie'). It is still a private duel between Eboli and Posa, she evincing all the fury of a woman scorned in those rapid staccato gestures so dear to French grand opera, and in a snarling use of the lower register; he more composed, replying in long, measured phrases ('Parlez, parlez et dévoilez') though soon to become as agitated as the princess. Carlos, though the subject of their dispute, takes no part in it; his voice soars above the other two in a long-drawn-out cry of bewildered innocence ('Qu'ai-je fait, qu'ai-je fait, ô douleur amère!') that becomes more and more poignant as the music moves from F minor to F major then dies away in a coda. (Ex. 63) As in so many of Verdi's ensembles the emotional elements of the scene are resolved in a lyrical whole without ever losing their separate identity. Verdi will use a similar method to this in the trio of *Aida*, Act I; but there it will be the soprano who rides high above the storm, and the orchestral colouring will be much lighter, without the sombre tones of a score from which four bassoons, lower brass and timpani are rarely absent.

63

But it is for Elisabeth that Eboli reserves the full weight of her contempt – that 'new saint' who would 'sup at both tables'. Here, as in Melitone's part, the inflexions of ordinary speech have been harnessed to the purposes of music drama. In her sneering contempt for the 'sham' of Elisabeth's virtue Eboli anticipates Falstaff's diatribe against honour. Note too the unison trill as an expression of anger.

64

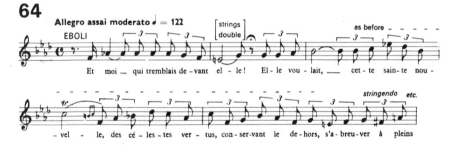

Posa has to be restrained by Carlos from dispatching Eboli on the spot. He throws away his dagger and declares that he will be guided by God; whereupon all three take up their positions for the final stretta-like allegro ('Malheur sur toi, fils adultère'). Eboli's is the opening theme, unaccompanied except for the final note of each phrase, which is underpinned by oboes, clarinets, horns and bassoons with a unison sneer. Later the same melody is taken up by all three soloists with oboes, clarinets, cellos and basses doubling; against this the cornets and violins hammer out a pattern of quavers which conflicts strikingly with the triplets implied in the melodic line. The four-note pattern that returned with Posa's entry assumes a new prominence (x).

65

After a stormy più mosso Eboli sweeps out, leaving Carlos and Posa to conclude the scene. Having reorganized the dramatic events, brought together incidents which were originally separate and in general reformed the plot to his own requirements, Verdi has penetrated to the heart of the drama far more successfully than if he had tried to follow Schiller's text. The ending, however, was marked down by him as a possible cut; and though he eventually changed his mind it is easy to see why. Posa's request for the private letters, Carlos's hesitation ('À vous, le favori du roi?'), Posa's reproach ('Carlos, tu doutes de moi?'), the prince's change of heart ('Non, non, mon appui, mon espérance'), and the fervent reconciliation of the two friends are all conveyed adequately, perhaps, but through the most conventional of 'scena' material. It could have been foreseen that Ex. 30 on full orchestra with trumpets and cornets prominent would ring down the curtain.

Scene 2 (Finale) A great square in front of the Cathedral of Valladolid. On the right the church with a great stairway leading up to it. At the back another stairway descends to a lower square in the middle of which a stake has been erected, whose pinnacle is visible. Huge buildings and distant hills form the horizon. Bells are ringing at full peal. A crowd swarms onto the stage, restrained with difficulty by halberdiers.†*

This is the scenic climax of the opera, a central act-finale laid out on a larger scale than anything Verdi had attempted before. By comparison the coronation scene of *Giovanna d'Arco* seems intimate. Both, however, have this in common: they begin with a certain amount of garish musical pageantry for which Verdi's biographers have thought it necessary to apologize even when they do not condemn it outright.‡ It is an understandable point of view. Vigorous, tuneful, showing considerable craftsmanship, the opening choruses and marches lack the nobility and depth that the rest of the score might have led one to expect. Some would have it that the note of vulgarity is intended by Verdi to show his feelings for the *auto da fé* which would doubtless have affected him as a bull-fight affected his compatriot Busoni. But that is the technique of the pamphleteer, not the serious composer. No one was less objective in his treatment of villains than Wagner; his Beckmessers and Mimes are mere footballs to be kicked around. Yet the music he writes for them restores their dignity and with it the human equation of the drama. To blacken a character by devaluing his music is a measure calculated to rebound on the composer himself.

A better defence will be found in the state of public music in nineteenth-century opera. The romantic age was one of private thoughts and feelings; public emotion meant nationalism, which is nothing more than the projection of individual feelings on a group of humanity. The various folk-idioms of the time, whether genuine or invented, proved to be fertile territory for composers to exploit, with results that vary from the merely picturesque, as in *Russlan and Ludmilla*, to the near mystical, as in *Boris Godunov*. In countries whose folk-music lies nearer the main classical tradition, a nationalist conviction is enough – as in Verdi's *Nabucco* and in that most splendid of all musical pageants, Act III, scene ii, of *Die Meistersinger*. But grand opera on the Scribe model was, if anything, anti-national; indeed its ideals of grandeur are cramped rather than enhanced by a local flavour unless applied as discreetly as in *Guillaume Tell* or *La Muette de Portici*. For ceremonial climaxes composers for the Paris Opéra were often content with a few neutral flourishes, so allowing the musical interest to yield to the visual. Meyerbeer could be guaranteed to improve on tradition by some rare combination of diverse scenic elements each with its appropriate musical representation. But attempts at a melodic solution produced at best the Wartburg scene from Wagner's essentially Paris-oriented *Tannhäuser*, at worst the pretentious banality of 'O divine justice' from Bizet's uncompleted *Ivan IV*. Only Berlioz, as so often, reaped the benefit of his lonely position, writing in *Les Troyens* scenes of genuine grandeur without the prop of nationalism.

Don Carlos, written expressly for the Paris Opéra, was inevitably bound by some of its limitations. This said, the present finale can be considered a remarkable

---

* 'Our Lady of Atocha' in the Italian score.

† The production books add a palace L. with large portico and a terrace for the stage bands. They also prescribe brilliant illumination and huge depth of stage.

‡ For instance, Hussey, p. 160 – 'on the lowest level of achievement'.

specimen of its type. Unlike those Meyerbeer tableaux to which it is so often compared, it is conceived with a sure sense of musical architecture which the by now traditional cuts serve only to obscure. On the one hand it can be called a rondo with the opening chorus (Ex. 66a) as its principal theme; on the other it falls into four clearly defined sections, each with its own special tonal area. These may be described for want of a more precise terminology as: Backcloth; Procession; Ceremony; and Incident.

A. *Backcloth*. This is composed of three ideas (Ex. 66a, b, and c) so contrasted as to produce a vivid chiaroscuro; the first is the opening chorus ('Ce jour heureux') preceded and mostly accompanied by the pattern ♪♫♫♪♫♫ which is the composer's sole concession to local colour. This is the populace en fête – a wide-spanned melody that leaps and plunges backed by full orchestra in various brilliant guises. The opening figure (*x*), a major-key variant of one of the opera's basic patterns, carries within it possibilities of contrapuntal working which are duly exploited later.* Sweeping scales from the woodwind bring the chorus to a close; after which a marcia funebre (Ex. 66b) strikes in with a sudden chill. The monks of the Inquisition are conducting heretics to the stake.† The melody on low clarinet, bassoon and cello is so cramped as hardly to deserve the name; while the bunching of divided basses and bassoons on a third of E minor below the stave is a notable instance of percussive scoring pre-Stravinsky. More sinister even than the death figure on bass drum is the menacing growl of unison trombones in the fourth bar. The third element (Ex. 66c)

66a

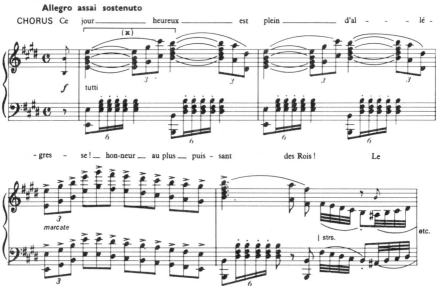

* See Ex. 19 and Ex. 65. The connection is surely structural rather than dramatic.

† *14 inquisitors (basses) enter two by two R. They sing while walking and halt in the centre at the words 'Un jour d'effroi! Malheur, malheur!' Enter after them 2 Dominican monks carrying torches, 2 guards, 2 condemned men, one condemned man, 2 guards. They cross the stage slowly behind the inquisitors, moving diagonally so as to exit backstage L. During the funeral march all present form a large stationary group. After their last words the Inquisitors exeunt R. The chorus return to their positions for the reprise of the joyful chorus. (Disp. scen. (1867), pp. 31–2; (1884), pp. 24–5.)*

66b

66c

is one of those simple snatches of melody that contain a wealth of meaning and to which the high cellos give a special eloquence, as the monks promise salvation to all those that repent at the last. It could be called in sonata terms a 'second subject'; and like all the best second subjects it will take on a slightly altered sense in the reprise.

The section is rounded off with Ex. 66a developed contrapuntally and rising to a peak from which it descends in a spiral of Gounodesque dominant sevenths that has set many a fastidious listener's teeth on edge; then turns aside briefly to C major before descending to an emphatic cadence, driven home with repeated rat-tat-a-tat-a-tats from full orchestra.

B. *Procession.* 'The cortège issues from the palace [*so run the directions in the French score*], all the state corporations, the deputies of all the imperial provinces, the grandees of Spain with Rodrigue in their midst; the Queen surrounded by her ladies. Thibault carrying her train, pages, etc. [*to which the Italian score adds the Count of Lerma and royal heralds*]. The cortège ranges itself in front of the steps of the church.'* Here a stage band was obviously *de rigueur*; and for the great exhibition of

* At the start of the military band music 4 trumpeters enter and play from the top of the steps that lead from the portico L. . . . then gradually the whole procession enters from the portico, comes down C. and retires backstage.

Order of Procession

1. 4 Trumpeters proceed to the flight of steps leading up to the church and remain there forming a single line.

1867 only the very latest model of Fanfares Théâtrales Adolphe Saxe would do. As always, neither the printed nor manuscript score tells us anything about its composition, since they confine the band music to two staves of short score. However, from the two specifications jotted down on Adolphe Saxe's guida banda (in pen and pencil respectively)* it is clear that as in *Jérusalem* there are no clarinets to smooth over the top in the Italian banda tradition. The melody is carried by the cornets and trumpets as designed by Saxe. If the sound was not particularly pleasing to Verdi, he at least never treats the banda in cavalier fashion. On the contrary, in weaving it together with the orchestra he performs remarkable feats of engineering in sound. At the same time he anticipates in embryo certain solutions adopted less ambitiously but more successfully in *Aida*. But their effect frequently goes for nothing when the band is discreetly placed behind the scenes. It has its own balcony in view of the audience and

---

2. *A platoon of Halberdiers — 8 men and a captain.*

3. *A platoon of Archers (ditto).*

   The first platoon takes up a position on the right of the steps, the second on the left. The rest of the procession do likewise, each taking up a position as indicated below.

4. *2 Mace-bearers, R. of steps.*

5. *8 University students; the first 2 carry a banner each, R. behind the mace-bearers.*

6. *2 Mace-bearers, L. of steps.*

7. *6 Doctors, L. behind the mace-bearers.*

8. *6 Magistrates, R. beside the first 2 mace-bearers.*

9. *4 Heralds, on the steps, 2 L, 2 R.*

10. *Great banner of the Inquisition carried by 3 Dominicans, R. in front of magistrates.*

11. *6 Alcadi, R. behind the magistrates.*

12. *1 Trumpeter with the royal coat of arms, beside the mace-bearers L.*

13. *1 Flag-bearer from the Indies, beside the trumpeter.*

14. *4 Lords each carrying a provincial standard, 2 R. behind the Alcadi, 2 L. behind the flag of the Indies.*

15. *4 Members of the Council of Castile, R. beside the magistrates.*

16. *2 Constables, L. facing the audience.*

17. *1 Sword-bearer, L. beside the constables.*

18. *4 Lords of the Golden Fleece, R. behind 4 members of Council.*

19. *4 Arabian ambassadors, L. behind the flag of the Indies.*

20. *1 Platoon of guards — 6 men and a captain, R. behind Lords of the Golden Fleece.*

21. *Royal Herald, proceeds to the lower steps; at this point the 4 trumpeters divide themselves into 2 pairs L. and R.*

22. *2 Royal pages, remain L. by chorus.*

23. *Elisabeth conducted by Rodrigue, C. of stage.*

24. *2 Pages holding the Queen's train, proceed to C. of stage, then leave hold of the train and take up a position by the King's pages.*

25. *Thibault, behind Rodrigue.*

26. *6 Ladies-in-waiting, L. by pages.*

27. *1 Grand Officer, L. by Thibault.*

28. *4 Halberdiers, they remain by the portico and join the other 4 who were stationed there at the beginning of the scene.*

29. *8 Arquebusiers bring up the rear.*

   Disp. scen. (1867), pp. 32–4; (1886), pp. 25–6.

   * The pencilled list reads: *Cornets à 6 pistons [sic!] 2; trumpets (ditto) 2; trombones (ditto); Saxhorns; B flat contralto, F alto, C or B flat baritone, B flat bass; E flat and C or B flat contrabass.* The list written in ink begins with two entries which must be guessed at since the corner of the page is torn away. They probably refer to cornets and trumpets. Then follow: *2 Saxhorns in D alto, 4 saxhorns in A baritone, 4 trumpets in C, 4 bass [saxhorns?] in A, 4 contrabass saxhorns in D.* To judge from the keys mentioned in it the ink-written list would seem to be the definitive one.

should, according to the production book, take up its position there during the opening chorus.

The best banda music – such as Berlioz's Trojan march – though it may modulate widely and contain moments of brilliant passage work, has a basis of arpeggios and chords, plain, solemn or hard-hitting as the case may be. Conventional lyrical writing too often gives the impression of a bad arrangement. Unfortunately the cornet-à-piston, the banda's chief melody-carrier, was popularized during the nineteenth century as a bel canto instrument and composers were expected to take this into account. Hence the hilarious vulgarity of Gounod's 'Gloire immortelle de nos aïeux' and the absurd trio which disfigures the otherwise dignified Coronation march from *Le Prophète*. In the present finale the entry of the banda in C sharp minor in a passage of nine bars shared out with orchestra is impressive enough; but the twelve-bar cantabile (Ex. 67a) which follows hardly avoids the pitfalls of its genre.

67a

67b

By echoing it a minor third higher on the orchestral strings Verdi raises the musical tension by contrasts of texture and tonality and even direction of sound. The banda's second idea (Ex. 67b) is essentially a pendant to the first, and benefits from its lack of thematic interest. If the sound is unlovely in itself, it exploits effectively the peculiar quality of brass-band legato. This too is taken up by the orchestra; until by a stroke of ingenuity the banda is made to emerge from the heart of the orchestral web with a variant of Ex. 66a which in turn leads to a triumphant resumption of 'Ce jour heureux' with both instrumental forces uniting and separating in a blaze of colour. In a short coda trumpets of banda and orchestra hurl brilliant arpeggios at one another – Verdi's first essay in that stereophonic trumpet writing which is such a notable feature of *Aida* and the Requiem.

C. *Ceremony* and D. *Incident*. In this crucial scene, the forces remain as before, but the atmosphere changes at once from secular to ecclesiastical. The herald who gives orders for the doors of the cathedral to be thrown open ('Ouvrez-vous, ô portes sacrées') carries the same precentor-like overtones as his Genoese colleague in the revised *Simon Boccanegra* when he orders the lights to be extinguished. The chorus take up his melody unaccompanied and with appropriately modal harmonies; whereupon 'The doors of the church are flung open, Philip is discovered, a crown on his head, marching beneath a canopy held aloft by monks.' The same modal inflections stamp the slowly marching orchestral motif punctuated by fanfares from the banda, from which all hints of worldliness have been purged.

There is genuine religious awe in the eight bars of declamation with which Philip pledges himself to avenge God by fire and the sword ('En plaçant sur mon front cette couronne'), a suggestion too that like another sixteenth-century tyrant's his soul is dark. The chorus comment approvingly ('Gloire à Philippe, gloire à Dieu') bringing the music into the sunlight of E flat major. A few bars of solemn procession follow to a restful theme on the strings, whose cadence is interrupted in an unobtrusive but exciting way – a rustling diminished seventh on violins and violas, as Philip suddenly sees six men dressed in black kneeling before him. It is the Queen who reacts first on seeing Carlos with them ('O ciel, Carlos!'). To his outraged father, Carlos explains that these are the deputies from Flanders and Brabant come to sue for protection from Alva's persecuting troops. All six are basses and their unison chant ('La dernière heure a-t-elle donc sonnée pour vos sujets flamands?') forms the principal idea of the huge concertato which now builds up.* Like most Verdian concertati this one sets forth a number of contrasting attitudes within a large choral and orchestral canvas; but for once the elements are not individuals but groups, with the exception of Philip, who in consequence predominates more powerfully than ever. The deputies make their appeal in a warm dignified melody of the type that Elgar would have marked *nobilmente*.† Cellos and violas playing on their lowest string

68a

* The demands of this scene had stretched the choral resources of the Opéra to such an extent that the Flemish deputies had to be supplied by Auber from senior students at the Paris Conservatoire. Among the names listed is that of Maurel, almost certainly the future creator of Iago and Falstaff. For the Neapolitan performance of 1872 Verdi asked for the number of deputies to be increased to 8 or even 10. Letter to Giulio Ricordi, undated (1872). (Abbiati, III, p. 607.)

† The resemblance of Ex. 68a to the opening theme of Elgar's A flat major symphony is even more marked in the original scoring which has violins marching in off-beat crotchets instead of the pattern of staccato bassoon quavers.

impart a ripe sonority while the acciaccatura sob on the oboe sounds just after the first and third beats of each bar as a reminder that the deputies are in mourning.

The melody flows on in twenty-three bars of apparent freedom but in fact skilfully varied symmetry. Philip's minor-key reply (Ex. 68b) contains a bunch of staccato semiquavers like an angrily shaken fist ('À Dieu vous êtes infidèles') while the six monks of the Inquisition add a dismissive comment of their own (Ex. 68c, 'Les Flamands sont des infidèles'). Against them Elisabeth, Thibault, Carlos, Rodrigue and the rest of the chorus plead in a triplet motif (Ex. 68d, 'Etendez sur leurs fronts votre main souveraine') that rises a minor third with every repetition until it flowers into a lyrical theme in the dominant in which Carlos and Elisabeth figuratively speaking join hands, as did Elvira and Ernani in the Act I finale of *Ernani*. As the ensemble builds up the use of conflicting rhythms (quavers against triplets, triplets against semiquavers) adds a special dimension to the clash of wills. There is a reprise in which the musical ideas are telescoped and where necessary manipulated in order to fit as counterpoints to Ex. 68a, now supported by a fuller orchestration that includes cornets. The deputies now have to run the gauntlet between Philip above and the monks below. The rest of the chorus and soloists, after a single statement of Ex. 68d, confine themselves to the 'weeping' broken triplets which had accompanied the lyrical melody of Carlos and Elisabeth. Only Posa has a melodic phrase of his own ('Qui va sanglant traînant sa chaîne'). The coda brings in a new idea announced first by the 'good' soloists then by the full chorus, to which Philip opposes his inexorable Ex. 68b. Up to this point Philip, though on the side of the monks, has never sung the same line as they; only in the final bars where the essence of the struggle is laid bare, does he merge with them; while Elisabeth and Carlos join the deputies in a final phrase based on the opening of Ex. 68a.*

In a rapid 6/8 tempo-di-mezzo Carlos complains to his father that he is wasting his youth at court ('Sire, il est temps que je vive'). If he is one day to wear the Spanish crown — and here horns sound an appropriate fanfare — he must be given responsibility. Let him be sent as governor to Flanders and Brabant. The words are taken largely from Schiller's Act II, scene i, where Carlos obtains a private audience with the King. Here their timing is unfortunate, to say the least, and would seem to justify Carlos's historical reputation as a near lunatic. His request meets with the reception it deserves. Carlos draws his sword; Philip orders first his guards then the gentlemen of the court to disarm him; but none dare lay a finger on the prince. At length Philip himself seizes a sword; father and son are about to join battle when Posa intervenes and demands Carlos's weapon. All this takes place to action music at its most economical with a three-note arpeggio figure hammered out over tremolando strings at irregular intervals, each time a semitone higher than the last. As Carlos, dazed, hands over his sword muttering brokenly, 'O ciel . . . lui . . . Rodrigue' Ex. 30 sounds softly on clarinets over a C major 6/4 with an acciaccatura sob on flute and bassoon; and for the first time we notice the drooping line of the theme itself.† All

---

* The production books prescribe the following routine: *The church doors open; the 4 heralds descend to the foot of the steps: likewise the Inquisitors who take up a position to left and right.*

Philip appears at the door beneath a richly appointed palanquin borne by 4 Dominicans; he comes down the steps and halts to say, 'En plaçant sur mon front cette couronne.' The 4 Dominicans remain at the head of the steps with the palanquin.

When Philip appears the soldiers raise their arms, and the flag-bearers their flags.

During the chorus 'Gloire à Philippe' the King comes down the steps and proceeds to the centre of the stage. Rodrigue takes Elisabeth by the hand and they both proceed towards Philip.

At this moment enter Carlos rapidly, followed by the 6 Flemish deputies who line up in two ranks and fling themselves at Philip's feet.

The chorus move forward slightly; the Inquisitors line the back of the stage; the sword-bearer comes downstage left of the Inquisitors. The Grand Officer moves to the right, and the two platoon commanders come forward. All the extras on the steps, back of stage and on each side, should turn towards the audience.

After saying the words, 'Que votre fils amène,' Carlos passes behind the King L. and approaches Rodrigue with whom he exchanges a swift glance.

The 6 deputies rise, exclaiming, 'Sire, Sire!'

Philip replies forcefully, 'A Dieu vous êtes infidèles,' and at his words, 'Gardes, éloignez-les de moi,' the officer comes forward, moves the deputies away and returns to his position.

The Inquisitors approach the King to say forcefully, 'Les Flamands sont des infidèles': everyone else likewise takes a step forward to sing the ensemble, at the end of which People, Deputies and Lords bow before the King. (*Disp. scen.* (1867), pp. 37–8; (1886), pp. 27–9.)

† Verdi's own directions on the performance of this passage are worth quoting. *At the end of the third*

the tension so carefully screwed up over forty bars collapses as Carlos is led away by guards and Posa kneels and presents the Infante's sword to Philip, who creates him Duke on the spot. The music then moves back from C to E major for a recapitulation, in the technical sense, of the opening 'Backcloth', Ex. 66a, its sonority increased, not to say aggravated, by the banda. Ex. 66b duly follows; then comes the surprise: Ex. 66c not in G major played by cellos, but in E major, sung by a Voice from Heaven, 'High up and in the distance,' Verdi said, 'so that the audience can understand straightaway that it is something not of this world.'* Harp and harmonium surround it with a soft halo. 'Of course, everyone on stage will pay attention only to the *auto da fé*,' Verdi continued, 'just as if they hadn't heard the voice.' Indeed the Flemish deputies, who alone might be expected to have heard it, merely murmur at the barbarity they are about to witness ('Dieu permet ces forfaits . . .'). To those who see in *Don Carlos* a rationalist drama of personalities and causes, this intervention from above, though it has a precedent in Rossini's *Moïse*, may seem a little shocking. But *Don Carlos*, as treated by both Schiller and Verdi, is a myth; and as such can be stretched to include the supernatural whether in the form of a ghostly monk or of a heavenly voice. Neither amounts to an attempt at mysticism; but both have a vital part to play as musical reagents. The heavenly voice imposes on the finale to Act III a wholly unexpected denouement involving as it does a classical use of tonal values. In its original key and context Ex. 66c offered consolation, but on conditions; it was a silver lining to clouds which refuse to disperse. In E major the consolation is absolute, since in this key it negates what has gone before. The heretics will go to their horrible death assured of a martyr's crown. Again we hear the funeral march, its brutality softened by the major tonality; and as the flames from the stake light up the scene in a rosy glow the Heavenly Voice rises in rippling trills like some celestial lark to the final noisy cadence.

If modern taste has been in general unenthusiastic about this finale, that of 1867 was entirely in its favour. The opera itself may have had a mixed reception; but the press united in singling this scene out for particular praise. Even the hostile critic of *Le Figaro* who found in the refinements of Verdi's later style only the misplaced determination to atone for the imagined sins of his youth could write of it: 'This scene . . . is admirable from beginning to end. It is a tremendous "page" which will ensure that *Don Carlos* will not die.'† Verdi himself in a letter to his publisher described it as 'without doubt the best thing in the opera'.‡ Doubtless this was to some extent an *argumentum ad hominem*, since he knew that to mount it properly would cost far more

---

act when the King has his son arrested, after the words, 'Disarmato ei sia,' there are three fortissimo bars for full orchestra of the utmost violence, especially the final A where there is bass drum and percussion. Then, after the words, 'A me il ferro,' I would like a very long silence, and when the clarinets take up the tune of the duet I would like a very soft, veiled sound – almost as if behind the scenes – quite smooth, without accent . . . I need hardly say that the singers' 'note tronche' should be sung senza voce. Letter to Mazzucato, 17.3.1868. Ghisi and De Bellis, *Atti del II° Congresso del I.S.V.*, p. 539.

* For the production in Naples in 1872 he expected the Voice to be sung by Thibault. See letter to T. Ricordi, undated (1872). Abbiati, III, p. 606. And in fact the production book of 1886 (though not that of 1867) instructs him to make his exit after the ensemble with this in view.

† Notice in *Le Figaro* after the second performance. Quoted in Programme book of La Fenice, 73–4, p. 84.

‡ Letter to Giulio Ricordi. Abbiati, III, p. 327.

than most impresarii were prepared to spend. Yet he was surely right to stress its importance. For all its occasional coarseness the finale to Act III remains a splendid specimen of grand operatic architecture.

ACT IV

Scene 1 (all versions): The King's cabinet in Madrid. The King is absorbed in deep meditation leaning upon a table strewn with papers; two large candles are just burning out; the dawn shows light behind the window-panes.

As in most grand operas in five acts, the fourth brings a shift of emphasis from the public to the private plane. Here the progression from aria to duet to quartet has a forerunner in Act IV of *Les Vêpres Siciliennes*, whose Act III also has an aria of loneliness sung by a man of power. But it is a fair measure of the distance between the two operas that whereas Montfort's 'Au sein de la puissance' is hardly known, Philip's 'Elle ne m'aime pas', under its Italian title of 'Ella giammai m'amò' is one of the most famous arias in the Italian repertoire. Here is the classical Verdi, shaping the traditional components and forms of a French 'scène et air' with a sculptor's hand and transforming them into the purest gold. The introduction to many a grand aria of Meyerbeer's would normally contain a number of piquant orchestral figures designed to stir the audience into attention. Here every gesture is charged with a profound significance, and each fills out an important detail of the canvas. The heavy acciaccatura sobs on horns, bassoons and strings convey that iron grief which lies at the heart not only of Philip but of the opera as a whole (see the original prelude and introduction to Act I); the solo cello conveys weariness as eloquently as when Siegmund falls exhausted into Hunding's dwelling. Muted violins begin an obsessive, circling motif that extends itself in a frieze-like pattern which like the accompaniment to Rossini's 'Sois immobile' never loses its emotional force. The three ideas are then combined vertically in a limpid sonority (Ex. 69a). All this is a preparation for the melodic idea which both frames the aria and forms the emotional kernel of the scene (Ex. 69b). 'She does not love me; her heart is closed to me; she has never loved me.' Philip speaks the words 'as in a dream'.* To a reprise of the foregoing Philip remembers how at his wedding Elisabeth looked with dismay at his grey hairs. 'No, she never loved me,' he repeats to the last three bars of Ex. 69b with a characteristic heightening of the apex of the phrase and an emphatic triplet in the penultimate bar. He awakes from his reverie to realize that it is already dawn and he has not slept all night. His muted exclamation in F sharp minor ('Hélas, le sommeil salutaire, le doux sommeil a fui pour jamais ma paupière') is his nearest approach to a cry of despair. A harmonic ellipsis which never loses its power to surprise brings the music back to D minor for the aria ('Je dormirai', Ex. 69c). The sombre, evocative use of two horns in the minor key is new in Verdi; it will be recalled in Ford's monologue in *Falstaff*. The melody with its broad flow of crotchets is very much in the French grand opera tradition; but quite apart from its truthfulness of expression

* It is worth noting that the immense personal grief of Philip, reported by his young wife, is an invention of Verdi and his librettists. Schiller's monarch in the equivalent scene feels only a kind of selfish humiliation. 'I could never give her love; yet did she even seem to feel the lack?' (*Don Carlos*, III, i.)

what gives it individuality is the skill with which its harmonic rhythm is varied. The wide intervals of the final phrase with each note harmonized separately are like a symbol of the cavernous vaults of the Escurial in which Philip hopes one day to find rest. The central idea strikes a more heroic attitude (Ex. 69d, 'Si la royauté nous donnait le pouvoir'); and here the King was supposed to rise to his feet.* Just as F sharp minor was the furthest point of his agitation, so B flat major represents a corresponding area of self-command. Both keys being a major third respectively above and below the D minor-major tonic balance each other within the total scheme. 'If only royalty conferred the power to see into men's hearts!' But once the ruler relaxes his vigilance, treachery is at work seeking to rob him of his kingdom – and his wife. As the music begins to modulate homeward so Philip's voice sinks to a muttered declamation 'à demi-voix'. A reprise of Ex. 69c, according to the usual French ternary plan, is followed by Ex. 69d, given out in the tonic by lower strings and bassoon, over which Philip repeats the appropriate words but in a parlante. His voice then gathers strength for an assertion of will that falls on the end of the second phrase of the melody. There is a long silence which says clearly, 'What is the use?' And Philip relapses into despondency. The tormenting thought 'She loves me no longer' (Ex. 69b) rounds off the scene, bringing the musical argument back to the point at which it began. All of Philip is in this scene – his dignity, his pathos, his obsessive suspicions, his gloomy fanaticism. If Verdi had ever succeeded in writing the *King Lear* that tempted him for so long, could he ever have achieved a more moving portrayal of desolate old age than this?

The Count of Lerma announces 'Le Grand Inquisiteur'. Enter a blind man of ninety supported by two Dominican friars. Like the dialogue between Philip and Posa, the duet with the Inquisitor (referred to by Verdi rather quaintly as the 'Inquisition Scene') is differently situated in the opera and the play. Schiller's King Philip sends for the Inquisitor firstly to ease his conscience for having had Posa murdered and secondly to find out if he is justified in asking for the extreme penalty for his son. In the opera the murder of Posa has not yet taken place. The ostensible object of their

69a

*Disp. scen. (1867), p. 41; (1886), p. 32.

69b

69c

meeting is Carlos; though here too it becomes apparent that the real bone of contention between them is Posa. But the sequence has been changed. In Schiller the discussion of Carlos is thrown away at the end as a deliberate anti-climax. In the opera it
constitutes the preliminaries of a musical battle unique in Italian opera.

Verdi had only once before written a duet for two full basses – that for Worm and
Count Walter in *Luisa Miller*: a melodramatic piece for partners in crime who
recollect their misdeeds with a mixture of bravado and fear. Though it served to in-
tensify the aura of villainy this combination of low sonorities was in the last resort
fortuitous. Here it serves a very definite purpose: to embody the conflict of two
superhuman, patriarchal forces, Church and State, nothing less than two full basses
will suffice. Doubtless taking his cue from the finale to Act I in Meyerbeer's
L'Africaine, Verdi is not afraid to stress the bass timbre to the point of exaggeration,
for the sinuous orchestral theme which serves as framework to the dialogue, like a
symbol of the Inquisitor's baleful presence.

70

To this theme Philip puts his questions in an offhand parlante that betokens his mood
of accidie. The Inquisitor replies to hierophantic chords for trombones and
ophicleide with his casuistical arguments as to why Philip should not scruple to
sacrifice his son. The first section is a free discourse based on Ex. 70, modulating
through related keys and concluding in the tonic major. Then the Inquisitor takes the
initiative, with the demand that Posa be handed over to the 'secular arm' as a heretic
far more dangerous than Carlos. Here he inevitably loses some of the monstrosity of
Schiller's original, whose particular strength lies in his ability to score points, so to
speak, from a sitting position, twisting back every question with a ferocious rebuke.
None the less, the mounting eloquence of the solo 'Dans ce beau pays pur d'hérétique

levain' is highly impressive, and all the more so for maintaining a deceptive quietness over the first fourteen bars. Then the Inquisitor's anger rises phrase by phrase, culminating in an outburst ('Pour les puissants du monde, abjurant mon courroux') declaimed over tremolando strings with sweeping upward scales on the cellos and punctuated by blasts from cornets, trumpets and trombones. But Philip in his present mood can only see his life as a vast desert stretching out before him with nobody in whom to confide except Posa ('Pour traverser les jours', etc.). The musical imagery here is almost modern in its austerity. Oboe and piccolo sustain a succession of high semibreves (*pp*) while a thin line of strings descends (*ppp*) in crotchets over three and a half octaves. The scale is that of F major but the tonal orientation is curiously vague. The Inquisitor brings the monarch down to earth. How can Philip consider himself a king if he requires another equal to himself? Only the orchestration of trombones, ophicleide, bassoons and rolling timpani can give an idea of the sarcasm that causes Philip to exclaim, 'Tais-toi, prêtre.' The Inquisitor's reaction is unexpectedly mild ('L'esprit des novateurs'), though the marking of allegro agitato indicates a certain urgency. The thematic cell of the next solo is a three-bar orchestral motif repeated according to the ritualistic 'rule of three' with the rise of a tone each time, then taking a wholly unexpected turn with an enharmonic modulation from G minor to G flat and a change of orchestral colour to solo woodwind. Here the theme is transformed so as to take on a false wheedling character ('Rentrez dans le devoir. L'Église en bonne mère peut encore accueillir un repentir sincère', Ex. 71a). This is the voice less of Schiller's iron cardinal than of Dallapiccola's gaoler-Inquisitor in *Il Prigioniero*. Only when Philip opposes a brusque 'non, jamais!' does the Inquisitor unsheathe his claws with a theme which in the original scheme had a far-reaching importance (Ex. 71b). The words are taken directly from Schiller:

INQUISITOR   If I did not
          Stand before you now, by the living God!
          You would have stood before me thus tomorrow.

Musically this has the force of an anathema, and though its fulfilment was removed before the first performance and never reinstated, the connection between the passages concerned is too patent to be overlooked. For the present, it will be sufficient to note the key (B flat minor), the scoring for cornets and trombones, and the outline of the opening phrase (x). The Inquisitor's concluding arpeggio descant over an octave and a half appropriately recalls Pastor Moser's denunciation of Francesco in *I Masnadieri* (see Ex. 71b on p. 126).

Philip's reply ('Prêtre, j'ai trop souffert ton orgueil criminel') is softened in the Italian into 'Prete, troppo soffrii il tuo parlar crudel', to which the Inquisitor retorts, 'Why have you called up the shade of Samuel?' – a key phrase in Schiller, reminding us that the paradigm of Saul, David and Jonathan underlies the relationship of Philip, Posa and Carlos. The section comes to an end, as might be expected, with a regular period of sixteen bars, though split up into short orchestral and vocal motifs. As Schiller puts it:

Two kings have I
Placed on the Spanish throne and I had hoped

> To leave a firmly founded work behind me.
> I see my life's fruits lost. . . .*

Again the musical argument comes full circle with a resumption of Ex. 70 ending first in the relative, then in the tonic major. Philip, totally defeated, begs the departing Inquisitor to be reconciled with him. But the Inquisitor's reaction is one of frigid indifference ('La paix . . . peut-être'). Philip reflects bitterly that the pride of kings must always yield to that of the Church, and his arpeggiated descent through two octaves can be regarded as the submissive major-key reply to the Inquisitor's 'Vous seriez devant nous au tribunal suprême'.

If in contrast to the Philip–Posa duet this one succeeded at the outset, surely it is because, beneath the cut and thrust of logic, it deals in feelings rather than intellectual ideas. In the discussion of Carlos's fate the force of the Inquisitor's arguments is in the last resort irrelevant. Philip's questions are mechanical; what counts in the Inquisitor's replies is not their sense but the chill authority with which they are uttered. The central section is concerned with the gradual ascendancy of the Inquisitor, spiritually armour-plated, over the vulnerable Philip. Twenty years before, this would have been written not as a duet but as an 'aria con pertichini'. As it is, the Inquisitor has the lion's share of the music in every sense; and his part requires an energy remarkable in a man of ninety. In all other respects this dialogue represents the kind of victory over convention that derives from as scrupulous an adherence to Schiller as the context will allow. It is a far cry from the scheme propounded in the prose project, which envisages the King – pen poised to sign Carlos's death warrant like many a Donizettian monarch – seeking counsel from Lerma and the Inquisitor respectively, with no mention of Posa at all.

The scène et quatuor that follows was altered and improved in 1884; but the differences between the two versions are not such as to warrant a separate discussion of either.† Here the opera has been forced to take for granted certain events that are recounted in the play. After her rebuff by Carlos, Eboli has decided to fall in with the schemes of Alva and Domingo. Not only has she at last yielded to the King's importunities (adultery may be condoned by the Church in certain cases, Father Domingo tells her); she has agreed to steal the Queen's jewel-case and bring it to Philip. Having discovered the theft, the Queen bursts angrily into the cabinet, demanding redress ('Justice, justice, Sire'). The agitation of her melody ('Je suis dans votre cour indignement traitée') is pointed up by anticipating violins, by busy violas, cellos and bassoons, who proceed to follow its chromatic course a tenth below, and by the wealth of appoggiature in the cadential phrase. Originally Verdi had wished to

* The chromatic scale for strings with sustaining woodwind that forms the first of these motifs is quite differently marked in autograph and printed full score. But the reason for the discrepancy is not editorial licence. In a letter to the conductor Mazzucato, Verdi wrote: 'In the Inquisition scene in Act IV, after the words "L'ombre de Samuel" there's a gesture for strings ( )which I've marked with a slur. At the Opéra, where the variety of bowing is excellent, I had it played staccato and this together with the hairpin on the wind and the roll of the timpani made a most powerful effect.' Letter to Mazzucato, 17.3.1868. Ghisi and De Bellis, *op. cit.*, pp. 539–40. Here at any rate the printed copy, not the autograph, represents the composer's last thoughts.

† For a fuller examination of this scene and its later corrections, as well as the composer's first thoughts, see Günther in *Acta Musicologica*, XLIII (Basle, 1971), 'Problèmes de création musicale au XIXe siècle', pp. 171–89.

71a

71b

include this theme in the orhcestral preamble; later he struck it out of the autograph, rightly allowing Elisabeth to come to the point as quickly as possible.

72

For answer Philip produces the case and asks Elisabeth to open it. She refuses with a gesture of contempt; whereupon the King opens it himself and takes out a portrait of the Infante. In the original version of this scène-à-faire Verdi twice employs the 'rule of three' first with a richly scored motif of thirds which has a curiously eighteenth-century flavour, suggesting a moment in some buffo finale;* secondly with a sinuous climbing motif for cellos and bassoon. (Ex. 73a, b)

The first of these is repeated half a tone down each time, the second half a tone up. Elisabeth coolly admits that the portrait is hers and that she brought it with her from France. The cantabile with which she reminds Philip of her former engagement to Carlos ('Lorsque Dieu vous fît mon époux') is a logical major key complement to Ex. 72. But Verdi, as we have seen, disliked it for being too mild. No doubt he also wished for a stronger contrast with Philip's next utterance ('Vous me parlez avec hardiesse') which in the original opera follows Elisabeth's self-justification without a break. First he sharpened the conflict by reducing the statements of Ex. 73a from three to two, a tone apart, bringing the unison forward two beats so as to make it part of the melody, and drawing the dialogue over it. Then he re-wrote Elisabeth's solo in a manner that is both more varied and more concentrated – four bars of plain unemotional statement in F sharp minor (vous le savez . . . j'étais promise') – a gentle cantabile in the dominant major ('vous osez frapper de démence') leaving an ominous pause in its wake. To be noted here is the motif of an ascending scale from

* Compare the theme from Martini's *Una Cosa rara*, which Mozart quotes in the finale of *Don Giovanni*; this may well have been the unconscious source.

73a

73b

mi to doh. It has first been heard at the point where Philip decided to open the jewel case himself.

74

PHILIPPE

Je l'ouvrirai donc, moi!

This simplest of all nineteenth-century commonplaces plays a vital role in the structure of the scene as a whole, both before and after the quartet.* Philip replies with a silky suavity ('Vous me parlez avec hardiesse') in a melody in which Ex. 74 figures prominently. In both earlier and later versions his passion soon breaks through the surface, expansively in 1867, with great pungency in 1884, largely because the new vocal line follows the natural inflections of human speech. 'I pity you,' Elisabeth replies. 'You pity me! the pity of an adulteress!' This too is differently set in the 1867 and 1884 versions. Originally 'La pitié d'une adultère' was sung to Ex. 74 culminating on a high F. Later it became an angry parody of Elisabeth's line at 'Je vous plains'. The Queen swoons; the King calls for help; Eboli and Posa enter, the first aghast at seeing the effect of her machinations, the second sententiously rebuking the King for being the only man in his vast empire who is unable to master his feelings. All this to a long decrescendo with a repeated semiquaver pattern. The improvements of 1884 consist principally of a greater harmonic variety and a more easy and natural declamation for Posa.

* See M. Chusid, 'Schiller revisited', in *Atti del II° Congresso del I.S.V.*, pp. 156–69.

The two versions of the quartet proper provide one of the most fascinating instances of an idea defined and sharpened at many years' distance from its origin without ever departing from the initial conception. Basically the form is traditional. The shock of the Queen's collapse brings about one of those moments of lyrical expansion so dear to the heart of the Italian romantic; and as usual the ensemble which builds up divides itself into two sections: the first in which the several characters propound their own mutually contrasted feelings successively; the second in which these feelings are comprehended within a single lyrical idea. Philip and Eboli are preoccupied with remorse; Elisabeth is returning to her senses; while for Posa the moment of truth has arrived – he must sacrifice himself for Carlos. (The timing of his decision, different in play and opera, is as inexplicable in one as in the other.) Throughout, it is Philip who dominates the canvas, and his is the initial solo. Such then are the terms of reference for both versions. That the later one should be more concentrated is not surprising; but it is also simpler than the original, clearer in its texture and far more moving in its effect.

In the 1867 score the King's solo ('Maudit soit le soupçon infâme', Ex. 75a) begins as a fragmented line which coalesces into a smooth cantabile to form a period of twelve bars. It remains poised ambiguously between major and minor until the last phrase, a magniloquent assertion of the major key (Ex. 76a) which at once proclaims itself as the main melodic feature of the ensemble. Posa now follows with an idea ('Il faut agir . . . voici l'heure', Ex. 75b) of the same rhythmic mould as Alfredo's 'Ah sì, che feci? Ne sento orrore'), with subdued chattering semiquavers. Then come six bars of ensemble dominated by Eboli ('O remords, ô amère tristesse'); and finally Elisabeth herself awakes to ethereal arpeggios on flute. Her melody ('Hélas, ma pauvre mère') is distinguished by some delightful harmonic sideslips (Ex. 75c).

The first section ends with a resumption by Philip of Ex. 75a with semiquaver interventions for Posa in the manner of his previous solo. The second, more strictly concertato section starts with a smooth motif sung by Elisabeth and Eboli an octave apart with clarinet arpeggios, mounts with a familiar ground-swell to a climax, then subsides into a coda in which Philip's opening phrase reappears in a pithier form, condensed from four bars to two.

When Verdi came to revise the movement he evidently took this coda as his starting-point since the new opening conforms to it in everything apart from an unequivocal minor tonality.

Philip's solo is now contracted from a twelve- to a six-bar period, with an agonized aside for Eboli during the fourth bar ('Je l'ai perdu . . . je l'ai perdu, ô remords fatal'). But the most significant change is reserved for the final phrase (Ex. 76a), which is thrown far more sharply into relief, partly because it bulks larger in the smaller period, partly because it is approached less ambiguously than before. Now the initial B flat has an uncompromisingly tonic sense where in the earlier version it had been tinged with dominant. It is announced not by the voice but by the orchestra – a not uncommon transference in the course of Verdi's revisions; while a much lighter supporting orchestration replaces the sustaining horns, marching bassoons and timpani beats of the original. Finally, the apex of the phrase is lowered from F to E flat. Had this been a case of substituting harmonic tension for a melodic high point it would not have been unusual, as the revisions in La Traviata have shown; but the revised phrase (Ex. 76b) is actually blander than the original, in which the high F

75a

75b

75c

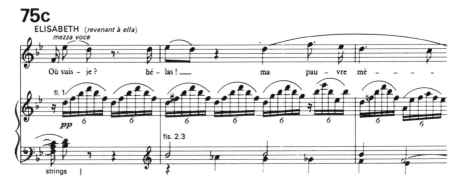

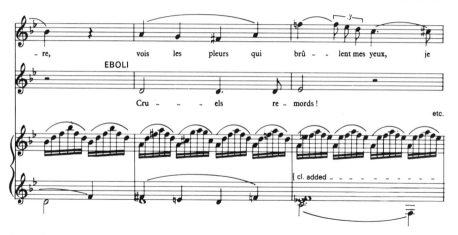

formed an appoggiatura. Here the change is surely designed to heighten the consolatory effect of one of those transcendental melodies that Verdi sometimes pours on situations of deep stress. By a neat stroke of economy Eboli, despite her agitation, is made to contribute to that effect with her soothing G flats in the second bar.

76a

During Ex. 76b Eboli and Philip contribute 'parlanti' appropriate to their states of mind. These continue during the latter part of Posa's solo, which now concludes more strongly with a bar of 2/4 leading to a resumption of Ex. 76b, sung by Philip with a counter-melody for Eboli. Elisabeth's awakening (Ex. 75c) follows as before; and there is yet another reprise of Ex. 76b. Since this is its third appearance a new orchestration is needed; Philip is now doubled by clarinets and horn while cellos join the rest of the strings and woodwind, gently pulsating triplet chords (*pp leggero*) that cover a stretch of four octaves. The second part of the quartet is also simplified by the omission of a few bars where the music turned aside into G flat major, and a rewriting of the voice parts so as to avoid the rather fussy semiquaver motion of the original. The new version of the quartet is in fact only eight bars shorter than its predecessor, but it is much more taut. The chief loser is Eboli, who in 1884 is deprived of a six-bar melody with which she made her entry into the ensemble while Philip and Posa declaimed beneath her. But Eboli's great moment of lyricism has yet to come; and in

76b

(1884)

the meantime she can afford to express herself in broken incoherent phrases. The extra repetition of Ex. 76b brings two gains: it allows the melody to assume due pride of place; and at the same time it gives stronger support to the otherwise diffuse chain of melodies of which the first part of the quartet is made up. Everything inessential has been pruned away; and a new warmth and humanity have penetrated the musical fabric.

Exeunt Philip and Posa to an orchestral postlude based on Ex. 75a, leaving Elisabeth and Eboli to play a scene which once again derives from a different point in the drama; hence a slight shift of emphasis. Schiller's Eboli is motivated first and foremost by her fears for Carlos, whom she has just seen arrested by Posa; Verdi's by her remorse at having, as she thinks, destroyed the Queen. In both play and opera she makes a double confession: first that it was she who stole the Queen's casket, partly to be revenged on Carlos for having rebuffed her and partly out of jealousy of Elisabeth; then that she herself committed the crime of which she has caused Elisabeth to be accused. The first of these confessions is made in an agitated 'scène' ('Pitié, pardon pour la femme coupable') in which Ex. 74 is prominent, beginning as an inner part in the orchestra then appearing as a triple sequence in the vocal line as Eboli's confession gathers strength ('Oui, l'amour, ma fureur, ma haine contre vous . . .') At her words 'L'Infant m'a repoussée' there is a long silence; then the versions begin to diverge.

1866

In the original scheme there was to have occurred that sure-fire device of romantic opera, a duet for two women in love with the same man. Verdi, as always intent on capturing the unique quality of the dramatic moment, gave it a certain sense of constraint. Elisabeth, sorrowful, compassionate, is struggling to repress her own feelings; Eboli is aware that she has told only half the story. Therefore the duet ('J'ai tout compris') takes shape from a hesitant motif, scored, like so much of *Don Carlos*, for a combination of lower instruments with many a pregnant pause (Ex. 77a). The voice parts begin as isolated fragments which move closer and closer together, overlap and finally join in a cantilena ('Ah, que le ciel pardonne') with delicate harp and woodwind scoring (Ex. 77b).*

The radiance dims, however, for the seven bars of hushed tremolando strings and a nervous triplet motif for cellos in which Eboli admits her adultery with the King ('Point de pardon. . . . Encore un aveu terrible . . .') Elisabeth retires murmuring, 'Horreur!' 'Je suis du ciel abandonnée!' Eboli cries; the music which seems to spin itself out in cadential repetitions reflects the stage directions of the play, which enjoin a long pause while Eboli waits with her face pressed to the floor, unaware that the Queen has left her.

In accordance with court etiquette it is the Duchess of Olivarez, chief stewardess, who in Schiller enters and demands Eboli's cross. In accordance with operatic 'convenienze' the task in Verdi must be entrusted to an accredited secondary or com-

* Unfortunately the music of this duet is not complete in all its orchestral detail: parts are missing for harp and second flute, though the presence of the former is clearly indicated by cues in the singers' rehearsal books. The harp part has been reconstructed differently by Andrew Porter and by Ursula Günther, but it will always be a matter for speculation where it is supposed to leave off. Thus Elisabeth's 'Vous l'aimiez; levez-vous; j'ai déjà pardonné' is declaimed gently to Ex. 77b on flute with accompaniment of clarinet and probably second flute and harp; but only first flute and clarinet parts have survived at this point (see, however, p. 157 *n*.).

77b

(1866)

primario role. Thibault would be unsuitable; the royal herald even more so. The only character available is the Count of Lerma. Between phrases of a somewhat forlorn conversation theme he tells Eboli to choose between exile and the veil. When he has left Eboli bursts out, 'Ah, je ne verrai plus la reine' in one of those swooping lines that sound so effective in the mezzo-soprano voice; there will be plenty more of them in *Aida*.

1867, 1872

The duet for Elisabeth and Eboli was one of the first passages to be cut before the first performance. The suture of three bars which joins 'L'Infant m'a repoussée' to the second phrase of the conversation theme is neatly managed; but it removes Eboli's second and more important confession as well as Elisabeth's gracious forgiveness of the first. However, she no longer needs to leave the room and therefore can take over Lerma's lines. Doubtless it was felt that as the theme of Eboli's adultery had been played down so much in the opera it could well be left out altogether. Yet Elisabeth loses by the omission since she now punishes Eboli for a sin that she had previously pardoned. Not surprisingly Verdi was concerned to remedy this in his later revision.

1884, 1886

Here Eboli is more frank and Elisabeth, though magnanimous, more formidable. To Eboli's 'L'Infant m'a repoussée', which no longer comes to a full close, the Queen extends a pardon that is almost offhand ('Vous l'aimiez! levez-vous'). What follows is almost more veristic than 'verismo', since at such moments Mascagni and his successors could rarely bring themselves to abandon that highly charged lyricism which is their stock in trade. There is nothing lyrical about Eboli's broken confession, an austerely unthematic sequence using the fewest possible notes, yet matching to perfection the singer's halting, barely coherent delivery. The exclamation 'Ne me maudisse pas!' exemplifies Verdi's ideas about the 'parola scenica' – the utterance which cuts through all the conventions of music and poetry in the name of dramatic truth.

78

Again Elisabeth does not leave, outraged; yet the C thundered out by full orchestra and sustained through a crawling motif for violins and basses conveys the full weight of her stony disapproval. She asks for Eboli's cross and pronounces her sentence in an expressionless monotone. The only orchestral accompaniment consists of a long held note on the horn and the chromatic figure on cellos and basses. Neither is related harmonically; they remain two musical patterns suspended in mid-air, an expression of sheer blankness. By contrast Eboli's 'Ah, je ne verrai plus la reine' takes on a new force, partly because it is now elaborated with syncopations, but most of all because of its unequivocally melodic character in relation to what has gone before.

All versions

The first verse of Eboli's 'O don fatal' may seem a little odd; for the fatal gift of beauty which she so heartily curses has not been especially evident in her case; nor have her sentiments any echo in Schiller. But then Schiller's and Verdi's Ebolis are differently drawn and for obvious reasons. To convey in music the subtleties of a nature such as Posa describes in Act I, scene v, of the play would have been difficult. Verdi and his librettists preferred to make Eboli a 'coquine' of limitless vanity. She believes in her own beauty as in a religion. If it proved insufficient to attract Carlos, it ensnared his father none the less, and as if to stress this aspect, Verdi recalls a motif (Ex. 8) last heard at the beginning of Act I, where Carlos first mentions Spain and Philip's court. Then it had been no more than a faint cloud on the horizon. Here it peals out, fortissimo timpani reinforcing the strings, and flutes, obòes and clarinets playing the arpeggios. In the 1884 version, it is further strengthened by triplet blasts from cornets, trumpets and horns as the screw of Eboli's remorse is given yet another turn. The opening melody (Ex. 79a) is one more variation of the opera's principal thematic nucleus, which appears in its original form at the words 'Je te maudis'. The final sentence, punctuated by tutti chords with a constant hammering of triplets on the trumpet, generates a wave of energy that carries the melodic line to G flat and a cadence in which the singer has to parade a compass of two octaves. The central section ('Adieu, Reine') (Ex. 79b) is Verdi's first essay before the Requiem in pure contralto sonority; nor was he prepared to modify it when he knew that he would not have a full contralto for the first performance. His only concession to Mme Gueymard-Lauters was a highish cadenza which has not found its way into printed scores. The form of the movement is regular, its motion smooth and measured like Philip's 'Elle ne m'aime pas'. The scoring is warm yet delicate with a skilful use of sustaining wind; but if any feature could be said to stand out from the general synthesis it is the harmonic scheme. The piece is, essentially, pivoted on the parallel 6/4 chords of A flat major and G major, and from the chromatic relationship of the two keys spring the chromatic inflections which give that touch of velvet to the singer's line.

79a

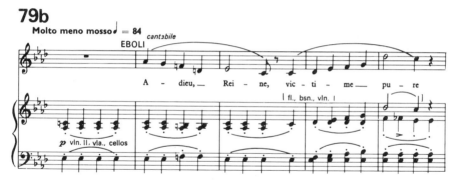

79b

For the final movement Eboli turns her thoughts to the need to save Carlos's life. Such is the intention of Schiller's Eboli also, though she is unable to do anything very effectual. One suspects that once she had shot her bolt of villainy Schiller lost interest in her. Verdi's Eboli means to act and does. Her resolution ('Et Carlos? . . . Oui! Demain peut-être il tombera sous le fer sacré. . . . Ah, un jour me reste. Ah, je me sens renaître') would once have prompted a cabaletta; and indeed the outlines of such a solution are discernible in the earliest stages of the movement's composition. This would have had the effect of uniting Eboli's disjointed thoughts in a formal scheme, in which it would have been impossible to give appropriate musical expression to each. What Verdi has done is to treat the opening bars as far as the first statement of 'Je me sens renaître' as a preparation – almost a *tempo di mezzo*. Then follows a single sweeping phrase which contains the whole of Eboli's resolution – and indeed her redemption (Ex. 80). The rest is coda.

80

It is the logical outcome of Verdi's emancipation from the solo cabaletta.

> *Scene 2: Carlos's prison: a cellar into which a few magnificent pieces of fur-*
> *niture have been hurriedly moved. At the back an iron grille separates the*
> *prison from a courtyard which overlooks it and in which sentries can be seen*
> *pacing to and fro. A stone staircase leads into the courtyard from the upper*
> *floors of the palace. Carlos is seated, his head in his hands.**

The opening motif for strings, spread out in six-part chords, is related partly to the chant of the monks at the start of Act II, partly to the music of the coronation ceremony. Here the effect of modal harmonies is wholly oppressive – a leaden weight of melancholy.

81

The oboe's forlorn reminiscence of Ex. 13 from the love duet in Act I has only one clear precedent in Verdi: in the third act of the much-despised *Corsaro* where Medora is waiting but without hope for Corrado's return. As Ex. 81 is resumed Posa enters unobserved by Carlos and speaks quietly to the sentry standing by the door; the sentry immediately retires. Posa looks sorrowfully at Carlos, who starts on becoming aware of his presence. The Infante's first words

> 'Tu l'as compris; ma force est abattue.
> L'amour d'Elisabeth me torture et tue'

need a little explanation for those unfamiliar with the play. They are not a statement of fact, so much as an attempt to justify Posa for having had him arrested. In the opera this justification makes no sense since Carlos has been arrested under circumstances which have nothing to do with his stepmother. Nor is there the same reason why he should go to such tortuous lengths to state his belief in Posa's integrity, since a moment's reflection would convince him that in acting as he did Posa was saving his life. But as so often, the librettists had recourse to sentiments expressed in the original play without considering how much sense they made in their new context. Just as the theme of Posa's apparent betrayal of Carlos is minimized in the opera, so is his very real betrayal of Philip. Indeed, since earlier in the act Philip has already agreed, reluctantly, to hand Posa over to the Inquisition, he himself is no less the betrayer. Posa briefly explains how he has written letters to William of Orange stating that he himself is the Queen's lover and the fomenter of rebellion in the Netherlands – and he has added a few of Carlos's private documents for good measure. He has taken care that the letters will be intercepted and brought to the King; he is now a marked man, but he will have laid down his life for Carlos.

* From the foregoing directions in the French score it is clear that Carlos is imprisoned in the royal palace, as in Schiller and, for once, in history. On the other hand, both production books describe a state prison, with Carlos seated on a stone bench.

Posa, as Verdi later admitted, was an operatic problem with which he would gladly have dispensed. His ideals, being intellectual, cannot be conveyed in music, only his idealism; and this together with his unswerving selflessness makes him musically rather uninteresting. Even at the height of his greatness Verdi can find for him nothing more impressive than a stream of generically noble baritonic melody.*
In effect this means two consecutive 'romanze' – a very unusual procedure. The first of these, a non-repeating melody ('C'est mon jour suprème'), in which second violins *tacent* throughout, is touching by reason of its restraint, especially where the regular flow of the melody is broken by gestures of a helpless affection.

82

Posa's explanations follow in a fast-moving 'scène' during which two men are seen to take up their positions behind the grille unnoticed by Carlos and Posa. One carries an arquebus; the other wears the uniform of the 'Holy Office'. At the mention of Flanders the music takes on a martial character for twelve bars. Then a shot rings out and Posa collapses, mortally wounded. Very striking is the motif that accompanies his agony (Ex. 83); it not only contains the ubiquitous acciaccatura sob but exploits to good purpose the essentially tired quality of cornet cantilena when unenlivened by a rapid vibrato. Not for nothing is the cornet's first cousin, the trumpet, the instrument par excellence of the blues.

This leads to the second romanza. 'Ah, je meurs, l'âme joyeuse' – a two-verse affair with harp prominent in the approved deathbed manner. The second verse adds trilling flutes and a few small elaborations to the melody. Between the verses there is a reminiscence of Ex. 30 played by a banda-like combination of wind – flutes, piccolo and oboes on the melody, bassoons, trombones and ophicleide on the accompaniment, timpani and bass drum marking the first beat of each bar. But it has an elegiac ring to it further emphasized by the tonality – A major against the D flat of the romanza. It would be pleasant to say that nothing in Posa's life became him like the leaving of it; but, alas, the tune of 'Ah, je meurs' is plain to the point of cliché. Even the final gathering of strength ('Souviens-toi . . . ah, la terre me manque . . . Carlos, ta main . . . sauvez la Flandre') and the cadenza – both of them afterthoughts on the

*Massimo Mila, *Verdi* (Bari, 1958), pp. 79 and 248, has declared that there is nothing in Posa's part which could not have come out of *La Battaglia di Legnano*. Allowing for the rhythmic cut of his melodies, always more French than Italian, and the greater variety of harmony, this is not an altogether unfair judgement.

83

evidence of the rehearsal books – do little more than follow the well worn paths of conventional melodrama.

1866, 1867, 1872

As Philip enters with a suite of grandees, cellos and basses recall Ex. 41a from the first version of the Philip–Posa duet in Act II. It is a benign, smiling phrase, a gesture of reconciliation; for Philip has come to restore Carlos's sword to him and with it his freedom. But evidently Verdi set little store by the back reference since in the version of 1872 he had already removed the theme's first appearance. Carlos's reaction ('Arrière! De ce mort le sang a rejailli jusqu'à votre visage') is a fifty-bar solo of allegro mosso, corresponding to the great denunciation of Schiller's Act V, scene i. If not the climax of the play it is certainly its most impressive moment when performed on stage. Accordingly this is Carlos's most forceful utterance in the opera, though not the most interesting musically. Twice he breaks into those hysterically savage downward arpeggios ('Dieu marque votre front' . . . 'O Roi de meutre et d'épouvante') with which Stiffelio had inveighed against his wife's seducer. It is one of the few passages in *Don Carlos* in which the composer reverts to the barnstorming style of his youth and must have sorely taxed Morère, who was no Fraschini. 'My kingdom is here,' Carlos concludes, indicating Posa's corpse.

1866 only

The original scheme allowed for a duet at this point between Philip and Carlos with chorus of grandees ('Qui me rendra ce mort'). Philip's first words are taken from the second scene of Schiller's Act V where the King is alone with his counsellors.

> Give me back this dead
> Man. I must have him back.
> I held him dear! I held him very dear.
> In that youth rose for me a fairer morning.

The chorus takes over Alva's words from the same context:

> Then we have lived in vain! Let us
> Go to our graves, then, Spaniards, even in
> His death this man[i.e., *Posa*] is robbing us of our
> King's heart.

Carlos, who has no part in Schiller's scene, is accommodated with a prayer to be granted Posa's greatness of soul – or else a place beside him in the grave. All three soliloquies are woven into an impressive threnody, whose principal theme (Ex. 84) owes its origin to the Inquisitor's denunciation in the previous scene (Ex. 71b), as has been noted. But the first was merely a demonstration, a musical placard held up menacingly. Now the same idea returns in the form of an experience, and therefore filled out and expanded. The Inquisitor has insisted that Philip must lose Posa; now he has lost him and would give anything to have him restored to life. The choral motif ('Ah, c'est en vain que nous vivons encore', Ex. 84b) backed by a bass-heavy accompaniment in which four bassoons are prominent, suggests the effect of a muffled side-drum, indicating surely the origin and raison-d'être of this famous 'topos'. Carlos's melody (Ex. 84c) takes shape more gradually, finding its way into A flat major instead of the D flat that one might expect. Ex. 84a, is then resumed with sustained counter-melodies from Carlos and the grandees; and later it forms the basis of the major-key coda to which Carlos's melody (Ex. 84c) is joined with an indescribably moving effect, offset by new figuration from the chorus basses.*

For all its grave beauty this duet has the disadvantage not only of protracting the scene beyond reasonable lengths but of leaving the baritone lying on the floor for far longer than the average star singer would be prepared to tolerate. Hence it became an early candidate for removal. However, as the music was too good to be lost entirely Verdi reworked the entire period of Ex. 84a into the Lachrymosa of the Requiem, keeping the harmonies intact and altering the melodic shape only so far as was necessary to accommodate the new text (Ex. 84d).†

1866, 1867, 1872

A tocsin sounds the alarm, and the strings set up an agitated prestissimo 6/8 in F minor. Lerma, mysteriously transformed into a baritone, hurries in to announce that the people are in revolt. Elisabeth arrives next, frightened about her husband's safety ('Sauvez le roi; sire, je tremble pour votre majesté'). Then the crowd is heard baying for blood in an unaccompanied chorus ('La mort! La mort à qui nous arrête!') recalling perhaps a little too obviously the furious conclusion to the 'Bénédiction des

---

* One curious feature of the reprise is the very obtrusive fifths between Philip's line and that of the chorus at the reprise of Ex. 84; these serve to confirm the suspicion held by more than one Verdian that the unconscious model for this number may have been the funeral march from Chopin's B flat minor sonata.

† As in the duet between Elisabeth and Eboli some of the orchestral parts are tantalizingly incomplete. Two pages of oboe and clarinet are missing – which suggests that they had a good deal to play. It may readily be supposed that this included the repeated acciaccatura lament that enters at the ninth bar of the 'Lachrymosa', especially as it figures so prominently throughout the opera (but see p. 157 n.).

84a

Andante sostenuto assai

PHILIPPE

Qui me rendra ce mort, qui me ren — — dra ce mort? O fu-nè-bres a-

— bî-mes! ce-lui-là seul...par-mi tant de vic-ti-mes! Un hom-me, un

(1866)

84b

COURTIERS   PHILIPPE

Ah! c'est en vain que nous vi-vons en — core. Cet hom — me — — fier,

(1866)

84c

DON CARLOS

Rem-plis mon cœur de la di-vi-ne flam-me… ou fais moi près de toi pla-ce dans le tom-beau. (1866)

84d Largo ♩ = 60

M. SOP.

con molta espressione

La-cry-mo-sa di — es il-la, Qua re — sur-get ex fa-vil-la, Ju — di (-candus)

(REQUIEM)

poignards' from Meyerbeer's *Les Huguenots*. Lerma calls on the grandees to defend their King; and the populace, breaking in, find Philip surrounded by the nobles with drawn swords. Between cries of 'Frappons!' from the people and 'Vive le Roi!' Philip calls on his subjects to strike him down, march over his bleeding corpse and do homage to his son, clad in the royal robes. It is an exciting piece of action music culminating in a solo for Philip of thirty bars, with a long baritonic high F before its final cadence ('à mon fils revêtu de mon manteau royal').

1866 only

At the end of the B flat cadence on the words 'royal' the 6/8 quavers become triplets within a new 4/4 as the rebellion begins to run out of fuel. The people recoil in the face of Philip's vehemence, and the music ebbs away to a long-drawn-out close in this same key of B flat minor based on the second phrase of Philip's solo. During all this Eboli, dressed as a youth, approaches Elisabeth, and explains briefly that it was she who roused the populace, so that she could save Carlos's life; that having thus proved her love for him, she is ready to enter a convent. ('Adieu, Reine.') The calming of the storm, the slackening of tension are certainly carried out by a master hand. But there are good reasons why the episode should be removed. Musically, it is static and repetitive – thirty or so bars of B flat minor relieved by a six-bar episode in the dominant, based on the principal theme. Throughout this Philip must stand his ground repeating, 'Frappez!' and, 'Du courage!' against an attack which becomes more unlikely every minute. Worst of all the impact of the following coup-de-théâtre is diminished. So this too was dropped. A note in the first Italian edition of 1867 under the first words of Philip's solo tells us that Eboli appears at the foot of the step 'preceding Carlos, who is being dragged away by the crowd'. Unfortunately, it remains a general rule that an audience rarely removes its attention from a character who is singing to one who is not, and the chances of this incident being noticed would be slim indeed.*

1866, 1867, 1872

Over the last chord of Philip's B flat minor cadence ('Frappez-moi donc' in 1866, 'manteau royal' in 1867 and 1872) a mighty voice cries, 'À genoux!' and a general cry goes up: 'Le Grand Inquisiteur!' Like a deus ex machina in the classic tradition of Verdian basses the Inquisitor orders the people to kneel before the Lord's anointed. Tremolando strings, sweeping scales on cellos, basses and bassoons, sustaining wind all add force to his pronouncement. The atmosphere becomes calm, almost radiant as the people fall on their knees and ask for forgiveness in a sequence of cadences descending by fifths from D major to B flat. 'Gloire à toi, grand Dieu!' Philip cries, joined later by the Inquisitor; 'Vive le Roi!' reply Lerma and the grandees; 'Pardonne,' murmur the people – all this on a long chord of B flat major which swells to a climax embellished by fanfares on cornets and trumpets.

---

* In 1867 the 'sommossa' proceeded as follows: *Enter R. the Count of Lerma with sword in hand crying, 'Rebellion!' Enter Elisabeth R. in great agitation and followed by two women. She approaches the King and says to him, 'Fuyons!' Philip takes her by the hand and leads her R. and reassures her with a gesture; then proceeding to the centre of the stage he orders the gates to be thrown open.*

The 4 sentries open the gates; at that moment Eboli, wrapped in a cloak and masked, enters hurriedly, followed by 8 men of the people, who are armed; and pointing out to them the door, she enters; the rest follow her.

At Lerma's words, 'Grands d'Espagne, sauvez le Roi!' the other lords unsheathe their swords.

The chorus, 'La mort!', is sung very distantly from the wings, and draws gradually nearer.

After the chorus the people burst in on stage from all directions; some remain on the terrace.

At the reprise of the chorus Eboli appears on the terrace leading Carlos; she is followed by the 8 men of the people, who make gestures of satisfaction. (Disp. scen. (1867), pp. 50–1.)

1884, 1886

Although by the time Verdi revised the opera into four acts it had long been the practice to end Act IV with Posa's death, he nevertheless felt that an uprising of some sort was necessary if only to justify Eboli's promise.* His concern was therefore to include all the important sentiments, especially those removed in 1867, in the least number of bars so as not to delay the fall of the curtain unduly. Inevitably, in so doing he starved some of the text of the musical expression it had previously enjoyed. Philip now restores Carlos's sword to him in a snatch of neutral unaccompanied recitative declaimed throughout on C sharp. Carlos's outburst is condensed from fifty bars to sixteen; Philip's 'Qui me rendra ce mort' is dispatched in a mere three-bar cadential phrase. The new 'sommossa' is based on the old, but the writing is more diversified and nimble in its effect, and all likeness to *Les Huguenots* has vanished with the remoulding of the principal theme. The King no longer challenges the people to attack him; he merely asks them what they want. 'The Infante,' they reply; and Philip points to him. Elisabeth is not present at all. But Eboli, masked, though no longer 'en travestie', approaches Carlos with the words 'Ah . . . fuyez!' and is just in time to spirit him away before the Inquisitor enters with a new and more powerful cry of 'Sacrilège infâme!', after which the scene proceeds as in the early versions. However, honour has been satisfied; Eboli has been seen and heard to fulfil her promise. But whether those two words are sufficient to wrest the audience's attention from Philip may be doubted. Even in its final version Eboli's rescue tends to slip by as unnoticed as the final, fatal exchange between Macduff and Macbeth in the revised version of that opera.

ACT V

Scene: The Monastery of St-Just. It is a moonlit night.

After the hurly-burly of the previous scene the last act moves on to the level of contemplative poetry. The air for Elisabeth ('Toi qui sus le néant'), as we have seen, had its origins in one intended for Carlos. Although the number of solo rehearsals arranged for Morère suggests that he was stupid to the point of autism, that was not the only reason for depriving him of a second scene to himself. Elisabeth needs this aria if only to achieve parity with Eboli. She has been the noble sufferer for too long. Now at last she will reveal herself as a woman of real spiritual stature. The orchestral prelude alone is remarkable. It begins with the chant of the monks (Ex. 20) from Act II set out on three trombones with two horns and ophicleide supplying the bass; at the fifth bar horns give way to the four bassoons; at the seventh a long timpani roll begins, persisting throughout a new answering phrase for cornets and horns. 'New' is perhaps not strictly correct, since, allowing for the alteration of key and the added tonic pedal, this is essentially a variation on the Monk's second entry ('Dieu seul est grand'). The curtain rises to reveal Elisabeth on her knees before the tomb of Charles V.† The reprise of Ex. 20, accompanied by a descant of broken phrases for violins

* The score from which Michele Costa conducted the first English performance ends Act IV with Posa's romance ('Ah, je meurs, l'âme joyeuse').

† According to the French score. The Italian score and both production books have: *Elisabeth enters, approaches the tomb of Charles V and kneels before it.*

and cellos at the octave, suggesting the kind of instrumental speech to be heard in the scène d'amour from Berlioz's 'Roméo et Juliette'. The corresponding variant of 'Dieu seul est grand' now takes the form of one of those self-torturing melodies so typical of the late romantics whether in France, Italy or Russia, with cellos adding their characteristic groan at the lower octave (Ex. 85a). There follows a brief *agitato* episode (Ex. 85b) to be recalled in the aria's central section.

Ex. 85a returns, more subdued, on violins and clarinet over chromatic harmonies on the lower strings tremolando; and the violins round off the statement with three bars of unaccompanied melody that descends over more than three octaves; a soft wind chord underlines the cadence that leads to Elisabeth's first words. For an aria prelude this is substantial indeed – as vivid and eloquent as the prelude to Act III of *La Traviata*. But there is an important difference. The earlier prelude presents Violetta in her sickroom; but the sickroom has no separate existence apart from her. The present introduction unites two contrasted scenic elements, each with its own identity, in a single piece – the chill, impersonal grandeur of the monastery and the agony of Elisabeth (Ex. 85a), which overflows into the momentary panic of Ex. 85b. Nor is the picture too strongly drawn. Elisabeth's situation is indeed desperate. From a wife and stepmother, nobly resisting her own feelings, she has willingly become an instrument of Posa's idealism; so much would be clear if the opera had included the substance of Schiller's Act IV, scene vii. If she succeeds in helping Carlos on his way to Flanders she herself will reap the whirlwind whether as heretic or suspected adulteress. As she herself puts it in the course of her aria, 'I have promised Posa to watch over [Carlos's] life. May he go on his way, glorious and blessed. As for me, my task is done and my life at an end.' The aria stretches the French ternary form beyond its usual limits; but the principal idea is so overwhelmingly strong that all danger of diffuseness is avoided. The opening part, formal as always, unites two opposing thoughts in the same musical period. The first apostrophizes the Emperor as one who knew the vanity of all earthly things; the second begs him to carry Elisabeth's tears to the throne of the Almighty 'if tears are still shed in Heaven'. 'Toi qui sus le néant' (Ex. 86a) is plain and severe, unaccompanied at its first appearance apart from soft percussion beats and unisons on lower brass between phrases, underpinned at the reprise by reiterated semiquaver chords on cornets and trombones. It is the prayer of an agnostic forced to contemplate first and last things. The first statement of 'Si l'on répand' (Ex. 86b) is backed by three flutes, violins and violas; the reprise by an even more delicate pattern of divided strings and woodwind. Both ideas are based on an arpeggio, the second moving up where the first moves down; and both break the chordal outline with a melodic curve linked however tenuously to the four-note nucleus so often observed elsewhere in the opera. At the same time the three-note patterns (x) at the words 'néant' and 'encore' respectively, though they occur at different points of each phrase, are like question and answer. Elisabeth's doubt in Ex. 86a is countered in Ex. 86b by an assertion of faith – whether in herself, in love, in God, it hardly matters. Both musical ideas span a wide vocal range; but the second always outreaches the first at vital points in the structure, as though to suggest the triumph of will over despair.

A reprise of the bitter Ex. 85a, low on tremolando strings, leads to the central section, which begins with a snatch of recitative such as one might have expected at the start of the scene. But how much better that Elisabeth's musical assertion should spring directly out of the conflict of the prelude. Once this is over she can afford to relax into free informal declamation over music which gradually forms itself into a thread of reminiscences, but not before there has been an outburst of spontaneous lyrical warmth as she thinks of Carlos's future ('Qu'il suive son chemin glorieux et béni!') in contrast to her own imminent fate. Then her thoughts turn to France. The love-duet (Ex. 13) is heard on three flutes and clarinet in the fullest version since Act I. Next, beneath tremolando violins and violas, flute, clarinet and oboe (a favourite Verdian reminiscence-combination) discourse in mounting sequences on the theme associated with Carlos's delirium (Ex. 36e) as Elisabeth calls on the birds and the fountains to sing aloud their memories of love to Carlos if he should ever return to them. A new darting motif starts up over bassoon arpeggio, twice bringing the turbulent Ex. 85b in its wake. Here Elisabeth bids farewell to her youthful dreams; now she longs only for death. And so to the reprise of the principal section (Ex. 86a and b) with enhanced scoring. Again Ex. 86a returns, to be finally vanquished by what could be called a cadenza substitute: three bars of free declamation 'a piacere' touched in with a light orchestral accompaniment. So with an extended aria on the highest spiritual plane does Elisabeth more than redress the balance that has been tilted in favour of her rival. If the singer needs more than average talent to be applauded after the Aremberg aria in Act II she must be poor indeed not to receive an ovation here.

Carlos enters unobtrusively ('C'est elle'). Throughout the following scene he and Elisabeth remain outwardly composed. Carlos will go to Flanders where he will erect a monument to Posa such as no monarch has ever been granted. Elisabeth, never at a loss for the transfiguring phrase, murmurs enchantingly 'les fleurs du paradis ré-jouiront son ombre'.

1866, 1867

Carlos tells how his fair dream of love has faded before a vision of a land laid waste ('J'avais fait un beau rêve'). He must go to the rescue. 'You will either sing of my triumph or mourn my death.' In his first, Parisian version Verdi had taken his cue from the word 'incendie' and portrayed a spreading fire through a developing motif which, as it gathers force, produces some bold combinations of horizontal patterns.

Elisabeth, fired by Carlos's determination, launches an allegro marziale ('Oui, voilà, l'héroisme', Ex. 88a) which for some reason has provoked the wrath of many of the most devoted Verdians, though it is hard to see why, as this is in purest *Aida* vein. Is it the strumming harp that offends? But the harp as a martial instrument had been an operatic convention in France since the Ossianic vogue at the beginning of the century and had even found its way into Rossini's *La Donna del lago*. Is it the square-ness of the melody? But this is effectively broken at Carlos's intervention ('Oui, c'est par votre voix que le peuple m'appelle') with its three-bar structure. True, there is no equivalent in Schiller's last act; but here as elsewhere Verdi has achieved his own synthesis of the drama by reshuffling the dramatic events. Schiller's Elisabeth does indeed spur Carlos to action but much earlier in the story, during the previous meeting arranged by Posa. But, as we have seen, Verdi's duet between the thwarted lovers in Act II took a very different course. Therefore it was necessary at some later point to recover that aspect of Elisabeth's character that he had suppressed earlier on. And is it not consistent with the dialogue that with Posa's death something of his spirit should have entered Elisabeth?

The tempo quickens for a new idea (Ex. 88b, 'Hier, hier encore aucun pouvoir humain') of which the gist is that Posa's death has turned Carlos's thoughts from hopeless love to honour. 'See, I embrace you without faltering,' he says; and the music comes to a firm cadence in C. But immediately a huge sadness wells up in the form of a weeping motif (Ex. 88c). Carlos sees that his stepmother is in tears. 'The

88d

88e

[vlas. added   (1884)

tears that women shed for heroes,' she replies proudly; the music, however, goes to strange harmonic lengths to portray a sorrow too deep for speech. (Ex. 88d)

1872

In order to shorten the duet Verdi omitted the two sections based on Ex. 88a and b. This was made possible by rewriting the last nine bars of the 'conflagration' passage based on Ex. 87 so as to bring the final cadence into C major; Ex. 88c then follows as before; but meanwhile Carlos has not embraced Elisabeth without flinching. Musically this works well enough but it relegates Elisabeth to a more passive role.

1884, 1886

Here the section beginning 'J'avais fait un beau rêve' is radically rethought so as to present two images rather than one. Ex. 87 is discarded altogether. Instead the 'beau rêve' is conveyed by means of Ex. 36c played by three flutes over pizzicato violin triplets. As the 'rêve' is Carlos's the key of D flat is especially appropriate. The crumbling of the vision is suggested by making chromatic scales on the violins which gradually invade the texture, until the suave sequences of Ex. 36c are swallowed up in a tutti of triplets over a rising bass. The effect is less novel than it sounds; Verdi has already used it in a more unsophisticated, schematic form in the sung dance of the Druidesses from the Act II finale of *Attila*.

The marziale allegro and its sequel are both reinstated; but the scoring of Ex. 88a is enhanced by the addition of cornets and trumpets which reinforce the melody (pianissimi) in four-part harmony. Elsewhere too the texture is richer in the later version; and it is amusing to note how the *Trovatore*-like ♪♪♪ ♪♪♪ ♪♪♪ ♪♪♪ at the end of the second statement of Ex. 88a becomes *Aida*-ized into ♪♪♪♪♪♪ – an inspired effect. Ex. 88b no longer remains rooted in A minor for most of its length but is developed in sequences towards E major, the key in which Carlos reaches his now defiant cadential phrase ('Et le vertu me reste et je ne fléchis pas').

Originally in C major, it had been interrupted by Ex. 88c in C minor; now the same theme interrupts it in C sharp minor. To a Wagner these two modulations would have been so totally different in their emotional implications that it is hard to imagine him ever substituting one for the other in the same dramatic context. Verdi employs another musical and dramatic convention; but even here the hard musical fact remains that a shift from tonic major to tonic minor suggests a negation of what has gone before, whereas a move to the relative minor implies a mere diversion from it. In the revised score, therefore, the tears of Ex. 88c are more compatible with the previous mood of heroic resolution than they were in the old; and the revised key scheme represents an unqualified improvement. Note too an extra touch of eloquence in the prolongation of the cello's final sob. (Ex. 88e)

All versions (with minor variants in 1884 and 1886)

The final movement of the duet ('Au revoir dans un monde') has the formality of a

'similar' cabaletta without ritornello. For once the later version is the higher (B major as against the B flat major of 1866, 1867 and 1872). (See Ex. 89a.)

It is a far cry to the brilliant cabalettas that ended the duets of Rossini's day. The melody is calm and poised, moving within the narrowest compass, vertical and dynamic; only the inner lines of violas and clarinets disturb the serenity like a faint but profound sigh, to which in the revision of 1884 Verdi added a reply from the cellos (*x*). Elisabeth and Carlos are confident that they will meet again in a better world; and when Carlos sings the melody after her, Elizabeth repeats his words as a pertichino. Unusually this second statement of Ex. 89a is extended by a short two-and-a-half-bar diversion into G sharp minor (originally G minor) before returning to a cadential phrase which is likewise protracted so as to absorb the extra half bar. This same episode is incorporated into a coda whose theme, contrary to Verdi's usual practice, is carried by instruments (bassoon and violins on the G string) in the earlier versions and by voices in the latter (Ex. 89b). The final bars melt away chromatically to a dying fall; but the bad habits of singers have a way of conditioning the professional composer's thoughts. To have expected a soprano and tenor to sing a long duet-movement pianissimo without a single phrase 'a voce spiegata' was un-realistic in the 1860s. Therefore in the early version of the opera stepmother and stepson bid each other a chaste farewell in a *fortissimo* outburst for which acciaccatura sobs on the horn and weeping figures on oboe and clarinet have already prepared us. In 1884 all these unwanted accessories are removed, leaving only the bass line of cellos, basses and bassoons and the broken triplets of the upper strings. The farewell itself ('Adieu pour toujours') has only the smallest of 'hairpins'; and is infinitely more moving in consequence. More startling too is Philip's cry of 'Oui, pour toujours!' as he enters with the Grand Inquisitor and several of the monks of the Holy Office (all basses). He adds in the words that conclude Schiller's play, 'I have done my part'; (to the Inquisitor) 'Now do yours.' The opera, however, does not end there, though many people appear to wish that it did. The denouement takes two forms.

1866, 1867, 1872

Carlos is subjected to a summary trial similar to that of Gaston in *Jérusalem*. The text, drafted by Verdi himself, clearly envisaged the ritual rule of three. Philip, the Inquisitor, then Philip again accuse Carlos by turns of three crimes: of nurturing a 'detestable love'; of subverting the Catholic faith; and of inciting Spanish subjects to rebellion. To each of the accusations Elisabeth and Carlos reply in unison 'God will be our judge'; while the monks of the Inquisition retort, 'God has spoken; may the traitor be accursed!' Each charge is preceded by a cataclysmic orchestral tutti, successively in D flat minor, D minor and E flat minor. The monks then strike up a solemn chant of commination: 'Ah, sois maudit, artisan d'une oeuvre détestée' (A minor–A major), with an accompaniment that uses all the resources of blatant brutality that Grand Opera can muster – reiterated semiquaver chords on the brass, sweeping scales on strings and woodwind, and at one point a savage semitonal clash between voices and trombones. (Ex. 90)

There is a reprise of the maggiore section. Then as Carlos retreats fighting towards the tomb of Charles V ('Ah, Dieu me vengera') the grille opens and the Monk

90

appears and covers Carlos with his cloak.* There is a crash on the gong, for the only time in the score. 'Mons fils, les douleurs de la terre nous suivent encore dans ce lieu . . .'. The monk repeats his moralizings from the second act to the same music as before, and scored for the same combination of trombones and ophicleide; then he draws Carlos into the depths of the monastery. 'La voix de l'Empereur.' 'C'est Charles V.' 'Mon père!' 'Grand Dieu' – cry severally the Inquisitor, the monks of the Holy Office, Philip and – with infinite relief – Elisabeth. All fall on their knees to the solemn chanting of distant monks that Charles V is naught but dust and shadow. The final chords on the orchestra recall almost literally the end of *Simon Boccanegra*.

1884, 1886

After Philip's pronouncement a few bars of rapid action music with appropriate exclamations from Carlos, now fighting for his life, lead to the appearance of the Monk, whose pronouncement is now a tone higher than before, while the score indicates clearly 'Charles V with royal robe and crown'. From here the music proceeds to a strong fortissimo ending with the chant of the monks no longer sung but thundered out as a brass chorale. The resemblance to the end of *Simon Boccanegra* vanishes completely. The removal of the judgement is welcome for various reasons. It is artificial in its context; it makes for too steep a descent from the high spirituality of the previous duet, and in any case Verdi had done the same thing very much better in the fourth act of *Aida*.

* The French score of 1867 refers to him throughout as 'the Monk'; the Italian score of the same date and the production book describe him unequivocally as 'Charles V'; neither makes any mention of the imperial regalia.

*

Of all Verdi's operas *Don Carlos* remains the most ambitious; not, however, the most successful. In its original form it had been hedged around with a number of données, mostly imposed by conditions at the Paris Opéra. His irritation with these transpires clearly enough from what he wrote and said both at the time and afterwards. It is in the context of *Don Carlos* that Monaldi places the composer's famous dictum that 'to write well one should write in a single breath, so to speak, leaving till later the matter of filling out, and modifying and polishing up the general sketch. Otherwise you will be liable to write an opera . . . in the manner of a mosaic; lacking both style and character. The exception of Meyerbeer doesn't apply; and besides for all the power of his genius even Meyerbeer had to waste a great deal of time in setting his libretti to music, and not even he was able to avoid that slackening of style that at times is so palpable in his masterworks as to make one think them the work of two composers. There's no getting away from it; excessive length in a libretto damages the total effect of an opera, even when it's entrusted to a composer of genius.'*

In his revision of 1884 Verdi set himself to remedy the debilitating effect of the Paris Opéra, to give it more 'sinew'. Certainly the four-act version is not only shorter; it is more compact and faster moving. The replacements are without exception superior musically to what they replace. The start and the finish mirror each other neatly. But there are two disadvantages – the love interest is no longer so firmly 'planted'; and there is at times a disparity of style between old and new. The five-act version of 1886 overcomes the first, but if anything aggravates the second. The prelude to Act III here recalls Carlos's romance in a form in which it has not been heard, since this last revision restores the romance to its original place and its original form.

It is to problems such as these that we owe the existence of at least two posthumous editions that made their way round the theatres of Europe during the Verdi renaissance of the thirties. First there is the German Ricordi edition of 1932.† This begins with a drastically reduced Fontainebleau scene presented as a flashback – a reminiscent dream in the mind of Carlos as he sits alone in his room in Madrid, before a tapestry depicting Fontainebleau. He falls asleep to five bars lifted from the 1884 prelude to Act III and slotted in where the cavatine should be; and the scene on the tapestry comes to life. A further short cut leads to the entrance of Elisabeth and Thibault; after which the duet follows, shorn of its episode in E major. Thibault returns with the plain announcement that Elisabeth is to wed the King and not the Infante. The dream then starts to fade over two pianissimo statements of the march ('O chants de fête', Ex. 17), and Carlos's final broken exclamations are those of one who has awakened, like the hero of Schubert's *Winterreise*, from a dream of spring. The start of the second act is untouched except that the Monk is Charles V in the flesh who is at that moment solemnly putting aside his imperial orb and sceptre to a chorus of approving monks. Carlos enters to sing his cavatine in the 1867 form but transposed down to B flat – a touch of ineptitude which shows how much Verdi's most enthusiastic admirers of 1932 had still to learn about his musical style. The monks' intervention is removed from the end of the scene. In Scene 2 there is no Veil song; Rodrigue is allowed one verse of his romance, Elisabeth one of her Aremberg

---

* Monaldi, 4th edition, p. 208.

† *Don Carlos: Oper in einem Vorspiel und vier Akten, textlich neu gefasst und unter Mitwirkung von Franz Werfel für die deutsche Bühne bearbeitet von Lothar Wallerstein* (Leipzig, 1932).

couplets. The duet between her and Carlos omits the D flat section. The final movement of the duet between Philip and Posa is deprived of its reprise. The first scene of Act III begins with the offstage chorus ('Que de fleurs et que d'étoiles') that precedes the exchanging of the masks in the 1867 version; but neither Elisabeth nor Eboli participates. The second scene of Act III was rearranged musically so as to fit the current production by Lothar Wallerstein at the Vienna State Opera. The scene was a courtyard in the palace through which the heretics were being conducted to the *auto da fé*. The general procession with the banda melodies (Ex. 67a and b) is left out and Philip's coronation reduced to thirty-two bars. But the fanfares are repeated after the arrest of Carlos, and with them the hymn ('Ouvrez-vous les portes sacrées'). But it is sung by the chorus behind a drop curtain to words approving the sentence of the Holy Office. A transition back to E major for the final reprise is effected by using material from the instrumental introduction – another clumsy expedient; the curtain then rises to show the Inquisition at its nefarious work. The heretics are bound to stakes; the fire is lit; and clouds of smoke gradually obliterate the scene, so that the voice from heaven is sung to a completely darkened stage. From this point to the end all the other vocal parts are omitted; but an appendix to the vocal score gives the original ending. Act IV, Scene 1 is mercifully allowed to stand as Verdi wrote it. Posa, however, is deprived of the second verse of 'Ah, je meurs, l'âme joyeuse' and the reminiscence of the friendship theme. In the duet of Act V the allegro marziale and its sequel are removed by a piece of surgery which has nothing to do with the version of 1872, but which has served many a performance in our own day. The ending is basically that of 1884 and 1886, but eight bars of string tremolando are added to allow the monks to sing their chant before the brass thunder out an orchestral echo of it. Meanwhile, at the appearance of Philip and the Inquisitor, Carlos has stabbed himself; whereupon Charles V appears, moralizes once more on the vanity of earthly things and commands the monks to take up the body of the Infante. All fall on their knees except the Inquisitor who remains erect gazing towards heaven. His last words are 'Hört die Stimme des Kaisers'. It would seem that Werfel and Wallerstein intended the moral victory to be his rather than Carlos's.

Somewhat less ruthless is the version published by Peters.* Here too it is the Fontainebleau scene which suffers most. While the Ricordi edition removed the opening chorus of huntsmen, leaving only the fanfare, this one retains the chorus but leaves out Carlos's recitative with the solo clarinet. Again there is no cavatina, the music passing straight to the second offstage fanfare. The duet remains intact; but the chorus 'O chants de fête' is reached in the same way as in the Ricordi German score. It is, however, allowed to proceed in a crescendo and to include the moment of Elisabeth's renunciation. But there is no decrescendo with expostulation from Carlos as the crowd moves away. The scene ends with a statement of Ex. 17. In the first scene of Act II the monks chant only once, so depriving their imperial brother of his impressive solo, 'Il voulait régner sur le monde'. The cavatine appears in its 1884 guise complete with preceding reminiscence. Philip and Elisabeth make no appearance at the end of the friendship duet. The second scene of Act II proceeds normally apart from the excision of the D flat major episode in the duet between Elisabeth and Carlos. Act II (III) begins with the entire episode in which Elisabeth and Eboli

* *Don Carlos: Oper in einem Vorspiel und vier Akten für die deutsche Bühne neu bearbeitet von Julius Kapp und Kurt Soldan.* Martin Chusid dates it 1961 (*Catalog of Verdi Operas*, Hackensack, NJ, 1974, p. 55).

exchange masks and continues with the 1884 prelude. Nothing else is added or omitted to the score until the last act. The solution of Kapp and Soldan to the final tableau is if anything worse than that of Werfel and Wallerstein, since it omits the Monk altogether and with it the music of 'Mon fils, les douleurs de la terre' which helps to close the act with a mirror reflection of Act I (II). Instead of 'La voix de l'Empereur!' the Inquisitor cries out, 'Nun hat Gott selbst gerichtet,' since once again Carlos has stabbed himself rather than fall into the hands of the Holy Office.

Finally mention should be made of the three-act version prepared by Norman Tucker for Sadler's Wells Theatre and given its première there during the Verdi year of 1951. Of this only the libretto was printed – which is hardly surprising since by comparison the Werfel–Wallerstein edition is a model of fidelity to Verdi's intentions. Much was omitted, much of what remained was redistributed throughout the opera and in certain cases given an entirely different sense by the English text. At one point a scene was invented in which Eboli brought Elisabeth's casket to the King, the music being taken mostly from the scene in the 1867 version in which Elisabeth and Eboli exchange masks. Carlos sang his cavatine at Fontainebleau but in the 1884 nostalgic version – the Werfel–Wallerstein folly in reverse! Considering how little the opera was known in England at the time, and the relatively low esteem in which it was held by Verdi's English biographers, this was a courageous attempt at rescuing a good deal of fine music that ran the risk of being buried. Not until the great Giulini–Visconti revival of the 1886 version at Covent Garden in 1958 was the opera rated by British music-lovers at its true worth.

Indeed, no single opera of Verdi's has undergone such a drastic reappraisal over the last twenty-five years as *Don Carlos*. From being regarded as gloomy, diffuse and musically unequal, despite many fine moments, it is now considered by many as Verdi's masterpiece. Already during the 1950s there were signs that the opera was assuming a new place in the Verdi canon. Massimo Mila in 1958 was already exalting it above *Aida*. The Second Verdi Congress of 1969, associated with star performances at Verona of both Verdi's opera and Schiller's play, called forth from scholars and musicians all over the world a spate of learned and enthusiastic papers devoted to this once neglected work. It is no longer heard in truncated, 'specially arranged' editions. It might even be thought that nowadays we go too far in the other direction. For the discovery of the music cut before 1866 has led to several permutations and combinations of the different versions, in which the rediscovered pieces are variously grafted on to the scores of 1867 – which is sensible – and 1886, which is less so since the four-act version mostly recoups the sense of what was lost by the original cuts.*

* Andrew Porter was the first to examine the orchestral material at the Bibliothèque de l'Opéra, Paris, in 1970. He found several pages stitched together, cut open the stitches and prepared full scores of the missing passages, reporting his findings in the *Financial Times* of 6 February 1970. His reconstruction of the Prelude to Act I was first performed the following year by the Chelsea Opera Group, London, under John Matheson. Since then, there have been performances in Boston, Mass. (1972), Venice (1973), Brussels (1973) and by the English National Opera (1973), in which the reclaimed music has been drawn upon wholly or in part. In June 1973 the B.B.C. broadcast the first complete performance of what could be called the 1866 conception in French with the addition of the ballet. The singers were André Turp (Carlos), Edith Tremblay (Elisabeth), Michèle Vilma (Eboli), Joseph Rouleau (Philip), Richard Van Allan (Grand Inquisitor), Robert Savoie (Posa), Robert Lloyd (Monk), Gillian Knight (Thibault), Geoffrey Shovelton (Herald), Emile Belcourt (Lerma), Prudence Lloyd (Voice from Heaven), with the B.B.C. Chorus and Concert Orchestra conducted by John Matheson. The edition used was Andrew Porter's which, as the author readily admits, contains one or two gaps which have

What then is the ideal form in which to give *Don Carlos*? Alas, there can be no simple answer. If stylistic consistency is the main consideration then one would choose the five act with ballet form of 1867, with or without the cuts made before the first night; but apart from its excessive length there would remain the problem of those passages such as exist in the original *Macbeth* and *Simon Boccanegra* which the later revision immeasurably improves without departing from the original style (e.g. the quartet of Act IV). The same problem exists with the version of 1872; while the local improvement of the Philip–Posa duet is offset by a nonsense in the text. There is much to be said for either the 1884 or 1886 versions. If length is no object the second will doubtless be preferred together perhaps with the original prelude and introduction to the Fontainebleau act but no other additions from the discarded material.*
Otherwise the four-act version, with its symmetrical opening and close, makes a satisfying evening's experience; but there is no evading the fact that whichever edition is used something is lost. A combination yet to be tried outside Russia, though sanctioned by Verdi, would be the four-act version *with* ballet and with the original opening to Act III replacing the prelude of 1884. It would be interesting to hear.

Then there is the question of language. We have already seen that it is nonsense to refer to the *Don Carlos* of 1867 as 'French' and that of 1884 as 'Italian', since the latter was reworked to a French text. Yet how much store did Verdi himself set by the original language? Certainly he never imagined that it would be performed outside France in any other language than Italian, unless it were the vernacular of the country concerned. But it should be borne in mind that Italian was still in most theatres the accepted lingua franca of opera. All over Europe and America Fausts greeted Marguerite's cottage with a 'Salve dimora!', Lionels apostrophized their Marthas with 'M'appari tutto amor'; Lohengrins would address their aquatic guides as 'Cigno gentil'; even Queens of the Night would proclaim to their daughters 'Gli angui d'inferno sentomi nel petto!' To have expected the international opera houses of Vienna, London or Berlin (let alone Milan) to give *Don Carlos* in French would have been unrealistic. However, there is at least one indication that Verdi was attached to the French text. Writing to Ghislanzoni about the opening chorus of Act II of *Aida* he held up as a model the chorus of women that begins the second act of *Don Carlos* and which, he said, 'in the French poem has colour and character'.† True, the best Verdi singers are rarely the best singers of French; the average Italian indeed often shies away from French vowels, being afraid that they will interfere with his voice production. But assuming an equal degree of vocal prowess in both languages there can surely be no doubt that a French performance is preferable to an Italian. Words and music fit better together; the drama in every situation leaps out with far greater force.

Finally there is the problem of the ending, generally considered in Germany as an

---

been made good in that edited by Ursula Günther, to be published by the Casa Ricordi. The edition made by Charles Mackerras for the English National Opera differs slightly from those of Porter and Günther.

* Maestro Claudio Abbado's recent inclusion of the Carlos–Philip duet in the Modena version of 1886 has modified my view on this point. When performed with sufficient musical and dramatic understanding any combination of versions can be made to sound convincing.

† Letter to Ghislanzoni, 14.8.1870. Abbiati, III, p. 382.

insult to Schiller. Such feelings might be justified if *Don Carlos* were a truly historical play. But it is nothing of the kind; it is a myth; and in myths the deus ex machina is perfectly acceptable whether he be a dead Emperor or a Voice from Heaven. That the ending should be swallowed up in the mysterious vaults of the Monastery of Saint-Just, whose atmosphere dominates so much of the opera, is surely not out of place. There is no need therefore to graft on to the music Schiller's own, no less un-historical ending. It may be felt, however, that the quiet close of 1867 has more to recommend it than that of 1884 with its pealing brass – that the opera should fade away as a dream rather than jolt us awake as from a nightmare. Indeed the original ending has been restored occasionally both in the theatre and on records with some success.

So *Don Carlos*'s place in the Verdi canon will probably fluctuate for many years to come. One can never over-estimate its importance in the evolution of the composer's style. Like *Les Vêpres Siciliennes* but to a still greater extent it set him new problems of scale and provided new varieties of metre on which to build. It must be said that the problem of scale in the last resort eluded Verdi. Even in its four-act version *Don Carlos* feels its length. Yet one can well understand why for many devoted Verdians it remains their favourite opera. No other work of his explores such a variety of human relationships. Each of the principals has a rounded individuality, that is nowhere sur-passed in the Verdian canon. Nor is it only the humans who spring to life. The monastery, the royal palace, the square of Valladolid, or the gardens, all have a real, musical existence as vivid as Klingsor's flower garden or the depths of the Rhine. The opera scales heights unheard of in Italian opera, even if it does not always attain the summits. The greatest geniuses do not always need classical perfection to make one aware of their greatness. Indeed Verdi himself had not achieved this quality since *Un Ballo in maschera*. But he would do so in the opera which now follows.*

* Since the above chapter was written all the orchestral material missing from the Elisabeth–Eboli and Carlos–Philippe duets has been rediscovered in the Bibliothèque de l'Opéra, so that Verdi's intentions for their detailed scoring are no longer a matter for speculation.

2 AIDA

AIDA

Opera in four acts
by
ANTONIO GHISLANZONI
(after a scenario by Auguste Mariette)

first performed at the
Opera House, Cairo
24 December 1871

THE KING	BASSO	Tommaso Costa
AMNERIS, his daughter	PRIMA DONNA MEZZO-SOPRANO	Eleonora Grossi
AIDA, Ethiopian slave	PRIMA DONNA SOPRANO	Antonietta Anastasi-Pozzoni
RADAMES, Captain of the Guards	PRIMO TENORE	Pietro Mongini
RAMFIS, Chief of the Priests	PRIMO BASSO	Paolo Medini
AMONASRO, King of Ethiopia and father of Aida	PRIMO BARITONO	Francesco Steller
The High Priestess	SOPRANO	Marietta Allievi
A messenger	TENOR	Luigi Stecchi-Bottardi

Priests – priestesses – ministers – captains – soldiers – functionaries – slaves
– Ethiopian prisoners – Egyptian populace, etc.

The action takes place in Memphis and Thebes, at the time of the reign of the
Pharaohs

One of the more pleasant by-products of *Don Carlos* was, as we have seen, the warm friendship that sprang up between the Verdis and the du Locles. In the years that followed the Parisian première du Locle never despaired of tempting Verdi back into another collaboration. But the late 1860s were difficult times for the composer, with one misfortune following another: the death of his father, then of his father-in-law and benefactor Antonio Barezzi, and the stroke which condemned his faithful librettist Piave to eight years of a vegetable existence. To help the distressed family Verdi persuaded Ricordi to publish an *Album Piave* of six romances to which the leading composers of the day should contribute, himself and also – he rather naïvely hoped – Wagner included. The volume duly appeared, though the list of represented composers, Verdi apart, is a more modest one than had been intended – Auber, Cagnoni, Mercadante, Federico Ricci and Ambroise Thomas. However, a composite Requiem Mass, planned by Verdi to commemorate the anniversary of Rossini's death, foundered on the intransigence of the impresario at Bologna, where it was to have been performed.* Verdi threw much of the blame on the conductor Angelo Mariani, for no better reason, it seems, than that this friend of twelve years' standing was beginning to get on his nerves.

On the happier side, this same period saw Verdi's meeting with Manzoni, and the wholly successful performance of the revised *Forza del destino* at La Scala, Milan, which in turn re-established the composer's relations with Italy's leading opera house after twenty-five years. Nor would it appear that he still cherished any thoughts of retiring. On the contrary he read with interest all the plays and scenarios submitted to him by du Locle. Their correspondence begins after du Locle's return from a voyage to Egypt, 'a land', Verdi said with a touch of unconscious irony, 'which once possessed a grandeur and a civilization which I could never bring myself to admire'.† The list of subjects ranged very widely, from tragedy to comedy, with a special eye to the latest master of the well-made play, Victorien Sardou. Was it true, Verdi wanted to know, that du Locle was collaborating with Sardou on the operatic version of *Le Cid*? If so he himself would give up any ideas he had for such a project, which had been suggested to him from St Petersburg during the work on *Don Carlos*.‡ After a visit to S. Agata in the late summer of 1868, du Locle sent a batch of

---

* The various pieces were in the meantime composed and copied, and the Mass could easily be resurrected from material in Ricordi's archives in Milan. See C. Hopkinson, *Bibliography of the Works of Giuseppe Verdi*, I (London, 1973), p. 85. The contents are as follows: 'Requiem' (Buzzolla); 'Dies irae' (Bazzini); 'Tuba mirum' (Pedrotti); 'Quid sum miser' (Cagnoni); 'Recordare' (F. Ricci); 'Ingemisco' (Nini); 'Confutatis' (Boucheron); 'Lachrymosa' (Coccia); 'Domine Jesu' (Gaspari); 'Sanctus' (Platania); 'Agnus Dei' (Lauro Rossi, who replaced Petrella); 'Lux aeterna' (Mabellini); 'Libera me' (Verdi). See *Copialettere*, p. 212. The last item was eventually transformed into the 'Libera me' of Verdi's own Requiem of 1874. (See, however, Preface to the Revised Edition, in Volume I, p. x.

† Letter to du Locle, 19.2.1868. J. G. Prod'homme, 'Unpublished Letters from Verdi to Camille du Locle' (tr. Theodore Baker) in *Musical Quarterly*, VII (1921), p. 77.

‡ Letter to du Locle, 8.5.1868. *Ibid.*, p. 78. In fact a *Cid* had been announced by both writers to be set to music by the Belgian composer Gevaert, but it never materialized.

plays to the composer – 'but, alas, not one of them is for me. The best of them are too long, too grim, and just at present I do not care to deal with that kind. The exception might be *Adrienne Lecouvreur*. . . . Might I dare ask you to send me some others? . . . Please remember that I should not know what to do with dramas like *La Tour de Nesle* or *L'Abbaye de Castro*. I want something more simple, more *in our style*.'* Then came Rossini's death, the Requiem project and the revised *Forza del destino* to which both du Locle and Perrin were cordially invited. Soon after, du Locle's appointment was announced as director of the Opéra Comique for the following year; and Verdi's thoughts extended to the lighter genre as well. Of two subjects by Sardou, who was more than delighted at the prospect of mating his genius with Verdi's, '*Piccolino,*' wrote Giuseppina Verdi, 'makes you neither laugh nor cry. There are no sharply drawn characters in it; in a word it lacks the inventiveness and originality that Verdi looks for in a comic opera.'† *Patrie*, on the other hand, was a complex, more sophisticated *Battaglia di Legnano*. Verdi himself pronounced it 'A fine play; vast, powerful and above all theatrical. A pity that the prima donna's part is necessarily a repulsive one. Amongst so many there's a situation that I find particularly novel: where the conspirators escape and bury the Spanish patrol under the snow.'‡ He went on to thank du Locle a thousand times for having sent him the play, 'which has made me admire Sardou's genius more and more'. But to Giulio Ricordi he was less enthusiastic. 'A powerful drama, and there are one or two novel scenes, but quite apart from the repulsive character of the woman there's no music there. There are two, three or four numbers ready made, but not an opera.'§ He offered to obtain Sardou's permission for the young Faccio to set it instead; but this was not what the playwright wanted, so the matter went no further for the time being. Eventually *Patrie* was set by Lauro Rossi under the title *La Contessa di Mons* (1874). *Froufrou*, by Meilhac and Halévy, authors of many an Offenbach comedy, 'would be extraordinarily fine if it were all as distinguished and original as the first three acts, but the last two lapse into the commonplace, though they're tremendously effective!'¶ Thence he proceeded to his well-known diatribe against the French theatre and French savants, and their disastrous effect on a composer's self-confidence. Nevertheless, the following month he was demanding from du Locle, together with the prose works of Wagner in translation, a copy of Dumas père's *Acté et Néron*, adding, 'I still believe that Nero might be a subject for a grand opera – always provided that it were done according to my ideas. So it would be impossible for the Opéra but highly possible here.'‖ Giulio Ricordi, apprised of these views, immediately thought of the *Nerone* on which Boito had been desultorily at work since he first conceived the idea in 1862. 'Today,' he wrote to Verdi, 'I managed to find out by adroit questioning that Boito has not yet started to set *Nerone* to music – indeed he hasn't even finished the libretto. Now the next task is to work out a means of finding out how he intends to treat it. Certainly *Nerone* is a splendid, grandiose and exciting subject; and before putting it on one side, don't you think, Maestro, you might try

---

* Letter to du Locle, 12.11.1868. *M.Q.*, VII, p. 80.
† Letter from Giuseppina Verdi to du Locle, October 1869. *Ibid.*, p. 82.
‡ Letter to du Locle, 6.10.1869. *Ibid.*, p. 86.
§ Letter to Giulio Ricordi, 29.11.1869. Abbiati, III, p. 323.
¶ Letter to du Locle, 8.12.1869. *M.Q.*, VII, p. 83. See also *Copialettere*, pp. 218–23.
‖ Letter to du Locle, 23.1.1870. *Ibid.*, p. 86.

something in that direction? . . . Please let me know how you feel about this.'* But Verdi did not rise to the bait, fortunately for Boito; and it was probably of Dumas's play that he wrote, 'In *Nerone*, as *Alarico*, there are great tableaux, characters, costumes, spectacle, etc., but what's needed is an original creation like for instance Fidès in *Le Prophète* or Valentine in *Les Huguenots*. . . . Send to Madrid for the following two plays: *La Vengeance Catalane* by Gutiérrez and *El Zapatero y el rey* by Zorilla.'† (The latter, it may be remembered, had been under consideration in 1857 and was one of the projects shelved in favour of *Don Carlos*.)

It is to this period (1868–70) that Luzio ascribes one of the most interesting of Verdi's plans for a comic opera, namely a version of Molière's *Tartuffe*, of which a detailed scenario exists at S. Agata, copied out in Verdi's hand.‡ The author is supposed by Abbiati to be Adolphe Dennery, who would indeed write one day to Verdi suggesting a collaboration. Dennery or not, the man who could state, 'Music is the only art . . . which possesses the remarkable faculty of expressing simultaneously such widely different things as Tartuffe's honeyed and caressing speech and the black perfidy of his thoughts,'§ was no novice in matters operatic. But this project too was destined to remain on the drawing-board.

At the end of March 1870 Verdi paid a three-week visit to Paris, evidently with a view to seeing for himself how the Opéra Comique was faring under du Locle's management. The reports he sent to Giulio Ricordi are all highly favourable, especially regarding the orchestra and chorus. It was all so different from the 'grande boutique'. Yet still a suitable subject eluded him. On his return to S. Agata he promised to study Zorilla's drama in translation; and he also asked for a copy of the comedy *El Tanto por ciento* by López de Ayala, a summary of which in *Etudes sur l'Espagne contemporaine* had mightily impressed him. But, alas, it turned out to be *Piccolino* all over again: 'You neither laugh nor cry. It's dull and doesn't seem to me suitable for music.'¶

Meanwhile a seed that had long lain on stony ground suddenly began to put out shoots. In November 1869 the Khedive of Egypt planned to inaugurate a new opera house in Cairo as part of the festivities celebrating the opening of the Suez Canal; and Verdi was invited to compose an ode in honour of the occasion, but he declined, 'partly because I am not accustomed to compose *morceaux de circonstance*'.‖ For the opening of the theatre the Viceroy had to be content with a performance of *Rigoletto* conducted by Muzio. But he had still not given up hope of a new composition from Verdi's pen. Particularly zealous in the affair was the celebrated Egyptologist Auguste Mariette, who had an Egyptian subject ready to hand culled from his own researches.

Mariette was a famous name in nineteenth-century archaeology. Appointed

* Letter from Giulio Ricordi, 10.2.1870. *Carteggi Verdiani*, IV, p. 186.
† Letter to Giulio Ricordi, 13.2.1870. Abbiati, III, pp. 331–2.
‡ See *Carteggi Verdiani*, II, p. 361.
§ *Ibid.*, p. 359.
¶ Letter to du Locle, 26.5.1870. M.Q., VII, p. 88.
‖ Letter to Draneht Bey, 9.8.1869, in *Quaderni dell' Istituto di Studi Verdiani*, IV, a cura di Salek Abdoun (Parma, 1971), p. xv. This invitation may well be the source of two often repeated myths: first, that Verdi composed *Aida* for the opening of the Suez Canal; secondly that he was the author of the instrumental march that served until recently as the Egyptian national anthem. (See Hughes, p. 397.) Nowhere is there any confirmation of this last assertion though many Egyptians believe it to this day.

Egyptologist to the Louvre Museum in 1849, he went two years later to Egypt in search of Coptic manuscripts, to discover, almost by accident, the Temple of Serapis and the tombs of the Apis bulls. After several further important finds he was taken into the service of the Khedive, given the title of Bey and put in charge of the excavations being conducted throughout Egypt. Yet his life was unexpectedly hard. A diabetic, by 1864 he had lost his wife and five of his eleven children. Moreover for a man of such eminence his vice-regal employer kept him on a tight rein. In the operatic project he saw a heaven-sent opportunity to take his family on a trip to Paris at the Viceroy's expense, and he counted on the help of his friend du Locle both to provide the libretto and to find the right composer. It seems that du Locle talked it over with Verdi both during a visit to Genoa at the beginning of 1870, and later during the composer's three-week stay in Paris in the spring. But Verdi preferred to concentrate on the search for an *opéra comique*. Still Mariette kept up the pressure. If Verdi was not interested he was empowered to approach Gounod or even Wagner. Meanwhile he enclosed a synopsis of the opera proposed, which, he said, had the Viceroy's complete approval. He continued:

> Now, if the scenario seems to you suitable and you agree to do the libretto, and if you find a composer, this is what you must do. You must write to me that the subject chosen is so archaeologically Egyptian and Egyptological that you can't write the libretto without a full-time policeman at your side; and besides that my presence in Paris is absolutely necessary for the decors and costumes. . . . If I could get to Paris this summer my goal will have been attained.
>
> It goes without saying that I have no kind of amour-propre in the matter and that you can modify, improve, turn upside down the scenario as you think fit. . . . Don't take fright at the title. Aida is an Egyptian name. By rights it should be *Aita*. But the name would be too harsh and the singers would inevitably soften it into Aida. Anyway, I don't set much store by that name more than any other.*

However, if Mariette was unconcerned as to which composer should write the opera du Locle was determined it should be Verdi. For some weeks after his return to Italy the composer continued to receive letters describing the chagrin of the Khedive at his obstinate refusals, offering ever better conditions – unlimited rehearsal time, in Paris, in Genoa, wheresoever Verdi wished. Du Locle even volunteered to supervise the production himself to save Verdi the sea voyage to Cairo. Finally, with the copy of *El Tanto por ciento* he enclosed Mariette's synopsis, together with his letter urging du Locle, should Verdi continue obdurate, to 'knock at another door . . . Wagner,' it ended, 'if he were willing, might do something really grand'.† This time the effect was immediate. In the same letter in which he rejected the Spanish play, Verdi wrote, 'I have read the Egyptian programme. It is well made; the setting is splendid and there are one or two situations which, if not entirely novel, are certainly very fine. But who wrote it? Behind it all is the hand of an expert . . . thoroughly familiar with the stage. Now let us consider the financial situation in Egypt and then we'll decide.'‡

* Letter from Auguste Mariette to du Locle, 27.4.1870. U. Günther, 'Zur Entstehung von Verdis *Aida*', in *Studi Musicali*, Anno II (Florence, 1973), No. 1, pp. 15–71.

† Letter from Mariette to du Locle, 28.4.1870. *Carteggi Verdiani*, IV, p. 8.

‡ Letter to du Locle, 26.5.1870. *M.Q.*, VII, p. 88; *Carteggi Verdiani*, IV, p. 9.

Du Locle replied, 'The Egyptian libretto is the work of the Viceroy and Mariette Bey; no one else has had a hand in it.'*

The mention of the Viceroy was misleading, if not downright false, and was doubtless intended to hook the composer still more firmly by appealing to his sense of snobbery. Certainly by his deliberate self-effacement in the matter Mariette created a quite unnecessary mystery about the paternity of *Aida*. True, in letters to his brother Edouard and to Draneht Bey, intendant of the new Cairo theatre, he claimed it as his own original work; likewise the critics Ernest Reyer and Filippo Filippi who went to Cairo for the first night both give Mariette as sole author of the story.† But as early as 1873 Clément and Larousse in the *Dictionnaire des Opéras* amongst their many inaccuracies attributed the plot of *Aida* to one Vassali, curator of the Museum of Boulaq. In the course of a controversy in the press in 1880 du Locle, then living in Rome, felt obliged to set the record straight with a letter to the editor of the French journal *L'Italie* stating roundly that 'the original idea for the poem belongs to Mariette Bey, the famous Egyptologist'.‡ In a letter to his wife, undated but clearly from the same period, du Locle was still more explicit: 'The true author of the libretto is Mariette Bey, who invented an Egyptian story of a kind and gave the Viceroy the idea of having it made into an opera. . . .'§ This should have settled the matter, but it did not. In 1891 Mariette's son claimed from Nuitter and du Locle a share in the copyright of the opera, as du Locle, now restored to Verdi's favour, wrote to the composer in high indignation. 'I'm utterly taken aback,' Verdi replied; 'I think you will remember yourself that you sent me four little printed pages without any author's name; you told me that the Khedive would like an opera on that subject because it's an Egyptian one and I supposed that the author of those pages was the Khedive himself. All I knew about Mariette Bey was that he had been commissioned to look after the costumes, etc. . . .'¶ At all events Mariette's son failed in his claim; and we hear no more about the authorship of *Aida* until, in his volume of reminiscences of his brother, Edouard Mariette stated that the subject was in part plagiarized from an unfinished novel of his own, called *La Fiancée du Nil*.‖ Amid the general uncertainty, which has lasted well into the era of Verdian scholarship, a certain Matteo Glinski advanced a hypothesis in the columns of *La Scala* which is discussed briefly by Abbiati and at length by Charles Osborne.** This traces the origin of the opera to Metastasio's *Nitteti*, 'musicked' by thirteen composers between 1756 and 1812, which its author claimed to have derived from Herodotus and Diodorus Siculus. This is surely the reddest of herrings. The plot of *Aida* is relatively simple;

---

* Letter from du Locle, 29.5.1870. *Carteggi Verdiani*, IV, p. 9.

† For relevant sources see J. Humbert, 'A propos de l'égyptomanie dans l'oeuvre de Verdi: attribution à Auguste Mariette d'un scénario anonyme de l'opéra *Aida*' in *Revue de Musicologie*, LXII (1976), pp. 229–56.

‡ Letter from du Locle to the editor of *L'Italie*, 28.3.1880. Quoted by A. Pougin, *Verdi* (Paris, 1881), p. 219.

§ Letter from du Locle to his wife, undated. *M.Q.*, VII, p. 103.

¶ Letter to du Locle, 9.12.1891. *Copialettere*, p. 374.

‖ E. Mariette, *Mariette Pacha, Lettres et souvenirs personnels* (Paris, 1904), pp. 77–8. However, from the relevant passages, quoted as Document I in H. Busch, *Verdi's* Aida: *the History of an Opera in Letters and Documents* (Minneapolis, 1978), pp. 435–9, it is clear that there were only a few similarities of situation between *Aida* and Edouard Mariette's novel.

** M. Glinski, *La Scala* (May, 1954), pp. 17 ff: see also F. Pérez de la Vega, *La Presapia de Aida* (Mexico City, 1950). Abbiati, III, pp. 520–30; Osborne, *The Complete Operas of Verdi* (London, 1969), pp. 377–82.

that of *Nitteti* infinitely complex, with an antefatto, a large cast and more than one mistaken identity. Certain situations in the two libretti can be paralleled; but, as Osborne himself points out, this likeness is shared in varying degrees by more than one drama of a previous age. To Racine's *Bajazet* he might have added Mozart's *Idomeneo*, where the triangle of Idamante–Ilia–Electra matches that of Radames–Aida–Amneris. In other words the plot of *Aida* is an old-fashioned and generic one and a surprising choice for Verdi, whose cry was usually for new and original subjects, with specific, unrepeatable characters such as had by this time become the norm even in Italy. Compared to the plots of *Michele Perrin*, *Ruy Blas* and *Un Capriccio di donna*, that of *Aida* seems like a throwback to an earlier century. When Verdi described its situations as 'not entirely new' he was scarcely exaggerating. But its immediate ancestry cannot at present be taken beyond Mariette.

The epoch is described vaguely as 'the time of the Pharaohs'. The Ethiopians are reported to be on the march; and the young general Radames is appointed to the command of the Egyptian armies. Loved by the Pharaoh's daughter Amneris, he himself is in love with Aida, Amneris's Ethiopian slave, captured during a previous campaign; she in turn is torn between patriotic sentiment and love for Radames. By a ruse Amneris discovers that Aida is her rival in Radames' affections. What she does not know is that Aida is also the King of Ethiopia's daughter. Radames returns in triumph from the war, bringing with him a number of captives, among them Amonasro, Aida's father. His reward is to be the hand of Amneris in marriage; meanwhile he obtains the release of his prisoners, all except for Amonasro, who, though his royal identity is still unknown, is held captive at the Pharaoh's court. Eluding the guards, Amonasro contrives to meet his daughter just as she is about to keep a tryst with Radames; and he bullies her into persuading Radames to betray an important military secret. For this the general is taken into custody and condemned to death by immurement. All Amneris's attempts to have him pardoned are frustrated by his own obduracy. Aida creeps into the tomb to die with him.

Few Verdian plots can be summarized as simply as this one, whose appeal to Verdi must have been similar to that of *Un Ballo in maschera* more than ten years before. Then as now the time had come for a work of consolidation. After the labyrinthine convolutions of *La Forza del destino* and *Don Carlos* he felt the need for an opera of clear, straightforward outline. It is possible to feel that *Aida* nowhere reaches the greatest moments of *Don Carlos*. What cannot be denied is that wherever a similar device occurs in both operas it is always carried out more perfectly in the later one. As Proust observes, there is often something rather disappointing about perfection. Hence no doubt the coolness sometimes shown towards *Aida* by a generation of opera-goers who have come to regard the earlier work as one of the great pinnacles of romantic musical theatre. For this is the work of Verdi the classicist. If *Don Carlos* is his *Don Giovanni*, *Aida* is his *Così fan tutte*.

Once Verdi had accepted the project in principle, events moved with remarkable speed. In a letter of 2 June he set out his conditions, one of which was that he should be allowed sufficient time, 'since we shall be dealing with a work of vast proportions, as it might be for the "Grande Boutique"'.* He would have the libretto done at his own expense, and pay for a conductor of his own choice to go to Egypt to give the first performance. His own fee would be 150,000 francs – four times what he had

---

* Letter to du Locle, 2.6.1870. *Copialettere*, pp. 224–5.

received for *Don Carlos*. But the Khedive made no demur. Next du Locle invited himself to S. Agata for about a week, where, as he put it, 'I wrote the libretto scene by scene, réplique by réplique, in French prose under the eye of the Maestro, who took a large share in the work. The idea of the finale of the last act with its two superimposed scenes belongs particularly to him.'* Verdi's account to Ricordi tallies with this.

> Some time last year I was invited to write an opera for a very distant country. I replied no. When I was in Paris du Locle was enjoined to speak to me about it again and to offer me a large sum. I still said no. A month later he sent me a printed synopsis saying it was the work of a person in high authority (which I don't believe), that he thought it good and that I should read it. I found it excellent and replied that I would set it to music on such and such terms, etc. Three days later a telegram: ACCEPTED. After that du Locle came here and I drew up the conditions with him; we studied the programme together and made the modifications we thought would be necessary. Du Locle then left, taking the conditions and modifications with him to be submitted to the powerful and unknown author. I've been studying the programme further and I've made and am still making more changes. Now we must think about the libretto, or, to be more precise, about writing the verses since verses are all that are required. Would Ghislanzoni be able or willing to do this job? It wouldn't be original work, make that quite clear to him; just a matter of writing the verses, which – let me tell you – will be very generously paid.†

Giulio Ricordi replied enthusiastically.‡ Ghislanzoni would come with a Nubian slave as dog-meat, so as to protect his own legs (the dogs at S. Agata being famous for their ferocity, although on one occasion they seem to have disgraced themselves by fawning on the Mayor of Busseto). By 8 July the visit had already taken place, and Verdi with the help of Giuseppina was hard at work on the prose synopsis, translating it into Italian, cutting here, filling out there. The contract, signed on the Viceroy's behalf by Mariette, was dispatched to S. Agata on 29 July and straightway signed by the composer. It contained the ominous clause that if for some reason other than his own fault the première in Cairo could not take place on the date planned, Verdi would have the right to mount it in an Italian theatre of his own choice after six months.§

So far all had gone smoothly for the two promoters of the scheme, Mariette and du Locle. Verdi had been hooked; the Khedive's wish had been fulfilled and he was prepared to grant Mariette his trip to France. True, even as he prepared to set sail for France, the Egyptologist began to have misgivings. It would be the Great Exhibition all over again, so he told his brother Edouard; he would spend his time pulling other people's chestnuts out of the fire and getting nothing in return. Verdi would have his

* Letter from du Locle in the Roman periodical *Italie*, 28.3.1880. Quoted in *Carteggi Verdiani*, IV, pp. 5–6. True, in an undated letter to his wife, probably written a year or two earlier, du Locle seems to make out that his share of the work had been more substantial (see *M.Q.*, VII, p. 103), but Luzio is surely correct in ascribing this to his feelings of bitterness after his own bankruptcy and Verdi's unyielding demands for the the repayment of the money deposited with him.

† Letter to Giulio Ricordi, 25.6.1870. *Quaderni*, IV, pp. 1–2; *Copialettere*, pp. 635–6.

‡ Letter from Giulio Ricordi, 3.7.1870. *Ibid.*, p. 636.

§ See *Stud. Mus.*, 1973, Doc. 37, pp. 62–3.

150,000 francs, du Locle his *droits d'auteur*, while he himself who had conceived the idea of the opera in the first place would merely ruin himself with hotel-bills, since the Khedive was not prepared to pay for his subsistence in Paris. Only the thought of seeing again his family and friends persuaded him to go through with the voyage – not to mention the clamourings of his daughters Joséphine and Sophie, who 'keep crying to me with mouths wide open, "Daddeeeeeeee; when do we start?" '*

He was right about his own expenses, as a number of letters written to the Intendant that summer hint,† but wrong about the benefits to be enjoyed by du Locle. Indeed, what the new director of the Opéra Comique had to gain from the entire transaction it is difficult to see. Throughout, du Locle presented himself as a disinterested intermediary, nothing more. If Mariette had assumed that the libretto would be in French, Verdi had made it quite clear in his letter of 2 June 'crisp and dry as a cheque'‡ that it would be in Italian. Possibly du Locle expected to receive from Cairo the kind of commission that was granted to Piave by the management of the Teatro la Fenice, irrespective of his work as a librettist. He undoubtedly still cherished the hope that he and Verdi might find 'something for the "petite boutique" by way of an entr'acte. . . . Now that you are putting pen to paper it wouldn't cost you anything more!'§ Nor did Verdi himself discourage such a notion, though he continued to reject everything that was offered to him: Octave Feuillet's *Redemption* and *Le Roman d'un jeune homme pauvre* ('too serious and too little action'); and *Les Premières Armes de Figaro* by Vanderbach and Sardou ('too much striving for effect, too many forced witticisms').¶ Meanwhile at the Opéra Comique Flotow's latest piece, *L'Ombre*, was playing to packed houses. No one was unduly worried when in early July a cloud appeared on the horizon no bigger than a man's hand: the designation of a Hohenzollern Princess as successor to the throne of Spain. Little more than a fortnight later France and Prussia were at war. Everyone expected the outcome to be in France's favour. Amid the general spirit of patriotic fervour that took hold of the French capital the aged Auber was able to see his *Muette de Portici* performed with the 'Marseillaise' interpolated into the third act and sung by Mme Sass with far more commitment than she had ever brought to Verdi's Elisabeth. Then came the defeat of Sedan; and soon the Prussian armies began to close in on Paris. Preparations were made to turn the new Opéra, the Palais Garnier, into an emergency hospital. Verdi, whose sympathies were entirely on the side of the French, instructed du Locle to put aside 2,000 francs from the first instalment of his own fee for the benefit of the French wounded; with the remaining 48,000 he was to buy on Verdi's behalf Italian government bonds (*cartelle di rendita italiana*), with consequences which have been described in the previous chapter.‖ Mariette was still haggling with Draneht Bey over the money due to the couturiers of the rue de Rivoli when all communication with the capital was cut off. Such then was the outcome of a deal made by two charmingly unbusinesslike Frenchmen for their mutual advantage: Mariette was to find himself trapped in Paris during the long cold winter of the siege; while to du Locle *Aida* not only brought no pecuniary benefit but was indirectly the cause of an action brought

* Letter from Mariette Bey to Edouard Mariette, 21.6.1870. *Stud. Mus.*, 1973, Doc. 30, pp. 37–8.
† See *I.S.V. Quaderno*, IV, pp. 3–7; 11–12.
‡ Letter to du Locle, 2.6.1870. *Stud. Mus.*, 1973, p. 31.
§ Letter from du Locle, 13.6.1870. *Stud. Mus.*, 1973, Doc. 26, p. 55.
¶ Letters to du Locle, 9 and 18.6.1870. *Ibid.*, pp. 53 and 56.
‖ See letter to du Locle, 26.8.1870. *Ibid.*, Doc. 40, p. 65.

against him by Verdi in 1876. Neither he nor Mariette was ever publicly associated with the opera, which to this day bears only the names of Verdi and Ghislanzoni.

Of the true state of affairs in France and their implication for the performance of his opera Verdi remained unaware until late in the year. Meanwhile work on the libretto had been proceeding rapidly since July. Of Mariette's synopsis – which, needless to say, has been hunted by musicologists as assiduously as if it were the 'black box' of a crashed aeroplane, in the hope that it might provide a vital clue to the story's provenance – no copy was found until quite recently, when the French scholar Jean Humbert turned one up in a place where no one had ever thought of looking, though given the clearest indications by du Locle's letter to his wife, mentioned above: 'This story of Mariette's which was printed in Cairo in a limited number of copies, is in Nuitter's files. For I gave my copy to him.'* Conscientious archivist that he was Charles Nuitter never threw anything away; and sure enough in the Bibliothèque de l'Opéra under the shelf-mark *Réserve III2* there exists a scenario entitled: *Aida, opéra en quatre actes et en six tableaux*. But it consists of twenty-three pages, not four.

This is not such a fatal objection as it seems. The only person to mention four pages is Verdi himself, in a letter written more than twenty years after the event, in which he was perhaps unconsciously trying to minimize Mariette's part in the affair if only to thwart the pretensions of his son.† Side by side with this scenario Humbert published a word-for-word Italian translation which is kept at S. Agata, and of which the first two acts are in Verdi's hand, the remainder in Giuseppina's – a document seen and described, together with other drafts of individual passages, by Luzio in his essay 'Come fu composta l'*Aida*'.‡ Finally there is a further prose draft in French, part summary, part dialogue, set out in du Locle's not always legible handwriting with erasures made by him or Verdi, which was evidently the fruit of the poet's visit to S. Agata in June. This too is described and quoted from by Luzio, and has recently been published in its entirety in Professor Hans Busch's monograph.§ It now becomes easy to trace the shaping of the libretto up to the time that it was consigned to Ghislanzoni to be put into verse.

A striking feature of Mariette's synopsis is its wealth of scenic detail. 'Splendid as regards mise-en-scène,' Verdi had said; not surprisingly therefore the scene descriptions find their way word for word in their Italian translation in Giulio Ricordi's *disposizione scenica*. The cast list includes as well as Ramfis, 'head of the college of priests', a certain Termouthis, 'grand priestess of the temple of Vulcan'. For the start of the opera Mariette envisaged the eminently orthodox gambit of a grand chorus of officers and priests about to wait upon the King. As they leave, enter Princess Amneris, who detains Radames with an imperious glance. From then on the scene proceeds as in the opera, beginning with the triple confrontation of Radames, Amneris and Aida. The only divergence is an otiose officer of the court who announces the King's arrival to give audience to a messenger (here a herald). Likewise Mariette presents Scene 2 of the opera in all essentials ready made – even down to

---

* Letter from du Locle to his wife, undated (*c*. 1880). *M.Q.*, VII, p. 103.

† In fact Italians often use the word 'quattro' to mean 'a few' as in the expression 'Facciamo quattro passi' ('Let's take a short stroll').

‡ *Carteggi Verdiani*, IV, pp. 5–27.

§ Busch, pp. 448–71.

the prescription of harps for the chant of the priestesses, in which presumably Termouthis would have had a part. While Radames walked to the altar they were to dance to the sound of timpani, a suggestion which Verdi did not follow up.*

The whole of Act II is set in the main square of Thebes; here it is that Amneris sends for Aida and worms her secret out of her by pretending that Radames has been killed in action. 'From this moment on there are no more doubts. For Amneris, Radames' lover is Aida. Aida will die.' For the second scene Mariette's outline would be faithfully followed down to the appearance of Amonasro among the Ethiopian prisoners. At that point Aida cries out, 'O, all-powerful king, may the gods open your heart to clemency; this man who stands before you, a humble slave, is my father.' 'But just as she is about to reveal that he is also the terrible Amonasro he stops her and tells his daughter that he is disguised as an officer of his own troops so that he can carry out the vengeance he has planned. Won over by Aida's pleas the King grants the prisoner's life; the defeated Ethiopian will take his place among the slaves assigned to guard the palace.'† All very plausible in the days of artificial asides and acres of dry recitative; but it was to be a long time before Verdi managed so clumsy an 'anagnorisis' to his satisfaction.

Act III is simpler than it later became, both in incident and motivation. Aida is waiting by the Nile for a tryst with Radames, who fortunately for her has not been ordered to marry Amneris. Amonasro arrives and persuades his daughter without difficulty to tempt Radames into betraying his country's military secrets. Accordingly 'she fascinates her lover, she wins him over, she captivates him. Lost in love, Radames throws himself at her feet. Not his country, not the world, not the sacred vows that bind him are worth one look, one smile from her. Honour calls to him in vain. . . .' True, he hesitates when Amonasro appears, but only for a moment, before telling him of the gorges of Napata through which the Egyptians plan to march and where they can be destroyed in an ambush. As all three leave the stage Amneris enters in great agitation from a place of concealment and swears vengeance both on her rival and on the lover who has spurned her.

For the start of Act IV Mariette again has a chorus of officers whose purpose is to detail the later news; how on hearing of Radames' treachery the King himself took command of the army; how once again the Ethiopians were defeated, Amonasro overtaken and slain, and Radames recaptured; but what has happened to Aida is still a mystery. Then come Amneris's scene with Radames, his readiness to die for Aida, his condemnation by the priests and Amneris's impotent grief. The course of the final scene differs from that of the finished opera only in the absence of Amneris.

From Mariette's synopsis we pass to the scenario of du Locle. Here the opening chorus is replaced by the dialogue between Ramfis and Radames that we know today; but there is as yet no 'Celeste Aida' for Radames. The officer of the court is eliminated; but the herald, rather awkwardly, gives utterance before the King's entrance. There are no changes to the second scene; but the first scene of Act II has now been moved to the apartments of Amneris, with a preliminary chorus of hand-

---

* *Revue de Musicologie*, p. 247.

† For this and the following excerpts I have had recourse to Professor Busch's translation of the documents concerned. Verdi's and Giuseppina's translation of Mariette's synopsis is reproduced as Document II, *op. cit.*, pp. 441–7.

maidens added. Her dialogue with Aida, worked out in two drafts, shows the princess in a slightly more favourable light than before. She no longer wishes to kill Aida, merely to humiliate her. In the course of three drafts the triumphal scene is further defined in the direction of the finished opera. Aida's intervention at the sight of her father is shortened, Radames is granted his magnanimous wish to set free the Ethiopian prisoners, and for the first time he is promised Amneris's hand in marriage by the King. This last fact naturally alters the content of Aida's romanza planned for the opening of Act III, which is now full of melancholy and the threat to end her existence in the 'cold waters of the Nile'. A second draft brings in the short scene of Amneris and Ramfis framed by an unseen chorus of priests in the temple. Amneris has come to pray to the Gods for Radames' love on the eve of her wedding; and it is from the temple threshold that she and the high priest witness Radames' betrayal. Indeed the three culprits give her plenty of time to do so since they all join in an inopportune trio before making off. Finally there is a brief scene for Amneris and Ramfis, she pleading for Radames' life, the priest determined on his execution. More than once in the heat of the moment du Locle writes Ramfis where he means Radames. There is nothing on the first scene of Act IV in his scenario, though according to Luzio there are subsidiary drafts in Giuseppina's hand, in one of which Amneris inveighs passionately against her rival.* The last scene of all mentions the divided stage, which du Locle tells us was Verdi's idea, and introduces Amneris into the temple for the conclusion.

The next stage, according to Luzio, was a more extended prose libretto of thirty-seven pages in Verdi's own hand.† Indicated in the margin were the ways in which each passage was to be set – 'lirico', 'cantabile', 'concertato', 'recitativo', and so on. Here for the first time Radames' betrayal of his country's secrets became an involuntary one. 'In this way,' Verdi informed du Locle, '[it] is no longer so repulsive, yet the theatrical effect is in no way diminished.'‡ Likewise the dialogue between father and daughter in the same act was redrafted into something like its present form. Verdi himself conceived the famous 'Celeste Aida' as a 'romanza' to be introduced at the singer's pleasure§ – a description of it which early exponents were to take rather too literally. The first scene of Act IV ends with a short dialogue between Amneris and the King during which she begs him to spare Radames' life, but in vain. 'He is condemned; he will die,' her father replies; collapse of Amneris in the arms of her handmaidens.¶ In the margin Verdi at some stage wrote, 'Pointless'; and the dialogue was duly discarded, apparently at Ghislanzoni's suggestion.||

During this time Verdi had been making various inquiries regarding Egyptian antiquities. Giulio Ricordi supplied him with the answers he needed, provided by 'an experienced man of letters, a friend of mine, who is entirely at our disposal'.** The in-

---

* *Carteggi Verdiani*, IV, p. 20.

† See *Carteggi Verdiani*, IV, pp. 16 ff. Of this the first thirty pages appear to have been lost; but the final seven are reprinted as Document VIII in Busch, pp. 487–93.

‡ Letter to du Locle, 15.7.1870. *M.Q.*, VII, p. 91.

§ *Carteggi Verdiani*, IV, p. 17.

¶ Busch, p. 491.

|| See letter to Ghislanzoni, 4.11.1870. *Copialettere*, pp. 664–7.

** Letter from Giulio Ricordi, 21.7.1870. Busch, pp. 36–7. Luzio in *Carteggi Verdiani*, IV, p. 15, identifies him as Michele Lessona without giving any reasons for doing so.

formation, published as Document VI in Busch's monograph,* would be of greater interest if Verdi had seen fit to take the slightest notice of it; nor was this either the first or the last time that he would ask for details of authenticity only to scout them, as the history of *Les Vêpres Siciliennes* and the *Otello* ballet music makes clear. Doubtless he also found out that Mariette himself, for all his insistence on correctness of dress and appearance, was not a great stickler for accuracy in matters of custom. His original synopsis is full of anachronisms and historical impossibilities: the Pharaohs always commanded their armies themselves, never attacked by surprise, never erected triumphal arches, never employed ceremonial trumpets and never worshipped the god Vulcan.† Fortunately such solecisms are for the Egyptologist rather than the music-lover to worry about.

From July onwards the work in progress was halted by an important series of letters from Verdi to Ghislanzoni, reproduced in the appendix to the *Copialettere*,‡ the originals of which, once in the possession of the tenor Masini, disappeared at his death. Since then nearly half have found their way to the Pierpont Library, New York. All these are supplemented by one or two of Ghislanzoni's early drafts together with a few of his replies. §

In writing to Ghislanzoni Verdi adopted a tone similar to that of his letters to Cammarano, tempering directness with the respect due to a witty and versatile man of letters as well as Italy's most sought-after librettist since the mid-1860s. Although he had been responsible for the changes made to *La Forza del destino*, Verdi does not seem to have worked with him in the theatre, to judge from the fact that throughout their correspondence he addresses him with the polite 'Ella' or 'Lei'. Unstinting with his comments, he always found a courteous way of rejecting Ghislanzoni's more platitudinous ideas ('Let me say once and for all that I never mean to criticize your verses, which are always good, but merely to tell you my opinion as regards the theatrical effect.').¶

Unlike *Don Carlos*, *Aida* was composed 'di getto', as fast as the librettist could provide the verse. Ghislanzoni cannot have sent his first draft before mid-July. By mid-September Verdi was already becoming impatient. 'The last sentence in your letter,' he wrote, 'gives me the shudders. "Can I start on the third act?" What? Isn't it finished yet? And I've been waiting for it to arrive hourly.'|| By November Giuseppina was able to note that the work was complete; though, as usual, there were various adjustments to be made, and, as it turned out, two new numbers to be added. Generally speaking the opera was composed in order, apart from the second scene of

---

* Busch, pp. 475–82.

† See Adriano Vargiù, 'Il libretto dell' *Aida*', in *Rassegna Musicale Curci* (1968), XXI, No. 3, pp. 140–50. The relation of Vulcan to Phta is purely etymological, Phta being a variant of Hephaestus, Vulcan's Greek counterpart. Needless to say Vulcan was never a god of war, though doubtless as a husband he wished he were!

‡ *Copialettere*, pp. 638–75. I have followed the revised dating set out in P. Gossett's 'Verdi, Ghislanzoni and *Aida*; the uses of convention', in *Critical Inquiry*, I, No. 2 (Chicago, 1974), pp. 291–334, which Busch also adopts.

§ The most substantial of Ghislanzoni's drafts is one which concerns Act I, Scene 1, printed as Document VII in Busch, pp. 483–7. Others are given in the context of the correspondence and in *Carteggi Verdiani*, IV, p. 17.

¶ Letter to Ghislanzoni, 8.10.1870. *Copialettere*, pp. 651–2.

|| Letter to Ghislanzoni, c. 14.9.1870. *Copialettere*, p. 645.

the first act which was held over for a while, partly because Verdi found the lines un-theatrical ('The characters don't always say what they have to say and the priests aren't sufficiently priestly . . . there is no parola scenica, or if there is it is buried under the rhyme or the verse and therefore doesn't leap out clearly and cleanly as it should'),* but also since at the time of writing them Ghislanzoni was uncertain whether it would be in order to include priestesses in the scene. Strictly speaking, it was not, as Verdi well knew. Mariette, however, as always, was willing to relax the rules of Egyptology in the interests of music and let Verdi know via du Locle that he could have as many priestesses as he wished.† The information was duly passed on.‡

As the correspondence proceeds we find Verdi taking an increasing part in the final shaping of the libretto, without ever usurping the librettist's function. Thus the opening recitative for Radames and Ramfis was shortened from thirteen lines to eight, merely by the removal of superfluous words and expressions. The text of 'Celeste Aida' was rewritten in several variants each derived from Verdi's and Giuseppina's extended prose draft and each implying a different form. § In the terzet-tino: 'It would be better to leave out the first lines, so as not to give Aida too much to say, and I don't like Amneris's threat either. . . . The hymn which follows is all right as you have adjusted it, only I would like Radames and Amneris to take part in the scene so as to avoid the two asides which are always ineffective. Radames will only have to change a few words. Amneris can take up a sword or a banner or some other piece of nonsense and address her verse to Radames, all warmth and love and fighting spirit. . . .'¶

Passing on to the chorus of attendants with Amneris which begins the second act he found it 'dull and insignificant, the kind of narration that any messenger could sing'. Clearly the habit of giving straightforward narrative to a chorus – in this case, the news of Radames' victory – died hard with Ghislanzoni, as may be seen from his libretto to Petrella's *Giovanna di Napoli* (1869). But for the Verdi of 1870 this would not do. He wanted something more colourful on the lines of the scene for Eboli and the ladies-in-waiting at the start of Act II, Scene 2, of *Don Carlos*, which, he said, despite the lack of action succeeds as a 'real little scene. Here too we must have a scene with a very lyrical chorus for the handmaids who are dressing Amneris and a dance of little Ethiopian blackamoors.' He then sketched out the text in detail: two quatrains for the slaves of contrasted character; then a couplet for Amneris.

CHORUS   Who is he, who is he who comes shining with glory, beautiful as the God of battle? *(Verse)*

(2)   Come, Radames, Radames; the daughters of Egypt await you and chant hymns of glory, hymns of love. *(Verse)*

AMNERIS *(aside)* Oh come, Radames. For thee alone the King's daughter sighs; thee only she loves. *(2 lines)*

---

* Letter to Ghislanzoni, 15.8.1870. *Copialettere*, p. 639.
† Letter from du Locle, 26.7.1870. *Stud. Mus.* (1973), p. 62.
‡ See letter to Ghislanzoni, 12.8.1870. *Copialettere*, p. 638.
§ See *Carteggi Verdiani*, IV, pp. 17–18, also Busch, pp. 484–5.
¶ Letter to Ghislanzoni, 12.8.1870. *Copialettere*, pp. 638–9.

Evidently Verdi's taste for biblical language, so apparent in *Nabucco*, had not lessened with the years. Here the model is not the Book of Daniel but the Song of Solomon, with judicious aid from that great forger of a more northern antiquity, James MacPherson. He was no less specific about the metre to be employed: double settenari, i.e. with the rhymes limited to every second line. 'And if it doesn't go against the grain, make some of the lines "tronchi"; this can sometimes be very pretty in music.' The melody in *La Traviata*, 'Di Provenza', would have been much less bearable if the lines had been 'piani'.* In the event Ghislanzoni made the lines alternately 'tronchi' and 'sdruccioli'.

In the duet between Amneris and Aida it was the 'parola scenica' that was lacking, notably where the Egyptian princess rounds on her rival after having forced her confidence by a trick. Almost apologetically Verdi asked his librettist for irregular lines ('verse sciolti') of which he himself provided the pattern ('Tu l'ami', etc.) 'so as to be able to say clearly and plainly what the action requires,'[dagger] and he stated his favourite maxim that sometimes, in the interests of good theatre, poets and composers should show a talent for writing neither poetry nor music. The final cabaletta seemed to him too long for the situation, but he would try to put this right in the setting. By the next letter he had at last devised a scheme for the consecration scene of Act I. His original specification had been:

> Religious chorus; chorale in the style of Palestrina (the Palestrina of those days, obviously).
> The sound of harps heard mingled with the singing of the priestesses.
> Religious chorus of priestesses. Another chorale (idea).[double dagger]

Now he set out the scene in greater detail. 'A "litany" chanted by the priestesses to which the priests reply; a sacred dance with slow, sad music; a short recitative, solemn and vigorous like a biblical psalm; and a prayer of two verses spoken by the priest and repeated by all present. And I would like it to have a calm and melancholy character, so as to avoid any resemblances to the chorus towards the end of the introduction (i.e. first scene) which has a slight feeling of the "Marseillaise" about it.' The 'litanies' were to consist of two ottonari and a quinario; this last would be the 'Ora pro nobis'.§ Ghislanzoni did as he was told, apart from sending settenari instead of ottonari, a mistake that he put right the following day, only to be told 'happily – I'm not sure – I've already set the settenari. Now we must keep to the settenario chorus which seems to me excellent.'¶ In the same letter Ghislanzoni was invited to S. Agata to put the last two acts in final order. But when he had left early in September the finale of Act II still needed some adjustment, partly for the musical architecture, partly for dramatic effect. Aida's recognition of her father needed more preparation and more prominence; 'and it should be made clear to the audience that Amonasro speaks only when he is afraid that his royal identity will be disclosed.'‖ In general it was the part of Ramfis and the priests that needed filling out. After the con-

---

* Letter to Ghislanzoni, 16.8.1870. *Copialettere*, pp. 639–40.
[dagger] Letter to Ghislanzoni, 17.8.1870. *Ibid.*, pp. 641–2.
[double dagger] *Carteggi Verdiani*, IV, p. 18.
§ Letter to Ghislanzoni, 22.8.1870. *Copialettere*, p. 642.
¶ Letter to Ghislanzoni, 25.8.1870. *Ibid.*, pp. 642–3.
‖ Letter to Ghislanzoni, *c.* 13.9.1870. *Ibid.*, p. 672.

certato Verdi wanted a full strophe for Ramfis warning both King and general of the dangers of releasing the prisoners. The priests were to have a special verse to themselves in the opening chorus, whose sense was to be modelled vaguely on that of Kaiser Wilhelm's telegrams ('We have conquered with God's help, etc.'). And: 'Don't be afraid of religious antiphonies, laments and so on. When the situation calls for them one should have no scruples. At this point [i.e., the closing chorus] the priests can do no more than call upon the gods to be propitious to them in the future.'* Still later he remembered that there were a score of prisoners on stage who would have to be accommodated with a verse. 'They can't keep silent, nor can they sing the same words as the people.'†

Act III, it will be remembered, contained Verdi's most important modification of the original scenario; and it is here that his hand on the helm is most clearly felt. From the clutch of letters written between 28 September and 22 October we can deduce not only that it took him a long time to hit upon a plan that struck the right balance between freedom and formality, but that he changed his mind more than once during the correspondence (a valuable corrective, this, to the view that Verdi always had the basic scheme in his mind from the start, as suggested by the *Traviata* sketch). He approved the opening hymn to Isis, but wanted it shorter and with the sense changed so as to avoid any resemblance to the consecration scene of the first act.‡ He also approved at first a romanza for Aida beginning:

> Schiava deserta ed orfana
> Della materne cure,
> Tutta l'amaro calice
> Vuotai delle sventure . . .

Then he attacked the two duets, going straight to the dramatic crux of each: in the first Aida's reaction to her father's curse, in the second Radames' reaction to the presence of Amonasro. 'I see that you are afraid of two things,' he wrote to Ghislanzoni; 'of certain what I might call theatrical *audacities*; and of not writing cabalettas! I am always of the opinion that cabalettas should be written when the situation requires them. Those of the two duets are not required by the situation, and the one in the duet between father and daughter seems to me particularly out of place. Aida in her state of terror and moral prostration cannot and must not sing a cabaletta. . . . After Amonasro has said, "You are the Pharaohs' slave," [she] can speak only in broken sentences.'§ Likewise at the point where Amonasro steps out of hiding Radames would have to stutter out words of half-crazed astonishment. He should not speak in coherent lines. In this way the conflict lacking in the original synopsis would be firmly planted. Aida and Radames would no longer be unthinking puppets with Amonasro pulling the strings. A patriotic cabaletta for father and daughter, like that of Arnold and William Tell, might do for grand opera of the late 1820s; not for a drama that aspires to the psychological insight of *Aida*.

The next two letters find further fault with the duet between Radames and Aida, chiefly in the articulation of the action and the distribution of recitative and can-

---

* Letters to Ghislanzoni, 8 and 14.9.1870. *Copialettere*, pp. 643–5.
† Letter to Ghislanzoni, 28.9.1870. *Ibid.*, pp. 646–8.
‡ See letters to Ghislanzoni, 28 and 30.9.1870. *Ibid.*, pp. 645–8.
§ Letter to Ghislanzoni, 28.9.1870. *Ibid.*, pp. 645–6.

tabile. Aida's reproaches were to be set as recitative, so as to stand out in due relief. The cantabile in which she cajoles Radames with visions of 'virgin forests' was to be set out in parallel stanzas for each singer; there was to be no terzetto after Radames has taken his fatal decision, and so another piece of conventional operatic nonsense was avoided. Evidently Verdi had to fight his librettist over the way in which Aida elicits the military secret from her lover. ('I would point out that Aida is justified by her duet with her father, and I would be inclined to say by the presence of her father himself, whom the audience knows to be in hiding and listening. Not only that. Aida can quite naturally stop to ask Radames a question; but after that duet Radames can't.') He insisted again on the importance of Radames' part at the moment when he realizes that he has betrayed his country.*

By 7 October he had received Ghislanzoni's revisions; and still the second duet was not right; but for the moment he wanted to concentrate on the first so as to lose no time. Where Amonasro had alluded to Aida's love for Radames with the words 'Io del tuo core leggo i misteri', Verdi preferred 'Nulla sfugge al mio sguardo' as being more in character. In the final section Aida's part was to be further developed at the expense of Amonasro's. But his insistence on the latter's 'Pensa che un popolo vinto e straziato' suggests that the broad melodic phrase that lights up the conclusion of the duet had already taken shape in the composer's mind. At this point he decided to remove the 'romanza' and replace it with a brief recitative, partly for fear of fatiguing the prima donna, partly because it would result in too much slow music which would bore the audience, and partly because its sense was somewhat commonplace and he was dissatisfied with his own setting of it.†

In his letter of 8 October Verdi returns to the second duet. 'Certainly this row of cantabili of eight lines sung by one character and repeated by the other isn't going to keep the dialogue alive. Besides the transitions between the cantabili are rather dull.'‡ By 'transitions' (*intermezzi*) he was referring once more to Aida's taunts ('Prode t'amai, benche nemico; non t'amerei spergiuro' and 'E non temi il furor d'Amneris?') which he set out, somewhat apologetically, in prose together with the dénouement. Once these had been accepted Verdi proceeded, rather inconsistently, to waive his objections to the 'row of cantabili' and even to reject his librettist's well-meaning revisions. 'Now that we've started along the path of cantabili and cabalette we must continue along it, and it's right that Radames should answer Aida's eight lines with eight of his own.'§ In fact the strophes in which Radames puts up a token resistance to Aida's wheedling are, as Spike Hughes points out,¶ scarcely logical. But in one of his drafts Ghislanzoni had thrown out the lines

> Il ciel de' nostri amori
> Come scordar potrem

and Verdi seized upon them avidly.‖ Doubtless he liked their sound. The final movement of the duet ('Ah, fuggiam da queste mura') is, after all, a cabaletta with

---

* See letters to Ghislanzoni, 30.9 and 6.10.1870. *Copialettere*, pp. 646–9.
† See letters to Ghislanzoni, 7 and 16.10.1870. *Ibid.*, pp. 650–1, 653–4.
‡ Letter to Ghislanzoni, 8.10.1870. *Ibid.*, pp. 651–3.
§ Letter to Ghislanzoni, 16.10.1870. *Ibid.*, pp. 653–4.
¶ Hughes, p. 410.
‖ See letter to Ghislanzoni, 18.10.1870. *Copialettere*, pp. 654–5.

parallel stanzas for both singers and to the most commonplace of texts (the opening line is identical with Gulnara's in a duet cabaletta in *Il Corsaro*). Here was a volte-face indeed.

The duet between Radames and Amneris had been discussed during Ghislanzoni's visit to S. Agata with Giulio Ricordi in September. The librettist had felt the final prose draft to be too extended and had proposed various cuts. Verdi resumed the argument in his letter of 16 October.

> Your notes and your cuts are perfectly right, but we shall have to put something in place of these cuts and notes because this scene should be very, very well developed. Perhaps I haven't got it quite clear in my mind, but the situation seems to me extremely good and extremely theatrical, and the part of Radames cannot be watered down. So develop this situation in the way you think best, and develop it fully; let the characters say what they have to say without worrying in the least about the musical form. Of course if you were to send me recitative from beginning to end I would be unable to write rhythmic music, but if you begin straightaway in a rhythm of some sort and keep it going until the end I shouldn't complain at all. You might just have to change it so as to make a little cabaletta at the end.*

The suggestion of making the duet lyrical throughout was more than a hint on Verdi's part; but he clearly had difficulty in persuading Ghislanzoni of its validity, since he returns to the subject more than once in the letters that follow. He began by sending Ghislanzoni part of the fourth-act scenario 'revised according to the observations you made and the cuts you proposed'.

Comparing it with the original† we find that here for the first time Radames accuses Amneris of having caused Aida's death only to be told that Aida is alive, having escaped when her father was overtaken and killed. Among various notes in the margin Verdi writes, 'There is no danger of recalling *Norma* to mind provided the lines have a different form.' He was, of course, referring to the duet 'In mia man alfin tu sei' from the second act of Bellini's opera, where the priestess is offering to have Pollione's life spared on a similar condition. Also in the margin: 'I think we could begin immediately with lyrical lines.'‡ Later: 'At the start of this duet there is if I am not mistaken something lofty and noble in Radames' part – something that I would like to have sung out. A melody *sui generis*, not a melody of romanze and cavatine, but a declaimed melody, sustained and lofty. The metre can be as you like, and do break up the dialogue if you think it will make it more lively.'§ But irregularity, like the initial romanza for Amneris in the unoperatic metre of 'novenari' which he suggested half-jokingly in the same letter, was not really what the scene required; Verdi realized this two days later and duly complained of a 'choppy' effect. From then on he urged the need for solemn, expansive verse in symmetrical stanzas interwoven with dialogue ('Don't be afraid that these lengthy stanzas will seem dull. Let the verse be as sustained and beautiful as you can make it. . . .'¶ Meanwhile, since

* Letter to Ghislanzoni, 16.10.1870. *Ibid.*, pp. 653–4.
† Busch, Document VIII.
‡ Letter to Ghislanzoni, 15.10.1870. *Copialettere*, pp. 657–9.
§ Letter to Ghislanzoni, 25.10.1870. *Ibid.*, pp. 659–60.
¶ Letter to Ghislanzoni, 27.10.1870. *Ibid.*, pp. 661–2.

Ghislanzoni was still unrepentantly beginning with recitative lines, 'I am ever more convinced that it must be written from the start in lyrical form. With the very first words of this recitative I scribbled some "settenari" and I am sure that a melody can be made of them. A melody based on words that seem to be spoken by a lawyer will seem strange. But beneath these lawyer's words there is the heart of a desperate woman consumed with love. Music is splendidly able to depict this state of mind successfully and, in a certain way, to say two things at once. . . .' and he appended yet another scheme for the duet.*

The cabaletta continued to worry him slightly as being too long for the situation ('Oh, those confounded cabalettas which all have the same form and are all alike!');† and as late as 5 November he suggested an alternation of long and short lines for the sake of novelty.‡ But the suggestion was not followed up, each line remaining in standard ottonari. The opening words 'Chi ti salva, o sciagurato?' are apparently Verdi's – or rather Piave's, since they are taken directly from the stretta of the Act I finale of *Stiffelio*.§

Metre also played a vital part in Verdi's ideas for the judgement scene – a dramatic moment to which he attached great importance. ('I may be mistaken, but this scene seems to me one of the best in the drama and not inferior to that of the "Miserere" in *Trovatore*. Perhaps you wouldn't agree and perhaps you are right. But if I am wrong, it's wise to leave me in my error. . . .'). The idea of having Radames tried and condemned off-stage but within hearing of Amneris and the audience first surfaces in Verdi's extended draft of Act IV.¶ But so far Ghislanzoni had not found the appropriate lines.

> The off-stage chorus is beautiful, but the senari lines seem to me too short for the situation. Here I would have liked the grand line, Dante's line, and also in tercets.
>
> Your 'Taci? Taci?' is so dry that it's impossible to make it musically interrogative. I think the tercet form would have been all right, because we could have repeated 'Radames' twice if we wished, and because we could have divided up the line, as for example:
>
> > Difenditi!
> >
> > Tu taci? Traditor!
>
> I know very well that the *ti, tu, ta* is bad (you will put that right); but this dreadful line says what the situation demands. You want to say 'Nel dì della battaglia' – There was no battle.

Ghislanzoni had couched the charges against Radames in ottonari (e.g. 'Alla patria, al re spergiuro'). Verdi wanted these changed to decasillabi. 'Some time ago I advised you to avoid that metre because in allegro movements it becomes too bouncing; but in this situation the accent *by threes* would strike like a hammer and be quite terrifying.' 'By threes' is a description which will apply to almost every aspect of the

---

* Letter to Ghislanzoni, 26.10.1870. *Copialettere*, pp. 667–8.
† Letter to Ghislanzoni, 27.10.1870.
‡ Letter to Ghislanzoni, 5.11.1870. *Ibid.*, pp. 662–3.
§ For a detailed analysis of the correspondence on this duet see Gossett, *op. cit.*, pp. 313–28.
¶ See Busch, Document VIII, p. 490.

judgement scene, as the analysis will show. Meanwhile, 'I have an idea which you may perhaps find too bold and drastic. . . . I would have the priests return on stage, and on seeing them Amneris like a tigress would hurl the bitterest reproaches at Ramfis. The priests would pause for a moment to reply, "È traditor! morrà!" Then they would continue on their way. Left alone Amneris would exclaim in just two lines of either ten- or eleven-syllable verse, "Sacerdoti, crudeli inesorabili, siate maledetti in eterno!" Here the scene would end.' As so often he enclosed a rough plan with the metrical scheme jotted in the margin.* Finally Amneris's emotions needed heightening: 'Omit . . . that "morrò d'amore". Instead we need two more anguished lines written in such a way that I can take bits of them for Amneris to repeat every time she hears an accusation from the underground chamber. Amneris can't remain so long on stage hearing these terrible indictments without crying aloud some despairing phrase.' Then too Ghislanzoni must find some way of conveying her terror at the prospect that the man she loves is to be buried alive.† All the lines suggested are in the long metres of decasillabo or endecasillabo.

For the final scene Ghislanzoni needed some guidance early on, having found himself embarrassed by a passage in Verdi's own detailed draft‡ 'The situation of the lovers is so desperate, so terrible, that the "Ah, vivi!" seems out of place to me and so even more does the "godiamo un'istante di felicità". These last words could even lend themselves to an erotic interpretation, which would certainly not correspond to the author's intentions.'§ Yet Ghislanzoni saw nothing wrong in making Radames exclaim over Aida's corpse like the Conte di Luna, 'And I live on!'; to which one is tempted to answer, 'Not for much longer!'¶ Verdi had a better solution. 'I would like to remove the usual death-agony. . . . I would like something sweet and ethereal, a very short duet, a farewell to life. Aida would gently fall into Radames' arms. Meanwhile Amneris, kneeling on the stone above the vault, would sing a "Requiescat in pace".'‖ In the same letter he asked the poet to shorten Radames' opening recitative and make it more direct in expression, and to set out the opening movement of the duet in two parallel stanzas. Next day, however, he changed his mind, having by now realized that the scene was a very special one. 'In inexperienced hands it could turn out too abrupt or too monotonous. It must not be too abrupt; with such an elaborate setting it would be a case of *parturiens mons* if it were not well developed. Monotony must be avoided by finding unusual forms.' Which meant that he now wanted the two opening stanzas of Radames and Aida to be in different metres. 'The French, even in their poetry for singing, sometimes use longer or shorter lines. Why shouldn't we do the same? The entire scene cannot and must not be anything but a scene of song pure and simple. A somewhat unusual verse form would oblige me to write a different kind of melody from those that are usually written on settenari or ottonari, and I would also have to change tempo and time

* Letter to Ghislanzoni, 4.11.1870. *Copialettere*, pp. 664–7.
† Letter to Ghislanzoni, probably 9.11.1870. *Ibid.*, pp. 660–1.
‡ Busch, Document VIII, p. 493.
§ Letter from Ghislanzoni, 31.10.1870. Busch, p. 89.
¶ See *Carteggi Verdiani*, IV, p. 22.
‖ Letter to Ghislanzoni, 12.11.1870. *Copialettere*, pp. 669–71. That this last idea was Verdi's alone we know from an earlier letter written to Giulio Ricordi, 7.11.1870 (Busch, pp. 97–8), in which he asked the publisher to find out from his knowledgeable friend what were the Egyptian prayers for the dead. In the event Amneris would be given a simple 'Pace t'imploro'.

signature for Aida's solo, a kind of semi-aria.' He then set out his scheme for Radames' 'Morire sì pura e bella' in which no less than three varieties of metre are employed, adding, 'You cannot imagine what a fine melody can be written within so unusual a form, or how much charm there is in the quinario after the three settenari, and how much variety is given by the two endecasillabi which come afterward; it would be as well, however, that these last should either be both piani or both tronchi. See if you can make real lines of them and if you can keep "tu sì bella" which fits the cadence so well.'* After this Aida's 'semi-aria' ('Vedi, di morte l'angelo') is in plain settenari. For the final movement Verdi had already specified endecasillabi with the accent on the fourth and eighth syllables, as though he had already thought of the melody of 'O terra, addio'. Here, be it noted, novelty of metre is not being used to create a novel design but rather to mask the features of an old one. Given its essentially classical nature it is logical that *Aida* end with a chain of symmetries culminating in a cabaletta of pure Bellinian stamp with three full melodic statements. But a cabaletta in hendecasyllabic rhythm could never sound conventional.

As Verdi did not intend to go to Cairo for the première, *Aida*, like *Il Corsaro*, was scored at home and not during rehearsal as was his normal practice. 'A month's work', he told Ghislanzoni; and in the course of it he returned once more to the moment in the finale of Act II at which Aida recognizes her father. ('Don't be afraid! It's a tiny matter. . . . The situation is very fine but perhaps the characters aren't properly realized in stage terms; that is to say they don't react as they should.')† In fact the passage proved more difficult to adjust than Verdi had supposed; not until mid-January was it patched up to his satisfaction with various short exclamations and audible asides. The final touches to the opera were not given until the following August, just as the score was about to be engraved. 'I want to re-do the music of the opening chorus in the third act, which hasn't sufficient character; and while we're about it I would love to add a little solo for Aida, an idyll as you suggested before; only the lines that you wrote then weren't really suitable. . . . It's quite true that Aida's personality doesn't really lend itself to one at this point; but digressing a bit with a reminiscence of her native land you could make a calm tranquil piece which would be like balm at that moment.'‡ And he sketched out the text of Aida's romanza as we know it today, in two stanzas with the refrain 'O patria mia, mai ti rivedrò', which was to be grafted also onto the end of the preceding recitative. Once again he wanted eleven-syllable verse ('I like the long line'). An unexpected change of mind, certainly, and perhaps to be explained by the fact that he had found meantime the ideal interpreter of Aida herself, Teresa Stolz. The following day he asked for a few more lines with which to expand the triple encounter of Aida, Radames and Amonasro in Act III without turning it into a formal terzetto.§ With that the opera was for the time being complete.

From the start Verdi had been turning over in his mind various ideas for an ap-

---

* Letter to Ghislanzoni, 13.11.1870. *Copialettere*, pp. 663–4. The effect of a quinario following three settenarii is less unusual than Verdi seems to think. He himself knew at least one specimen of it, namely Donna Elvira's 'Ah, fuggi il traditor' from *Don Giovanni*.

† Letter to Ghislanzoni, 21.12.1870. *Copialettere*, p. 673.

‡ Letter to Ghislanzoni, 5.8.1871. *Ibid.*, pp. 674–5.

§ See letter to Ghislanzoni, 6.8.1871. Busch, pp. 198–9.

propriate instrumental colour. He would have liked a stage band of old Egyptian instruments but doubted whether they would make an effect. 'I can assure you,' he
wrote to du Locle, 'that I would be loath to use Saxe's instruments. In a modern
subject they might be tolerable . . . but amongst the Pharaohs!'* Following a hint of
Fétis's in his *Dictionnaire universelle de musique* that the ancient Egyptians possessed a
highly sophisticated kind of flute he paid a visit to the Archaeological Museum in
Florence, only to discover that it was little more than a shepherd's pipe, as he
reminded his friend Arrivabene with great glee some years later† (he was always
pleased to be able to fault the Belgian pundit, to whom his own music was
anathema). Much later, with the Milan première in view, he experimented with an
A flat flute designed to his own specification (he had originally wanted one in A but
was told that it would be impossible to make) and though he professed himself
satisfied with the sound, especially in the middle and lower register, the stage effect
must have fallen short of his expectations; in the event he made do with the standard
orchestral instrument.‡ Meanwhile, even before completing the final act he had
begun to think about the trumpets required for the ceremonial march of Act II. They
were to be long and straight, three pitched in A flat and three in B. Giulio Ricordi
ordered the appropriate specimens from the firm of Pelitti in Milan only to find that
in order to reach the notes Verdi required a small valve would be necessary; this,
however, could be masked by a 'gauntlet' which the player would cover with his
hand and so shield it from view. Verdi was satisfied, provided that no one could see
the movement of the player's hand, since 'it's a question of showing what the
trumpets were like in ancient times'.§ Once again it was false antiquity; the trumpets
are Roman.

During this time Verdi came under increasing pressure from the management of
directors of La Scala, Milan, to allow the Italian première in that theatre during the
imminent carnival season. His contract with Mariette stipulated that once the Cairo
performance had taken place he was free to have the opera mounted in whatever city
he liked. Meanwhile the score was to be delivered to Cairo or Paris at a convenient
time and the composer paid the final instalment of his fee¶ from a Paris bank. With
the French capital still under siege and the opera practically completed Verdi wrote
to Mariette via his parliamentary friend Giuseppe Piroli asking where he was to send
the score and from what bank he was to draw his remuneration. The letter was to be
sent to Cairo on the assumption that Mariette had already returned there. But if, as
Verdi suspected, he was shut up in Paris together with the scenery and costumes then
it was to be forwarded to the management of the theatre or even to the Viceroy
himself.‖ Evidently communication between Cairo and Italy at that period was
slow; and it was over a month before Verdi heard from the Intendant of the theatre,
Paul Draneht, what by now he had learned from a letter of du Locle's, flown out of
Paris by balloon – namely that Mariette was indeed in Paris and that all work on the

---

* Letter to du Locle, 15.7.1870. *M.Q.*, VII, p. 91.

† Letter to Arrivabene, 8.8.1878. Alberti, pp. 209–11.

‡ See Letters: to Giulio Ricordi, 10.10; from the same 13.10; to the same, 14.10, 15.10, 26.10, 31.10,
2.12.1871. Busch, pp. 235–59.

§ Letters: from Giulio Ricordi, 13.11.1870; to the same, 15.11.1870. Busch, pp. 104–9.

¶ See Busch, Document V, pp. 473–4.

‖ Letter to Piroli, with enclosure to Mariette, 12.11.1870. *Carteggi Verdiani*, III, pp. 71–2; Busch,
p. 100.

sets for *Aida* had been suspended due to lack of workmen. Draneht could give no satisfactory answer about Verdi's score or his fee since he had never seen a copy of his contract with Mariette (Verdi had given his own copy to du Locle for safe-keeping). It was clear, however, that *Aida* could no longer be given on the date scheduled or even during that season. Verdi accordingly proposed to score the opera at his leisure with a view to a première the following winter.

Meanwhile from the safety of Brussels Muzio in a letter of extraordinary pomposity presented himself to Draneht as the man chosen by Verdi to direct the new opera, adding that a performance at La Scala, Milan, with the tenor Tiberini and the soprano Fricci was already in preparation for February 1871.* Whereupon Draneht wrote to Verdi in the utmost alarm pointing out the offence that would be given if the première of *Aida* were to take place outside Egypt. 'In choosing you, dear Maestro, to write the score for an unpublished work, in which the action takes place in his own country, His Highness had conceived the idea of creating a national work which would be one of the most precious souvenirs of his reign. Must it become the victim of a matter of dates due to circumstances beyond our control? I have no wish to invoke our right of priority, nor the case of *force majeure*. . . . It is to your loyalty, dear Master, to your tact and to your sense of delicacy that I wish to appeal. . . .'† Nor did he appeal in vain. Verdi wrote back agreeing to defer the première of *Aida* to the winter season of 1871–2 – even though his contract had authorized him, should the performance scheduled for January 1871 not take place, to mount it six months later in any theatre of his choice.‡

Paul Draneht, the lynch-pin of the *Aida* arrangements, was a man of uncommon ability and diplomatic skill. A Greek Cypriot by birth, he fled with his family to Egypt to escape persecution by the Turks. He himself was taken into the service of Mohammed Ali, the ruler, while still in his teens and sent to study chemistry in France under Baron Thénard, who was so pleased with his pupil's progress that he allowed him to change his family name of Pavlidis into an anagram of his own ('Draneht' being 'Thénard' spelt backwards). After his return to Egypt Draneht rose to ever higher office under Mohammed and his successors, becoming like Mariette first 'Bey' and eventually 'Pasha'. A friend of de Lesseps, he had a hand in negotiations for the opening of the Suez Canal, as well as for most of Egypt's foreign loans. To him was also due the laying of the Egyptian railways. But it is as Superintendent of the Viceregal Theatres that he enters the history of *Aida*. In the months that preceded the abortive première he had handled the various intrigues and contretemps with cool competence. He was sympathetic and helpful to Mariette but careful not to give him a blank cheque in his dealings on the Viceroy's behalf. He resisted pressure from the father of Giuseppina Vitali to recommend her for the part of Amneris once Verdi had indicated another singer; yet he did not hesitate to suggest that the principal bass role should be expanded so as to exploit the talents of Paolo Medini.§ A suitable cast had already been arrived at – Isabella Galletti-Gianoli (Aida), Ginevra Giovannoni-Zacchi (Amneris), Emilio Naudin (Radames), Paolo Medini (Amonasro), Giovanni Marè (Ramfis)¶ – when the unfortunate Mariani

---

* Letter from Muzio to Draneht, 5.12.1870. *Quaderno*, IV, p. 27. Busch, p. 112.

† Letter from Draneht, 22.12.1870. *Ibid.*, p. 30. Busch, pp. 117–18.

‡ Letter to Draneht, 5.1.1871. *Ibid.*, IV, p. 33–4. Busch, p. 125.

§ Letter from Draneht to Mariette, 4.8.1870. *Ibid.*, p. 10.

¶ At this stage Amneris was envisaged as a soprano and Amonasro as a bass.

made a last incursion into the composer's affairs. Gianoli, husband of the prima donna, had written to one Antonelli, Mariani's host at Bologna, that he understood that Mariani had been engaged to conduct the première of *Aida* at a fee of 50,000 francs. This letter Mariani forwarded to Verdi together with one of his own. 'If what Gianoli writes is true I should owe my fortune to you and I should cease to lead a financially cramped and highly dependent life. But let's set aside the 50,000 francs; half of that would be enough for me. And then what about the honour that would be mine in being sent by *you* to Cairo on such a solemn occasion? I'll speak frankly and tell you that I should consider myself the most fortunate of men if such a benefit came to me through you. You are all-powerful, and to your proven generosity I leave my fortune. Truly, last night, after reading Gianoli's letter I could not sleep for excitement . . .' and more to the same effect.* To which Verdi replied: 'Gianoli would do well to look after his own affairs and not interfere in mine. . . . You wrote to me once before that you wanted to go with me to Cairo; I replied that I wasn't going. If I had thought fit to send you in my place I would have asked you; if I did not, that is proof that I didn't think fit, and that I had entrusted the task to someone else. In a word this letter of Gianoli's is an ugly business for him, for you and for me.'† With its curt tone and shabby insinuation this was all too typical of the kind of letter that the conductor was now receiving from S. Agata. Clearly Verdi wanted none of him for the present. Events, however, would soon induce him to change his mind.

If ever there was a time that needed all Draneht's qualities it was the year preceding the première of *Aida*. By the terms of his original contract Verdi had bound himself to cast the opera from the company's current roster of singers. With the first performance deferred to the following year he was now able to give advice as to how that roster should be made up. Nor was there any obstacle to a second performance in Milan in the early months of 1872; and it was clear that Verdi himself set far more store by this than by the original première in Cairo, though the Khedive could offer higher fees than the management of La Scala. Hence some rather odd dealing.

For La Scala Verdi hoped to have the two leading sopranos of the day, Antonietta Fricci as Aida and Teresa Stolz as Amneris. Stolz was now engaged to Mariani, and the two of them frequently appeared together. But Giulio Ricordi was asked to approach her directly otherwise 'Mariani will ruin everything'.‡ In fact Teresa Stolz first consulted Mariani, and as he and Verdi were both in Genoa at the time as fellow tenants of the Palazzo Sauli it was through Mariani that the composer heard that she was disposed to accept; nor did Mariani make any objection. At the time Giulio Ricordi seems to have assumed that Mariani himself would be the conductor; failing that he would prefer Faccio. Verdi urged him to think 'very very very carefully' and implied that to have anything to do with Mariani was to court disaster.§ When Teresa Stolz's official letter of acceptance arrived hedged around with conditions which the board of management could not possibly accept Ricordi wrote to Verdi in

---

* Letter from Mariani. U. Zoppi, *Mariani, Verdi e la Stolz* (Milan, 1947), pp. 213–14. Walker, pp. 365–6.

† Draft letter to Mariani, 13.11.1870. *Carteggi Verdiani*, II, p. 34: Walker, pp. 366–7. 'Ugly' for Gianoli since his wife was notoriously flirtatious and he might be suspected of conniving in an affair between her and the equally susceptible Mariani.

‡ Letter to Giulio Ricordi, 30.12.1870. Busch, p. 121.

§ Letter to Giulio Ricordi, 7.7.1871. Busch, p. 128.

high indignation, throwing the blame on her fiancé for having advised her badly. At the same time he informed La Stolz that he would withdraw from the whole affair and that she would have to deal directly with the management. With matters thus at a stalemate Draneht was able to make a bid for the services of Mariani and Teresa Stolz through the agent Lampugnani. Sensing a gold-mine in the Cairo theatre (as did all the singers approached by Lampugnani on Draneht's behalf) Teresa Stolz raised her sights accordingly. From La Scala she had demanded 40,000 francs for the whole season; for Cairo she wanted 30,000 per month for herself and for Mariani 45,000 for the season – a neat illustration, this, of the huge discrepancy in those days between ratings of a star conductor and a star singer. Teresa Stolz would have received 120,000 francs by the time she left Cairo.* After some haggling Draneht offered both artists a joint fee of 125,000 for the season, with a benefit concert included, from which the takings could amount to a further 40,000 francs. Eventually Lampugnani received two telegrams: one from Mariani declining the offer from Cairo, the other from Teresa Stolz asking him to wait for her final decision. Two days later he heard that the soprano had signed an option with La Scala for the same season. 'It seems that Verdi is somehow involved in this affair,' he wrote to Draneht; and later, 'It is Verdi alone who has blocked the Cairo engagement – Verdi, the world's foremost Jesuit.'†

The problem of a prima donna for Cairo, however, was easily settled. Persuaded by Draneht that Isabella Galletti-Gianoli was no longer reliable, Verdi took the opportunity of an official visit to Florence as part of a committee advising on the reform of the conservatories to hear the soprano Antonietta Pozzoni-Anastasi at the Pergola Theatre. 'She has great talent,' he pronounced, 'a good deal of feeling, and she's very beautiful, which never does any harm.'‡ She was accordingly engaged for Cairo.

The choice of conductor was more difficult. Verdi had wanted Muzio as before, but soon understood from Draneht's silence on this point that since his last season in Cairo Muzio was no longer persona grata in that city.§ His thoughts turned once more to Mariani, especially since there was no longer any question of his appearing with Teresa Stolz. 'If, as you say, you want for your conductor a sure and recognized talent,' he wrote to Draneht, 'Mariani is absolutely the only one. The others are all much the same.'¶ After his ungracious behaviour of a few months before Verdi was hardly in a position to carry his point with the conductor himself; nor did he. Chronically indecisive and by now thoroughly afraid of the composer's changes of mood, Mariani prevaricated . . . and finally declined. Verdi none the less at first urged Draneht to wait before engaging someone else in case Mariani should change his mind. Draneht meanwhile was already half committed to Bottesini, whom he had approached as an alternative through his stage manager (Verdi's first tragic hero) Ignazio Marini. Bottesini had wired back enthusiastically, to be told by Draneht to wait for his final decision. By the end of April even Verdi began to realize

---

* See letters from Teresa Stolz to Lampugnani, 25.2.1871. (Busch, p. 140) and 13.3.1871 (Walker, p. 368).
  † Letters from Lampugnani to Draneht, 9.4.1871 and 16.4.1871. Busch, pp. 150 and 153.
  ‡ Letter to Draneht, 30.3.1871. *Ibid.*, pp. 148–9.
  § See also letter from R. Vitali to Draneht, 21.8.1870. *Ibid.*, pp. 53–4.
  ¶ Letter to Draneht, 14.4.1871. *Copialettere*, p. 259.

the futility of further delay and authorized Draneht to engage whom he thought fit.*
So he could not reasonably complain when Draneht closed a deal with Bottesini. Yet
complain he did, in two letters to Lampugnani.† He had not dared, he said, to
propose Muzio to Draneht; but could Lampugnani himself bring his influence to
bear in that direction? Lampugnani tried‡ but understandably failed. Bottesini
remained firmly in the saddle.

The casting of Amneris proved still more troublesome. One reason was that from
being in Verdi's original conception a soprano with good low notes she had become
a mezzo-soprano with good high ones; but at the time he never saw her as a full contralto and he firmly believed that the part would lie outside the compass of the
mezzo-soprano under contract to Cairo for the season, Eleonora Grossi. At the end of
April Draneht informed Verdi that he was negotiating with Marie Sass, former
heroine of *Don Carlos*.§ Verdi replied not to him but to Lampugnani that he had no
use for her 'either as Amneris, who is a mezzo-soprano, or as Aida, for other
reasons'.¶ During a visit by Draneht to S. Agata towards the end of May there was a
further discussion about Marie Sass, of which Verdi and Draneht had very different
recollections. Draneht assumed that Verdi approved the engagement of La Sass as
Amneris and signed her up accordingly. Verdi gave his explicit veto, firstly because
the role lay too low for her, secondly because 'I know from experience that it is in the
interest of both the management and the composer to give her operas in which she is
the only soprano, or at least an opera which has no other role equal or superior to
hers'.‖ To him the problem was simple: Draneht must engage another mezzo-
soprano of Verdi's own choice. But this Draneht was not empowered to do without
explicit instructions from the Viceroy, since the season's tally of singers was now
complete and the budget exhausted due to the excessive pretensions of the artists.
Verdi tried to enlist the support of Lampugnani and even du Locle; but in the
meantime Mariette returned to Egypt bringing with him his copy of Verdi's contract, from the terms of which Draneht would see that he himself was in an even
stronger legal position than he had supposed. He therefore alerted Eleonora Grossi to
the possibility that she might be required for Amneris, and at the same time
endeavoured to persuade Verdi of her suitability. 'She is now singing *La Favorite* as
written, and she has also performed the role of Fidès in *Le Prophète* without making
any changes. I can assure you that as far as talent goes Signora Grossi is second to no
other artist; and I can assure you of this with a clear conscience, having admired her
for two seasons in more than one opera in the theatre. . . .'** Verdi was unimpressed.
'Alboni too sang *La Gazza Ladra* some time ago, and I think *La Sonnambula*, and even
the part of Carlo in *Ernani*! But what of it? All this means is that singers and
managements have no scruples about tampering with or allowing others to tamper
with an author's creations.'†† Finally Verdi played what he intended as his trump

* Letter to Draneht, 28.4.1871. Busch, p. 154.
† Letters to Lampugnani, 1 and 4.5.1871. Busch, pp. 155–6.
‡ Letter from Lampugnani to Draneht, 4.5.1871. *Ibid.*, p. 155.
§ Letter from Draneht, 24.4.1871. *Ibid.*, p. 153.
¶ Letter to Lampugnani, 4.5.1871. *Ibid.*, pp. 155–6.
‖ Letter to Draneht, 8.6.1871. *Ibid.*, p. 170. Verdi was doubtless alluding to her behaviour towards
Pauline Gueymard-Lauters during rehearsals of *Don Carlos*.
** Letter from Draneht, 17.7.1871. *Ibid.*, pp. 184–5.
†† Letter to Draneht, 20.7.1871. *Copialettere*, pp. 265–6.

card. Asked for the libretto so that the sets and costumes could be ordered he sent it not to Draneht but to du Locle, with strict instructions to hold it until the dispute with Cairo over the mezzo-soprano had been solved. Draneht was now in a position to sue the composer had he thought fit; but, as he wrote to Barrot, the Viceroy's secretary, 'M. Verdi is a very rich man and has staunchly resolved to endure anything which might be done against him.'* Meanwhile to Verdi: 'I shall certainly not be the one to continue a pattern of resistance that might affect the good rapport we have enjoyed up till now. I know that by engaging the mezzo-soprano I am acting against the interests of the administration entrusted to me – and may not even be within my own rights in so doing. . . . But never mind. I promise you that I shall engage the mezzo-soprano in the hope that His Highness will come to approve my action; if he does not I am ready to suffer the consequences.'† But in the end it was Verdi who let go of the rope. Having received encouraging reports about Eleonora Grossi from Franco Faccio he declared himself happy after all to entrust her with the role of Amneris 'even though certain passages might lie rather high for her'.‡ So another crisis passed and preparations resumed their smooth course. It is interesting to note that after thirty years as a leading dramatic tenor Gaetano Fraschini had been under consideration for the part of Radames, and that only his unwillingness to go to Cairo prevented his being engaged. He had a more than worthy substitute in the swashbuckling ex-dragoon Pietro Mongini, already a famous figure to the audiences of Her Majesty's, London.§ Francesco Steller, the baritone, would never create a part more important than Amonasro; Paolo Medini, now Ramfis, was to be Verdi's favourite bass for his Requiem. In the absence of Ghislanzoni the stage direction was to be entrusted to one of Italy's more distinguished librettists, Carlo d'Ormeville.

A few weeks before the première of *Aida* there occurred an event of more than passing interest to Verdi. Heralded by a barrage of publicity, the first Italian production of *Lohengrin* took place at Bologna on 1 November under the baton of Mariani. Verdi went to hear one of the performances and received mixed impressions, to judge from his comments scribbled in the margins of the published libretto. True the execution suffered, mainly because Ricordi's agent, Luigi Monti, had tactlessly made known Verdi's presence in the theatre, so causing consternation among singers and players alike.¶ Nor did the various faults of imprecision and intonation go unnoticed in Verdi's jottings. There was much that he liked, however: the prelude, despite what he considered the composer's over-use of violin harmonics; the combination of cor anglais and bass clarinet in Act II in the theme of Ortrud's warning; and in general the instrumentation. His most frequent criticisms are reserved for the slowness of the action, the drawn-out word-setting and the excessive use of sustained chords and pedal points.‖ *Lohengrin* was not ideal opera as he himself understood it, but he was prepared to learn from the music. What annoyed him was the spate of articles and advertisements to which the occasion had given rise –

---

* Letter from Draneht to Barrot, 21.7.1871. Busch, pp. 189–90.

† Letter from Draneht, 21.7.1871. *Ibid.*, p. 189.

‡ See letter to Draneht, 2.8.1871. *Ibid.*, pp. 194–5, *Copialettere*, pp. 267–8.

§ For somewhat far-fetched anecdotes about this dangerous character, see J. Mapleson, *The Mapleson Memoirs* (ed. H. Rosenthal, London, 1966), *passim*.

¶ See letter from Mariani to C. Del Signore, 20.11.1871. Zoppi, pp. 302–3.

‖ Verdi's notes are reproduced in Abbiati, III, pp. 509–11.

'Lohengrinades', to use his own term.* Hence his irritation when the critic Filippo Filippi, invited by the Viceroy to Cairo, offered to put himself at Verdi's disposal for any commission he might want carried out or even merely to report on the progress of rehearsals. To Verdi himself it was nothing short of a scandal that he should have been sent there in the first place for the sake of a 'puff preliminary'. 'It seems to me that when art is treated like this it is no longer art, but a pastime, a popular sport, a hunt, something to draw the crowds, to be granted if not a success, at least notoriety at all costs. . . . What I feel about it is disgust and a sense of humiliation. I always remember with pleasure my early days in which I appeared before the public with my operas, with hardly a friend, with no one to talk about me, without preparations, without influence of any kind, ready to be shot at and very happy if I managed to make a favourable impression. . . . Nowadays, what an apparatus for an opera!'†

For a progress report Verdi referred to Bottesini himself. ('I beg you earnestly to give me news of the final duet as soon as you have had one or two orchestral rehearsals. You will have gathered from reading the score that I have taken great trouble with this duet, but since it belongs to what I would call the *ethereal* species it is possible that the effect is not quite up to what I would have wished. . . . Just tell me about the 3/4 in D flat [Aida's melody] and the other duet melody in G flat. . . .')‡A week later he informed the conductor about his final alteration to the score, which concerned the end of the duet in the first scene of Act II. 'The stretta which was there (originally) always seemed to me a bit commonplace. This one that I've redone is not, and it will make a good ending at the return of the theme of the scene in Act I; La Pozzoni sings it walking with faltering steps to the front of the stage.'§

The only remaining problem was the divided stage of Act IV, Scene 2, on which Verdi had insisted. Mariette, chiefly concerned about the view from the Viceroy's box and inclined always to dramatize a situation, proposed a solution whereby the lower level with Aida and Radames should be set forward and the upper with Amneris and the priests set back.¶ Nowadays the staging is no more problematic than that of Act I, Scene 2, of *Rigoletto*.

The première was predictably a success and earned the composer the title of Commendatore of the Ottoman Order. He was now free to turn his full attention to the Italian première, for which he had been laying down his requirements as early as the previous spring. In May Giulio Ricordi sent him the tally of players and choristers engaged at La Scala the previous season: strings in the strength of 15.12.8.7.10; double woodwind with extra piccolo, standard distribution of brass with the addition of two cornets and with a bombardon by way of bass; two harps. Male singers, 16.11.10.16; female 12.10.9, including augmentation from the school

---

* See letter to Giulio Ricordi, 24.12.1871. Busch, p. 268.

† Letter to Filippi, 8.12.1871. *Copialettere*, pp. 272–3.

‡ Letter to Bottesini, 10.12.1871. *Copialettere*, p. 678.

§ Letter to Bottesini, 17.12.1871. *Copialettere*, p. 677. Verdi had already mentioned this change to Giulio Ricordi in a letter of 2.12.1871. Busch, pp. 258–9. See also M. Conati, 'Aspetti di melodrammaturgia verdiana. A proposito di una sconosciuta versione del finale del duetto Aida–Amneris', *Studi Verdiani*, III (1985), pp. 45–78.

¶ See letter from Mariette to Draneht, undated. *Quaderno* IV, pp. 77–8. Busch, pp. 233–4. Abdoun gives 2 September as the date; Busch prefers 6 October, but very plausibly suggests December as a possible date.

attached to the theatre; a stage band of 26 players.* All this was changed by the committee of which Verdi was the president and which, though appointed to draw up rules for the reform of the conservatories, also took upon itself the reorganization of orchestra and chorus at La Scala, Milan, and the San Carlo, Naples. For La Scala they ruled a string section of 14.14.12.12.12. ('The author of *Aida* could make do with just 10 violins, 10 cellos and 11 double basses; but the president of the committee must not know that,' Verdi remarked slyly.)† The chorus was to consist of 64 men evenly divided into four, 36 women likewise divided into three. ('As to the chorus, it is the greatest mistake to reduce the number of middle parts. That way we would never have the full, robust, powerful wave of sound that tempers the high voices.') Next month Verdi wrote to his publisher a letter that was to become famous:

I beg you to tell me categorically,
1. Has the conductor been appointed?
2. Have the number of choristers I asked for been engaged?
3. Will the orchestra be composed in the way I indicated?
4. Will the timpani and bass drum be replaced by instruments a good deal larger than those that were there two years ago?
5. If standard pitch will be observed.
6. If the stage band has adopted that pitch so as to avoid the bad intonation I heard some time back?
7. If the orchestra will be set out in the way I indicated by a kind of diagram last winter in Genoa?

This arrangement of the orchestra is much more important than is generally supposed as regards instrumental colour, sonority and effect. These refinements will open the way to other innovations which will certainly come about one day; and one of these will be the removal of boxes from the stage, bringing the curtain right down to the footlights; another will be to make the orchestra invisible. This isn't my idea, it's Wagner's, and it's excellent. It seems impossible that in this day and age we still put up with the sight of our wretched dinner jackets and white ties mixed up with an Egyptian or a druid or an Assyrian costume, etc., etc., and, even more, the sight of the entire orchestra, *which is part of the imaginary world*, almost in the middle of the floor, among the booing or applauding crowd. Add to all this the unbecoming sight of the tops of the harps sticking up in the air with the necks of the double basses and the whirling baton of the conductor. . . .‡

The casting of the principals was more easily settled for Milan than for Cairo. Originally Verdi had had Antonietta Fricci in mind for the title role with Teresa Stolz as Amneris. Fricci, however, had been contracted for Lisbon and all efforts to get her released were fruitless. Having made sure of Teresa Stolz, Verdi then switched her to the role of Aida and allowed himself to be persuaded by the Ricordis into accepting as her rival the young and relatively untried Austrian mezzo-soprano

---

* Letter from Giulio Ricordi, 23.5.1871. Busch, pp. 160–1.

† Letter to Giulio Ricordi, 24.5.1871. *Ibid.*, pp. 163–4. He must surely have meant 10 first and 10 second violins together with 10 violas; but it is interesting to note his instinctive penchant for weighting the double basses, doubtless influenced by memories of the three-string basses of his youth.

‡ Letter to Giulio Ricordi, 10.7.1871. *Copialettere*, pp. 263–5.

Maria Waldmann. True, he expressed misgivings about entrusting such an important part to a beginner, and the financial pretensions of Waldmann herself at one point nearly brought negotiations to a halt. But 'as long as there's voice and feeling there, I'm always for the young ones', Verdi wrote to Tito Ricordi.* Nor was he to be disappointed. Until her marriage into the Italian aristocracy this beautiful and accomplished singer was to prove the outstanding exponent of all Verdi's great mezzo-soprano roles.

For Radames the management had engaged Giuseppe Capponi, who had already proved his worth as an excellent Don Carlos in the famous Bologna performance of the opera under Mariani. Unfortunately due to illness he had to be replaced at the last minute by Giuseppe Fancelli, 'a good voice but a noodle',† whose stock gesture – arms outstretched before him with all fingers extended – earned him from Massenet the nickname 'cinq-et-cinq-font-dix'. It was feared that the great baritone Francesco Pandolfini might find the part of Amonasro too small for him; but 'it cannot be otherwise. . . . If Pandolfini is intelligent, however, and likes to interpret a *character*, Amonasro is a character – perhaps the finest even though the shortest.'‡Fortunately Pandolfini was not one to make difficulties. As conductor Verdi was happy to accept the young Franco Faccio, who had just succeeded Terziani as La Scala's musical director and was soon to prove himself Mariani's successor as Italy's chief virtuoso of the baton.

Verdi began his coaching of the singers as early as September with the first of those visits of Teresa Stolz to S. Agata which were to cause Giuseppina such anxiety. The soprano was still Mariani's fiancée though their engagement had never been made public. By November it was definitely over.§ The problem of Verdi's domestic life over the next few years has already received as much and as fair treatment as it deserves from Frank Walker.¶ For the purpose of this study it will be sufficient to note that though not an international artist of the order of Patti or Tietjens, Teresa Stolz remained throughout the 1870s the ideal Verdian dramatic soprano, gifted with a phenomenal dynamic range and sensitive to every nuance of the composer's thought.‖

In a word no effort was spared to ensure the best possible elements, musical and scenic, for the Milan performance. Verdi himself wrote to the designer Girolamo Magnani urging him to accept a contract for the Carnival season at La Scala. If he were not disposed to shoulder the burden of the entire *cartello* would he please

---

* Letter to T. Ricordi, 22.5.1871. *Ibid.*, pp. 260–1.
† Letter to Arrivabene, 13.1.1872. Alberti, p. 137.
‡ Letter to Giulio Ricordi, 15.10.1871. Busch, pp. 1241–2.
§ See letter from Mariani to C. Del Signore, 14.11.1871. Zoppi, pp. 278–83.
¶ Walker, pp. 393–446.
‖ In 1875 after a performance in Paris of the Requiem, the American journalist Blanche Roosevelt gave the following account of her to the *Chicago Times*: 'Signora Stolz has a pure soprano voice with an immense range and a perfect tone; an unheard-of range which reaches from the lowest note to the highest. Her phrasing is really superb and I never heard the slightest fault of intonation. She sings a note and then holds it until it seems that her breath must be quite exhausted, but in fact she has only just begun to sustain it. Her notes are beautiful, bright, with a diamond-like edge to them, while the power she brings to a high C is quite astonishing. It is said that she is the greatest singer in the world and I think this may well be true since I cannot imagine there could be a greater.' The writer goes on to speak of her exquisite musical taste and striking appearance. The notice is quoted in Italian in Abbiati, III, p. 184.

consider mounting at least the scenes for *Aida*.* Magnani consented and was furnished with copies of the Cairo costume designs obtained via du Locle. For the ballet he secured the services of Hippolite-Georges Monplaisir, at the same time making sure that his ballet, *La Figlia di Cheope*, with music by Costantino Dell'Argine, scheduled for the same season, should bear no relation to the plot of *Aida* in the matter of either costumes or locale. A letter to Giulio Ricordi written in December bears witness to the composer's unceasing preoccupation with the visual side of the opera.

> I have seen the costume sketches. . . . They have much character and are beautiful; nevertheless I would make a few changes:
> 1. On those of the *little Moors*. Why that colour? I would like them completely black, and in that way we could also do away with the display of nudity.
> 2. *The insignia bearer*. I think you mean to say the flabellum bearer. I don't think that is the form of the *flabellum* but even if it were, I would modify it, and make it more theatrical by making it like the one which (if I remember rightly) they carry in Rome at papal ceremonies.
> 3. I don't know what effect the other *female chorister* will make; it is somewhat unusual for the theatre. Remember that at the Opera, which has the reputation of scrupulous consistency in the style of their costumes, this rule is never observed to the letter. . . .
> 4. I would also make Amneris's mourning dress sadder. I would make it plainer by removing several decorative ornaments that make it too cheerful for the occasion. . . .†

The orchestra drawn up for the season was a compromise between Verdi's own requirements and the recommendations of the Florence committee.‡ Verdi's only objection was to the use of the bombardon as the brass bass. 'I would like a *bass trombone* from the same family as the others, but if it is too tiring or too difficult to play get one of the usual ophicleides that go down to low B. In a word do what you like but not that devilish bombardon that doesn't blend with the rest.'§ For the choruses he urged the importance of a full bass sonority especially for the priests ('It might even,' he said, 'be necessary to engage six extra basses for the purpose') and a good, vigorous attack ('the general fault of all Italian choruses is to attack weakly or not at all').¶

It was possibly at Ricordi's suggestion that he agreed to write an overture for the Italian première and to dispatch a copy of it to Bottesini in Cairo if it should turn out to be effective.‖ If a first run-through revealed it as a *pasticcio* there was still the prelude. 'You will see,' he wrote to Ricordi, 'that at the end of the overture, when the trombone and double basses shout out the melody of the priests and the violins

---

* Letter to Magnani, 25.5.1871. Busch, p. 165.

† Letter to Giulio Ricordi, 13.12.1871. Busch, pp. 264–5.

‡ See letter from Giulio Ricordi, 4.9.1871. Busch, pp. 213–14: 16 1st violins, 14 2nd violins, 10 violas, 10 cellos, 11 double basses, double woodwind with piccolo, brass and percussion as previously listed. For the ballet an extra trumpet and one each of the woodwind instruments were available.

§ Letter to Giulio Ricordi, 25.12.1871. Busch, pp. 266–7. An interesting comment this, which raises the possibility that Verdi might have preferred the bass trombone to the bass tuba which is regularly used in modern performances of his operas.

¶ Letter to Giulio Ricordi, 10.12.1871. Busch, pp. 262–3.

‖ See letter to Bottesini, 13.1.1872. *Copialettere*, pp. 679–80.

and woodwind scream Amneris's jealousy, Aida's melody is played fortissimo by the trumpets. That moment is either a mess, or an effect. But it cannot be an effect if the trumpets don't have attack, sonority and brilliance.'* This shows how nearly Verdi was approaching the concept of Wagnerian leitmotiv without ever following up its structural implications.

In the event he was to be disappointed. As he wrote later to the conductor Emilio Usiglio, 'The orchestra was good, alert and responsive, and the piece could have reached port safely if it had been more solidly constructed; but the orchestra's excellence only revealed more clearly the pretentious tastelessness of this so-called overture.'† However, he did not destroy it. In 1913, the centenary of the composer's birth, the manuscript was shown to Toscanini who described it in more than one interview to the press but at the time respected Verdi's wish in not giving a performance of it. However, he must have copied it down, for on 30 March 1940 he performed it with the N.B.C. Symphony Orchestra in New York. Not to be outdone by a traitorous renegade Bernadino Molinari conducted the overture on 4 June of the same year before Benito Mussolini at the opening of a Verdi exhibition at the Villa Farnesini in Rome.‡ Of the two copies at present available one, the copyist's manuscript score, is in the possession of the Casa Ricordi and is presumably the one from which Faccio conducted the single rehearsal. The other is published by the firm of Suvini Zerboni in an edition by the pianist Pietro Spada, who claims to have taken down the music by ear from the pirate recording of Toscanini's performance of 1940. Spada's version, like Toscanini's, is set in E flat major, a tone higher than the original. Of the piece itself, more at the end of the chapter (see p. 255).

Apart from his own opera, Verdi was lavish with advice about the planning of the season as a whole. It began, as usual, on 26 December, with a revival of *La Forza del destino*, with Stolz as Leonora and Waldmann as a not very successful Preziosilla. If the box-office returns were poor he suggested replacing it by Donizetti's *Poliuto*, to be followed by the new *Macbeth* so as to allow time for *Aida* to be adequately rehearsed. His remark 'I'm always for *Poliuto*' is worth noting.§ No one was to be admitted to the dress rehearsal. If the conductor was Faccio the presiding authority was Verdi himself. Here one should perhaps mention the libretto annotated by him with stage directions. It was discovered by Gino Roncaglia, who reproduced its contents in an article 'Giuseppe Verdi. La regia e un libretto di *Aida* con annotazioni e schizzi del musicista'.¶ The annotations cover the first three acts only; and the libretto, which is dated 1872, is associated with a production in Parma that year. But since most of the instructions are carried over word for word into the production book published by Ricordi with the by-line 'come fu messa in scena al Teatro alla Scala, Milano' it is more likely that they were first jotted down during rehearsals for the Italian première, and merely served the composer as an aide-memoire for the Parma performance. They will be referred to together with other passages from the production

---

* Letter to Giulio Ricordi, 28.12.1871. Busch, p. 271. Curiously enough there is no point in the overture at which the three themes are combined vertically in the manner described.

† Letter to Usiglio, *c.* 26.1.1875. *Ibid.*, pp. 375–6. Draft published in *Carteggi Verdiani*, II, pp. 41–2.

‡ *Ibid.*, p. 250.

§ Letter to Giulio Ricordi, 26.12.1871. Abbiati, III, pp. 537–8.

¶ See G. Roncaglia, *Galleria Verdiana* (Milan, 1959), pp. 49–75; and Abbiati, III, pp. 548–52. The document itself and a set of production notes for the opera made by Franco Faccio have been reproduced as Documents X and XI respectively in Busch, pp. 500–58.

book in their respective contexts. For the present we may just note Ricordi's description of the leading characters.

> The King – about 45; majestic, imposing deportment.
>
> Amneris – 20; very lively; impetuous; susceptible.*
>
> Aida – Ethiopian slave, olive skin, dusky reddish complexion; 20; a loving nature; meekness and gentleness are her chief qualities.
>
> Radames – captain of the guards; 24; full of enthusiasm.
>
> Ramfis – Chief of the Priests; 50; unyielding, autocratic, cruel; majestic bearing.
>
> Amonasro – olive skin, dusky red complexion; 40; untamed warrior, deeply patriotic; violent, impetuous in character.

The Milan première on 8 February 1872 was to all appearances as successful as Verdi could have wished. Ticket prices, it was said, had been a matter of speculation on the stock exchange. In the event seats were shared, boxes crammed to bursting point. If applause was slow at first this was partly due to a sense of awe, partly to the rapt attention that was focused on every note. At the end of the second act Verdi's admirers presented him with a symbolic sceptre of gold studded with gems, and a parchment scroll. At once theatres throughout Italy and abroad applied to Ricordi for permission to perform the opera. But for the first two years Verdi himself withheld it from any theatre that in his view lacked the proper elements for its success. One reason was no doubt the curiously ambivalent attitude of the critics. Filippi, in *Perseveranza*, while paying tribute to the vitality of the score, recording dutifully the public enthusiasm and finally defending the composer against those like Ernest Reyer of the *Journal des Débats* who wished to teach him his job, launched an unexpected torpedo:

> No one who concerns himself seriously with art has failed to notice in *Aida* a strange duality, or rather an inner conflict. On the one hand there is a tendency to accept the operatic ideas, principles, tendencies and even the scientific procedures of the modern school (to deny that Verdi has been influenced by Gounod, Meyerbeer and Richard Wagner is like denying light to the sun); on the other hand the composer has retained a huge affection for his own past; as a result the transitions from one style to the other are curiously abrupt.
>
> In *Don Carlos* I found that this experiment brought about a very happy fusion; in *Aida* it seems to me to result in a certain disparity. . . .

What was new in the opera Filippi found too daring; what was traditional, too old-fashioned. The cabaletta of the duet between Aida and Radames in Act III he described as 'a cabaletta of the old stamp, based on a high, convulsive theme which Verdi has tried to dress up with harmonic tricks but without being able to make it please'.† This accusation, coming from so weighty a pen, seems to have impressed even the composer's friends. 'Let's leave in peace the cabaletta that you don't like,' Verdi wrote to Arrivabene. 'Certainly it isn't a masterpiece, but there are so many a

---

* 'Bear in mind that this Amneris has a bit of a devil in her, needs a powerful voice, is very emotional and very, very dramatic.' Letter to Giulio Ricordi, 24.5.1871. Busch, pp. 163–4.

† Review by Filippi in *Perseveranza*, 10.2.1872. Quoted in part in Alberti, pp. 138–43.

good deal worse. It's merely that it's now become the fashion to shout that we don't want to listen to cabalettas. That's just as much a mistake as when people wanted only cabalettas. They cry out against conventionality only to give up one sort for another. Oh, what utter sheep!'* But in the meantime he had already asked Giulio Ricordi for the score of 'that utterly horrible cabaletta which has brought me so much admonition, such wisdom and such benevolence from your critics' so that he could refurbish the instrumentation in time for the first revival, planned for Parma during that month.† Whether he did in fact rescore the music or whether, as in the case of 'Ah, la paterna mano' from *Macbeth*, he decided to leave it as it was we cannot tell since no variants have yet come to light. But whatever changes he may have made were insufficient to save the cabaletta from a similar criticism in a Neapolitan paper the following year.

It was probably for the Parma performance that he provided an alternative ending for the romanza 'Celeste Aida', designed for Giuseppe Capponi, the new Radames, who like most tenors found it impossible to sustain the high final B flat pianissimo.

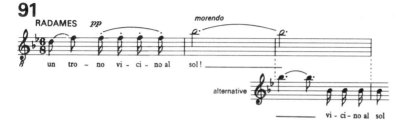

Later he was to recommend it via Usiglio to Adelina Patti's husband, Ernest Nicolini, who had asked (and been refused) Verdi's permission to lower the whole romanza by half a tone.‡ Richard Tucker, the tenor in Toscanini's recording, adopts the same solution, as do the French tenors Gustarello Affre and Paul Franz on their now unobtainable records of the romanza with piano accompaniment – a fact doubtless to be explained by the inclusion of this ending in the French score of 1880. Unfortunately it does not provoke applause; it also spoils the effect of the 'madrigalism' which matches the hero's vision of erecting a throne beside the sun by a soaring vocal line. The drop of an octave could easily imply the fate of Icarus.

The performance at Parma took place on 20 April with the same two female principals as at Milan, Fancelli and Pandolfini replaced by Capponi and Adriano Pantaleoni respectively, and Faccio's place taken by Giovanni Rossi. Once again Verdi was satisfied. 'Last night, *Aida* excellent. Good mise-en-scène and scenery, good orchestra, very good chorus. In other words, a rare success. So *amen.*'§ Such, however, was not everyone's opinion. A young man by the name of Prospero Bertani, living with his parents at Reggio Emilia and dependent on them for money, went to one of the later performances and found the music very inferior. So convinced was he that he had been conned that he wrote to the composer asking him to refund the price of his ticket, his train fare to Parma and his supper bill. Verdi sent the

---

* Letter to Arrivabene, 27.4.1872. Alberti, pp. 144–5.
† Letter to Giulio Ricordi, 6.4.1872. Abbiati, III, p. 570; Busch, pp. 294–5.
‡ See letter to Usiglio, 26.1.1875. Busch, pp. 375–6, drafted in *Carteggi Verdiani*, II, pp. 42–3.
§ Letter to De Sanctis, 21.4.1872. Busch, p. 297.

letter on to Giulio Ricordi with instructions to pay Bertani the first two items but not the third, since he could perfectly well have eaten at home before beginning his journey. In return Bertani must sign an undertaking never to attend one of Verdi's operas again. All this, together with the original letter, Ricordi was to publish in the *Gazzetta Musicale di Milano*. At once Bertani found himself the object of general derision; he even received anonymous letters threatening him with the fate of Colonel Anviti, the hated police chief of Parma who had been murdered by an enraged mob. At last he applied again to Verdi in a letter intended to be full of dignified reproach. He had wanted to see Meyerbeer's *L'Africaine* but dared not show his face in the theatre at Reggio after what had happened. He was being forced to live like a pariah. If he were to be lynched his ghost would haunt the composer who had brought this fate upon him. He was sure that Verdi would see the justice of his argument and send him a personal letter which he could publish and which would uphold his original judgement of the merits of *Aida*. Evidently Verdi thought the joke had gone far enough, and the letter remained unanswered.* The last Italian performance with which Verdi was personally associated was given in Naples in March 1873. It was only the fourth time the opera had been mounted anywhere – and it would have been the third if Verdi had not let himself be persuaded (against his better judgement, as he thought) to sanction a performance at Padua under Faccio's baton the previous June. Attended by every kind of contretemps at rehearsal – failure of the props to arrive from Milan, illness of principals, inefficient organization on the management's part – this too turned out a triumph. As he told Clarina Maffei:

> The success of *Aida*, as you know, was outspoken and decisive, untainted by *ifs* and *buts* and such unkind phrases as *Wagnerism*, the *Future*, the Art of Melody, etc., etc. The audience surrendered to its feelings and applauded. That's all!
>
> It applauded and even gave way to a hysteria that I don't approve of, but, after all, it expressed its sentiments without inhibitions and without arrière-pensée. And do you know why? Because there are no critics who behave like apostles, no crowd of composers who know about music only what they have studied in the *copybooks* of *Mendelssohn, Schumann, Wagner*, etc., no aristocratic dilettantes who are fashionably attracted to something they don't understand.†

Clearly critical reaction still worried him. At the beginning of that same year he had vented his feelings to Tito Ricordi: 'Stupid criticisms and even more stupid praise; not one noble idea; no one who wanted to point out my intentions; always absurdities and blunders and at the back of it all a certain sense of grudge as though I had committed a crime in writing *Aida* and getting it performed properly. No one indeed who was even willing to draw attention to the material fact of a performance and a production quite out of the ordinary. Nobody who has said to me, "Thank you, dog!"'‡ Certainly the intellectual climate of the 1870s was unfavourable to Verdi, for reasons which may become clear in the following chapter. But the theatres were clamouring for *Aida*, and Verdi had no further reason to withhold it from them, even if each performance caused him fresh annoyance.

* See 'Le vicende umoristiche di Prospero Bertani', in *Carteggi Verdiani*, IV, pp. 43–4.
† Letter to Clarina Maffei, 9.4.1873. Busch, p. 339.
‡ Letter to T. Ricordi, 3.1.1873. Abbiati, III, p. 553; Busch, p. 333.

Ever since the late 1840s he had campaigned for literal integrity in the performance of his works. He had asked Ricordi to include in all his contracts with the Italian theatres a clause which expressly forbade the omission or alteration of a single number whether by transposition or 'puntatura' under penalty of a fine. Only the ballets, if any, could be left out if the necessary resources were lacking. Of course it was an unrealistic notion. To this day conductors and managements reserve the right to cut according to their own judgement in the composer's absence, or even with his reluctant co-operation. Not even the name of his grandfather nor the almost religious atmosphere of Bayreuth prevented Wieland Wagner from cutting a sizeable passage from the third act of *Götterdämmerung* in his production of 1967. Imagine whether in an age when the rule of star singers, though no longer un-challenged, still persisted it was possible to enforce literalness of execution, in the way that Verdi wanted. But he could never see the matter in that light. To the aforementioned Usiglio who asked permission to lower 'Celeste Aida' he replied, 'It is not that I attach any importance to the romanza which you ask me to lower . . . but it is for me a matter of artistic principle not to allow an alteration.'* As reports came to his ears of pieces cut, shortened, or transposed, Verdi bombarded Ricordi and his agents with increasingly wrathful letters and telegrams. Typical are his reac-tions to a performance in Rome:

Nicolini has continually omitted his piece!!!
Aldighieri [a baritone] has omitted the third act duet at various times!!
Even the second act finale was cut one night!!!!!!!!!
As well as transposing the romanza down they changed several bars.
A mediocre Aida!!!
A *soprano* for Amneris!!
And what's more a conductor who takes the liberty of changing the tempi!!†

He would have liked to go to law. But there was no remedy. Ricordi could only shrug his shoulders helplessly and point to the box-office receipts by way of consola-tion.

By 1874 *Aida* had begun a triumphant career outside Italy, with prestigious perfor-mances in New York (under Muzio), Berlin and Vienna. But though his old friend Léon Escudier continually pestered him for permission to have the opera mounted in Paris and had even commissioned a French translation from Nuitter and du Locle, two years were to pass before Verdi gave his consent. *Aida* might be tailor-made for the Paris Opéra, now settled in its new (and present) home, the Palais Garnier; but the première of *Don Carlos* had left behind too many memories of slack perfor-mances, routine playing and a certain superior attitude to the foreigner for Verdi to risk repeating the experience. At first he even set his face against a performance in Italian at the Théâtre des Italiens, on the grounds that it lacked the necessary scenic resources.‡ However, in 1876 with the theatre under Escudier's personal manage-ment and Muzio at the helm he changed his mind. Indeed, having arrived in Paris in circumstances which have been described in the previous chapter, he agreed to help

---

* Letter to Usiglio, 26.1.1875. Busch, pp. 375–6.
† Letter to Giulio Ricordi, 25.3.1875. Busch, p. 380.
‡ Letter to Escudier, 7.3.1874. Busch, p. 364.

with the production. Needless to say difficulties occurred. ('What I said last night in a moment of anger I repeat now with my head perfectly clear: *I will not return to the theatre unless I am sure, materially sure, that the indecencies of the scenery in the fourth act have been put right.*')* But at least Verdi could count on a musical success and well filled houses. Even the criticisms irritated him less than usual. 'Here of course, as in Germany,' he wrote to the Ricordis, 'I have only learned to write well in the last three or four years; but at least they have not accused me of Wagnerism, as the Italian press so graciously did, especially in Milan.'†

Meanwhile, however, trouble had arisen over the French rights and in particular over Nuitter's translation, with which Verdi declared himself profoundly dissatisfied. After some correspondence with Tito Ricordi a fresh contract was arranged with Escudier and for the time being peace was restored, only to be shattered the following year when Escudier was unable to pay the composer the money due to him. His business was doing badly; and even the box-office receipts for *Aida* were unable to restore the fortunes of the Théâtre du Ventadour, which for the first time in thirty-five years was obliged to close its doors, leaving Muzio deprived of a job which he had held since 1870. So Escudier joined du Locle and De Sanctis among the defaulters for whom for the present Verdi had no further use; and a couple of stinging letters brought their friendship to an end. No economist, Verdi could hardly be expected to realize that the 1870s were a time of recession throughout Europe, when many a fortune was lost and its owner driven to suicide.

Nuitter revised his translation under Verdi's supervision; but still the composer withheld his score from the Opéra despite pressure from all sides.‡ The miracle was eventually accomplished by Auguste Vaucorbeil, who succeeded Halanzier as director in 1879. Formerly a répétiteur, he had made Verdi's acquaintance during the rehearsals for *Don Carlos*. In the autumn of 1879 he visited Verdi at S. Agata; and somehow carried the day. 'Seeing how far things had gone,' Verdi wrote to Muzio, 'I realized I could not refuse *Aida*, but *inter nos* I'm not very happy about it. Either I don't go to Paris and the opera is performed in a feeble, lifeless manner, without any effect, or else I do go and wear myself out body and soul.' A further disincentive was the presence of Escudier. 'After an association of more than thirty years between composer and publisher it is difficult to make a break. All the people who say now that he's a "fripon" would cry out against me if I changed my publisher. That's the way the world goes!'§ In the end Verdi went to Paris to supervise the production, which took place on 22 March 1880 with Gabrielle Krauss in the title role, Rosine Bloch (once destined for Eboli) as Amneris, Henri Sellier as Radames and Victor Maurel as Amonasro. He also used the occasion to put the finishing touch to the score. Vaucorbeil had asked with all due deference whether Verdi might see his way clear to enlarging the ballet music 'so that I could employ all my large ballet

---

* Letter to Escudier, 16.4.1876. Busch, p. 393.

† Letter to T. & Giulio Ricordi, 28.4.1876. Busch, p. 397.

‡ Among the many fascinating documents brought to light by Busch's monograph are three letters from Verdi to the French playwright Adolphe Dennery, giving cautious assent to the idea of collaborating with him on a piece for the Opéra, but always provided that he liked the subject and that he could withdraw the score if rehearsals should not go according to his wishes. See letters to Dennery, 19.6., 9 and 23.7.1878. Busch, pp. 411–12. The proposition went no further.

§ Letter to Muzio, 7.10.1879. *Copialettere*, pp. 312–13.

company, which would only add to the splendour of the spectacle'.* Verdi had replied that by adding anything else he would merely spoil the architecture of the whole.† None the less he was to find a solution that would satisfy Vaucorbeil without impairing in any way the balance of musical proportion. The original form of the six-minute ballet may be described as *a–B–a*. Verdi was to raise the height of what may be appropriately called the pyramid to *a–B–C–B–a*, so almost doubling the length of the music.‡

This time the success was unqualified from every point of view. Having agreed to conduct the first three performances himself (an unusual arrangement, this, at the Opéra), Verdi remained at the podium for a further two in order to satisfy the regular subscribers. Every appearance was a personal triumph, greeted with prolonged ovations. The press was unreservedly friendly and appreciative. Whether for this or for other reasons the Paris *Aida* of 1880 seems to have brought to an end the bleak despondency that hung over the 1870s. Verdi no longer felt out of touch with the times. His Indian summer of composition was already at hand.

That it should have taken the critics nearly ten years to bring *Aida* into focus is understandable.

In an age that believed in evolution and progress composers were expected to develop in a straight line, when more often they have proceeded by a chain of reactions. Hence disappointment and carping when Brahms's turbulent first symphony was followed by his more relaxed and apparently facile second. Verdi likewise has seemed to many of his admirers to have taken a backward step when after breaking the bonds of convention and closed forms in the last act of *Rigoletto* he returned to them in *Il Trovatore*. *Don Carlos* and *Aida* present a parallel case, the first an adventurous 'questing' work (to use Schiller's term), the second, as we have noted, a moment of the purest classicism in Verdi's output. If the merit of *Don Carlos* is that it carries grand opera into regions of which not even Meyerbeer dreamed, that of *Aida* is that it is the only grand opera from which you cannot remove a single bar.

Despite their very different natures a comparison of the two operas as to basic premises will prove illuminating, since so much of *Aida* seems like *Don Carlos* through the looking-glass. Both works are played against the background of a closed society: both take as their starting-point the same tragic conflict – that of private emotion versus public duty – but propound it very differently. Like the play from which it derives *Don Carlos* bears lingering traces of the values of 'Sturm und Drang' in which the claims of individual feeling threaten the disruption of society. Behind every confrontation (Philip–Posa, Philip–Inquisitor, Philip–Carlos, Carlos–Eboli) the menace of chaos looms. Yet our sympathies are weighted overwhelmingly on the side of private feeling – the loneliness of King Philip, the frustrated idealism of Posa, the agonized sensibility of Carlos, whose tragic stature is no greater than that of Marlowe's King Edward or Shakespeare's Richard II, and who scarcely measures up to the end devised for him either by Schiller or by Verdi and his librettists. In *Aida*, on the other hand, the two opposing forces are held in equilibrium, and the conflict arises only through special circumstances. At no point is society or government put at

---

* Letter from Vaucorbeil, 18.11.1879. Busch, p. 417.

† Letter to Vaucorbeil, 24.11.1879. *Ibid.*, pp. 471–8.

‡ This alteration was first noticed by Andrew Porter in 'Verdi's ballet music and *La Peregrina*', in *Atti del II° Congresso dell' I.S.V.*, pp. 355–67.

risk through the deliberate actions of the principals. To take two instances: when Eboli discovers Carlos's secret love for Elisabeth her jealous fury threatens the Queen's disgrace, a possible war with France, destruction all round; when Amneris has elicited Aida's confession of love for Radames, she can achieve nothing worse than the humiliation of her rival. Similarly when Eboli is overtaken by remorse she can accomplish a genuinely subversive action – the rescue of Carlos from prison. Amneris in a similar frame of mind can only bang her head, figuratively speaking, against a brick wall. Likewise with the respective heroes. Carlos's fate is forced upon him; Radames chooses his. By refusing Amneris's offer of help and by accepting his own guilt he reconciles both his love for Aida and his duty to the state which he serves. He would no more protest against his own immurement than Sophocles' Antigone. In contrast to *Don Carlos*, *Aida* is the stuff of classical tragedy. Certainly Verdi himself was in no doubt as to which opera he preferred. Asked that very question by Ferdinand Hiller, he replied 'in *Don Carlos* there is perhaps a passage (*frase*) here or a piece there which surpasses anything in *Aida*, but in *Aida* there's more bite and (if you'll forgive the word) more *theatricality*. Don't take theatricality in the vulgar sense. . . .'*

The balance of the plot finds a corresponding balance in the musical structure which for the Verdi of 1870 is surprisingly symmetrical, abounding in eight- and sixteen-bar periods with very little extension. On the other hand the richness of harmony and the swiftness and variety of harmonic movement are greater than ever before. The touches of exoticism are as new in Italian opera as they are in Verdi, being more than a matter of triangle, cymbals and bass drum. In 'invented' orientalism (if we discount *Russlan and Ludmilla*, which was unknown outside its native Russia for many years) it was France who led the way with such works as Félicien David's *Le Désert*, Saint-Saëns's *La Princesse jaune*, Bizet's *Les Pêcheurs de perles* and above all Meyerbeer's *L'Africaine*. Yet despite the enormous popularity of this last in the late 1860s Italian composers were slow to follow its example. The idiom of Pedrotti, Petrella and their contemporaries remains stolidly Euro-Italian. Only Gomes in *Il Guarany* and much later *Lo Schiavo* ventures occasionally to warble his native Brazilian woodnotes. Verdi himself was never opposed in principle to the use of folk tunes in an opera; indeed he sometimes asked his friends to hunt them out for him, even if he usually ended by rejecting what they provided. Here there was no question of seeking out an authentic Egyptian folk melody, which even if discovered would hardly have fitted into a modern opera. So Verdi invents his own Egyptian music, which owes surprisingly little to the commonplaces of French exoticism such as the pentatonic scale, and the augmented interval between ti and flattened lah. Rather it depends upon a subtle use of flattened re, a device that had occurred to him as early as *I Lombardi*, in the chorus of Saracen envoys. Here not only does it sound Egyptian and exotic where previously it had seemed merely provincial; it lends a delicate colour to the entire score, rather as the Swiss and Tyrolean elements colour *Guillaume Tell* and *La Wally* respectively. For his orchestral palette Verdi is content with three flutes as in *Don Carlos*, and at one point four old-fashioned, straight trumpets; otherwise his resources are those of the average Italian orchestra of the period with only two bassoons and no cornets.

* Letter to Hiller 7.1.1884 (unpublished) in the archives of the New York Philharmonic Society.

Finally in *Aida* Verdi succeeds for the first time in integrating a ballet within the operatic structure. To many at the time this seemed impossible for an Italian, as well as undesirable. After the first performance of *Don Carlos* at Turin a critic reproached the composer with having deferred to the outlandish custom of including a ballet; and of course he himself had no objection to the removal of *La Peregrina* in theatres that lacked the resources to do it justice. There is no question of removing the dances from *Aida*; they are far too firmly welded into their context. For the next two decades grand opera with a central ballet would be the norm in Italy. But of subsequent opera ballets only that of Ponchielli's *La Gioconda* would prove similarly indispensable.

PRELUDE

This is based on two ideas. The first (Ex. 92) with its suggestion of repressed yearning is associated throughout the opera with the heroine.

Only very gradually does it reveal the sensuousness of its harmonic implications. This is hinted at in the two-part writing of bars 4–6, where a momentary D minor harmony reveals itself not as a change of mode but as the first step in a chromatically rising pattern. The period ends with a turn towards the relative minor, whose melodic contour (*y*) forms an important element in the opera's 'tinta'. But for the moment B minor is withheld as a second period, based entirely on the figure (*x*), leads from B major to a melting cadence on F sharp. So far all has been muted four-part violins and violas, with a delicate touch of colour from low clarinet and flute in bars 13–15. Now the prelude's second theme, associated with the priests, sounds a more minatory note. Beginning in strong contrast to Ex. 92, moving down where the other had moved up, it ends here with its own variant of the figure (*y*), though it will not always do so. It is in fact the most flexible motif in the opera and will appear in more than one guise. (Ex. 93)

At first it seems no more than a faint cloud of unease on the horizon; and its initial extension as a canon at the octave is as free in its two-part writing as Ex. 92. But

93

stricter canonic entries at the third and fourth follow, and as the harmony and scoring fill out so the feeling of menace increases. The energy of the string writing would seem to recall Brahms's symphonies, though the first of these was five years in the future when *Aida* was written. Both these main themes, it will be noted, begin in different parts of the bar. In this way Verdi averts the threat of over-regularity which necessarily hangs over an opera so classically conceived; at the same time he can combine them vertically with perfect clarity over a dominant pedal in F sharp major at the prelude's central climax. Immediately afterwards woodwind and brass fall silent while further sequences of Ex. 92(x) on muted strings return to the area of D major by way of B flat. (Just as in Rigoletto's 'Pari siamo' the home key is reached by moving in the same direction round the circle of tonalities.) But barely has D major begun to be established than there is a brutal interruption, as though B minor, by-passed in the previous transition, were determined to assert its rights (it is of course the key of Ex. 93 and therefore, in this context, of the priests). During this new episode the music proceeds by contrapuntal sequences of Ex. 92(y), rising to another climax on the dominant of F sharp major, only to evaporate in a passage of meandering, diaphanous two-part writing high up on the violins. Once again the figure (y) is the prevailing idea but it is less and less closely worked. For the last time D major is reached but now from the opposite tonal direction, with a touch of the subdominant to prepare for the final cadence.

In the perfection of its craftsmanship this prelude far surpasses any instrumental piece that Verdi had composed up to this time. Atmospheric preludes beginning quietly with unison or two-part writing were rather fashionable at the time (doubtless yet another legacy from Meyerbeer's *L'Africaine*, which had taken Italy by storm in the late sixties); and the present piece, with its open and close on high ethereal strings flanking sonorous episodes in the middle and lower registers, may owe a further debt to the prelude to *Lohengrin*, especially if, as usually happened, its composition was left to the last moment. But the tonal scheme, resting as it does on the two poles of D major and F sharp with B minor as an important intervening area, is wholly Verdian. Other keys are touched upon in the course of transition – notably B flat major, significantly a major third's distance from both principal keys. But the key which would have figured prominently in any German composition of the period, namely the plain dominant (A major), never appears at all.

ACT I

*Scene 1: A hall in the royal palace in Memphis. To right and to left a colonnade with statues and flowering shrubs. At the back a large door through which can be seen the temples and palaces of Memphis, and the Pyramids.**

The curtain rises to disclose Radames and the High Priest Ramfis in conversation. Word has gone about that the Ethiopians are once more on the march and are

* *The colours should be very rich and bright, and the scene very well lit. Disp. scen., p. 7.*

threatening the city of Thebes. Has Isis been consulted, Radames wants to know? She has already named the man who is to command the Egyptian army, Ramfis answers, and adds meaningly, 'He is young and brave.' He then leaves to inform the King.*

This short scene belongs essentially to Ramfis; so it is not surprising to find it carried forward across a backcloth of orchestral counterpoint, since counterpoint is associated in this opera with priestly power. However, it is no theatrical 'trompe l'oreille' in the Rossinian manner, nor yet a learned gesture à la Meyerbeer designed to impress a snobbish public, but rather the unobtrusive polyphony of a Mozart or Schubert quartet. Cellos divided in the ratio of 3,3 and 4 launch a three-part canon at the octave.

94

Of course the canon is not maintained in full academic strictness; indeed twice the cellos break off to allow important phrases from the singers to come across with due emphasis. None the less all three instrumental voices have genuine independence and vitality; only for four bars does the middle voice become a mere holding part, enlivened by Beethoven-like syncopations.

Alone, Radames reflects on his hopes and dreams; if he is appointed commander he will fight and triumph for Aida's sake. His recitative ('Se quel guerrier io fossi') is punctuated by fanfares on trumpets and trombones where he imagines the battle, and the victory by soft string chords and a melting modulation when he thinks of his

* The production book lays down that Ramfis and Radames should be well to the front of stage, facing each other diagonally and neither looking directly towards the audience except in the case of an 'aside'. *All Ramfis' words are spoken with the intention of instilling joyous hopes into Radames, who will pay the very closest attention to what the High Priest says. Disp. scen., ibid.* Gatti's *Verdi nell'Im-magini* (p. 186) carries a sketch for this dialogue and the start of Radames' recitative ('Se quel guerrier io fossi') with minor alterations both to the text and to the voice-parts which bring them into line with the definitive version.

beloved. The two absorbing passions of his life are thus effectively planted. A long muted F in altissimo on first violins introduces the romanza 'Celeste Aida', the last in a long line of gentle tenor cantabili in 6/8 that began with 'Dal più remoto esilio' in *I Due Foscari*.

Gone, however, are the predictably regular periods, the interventions of sustaining wind at the points of modulation, the old bipartite structure with coda. The

design is French ternary, by now in general use in Italian opera. The main section
(Ex. 95a) parallels Amelia's 'Come in quest' ora bruna' from *Simon Boccanegra*, with
the same modulation in the second limb and a similar quickening of harmonic rhythm
towards the end. But it is all much simpler and more finely chiselled; while the final
bars are enhanced by a chain of melting 6/4/3 chords that set the cadence in still
higher relief (Ex. 95b).

96

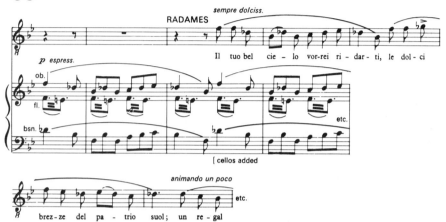

The episode (Ex. 96) does not wander, for unlike Amelia, Radames has no
mysterious tale to hint at; he is merely dwelling on Aida's 'native skies'. Yet the
melody is more than a mere minor-key counterpart to Ex. 95a with longer phrases
and a more regular bar-structure. It is one of several themes to be found in the minor
throughout the opera which begin with a descent from the fifth to the first degree;
and their connotation, as here, is always 'Ethiopia'.

The scoring of the romanza has a simple magic – the low-lying flute that persists
throughout with a variety of figuration, the plangent oboe and bassoon in the
episode and coda which seem to condole with the sadness of Aida's exile, the tracery
of three-part chords played by six muted violins over the reprise, with tenor reinforced by clarinet, bassoon and cellos; the tiny postlude of cellos and bassoons like
distant horn-calls. Only the somewhat frieze-like accompaniments of Ex. 95a and its
reprise hark back faintly to an earlier epoch. For once the flurry of flute arpeggios at
Radames' 'Un trono vicino al sol' do not betoken the approach of death. The hero's
vision of a throne beside the sun is very much of this world though viewed through
the rose-tinted spectacles of romantic love. Unfortunately, as noted earlier, most
tenors find it all but impossible to sustain a high B flat pianissimo when approached in
this way; hence Verdi's own faintly bathetic alternative (Ex. 91b).

The Princess Amneris enters to a gracious, ample melody, full of courtly triplets
(Ex. 97).

The instrumental colour – violins on the G string with horns, bassoons and lower
string accompanying – is well calculated to bring out the dark lights of the mezzo-
soprano voice. This is Amneris's theme just as Ex. 92 is Aida's, and will accompany
most of her appearances. But unlike Ex. 92 it is always instrumental with the vocal
line grafted onto it in what Basevi would call a 'parlante melodico'. Only here (if we

97

except the discarded overture) is it stated in full as a period of sixteen bars foreshortened to fifteen. Amneris is curious to know why Radames appears so eager and happy. Throughout their dialogue the orchestra expresses more of her feelings than does the vocal line, for she is a mistress of dissimulation. Radames tells her of the High Priest's hints. But still Amneris continues to probe. Has he no gentler aspirations, no other dreams or hopes, here in Memphis? (This to an expansive gesture from the full orchestra and a teasing acciaccatura on the oboe.)* Radames'

98

---

* See Vol. II, Ex. 20. *Amneris sings this recitative with great charm looking steadily at Radames; the words 'non hai tu in Menfi desideri . . . speranze?' should be spoken with marked meaning, smiling mischievously and moving slightly towards Radames. Disp. scen., p. 8.*

confused answer – 'Io? (Qual'inchiesta!)' – at once sparks off an allegro agitato whose main theme, though it is Radames who first sings to it, belongs unmistakably to Amneris. Verdi himself referred to it as 'Amneris's jealousy'; and Massimo Mila has aptly compared it to a caged beast pacing angrily up and down.* A simple suspension on horn and bassoon is sufficient to suggest an inward groan. (Ex. 98)

It is the old device of the double-aside, each singer looking away from the other even where at the end their voices join. Yet in a sense both are thinking identical thoughts. Radames is hoping desperately that Amneris has not discovered his secret – and so is Amneris. Again the regularity of the melody is striking: twenty-four bars with a twelve-bar coda.

Aida arrives heralded by Ex. 92, now on clarinet above tremolando strings. Before its eight bars have passed Amneris has noticed Radames start on seeing the slave girl; at once Ex. 98 starts to rampage softly in the orchestra with subtle alterations in harmony and scoring while Amneris exclaims, 'Aida . . . a me rivale forse saria costei?' But the final cadence breaks off into C major as she turns to Aida with an air of feigned tenderness. Her 'Vieni, o diletta, appressati' with its marching string crotchets and triplets on bassoon and cellos is strictly in the manner of Ex. 97; but violins, flute and oboe cannot suppress an involuntary twitching where Amneris brings herself to call Aida a sister.† What, she wants to know, is the secret sorrow which is making Aida weep? Aida answers in an agitated più mosso that she is upset at the thought of another war and more bloodshed. Again Amneris probes; has she no other cause for tears? Aida lowers her eyes and refuses to answer; whereupon Ex. 98 returns now in its original form ('trema . . . o rea schiava'), though with the vocal parts differently deployed. Then at the end of the twenty-four bar period comes the masterstroke. Aida, who has taken no part in the movement, pours on the tormented atmosphere the balm of lyrical melody in the major key ('Ah no, sulla mia patria') in the manner of Carlos in the terzetto 'De ma fureur' from that opera. It is her secret confession of love for Radames.

99

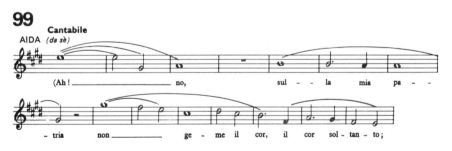

Here there is the additional contrast of pace, since Amneris and Radames are keeping up the rapid quaver motion of Ex. 98. But beneath the smooth surface of the high cantilena the sense of propulsion is enhanced by triplet 'flams' on the timpani (death figures, perhaps?) every second bar and towards the end of the period by a Tchaikovsky-like conflict of rhythm between quaver motion in the inner parts and minim triplets in Aida's line (compare the end of *The Queen of Spades*, Act III). In

* Mila, p. 256.

† *Aida comes forward again, with a bow; not without having first cast a loving glance at Radames who tries to hide his feelings. Disp. scen.*, p. 8.

1870 there is no longer any need for the movement to end in the major key; so a full coda follows based on Ex. 98 in the original E minor with rising chromatic lines and syncopations aggravating the mood of stress. Once again Verdi has combined dramatic truth and excitement with a musical structure of classical regularity – in this case the classical rondo.

Fanfares begin to mount on trumpets, horns and trombones as the King enters preceded by his guards and followed by Ramfis and by 'Ministers, Priests, Captains, etc., etc.'. Note here the effective role of the strings in building up the sense of consequence and solemnity with long, resolving unison trills. A powerful tutti flourish of double-dotted chords brings the procession to a halt; in a measured pronouncement accompanied only by the tramp of pizzicati cellos and basses ('Alta cagion v'aduna') the King gives warning of a national emergency and asks for the messenger to be summoned. The messenger enters, bows low before the King and tells of the Ethiopian invasion led by the fierce warrior Amonasro.* 'The King!' cry the ministers, priests and captains, divided into a double male chorus like that of di Luna's household in *Il Trovatore*. 'My father!' exclaims Aida, aside. The messenger's recitative ('Il sacro suol d'Egitto') is conventional enough but the orchestral motif which precedes and punctuates it has an air of sinister fatality as though Verdi and the messenger himself were aware of that ancient Egyptian custom mentioned in Shaw's *Caesar and Cleopatra* whereby the bearer of bad news was himself executed.

But that is unlikely. A comparison with Ex. 95b shows that it is essentially another signpost for Ethiopia. All present react with cries of 'Guerra!' over an orchestra which seethes like an immense cauldron.

In the rising scale of A minor formed by the cries of 'Guerra!' the B is flattened, so producing that Ancient Egyptian scale of Verdi's imagination; it will be very prominent in the next scene. Amid the shouting and the enthusiasm the King announces

---

* As soon as the trumpets begin the priests should enter two by two from the door at the back of stage and, crossing diagonally, should take up a position on left. (Diagram.) Immediately afterwards twelve guards enter backstage right and range themselves on either side of the door; after them the King, then Ramfis, then the King's Officer, then Ministers, captains, etc. etc. A diagram shows the courtiers and officials in three groups ranged from backstage centre to front stage right, with the principals forming a semi-circle in the order (L. to R.) Ramfis, Amneris, Officer, King, Aida, Radames. The King turns to the officer, saying to him 'Let the messenger come forward.' The officer, bowing, exits left and returns at once followed by the Messenger. . . . The latter approaches the King and salutes him, bowing low and carrying his right hand to his forehead. The messenger should carry a bow in his hand and a quiver at his side. Disp. scen., pp. 9–10.

that Radames has been chosen to command the Egyptian forces. He will straightaway be consecrated to victory in the temple of Vulcan.*

Before leaving all join in a battle hymn led by the King ('Su! del Nilo al sacro lido', Ex. 101).

To Verdi himself this melody smacked of the 'Marseillaise'. To most English listeners it is more likely to connote the Victorian bourgeois heroics of John Farmer's 'Forty Years On', italianized by the occasional martial bang on the last off-beat of the phrase. Yet its rather obvious uplift is given a certain distinction by the vigorous bass line and harmonies. The first period is answered by another one of equal length sung by Ramfis ('Gloria ai Numi, ognun rammenti') but modulating more widely until by an unexpected path it reaches a full cadence in the dominant, so launching the full chorus on a reprise of Ex. 101 with a busier accompaniment and counter-melodies from Ramfis and the King. Next Radames takes up the strain in C major ('Sacro fremito di gloria') beneath an anguished descant from Aida ('Per chi piango?') fraught with syncopations. It is like the agony of Elisabeth and Carlos during the festal chorus 'O chants de fête'; but here there is an additional subtlety. Take Aida's line by itself and it will immediately be found to suggest not C major but A minor. In other words there is an implied bitonality though no harmonic clash. During this verse Amneris has briefly left the stage. She now returns with a banner in time to take over the modulating strophe as she places her offering in Radames' hand ('Di mia man ricevi, o duce'); but by starting it a tone higher in relation to the newly established key she brings the final cadence into A major where previously it had been in E. Thereupon Ex. 101 is thundered forth by all present to sweeping scales from the violins, so rounding off the design in the manner of a sonata rondo. For once nationalist fervour is not expressed in a unison chorus. Only the King, Ramfis and the ministers and captains sing the tune: the priests double the bass, while each of the remaining principals, including the Messenger, contributes a separate counter-melody to the richly woven tapestry of sound. A minor returns together with cries of 'Guerra!' as before, this time driven home by a more melodic but no less fierce cadential phrase ('Guerra, guerra, sterminio'), during which the chorus are required

---

* Throughout the production book the stage directions for chorus frequently verge on the ludicrous. Thus when the King indicates Radames as supreme commander: *all are astonished: the various sections of the chorus cry out the word 'Radames!' and repeat it quietly but pronouncing it very clearly. While they say 'Radames' some of those who make up the various groups turn to each other passing on the news from one to another; others will point out Radames with their hands. Disp. scen.*, p. 11. Such a general reaction might do for the appearance of Lohengrin and the swan but hardly for a pronouncement (which everyone has heard).

to take three paces forward and raise their right arms in a salute.* The coda prolongs itself in the major key with trumpet fanfares; then amid the silence of an interrupted cadence Amneris expresses the thought that is uppermost in all their minds: 'Return victorious' ('Ritorna vincitor', Ex. 102a). Everyone else takes up the cry (Ex. 102b), and to the sound of Ex. 101 the stage empties, leaving Aida alone to ponder the implications of Radames' victory (Ex. 102c).

It is the perfection of a device intended to link two separate numbers that Verdi had first used in *Stiffelio* ('Tosto io riverrò' . . . 'Tosto ei disse'). Here, however, it is not confined to the repetition or carrying over of one word ('tosto'), but of the whole thought, which is stated three times with different harmonic and melodic inflections according to the speakers. With Amneris it seems to contain a faint question-mark; with the chorus it becomes an emphatic assertion. With Aida it is almost a cry of terror. Not only that. This simple scalic gesture, in itself a commonplace of Italian opera, especially useful for resuming a musical discourse after a full stop for applause† assumes unexpected prominence in *Aida*, recurring at several dramatic moments and so forming an important ingredient in the opera's 'tinta'.

The conflict of love and patriotism expressed in Aida's famous scena e romanza ('Ritorna vincitor') is common enough, but Verdi's treatment of it is entirely new, especially in the context of an exit aria. He conducts the inner dialogue in the manner of a duet, as a sequence of short contrasting movements, each of which becomes more 'formed' than its predecessor. The first is an eminently orthodox recitative

---

* *Disp. scen.*, p. 12.

† Walker draws attention to Mercadante's use of it in *La Vestale*. See *Grove's Dictionary of Music and Musicians*, 5th Edition, V, p. 713.

strengthened by repetition of the brusque figure that first occurs after the words 'empia parola', and by a short chromatic figure on oboe, basson and cellos repeated thrice, each time a semitone higher where Aida first mentions her slain brothers. Thence the scene proceeds as follows:

A. *Più mosso, E minor 4/4 ('L'insana parola, o Numi, sperdete', Ex. 103) 16 bars extended to twenty through an interrupted cadence*

Here remorse and patriotism have the upper hand. The first phrase and a half anticipate that doubling of vocal line and bass that is to become a hall-mark of Puccini's style.

103

B. *Andante poco più lento della prima volta, F major – A flat major–minor 4/4, 16 bars shortened to 15 then extended to 19 through an instrumental transition*

Ex. 92 given out by the gentle clarinet over tremolando lower strings indicates that Radames has taken possession of her thoughts; and indeed it is the idea of Radames' death which prompts the modulation to A flat in which the romanza finally settles. The four-bar transition on violins, first in unison, then in two parts, makes discreet play with augmented intervals.

C. *Allegro giusto poco agitato, A flat minor 4/4 ('I sacri nomi di padre', Ex. 104), 16 bars extended to 17*

According to the text Aida is now evenly balanced between the two claims upon her. But the contour of the melody, the tonality and the plangent oboe tone suggest the pull of her native Ethiopia.

D. *Cantabile, A flat major 4/4 ('Numi, pietà, Ex. 105), 32 bars extended to 34 and followed by an 8-bar coda*

This pathetic cry for guidance is expressed in one of those heartfelt transfiguring melodies of which Verdi never lost the secret. Its effect is enhanced by what amounts to rhythmic augmentation, since the section is roughly twice the length of its three predecessors. As in the terzetto, slow triplets heighten the lyrical expression; and, most remarkably, the voice is never once doubled by a wind instrument, even at its

104

105

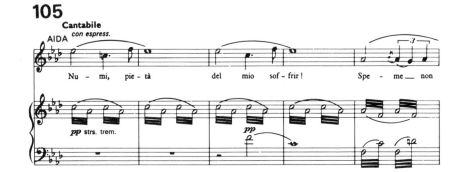

106

climax. The accompaniment is confined to tremolando strings and for three bars a roll on the timpani. Never had Verdi placed such faith in the natural resources of the soprano voice. A quotation from the coda (Ex. 106) will serve to show the bud from which sprang the romanza in Act III with its alterations of major and minor mode.

Both carry the Ethiopian 'tinta'. Clarinets, bassoon and cellos add a delicate postlude. Nothing could be further removed from the conventional noisy scene-ending which Verdi himself had once favoured and which was still the rule after an exit aria in the contemporary works of Petrella and Cagnoni.*

> *Scene 2: Inside the temple of Vulcan at Memphis. A mysterious light descends from above. A long receding row of columns loses itself in the darkness. Statues of various divinities; in the middle of the stage, on a platform covered with carpets, rises the altar, surmounted with sacred emblems. From golden tripods there rises the smoke of incense.†*

Described by Verdi as 'Grande Scena della Consacrazione e finale 1°', this scene has a purely ceremonial character – a solemn, awe-inspiring interlude in the development of the drama. The opening themes and ideas repeat themselves in the manner of an incantation: first the sound of distant harps; then the voice of the High Priestess behind the scenes invoking the God with a wailing melody that returns obsessively to the same E flat before sinking to the fourth below on a cushion of supporting female choristers ('Possente, possente Ftha', Ex. 107a). The 3-bar grace note, the diminished thirds and augmented seconds, the curling arabesques, all colour the music with a sense of strange Eastern ritual. By contrast the answering litany of

---

* At the word 'Pietà' 8 bars from the end Aida should move with painful effort, broken by grief, towards back of stage left, so that the last word 'soffrir' should find her in the wings. Disp. scen., p. 13. During this scene the stage director is asked to make arrangements for the chorus to change into priestly robes as quickly as possible since *any delay in the changing of the scene would spoil the entire musical effect.*

† The production book adds a huge statue of Vulcan in gold, various flights of steps and a glimpse of bright blue sky in the background. For theatres that lack the facility of steam there are directions for simulating smoke by pouring water on lime. *At the rise of the curtain Ramfis is on the left, standing on the altar steps holding Radames' sword; all the priests are ranged in double rows on either side of the altar* [diagram shows them forming an arc facing inwards]. *Round the golden tripods and on the steps leading up to each stand the ballerinas forming four pyramidal groups; they hold wide fans of white feathers. Offstage left two harps accompany the unseen female chorus. The solos of the invocation will be sung by the prima donna soprano* [i.e. Aida]. *The priests should hold their hands to their breasts but not crossed* [diagram]. *During the triple invocation to the god the most complete stillness is ABSOLUTELY ESSENTIAL. Disp. scen.,* pp. 14–16. Termouthis is no longer mentioned, presumably because her music is sung by Aida offstage.

the priests on stage (Ex. 107b) 'Tu che dal nulla hai tratto') is in orthodox, liturgical style apart from the 6/4 inversion in the second bar, which produces a 'mirror' movement between melody and bass. Here Ramfis, though a basso profondo, doubles the second tenors, presumably so that his voice should stand out with the prominence due to his rank.

107a

107b

The whole passage is a brilliantly imaginative variation on the traditional minor–major pattern. The melody of Ex. 107a is couched in an invented Phrygian mode in E flat with an augmented interval between the second and third degree; but because the harmonies are sited squarely within the area of A flat minor, it marries perfectly with the plain A flat major of the priests' chant, while at the same time surrounding it with a faint aura of ambiguity. Ex. 107b ends with what appears to be an imperfect cadence, which takes on a plagal quality in retrospect. Puccini achieves a somewhat similar result in the alternating sections of 'Nessun dorma' in *Turandot*.

The two melodies are stated three times to different but always mystical words ('Divinity who art the child and the father of thy spirit . . . fire uncreated and everlasting . . . life of the universe') and always ending with the refrain 'We call upon thee'. For once the repetitions are quite unvaried; since the addition of new elements would only spoil the effect of timeless stillness. Then the ballerinas lay down their fans and break into a slow dance set in the same Phrygian mode as before but with harmonies that remain unequivocally in E flat major, without any subdominant pull (Ex. 108a). It is here that the three flutes first come into their own. The second, longer section of the period contains an idea which, together with Ex. 107a, will play an important part in the last scene of all (Ex. 108b).

108a

108b

There is a C minor episode with deft modal touches in the French manner during which Radames is escorted in by four priestesses;* and the main theme is resumed, priestesses and priests joining in at the end with fragments of Ex. 107a and b respectively.

Ramfis, now an epitome of all the priests, prophets and hermits who have peopled Verdi's operas to date, steps forward, reminds Radames that he holds their country's fate in his hands and prays that his sword may bring death and destruction to his foes. The first phrase ('Mortal diletto ai Numi') is based on a minor-key arpeggio over tremolando strings; the second ('Il sacro brando dal Dio temprato') is backed by that time-honoured priestly combination of bassoons, trombones and brass bass. The cry is taken up more fiercely by the other priests with a still mightier emphasis on the word 'morte' (sung to a high F) – a fine example, this, of the 'parola scenica'. Then Ramfis leads the concertato with an invocation to the god ('Nume, custode e vindice'). Never have the three trombones sounded more solemn than here, despite their shameless parallel fifths in the fourth bar. (Ex. 109)

Note the figure (γ) which connects this theme with Exs. 92 and 93 in the prelude. Radames replies with the same melody in C minor over pizzicato strings and sustaining wind, while Ramfis contributes a counter-melody. The priests weigh in with

---

* *He proceeds to the altar, bows before it while the four priestesses hold a silver veil spread out above his head. Disp. scen.,* p. 16.

imitative entries, which vary the surface of what remains an essentially homophonic texture. But with each 'Nume, custode e vindice' the music swells, finally bursting into a restatement of Ex. 109 by everyone, fortissimo. But again the facile solution of a unison chorus is avoided, though the elaborate orchestral backcloth with its alternating scales in contrary motion might have justified it; instead chorus tenors provide a descant and Radames a counter-tune. The last cadence is interrupted by Ex. 107a chanted by the invisible priestesses in octaves, and the two ideas become yoked in a succession of dynamic contrasts, all the more effective in that while Ex. 107a is long and static, Ex. 109 is short and developing. Twice Radames' voice can be heard soaring to an A flat to the words 'Tu che dal nulla hai tratto il mondo'. There is a vigorous codetta in which the scale motif is shortened and tightened; then the same two themes are once more juxtaposed but with Ex. 109 now sung pianissimo. The music subsides to a pianissimo drumroll; then 'Immenso Ftha!' cry Ramfis and Radames in thirds, echoed by full chorus and orchestra in a blaze of orchestral sound which brings down the curtain.*

ACT II

Scene 1: A hall in the apartments of Amneris. Amneris, seated in a chair, is surrounded by women who are dressing her in preparation for the triumphal feast. Scented vapours arise from cups of gold and bronze. Young Moorish slaves dance and wave feather fans.†

The harp chords which open this scene with a steady crotchet tramp have a bardic ring, emphasized by the occasional notes for solo trumpet.

---

* It is difficult to show the same enthusiasm over the visual side as detailed in the production book, where the final tableau is set up as follows. *The priests have ranged themselves in two double rows extending diagonally from either side of the altar to front of stage left and right respectively, allowing a view of the ballerinas who are now grouped in front of the altar. During the pianissimo repetitions of 'Noi t'invochiam' the priests are required to bow very low. Ramfis and Radames who are standing mid-stage facing the altar turn to the audience and take four steps forward as they cry, 'Immenso Ftha!' At that precise moment all the priests straighten themselves swiftly, turn to face the audience and raising their arms above their heads reply, 'Immenso Ftha!' At the same time the ballerinas raise their fans so as to form a single huge fan. Disp. scen.,* p. 20. A curtain eminently worthy of the Folies Bergère.

† The production book prescribes *Light wooden columns and a wooden ceiling inlaid with gold, the walls formed by rich tapestries. All the chairs should be very high and accessible only by a stool. Amneris is to be dressed by four ballerinas. Disp. scen.,* pp. 22–3.

110

Mood and style hint at old unhappy far-off things; but the battles are recent; for it is of Radames' triumphant homecoming that the slaves are about to sing. If there are links here with the chorus of Bards from *La Donna del lago* (mentioned with approval by Verdi in a letter to Arrivabene)* as well as with the final scene of the revised *Macbeth*, the immediate ancestor of the chorus which follows is the 'Choeur des femmes', known to Verdi as 'Scorre legger sull'onde placide' from the third act of Meyerbeer's *L'Africaine*, as the following quotation may serve to show.

111a

Meyerbeer : L'AFRICAINE

111b

* Letter to Arrivabene, 25.7.1871. Alberti, pp. 132–3.

At the words 'shining like a sun' there is a graphic gesture from the full orchestra, followed by a pause and the last phrase of the melody. Voluptuous arpeggios on the harp and the occasional chromatic sigh mark the central idea of what is basically a 'couplet', where the hero is invited to receive the rewards of valour (Ex. 112a) – note here the upward scale of 'Ritorna vincitor'. Finally Amneris adds her own appeal (Ex. 112b) – a radiant, transfiguring refrain, beautifully balancing Ex. 112a with its downward motion. Subtle chromatic inflexions give a sense of painful longing.

112a

As with all couplets the design is repeated to a different set of verses. This time the tutti explosion illustrates the breath of wind which causes the foe to scatter. Hard on the heels of Amneris's final cadence comes a delightful Dance of the Little Moorish Slaves, to be performed by ballerinas – 'very lively and rather grotesque'.* As the music is Moorish, not Egyptian, all the usual nineteenth-century exotic devices are laid under contribution – flattened leading notes, 'Turkish' scoring with piccolo, side drum and cymbals, the progression by semitones from soh to la and back again in an inner part, so beloved of the Russians in their Oriental moods, a middle episode in C major where one would have expected B flat, a drone bass and an abundance of grace notes. The opening has a grotesquerie worthy of Tchaikovsky's Little Swans (Ex. 113).

* *Disp. scen.*, p. 23.

112b

Tchaikovsky again comes to mind with the scoring and harmonization of the C major episode. Other happy touches include its answering melody that proceeds entirely in harmonized sixths and the transference of Ex. 113 to the bass by way of coda.

The scene is rounded off by a partial reprise of the opening chorus, beginning with Ex. 112a. Amneris, her toilet now completed, descends from her chair and comes forward to sing her refrain supported by sustained chords from the chorus. As if by way of a postlude the Aida theme (Ex. 92) steals in on bassoon, violas and cellos as the heroine herself is seen approaching with Amneris's crown.* The princess dismisses her handmaidens and prepares to find out by a few well aimed questions and a little deception whether her suspicions are justified. A high solo horn projected from a diminished seventh chord conveys the thought that torments her; and her next

113

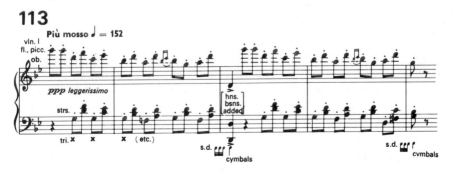

* *. . . holding in her hand Amneris's crown which she lays upon the table. Disp. scen.*, p. 24. There at least is a useful hint for producers who too often require Aida to carry the crown on a salver. As Amneris is frequently shown reclining on a couch, Aida seems to be bringing her mistress breakfast in bed.

phrase ('Il mistero fatal si squarci al fine') carries the appropriate tempo heading *allegro risoluto*. With this the music moves into the grand duet ('Fu la sorte dell'armi a' tuoi funesta').

As Philip Gossett has pointed out* the text is laid out as for a scena and three-movement duet, with the moment of drama situated before instead of after the central cantabile. But this proves to be no more than the starting-point for a scheme of rare originality. There is nothing in the setting that suggests recitative. The music proceeds straightaway in a steady rhythm, the irregular phrase-lengths and watchful pauses illustrating Amneris's insidious probings. The opening is typical of the false suavity with which the princess disguises her jealousy. The vocal line recalls 'Ritorna vincitor'; but the harmonies have a sense of effort about them while the death figure on the timpani is like a barely suppressed growl.

Aida replies tensely and in faster time ('Felice esser poss'io'). How can she be happy, knowing the fate of her people and of her own family? Amneris tells her that time will heal her wounds ('Sanerà il tempo') – here the text breaks into lyrical metre – and more than time, she adds, the God of Love.

Aida reacts immediately with the definitive exposition of Ex. 92 ('Amore, amore – gaudio tormento') for which all earlier appearances prepare; it is a vocal period of sixteen bars abridged to fourteen and a half with which great play was to have been made in the overture. Although sung as an aside with Amneris merely contributing the occasional 'pertichino' of observation, it is the central affirmation of the first, 'kinetic' part of the duet and, as such, establishes its tonal base of F major. (Ex. 115)

Amneris resumes her questioning with a leisurely conversational theme which recalls the coaxings of another mezzo-soprano, Eboli, through a similar insistence on an E flat over dominant harmony in B flat major. Amneris, being subtler than her predecessor, allows the orchestra to hint at her thoughts before she utters them. (Ex. 116) Why, Amneris asks, will Aida not confide in her? Could it be that an Egyptian soldier is occupying her thoughts? (Here the course of Ex. 116 is briefly diverted into four bars of G minor, with a delicate accompaniment of clarinets and bassoon.) Without waiting for an answer she adds casually (Ex. 116 again) that not all the army suffered the fate of its general. At once the bland surface of the music is shattered as Aida's world collapses about her, and she pours out her grief in a flurrying F minor

* Gossett, *op. cit.*, p. 321.

agitato. Still Amneris persists in feigned wonder. But she cannot keep up the pretence for long. A huge offbeat tutti halts the restless bass line and wrenches the tonality from its moorings ('Trema! In cor ti lessi'), as she now closes in for the kill. 'Look me in the eyes. . . . I lied to you. . . . Radames is alive.' For five bars she holds the musical argument suspended. Then her 'Radames vive!' rings out unaccompanied like the naked truth that it is; Aida responds with a cry of relief, falling to her knees to a 6/4 chord in F major. But neither mood nor tonality is permitted to last for long. Amneris sets out the position with brutal clarity. 'You love him; so do I. . . . I, a Pharaoh's daughter, am your rival.' To her accusation, marked *con massimo furore*, clarinets give a ferociously sarcastic smile.

117

AMNERIS
(nel massimo furore)

Si... tu l'a - - - mi... Ma l'amo an - ch'io... in-tendi tu?... son

tua ri - va - le... fi - - - glia de' Fa - ra - o - ni...

For a moment Aida shows a flash of spirit. She too is of royal blood – or so she is about to say; then she recollects her situation, falls at Amneris's feet and begs for mercy; at which point the duet, which had dissolved into rhythmic prose, now coalesces into a formal 'dissimilar' cantabile. Both singers have taken up fixed positions. Aida makes no attempt to deny her love for Radames, but entreats her mistress to show her pity and understanding. Amneris is determined to trample her into the dust. Each has her own orchestral palette; Aida's is made up of woodwind strands with low flute and a pattern of bassoon semiquavers that forecasts the 'Ingemisco' of the Requiem (Ex. 118a); Amneris's seething fury is expressed in tremolando strings and rolling timpani and a snarling descent to the contralto area (Ex. 118b).

Distant fanfares, then 'Su! del Nilo' (Ex. 101) played by stage band and sung by full chorus in unison, announce the returning army. Originally this was to have set the tone of a final cabaletta, composed of two independent themes in the same martial rhythm ('Alla pompa che s'appresta'). The attitude of the two women has not

118a

118b

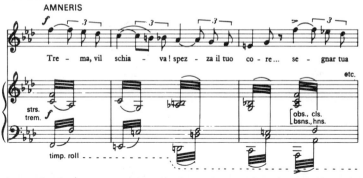

changed. Amneris is merely going to carry out her threat of humiliating her rival; Aida vainly offers to stifle her love for Radames. The contrast was to have been pointed thus (Ex. 119a and b):

119a

119b

120a

120b

Shortly before the first performance Verdi hit on a better solution. Instead of Ex. 119a he gave Amneris a counter-melody to Ex. 101 (see Ex. 120a), while setting Aida's reply in a faster, more agitated rhythm which effectively dissociates her from the march itself (Ex. 120b).

As in the grand duet from Act III of *Les Vêpres Siciliennes* all the forms characteristic of a cabaletta have been removed and doubtless for the same reason. There has been no change of attitude such as would justify this time-honoured 'clinching' design. For the closing of the scene Verdi had a better idea still – a reprise of 'Numi, pietà', shortened and with deliciously varied harmony, as Aida drags herself painfully in her mistress's wake.

> *Scene 2: (Grand finale secondo). One of the city gates of Thebes. In the foreground a group of palms. On the right the temple of Ammon. On the left a throne surmounted by a purple canopy. In the background a triumphal arch. The stage is crowded with people.**

This, the grand centrepiece of the opera, is made up of several of the same elements as the third act of *Don Carlos* – a celebration, a procession, a dramatic surprise, a concertato with contrasting pleas for mercy and punishment and a reprise replacing the traditional stretta; but the material is in general more distinguished and the structure far more economical with each new idea welded more firmly into its predecessor.

A volley of trumpet calls from the stage band is answered by the orchestra mezzoforte with an expectant march-like theme through which sporadic fanfares persist for a few bars. Then the music swells and quickens to arrive at a drawn-out emphatic cadence on the dominant. This introduction not only launches the ten-bar chorus ('Gloria all'Egitto', Ex. 121a) but also serves as an extension of it with choral participation. This so-called 'hymn', which the Khedive is said to have wished to adopt as the Egyptian national anthem (mistakenly, since it is far too short for the purpose), is accompanied by the stage band with the orchestra supplying those fortissimo punctuations on the empty off-beats which make many a sensitive spirit wince. Yet as Italian banda music goes it is good of its type, being plain and hard-hitting and unencumbered by those lyrical appoggiaturas that cheapen the march in *Don Carlos*. It shows too that even as late as 1871 Donizetti could still act as a germinating influence on the composer (Ex. 121b).

The printed score, Verdi's annotations and the production book all give a slightly different account of the opening stage manoeuvres. Where the score seems to indicate that the whole populace is on stage from the start, Verdi noted that they should enter gradually, followed by priests, ministers and the King himself, all of whom should be in position by the start of Ex. 121a, when Amneris should make her entrance. This suggests that as in the finale to Act II of *La Traviata* he underestimated

---

* *The backcloth shows the Pyramids in the far distance with the huge avenue of sphinxes leading up to them. To the right various temples and grandiose buildings; to the left palm trees. The principal backdrop centre represents one of the great gates of Thebes with huge columns extending to the wings either side. To these are attached bronze poles with flags. To the left the backdrop should be cut so as to allow a view of the rear backcloth; to the right it should reach only to the height of 4 metres, so as to represent a clump of palm-trees behind which those who are to perform the march can take up their positions. Front of stage right, a platform for the stage band. Mid-stage left, a semi-circular dais with three steps: two chairs, and three stools richly appointed in purple and gold with canopy to match; the dais covered by a rich, purple carpet. The scene should be very brightly illuminated, especially backstage. Disp. scen., pp. 7–8.*

Donizetti : POLIUTO

the time it takes to fill a stage. Far more realistic are the directions of the production book, according to which part of the populace is already on stage when the curtain rises; the rest filter in during the crescendo in time to sing 'Gloria all'Egitto'. During the opening statement Ramfis and the priests file in two by two and take up a position by the throne. When the introduction is resumed with cries of 'Gloria!' to powerful second-beat thrusts, enter the King followed by his suite. By the time the dominant cadence has been reached he will be seated on his throne.*

The chorus now divides into two, men and women each having a melody of their own – a scheme which faintly recalls that of the Wartburg choruses in *Tannhäuser* (an opera which at the time Verdi could not have seen performed though he certainly possessed the vocal score). But here the differentiation is much greater. The cadence of the preceding section is softened to prepare for the four-square lyrical tune ('S'intrecci il loto al lauro', Ex. 122a) to which the women call for a wreath of laurel and lotus for the victors. This is the cue for Amneris's entrance with suite.†

122a

---

* *The King should cross the stage and mount his throne, seating himself on the left: 4 ministers to the left, 4 to the right ranging from ground level to steps (diagram). Two fanbearers behind the throne. The eight ministers should be dancers. Disp scen., p. 29.*

† *Amneris with her suite should enter from the right slightly further to the front of stage than the King. She crosses the stage and mounts the throne assisted by the King who will rise and hand her to her throne. Disp. scen., p. 29. Her suite is to consist of Aida, 4 ladies, 2 pages and the little Moorish slaves. One of the pages carries a crown of lotus leaves.*

122b

The chorus of priests reply with Ex. 122b which is nothing more than a variant of Ex. 93 ('Della vittoria agli arbitri supremi'), its contours now confined to a stepwise motion. As usual it is developed in a tight canon: and though the priests are at present merely counselling the people to give thanks to the gods for victory their key of A flat minor in relation to the women's E flat major strikes a faintly ominous note. In due course, however, it works itself out into a triumphal E flat with the cadential phrase that ended Ex. 122a.

The first column of troops now enters at last, preceded by their trumpeters, and parade before the King to what is the most celebrated tune in the opera:

123

Its memorability is due to the masterly use of a few notes – soh, doh, re, mi with an auxiliary fa and the addition of an octave soh in the episode period. It is sufficiently unusual to suggest a distant era (note the three-bar structure of the main period); yet the melodic germ from which it springs can be traced as far back as the first buffo duet in *Un Giorno di regno*.* The melody is repeated by another trio of trumpets as a second troop of soldiers follows the first. The key is now B major and the accompaniment on four horns and pizzicato strings. The episode, however, returns to the original key with the melody played by the first set of trumpets and the second adding a decoration of triplets on the dominant, as in the duet 'Andrem raminghi e poveri' from *Luisa Miller*. The problem of combining the differently pitched

* See Vol. I, Ex. 28. And is it a coincidence that the opening idea of the celebrated 'Coronation March' from Meyerbeer's *Le Prophète* uses roughly the same nucleus of notes?

instruments is solved by turning the D sharp of the B trumpets into an E flat. Once again it is all very simple, very regular and supremely effective.*

At the conclusion the so-called ballabile is launched as from a bow – sudden, unexpected yet totally apt; no other ballet of Verdi's strikes in with such a sense of inevitability or maintains such a high level of musical quality, except perhaps the dances added to *Otello*. Originally it was quite short – a sequence of five piquant melodies each spiced with some exotic trick of harmony, scoring or contour (note the pentatonic colouring of Ex. 124 (d) and that obtrusive D flat in (e) with which Liza Lehmann embellished a melody from *Lakmé* so as to produce her famous song 'Myself when Young'.

Despite the vigorous, often masculine character of the music the dancers were originally all ballerinas who performed their steps round the idols and trophies taken from the conquered Ethiopians. At the second theme (Ex. 124b) with its popping bassoon and squeaking piccolo the little Moorish slaves of Amneris's suite were supposed to take part.†

In 1871 the dance was rounded off by a reprise of Ex. 124a. For the Paris production of 1880 Verdi expanded the scheme and for once instructed Ricordi to incorporate the Parisian version into all future editions of the vocal score.‡ As with *Macbeth* it is easy to see the join between old and new once it has been pointed out. The fresh material is less periodic, more brilliant in its scoring and crackles with harmonic quirks and epigrams. In Ex. 125a we encounter that somewhat pianistic figuration that often occurs in Verdi's late style; and the daring key-jump of Ex. 125b is very much of the 1880s. Exoticism had made great strides on the Parisian stage since *Aida* was first produced; and Verdi was doubtless eager to show that he too could match the flights of *Carmen*, *Samson et Dalila* and *Le Roi de Lahore*.

124a

---

* Nowadays producers place both sets of trumpets out of sight at either side of the stage, so producing an eminently Verdian stereophony (compare the 'Tuba mirum' of the Requiem). But this is far from what was originally intended. Both columns of troops were meant to make their entrance through the triumphal arch, with the trumpeters at their head, pass in front of the throne, then wheel round to take up a position to the rear of the stage band. In effect this meant that the second column had a longer distance to march than the first to the same number of bars while at the same time having to keep clear of the bells of the extended A flat trumpets. Elaborate cautions are given in the production book regarding the dangers of collision. As well as the three trumpeters each column was to consist of two officers (dancers), 6 ensigns (Moorish, in the second column), 18 soldiers with axes (first column) and lances (second column). See *Disp. scen.*, pp. 30–4.

† See *Disp. scen.*, p. 35.

‡ The original ballet can be found in first editions of the opera.

124b

124c

124d

124e

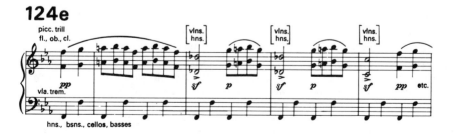

After the conclusion of the new music the ideas of Ex. 124 are all repeated with (a) placed at the end instead of the beginning, the altered perspective being sufficient to prevent any feeling of surfeit.

125a

125b

To a return of the introduction the triumph continues as more troops enter with war chariots, standards, sacred urns and statues.*

Ex. 121a is resumed to the words 'Vieni, o guerriero vindice', the priests now covering the interstices with fragments of their previous verse sung to powerful dominant unisons. The scene then winds briefly to a climax using previous material in stages of mounting grandeur. A più mosso based on a major-key variant of Ex. 93 played by the orchestra leads amid appropriate cries from priests and populace through part of the introduction to a grand pause and then a restatement fortissimo of

---

* In the course of 27 bars the following personnel, marching in double file, are required by the production book to have taken up their final position: *2 soldiers, drawing a war chariot, 2 ensigns, 4 soldiers carrying an idol on their shoulders, 2 ensigns, 2 soldiers carrying on their shoulders the statue of the Bull Bee, 4 fan-bearers, 2 soldiers carrying an idol on their shoulders, 2 ensigns, 2 soldiers drawing a war-chariot, 2 ensigns, 4 trumpeters (extras), 4 soldiers bearing Radames on his throne, 4 officers. Disp. scen., p. 30 . . . Radames' throne is set down in front of that of the King and Amneris. The officers, trumpeters and ensigns who had preceded it retire, as Radames steps down. The four soldiers then remove his throne from the stage. Ibid., p. 36.* At which point we may leave the complex manoeuvres enjoined by the production book, except to note that the prisoners enter backstage and move front of stage right, to allow Amonasro a suitably prominent position for his solo.

Ex. 122 over a tramping bass of quavers. The tempo quickens once more for a final reference to Ex. 93, now anchored to the key of E flat minor by a pedal bass, as Radames enters 'beneath a palanquin borne by twelve officers' (another divergence here from the production book); and a codetta in which triplet motion taken over in the orchestra concludes the grand parade. The King now descends from his throne and goes to greet the victorious captain, with the words 'Salvator della patria io ti saluto' – another variant of the ubiquitous Ex. 102. He commands Amneris to place the laurel wreath on Radames' brow; this she does in silence while violins on the G string give out Ex. 97 over a new bass line of rippling clarinet arpeggios with high sustaining flutes and piccolo. As a reward for his valour the King will grant Radames any wish he may care to express. Radames calls for the prisoners to be brought before him. As they are led in under guard the priests continue to chant their thanks to the gods *pianissimo* to yet another development of Ex. 93; but the curious 'groan' that enters the music at the ninth bar suggests that it is being used to depict the plight of the prisoners as well.

Then Aida catches sight of her father among the captives. The moment of surprise is conveyed much as in *Don Carlos* where the Infante leads in the Flemish deputies.* Tremolando violins charge the atmosphere with electricity; and here too it is a woman who cries out involuntarily. Aida's 'My father!' is echoed incredulously by all present; she herself runs to Amonasro, who whispers to her a fierce 'Non mi tradir!' The King commands him to stand forward and tell his story. Even before the start of his formal solo Amonasro is planted in all his formidable strength with a sure and economical touch. The usual paraphernalia of diminished sevenths and 6/4 chords associated with a scene of this kind is reduced to less than six bars. At Amonasro's first words bassoons, lower strings and brass bass catch the attention with a brusque gesture which halts the musical flow as it points a menacing finger towards D minor.

* See M. Conati, 'Verdi, il grand' opera e il Don Carlos', in *Atti del II° Congresso dell'I.S.V.*, pp. 265–6.

127

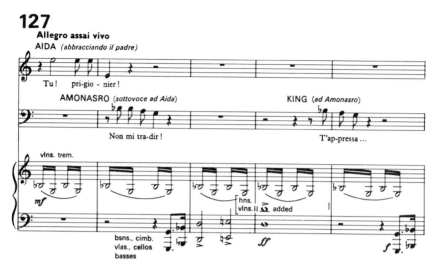

The harmonic stasis persists for twelve bars while the strings dwindle to *pppp*, as though the force of Amonasro's personality is causing all present to hold their breath. 'I too fought,' he says; 'we were beaten. . . . Vainly I sought death. . . .' and here the long prepared dominant of D minor strikes a hammer-blow. He fought beside his King but was powerless to save him from a warrior's death. For proof of his own courage he points to his torn and blood-stained garment in a measured cantabile ('Quest'assisa ch'io vesto'), the equivalent of the unison solo of Deputies in *Don Carlos* and, like it, destined to turn into the opera's central concertato. Not even in Renato's 'Eri tu' is so much unspoken meaning concentrated in a persistent domi-

128

nant. (Ex. 128) Surely too that weighty philosopher Colline had this solo in mind when he bade a portentous farewell to his own well-worn garment, or 'vecchia zimarra'.

The fortissimo tutti (*x*) shows again how a stock Verdian device can be transformed – in this case the explosion of ruthlessness (compare Pagano's followers in *I Lombardi*, the murderers in *Macbeth*, the courtiers in *Rigoletto*). Here entrusted to orchestra only, as the logical conclusion of the obsessive accompanimental pattern, and purged by its tonal context of all unintentional comedy it gives the effect of a flashing eye. Amonasro is proud and dignified in his humility. If it is a crime to be a patriot, he says, then we are all guilty. His 'Se l'amor della patria' is flung out like a challenge, all the bolder for being couched in the same note-pattern as the King's 'Salvator della patria', itself, as we have noticed, a variant of Ex. 102 ('Ritorna vincitor'). Then the musical argument turns aside from defiant dominant to placatory relative major; Amonasro begs the King to be merciful, remembering that the fortunes of war soon change and that he himself may one day require the same quality in others. The melody ('Ma tu, Re, tu signore possente') which forms the last section of Amonasro's cantabile and the first of the concertato, is typical of the Aida style – regular and periodic, with swift and unpredictable changes of harmony (note the E flat at the start of the second phrase – an almost sixteenth-century touch) and chromatic inflexions that caress without cloying.

Sung by Amonasro to strings alone the plea is specious and hypocritical; taken up by Aida and the four-part chorus of prisoners and female slaves (an ingenious disposition of sopranos and basses only), with wind accompaniment, it should have the ring of truth about it. But apart from the scoring and the vocal distribution the music is identical in each case and equally appropriate, and the question of sincerity as irrelevant here as in *Così fan tutte*. The priests, however, protest sharply with a contrasted theme in F minor marked by dotted rhythms and triplets ('Struggi, o Re, queste ciurme feroci'). Let the barbarians be put to death, in accordance with the will of the gods. From this conflict of ideas the concertato takes wing in a manner similar to that of *Don Carlos*, Act III; but the music is more complex and fetches a much wider tonal sweep, and rightly, since whereas in the earlier case the issue was decided from the outset here it hangs a long time in the balance. Here and there Radames and Aida emerge into prominence; the first with a lyrical D flat major phrase ('Il dolor che in quel volto favella') as he observes Aida's grief; the second with a succession of triplet phrases, like stylized laments. When Ex. 129 is resumed she shares the melody in octaves with her father. The general feeling is in favour of mercy; but martial gestures in the coda indicate that the priests are still putting up a fight, though ultimately forced to succumb beneath the weight of compassion. As usual there is a brief ensemble of soloists unaccompanied before the final bars. Aida crowns the final cadence with a high C.

Radames insists again that the Ethiopians should be set free; and the King, in accordance with his promise, must grant his request. The priests again object; the people still plead for mercy. Then Ramfis abandons the arguments of religion for a more pragmatic approach. If this savage horde is to be set free it will only be bent on revenge. His advice ('Ascolta, o Re') is set as a measured strophe over tremolando strings, as befits the weightiness of his words. Radames points out that with Amonasro dead there is little danger for the future. 'Nevertheless,' replies Ramfis, 'allow us for safety's sake to keep Aida's father.' This compromise is accepted, the King echoing Ramfis's cadential phrase. He then announces that he will bestow his daughter's hand on the victorious general. This tiny snatch of recitative with its descent by thirds is sufficiently unusual to draw attention to itself and so furnish material for a later reminiscence.

130

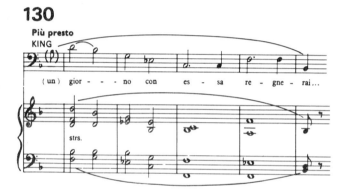

The princess has her brief moment of triumph ('Venga la schiava') in one of those downward sweeps that Verdi liked to give to his mezzo-sopranos. Then it is time to close the finale with a burst of pageantry. The problem was to find a way of balancing the magnificent conclusion of the processional music without mere inert repetition. The solution is brilliant and original. Essentially the music proceeds by variation. First comes a reprise of 'Gloria all' Egitto' (Ex. 121a) in full panoply, starting on Amneris's final note. The two variations that follow are so constructed as to give the impression of independent, contrasted melodies. The first (Ex. 131a, 'Inni leviamo ad Iside') is a joyous hymn of praise sung by Ramfis and the priesthood; the second (Ex. 131b) enables Aida and Radames to express their dismay – though to different words – at the King's latest decree, while Amneris in a counter-melody vents her satisfaction.

There is a minor episode in which Amonasro whispers to his daughter that the hour of revenge is at hand ('Fa cor! della tua patria i lieti eventi aspetta') – suitably stealthy but with death raps in the horns. The other principals repeat their previously expressed thoughts in a crescendo which leads yet again to Ex. 121a with both its variations superimposed. The vertical combination of different themes, as has been noted, was a speciality of Meyerbeer's first exploited in the Pré-aux-Clercs scene in *Les Huguenots* and developed to a preposterous degree of ingenuity in Act II of

131a
RAMFIS & PRIESTS

In – ni le -viamo ad I – – si-de — che il sa-cro suol di - fen – – de ! Pre-(ghiam)

131b
AIDA

D'av - ver – – so Nu-me il fol - go - re sul ca – – po mi-o di - scen – de
RADAMES

L'Étoile du Nord. But the effect is always slightly artificial. Likewise Verdi's own experiment in combining national anthems in his *Inno delle Nazioni* sounds contrived because there has to be a certain amount of harmonic manipulation to make it possible. There is no forcing in the present instance because all three melodies share the same harmonic basis; at the same time each is so designed as never to mask the salient features of the other two when played simultaneously with them. A final reprise of Ex. 122b launches the coda, and the curtain falls on Ex. 123 pealing out on banda and orchestra with the 'Egyptian' trumpets in A flat adding their dominant triplets.*

This finale is Verdi's last essay in musical pageantry, crowning a progress which started in *Giovanna d'Arco*. Had he continued further in the same direction he might have eliminated the residual brashness that can be sensed in the final pages. But he was never again to aim at this kind of surface grandeur. *Aida* remains his farewell to what may be called 'grand opera' in inverted commas.†

---

* During the last bars the production book prescribes an exeunt of the leading characters – the King with Amneris, Radames with Ramfis, Aida with Amonasro, the priests, prisoners and populace falling back so as to make way for them. *This movement needs to be executed quickly since there are only a few bars of music. Disp. scen.*, p. 42. This last statement is no exaggeration.

† The distribution of the chorus in the Milan production of 1872 is worth noting, since the production book insists that a similar proportion should be maintained even in theatres where the same numbers are not available.

PEOPLE	1st Sopraros	9			
	2nd Sopranos	7	28		
	Contraltos	12			
	1st Tenors	10	18	65	
	2nd Tenors	8			
	Baritones	8	19		
	Basses	11			
PRISONERS	1st Sopranos	4	8		107
	2nd Sopranos	4		18	
	Basses	10			
PRIESTS	1st Tenors	6	12		
	2nd Tenors	6		24	
	Baritones	6	12		
	Basses	6			

ACT III

Scene: The banks of the Nile. Granite rocks overgrown with palm trees. On the summit of the rocks is the temple of Isis, half hidden by the fronds. It is a starlit night. The moon is shining.

The opening of this act was radically transformed at a late stage. Had the Cairo première taken place as originally planned listeners might well have heard that 'Chorus à la Palestrina which would have earned me a "well done" from the bigwigs'.* The tapestry of strings which serves as backcloth to this night scene is formed from the note G played in a variety of ways and registers by muted violins and violas and unmuted cellos.† Only the full orchestral score can convey the effect of an idea which is texture and nothing else.

132

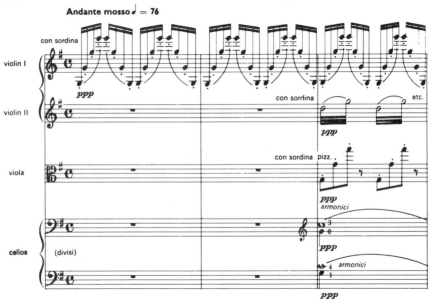

The effect is of a stillness that is intensely alive, like that of a tropical night. Even when the flute enters at the fifth bar it at first only plays round the open fifth implied in Ex. 132; then other notes steal in gradually: an E on the tremolando of the second violins; a trill, then an arabesque on the flute; a B flat begins to alternate with the B in the course of a rapidly repeated figure, which in its monotony and apparent inconsequence recalls the flute solo in Holst's 'Beni Mora' and so raises the possibility that Verdi like Holst may for once have taken a hint from an authentic Arabian folk melody. At the seventeenth bar a chorus of priests is heard chanting in the temple ('O tu che sei d'Osiride') answered by a priestess who here cannot be represented by the singer of Aida since the passage is far too close to her next appearance. The chant sung in unison is no more thematic than the prelude out of which it grows; but it uses the oscillation between B and B flat to achieve a suggestion of bitonality; the men singing in E minor, the priestess replying in G minor, while the cellos persist with

* Letter to Giulio Ricordi, 12.9.1871. *Copialettere*, p. 676. † Hughes, p. 403.

their sustained G harmonics. The entire passage of thirty-four bars shows Verdi reaching out far beyond the limits of traditional composition both in Italy and outside. For a comparable blend of timelessness with musical motion one can only turn to the opening of Wagner's *Rheingold*.

As priests and priestesses conclude their prayer to 'Isis, mother and bride of Osiris', a boat draws up to the shore; from it steps Amneris, handed by Ramfis and two women wearing thick veils.* Ramfis urges the princess to spend her night in prayer in the temple. After the austerity of what has gone before his words ('Vieni d'Iside al tempio') have a human warmth, being delivered in a beautiful arioso melody shared with the strings. Nothing could be simpler, more sparing of notes than Amneris's submissive reply ('Sì, io pregherò'); yet on the strength of it many an Amneris has stolen the audience's sympathy from her rival even though her own great scene is yet to come.

133

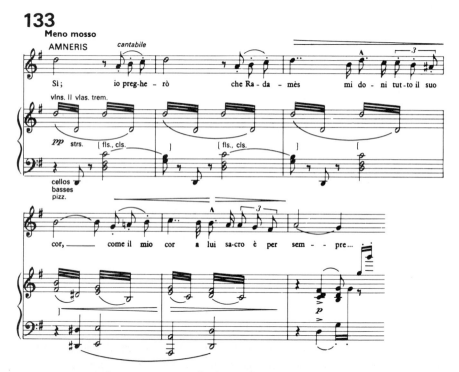

Previous material is now resumed; the violins and violas rustle, the priests and priestess chant, while a long flute trill over both brings the sequence to an end. But if Ex. 132 continues to pervade the scene, like some continuous sound which the ear no longer registers, this is because even after the musical idea has changed the high G persists on two violins, just on the limits of audibility, while in C major Ex. 92 played by flutes with a bare accompaniment of viola semiquavers announces the arrival of Aida. As in the prelude her melody turns aside from the home key in the eighth bar and the high held G vanishes as a result.

Aida is despondent and afraid. What if Radames had asked her to meet him merely to bid her farewell for ever? If so she will plunge herself into the Nile, whose

* The production book adds 4 soldiers and 2 oarsmen who remove the boat. See *Disp. scen.*, p. 46.

dark waters are painted in a swirling chromatic scale for cellos and basses combined with tremoli for low flute and clarinet. Her phrase 'Del Nile i cupi vortici' has all the guilt-ridden tragedy of Amelia's music as she approaches the gallows by night. But perhaps death will bring peace and forgetfulness. She thinks with longing of the homeland that she will never see again – its blue skies, green slopes and scented rills. Ghislanzoni had a pretty turn for nostalgic verse, as he had already shown in his poetry for Lucia's farewell to Como in Petrella's *I Promessi Sposi*. Aida's romanza 'O patria mia' is no less evocative in its language. It is set as a species of couplet-structure of two parallel verses, which is quite free from the formal tyranny of the quatrain. For here Verdi breaks with the time-honoured tradition of couplet writing whereby a new musical thought combines with new words to form a refrain. The 'punch-line' ('O patria mia, mai più ti revedrò') is scattered throughout the musical setting, preceding each verse as well as concluding it, and often split up into incoherent but expressive fragments. The romanza begins with what appears to be scena material:

The key is F major; but the desolate sound of the oboe, the modal inflexions which result in a bias toward the surrounding minor keys produce a twilight of tonality, from which emerges the 'false tonic' of A minor, just at the point where the formality becomes more pronounced: observe the 'Ethiopian' contour of the phrase and the vacillation between the major and minor third. (Ex. 135)

As in the 'Salve Maria' from *I Lombardi*, when next the real tonic is heard, at the words, 'O verdi colli, o profumate rive', it sounds like an episodic key. Not until the music has wound its way through F minor and D flat major does the F major 6/4 convey a sense of returning home. The second strophe is enhanced by various little refinements. Ex. 134 is shortened and concentrated; Ex. 135 given a more elaborate accompaniment; the final cadence reached three bars earlier, the vocal line mounting to a high C. If the exotic contours, the delicate scoring, the economy of the two-part writing all owe something to the example of Inés's 'Adieu, mon doux rivage' from

135

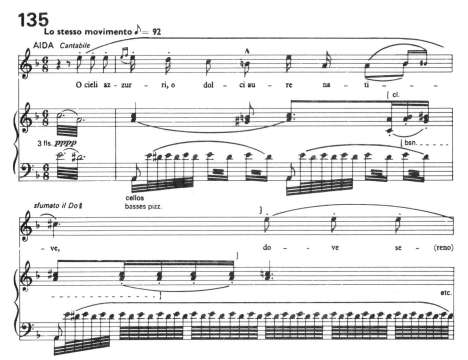

Meyerbeer's *L'Africaine* (a piece whose influence reaches as far ahead as the 'Willow Song' from *Otello*), the haunting poetic fantasy, the perfect formal balance born of varied symmetry owe nothing to anyone. Such effects as the flute tremolando in Ex. 132 have been adumbrated by Verdi himself as early as *I Due Foscari*.

A reflective postlude is abruptly broken off as Aida catches sight of her father lurking in the shadows. Amonasro loses no time in coming to the point.* In the briefest of recitatives he tells his daughter that he has observed everything.† She is in love with Radames; Amneris is her rival. He has a plan to enable Aida to get the better of her mistress. He follows up this stroke with an evocation of the fair land of Ethiopia to which he and his daughter may soon return ('Rivedrai le foreste imbalsamate'). This is the first formal movement of their duet, a cantabile of thirty-eight bars in dialogue to which the allegro pace, a prolonged dominant and throbbing viola semiquavers give a latent urgency (Ex. 136).

As the music pursues its way through D flat, B flat minor and major, one beautifully scored idea follows another, all generated by the initial one which is itself never repeated except at short range. The golden temples, the fragrant forests Amonasro cleverly associates with hatred of the Egyptian invaders. Then having worked Aida into a suitable frame of mind he tells her that the Ethiopians are ready to rise up ('In armi ora si desta il popol nostro'); victory is certain if only they can find out the route that the Egyptian army will take. In a short transition (*Poco più animato*) the

---

* *For this scene the music itself is the best instructor for the actors. Disp. scen., p. 46.*

† The phrase 'Nothing has escaped my glance' was suggested by Verdi himself as being more suitable to a fierce tribal warrior than Ghislanzoni's more commonplace 'I have read the secrets of your heart'. See letter to Ghislanzoni, 7.10.1870. *Copialettere*, pp. 650–1.

136 Allegro giusto ♩ = 100

AMONASRO   Ri – ve – drai   le   fo – res – te imbal-sa – ma – te,   le   fres – che

val – – li,   i   nost – ri   tem – pli   d'ôr ! ...

music takes on a swift, panther-like tread of dotted notes which slackens into a sequence of inchoate gestures ('Radames so che qui t'attendi. . . . Ei t'ama . . . ei conduce l'Egizii . . .') like so many meaningful hints. Aida realizes what is being asked of her; horrified, she refuses; whereat Amonasro bursts into a fiery 6/8 denunciation ('Su dunque sorgete, egizie coorti') – all blaring tuttis, rapping trumpets and trombones, rushing strings, savagely trilling flutes and piccolo. This is the pivotal movement of the duet, revealing the warrior king in all his formidable power. 'Just as a man in a towering rage oversteps all the bounds of order, moderation and propriety and forgets himself completely, so should the music likewise forget itself.' Thus Mozart to his father on the subject of Osmin's first aria, adding the proviso that music even in the most terrible situations should never offend the ear.* Both observations could have served as a maxim for this movement. The first two quatrains, calling upon the Egyptians to destroy the cities of Ethiopia, form a compact period of sixteen bars extended to nineteen, keeping strictly to C minor and ending on a half-close. Thereafter the metre changes from senario to the more flexible settenario and the piece begins to slip its tonal moorings, and to move in a steadily widening circuit of keys. 'A murdered nation,' Amonasro cries, 'will point the accusing finger at you.' Finally he evokes the vision of Aida's dead mother rising from her grave to denounce the daughter who has betrayed their people ('Una larva orribile, fra l'ombre a noi s'affaccia . . .'). Here a formal sequence embedded in the free-ranging melody provides the launching-pad for Amonasro's ultimate taunt: 'You are not my daughter; you are the slave of the Pharaohs!' Again the metre changes to the quinario as Amonasro's words are hurled with devastating effect between orchestral explosions ('Non sei mia figlia. De' Faraoni tu sei la schiava!') – one of the most remarkable instances of that 'parola scenica' so dear to the composer's heart.

Aida falls to the ground with a cry, then drags herself towards her father's feet, begging brokenly for pity. Her utter annihilation of spirit is portrayed by the stammering syncopations of the violins and the heavy, dragging line for cellos, basses

* Letter from Mozart to his father, 26.9.1781. *The Letters of Mozart and his Family* (tr. Emily Anderson, 2nd edn, London, 1966), II, pp. 768–9.

and bassoons which open the next movement (Ex. 137a). Aida is still her father's daughter; she will not be unworthy of her country. The slow painful theme is now transfigured (Ex. 137b) as Amonasro reminds her that only with her aid can an oppressed nation rise again ('Pensa che un popolo, vinto, straziato') – a soaring phrase which belongs in the succession of 'È puro l'aere' (*Giovanna d'Arco*) and 'Com'angeli d'ira' (*Macbeth*) but is more telling than either, partly because dramatically it coincides with a turning-point in the action, namely Aida's submission to her father's

137a

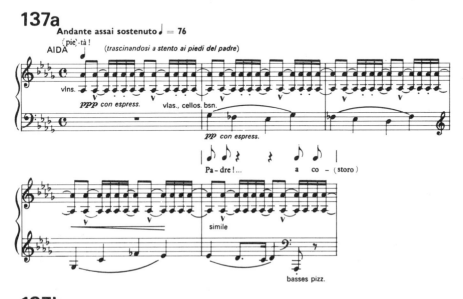

137b

137c

will, and partly because it is a musical development rather than a mere consequent of what has gone before. Once again the emotions of the moment appear transcended. There is more here than Amonasro's satisfaction at having got his way. Compassion, irony – who can tell? But it brings no comfort to Aida. While throbbing violins begin a slow twelve-bar climb she winds up the movement with that phrase to which Verdi attached so much importance ('O patria, quanto mi costi!', Ex. 137c), sounding all the more desolate for the ray of light which has preceded it. So ends a duet from which all convention has been purged in the interests of direct dramatic expression.

Radames' approach is heralded by fragments of his next melody ('Pur ti riveggo, mia dolce Aida') flung out over a drumroll. He seems, like Don José, to be entering with a song on his lips:

138

It is a melody well calculated to express the aura of easy heroic optimism that surrounds the singer up to the moment of catastrophe, and therefore to serve as a framework for the duet which follows. At once Aida begins to play the part assigned to her. The King has ordered him to marry Amneris; how could he possibly disobey?

She halts the confident flow of Ex. 138 with a contemptuous warning to Radames not to perjure himself. Her lover answers by unfolding his plan. The Ethiopians are preparing another attack; he himself will again command the Egyptian army and win the day. He will then be able to ask for Aida's hand in marriage which the King could not in all justice refuse him. This is unrealistic to say the least; but it inspires a gripping essay in tenor heroics ('Nel fiero anelito'), declaimed over a developing martial figure played by two trumpets.

139

After twelve bars this culminates in a restatement of Ex. 138. But what about Amneris? Aida asks; does he not fear her jealousy (recalled by Ex. 98 on the strings)? Aida herself, her father and her people would be the ones to suffer. But, she goes on, there is a way out; she and Radames must escape together; and she brings out the word 'Fuggir' with an abruptness which startles Radames into an incredulous echo. The oboe is again brought into play as Aida tries to seduce him with visions of a faraway land where they can be eternally happy ('Fuggiam gli ardori inospiti'). The structure of this movement is similar to that of Aida's romanza, with two parallel statements, the second of which is a modified repetition of the first. But here the modification goes much further, resulting in an expansion and re-orchestration of the material such as will be found in Nannetta's solo with chorus in Act III of *Falstaff*. As in the romanza there is a chain of ideas wandering away from the main key (B flat) and back to it, all clothed in the most delicate scoring imaginable with plentiful use of woodwind. This time, however, the opening declamation beneath winding oboe triplets (Ex. 140), modally inflected in G minor with some exotic diminished intervals, is essentially an introduction to the main body of the aria ('Là tra foreste vergini' – Ex. 141), to be recalled only in the most summary fashion between verses. The total design would be impossible without that equation of a major key with its relative minor already noted as a characteristic of Italian opera from Rossini's time.

140

Allowing for the modal flattened leading note of Ex. 140 the key is certainly G
minor; with equal certainty its reprise is in B flat major (see the final bar of Ex. 142)
yet the unharmonized melody is the same in each case.

Rarely have the three flutes sounded more caressing than at the point where Aida
herself moves from declamation into formal melody.

Whether there is any dramatic significance in the recollection of the trumpet march
(x), reinforced in the second verse by the addition of a triplet figure on four violins,
is difficult to say. Is she suggesting that Radames' triumphs will savour sweeter in
Ethiopia? More probably it is just one of those affinities which different parts of the
same opera might be expected to show to one another. Towards the end of the period
there is a beautiful and characteristic use of the non-functional 6/4 at the word
'estasi'. Radames is moved but not convinced. Here the ambivalent tonality, poised
between B flat major and G minor, can be made to express his vacillation. Each time,
he begins his reply to Aida in G minor; and each time he ends it with the same
melting phrase in B flat major enhanced in the reprise with the oboe triplets of
Ex. 140 and a simple descant from Aida. (Ex. 142)

As Radames still hesitates, Aida tells him to return to Amneris. 'Never!' he cries.
Well, then, Aida and her father will be executed. At this Radames makes up his mind
to escape after all. The 'similar' cabaletta that results ('Sì, fuggiam da queste mura')
is unquestionably of the old stamp, as Filippi had pointed out. But there is very little
of it – two identical sixteen-bar periods sung by each of the singers in turn, based on a
theme that is well designed to convey the release of tension felt by both. (Ex. 143)

142

RADAMES
dolcissimo.

il suol dov'io rac - col - si di glo - ria i primi al - lo - ri, il ciel de' no - stri a -

3 fls.   ob.

strs.

dolcissimo.

basses

[hns. pedal
dolce

- mo - ri   co - me scordar po - trem?

ob.

strs
only *pp*

143

Allegro assai vivo ♩ = 92

RADAMES (*con appassionata risoluzione*)

ppp

Si: fug - giam da que - ste mu - ra, al_ de - ser - to in - siem fug - gia - mo;

w.w. hns.   ] w.w. no hns.
p cresc.   *pp*
strs.

As was by now the custom there is no ritornello and no third statement by both singers;* instead, the main weight is taken by a reprise of Ex. 138 sung in unison and accompanied by a massive orchestral tutti. Then, just as they are about to leave together, Aida asks Radames the route that the Egyptian army will take so that they themselves can avoid it. 'The gorge of Napata,' he replies. 'The gorge of Napata!' repeats Amonasro triumphantly, stepping out of the shadows. 'Then my men will be there!' He reveals his identity: 'Aida's father and King of the Ethiopians.' In the heat of the moment Verdi has lapsed into an old habit – long since shed – of drowning the

* The only instance I have been able to find of a duet cabaletta of the period with a triple statement of the main idea is 'Ed ora, Contessa' in Cagnoni's *Un Capriccio di Donna* (1870).

all-important word 'Re' in a burst of orchestral sound. Wholly modern, however, is the unceasing tendency to express strong emotion in naturalistic rather than lyrical terms. The words 'Tu . . . Amonasro? . . . il Rè? . . . Numi . . . che dissi?' proceed as incoherent cries, first punctuated then backed by a more or less athematic semiquaver pattern in the orchestra. Indeed from here to the end of the act the music is never allowed to coagulate into a formal number; what looks like the start of a terzetto and even includes important melodic phrases remains strictly a scène-à-faire. Even in an opera containing two such magnificent female roles as this, Verdi's bias toward a world of masculine values asserts itself at the moment of crisis. Aida reveals herself for the mere pawn that she is, uttering helpless cries ('Ah no! ti calma, ascoltami! . . . all'amor mio t'affida'). It is the two men who dominate the picture, musically and dramatically. Radames, the sea-green incorruptible, can only dwell on the fact that he has disgraced himself by betraying his country; his eight-bar outcry ('Io son disonorato') has a desperate finality about it as it moves from B flat minor to its cadence in D flat minor (as in La Traviata, the passage of minor key to the minor of the relative major is like the closing of a door). Amonasro, hitherto the archetype of primitive patriotism, who has shown no sympathy for his daughter's feelings, now wastes valuable time by trying to comfort his country's enemy ('No; tu non sei colpevole!'). It is his one moment of humanity, for which he will pay with his life. For while the men have been arguing Amneris has come out of the temple. 'Traitor!' she cries; and here the orchestral cataclysm leaves her words clear. Amonasro makes to stab her with a dagger (apart from her inopportune presence she is a woman and therefore expendable), but Radames interposes himself. At that moment Ramfis appears with his guards. Radames tells Aida and Amonasro to escape while they can; Ramfis orders his guards to give chase.* Their hurried exit is marked by four bars of orchestral tutti; in the hush that follows Radames surrenders to Ramfis with the simple, ringing yet tragic 'Sacerdote, io resto a te!' after which nineteen bars of rapid D minor orchestral figuration wind up an act which is among the most dramatic as well as the most atmospheric that Verdi ever wrote. It is noteworthy that he should have asked Tito Ricordi to have it printed without any division into separate numbers, a request with which the publisher for some reason did not see fit to comply.†

ACT IV

Scene 1: A Hall in the Royal Palace. On the left a large doorway leading to the subterranean courtroom. A door on the right leads to Radames' prison.‡
The scene belongs essentially to Amneris; but Verdi, who had at one point considered the possibility of giving her a romanza, scouted the idea in favour of an

---

* For those who are not blinded by false piety there is something remarkably crude about the type of gesture recommended by the production book at this moment of catastrophe. On perceiving the Ethiopian King Radames *should incline slightly towards Amonasro, extending his left arm and pointing with his finger.* Later Amonasro *should put his right hand on [Radames'] shoulder saying, 'No; tu non sei colpevole!'* At their discovery by Amneris and Ramfis, *Radames turns to Aida and Amonasro and pointing towards the wings R. pushes them in that direction. . . . Disp. scen.,* pp. 50–2.

† See letter to T. Ricordi, 26.8.1871. Gossett, *op. cit.,* p. 327.

‡ *The backcloth represents a hall, half in darkness, formed by huge architectonic stones carved with sphinxes, deities, etc., in bas-relief. A dark reddish light . . . centre stage, a small column with an idol of porphyry. . . . This scene should be extremely shallow, and sited directly behind the curtain. . . . The stage band trumpeters and the*

extended scena with reminiscences. The first of these is a variant of Ex. 130 on woodwind in long held notes within a fast tempo – a reminder of the King's edict that Radames is to marry her. At once Ex. 98 supervenes with a waspish scoring of flutes, piccolo and first violins as Amneris is overwhelmed by anger and jealousy. This is the thought that torments her above all others.* Radames cannot be truly guilty . . . and yet the evidence cannot be denied . . . he wanted to flee the country with Aida and her father. . . . 'They are all traitors! To death with them!' Yet she loves Radames in spite of everything – and appropriately the strings murmur Ex. 97 in three-part harmony with a gently rocking bass. She decides to summon Radames from his prison and try to save him. The prisoner is led in, to a broad, shuddering theme, its rich scoring darkened by the presence of the cor anglais; and so the scene is set for a grand duet for tenor and mezzo-soprano. All musical resemblance to 'In mia man alfin tu sei' from *Norma* is successfully avoided; but if Bellini's duet is classical in tone Verdi's is still more so.† It is concise, densely packed with ideas and sculpted

144

player of the bass drum should be under the stage. . . . Amneris should be plunged in profound sorrow, leaning against the column with her head in her hands. At the beginning of her recitative she should take a few steps forward. The composer has indicated in two places in the recitative itself: PAUSA LUNGA; LUNGO SILENZIO; the actress is recommended to observe these indications literally without fear of exaggeration. These pauses have a very fine effect and portray very well the terrible perplexity of Amneris's thoughts. Disp. scen., pp. 54–5.

* According to Luzio one of the many sketches made for the draft programme that was eventually submitted to Ghislanzoni to be put into verse contains the following annotations in Giuseppina's handwriting: 'Ah, could the Gods but will that Aida should no longer live! . . . My hated rival has escaped my wrath, nor have they been able to track her down. . . . My love will turn to fierce, implacable hatred.' *Carteggi Verdiani*, IV, p. 20. None of these expressions found their way into the libretto.

† For a close analysis of this duet see Gossett, *op. cit.*, pp. 310–21.

with cool precision. Traces of an old tripartite scheme can be felt with its watershed at the point where Radames discovers that Aida is still alive. The opening movement is a 'similar' primo tempo with the two voices in different keys. The final one is a 'dissimilar' cabaletta, 1870s style. But underlying the Rossinian balance of contrasts that the form of the text might seem to imply is a steadily evolving musical argument. The theme with which it begins is simple and stark with sinister colouring from bass clarinet and trumpet. The colloquy is taking place under the shadow of death (Ex. 144).

The priests, says Amneris, are already gathering to pass sentence. If Radames will only justify his conduct she herself will plead with her father for his release. The whole of Amneris's melody is evolved Donizetti-fashion from the rhythmic pattern of its opening; during the second sentence, however, the triplet motif is spread to other woodwind instruments, the cor anglais echoes the voice-part, and finally the texture fills out, giving warmth to the modulation to G flat major which brings the period to its close.

Radames takes up Ex. 144 in F sharp minor, just where Amneris has left it. His conscience is clear, he admits, since he never intended to betray his country and his honour is therefore unsullied. The same modulation matches his assertion of innocence as the one that had accompanied Amneris's mention of a royal pardon. A brief transition of dialogue ends with a drooping, richly harmonized phrase in which Radames says that he has no longer the will to live. However the new idea to which it leads is not a separate movement but rather an episode within the previous one – an unheard-of departure from the post-Rossinian norm.

Amneris, no longer stately and controlled, pleads with him in a great upsurge of lyrical warmth, parading all the majesty of the mezzo-soprano voice ('Ah, tu dei vivere').

145

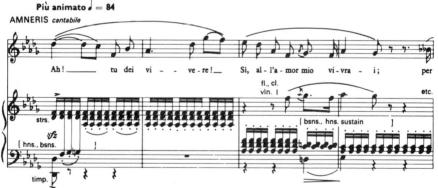

But she cannot keep the anguish out of her voice and the second phrase, torn by dissonances, ends in the minor. After a modulating third limb the melody returns to Ex. 145 altered and expanded so as to flower into a cadence of great lyrical beauty. Radames repeats it with a reference to Aida as the one for whose sake he betrayed his country. Amneris protests at the mere mention of her name. Radames with a return to Ex. 144, scored as before but with cor anglais giving an edge to the voice part, coldly accuses Amneris of taking Aida from him ('Misero, appien mi festi; Aida a me togliesti'), of killing her, perhaps.* Amid mounting excitement in the orchestra, Amneris tells him that, though Amonasro was captured and killed, Aida escaped. The flurry of semiquavers and syncopations is halted, and Radames in a haunting aside prays that she may return safely to her country and never know the fate that has befallen her lover. It is a byway from the main musical argument, but deeply moving in its simplicity.†

146

But if she sets him free, Amneris insists, will he renounce Aida for ever? No, he would rather die. At this Amneris's rage and misery erupt in the theme of the final cabaletta ('Chi ti salva, sciagurato?', Ex. 147a) to which Radames replies that he welcomes death as the highest good ('È la morte un ben supremo', Ex. 147b). Note the important D flat in the third bar of Amneris's theme, a harmonic subtlety employed by Verdi as early as *Luisa Miller*, whose heroine finds herself at that moment likewise caught in a trap from which there is no escape – and how much more powerful it is here, in the context of a searing upward climb in an inner part! Ex. 147b, moving up where Ex. 147a moves down, is not a mere major-key resolution of its predecessor but rather a proud defiance of it (Ex. 147).

Both themes share the same concluding limb, an inexorable slamming of the door in C minor. Amid a long-drawn-out tutti, fraught with syncopations and all the standard Verdian devices indicative of frantic despair, Radames is led back to his prison. Amneris is left to face the prospect of his death. Her thoughts are accom-

---

* It may be remembered that the combination of bass-clarinet and cor anglais in Ortrud's warning was one of the moments in *Lohengrin* that especially impressed Verdi.

† 'Much sentiment in this aside, so that a beautiful melodic phrase can be developed.' Letter to Ghislanzoni, 17.10.1870. *Copialettere*, pp. 657–9.

147a

147b

panied by Ex. 93 as it was heard in the prelude but in the major key and scored for
muted double basses only – a device to be used again to portray Otello's stealthy
entrance into his wife's bedroom. At the third, fifth and ninth bars the three trom-

bones sound a semibreve dominant pianissimo as in the march to the stake in *Don Carlos*, Act III. The theme is not, for once, built up contrapuntally, merely serving as a backcloth for Amneris's remorseful murmurings ('Ohimè . . . morir mi sento . . . Oh, chi lo salva?'). Extended to nine bars, it is stated three times, always with a new cadence and with a different bass-orientated orchestration. It is in her imagination that Amneris sees the priests, who do not actually enter until the third statement of Ex. 93 with its low clarinets and bassoon. They cross the stage to the entrance to the courtroom while Amneris covers her face with her hands. There is a faint suggestion of canon in the codetta, also based on Ex 93, a melting cadence formed by a see-saw of unrelated chords again repeated three times; then the prayer sounds from below chanted in unison by Ramfis and his fellow-priests ('Spirto del Nume, sovra noi discendi'). It is a special plainchant of Verdi's invention with pentatonic elements and ending in a melisma:

148 Lo stesso movimento

RAMFIS & Basses

Spir - to del Nu - me, so - vra noi di - scen - - - - - - - - di!

This too is built in three parallel, though not identical phrases. Amneris is given a snatch of distraught melody ('Numi, pietà del mio straziato core') after which Radames is conducted to the court room, as the orchestra declaims Ex. 93 in its second-act variant. The priests meanwhile chant their prayer, but on a single note, to be fortified by four trumpets and four trombones also situated in the subterranean hall; and Amneris continues her protests and lamentations, ending with a low 'Mi sento morir' over tremolando violas and a rolling kettledrum.

Then the trial begins. The rule of three which has already been in evidence since the end of the duet now emerges in the strongest possible relief in the most monumental of Verdi's judgement scenes.* The prisoner's name is called then echoed by a blast from stage trumpets and trombones. The charge is 'read' by Ramfis. 'Defend yourself!' he cries and the priests do likewise; there is a roll on the bass drum. 'He is silent,' observes the High Priest; and there is a general cry of 'Traitor!' followed by a howl of anguish from Amneris. The use of *terza rima* throughout this passage was as we have seen Verdi's idea. Whether or not he knew of it, the ghost's speech in Faccio's *Amleto*, also delivered from beneath the stage, furnished a suitable precedent (Ex. 149).

The entire pattern is twice repeated, each time a semitone higher as in the earlier judgement scenes; for the charge is three-fold. Radames has betrayed his country's secrets to the enemy, has deserted from the army on the eve of battle, and has broken his oath of loyalty to King and country. (If these do not strictly amount to three separate charges, it was in the interests of Verdi the musician to make them appear to do so.) Note the effectiveness of the interrupted cadence (*x*) in smoothing the transition from one statement to the next. As Radames remains silent the priests pronounce sentence in a unison strophe of triplets punctuated by orchestral blasts. The prisoner is to be walled up alive in the vault beneath the altar of Vulcan, whose godhead he has

---

* For a close analysis of this scene, see F. Noske, *The Signifier and the Signified* (The Hague, 1977), pp. 264–7.

dishonoured. At this pandemonium breaks loose in the orchestra (it is the moment
for which the tam-tam is reserved), and as it dies down Amneris is once more heard
inveighing against the bloodthirstiness of the priests who call themselves ministers of
heaven. The priests return to Ex. 93 flung out over diminished-seventh harmony.
Rolling timpani and bass drum, low notes on trombones, divided double basses all

149

amplify the bass resonances forbiddingly. The trial over, the rule of three gives way to that of two. As the priests cross the stage muttering, 'Traditor,' Amneris attacks them in one of those intensely concentrated musical periods which in mature Verdi does duty for a whole aria ('Sacerdoti: compiste un delitto!'). The second phrase ('Voi la terra ed i Numi oltraggiate') breaks unexpectedly into the major key, with a sardonic reminiscence of the 'Ritorna vincitor' pattern (Ex. 102).

'He is a traitor and will die,' the priests answer obdurately. Amneris next turns her accusation against Ramfis ('Sacerdote, quest'uomo che uccidi') to the same music, but he remains equally unmoved. Then she pours out her grief in an agonized phrase akin to Ex. 147a, in which the entire orchestra seems to groan with her.

The priests retreat into the distance still with words of condemnation on their lips. Amneris must be content with hurling an anathema at their backs with something of the hysteria of an Azucena. Fortified first by the brass choir, then by the full orchestra, the overwhelmingly powerful final phrase ('Empia razza! . . . Anatema su voi! . . . la vendetta del ciel scenderà') contains yet another ironical memory of Ex. 102. So to a vigorous curtain with the rule of three briefly re-established in the final bars.*

> Scene 2: The scene is divided on two levels. The higher represents the interior
> of the Temple of Vulcan, glowing with light and gold. The lower represents a
> vault. Long rows of arches lose themselves in the darkness. Colossal statues of
> Osiris with hands outspread support the pilasters of the roof.†

Radames is in the vault, standing on the flight of steps by which he has entered. Above, two priests are at work closing the entrance with hammers and pick-axes, miming the action so as not to disturb the music. The opening gesture for strings is first cousin to the phrase for clarinets and bassoons that begins the 'Miserere' scene in *Il Trovatore* — sombre and resigned. *Trovatore*-like too is the use of full orchestra

---

* *Thence exit hurriedly through the door L. This door should be closed quickly and the backcloth raised and the entire underground scene should be ready for the scene-change, which should take place immediately, as soon as the music finishes. Disp. scen., p. 60.*

† *The scenographer should take great pains to achieve the contrast between the two levels: the lower one gloomy, with stark colours, illuminated by a grey-green light; the temple glowing with light and warm colours; the columns will serve very well to mask the lighting mechanism which should preferably be gas jets. A great problem for the scenographer will be to suggest the grandeur of the Temple of Vulcan with less space available both vertically and horizontally. . . . The vault, lit by coloured glass, should be enclosed by two opaque curtains at either side to prevent the penetration of any other light.*

All the priests should form a circle round the altar of Vulcan, on their knees with their hands on their breasts as explained in the first act. See that both knees touch the ground. Disp. scen., p. 63. Again the most rigid immobility is prescribed until the priests rise to their feet for the invocation. The two harps, the female chorus and the harmonium (fisarmonica) to give them their pitch are all located offstage but at subterranean level. The production book envisages no less than three sub-conductors.

pianissimo, though here without second violins. What follows is scena music at its
most economical: tiny fragments of the opening idea interspersed with light
recitative. Radames is shut out for ever from the light of day. His thoughts are of
Aida; as in the previous scene he wishes that she may find happiness wherever she
may be and never learn of his fate. Flute and oboe give a faint octave groan. Radames
starts, suspects a ghost, then recognizes Aida's voice. From here to the end the duet
takes on purely lyrical form. Aida explains how she guessed that Radames would be
condemned; she had therefore stolen into the vault beforehand to die in her lover's
arms. Aida's verse ('Presago il core della tua condanna') maintains the bleak, barely
expressive tone of the preceding scena. Its only accompaniment is a succession of
minim D's played by low clarinets, bassoons, violas and cellos reinforced by bass
drum – a muffled death-knell. Only in the final phrase ('Nelle tue braccia desiai
morire') does a feeling of warmth break in, as the melody finally tears itself away from
D minor to E flat. From here on each successive idea in the duet follows at the key a
fifth below the one before, as though both singers were relaxing further and further
into an atmosphere of peace. At the same time the periods themselves become ever
more simple and traditional in their build and more sublime in their effect. Radames,
unbearably moved at the thought of one so young and beautiful dying for his sake,
taps a new vein of pathetic sweetness, in which, not for the first time, clarinets are
used to give a delicate shading to the vocal line ('Morir! sì pura e bella').*

* In a letter to Giulio Ricordi Verdi expressed unwonted scruples about the words of this strophe. 'It
is true that both the singers we have now are very beautiful. But what of future occasions?' Letter to
Giulio Ricordi, 7.9.1871. Abbiati, III, pp. 479–80. Ricordi referred the matter to Ghislanzoni, who gave
the commonsense reply: 'Apart from the fact that in the theatre all women are beautiful or at least are

But Aida's mind is already wandering. She sees the angel of death approaching and the gates of heaven being flung wide ('Vedi? Di morte l'angelo'). Her solo is constructed in an almost Bellinian form with first, second and fourth phrases all based on the same idea. But here too not only are the settenari set in an unusual rhythm; the scoring has a quality of translucence recalling that of Violetta's death-bed, with elaborately divided violins. Eighteen years' experience, however, had enabled Verdi to achieve an even subtler and more original combination of sonorities. 'Six or eight' of the first violins trace a pattern, mostly arpeggio based above the stave; six others double the vocal melody in three-part chords, one of each desk playing pizzicato the note that his partner plays coll'arco. The same chords are doubled by first flute and the two clarinets. Horn, bassoon and harp make up the rest of the texture, the last breaking into semiquavers where the gates of heaven are mentioned.

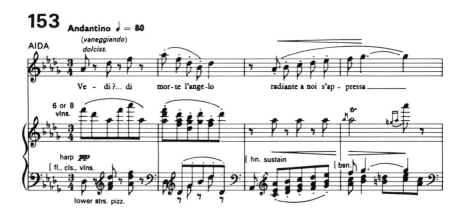

At the end of the long-drawn-out cadence the priests and priestesses in the temple break into song ('Immenso Ftha') with a recollection of the high priestess's incantation from the second scene of Act I (Ex. 107a) to the thrummings of the off-stage harps. It penetrates to the couple below; 'Our hymn of death,' Aida murmurs while Radames tries desperately to move the stone that covers the entrance. The end of the melody is neatly dovetailed into Ex. 108b played by flutes and harps;* and so the transition is effected gradually through the Phrygian ambivalence of the incantation from D flat major to the final movement of the duet in G flat major.

The lovers' farewell to life ('O terra addio') is in form the simplest and most elementary of cabalettas. In favouring the design $a1$–$a2$–b–$a2$ in his last operas Bellini was paring down the lyric melody to the limit of simplicity within the conventions of the time. In the final scene of *Aida* Verdi goes further, with a melody which can only be analysed as a–a–b–a with codetta phrase.

---

made so by musical idealism, I feel that any substitution of words whatever in this place would diminish the effect of the supremely beautiful phrase that the Maestro has written. Even if we had a monster from Lapland on stage the public would go into ecstasies.' Letter from Ghislanzoni to Giulio Ricordi, 21.9.1871. Busch, p. 223. Indeed if the public were unable to suspend its disbelief in such cases the opera houses would all have been bankrupt long ago.

* The production book makes it clear that the priestesses are expected to dance when this theme is played.

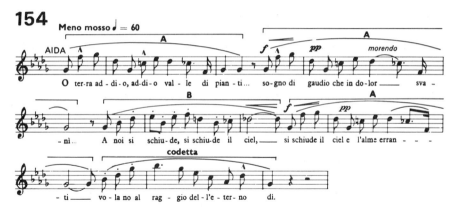

154

Not only that; the melody is repeated note for note by Aida, then after an episode based on Exs. 107a and 108b stated a third time in unison and even briefly recapitulated on the orchestra. Not even Bellini hazarded a design which involved the repetition of a phrase twelve times. Here the melody is everything. The shimmering harmonics on violins and cellos, the harp chords, the finely etched lines of woodwind have no other function than to set it in relief. Nor should familiarity blunt our response to what was new about it at the time and indeed gives it an abiding freshness to this day. Italian romantic composers have nearly always confined their melodic writing to the kind of intervals that a singer can encompass with only the most elementary harmonic imagination.* The wide arches of the main idea, though common enough in the vocal lines of Richard Strauss, are highly unusual in Italian opera of Verdi's time. Here they are designed to carry a cantilena based on eleven-syllable verse – a metre usually regarded as too long for lyrical setting but one to which Verdi was increasingly drawn in later years (compare Aida's romanza and the first movement of her duet with Amonasro). He was to achieve further wonders with it in the love-duet from *Otello* and Fenton's 'Sonetto' from *Falstaff*. In the central episode there is an effective use of the 'cutaway' technique, whereby the melody of 'Immenso Ftha' (Ex. 107a) is made to begin at the second bar, the implication being that it has continued unbroken during the duet. During the four bars of Ex. 108b Amneris enters dressed in mourning and kneels on the stone which seals the vault.† Her Requiescat for Radames' soul ('Pace t'imploro'), uttered in a monotone in a voice 'choked with tears', continues sporadically until the final curtain. As Ex. 154 dies away on two solo violins Aida falls dead in Radames' arms; the priests and priestesses back the last chord with a final 'Immenso Ftha'. It is one of the most magical endings to any opera.

OVERTURE

Although this was decisively repudiated by Verdi himself it merits a brief glance none the less. Like that of *La Forza del destino* it grows out of the original prelude,

* Bellini is again the exception here – but only on rare occasions, as in the terzetto 'No; non ti son rivale' in *La Straniera*, where at the words 'T'arrendi al prego estremo' he gives curiously pianistic figuration to the voice – another instance, no doubt, of that curious affinity with Chopin which so impressed the contemporaries of both.

† The production book helpfully warns against the danger of her dress catching fire from one of the gas jets!

diverging from it at the last cadence on the dominant of B minor before the priests have their final fling with Ex. 93(γ). Flutes, oboes and piccolo sound a warning on F sharp. There is a fidget in the violas, then over tremolando strings the clarinet gives out the melody of Aida's 'Numi, pietà' (Ex. 105) in B major, each of its 4-bar limbs shorn of its second, repetitive phrase, with curiously telescopic effect. The fidget is repeated, revealing itself as the beginning of the theme of Amneris's jealousy (Ex. 98), its angry agitated B minor contradicting the B major pleading of Aida. Begun by the full strings pianissimo in unaccompanied unison then breaking into harmony with sustaining winds, it runs its full 12-bar length before starting to develop in a restrained crescendo during which the rhythm of Aida's Ex. 92 emerges on cellos, bassoons, clarinet and horn, finally dissolving into rushing semiquaver patterns and a fierce cadence. From this, still in B minor, the priests' theme is launched in the form in which it occurs in the finale of Act II (i.e., Ex. 122b), here scored for bassoons, cellos and basses. True to its contrapuntal nature it evolves as a perpetual canon at the fifth above. The sequences tighten and eventually straighten out into a formal melody, curiously Elgarian in quality, which is interrupted by a series of three dominant flourishes (C sharp minor, E minor, A minor). There is a moment of repose as Ex. 105 is recollected with the same scoring as before and still haunted by the fidget of Ex. 98, but in a 'developmental' rather than a periodic form. After four bars of preparation new material is introduced with the suave theme of Amneris the princess (Ex. 97) on bassoon and unison strings (violins and violas using their G and C strings respectively with high accompaniment of woodwind pulsations). Immediately afterwards Ex. 98 reasserts itself, fortified by Ex. 122b darkly coloured by horns, trombones, bassoon and intermittently rolling timpani. After further development of both themes we hear Ex. 105 for the last time in unequal dialogue with the rhythm of Amneris's jealousy – the conflict between Ethiopian and Egyptian princess in orchestral dumbshow. When Ex. 105 has sunk defeated to its final cadence, Ex. 98 takes charge on unison strings punctuated by barks on lower brass, bassoons and timpani. Further developments of the opening phrase lead to a grand climax in the home key of D major based on the priests' motif, now in the form of Ex 93, in augmentation and decorated by exciting flute and piccolo trills. Amneris's vindictiveness is thus shown as the instrument of Ramfis's triumph.

Thence the music proceeds to a kind of reprise based not on Ex. 105 (with which Verdi has for the time being finished until its appearance in the opera) but Ex. 92, the generic Aida theme. This is reached in two stages. First a chain of sequences prepares for a climactic return of the opening phrase on lower strings and bassoons. The passage suggests the Venusberg music at its most hectic:

155

But this cannot be the real reprise because it is in the wrong key. Therefore further sequences are needed before, by a breathtaking modulation (*x*), the music finds its way back to the original D major. Note here the delightful extended phrasing of what was originally a one-bar unit.

156

The final cadence hangs in the air. Then woodwind and horn soloists announce Ex. 92, slower, *sempre pp e senza accento* with lower strings and brass touching in a discreet dominant harmony. Here for the first time we meet Aida's theme in the full, periodic form in which it will appear in the duet in Act II (Ex. 115, 'Amore, amore . . .'). It is repeated in its entirety with gathering momentum and the implied dominant pedal removed. First violins, upper woodwind and trumpet give a brilliant sheen to the melody while a group of middle instruments including second clarinet mutter Ex. 98. Thence to a very noisy combination of Exs. 93 and 98, the former once more in augmentation and forming the bass of the ensemble. Eventually the semiquavers of Ex. 98 dissolve into the Mozartian figuration observed in the overtures to *Luisa Miller* and *La Forza del destino*. A brief reference to Ex. 92 concludes the main body of the reprise. The tempo quickens yet again for the coda, which as so often introduces new material unconnected with the opera: a fierce D minor gesture is followed by a more gracious snatch of counterpoint with upward spiralling strings, ending with an epigrammatic cadence. After further winding up music of no great interest Ex. 92 is allowed the last word with an almost comically brassy flourish.

Although in no sense an orthodox sonata movement – much less so even than that of *La Forza del destino* – the overture to *Aida* is by no means formless. Its areas of exposition, development and reprise are all clearly defined, its contrasts of movement and stasis finely balanced. As an orchestral showpiece it could easily stand up in the concert hall. But as a *proemium* to the opera it will not do. For the analogy with the overture to *La Forza del destino* is a false one. The earlier opera benefits from an overture whose wealth of ideas and unexpected twists and turns foreshadows the epic complexities of the action. In relation to a drama as straightforward and measured in its pace as *Aida* the permutation and combination of themes amounts to a mere stirring of the pot-pourri.

In the years following Verdi's death *Aida* had no difficulty in entering the circle of steady favourites – witness the publication of a miniature score in 1914 alongside those of *Rigoletto*, *Il Trovatore*, *La Traviata*, *Un Ballo in maschera*, *Otello*, *Falstaff* and the Requiem.

It was a natural choice for the grand open-air performances instituted in Italy during the early years of this century in the arena at Verona and the Baths of Caracalla in Rome, and not only for its grandiose scenes. The third act can prove enchanting in the warm darkness of an Italian summer night. It has offered a wealth of possibilities to the scenographers of the world's leading opera houses; and can even make an effect on the lesser stages as English audiences were delighted to find when they attended the modest Vic-Wells performances in the 1920s. Since the last war, however, it has lost a little ground to *Don Carlos*; and not even Italian critics are as warm in its support as they once were. Massimo Mila and Andrea della Corte both find fault with the lack of human interest in the leading characters, notably Radames and Aida. True, these are not particularized in the manner of Carmen, or Hans Sachs, not to mention Carlos or King Philip; and it is understandable that the creator of Tatiana should find himself totally unmoved by the loves of Aida and Radames.* *Aida*, as has been said, is a classical drama; and its characters, with the possible exception of Amneris, too much a part of their respective backgrounds to be more than abstractions of the qualities they represent – heroic idealism, suffering and loving womanhood and wily primitive ferocity. Radames in particular is the eternal school captain, and school captains are usually too well adjusted to be interesting as people.

But there is another reason why *Aida* should have lost its pre-eminence in recent years. The present age, with its experience of totalitarian regimes, is suspicious of authority. In *Aida* state authority is never called into question except by Amneris, when the man she loves is condemned to death. But it is as a woman in love that she commands our sympathy, not as a fighter against oppression. By the standards of the story's convention Radames deserves his fate. It is the convention itself that has become faintly distasteful. Add to this the memory of blackshirted Radameses subduing Amonasro's hordes aided by all the resources of modern warfare while ever more spectacular performances in Verona and elsewhere proclaimed the glory of Fascist Italy, and it can be understood that despite a complete absence of racialist or fascist overtones the opera should have turned, even for Italians, just a little sour (compare the slump in Wagner's popularity among the present youth of Germany).

Yet with such a glorious stream of melodic invention *Aida* is unlikely to fall out of the repertoire. Unhappily, though by general consent a mezzo-soprano who fails with Amneris has no business on the operatic stage, and though the part of Amonasro is too short to overtax the average dramatic baritone, a certain mystique surrounds Radames and Aida. The former is assumed to require a heavy barnstorming tenor to be judged by the force with which he can deliver 'Nel fiero anelito'. As a result both 'Celeste Aida' and the final duet often fare badly. The poetic Radames of a Carlo Bergonzi or a Placido Domingo is often greeted with the comment 'Good, but not

* Letter from Tchaikovsky to S. J. Taneev 2 (14).1.1878. *Life and Letters of Tchaikovsky* (ed. R. Newmarch), p. 256.

really a Radames.' This is of course nonsense; neither of the tenors who created the Cairo and first Milan performances respectively was outstandingly heavy. As for Aida, so often assigned to singers of Turandot, Verdi's ideal choice after Teresa Stolz was Adelina Patti,* the singer of Amina, Lucia and the light florid repertoire. Roles as rich in musical variety as these will take more than one interpretation.

Aida is a milestone in Italian musical history, marking the perfection of *grand' opéra*, Italian style which had developed after the French model during the 1860s. Yet like many classical masterpieces it is not a forward-looking work. Though the drama is continuous the structure is basically that of formal numbers embedded within a con- tinuous musical texture; and though for a decade at least composers such as Ponchielli and Gomes would continue along this path with a similar amalgam of arias, duets, genre pieces and dances, future progress was to be towards a freer, more orchestrally based continuity in which the structural unit was the act rather than the scene. The leading spirits of the age were to be Wagner and Massenet. How and in what measure they were followed will be discussed in the next chapter.

* See letter to Giulio Ricordi, 5.10 (1877). Abbiati, IV, p. 37.

3 A PROBLEM OF IDENTITY
(ITALIAN OPERA 1870–90)

It is always tempting to find a historical turning-point at the beginning of a decade, and usually wrong. But the year 1870 provides a legitimate exception to the rule; enough happened then and immediately afterwards to give a new direction to Italian opera and Italian music in general. Not all the decisive events were concerned with music; nor were they confined to Italy. First and foremost was the shock of Sedan, felt throughout continental Europe and all the more powerfully because no one had thought it possible. True, the Europe that had existed since 1815 had been planned with a view to keeping France in her place. None the less successive French governments had been able to take advantage of tensions within the ranks of the Holy Alliance to acquire the prestige and influence from which their country was supposed to have been debarred. Napoleon III in particular was a master of the art of profitable semi-engagement in the affairs of Europe. With the indecisive battle of Solferino in 1859 he frightened the Austrians out of Lombardy and took Nice and Savoy as his reward. He had sent in his troops to fight alongside the British and Austrians in the Crimean War and so gained the good-will of Palmerston's England. His new Paris of 1860 with its boulevards designed by Baron Haussmann was regarded as the last word in modern urban planning. No one by this time begrudged him his title of Emperor; while those who looked with unease at Prussia's steady rise to prominence – her annexation of Schleswig-Holstein, her defeat of Austria at Königgrätz – were fully confident that if ever she were to tangle with Second Empire France her troops would be as soundly defeated as they had been by the Emperor's uncle. Napoleon III believed it no less firmly; indeed it was he who declared war, ostensibly to prevent the succession of a Hohenzollern to the Spanish throne. With the resulting defeat, the two sieges of Paris, first by the Prussians, then by the French government held at bay by the forces of the Commune, the exile of the Emperor and the collapse of a so-called Empire whose brilliance and gaiety had made Paris the cynosure of nations, it seemed that the face of Europe was about to be dramatically changed.

For fifty years and more what could loosely be called Germany had been the breeding-ground of illiberal, violently nationalistic sentiments and theories – as though its people were determined to be revenged not only on the humiliations of Jena but on the Peace of Westphalia of two centuries before. Such works as Kleist's bloodthirsty play *Die Hermannschlacht*, the defeated Romans symbolizing the French, the *Staatslehre* of Fichte, the curiously inhuman 'idealist' philosophy of Hegel, the aggressive pseudo-history of Treitschke – all these were symptomatic of an intellectual climate in which men consciously rejected conventionally enlightened principles; and many of them were to find an echo in the prose writings of Wagner. So long as such ideas remained 'in the mind' they could be looked upon as the charming aberrations of a fundamental innocence, the refreshing unreason of noble savages (for as such the Germans were regarded by Madame de Staël as by Tacitus). But now words were passing into deeds. The Prussian armies had been reorganized by Clausewitz and Scharnhorst. A new generation was being reared on the dour ideals and maxims of von Moltke with his talk of absolute obedience, 'blood and iron', and the constant reminder that man is not put on this earth for his pleasure alone. At the helm was one of the most astute of all European statesmen. As a young man Bismarck had greatly amused his Parisian hosts by announcing that he would like to explore the city to find out suitable gun-emplacements. They were certainly not laughing now.

No one viewed the turn of events with greater dismay than Verdi. In the past he had grumbled about French arrogance and artistic snobbery and the difficulty of pleasing a French public; but at the crisis he revealed himself a staunch Francophile. Hence his and Giuseppina's heartfelt letters of commiseration to the du Locles as enemy troops closed in upon Paris.* Nor was he alarmed on their account alone: '. . . I fear a terrible future for us,' he wrote to Arrivabene. 'Ah, the North! It's a country, a people that terrify me. . . . For my part I would have liked our government to take a more generous line and to have settled a debt of gratitude. . . . Yes, I know you will say, "And have a European war?" But a European war can't be avoided, and if France had been saved we should have been saved ourselves.'† To his old friend Countess Maffei he poured out his heart yet more fully . . .

> in the last resort France gave freedom and civilization to the modern world. And if she falls, don't let us delude ourselves, all our liberties and civilization will fall with her. By all means let our statesmen and men of letters sing praises to the knowledge, science and even (God forgive them) the art of these conquerors, but if they looked a little more closely they would see that the blood of the ancient Goths still flows in their veins; that their pride is immeasurable, that they are hard and intolerant and despise everything that isn't Germanic, and that their rapacity knows no bounds. Men of head but no heart; a powerful race but not a civilized one. And that King who always has the words 'God and Providence' on his lips, and with their help destroys the best part of Europe. He believes himself pre-ordained to reform the morals and punish the vices of the modern world. A fine type of missionary! Attila of old (another missionary of that ilk) halted before the majesty of the capital of the ancient world; but this one is about to bombard the capital of the modern one. . . .‡

However, few of Verdi's fellow-countrymen shared his fears. Their sympathies lay with Prussia, spearhead of a newly formed Germany as Piedmont had been of Italy, and with Bismarck seen as a northern Cavour. True, Prussia had never given material help to Italy as France had done, but neither had she imposed humiliating conditions as a recompense. Moreover, she had defeated Italy's old enemy, Austria, in 1866. Only two years before, Napoleon had allowed King Vittorio Emanuele to move his capital to Florence on condition that he made no attempt to enter Rome, where the Pope's authority was maintained with the help of a French garrison. Not surprisingly Italy's first action after the defeat of Sedan was to take advantage of

---

* See letters to du Locle, 22.8 and 24.10.1870. Günther, 'Zur Entstehung von Verdis *Aida*', in *Studi Musicali*, Anno II (1973), No. 1, pp. 63–4, 68.

† Letter to Arrivabene, 13.9.1870. Alberti, p. 121.

‡ Letter to Clarina Maffei, 30.9.1870. 'Il Carteggio di G. Verdi colla Contessa Maffei', in A. Luzio, *Profili biografici e bozzetti storici*, II (Milan, 1927), pp. 528–9.

France's discomfiture to march into Rome with complete impunity, and the following year to make the ancient capital the new seat of government. Even Ghislanzoni, who saw through the pretensions of the new Italy, made it politely clear to Verdi that he did not think the fault was all on one side. 'I like Napoleon,' he wrote. 'How ungrateful everyone is! And how base! Only a month ago all France was screaming for "war, war" with a single voice . . . and today they blame the Emperor alone for the disaster that has happened. The betrayed is called the betrayer. . . . We shall see how it will end. Napoleon is alive and the time will come when history will judge him and the republicans.'*

In fact it did not end as badly for France or Italy as Verdi had feared. For the pilot who would one day demand the suppression by violence of the German socialists (and be 'dropped' for it by an emotional young Kaiser) forbade the bombardment of Paris (much to the disapproval of Richard and Cosima Wagner);† and in the end all that France lost was an Emperor, Alsace-Lorraine and a good deal of face. Indeed, French music could be said to have benefited from the national defeat and the huge economic recession that followed in its wake, forcing theatre after theatre to close. Before 1870 opera was the only field in which a French composer could acquire fame and fortune; now a public began to be formed for the essentially untheatrical talents of a César Franck or a Fauré. Composers such as Saint-Saëns and Lalo were encouraged to spread their wings in the field of symphonic and chamber music, in which the excellent disciplines of the Paris Conservatoire could bear fruit. When after several years during which only the Opéra had been kept alive at the Palais Garnier by a strict diet of tried favourites,‡ a new operatic boom arose with Massenet as chief practitioner, French opera – and indeed French music in general – had acquired an identity and distinction which, Berlioz and Bizet apart, it had never known since the Revolution of 1789.

The recession of the 1870s was not confined to France. In Vienna bankruptcies and suicides came thick and fast; had Bayreuth been inaugurated at any other time we may be sure that it would not have had to wait six years before becoming a yearly or two-yearly event. In Italy one of the victims of the financial climate was Verdi's Neapolitan friend Cesare De Sanctis; here as in France the musical world was quick to feel its effects.

It may be remembered that in 1868 Emilio Broglio, Minister of Education, had propounded a scheme for relieving the State of the need to provide for the conservatories of music, so prompting an uproar throughout the peninsula and a stinging public reply from Boito.§ To their credit successive governments of the 1870s took a less blinkered view. For some time now the Italian conservatories had fallen into decadence and provincialism. Only that of Milan, under the admirable direction of Lauro Rossi for the past twenty years, had proved an exception.¶ The death in 1870

* Letter from Ghislanzoni, 11.9.1870. Busch, pp. 63–4.

† See Cosima Wagner's *Diaries*, I (1869–1877) (translated by G. Skelton) (London, 1978), p. 292.

‡ Saint-Saëns's *Samson et Dalila* was turned down by the directors and its première given not in Paris but in Weimar, 1877.

§ See Vol. 2, pp. 31–2.

¶ Rossi's *Guida ad un corso di armonia pratica orale* (Milan, 1858) is for its time an eminently practical book of instruction and well up to date in its harmonic notions. He himself was one of the first in Italy to revive the performance of renaissance and medieval music.

of Mercadante, still nominally Director of the Naples Conservatory though in-
capacitated by blindness, provided the occasion to review conservatory teaching
throughout Italy. For this a commission was appointed early in 1871. It was to sit in
Florence during March and Verdi was asked to preside. At first he refused as
categorically as he had refused the invitation to succeed Mercadante at the Naples
Conservatory; but in the end he agreed to take part in its deliberations. Meanwhile
he had made known his views on musical education to Florimo at Naples in a letter
which has become famous for the catch-phrase '. . . Return to the past; and it will be
a step forward';* and to the deputy for Parma, Giuseppe Piroli, who was acting as intermediary between him and the Minister of Education, he expressed himself in
similar vein. In a word, Verdi was for concentrating on the basic disciplines of
harmony and counterpoint and a study of the classics (only the Italian ones are mentioned and their selection is decidedly curious). There was to be no study of modern
music since this would only turn the pupils into bad imitators. In a long minute addressed to the minister he made his attitude still clearer.

> It is a strange thing, this conflict between the so-called men of learning and those
> who *do* (and a fruitless one because of the indifference of the second party and the
> arrogant obstinacy of the first); and what is even stranger is to observe that all the
> greatest achievements of this century of ours are hardly ever the product of
> Conservatories!
>
> The Bologna Liceo and the Naples Conservatorio boast the great names of
> Rossini and Bellini; but in my view they are quite wrong to plume themselves on
> these men. Rossini, to begin with, makes a mockery of the musical knowledge
> gained at the Liceo with his first operas in which you frequently come across
> musical solecisms and mistakes of grammar. And are not these sublime solecisms
> committed on purpose in other, later operas and even in *Guillaume Tell*, an opera
> from every other point of view most chastened and correct in all its parts? Bellini
> possessed exceptional qualities such as no Conservatory can impart and lacked
> those which a Conservatory ought to have taught him.
>
> From this you will understand that I would feel bound to leave the Conser-
> vatories as they are – apart from a few partial reforms regarding singing and com-
> position – and direct my concern to a surer, more useful and more practical
> purpose: the theatre.
>
> Let the Minister revive the theatres and there will be no lack of composers,
> singers or instrumentalists. Let him establish for instance three to serve later as
> models for all the others. One in the Capital, the second at Naples and the third at
> Milan. Orchestra and chorus to be salaried by the government.
>
> In each theatre a singing school for the public, free of charge, the pupils being
> obliged to work in the theatre for a given time. For every theatre a single
> Maestro-Concertatore-cum-Conductor who would be responsible for the entire
> musical side. A single Producer on whom would devolve everything that
> concerns the Mise-en-scène.
>
> Every year two new operas should be produced by composers at the start of

* Letter to Florimo, 5.1.1871. See Walker, 'Verdi and Florimo', in *Music and Letters* (October 1945),
pp. 201–8; for final version, *Copialettere*, pp. 232–3, where the epigram appears as 'Let us return to the
past; it will be a step forward' ('Torniamo all'antico: sarà un progresso').

their career (*debuttanti*); the scores should be examined by a commission of men who are learned without being pedants and who can't be accused of having preconceived ideas. . . .*

Such views were not peculiar to Verdi. They would be urged later in the decade by the critic D'Arcais both in the Roman periodical *L'Opinione* and in the Florentine *Nuova Antologia*.

But they were far from the government's way of thinking. Many deputies thought it morally wrong to expect the average peasant to contribute towards a form of entertainment from which he would never derive personal benefit.† The same arguments were urged by the radical members of the Milan City Council against the allocation of public moneys towards the first performance of Verdi's Requiem in the Church of S. Marco; and it took all Boito's eloquence to carry the day in Verdi's favour.‡ Faced as they thought with the alternative of having to support the theatres or the conservatories, the governments of the day did not hesitate to opt for the latter. Indeed their record in the field of musical education was a good one. The existing institutions were reorganized and their teaching methods brought up to date with more emphasis (too much in the opinion of Verdi and D'Arcais) given to training in instrumental composition. A new Conservatory founded at Pesaro with money left for the purpose by Rossini proved a model of its kind; and if no conservatory however good can be guaranteed to turn out a regular supply of geniuses, the Pesaro school would at least one day boast such well equipped musicians as Zandonai and Respighi.

With the theatres it was a very different story. While Italy had been divided into small states and provinces of Austria the theatres had been maintained by the central governments concerned and impresarios, singers, librettists and even composers forced to meet their obligations, if necessary, by the police. The first to break the system and withdraw the government subsidy – not as a matter of principle but merely to meet a particular financial crisis – had been Cavour in 1860. After the unification of Italy the responsibility of keeping the theatres alive gradually shifted from the government to the city councils, whose grants were often pitifully inadequate for their purpose. By a curious irony the 1870s, a period of poverty which saw the riots against the grain tax of 1877 and the floods of 1879, was also the period par excellence of Italian grand opera, or 'opera-ballo' as it was sometimes called – in effect the most costly type of opera outside Bayreuth. As D'Arcais pointed out, whereas an orchestra of fifty players and a chorus of thirty-two had been adequate for the opera seasons of fifty years before, present requirements were an orchestra of not less than a hundred, a chorus of eighty and a triple roster of soloists.§ And this at a time when fees demanded by front-rank principals had risen to astronomical heights: 25–30,000 lire

* Minute addressed to Correnti, Minister of Education and enclosed with letter to Piroli, 7.2.1871. *Carteggi Verdiani*, III, pp. 78–80.

† See F. D'Arcais, 'Rassegna Musicale', in *Nuova Antologia* (Sept.–Oct. 1881), pp. 145–56.

‡ See Gatti, *Verdi* (English edn. tr. E. Abbott, London, 1955), p. 256.

§ F. D'Arcais, 'Rassegna Musicale', in *Nuova Antologia* (Mar.–Apr. 1879), pp. 172–80. He makes no mention of the ballet dancers since most of the larger theatres had always employed a ballet company to give performances either before or after the opera and sometimes between the acts. Evidently the divorce of opera and ballet in Italy was a custom which died hard, since even in as revered a work as *Don*

for a prima donna soprano, 40–50,000 for a tenor, 10–15,000 for a mezzo-soprano or a baritone, 8–10,000 for a bass.* Inevitably the impresario found himself speculating with non-existent capital. Nor was he able to guarantee that the programme which he had announced to the subscribers could be carried through. If it appeared that a scheduled novelty did not please it must be taken off as quickly as possible and replaced by a tried favourite.

Not that it was easy to tell from its first-night reception whether an opera had pleased, due to a peculiar feature of the Italian scene – the war of the publishers. 'In no other country in the world,' wrote D'Arcais, 'does the publisher possess the power and authority that he has in Italy.'† He was alluding to the system initiated by Lucca in the 1840s whereby an opera would be commissioned by a publisher rather than a theatrical management, the publisher himself taking all responsibility for having it mounted in suitable style at whatever theatre he chose and allotting to the composer forty per cent of the subsequent hiring fees. Verdi's *Attila* and *Il Corsaro* were both commissioned in this way by Lucca; Ricordi was to do the same for *La Battaglia di Legnano*, *Stiffelio* and *Aroldo*. True, for most of his commissions Verdi still preferred to deal directly with the theatres concerned; but by the time he had made his peace with La Scala, Milan, which from 1869 onwards was to be the venue of all his Italian premières, the casting and production were looked after by Giulio Ricordi, who passed the composer's instructions on to the impresario. It was a system which the average composer was happy to accept since it relieved him of much tedious responsibility. At the same time it exposed him to the savage warfare waged between Lucca and Ricordi through their respective claques and house magazines (Lucca's *Italia Musicale* and Ricordi's *Gazzetta Musicale di Milano*). Francesco Lucca died in 1872, but he left a true Boudicca in his widow Giovannina, a formidable but large-hearted woman of whom Wagner graciously remarked that, 'Nature originally intended to make a man, then, realizing that Italian men are not up to much, she corrected herself.'‡ Among native composers Ricordi held the trump card of Verdi. Up till the 1870s Lucca could boast no one of greater distinction than Petrella; but he had been shrewd enough to acquire the rights in such influential foreign composers as Gounod, Meyerbeer and Wagner. Ricordi's chief sphere of influence was La Scala, Milan; Lucca's was the Teatro Comunale, Bologna. Here in 1871 *Lohengrin* was given its first performance in Italy under Mariani to general acclaim. Two years later the claque at La Scala managed to get this same opera whistled off the stage after a few performances. Meanwhile in the columns of the *Gazzetta Musicale di Milano* the aged Florimo thundered his denunciation of Wagner and all his works (of which he knew nothing), returning continually to Verdi's aphorism 'Torniamo all'antico; sarà un progresso', much to the composer's embarrassment. In 1876 *Rienzi* was performed in Bologna in Wagner's presence. The correspondent of the *Gazzetta* ventured to express his enthusiasm, only to be

---

Carlos Verdi's own ballet was often cut together with the original first act so as to make room for an extraneous ballet at the end. Only *Aida* and *La Gioconda* seem to have resisted this treatment.

   * For these statistics see F. D'Arcais, 'L'Industria musicale in Italia', in *Nuova Antologia* (May–June 1879).

   † *Ibid.*

   ‡ Cosima Wagner, *Diaries*, I, p. 489.

reproved by an editorial footnote to the effect that while the contributor was no doubt sincere in his views and there was no intention of censoring them the truth was that *Rienzi* had been very badly received by a discerning public.*

Such journalistic brouhahas could hardly benefit a genuine talent; but it could sometimes exalt a mediocre one. A spectacular case in point is the young composer Stefano Gobatti. In 1873 he produced at the Teatro Comunale, Bologna, *I Goti*, a number-opera of basically old-fashioned stamp showing all the faults characteristic of composers who tried to escape from the post-Rossinian prison-house without any idea of where to go – stiff, awkward gait (almost every number is an andante in 2/4), clogged harmonies, over-elaborate orchestral figuration. Its most memorable idea is a unison chorus 'Dell'impero de' Goti la stella' in Risorgimentali decasyllables of the type to which Verdi had bidden farewell in *Un Ballo in Maschera* with 'Dunque l'onta di tutti sol una':

157

Gobatti : I GOTI (1873)

Incredibly, this opera was hailed as Italy's finest essay to date in the 'music of the future'. Other theatres took it up only to find that they had a white elephant on their hands. A performance in Genoa the following year elicited from Verdi the observation that 'at present [Gobatti] is writing a language of which he simply has no knowledge, and though he may have the finest ideas in the world he will never manage to express them without having a better sense of melody, harmony, poetry and literature'.† Gobatti's next opera, *Luce*, was a failure despite all the attempts of the firm of Lucca to persuade the public otherwise; after which the name of Gobatti vanishes from the history of Italian opera. He wrote several more stage works but to no purpose. He died in 1914 having spent his last years in an asylum. To the end he ascribed his failure to the intrigues of others; in fact it was his early success, not his failure, that he owed to intrigue.

As the decade wore on and the economic situation worsened not all the 'puffs preliminary' could prevent the closure of theatre after theatre due to a lack of subsidy. By 1878 the seasons at Venice and Florence had become intermittent. In 1880 the Carlo Felice in Genoa closed its doors; next year it was the turn of Venice's La Fenice. Of the major theatres the Teatro Regio, Turin weathered the storm due to the intelligent management of Depanis and the ability of its chief conductor, Carlo Pedrotti; so, more precariously, did La Scala, Milan, bolstered by the energies of Giulio Ricordi and Franco Faccio. The seasons at the San Carlo, Naples, had become by common consent a disgrace.‡ Rome's leading theatre, the Apollo, could offer only four works for the carnival season of 1878–9 one of which (Marchetti's *Don Giovanni d'Austria*) had in the event to be postponed. Parma and Modena had

* *Gazzetta Musicale di Milano*, Anno XXXI, No. 46 (22.11.1876), p. 401.

† Letter to Arrivabene, 7.3.1874. Alberti, pp. 66–78.

‡ See F. D'Arcais, 'Rassegna Musicale', *Nuova Antologia* (Mar.–Apr. 1879), pp. 172–80.

declined into provincial status. All this must be seen as the background to Verdi's cri-de-coeur: 'Our theatre . . . is sick unto death and it must be kept alive at all costs. . . . If theatres close they won't open again.'*

By contrast non-theatrical music was in a much healthier state. By this time each of the big cities had its Quartet Society and its Orchestral Society which created a public for works not normally heard outside the walls of the Conservatories. At the same time the range of music studied in the Conservatories themselves had widened enormously; and in the pro-Prussian atmosphere of the 1870s that taste for the German symphonic repertory which Verdi so deplored continued to grow, encouraged by the presence in Italy of more than one distinguished foreigner from beyond the Alps. Following the break-up of his marriage, Hans von Bülow had taken up residence in Florence in 1869; and after it had been decided to send Lauro Rossi to succeed Mercadante in Naples he was being seriously considered for the vacant post of Head of the Milan Conservatory – to Verdi's intense alarm.† In Rome, where he spent several months of each year, Liszt became the centre of an artistic circle of which Baron von Keudell and his own pupil Sgambati were the moving spirits; while from his villa in Posilipo, where he had settled as a wine-grower, Liszt's former rival Thalberg exercised a powerful influence on the piano students of the Naples Conservatory, notably Giuseppe Martucci. It would be some time before the fruits of the new Italian instrumental tradition would ripen. But in the works of those who left the Conservatories in the late 1870s a more symphonic way of thinking is already apparent, of which the previous generation had been innocent. Bottesini's concerto for violin and double bass evinces throughout that mixture of operatic lyricism with sub-Paganinian virtuosity which passed for an instrumental style in Italy up till 1870; Martucci's Nocturne in G flat major for orchestra has the quality of a genuine tone-poem. Even Ponchielli's quartet for wind with piano accompaniment is little more than thinly disguised ballet music; whereas the quintets of Sgambati link hands with the chamber music of Schumann and Mendelssohn.

Inevitably this new direction in musical taste had consequences for opera as well. The older composers such as Cagnoni and Lauro Rossi now began to parade their schoolroom learning in the theatre in a way that would have seemed absurd twenty years before. The success of Meyerbeer's *L'Africaine*, Gomes's *Guarany* and Verdi's *Aida* had broken down that prejudice against exoticism which had marked the post-Donizettian tradition. In his *Contessa di Mons* of 1874 Rossi quotes the *Jota Aragonesa* at some length, for which his source could have been either Liszt's Spanish Rhapsody or Glinka's transcription. His younger colleagues were more disposed to draw upon the folk-idioms of Northern Europe; so it is no surprise to find Filippi, critic of *Perseveranza*, writing of Ciro Pinsuti's *Mattia Corvino* (1877) 'one can see that Pinsuti has studied to good effect the Rhapsodies of Liszt, Schubert's Hungarian Divertissement and the dances of Brahms. . . .'‡ The same critic had to say of 'Un'Estate a Perugia' by Luigi Mancinelli, for some years one of the white hopes of Italian music until like Faccio he devoted himself to conducting: 'It is very obvious that Mancinelli is in love, and very much in love, with Schubert, Schumann, Mendelssohn and

---

* Letter to Faccio, 1879–80. R. De Rensis, *Franco Faccio e Verdi*, pp. 182–5.

† See letter to Piroli, 24.2.1871. *Carteggi Verdiani*, III, p. 80. In the event Mazzucato was appointed to Milan.

‡ Quoted in Biaggi, 'Rassegna Musicale', in *Nuova Antologia* (July–Aug. 1877), pp. 970–90.

Gounod; he is very fond of reproducing Gounod's style of cadence with that blessed 6/4 chord which is the seasoning, the sine qua non, the vade mecum of all today's music.'*

Indeed Gounod, together with Meyerbeer and followed at some distance by Thomas, remained the strongest of strictly operatic influences during the 1870s. *Faust*, composed in 1859 and enlarged for the Paris Opéra, had already bid fair to replace *Il Trovatore* as the most popular opera in the European repertoire, though it still encountered resistance in Germany as a desecration of Goethe's play. *Roméo et Juliette* had also gained a firm foothold in Italy. Of Thomas's operas *Mignon* fared slightly better than *Hamlet*. By the end of the decade every one of Meyerbeer's French operas was in the repertory of the larger Italian theatres.

The most discussed of all foreign composers was Richard Wagner – 'the basin in which all the Pilates of music criticism like to wash their hands',† as Filippi put it with characteristic panache. An entire chapter could be devoted to the reception and influence of Wagner's music in Italy – indeed a German musicologist has recently made it the subject of a volume of more than five hundred pages.‡ The question is complicated by the fact that due to the circumstances of his life, the long gaps between the completion of his music dramas and their performance, the spate of theoretical and polemical writings that poured from his pen, and the entrenched position taken up by his enemies and partisans alike, the Italian musical world was already two steps behind Wagner the composer and one step behind Wagner the theorist by the time that his works began to be staged in Italy.

In 1848, having put the final touches to *Lohengrin*, Wagner had proceeded to embroil himself in politics, with the result that he was forced to flee from Saxony and to spend the next sixteen years in a life of hardship and dependence on others. In the first years of his exile he produced a number of artistic tracts of which the most widely read was *Oper und Drama* – 'the Sinai tablets of Wagnerian music-drama'.§ The theory here outlined may be described as Aristotelian; it is an elaborate extension of the principles laid down in that part of the Poetics that deals with music's role in tragedy – principles which had already inspired the Florentine Camerata and were echoed in Gluck's manifesto that accompanied the dedication of his *Alceste* to the Grand Duke of Tuscany. Like Gluck, Wagner complained that 'a means of expression [music] had been made the end; and that the end of expression [drama] had become the means'. This is the proposition on which his initial theory of music drama was founded and in the light of which he was to begin the great tetralogy that would exemplify the 'Artwork of the future'. Then in 1857 with *Siegfried* not yet complete he became converted to the philosophy of Schopenhauer, according to which music is the supreme reality in a world of illusion; and though he never retracted his earlier view in print the aesthetic of Schopenhauer begins from then on to colour both his compositions and his prose writings.¶ In the music the change occurs almost im-

---

* Quoted in *Gazzetta Musicale di Milano*, 6.2.1876. One wonders what Verdi, an avid reader of Ricordi's house magazine, would have made of that remark.

† F. Filippi, in *Perseveranza* (Milan, 19.3.1879). Quoted in Alberti, pp. 231–2.

‡ U. Jung, *Die Rezeption der Kunst Richard Wagners in Italien* (Vol. XXXV in *Studien zur Musikgeschichte des neunzehnten Jahrhunderts*, Regensburg, 1974).

§ G. Abraham, *A Hundred Years of Music* (2nd edn, London, 1949), p. 98.

¶ He did, however, mention in his open letter to Fr. Billot of 1860 entitled 'Zukunftmusik' that he

perceptibly. *Rheingold* was conceived strictly according to the tenets of *Oper und Drama*; but because of its purely expository nature it does not conflict with a theory of musical hegemony. In *Die Walküre* and *Siegfried* the music increasingly exceeds the brief originally laid down for it; so that Ernest Newman is surely right in asserting that Wagner's conversion to Schopenhauer, which certainly played its part in his decision to put aside *Siegfried* to write *Tristan und Isolde*, was due not to a sudden revelation but rather to the gradual emergence of ideas which had been subconsciously germinating for the past few years.* The miracle is that the unity of the *Ring*, written over a period of more than twenty years, should have survived not only the composer's stylistic development but also a radical change of viewpoint, so that the increased musical density from one opera to the next appears natural and logical.

But if it was difficult to keep pace with Wagner the theorist it was still more so as regards the composer. Since the performance of *Lohengrin* in Weimar under Liszt all the operas written before his exile were theoretically available. But sometimes Wagner himself put difficulties in the way of their performance; more often impresarios showed themselves reluctant to mount the works of a notorious revolutionary and so antagonize the ruler who paid their wages. In 1861 the revised *Tannhäuser* had failed spectacularly at the Paris Opéra.

Then in the mid-sixties the tide turned. Due to the beneficence of Wagner's new-found patron, Ludwig II of Bavaria, *Tristan und Isolde* was given in Munich in 1865, followed by *Die Meistersinger* in 1868 and both *Rheingold* and *Die Walküre* in 1869 and 1870 respectively – these last much against the composer's will, since he had already set his heart on launching the *Ring* at a special theatre of his own, the future Bayreuth Festspielhaus. Meanwhile he himself had become respectable in the eyes of Europe; *Rienzi*, *Der fliegende Holländer*, *Tannhäuser* and *Lohengrin* were circulating freely throughout Austria-Hungary and the German states, when Giovannina Lucca decided to acquire Wagner's Italian rights; and one by one these same operas made their Italian debut (*Lohengrin* 1871, *Tannhäuser* 1872, *Rienzi* 1874, *Der fliegende Holländer* 1877). No opera later than *Lohengrin* was heard in Italy until shortly after Wagner's death in 1883 when Angelo Neumann brought his touring company to give performances of the *Ring* in Venice, Turin, Rome and Bologna (Milan being pointedly excluded). The singers and conductor were German and for what must have been the first time on record Italian audiences were made to listen to operas given in a language other than their own. The first of Wagner's mature works to be given in translation was *Tristan und Isolde*, conducted by Giuseppe Martucci at Bologna in 1888. That same year the widow Lucca retired from business and ended a war of nearly half a century by selling out to Giulio Ricordi, who was thus forced to promote the works of a composer towards whom he retained a lifelong antipathy. In the following year he mounted *I Maestri Cantori di Norimbergo* at La Scala under Faccio, having previously travelled with him and the young Puccini to Bayreuth to decide upon suitable cuts. 'Not all of us have the good fortune to be able

---

was unable to read his earlier prose works without a feeling of nausea. R. Wagner, *Gesammelte Schriften* (4th edn, Leipzig, 1907) VII, p. 87.

* E. Newman, *The Life of Richard Wagner* (London, 1937), II, p. 291.

to travel abroad at our publisher's expense like Puccini,' wrote the envious Catalani, 'who has been provided with a fine pair of scissors and given by this same publisher the task of making the necessary cuts in the score of the *Mastersingers* so as to fit it to the figures of the good Milanese, just as though it were a suit. But the Milanese are beginning to rise in revolt and to say that they want to wear the suit just as it has been worn by the Germans up to now.'* During the 1890s individual operas from the *Ring* appeared separately in Italian translation. If an Italian *Parsifal* had to wait until 1914 before becoming a reality this was mainly due to the widow Cosima, who for years refused to allow the 'Sacred Festival Drama' to be performed outside the sacred walls of Bayreuth.

Not surprisingly, therefore, it was a long time before Italian critics, professors and leaders of musical opinion brought Wagner into focus. Very typical was the experience of the critic E. Panzacchi who reported on the Bayreuth Festival for the *Nuova Antologia*.† Having familiarized himself thoroughly with *Oper und Drama* and the notions of an Artwork of the Future which would unite music, poetry and spectacle in a transcendent whole, he went to the Italian première of *Lohengrin* prepared for the most bizarre extravagances and abstrusities, only to find that it was – just an opera; nobler, more spacious than most of its type, free from all stereotyped forms such as the couplet and the cabaletta, but still an opera. Next year a performance of *Tannhäuser* – that controversial work which the French had hissed off the stage – confirmed him in the view that the devil was nothing like as black as he had painted himself. With these considerations in mind he went to the first Bayreuth Festival of 1876, expecting a *Ring* in the style of the two operas that he had already seen; and of course *Rheingold* sent him reeling. Wagner *had* meant what he said in his early prose writings after all. Of course if he had read, say, the Wagner centenary essay on Beethoven of 1870 he might have viewed the completed *Ring* in a very different light. Similarly if he had been able to visit Munich in the 1860s and see performances of *Tristan und Isolde* and *Die Meistersinger* he would indeed have found the music difficult, too harmonically charged, too much conceived in terms of orchestra, too little in terms of the voice; but he would have realized that neither needs to be viewed through the spectacles of *Oper und Drama*. Those who missed the Bayreuth Festival met with a similar experience to Panzacchi's seven years later with the visit of Neumann's troupe. D'Arcais had looked forward to their appearance in Rome as an artistic event of major importance. Yet it was to leave him as disoriented as his colleague. Not until the mid-eighties did the Italians succeed in coming to terms with the mature Wagner and so learn to use with discrimination a term which they used to apply to such works as *Aida*, Goldmark's *Königin von Saba* and even Bizet's *Carmen* – the work which Nietzsche hailed as the perfect antithesis of everything that Wagner stood for.

All this explains why, for all the brave words that were bandied about on Wagnerism and the music of the future, traces of the mature Wagner's influence are hard to find in Italian opera between *Aida* and *Otello*. On the other hand certain mannerisms, and even snatches of melody, will recall the early operas, especially *Lohengrin*, which had become a repertory work within a few years of its Italian

---

* Letter to Depanis, 20.8.1889. Catalani, *Lettere* (ed. C. Gatti), pp. 100–1.

† 'La tetralogia di Riccardo Wagner' in *Nuova Antologia* 2nd series, III, 10 (October 1876), pp. 265–78.

première: the slow broad gait, particularly where the poet has provided eleven-syllable verse, the climactic insistence of the dominant major ninth, imperfect cadences with triple appoggiature, the occasional gruppetto. At one point Dardano, the father/villain of Catalani's *Dejanice* proclaims himself first cousin to Wolfram:

158

Catalani: DEJANICE (1883)

A few pages later he pronounces a decree of banishment on the hero in a rhythm which awakes inappropriate memories of Tannhäuser's passionate address to Venus. Likewise it is impossible to hear Elda's cry to the God of the Baltic without thinking of Elisabeth's 'Dich, teure Halle, grüss' ich wieder'. But nothing in Catalani's work or that of his contemporaries as yet approaches the world of *Tristan, Parsifal* or the *Ring* – unless it be their readiness to revel in orchestral sound. With their new-found mastery of the modern orchestra came a corresponding interest in pictorialism, which sometimes threatened to get the upper hand of dramatic expression. Hence their fondness during this time for northern myths and settings which gave them the opportunity for atmospheric tone-painting: Puccini's own *Le Villi*, Zuelli's *La Fata del Nord** and the entire dramatic oeuvre of Catalani except for *Dejanice*. The older generation shook their heads. 'An excellent musician,' was Verdi's verdict on Catalani, 'though he has an exaggerated idea of the importance of the orchestra.'†
Likewise on the composer of *Le Villi* shortly after its successful performance at the Teatro Dal Verme: 'I've heard the musician Puccini is being very well spoken of. . . . He follows the modern trends, which is natural, but he keeps steadily to melody, which is neither ancient nor modern. However, it seems that the symphonic element predominates in him! No harm in that. Only here you have to proceed with care.

---

* One of the two operas which won the competition for which *Le Villi* had been submitted in 1883.
† Letter to Giulio Ricordi *circa* January 1892 quoted in Abbiati, IV, p. 428.

Opera is opera; symphony is symphony, and I don't think it a good thing to insert a symphonic piece into an opera just for the pleasure of making the orchestra dance.'*

Not until the end of the decade do we find that tendency to organize acts or parts of acts through a network of short recurring themes which is the nearest approach to Wagner's mature style that the Italians were ever to attempt. If they never pursue it with Wagnerian principles the reason lies in the constant demand of Italian singers and audiences for the finite, autonomous vocal period which no composer could afford to neglect. It remained for Puccini to reconcile both principles by the use of motifs which can be incorporated quite naturally into set pieces. Here too his model was a Wagnerian one – *Die Meistersinger*. But to expatiate on this would take us beyond the limits of the present study.

A more immediate influence on the new generation born in the 1850s was that of Massenet, whose opera *Le Roi de Lahore* reached Milan in 1879. He was to be Ricordi's answer to Wagner and the host of foreigners who had made the fortunes of the house of Lucca. Ricordi even commissioned Massenet's next opera *Hérodiade*, to be composed to an Italian text by Angelo Zanardini. In the event the composer found this too difficult and preferred to work on a French version by Louis Gallet which was then re-translated into Italian by Zanardini, keeping Gallet's prosody. For years *Erodiade* proved more popular in Italy than *Hérodiade* in France, where the opera was first heard, incredibly, in its Italian version at Victor Maurel's newly opened Théâtre Italien in 1884.† Although Massenet never fulfilled Ricordi's hopes and his subsequent operas took much longer to penetrate south of the Alps, his influence on the younger composers remained decisive in the sphere of rhythmical articulation. As we have noticed, once fioritura began to disappear Italian vocal melody tended to become curiously stiff at the joints. The bones of the old Italian metres obtruded awkwardly. Whether handled skilfully by a Gomes or a Ponchielli, or bungled by a Gobatti, the musical periods remain fundamentally regular and ceremonious. Massenet, aided by the flexibility of the French language, was a master of the elastic vocal line whose varying pace and fluid irregularity would catch precisely the mood and character of the singer: Manon bubbling over with a mixture of excitement and shyness at meeting her cousin Lescaut at Amiens; Werther pouring out his romantic feelings at the sight of Charlotte and her infant charges; Thaïs hysterically begging reassurance from her mirror. In their attempts to assimilate this manner Italian composers faced two obstacles: the heavier accents of their own language as compared to French, and the lingering reluctance of their librettists to stray outside the traditional bounds of Metastasian verse. That the first score to show the influence of Massenet should be Catalani's eclogue *La Falce*, written three years before the Italian première of *Le Roi de Lahore*, as his graduation piece for the Milan Conservatory, is less surprising than might appear. For Catalani had spent half a year in Paris, where he had been able to hear Massenet's *Eve* and *Marie-Magdalène* in which the composer's style was already formed. As well as that the author of the text of *La Falce*, though described as N.N. (Non Nominatus), was Arrigo Boito, one of the few opera poets of the time who genuinely understood the importance for a young composer of metrical variety. To the end of his life Catalani vainly hoped that Boito would give him another libretto. But even with the help of Zanardini he was able in parts of

---

* Letter to Arrivabene, 10.6.1884. Alberti, pp. 311–15.

† Its first performance in French had been at the Théâtre de la Monnaie, Brussels, in 1881.

Dejanice to achieve a Massenet-like flexibility of phrase, as for instance in the prima donna's opening arioso ('Inni, lauri al nocchier'), which the composer unaccountably cut from later editions of the score:

159a

159b

Catalani : DEJANICE (1883)

Also to Massenet's example may be attributed those little flurries of semiquavers which will often give unexpected emphasis to a Puccini line and which are evident as early as *Le Villi*.

160

Puccini : LE VILLI (1884)

If Puccini's biographers have made little of Massenet's influence on their subject his teacher Ponchielli was in no doubt about it. Shortly before the première of his *Marion Delorme* he called on Verdi and in the course of their conversation talked about Puccini's *Le Villi* '. . . written in a style which we don't like because he follows in the footsteps of Massenet, Wagner, etc.'.* This reported comment, alas, is the only clue that we have to Verdi's sincere opinion of Puccini's music. The complaint that his younger contemporaries were 'germanizing' and selling their Italian birthright for a mess of ultramontane pottage which runs like a leitmotif through Verdi's correspondence is usually regarded as the perverse grumblings of a rugged patriot, of the self-made man who sees no reason why others should be exposed to a wider culture than he himself had enjoyed at their age. In fact his view was widely shared and not only in Italy. 'The anxious northern genius,' Shaw wrote, 'is magnificently assimilative: the self-sufficient Italian genius is magnificently impervious.'† An over-simplification, of course; yet, paradoxically it was precisely when Italian opera was at its most narrow, not to say provincial, in style that it won the readiest acceptance abroad. Throughout the mid-nineteenth century the Théâtre des Italiens and Her Majesty's (followed by Covent Garden) provided a prestigious shop-window for the latest Italian operas and artists in Paris and London respectively. If the Théâtre des Italiens was forced to close in 1876 the reason lay only partly in the financial recession of the time coupled with Escudier's mismanagement. For some years French musicians and critics had been calling for its closure on the grounds that, Verdi apart, Italy had nothing more of interest to offer the Parisian public. In 1879 the young composer Joncières protested in the columns of *La Liberté* against the 'barbarous practice' of sending winners of the Prix de Rome to study in Europe's 'Gehenna of music' – Italy.‡ In a letter to Marie Escudier written in 1851 Verdi had expressed doubts about the ability of Ferdinand Hiller to conduct Italian opera idiomatically ('. . . these great names, heads of conservatories, of lyceums, hurl anathemas against a fifth or an octave or a tune that is – "imagine" – "*popular*"').§ Thirty years later, far from berating Italian music for not being German, Hiller was finding fault with it for being insufficiently Italian. 'It is astonishing,' he writes, 'how seriously the Italians set about the important task of following in the harmonic footsteps of the Germans. Not only do they seek to propagate German instrumental music by means of orchestral concerts, set about performing oratorios and experiment with Wagner and Goldmark on their stages – they even write critical-aesthetic newspaper articles of a German profundity; they set up prizes for church and chamber music – found one musical periodical after another. . . . And yet! Far be it from me to feel displeasure at this peaceful victory – how recently did we Germans still count as barbarians in Italian eyes! And if this volte-face is more to be ascribed to Moltke than to Beethoven the result is the same and very beneficial to us – but is it quite so beneficial to the Italians?'¶

* Letter from Ponchielli to an unnamed correspondent, quoted Abbiati, IV, pp. 261–2.

† G. B. Shaw, *Shaw's Music*, ed. Dan. H. Laurence (London, 1981), III, p. 582.

‡ See G. A. Biaggi, 'L'arte musicale nell'anno 1879', in *Nuova Antologia* (Jan.–Feb. 1880), pp. 337–61. 'Such dear fellows, are they not, these young French composers?' is Biaggi's comment.

§ Letter to M. Escudier, 30.9.1851. Walker, 'Four unpublished Verdi letters', in *Music and Letters* (Jan. 1948), pp. 44–7.

¶ F. Hiller, *Erinnerungsblätter* (Cologne, 1884), pp. 70 ff.

In the short run, not at all. When he talked of a 'victory' Hiller was not exaggerating; and Italian composers were the vanquished – or so it seemed at the time.
When the recession was over and the theatres began to reopen, now mostly sub-
sidized by big business, it was the foreigners who held the field. The carnival season
of 1882–3 opened at Bologna with a revival of *Lohengrin*, in Milan with *L'Étoile du
Nord*, in Naples with *Le Roi de Lahore*, in Turin with *Rienzi*. The operas most in
demand during the 1880s were *Carmen*, *Lakmé*, *Die Königin von Saba*, and the early
Wagnerian canon. Native works were at a discount, and even those which, like
Marchetti's *Don Giovanni d'Austria* and Bottesini's *Ero e Leandro*, achieved a certain
success in the theatre for which they were written rarely went the rounds in Italy
itself; whereas a foreign work once introduced would be taken up by one theatre
after another. With the exception of *La Gioconda* and *Mefistofele* no opera written
between *Aida* and *Otello* ever established itself abroad. As D'Arcais remarked sadly,
'Nowadays the only Italians to set foot outside Italy are a few pathetic composers of
ditties and romances who go to London to teach singing to the English ladies and
their daughters.'* (The reference is of course to Paolo Tosti and Ciro Pinsuti.)

In 1890 a long bleak winter came to an end with the explosion of *Cavalleria
Rusticana*; after which Italian operas began once more to cross the Alps and fill the
leading theatres of Europe. At last the random breezes that had blown Italian opera
hither and thither had united to form a steady wind. After three-quarters of a century
a new robust Italian tradition had been founded and one which the entire operatic
world recognized as such; and by what sign? Simply by a reckless confidence for
which one will search in vain in the works of Ponchielli and Catalani. In *Cavalleria
Rusticana* the composer no longer parades his German lessons or makes self-conscious
display of schoolroom technique – a foible which turns Franchetti's *Asrael* of 1888
into an Italian equivalent of Rubinstein's *The Demon*. The musical expression is
direct, vivid, theatrical. The unexpected progression or modulation will be
motivated by the drama without undue regard to grammatical niceties. A passage
from the brief orchestral preamble to Santuzza's confession 'Voi lo sapete, o Mamma'
will serve to illustrate the point:

161

Mascagni : CAVELLERIA RUSTICANA (1890)

The 'Dorian' progression (x), even if we regard the C sharp in the melody as an appoggiatura resolved by the cello and bassoon on the changing-note principle, is
clumsy and over-emphatic in relation to the cantilena as a whole (compare
Massenet's more graceful working of a similar idea in his song 'Printemps dernier').
No matter; it conveys with a rare immediacy the anguish that Santuzza is vainly

* F. D'Arcais, 'Rassegna Musicale', in *Nuova Antologia* (Jan.–Feb. 1883), pp. 355–66.

trying to suppress as she tells her story; and it finds an echo in the still more powerful 'Io son dannata' with which her solo ends. With such an example before him Puccini, who had minded his manners in *Le Villi* and *Edgar*, would not scruple in *Manon Lescaut* to dwell with almost unbearable insistence on a chord of E flat minor, melodically embellished with an ungrammatical F flat, as des Grieux watches the roll-call of the prostitutes. In other words 'verismo' had been born.

Although it took Italy and Europe by surprise at the time hindsight allows us to distinguish some of the factors which helped its precipitation. One was the example of Bizet's *Carmen*. A failure at the Opéra-Comique, it had entered Italy by the back door. In 1880 the impresario Guillaume had opened the Teatro Bellini in Naples as a repertory theatre for opera buffa and semi-seria, both genres heavily in decline in Italian opera. Inevitably he had to fill out his season with French works, among which he included *Mignon*, Hérold's *Le Pré-aux-Clercs*, and *Carmen*. Faced with Bizet's masterpiece the critics were at first cautious, scenting some new form of Wagnerianism; but the public soon took it to their hearts; and even D'Arcais ended by declaring its composer to have been the most gifted of his generation in France, far out-shining Massenet.[*] The following year it was taken up with even greater success at the Teatro Dal Verme in Milan. True, a production on the larger stage of the Teatro Regio, Turin, failed with the subscribers; but a revival towards the end of the same season packed the house. It was left to the San Carlo, Naples, in 1885 to prove once and for all that *Carmen* could fill the larger theatres as well as the small; and this together with the success elsewhere of opéras-comiques such as Delibes's *Lakmé* and Bizet's own *Jolie Fille de Perth* helped to wean native composers away from that pointless grandiosity which had been Italian opera's besetting sin for nigh on two decades.

Another sign of the times was the announcement in 1883 of a prize for one-act operas instituted by the publisher Edoardo Sonzogno, an ex-scapigliato and political radical soon to succeed Giovannina Lucca as Ricordi's chief rival and ready to outdo both her and Giulio in unscrupulous warfare.[†] Among the competitors was Puccini, whose *Le Villi* failed even to get an honourable mention, due not to any obtuseness on the part of the judges but merely because the illegibility of his handwriting led them to put the score by with hardly a glance. None the less a number of friends and well-wishers, including Boito, subscribed towards a performance at the Teatro Dal Verme in May 1884, whose outcome was wholly favourable. Meanwhile the winning entries, Mapelli's *Anna e Gualberto* and Zuelli's *La fata del Nord*, given at the Teatro Manzoni, also excited sympathetic interest as pointers to the style of the future. Six years later it was this same competition which brought into being *Cavalleria Rusticana*. Nor is it a coincidence that the Italian publisher of *Carmen* was Sonzogno.

For the subject matter and ambience of the new Italian opera again the example of *Carmen* is decisive. It is an opera of ordinary people and primitive passions. If

---

[*] F. D'Arcais, 'Rassegna Musicale', in *Nuova Antologia* (Mar.–Apr. 1880), pp. 756–64.

[†] For an account of his dealings with Frederick Cowen over the première of his opera *Signa* at La Scala, Milan, and of his subsequent slandering of Boito which nearly led to a duel, see P. Nardi, *Arrigo Boito* (Verona, 1942), pp. 601–3.

Mérimée's Don José is a gentleman of rank his operatic counterpart is a man of the people with an old mother who lives in a humble homestead and a young village girl-next-door with whom he has an 'understanding'. This same opposition of innocent maid to femme fatale is exploited to good purpose in another important pre-'verismo' opera, Puccini's *Edgar*. If it be objected that there is nothing new in the situation, that it lies at the heart of several double prima donna operas of the time (Gioconda v. Laura, Fosca v. Delia, Dejanice v. Argelia) the difference lies in the realistic portrayal of the temptress. In the operas of Ponchielli, Gomes and Catalani the femme has long ceased to be fatale before the curtain rises; she is hopelessly in love with the man she has seduced; and in the end it is she who makes the supreme sacrifice. Carmen and Tigrana are redeemed by no such gesture: they are single-minded, without pity or remorse; and their victims remain wholly in their power. In discussing a performance of *Carmen* at Rome's Teatro Argentina D'Arcais wrote, 'Some people would like to consider [the composer] as head of some school or other of realism in France,' adding, 'a judgement which doubtless Bizet, were he still alive, would probably have been the first to repudiate.'* Perhaps; but this view, however erroneous, only stresses the importance of Bizet's example in the forming of the so-called 'veristic' style.†

However, 'realism' in opera was impossible without a drastic revision of the style and language of libretti; and indeed this rather than the subject matter gives 'verismo' its hall-mark. Composers saw no reason to follow the examples of *Cavalleria Rusticana* and *Pagliacci* in keeping to the lower end of the social scale; but they made their characters use the language of everyday in place of the stilted fustian that had obtained hitherto. If Puccini's Bohemians sometimes become high-flown in their expressions they do so by way of parody; it is all part of their world of half-humorous make-believe. But they soon descend to plain language under stress ('Ho un freddo cane,' exclaims Marcello – 'I'm hellish cold!'). In 1841, in *Luigi Rolla*, Cammarano's Michelangelo had taken leave of his carousing pupils with a lofty 'I go to take my customary nutriment of milk'. Pinkerton more briefly offers Sharpless, 'Milk punch or whisky?' without even the formality of a verb. A whole system of metres which had served Italian opera for two centuries quietly dissolved. Under the influence of Luigi Illica, who was to be to the 'giovane scuola' what Romani was to Bellini, and Cammarano to the mid-century romantics, quinari, senari, settenari, ottonari, decasillabi and endecasillabi gave way to casually rhymed – or even unrhymed – lines of irregular length referred to jokingly by Giuseppe Giacosa as 'illicasillabi'. Indeed, Puccini was unable to handle any other form of text; a romanza in regular metre, he used to say, brought on a semi-seizure.‡

It was the logical outcome of a campaign in which both Verdi and Boito had been engaged for over thirty years – Boito with his denunciations of formulae and his

* F. D'Arcais, 'Rassegna Musicale', in *Nuova Antologia* (Mar.–Apr. 1884), pp. 717–26.

† It would seem that the term 'verismo' and its derivatives were already vogue words in Italy by the end of the 1870s. Thus in the letter to Faccio already quoted (Jan. 1879) Verdi refers satirically to *Le Roi de Lahore* as a 'veristic' work in which there is not a trace of 'verity'. Boito, in his correspondence with Verdi over the revision of *Simon Boccanegra*, refers to Piave's words 'Stolido va' as being 'rough and ready and liable to raise a laugh with their vulgarity (or let us say verismo)'. Letter from Boito, 15.2.1881. II, p. 265.

‡ See Giulio Gatti-Casazza, *Memories of the Opera* (London, 1977), pp. 274–5.

praise of French texts as a means of liberating Italian composers from the tyranny of Italian metre, Verdi with his constant advocacy of the rights of the 'parola evidente e scenica' and the need for composers and poets to renounce the rules of their calling in the interests of the theatre. (He welcomed the decision of Nuitter and du Locle to make their translation into French of *Simon Boccanegra* unrhymed.)* Yet clearly neither relished the form which victory had taken. To the end of his life Boito was disposed to help younger composers. Zandonai as well as Puccini owed him the start of his career since it was Boito who first recommended him to the attention of Tito Ricordi, Giulio's son;† but he could never bring himself to praise their work. Camille Bellaigue, who asked his opinion on Franchetti, Leoncavallo, Puccini and the rest of the 'école moderne italienne', met only with evasiveness – until he himself confessed that a performance of *Pagliacci* at the Paris Opéra had disgusted him. To which Boito replied, 'Comme je vous plains d'avoir assisté à cet avilissant spectacle de l'opéra.'‡ The only member of the 'giovane scuola' for whom he could summon any enthusiasm was Faccio's pupil Antonio Smareglia, whose idiom, like Catalani's, was formed in the pre-'verismo' decade. Likewise Verdi might plead with Romilda Pantaleoni to undertake the part of Tigrana in *Edgar*; he might receive Mascagni kindly and give him words of encouragement; but his unenthusiastic comments on the libretto and music of *L'Amico Fritz* have already been noted.§ 'But then,' he concluded, 'I'm an old fogey [*codino*]. . . . Well, old certainly; perhaps not so much of a fogey as all that.'

Reactionary or progressive, Verdi had parted company with contemporary Italian tradition once it had taken the form of 'verismo'. But, if not precisely influenced by the composers of the 1870s and 1880s in his revisions of *Simon Boccanegra* and *Don Carlos*, he was at least aware that he was writing for the same audiences as they. So it will be useful to conclude this chapter with a brief survey of the three outstanding figures of the two decades under consideration, noting their attempts to adapt themselves to the changing tastes of the times in which everything good was held to come out of France and Germany. It may seem odd to exclude Boito from their number in view of the fact that his *Mefistofele* of 1875 (or, more accurately, 1876 since it was the Venetian version with its addition of the duet 'Lontano, lontano' that first gained the opera something like popularity) was one of the few operatic products of Italy that proved exportable. But *Mefistofele*, like the later, uncompleted *Nerone*, stands apart; it has no musical ancestors and no progeny. Likewise the veterans Cagnoni and Lauro Rossi can be left out since their best work, such as it is, belongs to an earlier period. Even Filippo Marchetti, despite the stout advocacy of D'Arcais, never followed up adequately his *Ruy Blas* of 1869. There remain Amilcare Ponchielli, Antonio Carlos Gomes and Alfredo Catalani.

Of these Ponchielli is the oldest and the most conservative. Here the example of his most famous composition, 'La Danza delle Ore' from *La Gioconda*, is misleading, since apart from those tell-tale woodwind chords sustaining at the point of modulation in the opening theme, and the sudden tutti explosions, it could easily pass as a piece of French frippery of the late nineteenth century – and indeed was rapturously

* Letter to Nuitter, 23.2.1883. *An. Mus.*, XV, pp. 394–5.
† See Nardi, p. 675.
‡ *Ibid.*
§ See Vol. 2, p. 46. Letter to Giulio Ricordi, 6.11.1891.

received by an otherwise blasé French audience when performed in Paris for the first time by the Turin Orchestra under Pedrotti at the Great Exhibition of 1878.* Many looked forward to hearing the opera from which it came. One could imagine their disenchantment the moment the curtain rose on a swift 6/8 chorus of basically Donizettian stamp though more grandly developed. Not even Verdi was as ready as Ponchielli to delve into the tradition of fifty years ago in order to enrich a contemporary style. Mention has already been made of his *I Promessi Sposi* of 1856 written for provincial Cremona, his refurbishing of it for Milan in 1872 with the help of Emilio Praga and Verdi's verdict on the result.† But the public were on the whole favourably impressed; the opera circulated and the composer's name was made, if somewhat belatedly (he was nearing forty). He felt emboldened to attempt a grand opera in a wholly modern style; the result was *I Lituani* to a libretto by Ghislanzoni based on Mickiewicz's *Konrad Wallingrod*, dealing with the subjugation of a northern people by the Teutonic knights. How seriously he set about it can be judged from one of his many voluble, self-doubting letters to Giulio Ricordi:

> I've never had to set a text requiring such novel and gripping musical forms as *I Lituani*. As you know, in the past people didn't pay much attention to thematic unity; now on the other hand it's regarded as something absolutely essential, and indeed I would almost say that too much is made of it altogether, and you know how difficult it is to adapt a musical idea to more than one context because so often the words are against it. To give you a notion: now that I've worked at the entrance of the prisoners in the first act I'm very keen to change the recitative in the prologue and also the other little recitative where Walter says, 'You see those fires below.' Here I need the theme of the *suffering Lithuanians*; we should hear the lash of the orchestra and I will need to find a dreamy melody for the violins or something else very sad which I can adapt to all three places – in the opening recitative in the prologue, in that of the duet finale of the same, and at the entrance of the prisoners. . . .‡

He was also exercised over the resemblance of part of Act III to the 'funeral march' in *Don Carlos*.§ *I Lituani* was produced at La Scala in March, 1874 to great critical acclaim, though Filippi found it overlong. For a revival the following year Ponchielli trimmed the bulk but added one or two dances and a battle scene and changed the baritone aria. Again the critics were favourable; yet the public never really warmed to the opera and, unlike *I Promessi Sposi*, it never went the rounds of the major Italian theatres. After Milan only Trieste took it up, though for years afterwards writers such as D'Arcais and Biaggi urged it on managements at home and abroad as the composer's masterpiece. It did, however, enjoy one unlikely revival in Ponchielli's lifetime at St Petersburg in 1884, where it was given together with a new soprano aria under the title of *Aldona*.

* See F. D'Arcais, 'La Musica Italiana all' Esposizione di Parigi', in *Nuova Antologia* (Sept.–Oct. 1878), pp. 325–45.

† See Vol. II, p. 28.

‡ Letter to Giulio Ricordi, 28.6.1873. *Amilcare Ponchielli—Notizie e incisioni raccolte da Giuseppe De Napoli* (Cremona, 1936), p. 114.

§ Letter to Giulio Ricordi, Nov., 1873. *Ibid.*, p. 115. There is no such resemblance in the finished score.

For his next and best known work, *La Gioconda*, Ponchielli was careful not to aim too high. 'I believe,' he wrote to Giulio Ricordi, 'that where the Italian public is concerned it's vital not to make too much of the drama otherwise you land yourself in rhythms that don't arrest the attention and you have to exploit the orchestra and finally you need the kind of artist whom we don't have today and who perhaps didn't even exist in Rossini's time. . . . Therefore in my opinion it's best to stick to the lyrical side even if it means struggling to avoid hackneyed rhythms and accompaniments.'* Strange words from the composer of *I Lituani*! He is ready even to countenance a cabaletta for the conclusion of the Barnaba–Enzo duet in Act I, having failed to devise such a novel solution as Verdi's for the end of his duet between Amneris and Aida.† But his instinct had not misled him. Aided by a libretto which shows Boito at his most luridly theatrical and with the age's leading dramatic tenor, Julian Gayarré, in the role of Enzo, *La Gioconda* scored a decided success. But Ponchielli had not finished with it by a long way. For a performance in Venice the following autumn he drastically altered the end of the first act and added to Act III a new grand aria for the bass, Alvise.‡ Boito's satanic text for the latter did not please him. 'The situation is doubtless well rendered,' he wrote to Ricordi, 'but I would have preferred that Alvise should be seized by remorse, by past memories, that he should ask himself for example whether he loved that woman enough to have deserved her love, etc. . . . Something less cynical, with a different colour to it, even with a trace of passion so as to make for a melody and then there would perhaps have been a contrast with the preceding scenes and with those that follow.'§ However, a few days later, 'For better or worse I've written the bass aria,'¶ and by all accounts it made a great effect. Filippi waxed particularly enthusiastic over Boito's 'fine Shakespearian lines' which he reproduced in full in his review. Nevertheless, though it survived his next revision for Rome in 1877 together with the Act III stretta-finale (later removed), Ponchielli saw fit to replace it in the opera's definitive version first given again at La Scala, Milan in February 1880. Boito was able to find a better context for two of his Shakespearian lines, as we shall see in the next chapter.

The years that followed *La Gioconda* saw Ponchielli again oscillating between the old and the new. In the autumn of 1877 he presented *Lina* at the Dal Verme, Milan, a half-hearted updating of his earlier *Savoiarda*, which in turn could be described as *Linda di Chamounix* with the comedy eliminated. All Donizetti's props are there – rustic choruses with an Alpine flavour, a love duet with a melody to be recalled at moments of poignancy and even (save the mark!) cadenzas at the end of arias. This time he did not repeat the success of *I Promessi Sposi*; and for his next opera Ponchielli set his face towards the future. *Il Figluol Prodigo*, written to a libretto by Zanardini and first produced at La Scala at the end of 1880, is the first of Ponchielli's operas to show the influence of Massenet, both in the use of orientalisms and in the attempt to create two contrasting ambiences – the frugal, pastoral world of the patriarchs of Judea and the debauchery of Nineveh. For the first he makes effective use of a pentatonic motif with a drone bass.

* Letter to Giulio Ricordi, 12.9.1874. *Ibid.*, pp. 151–2.
† Letter to Giulio Ricordi, 27.1.1875. *Ibid.*, pp. 158–9.
‡ For a detailed analysis of all the modifications introduced for Venice, see the article by Filippi quoted in *Gazzetta Musicale di Milano*, XXXI, 43 (22.10.1876).
§ Letter to Giulio Ricordi, 22.6.1876. De Napoli, p. 178.
¶ Letter to Giulio Ricordi, 1.7.1876. *Ibid.*, p. 176.

162 Andante sostenuto religioso ♩ = 63

Ponchielli : IL FIGLUOL PRODIGO (1880)

On Reuben's farm the melodies march like chorales; in Nineveh they leap and swirl. In no other opera of Ponchielli's is the harmonic vocabulary so rich and varied. Yet by the third week of the season it was being cut down to make room for a new ballet, since, as Teresa Stolz remarked to Giuseppina Verdi, '*The Prodigal Son* is not very prodigal towards the theatre's coffers!!'* A similar fate lay in store for Ponchielli's last opera *Marion Delorme*, again at La Scala, in 1885. Ponchielli prepared a new version for performance at Brescia, having sought and rather surprisingly obtained Verdi's advice as to the restructuring of the libretto; then in January 1886 he died and, as Boito remarked, 'Perhaps that unhappy soul will have found some respite from the torments inflicted upon him by his wife's relations.'† Ponchielli's earthly trials had included marriage to a very demanding prima donna.

Uncertainty had been his besetting weakness (the number of times the word 'forse' appears in his letters is revealing). Brought up in the post-Rossinian tradition, he was far more successful than Lauro Rossi, Cagnoni or Pedrotti in reconciling a basically national idiom with the sophisticated harmonic and orchestral style which modern taste was beginning to require – which is doubtless why D'Arcais considered him a latter-day Mercadante. His hall-mark was a sinuous melodic style seen at its most characteristic in the theme that symbolizes Gioconda's love for her mother. (Ex. 163)

Yet even in his most adventurous works he never escaped from the stifling weight

163 LA CIECA

Tu can - ti a - gli uo - mi - ni   le tue   can - zo - - ni,   io can - to a -

Andante flebile

- gli an - ge - li   le mie o - ra - zio - - ni,

Ponchielli : LA GIOCONDA (1876)

* Letter from Teresa Stolz to Giuseppina Verdi, 16.1.1881. Abbiati, IV, p. 152.
† Letter from Boito, 18.1.1886. *Carteggio Verdi–Boito* (Parma, 1979), I, pp. 96–7.

of grand opera, never overcame a tendency to prolixity. Even in *La Gioconda* after its fourth revision there is a certain disproportion of means to ends. Having seen his most deeply considered opera, *I Lituani*, coolly received, he was for ever tinkering with his scores to make them more acceptable. His main advance was in the sphere of pictorialism. He had a remarkable gift for defining an ambience through the association of images in sound – witness the beginning of *La Gioconda*, Act II. It was a gift which he would bequeath with interest to his pupil Puccini.

Although he was a man of very different temperament, the career of Antonio Gomes runs parallel to Ponchielli's in a number of ways. A native of Brazil who came to Italy to complete his studies, he made his name with *Il Guarany* of 1870, a swiftly moving drama, boldly scored and with a certain melodic naïveté which only adds to its charm.* Like Ponchielli he followed it up with a work of far higher aspirations and one which he long regarded as his masterpiece – *Fosca*, with libretto by Ghislanzoni based on a story by Luigi Capronica of medieval piracy on the Adriatic. Produced at La Scala, Milan, in 1873 it made little impression on the public. For his next opera Gomes accordingly lowered his sights. *Salvator Rosa* (Genoa, 1874) is a thoroughly old-fashioned grand opera with a Neapolitan setting and the scarcely unfamiliar character of Masaniello among the principals. Yet it proved to be Gomes's most successful opera (it opened the carnival season of 1876–7 in no less than six of Italy's leading theatres). If Ghislanzoni's libretto is clumsily built, if the dramatic interest is diffused among too many leading roles, the music is strongly coloured, and the opera full of rapid incident and, as in *Un Ballo in maschera*, the gloom of the tragedy is lightened by a pert trouser role, the young 'scugnizzo' Gennariello whose opening canzonetta 'Mia piccirella' was to become one of the hit-tunes of the day. But it is in the transitional passages that Gomes's skill is most evident. The scene that precedes the canzonetta is couched in that graceful conversational style of which Verdi had for so long held the secret; using the transitional 6/4 with an ease and assurance worthy of the opening scene of *La Forza del destino*.

164

Gomes: SALVATOR ROSA (1874)

* For a perceptive appraisal of Gomes's music, see M. Conati, 'Formazione e affermazione di Gomes nel panorama dell' opera italiana. Appunti e considerazioni', in *Antonio Carlos Gomes: Carteggi italiani raccolti e commentati da G. Nello Vetro* (Milan, 1977), pp. 33–77.

During the next six years Gomes worked on a revision of *Fosca* which he refloated at La Scala in 1878. The critics were kind, but again it failed to interest the public, and was not taken up elsewhere. Meanwhile he had begun work on a *Maria Tudor* with the 'scapigliato' poet Emilio Praga; but Praga died before the text was completed; the rest was the work of Boito. It was an unfortunate choice of subject. Not only is *Maria Tudor* one of those Hugo plays in which every character is a monster of depravity; the blackest villain of them all is an Italian, Fabio Fabiani (Pacini when setting the same subject at least had the good sense to turn him into an Englishman). Apart from its excess of grand opera paraphernalia Gomes's work has many of the virtues of *Fosca* and *Salvator Rosa*; but at its production at La Scala in 1879 the audience was implacable. The opera was withdrawn and never heard of again. As a result Gomes's Italian career was virtually finished. True, *Il Guarany* and *Salvator Rosa* remained in the repertoire and would provide stars of the future with a promising start to their career (Gemma Bellincioni first made her name as a sparkling Gennariello). But apart from a moderately successful revival of *Fosca* in Bologna in 1889 in yet a third version, the story of Gomes's life in the 1880s is one of blighted hopes, of libretti begun and never finished, of family quarrels and lawsuits. An annuity promised to him by the Brazilian government never materialized. He was obliged to sell the magnificent Villa Brasilia by Lake Como which he had built himself out of the proceeds of his two successes. His next opera, *Lo Schiavo*, after years during which he had vainly tried to place it in Italy, and even in London, finally reached the stage at Rio de Janeiro in 1889; and for the last time its composer experienced an unqualified triumph. Gomes returned briefly to Milan where his last opera, *Condor*, was brought out in 1891 before a public that had tasted 'veristic' blood. It failed to please and its composer left Italy finally for his native land where he ended his days as director of the newly formed national conservatory.

Compared to Ponchielli, Gomes is a bolder, more theatrical composer, even if his harmonic vocabulary remains basically that of Verdi in the 1860s; but he too remained tied to the grand opera convention which in the long run quenched the vitality of his music. True, in *Lo Schiavo* there is an attempt to break new harmonic ground; certain of the rhythms and progressions of the 'verismo' school are to be heard approaching in the distance; at the same time dramatic élan has begun to give way to a preoccupation with pictorialism, some of it, like the 'dawn prelude' of the fourth act, very striking. Yet somehow the central problem of music-drama, of providing a vivid theatrical experience, has been by-passed.

The career of Alfredo Catalani traces a very different graph. The signs of a new and original talent with a radical approach to music drama are already present in the oriental eclogue *La Falce* of 1876. In place of a prelude or an overture there is a 'prologo sinfonico' describing the Battle of Beda. At first glance this appears to be romantic battle music at its most naïf, the score being plastered with instructions, 'Mohammedans attack', 'the attack is beaten off', 'angels to the rescue' and so on like one of those Victorian piano pieces describing the Siege of Lucknow or the Battle of Alexandria. A closer look reveals it as a symphonic poem in miniature with a pronounced orchestral and harmonic colour of its own (the flattened leading-note is much in evidence). The themes are couched in free and flexible rhythms and are deployed very much in Liszt's manner, as a chain of ideas stated in one key, then repeated note for note in another – a procedure much favoured by Catalani for large choral or instrumental scenes. The main body of the eclogue is divided into the usual recitatives, romanze and duets and choruses, but of the six numbers only one, the *Tannhäuser*-ish 6/8 romanza 'Tutti eran vivi', is printed with that extra final bar which allows the option of a separate performance. The rest, mostly ternary in structure, are bound together in a seamless continuity with the aid of thematic and rhythmic recall. The range of harmony and modulation exceeds that of Ponchielli or Gomes; augmented fifths and secondary sevenths of every kind abound; the melodies show such features as the French cadential mordant (compare 'Je suis amoureuse' from Bizet's *Carmen* and 'C'est mon premier voyage' from Massenet's *Manon*) and that dipping fifth which was to be a fingerprint of Puccini's, expressive of the 'mestizia toscana' which both composers shared. The second duet ('Andiam, andiam vagabondi' (Ex. 165)) provides a foretaste of one of Catalani's most famous numbers – the 'Chanson groenlandaise' which he was to incorporate into *La Wally* as 'Ebben? Ne andrò lontano'. The form which it assumes in *La Falce* makes clear its descent from those wistful valedictory duets from *Belisario* and *Luisa Miller* where father and daughter resolve to wander through the world. True, Zora and her young reaper whom she had mistaken for Death are departing to a life of happiness; but Catalani's was always an elegiac muse.

165

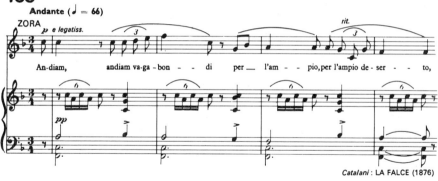

Catalani : LA FALCE (1876)

In *Elda* (Turin, 1880), his first full-length opera, Catalani's imagination is as rich as ever; but the individuality which had been precipitated in the miniature eclogue is somewhat diffused in the massive frame of Carlo D'Ormeville's four-act 'dramma fantastico'. The story, a Baltic version of the Lorelei legend with jilted maiden turning siren, offers Catalani full scope for pictorial effects, for ballets of winds and water-sprites and that northern local colour which was his special predilection. But the human interest is buried beneath a weight of ensembles (three of the four acts end with huge, elaborate concertati). And whereas Ponchielli and Gomes even at their least dramatically urgent had never slackened their structural grasp of the separate number, in reaching out towards a larger organic unit Catalani often allows the design of his set-pieces to straggle. Too many of his romanze follow a spacious ternary pattern whose effect is strangely casual; the central episode is usually too long and there is no cogency in the reprise.

The subject of Catalani's next opera, *Dejanice* (Milan, 1883; Turin, 1884, revised) set in the Eastern Mediterranean in ancient times, brings about a closer approach to the Massenet of *Hérodiade* and *Le Roi de Lahore*, hampered by the rigidity of the Italian metrical system which none the less Zanardini was clearly doing his best to modify.* Yet despite these and similar shortcomings, including a very clumsily designed libretto, *Dejanice* impressed at least one student from the Milan Conservatory. 'Last night I went to see Catalani's new opera,' wrote Puccini; 'it didn't send the public into raptures; but artistically speaking it's beautiful, and if they put it on again I'll go back and see it.'†

In his next two operas Catalani begins gradually to emancipate himself from the tyranny of grand opera. *Edmea* (Milan, 1886) derives from the same play by Dumas fils that furnished the libretto of Gomes's *Lo Schiavo*. Both composers, however, removed it to the locale of their choice, so that the Russia of *Les Danicheffs* becomes for Gomes the slave-worked plantations of America and for Catalani medieval Germany. Nowadays *Edmea* is chiefly famous for having provided Toscanini with his official debut as a conductor. Its prevailing tone of intimate pathos is established at the start by a delicate spinning chorus which had its origin in a piano piece. The dances and choruses are no more obtrusively grand than in *La Traviata*; while for the 'mad scene' of Act II, Catalani hit a style of expressive fioritura which is deeply pathetic yet owes nothing to the age of Donizetti. (Ex. 166a, b)

If, despite a use of thematic recall both subtler and more systematic than in earlier operas, *Edmea* still seems curiously old-fashioned in its design this is due to the effect of a conservative librettist such as Ghislanzoni on a composer who is still not quite sure of himself. (At one point that most complacently derivative of operatic poets had had the chorus sing 'Mesta così la tua canzon'!) Far more time and trouble went to the transformation of *Elda* into *Loreley* (Turin, 1890) with the help of Zanardini

166a

---

* Of this libretto Luigi Baldacci remarks, 'Finally what is still more licentious [i.e., than the hetaerae, the dancers and the cithara-players] is Zanardini's versification; which moreover is very like the kind that he adopts in his translations of Wagner's librettos, so that it is difficult to say whether one is dealing with metrical solecisms or . . . Wagnerisms.' L. Baldacci, *Libretti d'opera e altri saggi* (Florence, 1974), p. 241.

† Letter from Puccini to his mother, Mar. 1883. G. Adami, *Letters of Puccini* (tr. E. Makin: new edn revised M. Carner, London, 1974), p. 41.

166b

Catalani : EDMEA (1885-6)

and the guidance of Giuseppe Depanis, son of the impresario. If the finished result does not entirely overcome the opera's faults of origin it provides the first instance of that motivic working which will become the main principle of organization in Italian opera during the decade which follows. *Elda* had begun with a sunrise whose climax had been reached in an arpeggio theme for horns which was then loosely woven into Sven's following scena. In *Loreley* this same arpeggio provides a motivic base on which to float a chorus of eager conversation. (Ex. 167)

To compare this with the opening chorus of *La Gioconda* is to observe the crossing of a great divide between the old and the new. In Catalani's last work, *La Wally*, in which he had the supreme benefit of a libretto by Illica with no supererogatory choruses or dances in it, as well as the example of the first 'verismo' operas before his eyes, his liberation from grand opera is at last complete. The vocal lines are varied and supple with no hint of the ceremonial march about them; and the freely developing orchestral motif replaces the heterogeneous 'scena' as the principal means of carrying the action forward between lyrical set numbers. Above all the long, often busy, extendable orchestral melody which was so prominent a feature of mid-century 'parlanti', and of which Gomes continued to turn out some graceful examples as late as *Maria Tudor*, was rendered completely obsolete. The act, not the 'scena ed aria' or 'scena e duetto' or whatever, has finally become the main formal unit of the opera, though it may allow room for the smaller organism of the detachable romanza, 'couplets', or genre piece.

Whether if he had lived Catalani would have overtaken his fellow-Luccan Puccini

167

Catalani : LORELEY (1888-90)

as the front-runner of the 'giovane scuola' can only be guessed. Certain of their contemporaries, notably Toscanini, thought that Catalani had the finer sensibility of the two.* Yet there is a sense in which Catalani's music continues to the end to reflect the dilemma which beset Italian opera composers during the two decades under consideration – how to do something new without seeming to deck oneself in borrowed plumage. Though he finally solved all the problems of scale and dramatic continuity and won through to a new freedom of expression, his own artistic personality emerges curiously pallid and insubstantial. By the time of *La Wally* the direct echoes of Massenet, Wagner, Mendelssohn and Gounod have gone; but Catalani's own voice remains elusive and his ideas mostly unmemorable. Despite his life-long enthusiasm for German romantic music, very few German encyclopedias rate him worth a mention though they will contain exhaustive entries on Puccini and Mascagni. His greatest achievement, the conquest in *Loreley* and *La Wally* of that *Naturromantik* which Weber first introduced to the German theatre and of which French and Italian opera remained largely innocent, went unappreciated in

* J. W. Klein, 'Alfredo Catalani 1854–93', in *Music and Letters*, XXXV, No. 1 (London, January 1954), pp. 40–4. Two of Toscanini's children were named after characters in *La Wally*.

Germany, since Italians were not supposed to excel in this field. It was not reckoned to Catalani's credit that he had 'brought the high mountain into Italian opera'.*

Despite the different procedures employed by the composers just mentioned, the underlying trend towards greater continuity persists in the music of all three, and is gradually reflected in the successive editions even of such a conservative publisher as Ricordi, who as late as 1889 was still providing singers' rehearsal books in the form of a melody with figured bass.† Throughout the 1870s, not excepting Act III of *Aida*, which Verdi had vainly tried to persuade Ricordi to print without the interruption of subheadings, he continued to divide each act into separate pieces even where these merged into one another without a perfect cadence. As if to compensate for the meaninglessness of his subdivision the headings become ever more various and fanciful, so that to the traditional categories of 'scena e duetto', 'scena e romanza', 'scena e coro' are added 'dialogo e canzone', 'scena e frase', 'invettiva – coro' (*Fosca*), 'scena e strofe' (*Salvator Rosa*), 'scenetta dell'Ironia' (*Maria Tudor*), 'delirio' (*Il Figliuol prodigo*), 'monologo' (*Dejanice*) – an elaboration surely paralleling the inflation already noted in the terms used to classify singers. (In Gobatti's *I Goti* everyone in the cast has 'primo' or 'prima' in front of their voice descriptions, the real principals being distinguished by the term 'assoluto' or 'assoluta'. As in Lewis Carroll's Caucus race, 'everybody has won and all shall have prizes'. But by the time of *Edmea* (1886) the line of text quoted beneath the subheading is the first of the number itself, not the beginning of its formal section. In *Loreley* (1890) the subheadings are relegated to the index, where they indicate only the most important solos or ensembles. The musical text is presented as a continuity from the beginning to the end of each act.

The ever-lengthening reach of operatic design is the only important link between Verdi and his younger contemporaries. We have seen how in his revision of *Simon Boccanegra* he welded together the separate numbers of the 1857 opera, 'decabaletizing' the cabalettas where necessary. Yet he retained and even elaborated upon such old-fashioned features of the first version as the self-perpetuating accompanimental pattern and the orchestral 'parlante'. Thereafter he begins to go his own way. The forms of Italian opera throughout the 1870s and 1880s remained those of the grand Parisian genre as handed down by Meyerbeer and Gounod: the 'couplets', the French ternary aria, the rondo, the 'grand morceau d'ensemble' and multi-movement duet – the last two freer and more ample than their post-Rossinian counterparts. Beginning with the modifications to *Don Carlos* (1884), and especially the duet between Philip and Posa in the new Act I, we find Verdi having less and less recourse to traditional forms, French or Italian, but allowing the situation of the moment to suggest a purely individual solution. He does not disdain the use of 'motifs' which develop, but they are never purely orchestral as in most of *La Wally*; they always originate in some key-phrase of the sung text ('Dalle due alle tre', 'Te lo cornifico', etc.) which is made to reverberate in the music which follows. Mostly, however, the seamlessness of both *Otello* and *Falstaff* results from the composer's miraculous ability to transform one idea almost insensibly into another.

Just how untrammelled by preconceptions Verdi's mind had become, how completely he had emancipated himself from traditional formal thinking, while remain-

---

* The phrase is taken from Carlo Gatti's summing up of *La Wally* as 'L'alta montagna portata nel teatro di musica'. *Catalani: Lettere* (ed. Gatti), p. 40.

† Letter from Catalani to Depanis, 20.9.1889. *Ibid.*, p. 105.

ing a master of form, is illustrated by one of those unauthenticated anecdotes which has come down to us at second hand, recalled after a lapse of many years yet with the ring of truth about it. In his memoirs of the opera Giulio Gatti-Casazza, impresario successively of La Scala, Milan, and the New York Metropolitan Opera House, relates how Luigi Illica had told him of an argument he had had with Alberto Franchetti about a passage in the libretto for *Tosca* which he had originally prepared not for Puccini but for Franchetti himself. The passage in question was Cavaradossi's aria in Act III, later replaced by 'E lucevan le stelle'. Franchetti declared that the lines were unsettable; Illica maintained that there was nothing wrong with them and refused to change a word. Eventually it was agreed that they should refer the matter to the eighty-two-year-old Verdi. Much to Franchetti's mortification the old man praised Illica's work to the skies, adding, 'What on earth do you young composers want? Aren't you satisfied even with a piece of good fortune? If only I'd had such an excellent libretto! When I was young I had to put up with all sorts of stuff! Alas, what a misfortune it is to be old!' Abashed, but not prepared to give in completely, Franchetti returned, 'One moment, Maestro, that is all very well. The verses will be fine for the tenor. But how would you set them? Would you write recitative or an arioso or a real romanza?' 'My dear Franchetti, *I would simply make some music — a little music, that's all!*'*

* Gatti-Casazza, pp. 91–2.

4 OTELLO

OTELLO

Opera in four acts
by
ARRIGO BOITO
(after the tragedy, *Othello, or the Moor of Venice* by William Shakespeare)

first performed at the
Teatro alla Scala, Milan
5 February 1887

OTELLO, a Moor, general of the Venetian army	PRIMO TENORE	Francesco Tamagno
IAGO, ensign	PRIMO BARITONO	Victor Maurel
CASSIO, platoon captain	TENORE	Giovanni Paroli
RODERIGO, a Venetian gentleman	TENORE	Vincenzo Fornari
LODOVICO, ambassador of the Venetian Republic	BASSO	Francesco Navarrini
MONTANO, Otello's predecessor as Governor of Cyprus	BASSO	Napoleone Limonta
A herald	BASSO	Angelo Lagomarsino
DESDEMONA, wife of Otello	PRIMA DONNA SOPRANO	Romilda Pantaleoni
EMILIA, wife of Iago	MEZZO-SOPRANO	Ginevra Petrovich

Soldiers and sailors of the Venetian Republic – ladies and gentlemen of Venice – Cypriot populace of both sexes – Greek, Dalmatian and Albanian men-at-arms – children of the island – an innkeeper – four servants of the inn – ship's crew

The action takes place in a maritime city on the island of Cyprus

Epoch: the end of the fifteenth century

'As for your *dolce far niente* after all you've done – if it were really the case I might envy you; but I don't take you literally, and even if I attach no weight to the rumours that you're at work on a new score (some say *Nero*, others *Julius Caesar*, others something else again) I hope that you have not terminated your career and that your genius will manifest itself with new creations.'* Thus Piroli to Verdi nearly six years after the completion of *Aida*. Verdi was rising sixty-four and apparently robust. But he seemed to have entered his sixties in a mood of gloom and depression much as Rossini had done before winning through to the Indian summer of the last years in Paris. His letters at the time are full of complaints about the Italian theatre, Italian politics and Italian music in general, seen by him as sinking beneath a tide of Germanism which his own example had been powerless to stem. Bülow, then at the height of his fame as a pianist and conductor, had publicly sneered at his Requiem without even bothering to hear it. The reality of the new Italy after the euphoria of the Risorgimento produced its reaction in Verdi as in many of his contemporaries; while the swing eastward of the Italian left away from France towards alignment with Germany saddened him particularly. He even came to regret having declined to represent Italy on the organizing committee of the Paris International Exhibition of 1878. 'What a pity', he told Piroli, 'that we cannot get on with that country to whom we owe so much!'† While the Requiem was steadily gaining ground in Italy and abroad Verdi's domestic life and business affairs were in a troubled state. The early 1870s were the years of what seemed to Giuseppina a *ménage à trois*, with Teresa Stolz a permanent visitor.‡ They were years too of bankruptcies and failed friendships – for Verdi, in many ways a typical bourgeois of the Victorian age, had no use for those who were unable to manage their own fortunes, and still less if his own money was involved in their ruin. First du Locle, then Léon Escudier fell into disgrace. Next it was the turn of Cesare De Sanctis, from whom Verdi decided to call in a loan of 25,000 lire that he had made to him in 'urgent circumstances' some years before.§ Alas, De Sanctis, no more a businessman than du Locle, was unable to comply. Verdi allowed the debt to be liquidated in regular supplies of good Neapolitan pasta; but from then on it was Giuseppina who kept up the correspondence of the last twenty-five years until De Sanctis's death in 1884. She herself was to sustain a heavy blow when her friend, Mauro Corticelli, for many years bailiff to the Verdi estates, was discovered to have speculated with the savings of two of the servants at S. Agata and lost them. Verdi dismissed him without ceremony; a few days later Corticelli attempted to commit suicide in Milan. In the meantime, Verdi had discovered some irregularities in Ricordi's accounts regarding the hire-fees for his operas. After a long correspondence the firm agreed to pay him 50,000 lire by way of reparation. 'It is not what is due to me,' he wrote to Piroli, 'but it won't go

* Letter from G. Piroli, 12.3.1877. *Carteggi Verdiani*, III, pp. 124–5.
† Letter to Piroli, 14.10.1877. *Ibid.*, pp. 128–9.
‡ See Walker, pp. 433 ff.
§ Letter to De Sanctis, 14.12.1876. *Carteggi Verdiani*, I, pp. 183–4.

any higher than that. The trouble is that our relations will never again be what they have been in the past.'*

But there he was wrong; he had underestimated the qualities of the young man who, because of his father's ill-health, was now taking more control of the affairs of the House of Ricordi and was soon to possess a greater share of Verdi's artistic confidence than his father or grandfather had ever enjoyed – and indeed would play a vital role in his return to theatrical composition.

Giovanni Ricordi had decided from the start that his line should not be one of mere businessmen. Of his eldest son Tito he made a pianist and a painter of some skill; his grandson Giulio was likewise trained in music and painting and soon showed some aptitude for composition. By the age of seventeen he had had a number of piano pieces published by the family firm; and he was to write several successful operettas under the pseudonym of J. Burgmein. That he was also a shrewd critic became evident when he took over the editorship of Ricordi's *Gazzetta Musicale di Milano*. At first, by appearing to side wholeheartedly with Boito, the Società del Quartetto, and the cause of 'spherical music', he had incurred Verdi's displeasure; but thanks to the vigilance of Giuseppina, that inveterate peacemaker, an open breach was avoided. However, 'Giulio, who is very gifted, should begin to consider the fact that he has a wife and family,' she wrote to Tornaghi, Ricordi's agent, 'that two and two make four, and that however elastic you may be, a miscalculated leap can lead to a broken neck.'† Clearly she was in no doubt that if out of pique Verdi were to transfer his custom elsewhere the fall of the House of Ricordi would soon follow. But Giulio was less of a partisan than Giuseppina imagined. When *Mefistofele* was first produced at La Scala in 1868, amid the frenzied attacks, the spirited defences, the special pleadings and the fierce recriminations his own notice struck a refreshingly impartial note. He observed the lack of musical development in each number 'as though the composer had renounced all form of melody for fear of losing touch with the text'. He concluded thus:

> Boito has written an opera which does not lack a number of merits and equally is not free from many faults. Are the latter due to inexperience of the theatre and of its effects? In that case so much the better; we shall witness great advances from opera to opera and then I truly hope to be able to number Boito among the greatest of composers. On the other hand, are these faults due to a preconceived system, to an unshakable artistic conviction? Well, then I dare to assert openly with all the frankness that I associate with my deep and heartfelt friendship for Boito: you will be a poet, a distinguished man of letters, but you will never be a composer for the theatre.‡

A harsh judgement but not far wide of the mark. The same acumen enabled the writer to pick out Puccini among the struggling young composers of the 1880s, and to cast him as Verdi's successor on the strength of a one-act opera which had failed to win a place in the competition for which it was submitted; to hold fast to his opinion

---

* Letter to Piroli, 29.12.1875. *Carteggi Verdiani*, III pp. 115–16.

† See draft letter from Giuseppina Verdi to Tornaghi, 5.5.1865 (misdated 8.5.1865). *Carteggi Verdiani*, IV, pp. 183–4; Walker, pp. 456–7.

‡ See P. Nardi, *Vita di Arrigo Boito*, p. 290.

of him even after the explosion of *Cavalleria Rusticana* had convinced most of Europe that Italy's musical future lay with Mascagni; and to spare no effort in smoothing out Puccini's relations with his librettists, exasperated as they were with his perpetual demands for alterations.

Throughout his management he was always ready with helpful advice to the composers whose works he published. Ponchielli and Gomes poured out their troubles to him as a father-figure (he was considerably younger than either). His last good deed was to persuade Boito in 1912 that his opera *Nerone* was complete in the four acts which he had managed to set, without the fifth for which he had written only the libretto. Significantly it was after Giulio's death that same year that Puccini's troubles with the House of Ricordi began.

Giuseppe Depanis, son of the impresario of the Teatro Regio, Turin, and lifelong friend of the composer Catalani, has left a vivid portrait of 'Sör Giüli', as he was known to his Milanese intimates.

Small in stature, trim, spare, Giulio Ricordi . . . possessed a lively mind together with a vast culture. Gifted with a remarkable quickness of perception, he won laurels in various fields, including the field of battle, where he proved a brilliant officer in the national army. A writer of graceful, measured prose, a sharp and biting satirist, a fluent, elegant composer, anyone who had dealings with him realized at once that they had to do with a superior intellect. Firm in his likes and dislikes, tirelessly active, he was present everywhere and saw to everything. In his study there was a continual procession of composers, librettists, singers, conductors, agents and impresarios. His manner was somewhat reserved, with something of the aristocrat and the soldier in it; he would settle a business affair in a few words; from hearing a budding prima donna he would pass with a certain weary elegance to the sampling of a new score. First impressions were decisive; and he was rarely prepared to change his mind; artists and composers who were perfectly aware of this would solicit his judgement with a kind of holy terror. . . . A valued friend – and a formidable opponent.*

This last was certainly true. Hand in hand with the idealist went a ruthless man of business who threw himself heart and soul into the war with the widow Lucca and Edoardo Sanzogno. Nor was his influence confined to the world of publishing. At La Scala, impresarios might come and go, but until Sanzogno's take-over in 1895 the guiding hand in the theatre's counsels was that of Giulio Ricordi; and anyone who criticized the results would be trounced in the columns of the *Gazzetta Musicale*. We have noticed how throughout the 1870s and most of the 1880s he turned Milan into an anti-Wagnerian stronghold. Nor did his attitude change once he had acquired the Meister's publishing rights; indeed in the year of Verdi's death he would withhold all Wagner's scores from the theatres of the peninsula. But Catalani – so obviously not long for this world – whom he had inherited from the same source he seems to have regarded as a poor investment. He waited nearly two years before promoting the première of *Loreley*. *La Wally*, whose success in 1893 he had helped to bring about, could not compete in his eyes with *Manon Lescaut*; accor-

---

* G. Depanis, *I Concerti Popolari ed il Teatro Regio di Torino* (Turin, 1914), I, p. 175.

dingly it was Puccini's opera which he proceeded to force on theatrical managements as a condition for being allowed to give *Falstaff*.

If there is one merit above all others for which Giulio Ricordi deserves posterity's gratitude it is that of having foreseen the artistic partnership which would make possible the final, most glorious flowering of Verdi's genius, and thereafter to have set himself with infinite patience and tenacity to bring this about. On the face of it it was an unlikely event. Verdi and Boito were leagues apart in age, temperament and upbringing. Verdi was Italian through and through, a craftsman, never a philosopher of his art, a man of deeds not words, who taught by example rather than precept, and one whose learning hardly rose above the level expected of those of his social standing (in the matter of languages, for instance, Giuseppina was a long way his superior). Boito was half Polish and considered it his mission to open up Italian musical life to all those ultramontane influences which Verdi believed to be so harmful to it; to drag Italian music, however painfully, into the vanguard of European culture. He was, as Ricordi noted, at least as much a man of letters as a musician; he theorized about music more than he practised it and always in grand, idealized concepts. He was also an able and somewhat extravagant polemicist. What more likely than that Verdi, far more sensitive to adverse criticism than he admitted, should one day feel himself to be the target of one of Boito's shafts?

And so, of course, it happened. Only a year after he had supplied Verdi with the text of the *Inno delle Nazioni* Boito delivered his famous Sapphic ode, 'All'arte Italiana', a post-prandial tribute to Faccio's *I Profughi fiamminghi*, containing the verse 'Perhaps the man is already born who will raise up the art [of music] in all its chaste purity above that altar now befouled like the walls of a brothel.'* All the good will Verdi had shown to the young poet evaporated at once; and indeed the offending verse was to supply him with a fund of misquotations for the next fifteen years. Piave, whose application for a professorship of operatic poetry at the Milan Conservatory had been passed over in favour of the 'scapigliato' Emilio Praga, fed the flames of Verdi's resentment. Only Boito himself, it seems, remained in ignorance of the effect of his ode, since in 1864 he sent Verdi a copy of his grotesque poem, *Re Orso*, with a suitably modest and respectful inscription. But it was to be a long time before the two men returned to speaking terms. The failure of *Mefistofele* in 1868 played its part in bringing Boito out of the clouds of vague fantasy on to theatrical terra firma; while the notorious Broglio letter gave him the opportunity of breaking a lance on Verdi's behalf. Rehearsals for the revised *Forza del destino* at La Scala brought about a cordial friendship between Verdi and Faccio, who was assisting Mariani with the preparation of the opera. Surely a reconciliation with Boito would quickly follow.

During the search for an operatic plot which ended with *Aida*, Dumas's *Acté et Néron* was mentioned. Giulio Ricordi immediately thought of the subject which was now nearest to Boito's heart; having found out by indirect means that Boito had not even completed the text of *Nerone*, let alone begun to set it to music, he wrote to Verdi proposing that, Boito willing, he should set it himself. But his letter remained unanswered.† A year later, with *Aida* in all essentials complete and only awaiting the release of sets and costumes from beleaguered Paris, he tried again, this time enclos-

---

* See Walker, p. 449.

† Letter from Giulio Ricordi, 10.2.1870. *Carteggi Verdiani*, IV, p. 186.

ing a copy of Boito's libretto for *Amleto*. By now he had already broached his plan to Boito himself, who 'would consider himself the happiest and most fortunate of men if he could write this *Nerone* for you'.* Verdi gave a brief non-committal reply before answering at length. Yes, he liked the subject and would be loth to give up the plan completely; also he had been very impressed with the libretto of *Amleto*. But for the moment he had too much on his mind (this was the period of the Florence Commission on the Reform of the Conservatories). Could the matter be left open for a while? In the meantime Boito must on no account wait upon his convenience. Let him continue with his own opera on *Nerone* and they would resume discussion later.† In vain Giulio Ricordi exerted his eloquence, begging Verdi to strike while the iron was hot and not to hold back out of consideration for the poet. The Verdi–Boito *Nerone* which had seemed within easy reach of fulfilment was adjourned in perpetuity.

During the early 1870s Boito was earning his living by journalism, by writing libretti for other composers (*La Falce* for Catalani, *La Gioconda* for Ponchielli, *Iram* for Cesare Dominiceti and *Pier Luigi Farnese* for Constantino Palumba all belong to this period) and by making innumerable translations of foreign works, amongst them Wagner's *Rienzi*, *Tristan und Isolde*, *Das Liebesmahl der Apostolen*, Weber's *Der Freischütz* and Glinka's *Russlan and Ludmilla*, not to mention various collections of songs and romances. From all this hack work he was set free by the vindication of *Mefistofele* in its revised form at Bologna in 1875, and its even greater triumph in Venice the following year. But the moment for a collaboration with Verdi had receded. In his rage at the growing popularity of foreign music the older composer was continually recalling the offending Sapphic ode. To Giulio Ricordi in 1875: 'I cannot take as anything but a joke your sentence. "The whole salvation of the theatre and of art is in your hands!!" Oh no, never fear, composers for the theatre will never be lacking, and I myself will repeat what Boito said in a toast to Faccio after his first opera: ". . . and perhaps the man is born who will sweep the altar clean".'‡ To Clarina Maffei in 1878: 'You, of all people, advise me to write! Now let's talk about it seriously. For what reason should I write? What would I succeed in doing? What would I gain by it? The results would be quite wretched. I would have it said of me all over again that I didn't know how to write and that I've become a follower of *Wagner*. Some glory! After a career of nearly forty years to end up as an imitator!'§ A year later the tide would slowly begin to turn.

Indeed there are signs that during this time Verdi's morale was not quite so low as he had led his friends to believe. Several times during the mid-1870s he travelled abroad to conduct performances of his Requiem. On each occasion his letters to Italy are full of praise for the performance and delight at the audience's response, and nowhere more so than at Cologne, where the Mass formed one of the novelties of the Lower Rhine Festival of 1877. Founded by one Bischoff in 1811 and held in rotation at Aachen, Cologne and Düsseldorf, this festival had become as firm a stronghold of traditional German music as the Three Choirs Festival of English. Its director at the time was Ferdinand Hiller, no Wagnerian visionary, but a worthy and sensitive

---

* Letter from Giulio Ricordi, 16.1.1871. *Ibid.*, p. 187.
† Letter to Giulio Ricordi, 29.1.1871. *Ibid.*, p. 188.
‡ Letter to Giulio Ricordi, April 1875. Walker, pp. 469–70.
§ Letter to Clarina Maffei, 19.3.1878. Luzio, *Profili biografici e bozzetti storici*, II, pp. 541–2.

musical craftsman in the Mendelssohnian tradition (this alone, aggravated by his Jewish origin, would be sufficient to alienate him from the world of Bayreuth). A close friend of Rossini, he had always taken an interest in Italian music; he had had an opera, *Romilda*, produced at La Scala, Milan, in 1839, and in 1852–3 had been musical director of the Théâtre des Italiens in Paris. At the time Verdi had expressed strong reservations about the appointment,* but for the composer of the Manzoni Requiem Hiller represented everything that was most admirable in contemporary German music. The two composers became firm friends and corresponded at intervals until Hiller's death in 1885. So touched was Verdi by his reception on this first occasion of their meeting – poems and speeches in his honour, a magnificent rendering of his quartet, presents of a gold and ivory baton, a gold and silver wreath with the names of the donors inscribed on each leaf and an album containing views of the Rhine painted by one of the city's leading artists – that he at once wrote to Piroli asking him to obtain from the government a decoration for Hiller – 'not mere Cavaliere but Ufficiale. Fernando Hiller is a Doctor of Music; he's one of the greatest musicians in Germany; he's a very fine composer, Director of the Conservatory here and Director of these famous Rhine Festivals; also a very learned man of letters and an excellent writer'.† But there were the usual bureaucratic delays and difficulties; and eventually Piroli was told to forget all about it; to persist would be 'a humiliation for myself and my friend'.‡

Verdi showed an interest in Hiller's music which he never accorded to that of his younger Italian contemporaries; he asked to see the score of his new pastorale *Rebecca*, and having read it praised it very highly. In 1879 came the surprise. Hiller sent to Verdi his setting of the psalm 'De Profundis' as translated by Dante, with the request that Verdi might correct some of the faulty scansion. (It was to be published by Ricordi with a dedication to Verdi himself.) Verdi replied, 'The beauty of it is that last winter I had the idea of setting the same psalm to music, but fortunately I changed my mind and decided to do the 'Pater Noster', also translated by Dante, as a piece for five voices. . . .'§ That year saw the completion not only of the 'Pater Noster' but of an 'Ave Maria' for solo soprano and strings. Both pieces were performed at a concert given by the Orchestral Society of Milan on 18 April 1880. Clearly the mills of creation had begun to grind once more.

How the seed of *Otello* was planted was told by Giulio Ricordi to Puccini's last librettist, Giuseppe Adami, who in turn has left us a full account in his monograph on the publisher:

> The idea of the opera arose during a dinner among friends, when I chanced to turn the conversation on Shakespeare and Boito. At the mention of *Othello* I saw Verdi look sharply at me, with suspicion but with interest. He had certainly understood; he had certainly reacted. I believed that the time was ripe. Franco Faccio was my clever accomplice. But I had overestimated. Next day when on my advice Faccio brought Boito to Verdi's hotel with the scheme of the libretto already outlined, the composer, having examined it and found it excellent, had

---

* See previous chapter, p. 277.
† Letter to Piroli, 22.5.1877. *Carteggi Verdiani*, III, pp. 126–7.
‡ Letter to Piroli, 14.7.1877. *Ibid.*, p. 128.
§ Letter to Hiller, 21.7.1879. *Carteggi Verdiani*, II, pp. 330–1.

no wish to compromise himself. He said, 'Now put it into verse. It will come in handy for yourself . . . for me . . . for someone else.'

I encouraged Boito to finish it. But when I announced to Verdi that I would like to pay a flying visit to S. Agata with the poet I got a distinctly firm letter by way of reply: 'No, no . . . You've already gone too far, and we must stop before giving rise to gossip and petty annoyances. If you come here with Boito I would find myself of necessity obliged to read the libretto which he brings with him all complete. If the libretto is a good one I would find myself necessarily committed. If I find it good and then suggest modifications which Boito accepts I should find myself committed still more. And then suppose I don't like the libretto, however beautiful it may be, it would be too difficult for me to say so to his face. The best thing (if you are agreeable and it suits Boito) is for him to send me the finished poem so that I can read it and give my opinion at my leisure without either party being committed. Once these rather thorny difficulties have been smoothed out I shall be happy to see you arrive here with Boito.'*

The libretto would not have been ready in any case since Boito was impeded by bouts of ill health during the late summer and early autumn of 1879 and could only work by fits and starts, despite continual exhortations from Giulio Ricordi. 'I shall tell Giulio that I'm manufacturing chocolate,' he wrote to Tornaghi in July, using the term by which *Otello* was to be referred to by all those in the secret,† and on 21 September, 'If I don't send off to Giulio Desdemona strangled this week I'm afraid he may strangle me!'‡ To Ricordi himself, in the full knowledge that his words would be relayed to Verdi: 'I'm applying a very special type of rhythmic construction to this work (particularly to the lyrical parts) and that should, I think, be of great interest to our Maestro . . . and should prove a strong incentive to setting in motion the project that we all have so much at heart.'§ In the event only part of the libretto was sent to Verdi; but Boito had shown willing and Giuseppina was able to assure Giulio Ricordi that her husband was very pleased with what he had read so far; but that it would be unwise to apply any pressure. 'Let the river find its own way to the sea. It is in the wide open spaces that some men are destined to meet and understand one another.'¶ A meeting was suggested for Milan later that month where the question could be further discussed behind closed doors.

But secrets are difficult to keep in Italy; and already in the September–October issue of the *Nuova Antologia* of that year D'Arcais, deploring as usual the dearth of good contemporary Italian operas, asked his readers innocently why Verdi should not set *Othello* to music. True, Shakespeare presented many difficulties for the opera composer and even Verdi's own *Macbeth* fell short of the original in many ways. But surely *Othello* was tailor-made for an Italian opera and if written by Verdi could not fail to be a masterpiece . . . and so on.‖ Hence no doubt Giuseppina's discouraging

* G. Adami, *Giulio Ricordi, amico dei musicisti* (Milan, 1945), pp. 92–3; see also letter to Giulio Ricordi, 4.9.1879. *Copialettere*, p. 311; Abbiati, IV, pp. 86–7.

† See Nardi, p. 462.

‡ Letter from Boito to Tornaghi, 21.9.1879. *Ibid.*, p. 462.

§ Letter from Boito to Giulio Ricordi, 5.9.1879. See *Carteggi Verdiani*, IV, pp. 198–203 for the anxious correspondence between publisher, librettist and composer at the time.

¶ Letter from Giuseppina Verdi to Giulio Ricordi, 7.11.1879. Nardi, pp. 463–4; Walker, p. 476.

‖ D'Arcais, 'Rassegna Musicale', in *Nuova Antologia*, Sept.–Oct. 1879, pp. 155–62.

reply to an inquiry from her husband's old friend the Countess Negroni-Prati-Morosini. She admitted that Verdi had liked what he had seen of Boito's libretto and had decided to buy it 'but . . . he put it away in his briefcase beside Somma's *Re Lear* which has been sleeping soundly and undisturbed for thirty years. What will become of this *Otello*? We don't know at all' (this last a catchphrase in Milanese dialect).*

Significantly, however, when a month later Verdi received from his Neapolitan friend the painter Domenico Morelli a photograph of a sketch from *King Lear*, he wrote back suggesting that he try his hand at a scene from *Othello*: 'for instance: when Othello smothers Desdemona; or better still (it would be more novel) when Othello tortured by jealousy faints and Iago looks at him with a hellish smile and says, "Work on, my medicine, work!" Iago – what a figure ! ! ! Well, what do you say?'† The painter reacted at once. 'Iago looking at Othello who has fainted, what a fine situation! Iago with the face of an honest man. I've found a priest who seems to me just right – if I can manage him successfully I'll send him to you – not the priest, a canvas which I've scrawled on.'‡ To the anti-clerical Verdi this was heady stuff. 'Good, fine, excellent. Iago with the face of a gentleman! You've struck right home – just as I always knew you would. I think I can really see this *priest*, that is, this Iago with the face of an honest man. Quickly, then; a few brush strokes and send me that canvas you've scrawled on.' Then changing the subject to another painting of Morelli's, 'The scene of the kneeling monks is beautiful – "La Vergine degl' Angeli", etc., but it's an operatic subject. This Iago is Shakespeare, humanity, that is to say a part of humanity – evil!'§ Morelli was to prove highly dilatory in carrying out Verdi's wishes; and several more letters were to be exchanged between them before the painter completed his 'Othello fallen in a faint after Iago's insinuations'. For the moment it is sufficient to note that in Verdi's mind *Othello* was not sleeping the sleep of *King Lear*.

Why should it have taken so ardent a Shakespearian as Verdi so long to arrive at the idea of setting *Othello*? As D'Arcais remarked it is precisely suited to Verdi's means and to those of Italian opera in general. Of all Shakespeare's dramas it is the best constructed and the most vividly theatrical; it is also the one which most nearly conforms to the canon of Aristotle's *Poetics* in everything apart from its time-scale. There are no sub-plots, no episodes that fail to bear on the central action, none of those effusions of poetry for its own sake that sometimes clog the pace of a Shakespearian play. Even the most ardently lyrical passages are all harnessed to the dramatic purpose. Above all there is no superfluity of characters principal or secondary whose elimination would be essential if the *convenienze* were to be observed.

The truth is [*wrote Bernard Shaw with his usual mixture of brilliance and eccentricity*] that instead of *Otello* being an Italian opera written in the style of Shakespeare, *Othello* is a play written by Shakespeare in the style of Italian opera. It is quite peculiar among his works in this respect. Its characters are monsters; Desdemona

---

* Letter from Giuseppina Strepponi to Countess Negroni-Prati–Morosini, 18.12.1879. Nardi, pp. 464–5.
† Letter to D. Morelli, 6.1.1880. *Copialettere*, pp. 692–3.
‡ Letter from Morelli, 8.1.1880. Abbiati, IV, p. 111.
§Letter to Morelli, 7.2.1880. *Copialettere*, pp. 693–4. 'La Vergine degl'Angeli' of course refers to the finale of the second act of *La Forza del destino*.

is a prima donna with handkerchief, confidante and vocal solo all complete; and Iago, though certainly more anthropomorphic than the Count di Luna, is only so when he slips out of his stage villain's part. Othello's transports are conveyed by a magnificent but senseless music which rages from the Propontick to the Hellespont in an orgy of sound and bounding rhythm;* and the plot is a pure farce plot; that is to say it is supported on a desperately precarious trick with a handkerchief which a chance word might upset at any moment. With such a libretto Verdi was quite at home; his success with it proves not that he could occupy Shakespeare's place but that Shakespeare could occupy his . . .†

It is understandable that a playwright who consistently plays down the sexual drive should belittle a tragedy of sexual jealousy and imagined betrayal; nor is it necessary to point out with Aldous Huxley that one man's farce is another's tragedy or to recall Horace Walpole's 'Life is a comedy to those who think and a tragedy to those who feel'. Nevertheless, the operatic element in Shakespeare's tragedy is patent. What undoubtedly deterred Verdi and his contemporaries from treating it as such was the existence of Rossini's *Otello* of 1816, composed at a time when Shakespeare was barely known in Italy. Had it been a work of no importance it would not have proved an obstacle to Rossini's successors, but it is a minor masterpiece which held the stage for most of the nineteenth century, even if rarely performed as Rossini wrote it. The San Carlo in 1816 was almost unique in having on its roster three star tenors who could divide the principal roles between them. For revivals elsewhere it was usual to allocate one of them (normally Rodrigo, but occasionally Iago) to a mezzo-soprano, making the necessary transpositions and *puntature*, and even permitting the substitution or addition of an aria or two. For despite its structural inventiveness Rossini's *Otello* remains for its first two acts essentially a traditional number-opera of the kind that lent itself in those days to dismemberment and spare-part surgery. There are many gems – the spacious 'introduzione e cavatina', the duettino between Desdemona and Emilia, the oath-duet between Iago and Othello with its hammering rhythm that looks forward to Rigoletto's 'Sì, vendetta' – but they can hardly compensate for the degradation of Shakespeare's plot into the most commonplace of triangle dramas with Rodrigo a hot-headed brainless compendium of himself and Cassio, the scene laid in Venice throughout and an offstage duel to bring down the curtain on the second act. What kept Rossini's *Otello* alive and in general repute was the last act, which even today can rightly be viewed as one of the supreme achievements of ottocento opera, if the mind can be wiped clean of Verdi's still finer Act IV. All the traditional elements are there, but for once pressed into the service of a single organic design. With Rodrigo disposed of, the plot approximates quite closely to Shakespeare's Act V but with two accretions – a prayer for Desdemona before retiring and, earlier on, the distant song of a gondolier singing Dante's famous lines 'Nessun maggior dolore che ricordarsi d'un tempo felice nella miseria'. Here, as in late Puccini, a peripheral idea is used to define the central mood of the scene – one of haunting desolation. The folk-like melody, Rossini's own, was transcribed by

* Not really a fair comment, this, since the passage to which it implicitly refers – III, iii, 460–7 – does not appear in the earliest quarto edition and may not be definitive.

† *Shaw's Music*, III, p. 579.

Liszt to form the second movement of his *Venezia e Napoli*. So much more impressive than the willow-song ('Assisa al piè d'un salice'), the 'Canzone del Gondoliere' remained like a sentinel barring the way to any composer rash enough to attempt a subject that Rossini was considered to have made his own.

So we are not surpised to learn from a draft letter of Giuseppina recalling that famous dinner party in Milan with Faccio and Giulio Ricordi that 'The conversation turned upon Rossini's opera. . . . Angry sarcasms rained down on all sides at the expense of the librettist who had cobbled together such a hateful caricature of Shakespeare's drama. There were also some nice things said about the Jupiter of Pesaro's music beginning with that stupendous passage, the song of the gondolier. . . .'[*] Clearly the challenge of Rossini and his gondolier had to be faced and weighed up before there could be any question of setting the subject anew; and Verdi had allowed himself to be persuaded that the time had come when it was safe to make the attempt. Yet it is remarkable how often the image of Rossini's opera recurred to him as a model for certain details which he preserved as well as at least one which he discarded.

That Boito was the ideal if not the only imaginable partner for Verdi in this venture seemed obvious at the time and has seemed so almost ever since. 'Almost', because in recent years a fashion has sprung up of regarding Boito as a disaster for Verdi, as one who usurped his authority as a composer and led him on a trail of false intellectualism with a persistence which Verdi himself was too old and tired to check. 'The fact is', wrote the late Gabriele Baldini, 'that, with the single remarkable exception of Boito, Verdi's librettists could never influence him when he had discovered truly apposite musical material: they became merely secretaries, copyists, and though they were unaware of their position, they wrote their texts by dictation. Piave did this more than the others, and for this reason he is the greatest. By offering to cancel himself out completely Piave became the only one who found his own extraordinary, inimitable style – in reality the literary style of Verdi himself.'[†] Hence the startling judgement: '. . . *Macbeth* can be heard to be in the mainstream of Verdian masterpieces, and one can well understand how much more vigorous and powerful is the Shakespeare *re-invented* on that occasion than the Shakespeare watered down by the preciosity of Boito in *Otello*.'[‡]

It is true that Boito's literary reputation has vastly declined since his own day; but are Piave, Solera or Cammarano any more esteemed as men of letters? What counts in a librettist is his ability to aid and stimulate the thought of the composer. In collaboration with Boito men like Catalani and Ponchielli produced some of their best work, simply because he was more alive to their musical needs than such as D'Ormeville, Zanardini or Ghislanzoni. The apparently clumsy parentheses that sometimes hold up the flow of his verse in *Otello* will be found to have their raison d'être in the configuration of mature Verdian melody, so much more subtle and complex than in the operas written with Piave.[§] Above all, the years that had elapsed

[*] Draft letter from Giuseppina Verdi to the Countess Negroni-Prati-Morosini, 18.12.1879. *Carteggi Verdiani*, II, p. 95.

[†] G. Baldini, *The Story of Giuseppe Verdi*, trs. R. Parker (Cambridge, 1980), p. 127.

[‡] *Ibid.*, p. 137.

[§] Paradoxically Baldini did not extend his condemnation to *Falstaff*, which he seems to have regarded as Verdi's masterpiece. Unfortunately he never lived to explain how Boito's collaboration, apparently so harmful to *Otello*, was beneficial to its successor.

since the première of *Mefistofele* had turned the lofty visionary into a practical man of the theatre.

In trimming *Othello* for the operatic stage he made two notable modifications. The first and most important is the omission of the Venetian act and with it Brabantio. For this he has been much commended – and indeed as early as the mid eighteenth century Samuel Johnson regretted that Shakespeare had not designed his drama in that way. Othello's courtship and his initial security in Desdemona's love must therefore be conveyed by a long duet following the dismissal of Cassio. The heights from which the hero is finally brought down are thus clearly established. What the new arrangement fails to make clear is the reason for his vulnerability. Shakespeare was after all in Verdi's words the 'master of the human heart', or in other words a psychologist of rare skill. If Othello is naturally prone to jealousy he no more commands our sympathy than a natural miser or lecher. In fact during Shakespeare's first act he is made to sustain the kind of spiritual battering which a saint could hardly survive without a scar. The knowledge that Othello has married his daughter turns Brabantio from a kindly host into a primitive tribal chief screaming the crudest insults and threats at one who has dared to taint the purity of his stock. Nothing is held back; Othello's age is cast into his teeth as well as his colour. His marriage to Desdemona is denounced before the senate as an abomination in the sight of God and man. True, the senators take Othello's side; but it is Brabantio who has the last word:

> Look to her, Moor, have a quick eye to see:
> She has deceiv'd her father, may do thee.*

Tragic heroes are not interesting if they are saints. That Othello's morale should give way with the right combination of circumstances is absolutely logical. In the same way the hero of Euripides' *Hercules Furens* having acquitted himself from an ordeal with unswerving courage, finally suffers an inner collapse. Rightly does Othello describe himself as:

> . . . one not easily jealous, but being wrought
> Perplexed in the extreme.†

Now if motive were as serious a factor in opera as certain commentators would have us believe the omission of the Venetian act would be a serious flaw; for without it Othello responds too readily to Iago's insinuations. On the evidence of the libretto alone he is as naturally prone to jealousy as his Rossinian counterpart, who so repelled Stendhal for that reason. But this argument takes no account of the power of music to convey mood, emotion and even character with a directness beyond the capacity of words, which, as Bernard Shaw remarks, are the counters of thought, not feeling. In a spoken play the audience needs to know the motivation of a feeling in order to be convinced of that feeling's reality and force. Equally it needs to see Othello defending himself with dignity against the foul-mouthed insults of Brabantio if it is to be persuaded of his basic nobility of character. In the opera only a few deft musical strokes are needed to bring Othello before us in all his authority and poise, his gentle and loving nature. Music again will suffice to depict the agonizing horror of his fall. The soul is 'purged by pity and terror' without the aid of the

---

* Shakespeare, *Othello*, I, iii, 292–3.
† *Ibid.*, V, ii, 346–7.

Venetian act; though, as will be seen, Boito borrowed certain lines from it for his love duet.

The second modification is rather one of emphasis, and is due to Verdi's perennial need to find a suitable place for a concertato act-finale. In an age when opera was tending more and more in the direction of naturalism – in so far as the increasing resources of the operatic orchestra would permit – the largo concertato was the last bastion of artificiality. Here time is suspended; the singers lose all awareness of each other's presence and pour out their several feelings to the footlights in a glorious web of lyrical sound. From his celebrated letter to Florimo of 1838* it would seem that Mercadante was already irked by this tradition which compelled singers to stand around doing nothing. Yet to composers of his and Verdi's generation the concertato was an essential feature of operatic architecture, the centrepiece to which both eye and ear should be drawn. It was left to the 'veristi', following the example of Massenet, to abolish this cumbersome device and close their acts with the equivalent of a curtain line in a spoken play: 'She is another's!' (*Werther*), '. . . and before him all Rome trembled!' (*Tosca*), and many others. Even when Puccini ends an act with a grand tableau, as with the embarkation at Le Havre, it is never one in which time stands still. If he or Massenet had set *La Dame aux Camélias* as an opera, we may be sure that after Armand has thrown his winnings at Marguérite's feet there would have been no entry of Germont, and no concertato of sad sweet melody. Instead Baron Duphol would have struck Armand across the face with his glove and the curtain would have descended to Dumas's ringing phrase: 'Monsieur, vous êtes un lâche!'

Verdi's own attitude to the concertato, as to so many of the post-Rossinian conventions, is ambivalent. In *Rigoletto* he had in effect dispensed with it entirely (the ensemble at the end of the first scene is too short and occurs too early in the proceedings to count as an example). In *La Forza del destino* there are a number of static choral tableaux; but none of them has the complexity associated with this particular style of ensemble, except perhaps for the pilgrim's chorus in Act II; and that takes place in the middle of a scene. In all his other operas Verdi seems to have considered a central concertato to be a sine qua non; but he is increasingly concerned to give it some kind of motion. In the new Act I finale to *Simon Boccanegra* he would want the characters to talk to each other rather than at the audience, and so to break the illusion of suspended time. It was to the central finale that he and Boito first addressed themselves when they proceeded to revise that opera; and it is the first feature to be mentioned in the correspondence in *Otello*. As we shall see, in the case of both *Otello* and *Falstaff*, Verdi himself continued to worry at the concertati finali long after the premières of the operas themselves.

In Shakespeare's *Othello* there is no obvious situation for a grand operatic concertato unless it be the scene before the Venetian senate in the first act, which Boito had discarded. He fell back on the moment at which Othello strikes his wife in front of the ambassador† – not an especially important stage in the Moor's downfall. That Boito realized the extent of the problem and the importance of solving it at an early stage is indicated by a letter sent to him by Giulio Ricordi, dating from July 1880. The spring had brought distractions for both partners: for Verdi the première of *Aida*

* See Vol. 2, p. 6.
† *Othello*, IV, i, 210–74.

in French at the Paris Opéra; for Boito the first performance of *Mefistofele* in London. Both events had proved gratifyingly successful; and the publisher judged the time ripe to nudge the 'chocolate project' into motion once more. 'You will recall that at your request I wrote to [Verdi] to say that on your return you would apply yourself to that famous finale for which you had already outlined the idea, leaving only the versification to be done. Don't make me look a c——! By now the fumes of English bitter [*cervògia*] should have dispersed and your nerves should have recovered their calm. I have the feeling that Verdi has put the Moor to sleep for a little. An electric shock from your lines would do wonders!'*

Boito did as he was asked, but the shock was slow in taking effect. Not until 15 August did Verdi reply with a long letter, the first, it seems, in which he expounded his views to Boito without an intermediary. Certainly he preferred the finale as at present worked out to the original scheme; but he could not see his way to making it musically and theatrically effective.

> After Othello has insulted Desdemona there is nothing more to say – at the most a sentence, a reproach, a curse on the barbarian who has insulted a woman! And here we would either bring down the curtain, or else *invent* something that is not in Shakespeare! For instance, after the words: 'Silence, Devil!' Lodovico, with all the pride of a patrician and the dignity of an ambassador, could address Othello thus: 'Unworthy Moor, you dare to insult a Venetian patrician, my relative, and you do not fear the wrath of the Senate?' (a stanza of 4 or 6 lines):
>
> Iago gloats over his work (a similar stanza)
> Desdemona laments (a similar stanza)
> Roderigo (a stanza)
> Emilia and chorus (a stanza)
> Othello mute, motionless, terrible, says nothing. . . .

So far Verdi was merely filling out Boito's design as an eminently orthodox pezzo concertato led by Lodovico, as Germont leads that of *La Traviata* (Act II), Amonasro that of *Aida* (Act II) and the Flemish deputies that of *Don Carlos* (Act III). But if in 1880 the largo no longer required a full stretta to complement it, the need for a coup de théâtre to give a strong curtain remained. Here are Verdi's rather unfortunate first thoughts on the matter:

> Suddenly distant drums, trumpets, cannon-fire, etc., are heard. The Turks! The Turks! The stage is invaded by soldiers and populace; general surprise and panic. Othello shakes himself like a lion and draws himself erect; he brandishes his sword. 'Come on; I will lead you to victory again.' They all leave the stage except Desdemona. Meanwhile the women, gathering from all sides, fall on their knees in terror while offstage are heard the shouts of the soldiers, cannon-fire, drums, trumpets and all the tumult of battle. Desdemona, isolated and motionless in the centre of the stage, her eyes turned to Heaven, prays for Othello. The curtain falls.

---

* Letter from Giulio Ricordi to Boito, 24.7.1880. Nardi, pp. 465–6; Walker, p. 477.

Strange mixture of the now discarded ending to Act III of *La Forza del destino* and the finale to Act II of Rossini's *Otello*! Yet we should bear in mind that in 1880 grand opera was still the order of the day in Italy. This too was the period of the long, spectacular Umbertine ballets with titles like *Excelsior* and *Amor* set to supremely unmemorable music and with choreography reduced to a superior mixture of parade-ground drill and acrobatics. Verdi may have been prepared to meet his audience's tastes so long as the musical scope was not diminished. He continues:

> The musical piece would be there and the composer would be satisfied. The critic would have much to say. For example: if the Turks have been defeated (as was stated at the outset) how could they now fight? This, however, is not a serious criticism because one could suppose, and state in a few words, that the Turks had suffered damage and had been dispersed by the storm but not wiped out. There would be a more serious objection. Can Othello, crushed with sorrow, gnawed by jealousy, discouraged, physically and morally sick – can he suddenly pull himself together and become again the hero that he was? And if he can, if glory can still allure him, and he can forget love, sorrow and jealousy, why should he kill Desdemona and then himself?
>
> Are these needless scruples, or are they serious objections? I wanted to tell you what's going through my head. Who knows? Perhaps you'll find amongst these stupid ideas of mine a germ of which something could come.*

Possibly it was Boito's failure to reply at once that was responsible for a slight drawing-back on Verdi's part. Once again, through Giuseppina, he dissuaded Ricordi and the poet from visiting S. Agata together. As yet his ideas on the subject were not sufficiently crystallized for him to wish to work on the libretto and in any case he was too busy. 'I think frankly,' Giuseppina wrote, 'that the best thing to do is to leave matters as they are for the present and surround the Moor with the greatest possible silence.'† So Boito took the only possible course, which was to rewrite the ending of the finale, adding something along the lines that Verdi had suggested. There was to be no Turkish attack, however. Othello would merely throw off his black mood in a single stanza which may be rendered thus:

> 'What? On the day that celebrates our victory
> Shall dark cloud brood over Cyprus?
> I want the sound of joy and of glory.
> Let the cannon roar! Let trumpets sound!'
> *[A burst of fanfares: movement of crowds and banners. The curtain falls.]*‡

This time there was a reaction. 'Divinely well done,' Verdi wrote back. '. . . But now what do you think of the scruples manifested in my last letter?'§ Boito replied with that exquisite tact which native sensibility and good breeding combined with twenty years' experience in theatrical hurly-burly had taught the once brash young 'scapigliato'. He was embarrassed, he said, at having to contradict himself, since:

---

* Letter to Boito, 15.8.1880. Walker, pp. 477–8.
† Letter from Giuseppina Verdi to Giulio Ricordi, 6.9.1880. Nardi, p. 468.
‡ *Carteggi Verdiani*, II, p. 112.
§ Letter to Boito, 14.10.1880. Nardi, p. 468; Walker, p. 478.

. . . in my deeds I have agreed with the Maestro and the composer while in my words I am about to agree with the critic. When you ask of me – or rather yourself: Are these needless scruples or serious objections? I reply: they are serious objections. Othello is like a man moving in circles beneath an incubus, and under the fatal domination of that incubus he thinks, acts, suffers, and commits this dreadful crime. Now if we invent something which must necessarily rouse Othello and distract him from this incubus that holds him fast, we destroy all the sinister fascination created by Shakespeare and we cannot arrive logically at the climax of the action. That attack of the Turks is like a fist breaking the window of a room where two people are dying of asphyxiation. The close atmosphere of death, so carefully precipitated by Shakespeare, is suddenly dispelled. Vital air circulates again in our tragedy and Othello and Desdemona are saved. In order to set them once more on the way to death we must re-enclose them in the lethal chamber, reconstruct the incubus, patiently lead Iago back to his prey, and there is only one act for us in which to begin the tragedy all over again. In other words: *we have found the end of an act, but at the cost of the effectiveness of the final catastrophe.*

He went on to stress the perfection and homogeneity of Shakespeare's scheme and to point out the dangers of departing from it and the inevitability of falsifying the characters thereby. But he concluded:

An opera is not a play; our art lives by elements unknown to spoken tragedy. An atmosphere that has been destroyed can be created all over again. Eight bars are enough to restore a sentiment to life; a rhythm can re-establish a character; music is the most omnipotent of all the arts; it has a logic all its own – both freer and more rapid than the logic of spoken thought, and much more eloquent. You, Maestro, could with a single stroke of the pen reduce the most cogent arguments of your critics to silence. You have said: Act III is divinely well done; therefore you are in the right, since this exclamation of yours simply indicates to me that the musical conception is already strong and clear in your mind.*

No mere flattery, this, or sugaring of the critical pill, but an important statement of aesthetic principle, and yet another reminder of the foolishness of judging musical and literary drama by the same canons.

Boito then offered a fresh solution. He transferred Othello's fainting fit from its original position in the play to the Act III finale following the concertato. The court and the ambassadors have left; outside the crowd are hailing Othello as the victorious general. Only Iago remains behind, spurning the unconscious Moor with his foot. Thus the very scene which Verdi had singled out in his letters to Morelli as being especially gripping was now placed just at the point where, for operatic reasons, a powerful coup de théâtre was needed. No wonder the composer was pleased.

'Good idea, that third finale!' he wrote back. 'I like Othello's fainting fit better in this finale than where it was originally. Only I don't find, or feel, the big ensemble! . . . We'll discuss it later; at present, as Giulio will have told you, there is something else to think about.'† This 'something' was of course the rehabilitation of *Simon*

---

* Letter from Boito, 18.10.1880. Nardi, pp. 469–71; quoted in part in Walker, pp. 478–9.

† Letter to Boito, 2.12.1880. Nardi, p. 471; Walker, p. 480.

Boccanegra, for which Verdi hoped that Boito would be willing to provide some new verses. Boito agreed, but without enthusiasm, since however radical the musical revision the bulk of the text would remain Piave's and the resulting libretto a literary hotch-potch. 'Therefore,' he wrote to Giulio Ricordi, his task almost completed, 'the new *Boccanegra* must be given under the name F. M. Piave pure and simple, and my name must not be associated with it in any way.'* Verdi was in fact asking him to do a hack job; he understood the librettist's repugnance, but 'there are reasons, not commercial, but let me say *professional* which prevent me from giving up the idea of putting this *Boccanegra* in order without at least first having tried to make something of it.'† The overriding reason, one suspects, was the necessity he felt to get into training for the monumental task ahead. Apart from the few pages of extra ballet for the Paris *Aida* he had written no operatic music for ten years. The importance of the *Boccanegra* revision lies not only in the magnificent quality of the new music but in the proof it gave that Verdi could, in a sense, pick up from where he had left off. If there are occasional discrepancies of style between the best of the new and the weakest of the old, more noteworthy are the many places where by a few deft touches of harmony or rhythm the material of 1857 is transformed and modernized without any loss of its original character.

In the same letter Verdi added, with a sly tact worthy of his new collaborator, 'By the by, it's in everyone's interest that La Scala should survive. The schedule for this year is lamentable. Ponchielli's opera‡ is an excellent choice, but the rest? There is one opera which would arouse great interest in the public and I don't understand why its composer and publisher persist in withholding it! I mean *Mefistofele*. The moment would be opportune and you would be rendering a service to art and to us all.' Verdi's merest whisper was by now like a court order in Milanese musical circles; so it is not difficult to connect that letter with the fact that two months after the première of the revised *Boccanegra*, *Mefistofele* did indeed appear on the stage where it had failed so miserably twelve years before. Verdi telegraphed his congratulations to the composer, adding, 'Let's have *Nerone* soon;'§ though how far his private opinion of the opera had changed since he heard it in Genoa can only be guessed.

For obvious reasons, then, no work was done on *Otello* during the first half of 1881. Indeed what had so far been accomplished had been the merest groundwork. 'Let's not talk for the present of the wicked Iago,' Verdi had written to Arrivabene the previous September. 'Boito is writing me the book and I've bought it but I haven't yet composed a note.'¶ However, this did not prevent another calculated indiscretion on the part of their common acquaintance, D'Arcais, in the columns of the January issue of the *Nuova Antologia*: 'Everybody is aware that Verdi is writing a new opera, to verses by Arrigo Boito – *Iago*, taken from Shakespeare's *Othello*. Readers may remember an article in the *Nuova Antologia* advising him to do that very thing. Only he should call it *Otello*, not *Iago*.'‖ Five years were to pass before Verdi agreed

---

* Letter from Boito to Giulio Ricordi, 21.1.1881. Nardi, p. 473.
† Letter to Boito, 11.12.1880. Walker, p. 480.
‡ *Il Figluolo prodigo*, produced on 26.12.1880.
§ Telegram to Boito, 26.5.1881. Walker, p. 485.
¶ Letter to Arrivabene, 14.9.1880. Alberti, pp. 259–60.
‖ D'Arcais, 'Rassegna Musicale', in *Nuova Antologia*, Jan.–Feb. 1881, pp. 707–17.

to follow this advice. Meanwhile he had already found his ideal Iago in the new Boccanegra, Victor Maurel (of whom more anon), and is said to have exclaimed during a rehearsal, 'If God give me strength I'll write this *Iago* for you.'*

Correspondence between poet and composer was resumed towards the end of May, though there had clearly been some verbal discussion beforehand. Much yet remained to be done to the text of the Act III finale; in the meantime they turned their attention to a different problem – the need, felt strongly by Verdi, for a moment of light relief amid so much encircling gloom. Why not a chorus of women and children singing Desdemona's praises? As so often in Boito's scenic conceits the literary, musical and visual elements all neatly coalesce.

> See where I've thought it suitable to place this chorus: towards the end of the first fatal conversation between Iago and Othello, when Iago astutely steers the Moor's thoughts towards the precipice of jealousy. After Othello's words 'Away at once with love or jealousy'† the public hear a sweet-sounding chorus behind the scenes which gradually approaches, while Iago continues to play his hellish part. Shortly afterwards, through a wide opening in the centre of the stage which gives on to the garden, Desdemona will be seen surrounded by women and children attractively grouped who spread flowers and fronds in her path and move around her singing serenely. At this fateful moment of the drama it will be like a pure, sweet apotheosis of songs and flowers encircling the beautiful, innocent figure of Desdemona. Throughout the piece it is desirable that Desdemona and the chorus should remain framed within the arch of the central aperture. You will remember, Maestro, the plan of the stage – octagonal with a balcony; and it's a shallow scene.
>
> The chorus, then, together with Desdemona, should stand on the far side of the door in full view of the spectator . . . but no one should cross the threshold. Therefore as they will be rather far away from the orchestra they could be accompanied by harps; and these could be in view. The poetry also mentions 'mandolas', so mandolines could be used as well.
>
> Iago and Othello are on stage, that is on this side of the door, standing by the proscenium, while the gentle apotheosis of Desdemona proceeds.
>
> For the beginning and end of this chorus and in the refrains I've attempted a six-syllable line accented in an unusual way with alternating strong and weak stresses: the rhythm of the line implies a three-pulse measure. [*Here follow the lines precisely as in the definitive libretto.*] The moment Desdemona pronounces the name of Cassio the remembrance of the chorus which still haunts Othello's soul ceases, and the drama resumes its inexorable course.

His reason for using a trochaic senario, he hastened to add, was not merely a desire for novelty (and a senario that sounds like a truncated ottonario was certainly novel in an opera libretto) but the need to find a metre that would match and contrast with the quinario of the intervening verses. 'If this chorus seems to you to be satisfactory

---

* Walker, p. 485.
† Boito alters this to 'love *and* jealousy'; see below.

the hardest part of the retouching of *Otello* has been done: I will get down to work on the big ensemble.'*

Verdi replied:

I think the chorus you have sent me will do very well. I say 'I think' because as I haven't got the second act in front of me I'm not really clear about the position it will occupy. At all events that chorus could not be more graceful, more elegant or more beautiful. And then what a splash of light amidst so much darkness! Get busy, then, on the finale and make it a well developed piece, a piece *on a grand scale*, I should say. The theatre demands it; but more than the theatre, the colossal power of the drama demands it. The idea (which I still like) of setting *Otello* to music without a chorus was, and is, perhaps, a crazy one.†

And so back to the finale of Act III; and this, together with certain cuts in the part of Otello himself mentioned in their previous correspondence, evidently formed the main topic of discussion when at long last Boito paid his first visit to S. Agata early in July, together with Giulio Ricordi. 'Giulio will have told you that our visit to S. Agata was extremely useful as regards chocolate,' he wrote to Tornaghi on his return. 'We have now settled with the Maestro the last dubious point of the work and I am now occupied in giving form to the results of my ideas.'‡ His next letter to Verdi is of especial interest, since it shows a new approach to the problem of over-coming the traditional concertato 'freeze' to which Verdi had begun to object.

The pezzo d'insieme has, as we intended, its lyrical and dramatic parts *fused together*; that is to say, it is a melodic, lyrical piece beneath which a dramatic dialogue develops.

The principal figure on the lyrical side is Desdemona; the principal figure on the dramatic is Iago.

This Iago, after being for a mere instant overwhelmed by an occurrence right outside his control (the letter recalling Othello to Venice), at once gathers up again all the threads of the tragedy with incomparable energy and swiftness, takes charge once more of the catastrophe and actually makes use of the unforeseen circumstance to hasten the course of the final disaster at a dizzy pace.

All that was in Shakespeare's mind, and it emerges clearly in our work. Iago goes from Othello to Roderigo, the two tools of his felony that still remain to him; then he has the last word and takes up the final pose in the act.

Please look and see whether the two parts, the lyrical and the dramatic, seem to you to be well fused. See too whether the length of each is well calculated. I haven't been economical with my lines because I remembered your admonition: say everything which has to be said and let everything be explained. . . .

Indeed, in case the dialogue between Iago and Roderigo should seem cramped and insufficiently clear, here are four lines which can complete it and round it off. [*He then proposed the four lines beginning 'A notte folta', in which Iago offers to find*

---

* Letter from Boito, 17.6.1881. *Carteggi Verdiani*, II, pp. 107–8.
† Letter to Boito, 23.6.1881. Walker, p. 485.
‡ Letter from Boito to Tornaghi, 10.7.1881. Nardi, p. 481.

Roderigo a suitable occasion for disposing of Cassio.] I've an observation to make. The Iago–Otello and Iago–Roderigo dialogues follow each other in that order. During the Iago–Othello dialogue what is Roderigo supposed to be doing? Nothing. However, his voice could form an extra *real part* at the beginning of the melodic ensemble and he could continue to sustain that part until it's time for his dialogue with Iago. That being the case, I'm offering you four lyrical lines which Roderigo can sing with the others while Othello is talking with Iago and while the ensemble is getting under way. [*Here he added the quatrain beginning 'Per me s'oscura il mondo' which remained in the definitive text with one or two minor verbal changes.*] At this point it could be remarked: since we've concerned ourselves with Roderigo's attitude during the Othello–Iago dialogue, why don't we do likewise with Othello's attitude during the exchange between Iago and Roderigo? No. Othello's attitude is already indicated, predetermined by the drama. We have seen him in a state of collapse by the table at the words 'Fall to the ground! and weep!' And thus he should remain without rising to his feet throughout the duration of the piece even when he replies to Iago. He has no need to speak while Iago is conversing with Roderigo. Silent he is greater, more terrible, more lifelike.

He should only rise to his feet to cry out, 'Away from me!' And then he should plummet to the ground. So far, I hope we are in perfect agreement. But perhaps you will say that Desdemona (being as I said *the leading figure in the lyrical part of the ensemble*) should have four more lines than the rest, especially since her first four lines don't lend themselves to the development of lyrical melody. In that case here are four more lines to finish Desdemona's stanza. . . .*

And he set down an early but recognizable variant of Desdemona's second quatrain (see Ex. 221b). The remainder of the letter concerns the problem of metre in a concertato of so novel a cut. Verdi and Boito had agreed that the lyrical and dramatic parts would each need a different metre. For the first the orthodox settenario would serve; for the second Boito proposed eleven-syllable lines so devised that they could be broken up into quinari maintaining a perfect rhyme-scheme either way (a typical stroke of Boitian ingenuity). 'You are therefore free to use first one then the other wherever you like. I needed to do this since a hendecasyllabic line extended in its entirety beneath a lyrical movement might have turned out too heavy and a quinario too light.'

Verdi saw the point at once.

The finale is very well done indeed [*he wrote back*]. What a difference between this one and the first !

I shall add the four lines for Roderigo.

Perhaps the other four for Desdemona won't be needed. [*They were, though.*]

So true is it that a silent Othello is grander and more terrible, that my idea would be not to have him speak at all during the whole ensemble. It seems to me that Iago alone can say and more briefly everything that needs to be said for the spectator's understanding, without any reply from Othello.

IAGO: Hurry! Time is flying! Concentrate on your task and on that alone! I'll

* Letter from Boito, 24.8.1881. *Carteggi Verdiani*, II, pp. 112–16.

see to Cassio. I'll pluck out his infamous guilty soul. I swear it. You shall have news of him at midnight.

(Altering the lines, of course.)

After the ensemble and the words 'Tutti fuggite Otello!' I find that Othello does not speak or cry out enough. He is silent for four lines and it seems to me (scenically speaking) after 'Che d'ogni senso il priva' Othello ought to bellow out one or two lines: 'Away! I detest you . . . myself . . . the whole world!'

And it seems to me too that we could save a few lines when Othello and Iago stay behind together. [*Then by a procedure quite common in his previous operas he filleted Boito's original text so as to make it run as in the final version.*] A strangled cry on the word 'fazzoletto' seems to me more terrible than a commonplace exclamation like, 'Oh, Satana!' The words 'svenuto . . . immobil . . . muto' somewhat hold up the action. One stops to think, and here it's a matter of hurrying on to the end.

He would also have liked the chorus to react to Othello's proclamation of his successor with:

> . . . four lines, not of revolt but of protest: 'No. No, we want Othello!'
> I know perfectly well that you will reply at once: Dear Signor Maestro, don't you know that no one dared to breathe after a decree of the *Serenissima* and that sometimes the mere presence of the *Messer Grande* sufficed to disperse the crowd and subdue the tumult?
> I would dare rejoin that the action takes place in Cyprus, the *Serenissimi* were far away and perhaps for that reason the Cypriots were bolder than the Venetians.*

But the idea was never used.

The ground-plan had been laid, the thornier problems of operatic construction resolved. At least a month after his letter to Boito (his last for some time) we find Verdi writing to Morelli once more about the projected scene from *Othello* and developing his ideas about Iago's appearance.

> . . . If I were an actor and had to represent Iago I would think in terms of a tall, thin figure, with thin lips and small eyes close to his nose, monkey-fashion, a high forehead sloping backwards and a head that bulges at the back; a manner that is absent-minded, *nonchalant*, indifferent to everything. He should throw off good and evil sentiments lightly as if he were thinking of something quite different to what he actually says. Thus if someone were to reproach him, and say, 'What you propose is infamous,' he would reply 'Really? . . . I didn't think it was. . . . Don't let us talk about it any more!' A man like that might deceive anybody, even his own wife to a certain extent.†

But he was in no hurry to begin the composition. The next three Christmases were to

---

* Letter to Boito, 27.8.1881. Walker, pp. 486–7.
† Letter to Morelli, 24.9.1881. *Copialettere*, pp. 316–17.

see the delivery to S. Agata of a large cake with the figure of a Moor in chocolate icing on the top – Giulio Ricordi's way of reminding the composer of what they all had so much to heart. But a plea from the French critic Baron Blaze de Bury, forwarded through Boito, to be allowed to translate the libretto into French on the grounds that 'Un jour ou l'autre Iago existera' drew a very dry response from the composer. He was surprised, he said, at the Baron's certainty since even he himself was uncertain whether Iago would some day exist. He was still more surprised that the Baron should wish to attempt such a thankless task as the translation of an Italian libretto into French. 'We have free verse [verso sciolto]; they're obliged to have rhymes and masculine and feminine endings in alternation and that's why they hardly ever manage to preserve the literal sense together with the phrase and the musical stress. À propos of this I said a few months back to the translator of one of my operas, "Why do you write rhymed lines in the recitatives and at the theatrical moments?" But the nature of their poetry doesn't allow them to write blank verse – at least no one ever dares do so.'[*] Anyway Iago would not be suitable for Paris – it would have Italian proportions, Italian melody (save the mark!) and no ballet (or so he thought at the time).

In all this we can sense the aftermath of Verdi's recent discussions with Nuitter over the revision of Don Carlos. Begun in the late summer of 1882 it took Verdi much longer than the more thoroughgoing revision of Simon Boccanegra, partly because of his refusal to communicate directly with du Locle, the original author, partly because the problems of coming to grips with the thought of a great playwright such as Schiller were more arduous than the patching-up of a libretto drawn from a minor drama. Again, one may agree with Andrew Porter that the revised Don Carlos was something in the nature of a trial run for the infinitely greater task before him.[†]

So it was that with the première of the four-act Don Carlos out of the way, the composition of Otello (or Iago, as it was still called) was begun. . . . A letter to Boito of February 1884 alludes to a variant of the text which Verdi had asked for. ('How promptly you've done it! If only I could be as quick!')[‡] A week later Boito confidently informed Tornaghi that the Maestro was getting down to work, and that the manufacture of chocolate was going ahead. He spoke too soon.

In March Boito went to Naples for the first performance in that city of Mefistofele. At a banquet given in his honour he found himself parrying an awkward question from the journalist Marco Cafiero: would he not have liked to set Othello to music himself? The difficulty was to disclaim all personal interest in Shakespeare's play without seeming to decry it as an operatic subject. His answer convinced Cafiero, who made no mention of the matter in his own paper. Unfortunately Boito's words had been overheard by the correspondent of the Neapolitan paper Roma, who interpreted them as meaning, 'I never thought that Othello would make a good opera, but now that I have begun to write the libretto I regret not being able to set it myself.' In this form his reply was relayed through various local papers until it reached Il Pungolo of Milan and was read by Verdi himself. He at once wrote

[*] Letter to Boito, 16.8.1882. Carteggio Verdi–Boito, I, p. 65.
[†] A. Porter, 'The making of Don Carlos', in R.M.A. Proceedings, No. 98 (1971–2), p. 85.
[‡] Letter to Boito, 7.2.1884. Nardi, p. 490.

not to Boito but to Faccio telling him that he was perfectly willing to restore Boito's libretto to him 'without resentment or rancour of any kind. More, as that manuscript is my property, I offer it to him as a gift if he wishes to set it to music.'*

Unfortunately Faccio was away from home when Verdi's letter arrived. When at last he read it he was horrified and replied at once that Boito must have been mis-reported. But in the meantime Boito had already visited the Verdis at Genoa on his return from Naples. He had read the report in *Roma* and it had incensed him; but he doubted whether it had reached Verdi and thought it prudent not to mention the matter. It was not until after mid-April that he met Faccio at Turin where he was conducting concerts for the Italian Exhibition. Thus nearly four weeks elapsed before Boito became acquainted with the contents of Verdi's letter. His noble reply can be read at length in Luzio's *Carteggi Verdiani* and in English in Walker's translation.† He might or he might not write *Nerone*, but he would never abandon it for another subject; and he conjured Verdi in the name of the art which they both loved not to give up work on *Otello*.

The composer's reply had a touch of frost about it; he still could not quite under-stand why Boito had not mentioned the article on his last visit, meantime: 'You say, "I may finish *Nerone* or I may not." I say the same thing about *Otello*. There's been too much talk about it! . . . I'm too old! . . . I don't wish the public to have to say to me too evidently, "Enough!" . . . The upshot is that all this has cast a chill over this *Otello* and stiffened the hand that had begun to outline a few bars! What will happen in the future? I don't know.'‡ Clearly the future of *Otello* was still in the balance. Skilfully Boito steered the project back on to the rails by taking up the revision at the point where he had left off, but being careful to make clear that he was not trying to prod the composer into action, he was merely writing for his own comfort and pleasure. 'I remembered that you were not happy with a scene for Iago in the second act in double quinari and that you wanted a freer, less lyrical form: I proposed a sort of *Evil Credo*, and I have tried to write one, in broken metre, asymmetrical.'§ 'Most beautiful, this Credo!' was Verdi's enthusiastic reaction; 'most powerful and wholly Shakespearian. You'll naturally have to link it with a line or two to the preceding scene between Cassio and Iago; but you can think about that later. Meanwhile it would be as well to leave this *Otello* in peace for a bit, for he too is in a nervy state, as we are – perhaps you more than I.'¶ And so the summer and autumn of 1884 passed away with no further work done. But in the meantime an important area had been defined: the character of Iago.

Much has been written on this subject by Shakespearian scholars and more than one theory expressed. The traditional view is that of Coleridge, who saw in Iago a case of disinterested, motiveless malignity;‖ a man who has said, 'Evil, be thou my good,' and acts accordingly. Bernard Shaw, the Fabian rationalist, took a more prosaic view. To him Iago was the old soldier turned sour through lack of

---

* Letter to Boito, 27.3.1884. Nardi, p. 491; Walker, p. 489.
† Letter from Boito, 20.4.1884. *Carteggi Verdiani*, II, pp. 100–3; Walker, pp. 489–90.
‡ Letter to Boito, 26.4.1884. Walker, p. 490.
§ Letter from Boito, undated (April/May 1884). Walker, p. 490.
¶ Letter to Boito, 3.5.1884. Nardi, p. 496; Walker, p. 490.
‖ S. T. Coleridge, 'Notes on *Othello*', published in *Coleridge's Lectures on Shakespeare* (London, 1907), p. 172.

promotion.* M. T. Ridley finds him 'a power-seeking opportunist often propelled willy-nilly into further villainy by the unforeseen consequences of his own intriguing'.† Verdi and Boito clearly held to the Coleridge view. As early as 1876, before the idea of setting *Othello* had even been hinted at, Verdi wrote a famous letter to the Countess Maffei about the necessity of 'inventing truth' (something that his young friend the playwright Achille Torelli had in his opinion singularly failed to do in his comedy *Color del tempo*). 'Ask Papa,' he wrote, meaning Shakespeare. 'It is quite possible that he, Papa, might have come across a Falstaff of some kind; but it's most unlikely that he ever met a villain quite so villainous as Iago, and he could never have met women as angelic as Cordelia, Imogen or Desdemona, etc. Yet they are so true. . . .'‡ The same view is clearly reflected in the correspondence with Domenico Morelli already quoted. That Boito was of the same opinion is evident from the verses of the Credo; that he embroidered it unnecessarily by stressing Iago's resentment at Cassio's preferment (an argument surely designed to convince Roderigo only), emerges from his preface to the production book, and it explains a small, relatively harmless addition on his part to Shakespeare's plot.

Now the absence of motive, let it be said again, is far less problematic in an opera than in a spoken play; and for the born music-dramatist the polarity of Desdemona and Iago, as of Budd and Claggart, can be conveyed essentially by the power of music – but aided none the less by words; and when it is a matter of laying bare the depth of evil in the souls of such as Iago or Claggart an extended soliloquy of some kind is needed. There are two substantial soliloquies for Iago in Shakespeare's drama (I, iii, 381–402, and II, iii, 281–307). What is surprising about them is how little they tell us about the speaker. In both Iago alludes to the possibility that 'The Moor betwixt my sheets hath done my office' and Emilia admits in a later passage that her husband had indeed taxed her with adultery. Yet somehow the charge rings false even with Iago himself, especially since he is ready to acknowledge Othello as being 'of a most constant, noble and loving nature' who will prove to Desdemona 'a most dear husband'. Ridley suggests that by harping on the subject of his wife's infidelity Iago is deliberately trying to fan his cold nature into a passionate hatred which will give him the will to act. More probably both soliloquies are designed to reveal Iago as a spiritual void and therefore unable to justify himself even to himself. Indeed the word 'justify' had no place in his vocabulary, since a rationale of evil is a contradiction in terms. By the same token we should attach no weight to his claim to hate Othello for having promoted Cassio in his stead. A man who revenges himself on someone who has done him harm can claim to be a crude moralist; he believes that he is increasing the sum of 'right'. This Iago has no wish to do. Since total negation can give no account of itself, it is only when trying to corrupt the foolish Roderigo that Iago's bottomless cynicism achieves a kind of coherence:

'Virtue? A fig! 'Tis in ourselves that we are thus or thus; our bodies are gardens to which our wills are gardeners. . . . If the balance of our lives had not one scale of reason to poise another of sensuality the blood and baseness of our natures would

---

* *Shaw's Music*, II, pp. 402–3. In fact Shakespeare makes Iago explicitly give his own age as twenty-eight. (See Act I, scene iii.)

† M. T. Ridley in the introduction to *Othello* in the Arden edition (London, 1958), pp. lx–lxv.

‡ Letter to Clarina Maffei, 20.10.1876. *Copialettere*, p. 624.

conduct us to preposterous conclusions.' Love he defines as 'a lust of the blood and a permission of the will'.*

In his original version of Iago's principal solo, which can be found in the second volume of *Carteggi Verdiani*,† Boito had distilled from this speech the single line 'Son scellerato – perchè son uomo' which he would carry over into the revision. For the rest he was content to expand into four stanzas the sentiments of

> I ha't, it is engendered; hell and night
> Must bring this monstrous birth to the world's light.‡

For musical purposes – and perhaps with the theatrical effectiveness of Mefistofele's 'Son lo Spirito che nega' in view – Verdi required something more cosmic in utterance as well as freer in metre. Boito responded with the 'Credo' as we know it today – a piece of high-flown nonsense which has its entire justification in the musical setting, one of the most powerful depictions of evil in the operatic repertoire. Anyone who had been present at the revival of *La Gioconda* in Venice in 1876 might have noted something familiar about the conclusion:

> La morte è il nulla,
> E vecchia fola il ciel.

In fact these were the final lines of the new aria for Alvise for which Boito had supplied the text at Ponchielli's request (see previous chapter). In mid-December Boito was delighted to read that Verdi had resumed work and wanted four lines apiece for Iago and Emilia at the end of the Act II quartet ('It seems impossible – but it's true all the same! I'm busy, writing!! . . . without purpose, without worries, without thinking of what will happen next. . . .')§ Boito duly obliged, adding a few extra lines for good measure 'since the note and the word [*Verdi's phrase*] eat up a good many lines in a rapid metre such as the quinario'.¶ In February he sent a variant for the opening of the handkerchief trio in Act III; and there is mention of a personal consultation between poet and composer in Genoa later that month. The usual break occurred during the summer followed by another visit of Boito to S. Agata, during which the fourth act was slowly hammered into shape. Part of the process can be observed from the excerpts of various drafts published by Luzio.‖ Boito's first version kept strictly to Shakespeare's IV, iii and V, ii, though with certain omissions. Emilia, for instance, does not defend adultery in certain circumstances as in the play; but Desdemona is allowed her artless question:

> Dost thou in conscience think – tell me, Emilia –
> That there be women do abuse their husbands
> In such gross kind?

The original Willow Song lacked the 'salce' refrain and was indeed a rather commonplace affair in double quinari. The final scene included Othello's long speech beginning 'Soft you, a word or two' and ending with the description of the Turk

---

* *Othello*, I, iii, 319 ff.
† *Carteggi Verdiani*, II, p. 110.
‡ *Othello*, I, iii, 388–9.
§ Letter to Boito, 9.12.1884. *Carteggio Verdi–Boito*, I, pp. 78–9.
¶ Letter from Boito, undated (December 1884). *Ibid.*, pp. 79–81.
‖ *Carteggi Verdiani*, II, pp. 117–22.

stabbed in Aleppo. At Verdi's request Boito supplied a shorter, tighter version but with an extra cantabile quatrain for Desdemona written in the grand metre, the sense of which runs:

> My lord; have pity! I beg for my life as a boon;
> I beg it in the name of the love we once shared.
> Condemn me to exile, to live deserted,
> But yet allow me to live on.

If the first version of the final scene was too prolix the second had something of the absurd rapidity of the curtain of *Il Trovatore*. Verdi's solution was to make a rough conflation of both as a scaffolding for the music. On 5 October he wrote to Boito: I've finished the fourth act and I breathe again. . . . Writing the music for this terrible scene I felt the need to take out a strophe that I especially asked you to add (that for Desdemona); and I've had to take a line here and half a line there and above all to make use of a most beautiful verse which we had wrongly decided to abandon' (this was Othello's apostrophe to the lifeless Desdemona beginning 'Come sei pallida'). 'As a result there are a few disconnected lines for which you will have to supply the connection.'* Boito invited himself to S. Agata to hear the music for which he was required to make the textual adjustments. The outcome of his visit was the text as we know it today. Verdi proceeded to the instrumentation of this act at once 'so as to put it under seal and not to speak of it any more until . . . until . . .'†

Enough remained to be done to occupy most of the following year. First Verdi wondered whether he ought to include a part for Montano in the Act III concertato. He sincerely hoped not, since the concertato was written in twelve real parts and he did not see how he could work in another one; nor could he very well double Montano with another bass. Boito's reply is missing but it was evidently to the effect that as he had been severely wounded by Cassio in Act I it was reasonable to confine him to bed in Act III (by Act IV he could have recovered).‡

It was about this time that the title of the opera was finally chosen. So far it had been referred to indiscriminately as *Otello* or *Iago*. According to an unwritten law of the theatre whereby any opera written to a subject previously treated should have a fresh title, *Iago* was the more likely choice. But now Verdi decided otherwise. 'It's true,' he wrote to Boito, 'that he [Iago] is the demon who sets everything in motion; but it is Othello who acts: *he loves, is jealous, kills and is killed.* For my part I would find it hypocritical not to call it *Otello*. I would rather it were said "he tried to pit his strength against that of a giant and was crushed", than "he tried to hide behind the title of *Iago*".'§ An implicit allusion, this, to another unwritten law whereby if an opera is judged superior to its predecessor on the same subject it is allowed to usurp its predecessor's title. Thus Rossini's *Almaviva, ossia L'inutile precauzione* took over as by natural right the title of Paisiello's *Il Barbiere di Siviglia*, which it had ousted from the repertoire. Rossini himself, that 'giant' with whom Verdi had dared to wrestle, would thus share Paisiello's fate with his own *Otello*.¶

---

* Letter to Boito, 5.10.1885. *Ibid.*, p. 122.

† Letter to Boito, 27.10.1885. *Carteggio Verdi–Boito*, I, p. 92.

‡ See Letters to Boito, 11 and 14.1.1886. *Ibid.*, pp. 93–5.

§ Letter to Boito, 21.1.1886. *Ibid.*, pp. 99–100.

¶ Another instance of this rule, though rarely mentioned, is Verdi's own *Un Giorno di regno*, which,

In mid-March Muzio visited Verdi in Genoa and heard him play over the duet finale to Act I – 'the only piece which I hadn't yet heard because he only finished it during the last few days'.* Over the final bars Boito had written a couplet for Iago as he gloats over his plan to ruin the lovers' idyll, rather as in the second version of *Boris Godunov* Rangoni smiles upon the raptures of Marina and the false Dimitri as a triumph for Mother Church. It is one of those effects that are better in theory than in practice (it is usually omitted in present-day productions of Mussorgsky's opera), and Verdi with his vast experience of musical theatre wisely removed it. Later he found a place for Boito's lines at the end of the chorus of homage to Desdemona, with minor modifications supplied by Boito himself.

Indeed the scrupulous care which Verdi brought to his study of Shakespeare's Iago in all his facets can be seen from a letter written to Boito early in May. Following Rusconi's translation, Boito had made Iago say to Roderigo, 'Were I the Moor I would not wish to have about me an Iago.' But that, Verdi pointed out, is not what Iago says. The original text runs, 'Were I the Moor I would not be Iago.' Moreover both Maffei and F. Victor Hugo translate this literally.† Boito, however, defended the mistranslation. 'It tells us much more than the original text; It reveals Iago's evil soul, Othello's good faith and it makes clear to the listener that this is a tragedy of subtle deception. Now that we have had to give up the wonderful scenes that take place in Venice, where these sentiments were touched upon, Rusconi's sentence comes in very useful indeed.'‡ On Boito's side it must be added that Iago's original line has puzzled more than one Shakespearian commentator. As rendered by Rusconi and himself it at least makes unequivocal sense.

It was at this time that Verdi suddenly hit upon the precise form of one of the most famous entrances in all opera – Othello's 'Esultate!'§ Boito was delighted to shorten Otello's lines accordingly ('Now the entrance which we weren't happy about and which we've been searching for has been found, and it's splendid!').¶ In the same letter he developed his ideas about the settings and costumes with his usual thoroughness. The Italian writer Cinzio Giraldi, he pointed out, followed the precedents of Boccaccio and Chaucer in setting his *Ecatommiti* or *Hundred Myths*, one of which is *Othello*, in a definite historical framework, each tale being recounted by a fugitive from the sack of Rome in 1527. The events described should therefore be placed a few years before that date; but as fashions in dress changed slowly in those days the paintings of earlier masters such as Carpaccio and Gentile Bellini could serve as models for the Venetian dress of the time.

By July Verdi's concern was about the printing of the libretto. He wanted all the verses of the concertato apart from those of Desdemona's opening solo set out in three parallel columns so that the eye could take them in at a glance (clearly there was no question at this time of a darkened auditorium).‖ Boito meanwhile wanted to

---

for all its weakness, is so much more vital than Gyrowetz's original setting of the same libretto that it too was allowed to inherit Gyrowetz's title, *Il finto Stanislao*.

* Letter from Muzio to Giulio Ricordi, 14.3.1886. Abbiati, IV, p. 279.

† Letter to Boito, 8.5.1886. *Carteggio Verdi–Boito*, I, p. 103.

‡ Letter from Boito, 10.5.1886. *Ibid.*, p. 104.

§ Letter to Boito, 14.5.1886. *Ibid.*, p. 105.

¶ Letter from Boito, 16.5.1886. *Ibid.*, pp. 106–7.

‖ Letter to Boito, 17.7.1886. *Ibid.*, pp. 108–10.

make a further alteration to the preceding scena (he had already at Verdi's request shortened the dialogue of Iago and Otello by two lines). Now he wished to plant Desdemona's entrance more firmly.* 'Those lines go very well,' Verdi wrote back. 'They make things a little awkward for the composer who will have either to delay or to prolong that little concerto of trumpets behind the scenes. . . . But no matter.'†

There was a last spirited interchange about Iago's drinking song. Verdi: 'In the brindisi in the first act what should the women be doing? Should they be drinking as well? And if not why not??'‡ Boito:

Musical reasons in my view are what should decide the answer to your questions.

Will women's voices add to the effect of the brindisi? If so add them. . . . If not and you merely want to add them for no better reason than that they shouldn't remain on stage doing nothing, this argument doesn't seem to me sufficiently cogent to warrant devoting to them two lines of score . . . and especially if those two lines don't make a musical effect or worse still spoil the masculine boldness of this piece in the slightest degree. I repeat: if you want to add the women just out of consideration for the mise-en-scène don't do so. They won't be idle. The women at La Scala number forty-five: after the 'fuoco di gioia' twenty or so could just melt away gradually; those who stay behind we can divide into two groups; some could move backstage and stroll and sit about with their lovers; others could lay out their fishing-nets on the floor of the ramparts; the prettiest and the least decorous we could have sitting at the tables with their menfolk; these would amount to about ten or twelve and they would be fully occupied with eating and drinking and a bit of slap and tickle. These and the ones who have remained backstage – over twenty in all – will cry out the two 'Let's fly's' and 'they're killing each other's', the moment the quarrel starts, but if these are not sufficient to make the cry really powerful the other twenty or so who had dispersed in the wings could have rushed in on hearing the noises earlier on and then seeing the swords drawn they could cry, 'Let us fly!' with the rest.§

Verdi: 'I'll settle for the slap and tickle. In that way I'll be able to keep the women quiet in the brindisi (they would have spoiled it) and I'll have them giggle a couple of times in F sharp minor either on their own account or because of Cassio or because of the slap and tickle.'¶ Entertaining but irrelevant since he did include women's voices in the drinking song after all. In the same letter Verdi announced that the Moor was now three-fifths complete. 'I've been over one by one the three leading parts to see if they were clothed in seemly fashion without any patches; and whether they stand up straight and move well . . . and they do! A curious thing! The role of Iago apart from a few *éclats* could all be sung at half-voice.'

* Letter from Boito, 21.7.1886. *Ibid.*, pp. 111–12.
† Letter to Boito, 22.7.1886, *Ibid.*, p. 112.
‡ Letter to Boito undated (Sept. 1886). *Ibid.*, pp. 113–14.
§ Letter from Boito, 6.9.1886. *Ibid.*, pp. 114–15.
¶ Letter to Boito, 9.9.1886. *Ibid.*, pp. 115–16.

Then at long last on 1 November a laconic:

> DEAR BOITO
> It's finished!
> All honour to us! (and to *Him*!!).
> Farewell.
> G. VERDI[*]

By mid-December *Otello* had been consigned to the printer. 'The dream,' Boito said, 'has become a reality'; and since Verdi had regretted that the Moor would never return to his own home in Genoa, he added, 'You will go and visit the Moor at La Scala, Milan.'[†]

There remained the more prosaic reality of the performance. No sooner had word got about that *Otello* was well and truly on the stocks than all the leading sopranos, tenors and baritones of Italy were hammering on Giulio Ricordi's door. The most difficult role to cast was Desdemona – 'not a woman,' Verdi wrote on a later occasion, 'but a type. She is the type of goodness, resignation, self-sacrifice. There are beings who are born for others, who are quite unaware of their own egos. . . . Shakespeare translated them into poetry and made them divine when he created Desdemona, Cordelia, Juliet, etc. – types which cannot be matched anywhere except perhaps by the Antigone of the ancient Greek theatre.'[‡] A strong favourite for the part had been Gemma Bellincioni, the soprano who first played Violetta in a crinoline and who would create Mascagni's Santuzza in Rome in 1890. She had the support of Giulio Ricordi; but after receiving discouraging reports from Boito on her performance as Alice in *Robert le Diable* early in 1886, Verdi refused to consider her. He eventually settled, not without misgivings, for Romilda Pantaleoni, a lively dramatic artist who had recently enjoyed a great success in the revised version of Ponchielli's *Marion Delorme* – hardly the pattern of pure womanhood as described by Verdi above. But she had been urged by Franco Faccio who was in love with her; and Faccio would after all be conducting the opera. After giving her some preliminary coaching in S. Agata Verdi professed himself fairly satisfied. 'Signora Pantaleoni . . . knows the whole of her part very well indeed and will I hope produce some excellent effects in it. Only in her scene in Act I there is something lacking. It isn't that she doesn't sing her solos well but she gives them too much emphasis – makes them too dramatic. Anyway we shall have other rehearsals and I shall go on at her until she manages to find the right degree of emphasis for the poetry and the situation.'[§] In the event she fell short of expectations, and was much chagrined to be replaced in the revivals of *Otello* in Rome and Venice by Adalgisa Gabbi. Later correspondence between Verdi and Giulio Ricordi suggests that the 'protesta' lay rather heavily on the composer's conscience since he liked the soprano personally and admired her in what he called 'parti nervose'. (It was at his and Faccio's recommendation that she undertook the part of Tigrana in *Edgar*.) There is no evidence that Verdi ever found a Desdemona wholly to his liking.

As the most outstanding 'tenore di forza' of his day Tamagno seemed indicated for

---

[*] Letter to Boito, 1.11.1886. *Ibid.*, p. 117. 'Him' of course means Shakespeare.
[†] Letter from Boito, 21.12.1886. *Ibid.*, p. 119.
[‡] Letter to Giulio Ricordi, 22.4.1887. Abbiati, IV, pp. 331–2.
[§] Letter to Boito, 29.10.1886. *Carteggio Verdi–Boito*, pp. 116–17.

the title role. Not even Verdi could think of anyone more suitable. The danger spots would be those passages where Otello had to sing gently and softly, as in the love duet and the sequel to Desdemona's murder; Tamagno 'must always sing out in full voice, otherwise his tone becomes ugly and the pitch uncertain'.* Then there were personal problems. Tamagno would need far more coaching than the other principals. But how to suggest this without giving offence? Verdi would gladly invite him to Genoa to coach him privately; but to entertain him all day as a guest would be too fatiguing. 'He could put up at the Londra or the Milano, since both hotels are near by and come to me towards mid-day; then we could work for a couple of hours or so; then he could go for a walk and come back about six o'clock and have supper with us. After that he could have a nice coffee and smoke a good cigar and after nine o'clock we could go over the work we'd done in the morning. That would be an excellent arrangement, but I daren't suggest it to him. I wouldn't have the courage to get him to spend the odd hundred lire after having seen him travelling second class with his little daughter just from Genoa to Milan.'† Tenors were the most highly paid animals on the Italian stage, and Tamagno's meanness was notorious. Verdi had considered advising him to go and see the performance of Shakespeare's *Othello* given by the actor Giovanni Emanuele in Milan. Boito counselled against this, however, on the grounds that Emanuele was a mediocre actor, not to be compared with such as Salvini or Rossi, and that if any of Verdi's artists were to go and see him they would only pick up bad habits. Happily Tamagno surpassed himself on the night and was to remain till the end of his career the leading exponent of Verdi's greatest tragic hero.

From the outset there had been only one possible choice for Iago – Victor Maurel. Nearly a year and a half before the first performance, he had written to Verdi to remind him how he had promised him Iago at the time of the revised *Boccanegra*. This was not the kind of letter that Verdi cared to receive. However, he replied amiably enough, 'It is not my habit to make promises which I am uncertain of being able to keep. But I may very well have said to you that the role of Iago is one that perhaps no one could interpret better than yourself, and if I said that I will stick to it. But it doesn't amount to a promise: merely to a wish that should be very easy of fulfilment provided that unforeseen circumstances do not bar the way. . . .'‡

Verdi did indeed hold fast to his intention of engaging Maurel, despite the attempts of Giulio Ricordi to induce him to consider one Duveyod. He had good reasons for standing firm. Victor Maurel was one of the most remarkable artists of the century and one whose talents reached far beyond the normal bounds even of dramatic singing. Born in Marseilles in 1848 and trained as an architect he decided early on a singing career. After a local success in the title role of *Guillaume Tell* he entered the Paris Conservatoire in 1866. The following year the name Maurel figures among the list of students who were engaged to swell the chorus of Verdi's *Don Carlos*. At twenty he was sustaining important baritone roles at the Opéra, such as Nevers (*Les Huguenots*), Luna (*Le Trouvère*), Alfonso (*La Favorite*) and Nelusko (*L'Africaine*). But the presence of Faure, then at the height of his popularity as Paris's leading baritone, decided him to concentrate his career in Italy and the Italian theatres in London,

---

* Letter to Giulio Ricordi, 22.1.1886. Abbiati, IV, p. 274.

† Letter to Giulio Ricordi, 4.11.1886. *Ibid.*, p. 298.

‡ Letter to Maurel, October 1885. Abbiati, IV, pp. 267–8.

New York and even St Petersburg. Within ten years of leaving the Conservatoire he had built up a vast repertoire of leading roles ranging from *Don Giovanni*, about whose interpretation he has some valuable and remarkably modern observations to make in his booklet *A propos de la mise-en-scène du* Don Giovanni *de Mozart*★, to Telramund and Wolfram, and including most of the famous baritones of Italian romantic opera. His dramatic subtlety is reflected in many of the parts especially written for him, such as the protean Cambro in Gomes's *Fosca*. Tonio in *Pagliacci* with his triple persona of compassionate master of ceremonies, Nedda's would-be lover and Taddeo the fool could not have come into being without him. Bernard Shaw encouraged all those who cared for good operatic acting to attend not only his performances but his lectures as well. Having studied painting he was even commissioned to design the sets for Gounod's *Mireille* at the Metropolitan Opera House, New York, in 1919. Throughout his long career Maurel sometimes over-reached himself. His attempt in 1884 to revive the Théâtre des Italiens in Paris under his own actor-management was laudable; but to have included on his affiche the first French production of *Lohengrin* was asking for trouble from a nation that was still smarting under the tasteless satire of *Eine Kapitulation*, and the theatre soon closed its doors once more. In the early years of this century he tried to make a new career in the spoken theatre but without success. Even as an operatic interpreter he would occasionally fall victim to his own ingenuity, as when at Covent Garden in 1874 he insisted on playing Gounod's Mephistopheles† with a monk's grey habit and with a spirit lamp attached to his beret.

Inevitably he had his his own views about Iago. Muzio, with whom he was studying the role in Paris, reported to Giulio Ricordi: 'He would like to shave off his beard since he considers that a full beard makes his face too gentle. . . . In the second act he is playful, humorous, ironic, but from the "Credo" onwards very terrible and he says that the movement of his features needs to be clearly seen.'‡ A shrewd comment and one which would be supported by anyone who has seen the remarkable Iago of Tito Gobbi. Yet by Maurel's own account both Boito and Verdi opposed this idea.§ None the less Maurel seems to have had his way, judging from a photograph taken in his dressing-room during the Paris *Otello* of 1894 and showing a smiling, beardless Iago welcoming a singularly ungracious-looking Verdi.¶

The first night was a predictable triumph. The confluence of the mainstreams of Italian literature and music under the aegis of Shakespeare was enough to mark the occasion as one of the great events in Italy's cultural history. Correspondents came from all over Europe and wrote enthusiastic reports of this new unexpected step in Verdi's art. From England came Francis Hueffer of *The Times*, who would make the first English translation, and Joseph Bennett of the *Daily Telegraph*, whose account of the occasion shows that Verdi had not changed since the première of *Macbeth* in Florence almost exactly forty years before.

★ Paris, 1897. Maurel was one of the first to advocate a small-sized orchestra for the performance of Mozart's works.

† Although a bass part it was sometimes undertaken by baritones with appropriate transpositions. Faure, for instance, gave its first performance at the Opéra in 1869.

‡ Letter from Muzio to Giulio Ricordi, 22.11.1886. Abbiati, IV, pp. 296–7.

§ V. Maurel, *A propos de la mise-en-scène du drame lyrique* Otello *de Verdi* (Paris, 1888). (But see Preface).

¶ See *Verdi: A documentary study* compiled and edited by William Weaver (London, 1977), pl. no. 258.

The illustrious composer of *Otello* personally directed the preparation and production of his work. I have known other composers do the same but not in a like spirit. They have bowed to the will of an impresario, or listened indulgently to suggestions from the orchestral chief or yielded to the storm of public voices declaring that faith should be kept as regards a promise given. To none of these influences would Verdi respond. He was at La Scala to see that justice was done to *Otello*, and in comparison with that object, the pleasure of managers, *chef d'orchestre* and amateurs went for nothing. Again and again was the first performance put off and almost all day long were the performers kept severely to the point of duty. Probably Tamagno, if he ever swore, vented oaths in copious abundance; and Maurel, if given to invocations, may have called upon all the creatures in the Jardin des Plantes, but such exercises, if possible, were in vain. The old master went calmly on till he was satisfied.[*]

Here and there could be heard sighs of regret for the passing of a simpler, more artless kind of musical theatre which the birth of *Otello* seemed to signalize. Thus Antonio Fogazzaro:

Otello marks a new evolution in Verdi's style, a step to what is called music of the future. It could be argued whether or not it was a good thing to have taken this step; but certainly it could not have been more powerfully taken. I believe the operas of Verdi's second manner — *Rigoletto, Ballo in maschera, Traviata* — to be his best; none the less he has rendered one great service to art; from now on it will not be possible to set to music absurd dramas and lamentable verses. Since this type of music follows the words with strict fidelity, the words will have to be worthy of being followed.[†]

Bernard Shaw recalling the first London performance of July 1889, observed:

So long as an opera composer can pour forth melodies like 'La donna è mobile' and 'Il balen' he does not stop to excogitate harmonic elegances and orchestral sonorities which are neither helpful to him dramatically nor demanded by the taste of the audience. But when in process of time the well begins to dry up . . . then it is time to be clever, to be nice, to be distinguished, to be impressive, to study instrumental confectionery, to bring thought and knowledge and seriousness to the rescue of failing vitality.[‡]

This is rather like saying that Wagner took to 'music drama' in the manner of *Tristan* because he was no longer able to pour out melodies like Senta's ballad and 'O Du mein holder Abendstern'. The truth is that *Otello* is a difficult opera to 'place' in that it cannot really be compared with any that were being written at the time. It is strictly modern in that it is conceived in whole acts rather than individual numbers, and its tonal and harmonic range is as wide as in any composition of the 1880s. But nowhere do we hear 'verismo' approaching in the distance; nowhere does the post-

[*] J. Bennett, *Forty Years of Music* (London, 1908), p. 292.
[†] Letter from A. Fogazzaro to Mrs Starbuck, quoted by Nardi, p. 504.
[‡] *Shaw's Music*, III, p. 572.

Wagnerian tide begin to encroach. The musical language of the time is stretched in a purely personal way. This is not to say that music heard over a lifetime of more than seventy years does not leave an echo here and there. Verdi's growing mastery of the long, eleven-syllable melodic line which is first noticeable in *Aida* owes something to French models, which in their turn had influenced the rhythmic structure of parts of *Lohengrin* and *Tannhäuser*; and since *Lohengrin* had become an honorary Italian classic years before *Otello* was born it is no treason to discern affinities between the love-duets of the two operas. In the final act of Verdi's work there is even a near-quotation from *Parsifal*, of which he certainly possessed a score. Yet the synthesis remains as independent, sometimes as baffling in its modernity as that of a late Beethoven string quartet, deriving as it does from a phenomenal development of inner resources. From the start we are aware of a conscious putting forth of gathered-up strength, reflected partly in the Parisian-sized orchestra with two cornets as well as trumpets, three flutes with third doubling piccolo and four bassoons. But here Verdi is no longer encumbered by the traditions of grand opera spectacle and pomp. There are no parades or ceremonies in *Otello*. All the physical resources are placed at the service of the drama. For the first time too the brass bass is specified as a bass trombone.* Only one feature of the score remains curiously old-fashioned: Verdi continues to use the valve-trombones and to write for them chromatic flourishes which on modern instruments sound like glissandos. A revival of *Otello* with trombones of the period might add a new touch of interest to the storm.

The production book or 'Disposizione scenica' produced by Giulio Ricordi for *Otello* is the most elaborate of any we have considered so far. All the latest devices of theatrical machinery are drawn upon and exploited. In addition there is a substantial preface by Boito which it is worth quoting in full:

The Characters

All theatrical artists, even the greatest, should have engraved upon their memories the following words, which were written three centuries ago yet which still today remain the most perfect and the most modern lesson on acting that has ever been devised.

Here is the lesson:

'Speak the speech, I pray you, as I pronounc'd it to you trippingly on the tongue; but if you mouth it, as many of our players do, I had as lief the town-crier spoke my lines: Nor do not saw the air too much with your hand thus but use all gently; for in the very torrent, tempest, and, as I might say, whirlwind of your passion you must acquire and beget a temperance that may give it smoothness. O, it offends me to the soul to hear a robustious periwig-pated fellow tear a passion

---

* That the instrument may have been designed to Verdi's own specification is suggested by the presence among the exhibits in the Esposizione Teatrale of 1894 in Milan of a 'trombone basso Verdi' manufactured by the firm of Pelitti (see A. Soffredini in *Gazzetta Musicale di Milano*, 24.6.1894). At the start of the second act it is described in the autograph as 'in B flat at the lower octave'. No tonal transposition, however, was involved in its notation. The term 'piatti squillanti' given on the first page of all printed editions has been shown by Alberto Zedda to be a misreading of Verdi's 'piatti oscillanti', i.e. suspended cymbals.

to tatters, to very rags, to split the ears of the groundlings. . . . I would have such a fellow whipped for o'erdoing Termagant; it out-Herods Herod. . . .

'Suit the action to the word, the word to the action; with this special observance, that you o'erstep not the modesty of nature; for anything so overdone is from the purpose of playing, whose end both at the first and now, was and is to hold, as 't were, the mirror up to nature. . . .

'O, there be players that I have seen play – and heard others praise, and that highly – not to speak it profanely, that, neither having the accent of Christians nor the gait of Christian, pagan, nor man, have so strutted and bellowed that I have thought some of Nature's journeymen had made men, and not made them well, they imitated humanity so abominably.'

These words are Shakespeare's (*Hamlet*, Act III, scene ii) and three centuries have passed – not a year more, not a year less.* We have thought it useful to remind the artists of these words before indicating the main outlines of the characters of *Otello* very broadly and roughly so as to make ourselves understood by all who may read us.

Let us begin with the one who gives his name to the tragedy.

Otello

A Moor, general of the Venetian republic. He has passed his fortieth year. He presents the brave, loyal figure of a man of arms. Simple in his bearing and in his gestures, imperious in his commands, cool in his judgement – the scene that follows the duel in Act I should suffice to reveal these gifts of temperament. This act shows him in all his strength, in all his glory, in all his radiance. His first words proclaim victory in a voice of thunder amid the tempest; his last words exhale a sigh of love upon a kiss. First we should see the hero, then the lover; and we must perceive the hero in all his greatness if we are to understand how worthy he is of love and how great his capacity for passionate devotion. Then from that prodigious love a fearful jealousy will be born through the cunning agency of Iago. Reason and justice govern Otello's actions up to the moment at which Iago (who seems honest and is reputed to be so) succeeds in gaining an ascendancy over him. From that moment (and the actor must study this effect with the utmost care) the whole man changes, and it is precisely at Iago's false and treacherous words in the second act that the change becomes perceptible: 'If you should hold my soul within your grasp you should not know it'; and Otello lets out a cry, and Iago immediately adds, 'Beware, my lord, of jealousy.'

Jealousy! The word has been spoken. Iago has first stabbed the Moor to the heart and then put his finger on the wound. Otello's torture has begun. The whole man changes: he was wise, sensible, and now he raves: he was strong and now he waxes feeble; he was just and upright and now he will commit a crime; he was strong and hale and now he groans and falls about and swoons like one who has taken poison or been smitten by epilepsy. Indeed Iago's words are poison injected into the Moor's blood. The fatal progress of that moral blood-poisoning should be expressed in all the fullness of its horror. Otello should undergo, phase by phase, all the most fearful torments of the human soul – doubt, fury, spiritual overthrow. Otello is the supreme victim of the tragedy and of Iago. If the per-

* Modern scholarship, however, places *Hamlet* in the years 1600–1.

sonification of an abstract idea were not a frigid, false, puerile and altogether stale artifice in the theatre one could say that Otello is Jealousy and Iago Envy.

Iago

Iago is envy. Iago is a villain. Iago is a *critic*. In the cast-list Shakespeare describes him thus: *Iago, a villain*, and adds not a word more. In the square in Cyprus Iago says of himself, 'I am nothing if not critical.' He is a mean and spiteful critic; he sees the evil in mankind and in himself. 'I am a villain because I am human.' He sees evil in Nature, in God. He commits evil for evil's sake. He is an artist in deceit. The cause of his hatred for Otello is not very serious compared to the vengeance he exacts from it. Otello has appointed Cassio captain in his place. But this is enough; if it were more serious then his villainy would have been the less; this cause is sufficient to make him hate the Moor, envy Cassio and act as he does. Iago is the real author of the drama; he it is who fabricates the threads, gathers them up, combines them and weaves them together.

The crassest of mistakes, the most vulgar error into which any artist attempting this role can possibly fall is to play him as a kind of human demon; to give him a Mephistophelean sneer and make him shoot Satanic glances everywhere. Such an artist would make it all too plain that he had understood neither Shakespeare nor the drama which we are discussing.

Every word spoken by Iago is on the human level – a villainous humanity if you like, but still human. He should be young and well-favoured. Shakespeare makes him out to be twenty-eight. Cinzio Giraldi, the author of the story from which Shakespeare derived his masterpiece, says of Iago: 'An ensign of a most handsome presence, but of the most villainous nature that the world has ever known.'

He must be handsome and appear genial and open and falsely bonhomous; everyone believes him to be honest except his wife who knows him well. If he did not possess great charm and an appearance of honesty he could not be the consummate deceiver that he is.

One of his talents is the faculty he possesses of changing his personality according to the person to whom he happens to be speaking, so as to deceive them or to bend them to his will.

Easy and genial with Cassio; ironic with Roderigo; apparently good-humoured, respectful and humbly devoted towards Otello; brutal and threatening with Emilia; obsequious to Desdemona and Lodovico. Such are the basic qualities, the appearance and the various facets of this man.

Desdemona

We would beg the ladies who are called upon to play this role not to roll their eyes, wriggle their arms and bodies or take strides ten foot long, or to try for so-called 'effects'. If the artist is intelligent and has a respect for art, she will achieve these effects without trying, and if she is not intelligent she will strive for them in vain. Features, expression, diction – these are the three sources of the art of conveying dramatic emotion. Apart from those exceptional cases where horror borders on excess the whole range of joy and sorrow should be capable of being expressed without distorting the features, rolling the eyes or caricaturing the diction. A feeling of love, purity, nobility, docility, ingenuousness and resignation should pervade the most chaste and harmonious figure of Desdemona in the highest degree. The more simple and gentle her movements and gestures, the greater the emotion they will arouse in the spectator. The charm of youth and beauty will complete the impression.

Emilia

Iago's wife; devoted to Desdemona. She hates her villainous husband and fears him, and while she submits to his violence and bullying she knows the wickedness of his soul. But at the end she reveals his infamy with all the strength and courage of a downtrodden creature that rebels.

Cassio

Captain of the Venetian Republic. Handsome, very young, gay, witty, smart and successful with women of easy virtue; he is somewhat obsessed with his passing affairs and a little vain; but he is a brave soldier who knows how to defend himself with spirit, sword in hand: a skilful fencer and a jealous guardian of his own honour.*

Roderigo

A young Venetian, rich and elegant, hopelessly and platonically in love with Desdemona, quite without her knowledge. He is a visionary, a simple creature, a dreamer who allows himself to be cheated and dominated by Iago. Iago makes use of him as a passive and docile instrument for the accomplishment of his designs.

Lodovico

Senator of the Venetian Republic, Ambassador to Cyprus. Of grave deportment though still youthful. He has all the appearance of a man worthy of the high office to which he has been called. He has great authority both in his looks and in his speech.

Montano

Othello's predecessor as Governor of Cyprus. A man of war, faithful to his duty, a good swordsman, a brave soldier, and a strict officer.

ARRIGO BOITO

'Excellent!' Verdi wrote when he read it. 'It couldn't be better! But those gentlemen . . . will they read it, will they understand it . . . will they follow the advice it gives?'† He might with still better reason have doubted the efficacy of Giulio Ricordi's instructions for the staging which all the performers were required to know by heart and from which no departure, however slight, was to be allowed. As an instance of what could be achieved within the conventions of elaborate painted

---

* Maurel, however, cautions against making Cassio appear too much of a Don Juan (*op. cit.*, p. 71), and from the Shakespearian point of view rightly. Boito seems to have conceived him as a typical young Italian 'donnaiuolo'.

† Letter to Tornaghi, 13.8.1887. Abbiati, IV, p. 343; see also *Carteggio Verdi–Boito*, p.126.

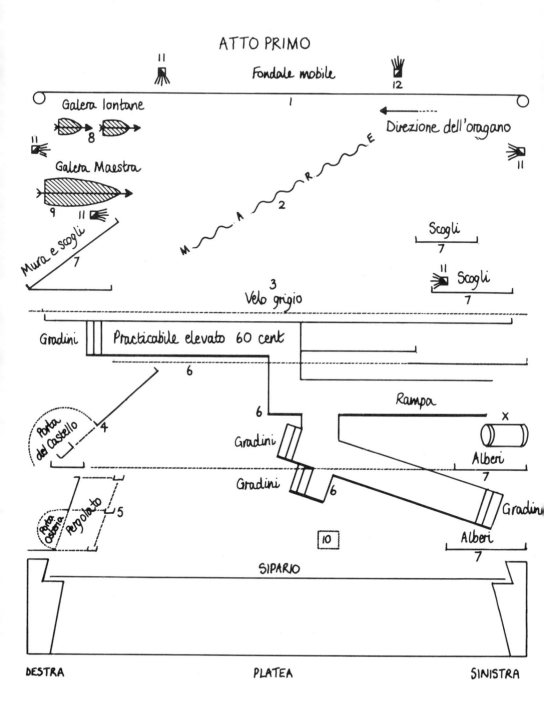

ATTO PRIMO

ESTERNO DEL CASTELLO

scenery, electric light and hand-operated stage machinery as it existed in the last decades of the nineteenth century, it is worth while to quote in their entirety the first two pages of the production book which concern the storm in the first act, together with the appropriate diagram (see opposite):

1. Moving backcloth (the equivalent of a modern cyclorama) mounted on two revolving drums (ab). It should be about three times the length necessary to cover the back of the stage. First of all, at the rise of the curtain it should represent a night sky with large, black swirling clouds; the lightest part of the clouds should be made of transparent material; so also the two streaks of forked lightning which should reach diagonally across the entire sky from top left to bottom right. . . . The backcloth will move from left to right as the clouds will be seen gradually to disperse until it comes to a halt depicting the cloudless serenity of a clear night; in due course two or three little stars (not more) should appear; the brightest and most conspicuous of them should be more or less in the centre, at half the height of the backcloth.

2. Fixed backcloth (Tela). This represents a stormy sea; it should be agitated by various capstans which will keep up a continuous movement until the end of the act. At the rise of the curtain it should be violently shaken by several stage-hands disposed at suitable points below, who should also move up and down a few wooden discs, not too rapidly, to form the crests of waves. The horizon must be made to appear as distant as the dimensions of the stage permit.

3. Gauze curtain. This should cover the entire stage; later it will move slowly from left to right.

4. Lateral parapet. This represents a wing of the castle with a practicable door.

5. Lateral parapet. This continues the castle wing together with an inn door, also practicable; in front of this is a trellis supported on one side by the castle wall, on the other by three slender columns. Beneath this trellis three steel wires should be stretched on which in due course coloured Chinese lanterns will be hung.

6. Practicable elevations, about 60 centimetres high representing the castle ramparts facing towards the sea.

7. Trees, rocks, walls, flats and cut-outs which will close the view on the left and mask the commanding galley on the right.

8. Distant galleys; they should be about a metre in length and cross the stage at the back from right to left with smooth simple motion.

9. The commanding galley. This should be four or five metres in length according to the width of the stage; it should cross the stage with a movement suggestive of pitching and tossing.

10. A trap door: this will serve for the bonfire as will appear later on.

11. Electric lamps for sheet lightning.

12. Electric lamp for forked lightning.

13. (X) Bass drum especially constructed for thunder: two metres in length, 1·25 in diameter.

Lighting and Electric Light

Before the orchestra begins the lighting in the hall must be very considerably lowered.

On the stage it must be darkest night, so that the effects of the storm can be all the more impressive. When Iago descends from the ramparts there should be a little more light at the proscenium – when the bonfire and the Chinese lanterns are lit the general illumination of the stage should be increased and the lateral lights at the back should be adjusted so that when the sky clears it should be appropriately lit.

In the larger theatres there should be four electric lamps placed high up in the wings; in the smaller theatres two should suffice. At the rise of the curtain they should produce repeated and prolonged flashes which gradually become less; when the overcast sky on the movable backcloth remains only on the right the flashes on the left will cease; those on the right will continue for a while, ceasing completely about a minute after the entire sky has become clear.

Behind the movable backcloth the electric lamp (11) will produce lightning flashes in the manner indicated for those in the wings, now in one place, now in another, wherever the clouds are transparent. Lamp No. 12 should emit a full flash across the entire backcloth. During the tempest it should be switched on no more than three times; at the same time a stage operator with a reflector of about 40 square centimetres will hold this toward the electric lamp and rapidly transmit the reflected beam from top to bottom along the transparent lines of the backcloth which represent the forked lightning.*

As in preceding chapters further quotations from the production book will be given in the footnotes when they either serve to elucidate the action or shed an interesting light on the staging methods of the time.

ACT I

Scene: Outside the castle. A tavern with a trellised harbour. In the background ramparts and the sea. It is evening. Lightning, thunder, hurricane.

The opening scene is stupendous from every point of view; vividness of description, harmonic boldness, matching of action and drama to musical development. In Shakespearian theatre there is no model for the physical presence of a storm; it must all be conveyed by language. Italian opera, however, abounds in noisy tempests – witness the storm and shipwreck which opens Bellini's *Il Pirata* and which may well have provided Verdi and Boito with a rough and ready framework for the present one. But superior craft and imagination have rendered the derivation, if it exists, quite unrecognizable. What in Bellini's score is a static tableau, not unlike the first scene of Verdi's own *Nabucco*, is here instinct with energy and movement, packing

* *Disp. scen.*, pp. 9–10.

more musical incident into its brief six and a half minutes than most composers could achieve in half an hour. Consider the opening cluster of ideas:

In the post-*Tristan* era there is nothing so intrinsically startling about beginning with a chord of the dominant eleventh; but one would at least expect it to resolve, however circuitously, instead of merely losing definition, as happens here. The harmonic outline is further blurred by sonorities that might be described as para-musical: two bass drums including one for the thunder, a gong, suspended cymbals, played with two sticks like a drum (a familiar enough modern effect but rare in Italian opera of that time) and three organ notes a semitone apart from each other 'to be played in the register of the basses and the timpani'.* About this effect, which lasts for 255 bars, a whole treatise could be written; yet it would be wrong to regard it as an instance of modern discordant harmony since it is not strictly speaking a harmonic device at all but rather an external colouring of the musical landscape, making its effect subliminally. The listener is aware of it only as part of the dark background against which Otello will make his entrance like a brilliant shaft of light.† One of those cases, Verdi might have said, where the musician, like the poet, must unlearn his calling in the interests of theatre. The opening of *Otello* is the parola scenica made music.

By the tenth bar (Ex. 168b) the tonality has become suspended completely, aided by chromatic and diminished-seventh harmony; high horns and upper woodwind take over the function of the wordless chorus in *Rigoletto*, representing the howling of the wind; the lightning, however, is, as in Mantua, traced by descending patterns of flute and piccolo to which oboe now contributes (Ex. 168c). The first flash reveals to some of the bystanders an approaching ship.‡ 'A sail, a sail!' they cry out, as in Shakespeare, during one of those tense lulls with which Verdi's storms are punctuated. At the second flash they make out the winged Lion of St Mark. Full orchestra peals out with a figure akin to Ex. 168a but for the moment in an unequivocal D minor. Then a trumpet signal is heard in the distance followed by a cannon-shot. 'The general's ship!' cries Cassio. In the subsequent succession of ideas the tonal physiognomy of the score becomes gradually clearer.

169a

* In theatres where there is no organ an instrument should be used that is made of three or four pipes of low pitch in the timpani register which will be made to sound by a pair of hand-operated bellows. This is very easy to construct and can be obtained from any organ-builder. The producer should be advised that it is absolutely essential where no proper organ exists. Disp. scen., p. 10.

† A note in the autograph requires that the organ be silent during Otello's opening solo ('Esultate', etc.) and resume thereafter. Presumably Verdi changed his mind during rehearsals.

‡ Cassio and Montano are standing on the rear rampart (R); Iago and Roderigo on the diagonal (L): behind the

169b

169c

The first (Ex. 169a) shows the ship labouring in heavy seas; it unfolds the pattern of piled-up thirds inherent in Ex. 168a in an area between B minor and D major. B minor, however, establishes itself at the start of Ex. 169b which is developed in orthodox sequences beneath more 'lightning' figuration from upper woodwind to another climax ('Lampi! Tuoni! Gorghi!') then settles down with an air of greater permanence in C minor for a new idea, again triplet-based and with an effective use of punctuating trombones (Ex. 169c). The leaping bass (*x*) of Ex. 168a with its Brahms-like energy forms the ascent to the next climax ('Fende l'etra un torvo e cieco spirto di vertigine') to which a crowd of women who have rushed out of the castle add a terrified 'Ah!' (Ex. 170)

Here the language of the 'Dies Irae' from the Requiem is bent to a new descriptive purpose. Note the vertiginous revolving round a three-note pattern (*x*) followed by the headlong plunge of the orchestral semiquavers. The single crotchet-triplets (in

---

former eight Cypriots; all are looking anxiously out to sea, gesticulating rapidly and repeatedly in the direction R: beneath the trellis another 10 or 12 chorus men (sailors, soldiers) are standing ready to come to the rescue; they too are looking out to sea and with much gesturing asking the others for news. . . . As soon as the curtain rises a few extras run out of the castle, cross the stage rapidly and exeunt along the ramparts. These extras, who should be in groups of 2, 3 and 4, are making for the harbour to give assistance to the ships in distress. . . . At the eighth bar of the opera the two distant galleys should be set in motion. After the trumpet calls the commanding galley should begin its passage, buffeted by the waves. According to the width of the stage its speed should be so calculated that it should have vanished into the wings by the time the chorus begin 'Dio, fulgor della bufera!'. Disp. scen., p. 11.

170

the Requiem there are four together) not only add further rhythmic variety to an already tightly woven complex of heterogeneous ideas; they also save an eight-bar phrase from any sense of regularity such as would be premature at this stage. (Nor was Verdi the only composer to find the slow triplet within a fast pulse a useful way of suggesting the surge of waves – witness the opening movement of Vaughan Williams's Sea Symphony.)

The climax subsides with a dizzy shift from E flat to E, while the start of Ex. 170 is developed on the horns, marked *come un lamento*. Within a few bars a fresh climax is being prepared, first by quaver triplets in the strings, then by terrifying whoops on high brass and trombones in unison, illustrating the 'Titanic trumpets blasting through the air' – Boito's own fanciful contribution to Shakespeare's 'great contention of the sea and skies'. Then, exactly as in *Rigoletto* but on a far more impressive scale, the storm reaches its height in a purely symmetrical melody, 'Dio, fulgor della bufera!' – a choral prayer of thirty-two bars with a clearly defined tonal centre of A minor. (Ex. 171)

This is the coping-stone of the design; the goal to which the preceding medley of ideas has been tending. Here too the orchestra is at its noisiest with trombone trills which strictly speaking require an instrument with valves. The period ends with an interrupted cadence and the music descends from its pinnacle with a free development of Ex. 169b as the bystanders describe the perilous progress of Otello's ship. 'The tiller is broken!' (Iago); 'The bow is hurtling against the rocks!' (Roderigo). The chorus call for help. In a vicious descending phrase Iago hopes that Otello may be drowned ('L'alvo frenetico del mar sia la sua tomba!').* But his A flat minor tonality

---

* *The chorus raise their arms to heaven crying, 'Aita!' while Iago, grasping Roderigo by the hand, comes hurriedly down the steps, clears a way through the crowd and comes forward in their midst to exclaim in tones of fierce hatred,*

171

CHORUS

Dio, ful - gor del - la bu - fe - - - - - - - ra!

(Lampi, tuoni e fulmini continui)

tutti *tutta forza*

Dio, sor - ri - so del - la

etc.

is obliterated by the orchestral diminished seventh which turns F flat into E natural and so prepares a triumphant resolution on an E major 6/4 to which the chorus exclaim that time-honoured cry of relief 'È salvo!'* The labouring motif (Ex. 169a) is heard again and with it the voices of Otello's crew (six basses) giving orders to lower the boats, pull at the oars and do whatever else the situation demands. At length Otello himself appears up the ramp followed by his suite, to make one of the most glorious entries in all opera.† (Ex. 172)

How characteristic that a musical idea which spans two keys a third apart should give the effect of a self-sufficient statement together with a sense of affirmation to be

---

'L'alvo, etc. . . .' *Disp. scen.*, p. 13. Clearly Iago's phrase can only make its effect if the singer somehow manages to deliver it from somewhere near the footlights.

* Whether the sounding of F flat in the first violins simultaneously with E natural in the lower instruments is a piece of hypersubtlety on Verdi's part or whether it merely reflects his essentially keyboard-trained ear only the listener can decide.

† The suite is indicated as follows: 2 soldiers with torches, 2 captains bearing Otello's shield and helmet, a standard bearer, 8 guards; 2 men-at-arms; 4 members of the crew carrying a stretcher on which are trophies: 10 sailors carrying bales of merchandise and chests. *Disp. scen.*, p. 13.

172

found only in such moments as the famous horn entry in the introduction to the finale of Brahms's First Symphony (indeed the two themes are curiously similar in construction as well as in the image they convey of light overcoming darkness). Otello's solo goes far beyond the mere announcement that the Turks have been defeated in battle and their pride laid low; it places Otello himself upon a peak of sublimity from which his descent will be all the more terrible; and it also establishes E (as so often with Verdi the key of power) as the tonal centre for the episodes that follow.

Otello's words elicit shouts of 'Evviva!' from the crowd and a peal of fanfares from cornets and trumpets. Then as he enters the castle followed by Cassio, Montano and those who had disembarked with him, the music settles down to a brisk E minor scherzo of rejoicing ('Vittoria! Vittoria!') in which excited chatter alternates with shouts of joy.* The quieter passages have a Queen-Mab-like delicacy; while the

---

* *Machinery. Scarcely has Otello entered the castle when the gauze curtain should begin to move very slowly from L to R. The movement of the sea should gradually become less, the lightning flashes weaker and less frequent. The pedal notes of the organ should have continued without interruption even during Otello's recitative. When the gauze curtain has disappeared, the intensity of the footlights can be raised very slightly. Disp. scen., p. 15.*

more demonstrative outbursts harness the by now intermittent fury of the receding storm to a more joyful purpose. The growling of the organ notes continues unabated, however. The central G major episode ('Avranno per *requie* la sferza dei flutti') combines a reminiscence of *La Battaglia di Legnano* (the Como scene) with an anticipation of the women's ensemble from Act I, scene ii, of *Falstaff*. As always, Verdi's unity of language preserved across so vast a musical development remains a continual source of wonder.

The movement ends with a long decrescendo which in an earlier work would merely have indicated an emptying stage. Here its main function is to depict the retreating tempest. The organ notes are first lightened in register, then cease altogether; the lightning flashes and the wind moans once or twice; the chorus murmur 'Si calma la bufera' to another E major chord, then retire towards the inn, leaving Roderigo and Iago near the footlights.*

Their dialogue has been spliced in from Shakespeare's Act I, scene i, 1–65 and scene iii, 301–80. Boito's hendecasyllabic verse (in Shakespeare it is all prose at this point) is set by Verdi as pure recitative, but of the kind which allows Iago's character to leap out of the notes — a curious mixture of offhand charm with equally offhand malignity. Roderigo wishes to drown himself. 'Whoever drowned himself for love of woman?' Iago asks with a triplet sneer on the word 'donna'. Soon, he continues, Desdemona will be disgusted with the 'dusky kisses' from those 'swollen lips'. All this in the bald, flat style of certain recitatives in *Rigoletto*, Act III. A false melodic warmth steals in as Iago proclaims himself Roderigo's true friend and he adds to a dancing, mocking little tune that women's vows are easily loosened by himself and by Hell.

173

* 5 or 6 extras should enter up the ramp carrying trophies, oriental jars, bales, etc., representing the booty captured from the Turks. They come down the ramparts and enter the castle. The chorus look on curiously, then stroll leisurely about backstage, forming small groups; a few young men approach the women and greet them in jocular fashion; some of the women should accept the arms offered to them. . . . In general the scene should be lively but without excessive noise such as will attract attention or disturb to the slightest extent the conversation between Iago and Roderigo at the front of the stage. Disp. scen., p. 16.

At the word 'inferno' the orchestra betrays the cloven hoof which Roderigo is too stupid to notice. Again in low-keyed recitative Iago explains that he hates the Moor, and points to Cassio, then conveniently crossing backstage, as his reason.*

> This counter-caster:
> He in his time must his lieutenant be,
> And I, God bless the mark, his Moorship's ancient.†

The setting of this last phrase is a masterpiece of graceful irony with only the unison accompaniment and the trill on the cadence to suggest the underlying spite.

174

But then, he adds in recitative once more, 'It is true that as sure as you are Roderigo, if I were the Moor I would not have men around me like Iago,' Boito's and Rusconi's gloss, not to say improvement, on Shakespeare's strangely meaningless:

> It is as sure as you are Roderigo,
> Were I the Moor I would not be Iago.

Chromatic scales in the strings suggest both Iago's sardonic humour and the clouds of smoke that start to billow from the bonfire. He leads Roderigo out of earshot ('Se tu m'ascolti') just as the fire bursts into flame.‡

The bonfire chorus ('Fuoco di gioia!') is another tour de force of Verdi's new manner (it was encored on the opening night) and another passage which looks forward to *Falstaff*. The traditionalists might regard it as essentially orchestral trickery with no trace of true melody; the more perceptive will see it as a kaleidoscope of melodies some of them so short that they disappear before you have time to grasp them, like the sparks which they describe. The E minor–G major–E major axis is familiar, as is the use of the flattened supertonic of the opening idea, which casts a momentary shadow of ambiguity over the tonality, otherwise firmly

---

* *Cassio comes out of the inn with a springing step, then seeing a few girls gathered beneath the trellised arbour goes up to them and enters into gallant conversation with them. The actor must make certain that all this is made clear to the audience. Disp. scen., p. 17.* As Cassio was last seen following Montano and Otello into the castle we must assume that there is a separate entrance from the castle to the inn.

† *Othello*, I, i, 31–3.

‡ *At the words 'Se tu m'ascolti' Iago takes Roderigo by the arm and they continue their conversation as they move away to R. of the chorus, pass under the trellis and are lost to view backstage. Disp. scen., p. 19.* The instructions which follow for the lighting of the bonfire envisage a device of twisted metal which can simulate a fire without the inconvenience of excessive smoke or the risk of a general conflagration.

underpinned by a tonic pedal like a distant reminiscence of the bourdon that persisted throughout the storm.* The principal theme (Ex. 175) effects the transition from free recitative to formal number by an irregular, telescopic pattern of phrases which coalesce into a normal eight-bar period with extension.

175

Two more ideas flit swiftly past, both in E major: five bars of unaccompanied chorus in triplet rhythm ('Fuoco di gioia!') which might have come from Windsor Forest,

---

* During the first chorus the stage director will arrange for the following to take place: the mobile backcloth should have begun to move very slowly so that the public are unaware that it is doing so. In this way the clouds will gradually disappear.

As soon as the chorus begins, three tables, two benches and two chairs should be brought out from the inn and placed outside and under the trellis, together with several cups and jars. Immediately afterwards 6 extras with 12 lighted Chinese lanterns (one in each hand) will come out of the inn and hang them on the wire beneath the trellis. . . . 4 extras will mount the practicable ramparts carrying large lighted Chinese lanterns on poles which they will affix to the ramparts themselves. . . . They will be followed by about 20 more extras and 8 or 10 boys and girls.

At this moment the lighting-hand should raise the lighting at the front of the stage and also by the backcloth so as to give the effect of a perfectly clear night. Disp. scen., pp. 20–1.

then a filigree of high woodwind in semiquavers with pianissimo interjections from the voices ('Guizza . . . sfavilla'). Ex. 175 returns, solidified into symmetrical phrases with a motif of triplets for voices and wind on the second and fourth bars ('Guizza, sfavilla, crepita, avvampa'). After a full stop a new theme surfaces ('Dal raggio attratti'), related to the second of the E major ideas. Boito's picture of bright young faces that appear and vanish in the flickering light is evoked by the combination of two-part voice writing and woodwind scales with piccolo prominent – all resulting not in a formal melody so much as in an adumbration of that same chord of the eleventh with which the opera began; but by the time the apex is reached the base has vanished.

176

At the words 'e son fanciulle' the violins take over the semiquavers and steer the music towards a more orthodox dominant. At once a longer, more substantial theme makes its appearance in G major ('Arde la palma'), a kind of trio in regular four-bar phrases with an element of antiphony about it. (Ex. 177) The pattern of four semiquavers alternating with two quavers will constitute an important rhythmic element in the scena which follows the chorus itself. (Ex. 178)

A brief digest of the first two E major ideas leads to a derivative of Ex. 177 with an attractive alternation of violins arco and pizzicato.

So to the reprise of Ex. 175 with a new superstructure of voices, after which there is a final decrescendo to match the dying bonfire.* On the heels of the last pizzicato Iago

---

* *Cassio comes out of the inn and forms a group near the table by the proscenium together with a few officers and the chorus; drinking with them he sits down on the chair nearest to the footlights. Iago and Roderigo come forward from backstage and place themselves C. by the footlights. Disp. scen., p. 21.*

calls out, 'Roderigo, let's drink!' and the motion continues as before, the texture now
reduced to pizzicato violas, later joined by violins with an occasional intervention
from the cellos. During this sixteen-bar pendant to the bonfire chorus ('pendant'
since its rhythmic gait derives from the chorus itself and especially from Ex. 177) Iago
urges Cassio to drink. Cassio is at first reluctant, until the proposed toast to
Desdemona elicits from him a long affectionate phrase ('Essa infiora questo lido')

that at once establishes him as a tenore di grazia. Shakespeare himself avoided developing Cassio as a character, being content to give him good manners, and an open, affable, slightly weak-willed disposition. It is enough that in Iago's words:

> He hath a daily beauty in his life
> That makes me ugly.*

This beauty Verdi has traced in Cassio's brief apostrophe; and if despite the characteristic displacement of bass notes to give 6/4/3 harmony (x) we hear a faint echo of Nemorino sighing for the unobtainable, this serves only to lend colour to the insinuations with which Iago continues to ply Roderigo.

179

Cassio's effusion has slowed down the tempo to one of these free declamatory passages over sustained chords that so often take the place of recitative in operas of this period. Iago then restores the pace with an accelerating parlando – typically offhand – that leads up to the drinking song.

Needless to say this is no mere set piece or 'stage item' to be marked off with orchestral ritornelli like the drinking songs of twenty years back, but a fully developed 'pièce d'action' firmly welded into its context and evolving in a variety of that 'bar-form-with-refrain' (ab–ab–cb) which Verdi had already employed in Amelia's 'Ma dall'arido stelo divulsa' and Carlo's 'Son Pereda, son ricco d'onore'. First, however, observe the skilfulness of the transition from what has gone before. Iago's call for wine is answered by an orchestral flourish whose spirit is that of the brindisi but whose rhythm derives strictly from Ex. 177.

180

---

* *Othello*, V, i, 18–19.

After eight bars and a half-close* four bars of tonic-dominant preludizing on cellos, basses and four bassoons give a plain, pulsating background to what will turn out to be a 6/8 melody:

181a

But the 2/4 is not immediately vanquished by the new pulse; and such has been the weight of Ex. 180 that there is nothing illogical about its return at the end of the first phrase; on the contrary, a highly emphatic cadence (x) at the end of the second is needed to establish the 6/8 beyond all possibility of contradiction. Cassio replies in character (Ex. 181b) with a lyrical phrase ('Questa del pampino verace'), his own personal 'antithesis' in the dialectic of the brindisi.

So to the refrain ('Chi all' esca ha morso') in A major where one might have expected B or D (though anyone familiar with Verdi's works from *Il Trovatore* onwards would be wary of expecting anything so predictable). The striding melody (Ex. 182a) with its vigorous bass line is as heady as the wine which it celebrates. After the tenth bar it begins to weave back on itself; the melodic line dissolves in a welter of chromatics, ending in a plunge down a scale of semitones to which strings give a spiralling motion.† A magnificently assertive cadence (Ex. 182b), in effect an expansion of that which ended Ex. 181a, restores rhythmic and harmonic equilibrium, Beethoven-fashion.

* On the fourth, fifth and sixth bars of the allegro con brio Iago fills one by one three cups; one he offers to Cassio, another to Roderigo, the third he keeps for himself.

† *On the chromatic scale at the word 'Beva' the chorus mime the act of drinking (closed fist, thumb pointing towards the mouth). Disp. scen., p. 24.*

181b

Que-sta del pam-pi-no ve-ra-ce— man— na di va—ghe an-

-nu-go-la— nebbie il pen - sier.

182a

Chi al-l'e— -sca ha mor-so— del di-ti-ram-bo spa-val-do e stram-bo

be— va con me, be— va con me, be— va, be— va,

etc.

182b

The refrain is repeated with chorus taking part but leaving the chromatic phrases to Iago. To reach the second strophe a short bridge is needed because of the unusual key-relationship of verse to refrain; and it allows for a gleeful interchange between Iago and Roderigo ('Un altro sorso e brillo egli è') as they note Cassio's growing inebriation. The second strophe ('Il mondo palpita') proceeds exactly as the first though with a fuller accompaniment of trilling figures on flute and strings and syncopated chords on the four horns. Cassio too is doubled by flute, oboe and later clarinet with three bassoons active in the bass. After an unaltered refrain,* Iago begins a third verse ('Fuggan dal vivido nappo') – the *c* of the bar form – to a hiccupping accompaniment of low clarinet, four bassoons, lower strings, timpani and bass drum. Cassio, now well in his cups, interrupts successively with phrases from his Ex. 181b, neither of which he is able to finish. Iago befuddles him still further with snatches of the refrain (Ex. 182a). Again Cassio tries to join in but without success. In musical terms this means a fragmentation and fugato development of previous material; and so artistic order is imposed in naturalistic fashion on a scene which is far from orderly. The crowd that has gathered round at the start of the brindisi begins to titter. Cassio next attempts the beginning of Ex. 181a in F sharp minor but cannot get beyond the first two or three notes. As the orchestra marks time with a motif of open fourths and fifths Iago whispers to Roderigo that the time is ripe to provoke him. Choral laughter is punctuated by those rapid descending scales on high violins and woodwind (here flutes and piccolo) which since *Les Vêpres Siciliennes* have come to symbolize a guffaw. From all this a new, Beethoven-like theme takes shape as the chorus urge Cassio to further potations. (Ex. 183)

This in turn leads to a reprise of the second half of the refrain (the final *b* of the bar form) and with this the brindisi as such comes to an end; but sufficient energy has been generated to carry both music and action forward in a pendant analogous to that which followed the bonfire chorus. The whole orchestra bursts into a boisterous rollicking unison; all present carouse until the arrival of Montano produces a

---

* By now *Cassio's legs are beginning to give way; he listens with his left hand on the table behind him, endeavouring to prop himself upright. Disp. scen.,* p. 24. Maurel, however (*loc. cit.*) insists that Cassio's physical control should remain unimpaired.

183

RODERIGO &
CHORUS

Be - vi, be - - vi con me, be - vi, be - - vi con me, be - vi, be - vi, be - vi,

momentary silence. The retiring governor, having finally located Cassio, tells him
that it is time for him to return on duty ('Capitano, v'attende la fazione ai baluardi').
He is shocked to find the captain in such a condition ("'Tis evermore the prologue to
his sleep,' Iago whispers). The music continues in the same tripping fashion,
dominated by a descending figure on violins but with the menacing tramp of trombones beneath. Roderigo insults Cassio, who draws his sword; Montano intervenes,
and while he and Cassio fight, Iago, in full command of the situation, tells Roderigo
to raise the alarm. The women flee, the men call on the combatants to desist, extras
hastily clear away the tables and chairs, the bells sound 'a stormo' and all proceeds in
a steady crescendo of reiteration and sequence which might have turned out

184a

IAGO
(a parte a Roderigo)

(Va al porto, con quanta più pos-sa ti re-sta, gri-dan-do: sommossa! som-mossa! Va!

184b

IAGO

(agli astanti)

Nes - sun più raf - fre -na quel nembo pu - gna-ce! Si gri - - di l'al-(larme)

CHORUS
Tenors
Basses
pa - - ce!

musically tedious but for Verdi's ability to match the growing tension with mounting thematic interest, with patterns that germinate and proliferate. This progress by motivic transformation, already encountered in parts of the revised *Simon Boccanegra*, is nowhere so apparent as in Verdi's last two operas. Only in his maturity was he able to arrive at the richness of Ex. 184b from the thin neutrality of Ex. 184a.*

As Montano staggers back wounded and two soldiers rush to his support enter Otello with his suite. 'Lower your swords,' he commands. There is immediate silence.

> Why, here now, ho! from whence arises this?
> Are we turn'd Turks and so ourselves do that
> Which heaven has forbid the Ottomites?

His speech is punctuated by fierce chords and a furious upthrusting gesture on the strings. Iago's hypocritical reply ('Non so, qui tutti eran cortesi amici') is a master-piece of the unspoken. Soft, bitten-off pizzicato chords, the occasional harmonic splash of colour, as at 'sguainando l'arme s'avventano furenti', all suggest a tale too terrible to be told. Cassio is tongue-tied. At the sight of Montano wounded, Otello's fury redoubles; he abruptly strips Cassio of his rank, just as Desdemona arrives on the scene, having been disturbed by the noise of fighting. Cassio lets fall his sword which Iago retrieves and hands, gloating, to a soldier ('O! mio trionfo!'). Otello sends him to restore order in the city and commands that Montano should be looked after. He himself will remain by the quayside until all is quiet; and he signs to the men with torches to leave him. During all this the orchestra has taken charge with two successive melodies in F major, of which the first (Ex. 185a) will be recalled in far more harrowing circumstances. Both are smooth and regular in form, both rise gently over a tonic pedal to an apex of E flat from which they descend languorously with harmonies that correct the resulting subdominant bias. The effect, aided by the hypnotic pulsations of Ex. 185b, is to pour a healing balm on the atmosphere of strife and tumult and so, within less than a minute of Cassio's demotion, establish the sense of tranquillity in which the most spiritual of all Verdi's love duets can unfold. At the end of the second period a muted cello takes wing to the distant region of G flat major where it is joined by three others in a chain of dominant ninths whose ellip-tical resolutions purge away all sense of the trite and sentimental, leaving a residue of pure sublimity. (Ex. 186)

The duet ('Già nella notte densa') has been said to defy analysis except as 'a string of exquisite tunes which meander through one unlikely key after another in the most unexpected but unchallengeably logical manner'.† True, there are none of those thematic signposts to be found in, say, the love duet from *Madama Butterfly* for which, in certain other respects, it surely served as a model. Essentially it belongs to the same order as the great dialectical duets of *I Due Foscari*, *La Traviata* and *La Forza del destino*, with a design of contrasted interlocking movements. But here the movements have been fined down to a single phrase, or, at the most, period, while the element of

---

* *The duel should be conducted so as to end with the wounding of Montano at the fourth bar from the foot of page 88. It should be directed by someone with technical knowledge and practical ability in the art of fencing as it was prac-tised in the fifteenth century; it is a mixture of cut and thrust, proceeding not so much by repeated strokes as by rapid movements on the part of the combatants together with timely leaps and changes of position. Disp. scen., p. 27.*

† Hughes, p. 440.

185a

Ja-go, tu va nel-la cit - tà sgo - men - ta con quel-la squadra a ri-com-por la

pa - ce. Si soccor - ra Mon - ta - no.

185b

186

contrast has been profoundly modified, since Otello and Desdemona are, in Iago's words, 'well tuned'. Yet that they are different people with different ages and outlooks is reflected in the passing to and fro of the melodic thread with corresponding changes in the harmonic and orchestral shading. As usual there is no neat keyscheme in the classical sense; but the duet can none the less be seen to fall into three main parts each with its special tonal area and each marked off by discernible transitions. The first part (I) centres on the lovers' present happiness. Otello in a long, non-repeating period evinces a calm inner security, enhanced by his thoughts of the tumult without ('Tuoni la guerra e s'inabissi il mondo'); and he finishes firmly in the key of G flat in which he began.*

Desdemona is more child-like and impulsive; and her twelve bars of melody ('Mio superbo guerrier!') wander more freely. Her subdominant cadence at the words 'soavi abbraccìamenti' suggest a happiness almost too great to be believed. Inconsequentially she wanders off on a pattern of sixths ('O! com' è dolce il mormorare insieme'). Two steep modulations bring her to the magical chord of C major,

* The autograph specifies four solo cellos only up to the entry of Desdemona ('Mio superbo guerrier'). Likewise in both the autograph and the first edition strings remain muted until the end of the duet. In later editions mutes are removed at the start of the central section ('Quando narravi', etc.). The second of the four cellists at the opera's première was a certain Arturo Toscanini.

set out on flute, piccolo, bassoon, harp and widely spaced strings ('te ne rammenti'). This is the gateway into memory and with it the central section whose tonal basis is F with excursions into related keys. For this Verdi darkens his orchestral palette, substituting cor anglais and bass-clarinet for a second oboe and clarinet respectively. The sonority at the start of the largo movement suggests a deep but limpid pool. Very striking here is the use of arpeggios in the bass register of the harp, a new effect for Verdi:

The text of this central section (II) is taken from Shakespeare's first act. Otello and Desdemona are recalling together the story of their courtship as it was recounted to the Venetian senate by Otello himself. No sooner has Desdemona reached her half-close in C* than Otello takes up the memory:

> Wherein I spake of most disastrous chances,
> Of moving accidents by flood and field;
> Of hair-breadth 'scapes i' th' imminent deadly breach.†

All this the orchestra reflects in six bars of busy figuration with death figures rapping on cornets, trumpets and high woodwind, rising to forte only at the cadence. After Otello's declamation Desdemona reasserts the lyrical manner as she turns away from

* The French version of 1894 gives a variant of the cadence on the words 'coll'estasi nel cor':

† *Othello*, I, iii, 133–5.

C major to A flat – always a relative of F in Verdi's scheme of things. Her discourse is now:

> . . . of antres vast and deserts idle,
> Rough quarries, rocks and hills whose heads touch heaven.*

Her melody (Ex. 189b), be it noted, is harmonized above, a method Verdi usually reserves for thematic reminiscence (e.g. that of 'Figlia, a tal nome' in Act II of *Simon Boccanegra*) and a simple transference of ideas renders it no less appropriate for summoning up remembrance of things past. The rhythmic structure has now taken on a marked resemblance to that of the love duet from *Lohengrin* (Ex. 189a), with this difference, however, that whereas Wagner's melody remains strictly regular, each

189a

189b

* *Ibid.*, I, iii, 139–40.

phrase confined within the straitjacket of his iambic pentameters, Verdi extends his final phrase by a bar without upsetting the equilibrium of the paragraph.

Otello responds with yet another melody, its arc rising through a poignant diminished fifth ('Ingentilìa di lagrime') which takes the music from F minor to D flat; Desdemona returns it to the main key by means of a two-bar pendant ('Ed io vedea fra le tue tempie'). The central section is rounded off with what we may call, prosaically, a cabaletta-digest set in an enchanted twilight between F major and minor to Shakespeare's words:

> She lov'd me for the dangers I had passed,
> And I lov'd her that she did pity them.*

The effect of formal tightening created by the repetition of the double phrase by each voice with different orchestral colouring is enhanced by a small coda in which the vocal lines overlap as in so many a duet cabaletta. After the cadence the tempo accelerates to *Poco più mosso* for the transition to the final section (III), its mood, like that of (I), the joy of the moment, its tonal centre E major with C as a subsidiary area (again the relation is a close one in Verdi's language). To flute tremolandos, like those in the 'scena' of Jacopo's cavatina in *I Due Foscari*, sustaining horns and middle woodwind and soothing bass-clarinet arpeggi Otello declares that he would be happy to die at such a moment of ecstasy ('Venga la morte! e mi colga nell'estasi di quest'amplesso il momento supremo!'). As in the previous transition the modulations are strong and wide-ranging; but eventually the music finds its way home to E major ('Quest'attimo divino nell'ignoto avvenir del mio destino').† At the same time the

* *Ibid.*, I, iii, pp. 166–7.
† *At the height of his emotion Otello feels his strength give way; Desdemona passes to the left and while he sinks*

stage directions tell us that the sky is now completely clear, stars are shining and on the horizon can be seen the reflected light of the rising moon. With Desdemona's intervention over an interrupted cadence there is a shift to C major ('Disperda il ciel gli affanni'). 'Let not love change with the changing years!' she prays in a melody of heartfelt simplicity. 'Let the host of Heaven reply Amen!' – a sentiment echoed by her husband. The music stirs into a semiquaver motion as Desdemona feels a wave of happiness sweeping over her ('Ah! la gioia m'innonda!') and finally a diminished seventh prepares the supreme moment to which the duet has been tending – the Kiss.

191

All of mature Verdi is in this theme. How fitting, too, that a duet which sports a greater variety of cadence than any love duet in tonal music should culminate in an idea which is little more than an expanded cadence in itself. The elliptical progressions (at one point the music seems to pull back from the brink of B major) merely add to the spontaneity of the expression with its sense of pent-up emotion sweeping forward like a tide. The final bars are especially striking. The consecutive dominant in keys a third apart are accompanied by an inflexion of the vocal line which makes unusual demands on the singer's harmonic sense. By many Italians of Verdi's day this passage would have been dubbed unvocal. Instruments might have been expected to pitch that diminished fourth but not voices. Its occurrence in the most important theme of the opera is yet another instance of how Verdi and Wagner so often reached the same goal by different paths. The final progressions of the theme epitomize the E–C–E pattern of the whole section (III) to which it forms the climax.

back she follows him and gives him support; at the words 'Mi giacio' Otello leans against the ramparts and sits down on one of the flights of steps leading up to them, almost in a faint. Disp. scen., p. 34.

But E major is not the end of the journey. A shimmering coda ('Venere splende') with tremolando violins, flutes and oboes and high rippling harp moves into D flat in the tonal region of the initial G flat. There is a final memory of Ex. 186 on the four muted cellos beneath trilling first violins as the lovers clasped in an embrace go slowly into the castle. Rarely has that romantic cliché, the semitonal descent from la to sol, sounded so magical as in the first cello's final phrase.

ACT II

*Scene: A hall in the castle on ground level. A glass panel separates it from the garden. There is a balcony.**

In Shakespeare's play Cassio's punishment has the effect of sobering him immediately. No sooner has Othello left with Desdemona than Iago is able to ply him with false comfort and suggest that he enlist Desdemona's support for his reinstatement ('The general's wife is now the general'). Boito and Verdi shift the scene to the following day, by which time Cassio might have been expected to have slept off the effects of his debauch. The dialogue between Cassio and Iago exploits a traditional device of Italian opera but in a highly compendious and dramatic fashion. The practice of beginning a 'scena' with a fully formed orchestral melody, fragments of which are then interspersed with recitative, is common enough in the works of Rossini, Donizetti and Bellini. This is the background against which Arsace makes his first appearance in *Semiramide* and Norma is tempted to murder her sleeping children. It is one of the many procedures whereby the organism of the 'scena ed aria' was expanded. In the present case the melody is of an unusually 'progressive' kind, beginning in rudimentary fashion (Ex. 192a) and bursting into full flower (Ex. 192b)

192a

---

* The lay-out of this scene, to which Verdi evidently attached great importance, is amplified in the production book approximately as follows: the backcloth represents the garden and the sea. In front of this is an avenue running laterally L–R in the form of one of those practicable elevations 60 centimetres high in which the scenery of the opera abounds. From this a ramp descends towards the front of the stage, flanked by bushes and trees. This terminates in a wide arch panelled with glass representing a window of the hall in which all the subsequent dialogue will take place. There is a balcony R. with a door leading to the garden. L. is the door by which Otello will enter. See *Disp. scen.*, p. 34.

192b

after a short D minor episode. Its basic constituents, however, are present from the start – a triplet gesture (*x*), neutral but with an undercurrent of savagery, and a suave, almost classical motif such as might have come from an opera semi-seria of Paer and which throughout the dialogue acts as a rondo theme, a refrain of gentle reassurance.

A second episode follows in F minor, modulating freely and chromatically before the voices enter ('Non ti crucciar'), to be succeeded by a comforting return to Ex. 192b. Musically it is a picture of Iago at his most falsely charming – for it is he who does most of the talking. 'Soon,' he assures the crestfallen young man, 'you will be able to return to the carefree embraces of Monna Bianca.'* As in Rossinian opera the main theme (Ex. 192b) is split up by vocal intervention; but apart from Iago's one bar 'senza misura' none of it can be called recitative, so there is no slackening of the rhythmic impulse; the melody is merely opened up and diversified. Another particularly caressing episode is added in G minor at the words 'Attendi a ciò ch'io dico' with the concomitant return of Ex. 192b; a reference follows to the F minor idea and a final repeat of the refrain sends Cassio away consoled.

At once the rhythmic gesture of Ex. 192a (*x*) is transformed as the mask slips from Iago's face.† The tonal centre remains F, however, both here and throughout the following 'Credo'. As he watches Cassio depart Iago exults in his power to ruin ('Vanne! La tua meta già vedo; ti spinge il tuo dimone'). And so to Verdi's most terrifying expression of evil, an expansion of Shakespeare's exclamation, 'Divinity of Hell!' Iago's so-called 'Credo' ('Credo in un Dio crudel') is a 'canto declamato' of the type already adumbrated in Fra Melitone's comic sermon in *La Forza del destino*; but it is more thematic, more solidly welded than the earlier example. Here the

---

* This is one of Boito's few gratuitous ineptitudes and it raises once more the vexed question of the time-scale of *Otello*, which has troubled many a Shakespearian scholar. If the succession of events in the play is closely examined it will be found that Cassio would not have had a moment in which to commit adultery with Desdemona. Yet although a stranger to Cyprus, by Act IV he has had enough time to form a liaison with the clinging Bianca, and one of sufficiently long standing to have become a joke between him and Iago. Boito brings in Bianca at a still earlier stage, before Cassio could even have met her.

† *Iago will have followed [Cassio] for two or three paces; then he stops, and following [him] with his eye, immediately changes his expression and mode of utterance. He is no longer the gay and openhearted character of a moment before; he reveals instead the most repulsive cynicism. As he says 'E il tuo dimon son io,' he turns towards the audience and at the words 'Inesorato Iddio' comes forward to the footlights and stands in an attitude of sardonic cruelty. Disp. scen.*, p. 37. In general he is required to make his effects less by his gestures, in which he should be sparing, but rather by the play of his features. Likewise Maurel: '. . . Mais encore faut-il une réserve assez grande dans les gestes; sans celà les principaux effets de cette superbe page de déclamation lyrique se trouvaient sensiblement amoindris.' (Maurel, *op. cit.*, p. 57.)

orchestra, as in Wagner, carries the structural burden, leaving the voice free to follow the inflexion of the words. Once again there are two motifs:

193a

193b

The first (Ex. 193a) has already been foreshadowed in the revised *Simon Boccanegra* where Paolo is forced to curse himself; it will be echoed at the outset of Puccini's *Turandot* where a crowd is baying for blood. But as a unison of negative emotion it remains unsurpassed in Italian opera. A constant feature (again not lost on Puccini) is the use of G flat as a flattened supertonic within the key of F minor; also characteristic is the savage trilling of violas and low clarinets. Ex. 193b has echoes of both Liszt's and Boito's Mephistopheles, with its suggestion of an infernal dance. Iago's creed has four articles of belief: in a cruel God who has created him in his own image; that to do evil is to fulfil his destiny; that virtue is a lie and the good man a contemptible dupe; and that man is the plaything of fate and can hope for nothing in this life or after death – 'for death is nothingness and heaven an old wives' tale'.

The piece is so designed as to fall into two sections: the first, short and expository, is framed by two massive statements of Ex. 193a and contains the first statement of Ex. 193b as well as a motif of repeated trills which we have heard as long ago as *I Masnadieri* in the music of that other double-dyed villain, Francesco Moor. All this conveys the first article of faith. The second section ('Credo che il giusto è un istrion beffardo') is based mostly on Ex. 193b, beginning in C minor and modulating freely so as to culminate in a B major climax at the words 'dal germe della culla' that dissolves straightaway into an orchestral guffaw of semiquavers. For the end of his discourse Iago employs the technique of crouch and spring, dwindling first of all to a veiled pianissimo in which the harmonization of Ex. 193a is especially telling. (Ex. 194)

The mention of death evokes the same terrifying void as in the 'Dies Irae' of the

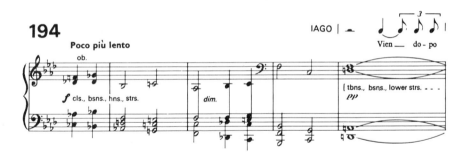

Requiem. Then a shrill Ex. 193b in the orchestra – all upper instruments and a cymbal roll without the usually accompanying bass drum – brings in Iago's final 'e vecchia fola il ciel', and the music swings around with surprise logic to the original tonic of F; after which by tradition (though there is no warrant for it in the score) Iago bursts into mocking laughter.* A similar shock effect of a protracted diminuendo followed by a sudden outburst will be employed at the end of the 'Willow Song' to a very different purpose. What in Iago's case is a deliberate assault on the sensibilities of his audience is with Desdemona an involuntary release of pent-up sorrow, like a rush of tears.

Iago's 'Credo' is sometimes compared to Mefistofele's 'Son lo Spirito che nega' from Boito's opera. The comparison is valid in so far as Boito had helped to set a new fashion in highly charged melodramatic villainy which was followed by Ponchielli in *La Gioconda* and Cagnoni in *Francesca da Rimini*, and by Verdi himself in the redrawing of Paolo in *Simon Boccanegra*, not to mention Puccini in *Tosca*. If this vignette of Iago surpasses anything of the kind previously attempted by Italian composers this is because it is a unique musical organism that develops from the implications of its material, while Barnaba and Cagnoni's Alberigo express themselves in 'off the peg' designs, and Mefistofele in a mechanically constructed 'couplet' – a mosaic *à la* Meyerbeer. The verbal text, it may be said once more, is nonsense – a conglomeration of sentiments which Shakespeare's villain would not have thought worth formulating. But if music drama is not dependent on the validity of intellectual concepts, it requires words to define the negative emotions immanent in the notes; and here Boito, with his wide-ranging and evocative literary vocabulary, cannot be faulted in aiding the realization of Verdi's tour de force.

Desdemona and Emilia are now seen to pass by in the garden. Iago goes to the terrace and over the next fifty bars reports on events which the audience can observe at a distance and in dumb show: Cassio approaching Desdemona, then talking with her earnestly as they pace up and down the garden. In the play this is managed more straightforwardly: Cassio pleads with Desdemona in the full hearing of Iago and the audience, leaving the stage just as Otello arrives. Yet the purpose of Verdi's scene is clear. The first dialogue between Otello and his 'ancient', which corresponds to Shakespeare's III, iii poses a problem for librettist and composer: how to prevent Othello's jealousy being awakened so quickly as to alienate the sympathies of the

* At the final words 'e vecchia fola il ciel' he shrugs his shoulders, turns away and moves upstage. Disp. scen., p. 37.

audience. In the play there is the Venetian act to explain the subconscious trauma on which Iago could work; then too the more rapid pace of a spoken drama offers the hero plenty of time to move plausibly from puzzlement to suspicion and finally to jealous despair. Boito is forced to compress; it remains for Verdi to compensate by enlarging the musical time-scale at the outset. First he turns Iago's commentary into a swift pattering interlude with one of those fleet bass lines accompanied by rapid changes of harmony that we encounter in part of the revised *Boccanegra*. There is nothing interesting thematically or orchestrally about this passage (all strings with the occasional bassoon to reinforce cellos); but in performance it offers a fine example of 'diffused' melody such as will form the stylistic basis of *Falstaff*, voice and orchestra sustaining irregular fragments of a continuous melodic tissue. The music whirls from F to C and related keys, settling for 10 bars in A minor, then once more on the move through C major, B minor, and easing conclusively into D major as Iago sees Otello approaching and takes up his stance behind a pillar, murmuring as he observes Desdemona and Cassio, 'I like not that' ('Ciò m'accora'), loud enough for Otello to hear; he then affects surprise at the general's presence. The fifty bars of allegro with rapidly changing harmonies are followed by an 'assai moderato' of which the first fifteen bars are built over a dominant pedal. At once time seems to slow down. Iago spills out his poison in drops of half-uttered phrases and vague beginnings of a musical idea which does not take shape until his question about Otello's courtship ('Cassio, nei primi dì del vostro amor, Desdemona non conosceva?'): it is a sinuous theme, falsely innocent, and Otello soon becomes entangled in its coils.

195

A spacious sixteen-bar period is adumbrated but never completed; the melody dissolves once more into inchoate fragments as Iago keeps repeating Otello's questions with a pretence at stalling. This produces the required result. Otello bursts out impatiently ('Pel cielo, tu sei l'eco dei detti miei'). Here Boito reflects the growing tension by changing the metre to one of 'settenari doppi' as in Azucena's 'Condotta ell'era in ceppi'. But Verdi no longer feels the need to set them regularly as in *Il Trovatore*, where the end of a phrase coincides with that of a line, and the rhyme leaps to the ear. In the two stanzas which follow Otello proceeds in irregular phrase-lengths. First a two-bar unit is followed by one of five bars. At the words 'Sì; ben t'udii poc'anzi mormorar' the phrases become shorter and more agitated before gathering strength in preparation for an implied cadence ('Suvvia, parla se m'ami'). His second outburst ('Dunque senza velami t'esprimi e senza ambagi') begins with a two-bar phrase and continues with one of three bars. In both cases the musical thought is caught up by Iago and with the fewest possible words directed into whatever key he chooses: from B minor to D minor, from A minor to B flat. A spine-chilling transition marks the first mention of jealousy, whispered into Otello's ear ('Temete, Signor, la gelosia'). The strangeness of the progression is underlined by the use of the full orchestra pianissimo. Note above all the dramatic use of a device which will become a mannerism in the hands of Puccini – the doubling of melody and bass.

196a

It is the green-ey'd monster which doth mock
The meat it feeds on.*

This for Verdi is a regular period of three phrases, standing out like a rock in the emotional rapids and therefore all the more memorable for future reference. There is an obvious similarity to the theme in which King Philip first confides to Posa his suspicions about Elisabeth and Carlos. Surely this is more than coincidence. The curling line and the unison voice and accompaniment are common to both. But Iago characteristically allows himself a snarling trill at the final cadence.

196b

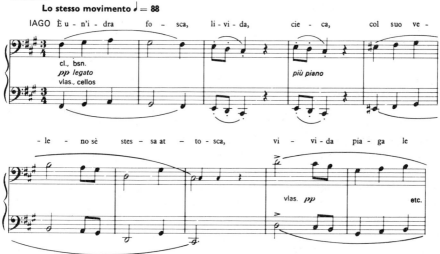

This again elicits from Otello a turmoil of irregular phrases ending with a magnificent cadential flourish involving an ascent of an octave and a half ('Amore e gelosia

* *Othello*, III, iii, 170–1.

vadan dispersi insieme'), in which energy of line and vigour of harmony are superbly combined:

197

The clumsy parenthesis ('Otello ha sue leggi supreme') can be defended as necessary to prepare the full detonation of Verdi's phrase, but by altering 'love or jealousy' to 'love *and* jealousy' Boito certainly introduces a note of irrational despair into Shakespeare's lines, in which Othello is lulling his own suspicions with a show of fair-mindedness:

> I'll see before I doubt; when I doubt prove;
> And on the proof there is no more but this –
> Away at once with love or jealousy.*

It is as though Boito's Desdemona could be proved guilty but not innocent.

If the drama is already threatening to move too fast, the next episode effectively applies the brakes. A distant chorus is heard ('Dove guardi splendono raggi') to a text curiously reminiscent of Pope's 'Where'er you walk'. Through the first verse Iago, swiftly declaiming on a dominant-bound monotone (since the simplicity of the choral melody will not allow anything more elaborate), warns Otello to be on his guard. Then Desdemona appears in the garden. She is surrounded by women from the island, children, and Cypriot and Albanian sailors, who come forward and offer her flowers, sprigs of blossom and other gifts. Some accompany themselves as they sing on the 'guzla, a type of mandolin',† others have portable harps strapped to their shoulders. In addition to a separate children's chorus – a single line of so-called 'voci bianche' singing at alto pitch – the piece requires extra instruments: a 'cornamusa', two mandolins and two guitars, though a note in the score states that where these in-

* *Ibid.*, III, iii, 188–90.

† Not so: a guzla is a type of rebab, a one-stringed instrument played with a bow, in common use among Balkan peasants.

struments are lacking they can be replaced by two oboes and four harps.* The chorus itself belongs to the genre of 'invented' folk music; but the alternating drones of the cornamusa, the delightful, if primitive counterpoint of violin and mandolin patterns that decorate the second verse give it a genuinely rustic character, not unlike the first trio in the scherzo of Beethoven's Pastoral Symphony with its comic bassoon bass. It is an idealized version of the kind of melody that could have been heard in any waterfront café along the Dalmatian or Greek coast in Verdi's day.

198a

Three episodes follow, all in 6/8, for the children, the baritones and the women respectively, and each in a different key. Despite the rustic instruments these are harmonically much more sophisticated, sometimes in the French, sometimes in Verdi's own individual manner – note in this connection the side-slip of a fourth in the first phrase of the children's verse ('T'offriamo il giglio soave'). The choral writing is varied in texture and so designed as to be self-sufficient. The women's and the

* The production book makes it clear that there are two quite separate choruses in this scene: (1) the 'coro speciale' (4 sopranos, 4 contraltos, 6 tenors, 6 baritones and basses, 8 boys) who will appear on stage together with the players of mandolins and guitars (5 or 6 apiece) and an extra who mimes the playing of the cornamusa. This choir will sing the solos in the episodes which follow; if the boys are weak their line can be reinforced by two of the contraltos. The main part (2) of the chorus, which should be invisible, stand in the wings backstage L. with a harmonium near by. They will sing the accompaniments. There is no mention of guzlas or portable harps. *Disp. scen.*, p. 41. *The boys have lilies in their hands, the women roses and geraniums, the basses coral necklaces and brooches of pearls. Disp. scen.*, p. 42. Some time later Verdi expressed the view that the three solos of the special choir should be sung by single voices – 'a good treble for the first solo, a good baritone for the second, a good soprano for the third . . . accompanied with a single mandolin and a single guitar with a chorus of only eight voices singing the accompaniment – perhaps not even as many' (letter to Giulio Ricordi, 1.1.1889; Abbiati, IV, p. 366). A few days later: 'Thinking about it still further I'm becoming convinced that in the second act chorus the solos must really be performed by solo voices with a small accompaniment of voices and sounds. It would be quieter, simpler, more modest – I would say, more innocent and in keeping with the personality of Desdemona. For instance one boy presenting flowers is doing a kindly and innocent act; six boys are a nuisance' (letter to Giulio Ricordi, 9.2.1889. *Ibid.*, p. 372). Evidently he did not press the matter since none of the printed scores, full or vocal, specify single voices for the solos.

children's episode is supported by pulsations from the rest of the chorus; the baritones' graceful derivative from Ex. 198a ('A te le porpore') is sung beneath sustained chords. In each case the instruments merely decorate.*

198b

Finally Ex. 198a returns, its last two phrases echoed by Desdemona herself. Otello's counter-melody ('Quel canto mi conquide') is Boito's equivalent of:

> If she be false, O! then Heaven mocks itself.
> I'll not believe it.†

Iago, taking up his stand on the dominant once more, delivers the phrase that Boito had originally intended for the end of the love duet:

> . . . O! you are well tuned now;
> But I'll set down the pegs that make this music.‡

During an instrumental coda Desdemona caresses some of the children on the head; some of the women kiss the hem of her dress; and she hands a purse to the sailors. The chorus retire. Desdemona, followed by Emilia, enters the hall and approaches Otello. She launches her plea for Cassio's reinstatement in a pathetic wheedling melody with a suggestion of a sob in the pattern of violin octaves that accompany her in semi-quavers ('D'un uom che geme').

199a

It is the language of Amneris as she tries to force Aida's confidence; and if there is no arrière-pensée in Desdemona's case, Otello is not to know that. The dialogue is that of Shakespeare III, iii, 43–4, suitably condensed. 'I have been talking with a suitor here, a man that languishes in your displeasure.' 'Who is't you mean?' 'Cassio.' 'Went he hence now?' 'Ay, sooth; so humbled that he hath left part of his grief with me to suffer with him. I pray thee, call him back.' With this Desdemona reaches the third and fourth phrases of the paragraph and in accordance with that traditional shaping of Italian verse-setting noted by Dallapiccola her eloquence attains a

---

* The women's and the baritones' verses are often left out in performance, and an element of variety is thereby lost.   † *Othello*, III, iii, 282–3.   ‡ *Ibid.*, II, i, 196–7.

piercing sweetness that to Otello only hints at a deep involvement with Cassio.

199b

The musical means are by now familiar: a chain of assorted dominant seventh inversions that never resolve in the expected manner and finally reach a melting cadence. 'Not now,' Otello replies angrily; but Desdemona continues to plead for Cassio's pardon, the oboe now colouring the cadential phrase. Otello's mood finds expression in a sudden unrelated 6/4 and a substantial allegro agitato transition follows. He complains that his forehead is burning; Desdemona produces a handkerchief, which he throws to the ground, whence it is retrieved by Emilia. Desdemona, reverting to the lyrical vein which is her natural element, begs Otello to forgive her if she has inadvertently annoyed him. The soothing descending phrase 'Se inconscia contro te, sposo, ho peccato' merges seamlessly into what in general outline will turn out to be an old-style concertato, in which four characters express their individual feelings within a closed form.

Yet the quartet ('Dammi la dolce e lieta parola del perdono') is both more and less than that. For Emilia and Iago it is a pure action piece, in which he tries to bully her into giving him the handkerchief while she retorts with some spirit that she is his wife, not his slave. In the end he has to snatch the handkerchief from her. Neither part has much musical interest; though each contributes a certain rhythmic vitality to the ensemble. Desdemona on the other hand carries the melodic burden of the entire piece, with what is perhaps the most sustained stretch of lyrical writing in the opera. Its range is formidable, extending from low B flat upwards for two octaves; and it all forms a monolithic melody of twenty bars (excluding the codetta) of largo 12/8 without any element of reprise. (Ex. 200)

Not even Bellini achieved such a span. Despite the somewhat complex harmonic scheme – possibly because of it – it is interesting to find Verdi buttressing the third double phrase with a pattern of flute and clarinet semiquavers rather in his early manner, except that in earlier days these would have been played on clarinet alone. The quartet is then first and foremost a concentrated expression of Desdemona's compassionate nature; all she can think of is soothing her husband's distress. But Otello, in the grip of suspicion, can feel none of this. Beneath her melody he keeps up an anguished soliloquy culled from Shakespeare's III, iii, 267–70.

> . . . Haply, for I am black,
> and have not those soft parts of conversation
> That chamberers have; or, for I am declin'd
> Into the vale of years . . .

200

The decline is reflected in the 'madrigalism' of a descending scale. All Desdemona's sweetness of disposition is summed up in her codetta phrase, in which she repeats her opening words, an ascending scale passage forming a counter-melody to Ex. 200 on the first violins. But Otello roughly sends her away, collapses on a chair and sits staring in front of him; muttering brokenly ('Desdemona rea. . . . Atroce idea!'). Strings and bassoon spin out a postlude based on fragments of the Largo, breaking off for two bars to allow Iago a moment of recitative as he slips the handkerchief into his doublet ('Con questi fili tramerò la prova del peccato d'amor'). Note here stabbing acciaccatura figures always on the offbeat, like a thought that continually gnaws at the brain. The music side-steps the full close to which it seems to have been leading, and Otello rouses himself and turns on Iago with savage fury ('Tu! Indietro! fuggi!!'). Not even Alberich's despair is expressed with more harmonic force.

> Avaunt! Begone! Thou hast set me on the rack.
> I swear 'tis better to be much abus'd
> Than but to know't a little. . . .
> What sense had I of her stol'n hours of lust?. . .
> I slept the next night well, was free and happy
> I found not Cassio's kisses on her lips.*

Most of this outburst is declaimed over a coiling F minor bass line not sufficiently formed to be called a theme, yet clearly akin to Ex. 196b. (Ex. 201)

* *Ibid.*, III, iii, 339 ff.

201

O now, for ever,
Farewell the tranquil mind, farewell content
Farewell the plumed troop and the big wars
That make ambition virtue.*

In the double strophe 'Ora e per sempre addio' the listener may be surprised to note the same key, tempo and scoring – even down to the instruction as to the proportion in which the double basses are to be divided – as in Renato's 'Dunque l'onta di tutti sol una'. True, the harps are now two instead of one and there is additional figuration on the middle strings. More importantly, however, Boito's use of the grand metre requires a more complex rhythmic articulation than Somma's plain decasyllabics.

202

* *Ibid.*, III, iii, 351–4.

Unlike the square melodies of the Risorgimento operas which seem to call one to action, Otello's farewell to glory, by the irregularity of its phrase within a formal unit, suggests the shattering of a dream. The 'Pomp and circumstance of glorious war' are all reflected in the orchestral accompaniment, but like Mahler's 'schöne Trompeten' they reach us in fragmentary gestures through a mist of sadness. In the second strophe which moves to C flat in the manner of the *Aida* trumpet march ('Addio vessillo trionfale e pio') there is a striking interplay of cornets and trumpet, with triplet fanfares for the first and for the solo trumpet a series of low 'death figures' pianissimo followed by a long G flat swelling in a crescendo while the rest of the orchestra remains variously at mezzo forte or pianissimo.

At 'Othello's occupation's gone' the sense of rupture is strengthened by a brutal inserted bar of 2/4; then Otello's fury with Iago starts slowly to come to the boil. The triplet pattern for violas and cellos tremolando which forms the basis of this huge groundswell seems at first harmless enough. But as it mounts to a climax scale passages in contrary motion clash fiercely.

203

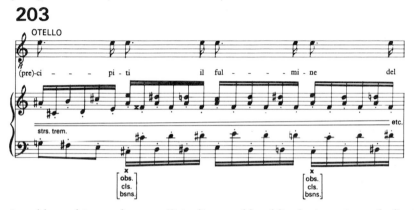

Iago blames his own honesty ('Meglio varrebbe ch'io fossi un ciurmador'): Otello thrashes round him in perplexity ('Credo leale Desdemona e credo che no lo sia; te credo onesto e credo disleale'). In all this Verdi avoids the pitfall of so many 'veristic' composers who make their heroes bluster continually. Even in the grip of strong emotion Otello is sparing with his fortes. His agitation is expressed partly in the disjointed, irregular phrasing of the voice part and also in an energetic bass line that drives forward at a great speed. Otello calls for proof of Desdemona's guilt. Iago inquires in more elegant language than Shakespeare's whether he expects to see them coupled; he then takes advantage of Otello's shock ('Morte e dannazione!') to introduce the subject of Cassio's dream. In his solo ('Era la notte') there is another echo from *Un Ballo in maschera*, this time of Ulrica's 'Della città all'occaso'; and once again what is symmetrical in the earlier opera has a freedom of design in the second which is very closely bound up with Boito's highly unusual metre of triple quinari. (Ex. 204) This progress by small units grouped in three allows for an infinite variety of expansion within the framework of what remains a formal set-piece. It is all superb narrative music, with rich harmonies adding to its insinuating character and cadences deployed like so many structural landmarks. Muted strings remain the basis of the scoring, discreetly coloured here and there by woodwind without oboes and horns (how useful is the third flute in this context!). Cassio's words ('Sweet Desdemona, let

204

us be wary, let us hide our loves. . . . Cruel, cursed fate that gave thee to the Moor')
are declaimed on a monotone pianissimo and underlined by woodwind alone. There
is a characteristically steep cadential modulation from E major back to C preceded by
a passage that anticipates Debussy in its impressionistic suspension of tonality.

205

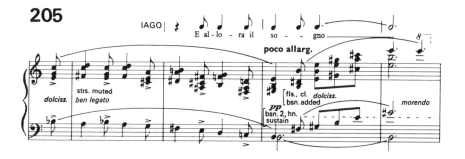

The narrative concluded, Iago prepares the coup de grâce. Does Otello recall
having possessed a handkerchief like the one Iago now produces? The Moor
recognizes it at once. 'This handkerchief I found in Cassio's lodging.' This has its
effect. A violent orchestral E major chord like a gash brings in Otello's:

> O, that the slave had forty thousand lives!
> One is too poor, too weak for my revenge!*

The music builds up in a succession of sequential patterns for the final duet of the oath
('Sì, pel ciel marmoreo giuro!') that Boito carved from Shakespeare's 'Now by yon
marble heaven'. The theme, traced in a thick powerful line by horns and lower
woodwind, swings back and forth like the blows of some vast hammer. (Ex. 206)

Iago's work has been accomplished; the act requires a 'clinching' design; and for
Verdi even in 1887 there was none better than the cabaletta with its formal
repetitions that drive home the point that has been made. Hence for the first time
since the choral episode a symmetrical melody with a self-propagating rhythmic
pattern. No wonder that the unsophisticated find this the most enjoyable moment in

* *Ibid.*, III, iii, 446–7.

206

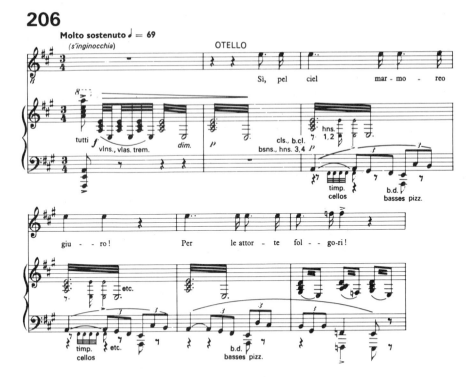

the opera. It is of course a cabaletta with a difference, since nobody at this time was writing the conventional Donizettian variety. Nor are Otello and Iago required to sing the melody in different keys according to their compass; instead the melody remains in A and is sung by Iago alone, Otello's verse being set as a counter-melody as in Ex. 206. The final statement where the two voices unite provides an instance of one of those thoughts which occur to the composer after a première. 'Please keep silent about this change,' he wrote to Ricordi, 'or else people will say I'm rewriting *Otello*.'* In fact the passage as we know it today was first heard when the opera was performed at Venice in May. The melody and thought are unchanged, but the accompaniment is vastly strengthened. Instead of the original cursive pattern of semiquavers in strings and upper wind, the timpani 'paradiddle' with its associations of death is reinforced by arpeggios on flutes, piccolo, oboes and clarinets, and also by bunched horns which then move in Beethoven-like thrusting syncopations. If the original version was more brilliant the second has far greater force.† The coda is full of abrupt modulations leading as always to an assertion of the tonic that is all the stronger in consequence. Logically enough the final bars bring back the doubling device noted in Ex. 196a with grinding effect. (Ex. 207)

---

* Letter to Giulio Ricordi, 2.5.1887. Abbiati, IV, p. 336.

† Curiously enough, the first version of this duet persists in a number of later vocal scores, including that relating to the Paris version of 1894.

207

ACT III

*Scene: The Great Hall of the Castle. On the right, a large portico which leads to a smaller room. At the back a terrace.**

The act opens with a short prelude based on Ex. 196b, almost a companion piece to that of Act III in the revised *Don Carlos*. The subject, like that of Carlos's love (Ex. 9), is expanded contrapuntally after a quiet start on the cellos beneath viola semiquavers; but instead of floating away into gossamer dreams it rises quickly, via pattering quavers which recall Iago's stage managing in the previous act, to a tutti reprise with heavy lower brass and a counterpoint of semiquavers in flute, piccolo and first violins. For Otello's incubus is only too real; the monster is already consuming him. So by summing up the swift progress of his malady the prelude prepares for the harrowing events of the act. It is the equivalent of Iago's:

> Not poppy, nor mandragora,
> Nor all the drowsy syrups of the world,
> Shall ever medicine thee to that sweet sleep
> Which thou ow'dst yesterday.†

The curtain rises on Otello and Iago still in conversation. The prelude is interrupted by an unrelated pianissimo chord of E on the brass as the herald enters to announce that the ship carrying the Venetian envoys has been sighted. Otello acknowledges the news and signs to him to leave; while the resumption of a phrase from the prelude indicates that his mind is returning to his obsession. He tells Iago to continue what he was saying. In free, lightly scored recitative Iago unfolds his plan to bring Cassio to the castle and trap him into compromising himself. Otello must meanwhile hide by the balcony and eavesdrop on their conversation. Seeing Desdemona approach he warns Otello to conceal his feelings. 'I leave you . . . the handkerchief!' Here Iago as he starts to leave should 'return to Otello to speak the last word'. Otello dismisses him brusquely ('Va! volontieri obliato l'avrei').

Desdemona's entrance (Ex. 208a) shows Verdi once more drawing on the idiom of

---

* The production book specifies a series of receding arches ending in the inevitable practicable elevation of 60 centimetres. The backcloth should give a view of the sea and a wing of the castle. *Disp. scen.*, p. 55. In 1889 Verdi mooted the idea of dividing the act into two scenes 'an interior for the dialogue between Otello, Desdemona, Iago and Cassio and a change for the rest'. (Letter to Giulio Ricordi, 1.1.1889, Abbiati, IV, p. 366.) But the directions for this do not appear in any subsequent edition of the vocal score; so Verdi must be assumed to have had second thoughts about it.

† *Othello*, III, iii, 327–9.

a classical age for dramatic effect. It might have been the introduction to any arietta sung at Vauxhall or Ranelagh in George III's time. Poise, grace, a simple nobility of heart – all these are connoted by the three bars of tripping string quavers, ending in a cadence whose rhythmic pattern is carried over into the main body of the duet (Ex. 208b, 'Dio ti giocondi, o sposo').

208a

Here Boito has made a skilful conflation of two different scenes (Act III, scene iv, and Act IV, scene ii), postponing a passage from the second so that it can function as a soliloquy ('Dio, mi potevi scagliar'). In the first Otello takes Desdemona's hand, mutters enigmatically about a 'moist and sweating devil that commonly rebels', starts to question Desdemona about the handkerchief and frightens her into lying about its loss. Desdemona, innocently returning to the subject of Cassio's reinstatement, then quite logically brings down upon herself the fearful denunciation that belongs to Shakespeare's following act. But the design that makes a logical unity out of the two parts is Verdi's. No composer was more skilful at investing a suave melody with emotional ambivalence. Already this is apparent in *Stiffelio* and *Aroldo*, both milestones along the road to *Otello*, and especially in those scenes where betrayal is suspected. Nowhere, however, is there a greater degree of polarity between the emotional states encompassed by a single melody than in Ex. 208b. As sung by Desdemona it is all innocence and charm; when taken over by Otello ('Grazie, madonna, datemi la vostra eburnea mano') and edged by the oboe it assumes a bitter sarcasm that sets the listener's teeth on edge. The entire movement is planned with a classical symmetry broken only by Otello's three-bar phrase 'Caldo madorne irrora la morbida beltà'. Like the prelude to Act II it is a rondo with a shorter then a larger episode, the whole forming an essentially bipartite structure, of which the second half begins with the second episode. (The relation of this to the traditional binary form of a 'cantabile' needs no stressing.) A restatement of Ex. 208a gives the final polish to a movement in which both characters express themselves 'con eleganza' and 'dolcissimo'; yet the context confers on it an irony and tension that is almost unbearable. Again Desdemona brings up the subject of Cassio. Otello pretends a 'salt and sorry rheum',* and asks for Desdemona's handkerchief, knowing that she will be unable to produce the one filched by Iago. Here a new idea presents itself, symbolic of Otello's barely controlled fury. Of its two elements the upper pattern of semiquavers is developed the more strictly, the lower crotchet motif being used for its rhythm more than its line.

209

That handkerchief
Did an Egyptian to my mother give;
She was a charmer and could read
The thoughts of people.†

The essence of Shakespeare's speech, so like the corresponding warning about the ring in *Aroldo*, is declaimed pianissimo to an ominous crotchet rhythm over the semiquaver figure of Ex. 209 in two five-bar phrases, each ending in a hierophantic cadence, its modal inflexions brought out by simple but wonderfully effective wind colouring (Ex. 210). At the sight of Desdemona's mild alarm Otello's fury threatens to break its bounds, when there is a sudden change of mood. Desdemona, whose conscience is clear, cannot think that anything serious is amiss between her and her husband.

This is a trick to put me from my suit.
Pray you let Cassio be receiv'd again.‡

This miniature aria of three phrases furnishes the rhythmic basis of what is to follow. As in Amneris's 'Non hai tu in Memfi' from *Aida* the acciaccatura figure is no longer a lament or a sob but rather an archly raised eyebrow (see Vol. 2, Ex. 22). In two subsequent phrases – 'È Cassio l'amico tuo diletto' and 'A Cassio, a Cassio perdona' –

---

* Boito changes the 'rheum' to a headache. In his preface to the first English translation, which takes the form of an elegant open letter to Boito, Francis Hueffer begs leave to change it back.

† *Othello*, III, iv, 54–7.

‡ *Ibid.*, III, iv, 87–8.

210

she tries to maintain the tone of lyrical wheedling; but she is powerless against Otello's mounting anger, reflected in flurries of demisemiquavers in the cellos and his repeated demands for the handkerchief ('Il fazzoletto! il fazzoletto!'). With the transition to Shakespeare's Act IV the tempo increases to Più mosso. Violins and cellos alternate in a figure that may recall the accompaniment to Rigoletto's 'Cortigiani, vil razza', while trombone triads growl in the background. Yet Otello is ominously calm as he asks Desdemona to look him in the face ('Alza quegl'occhi'). 'Why, what art thou?' 'Your wife, my lord, your true and loving wife.' 'Come, swear it, damn thyself.' During all this time the music drives forward in furious sequences toward a massive E minor close whose last note is reached across a terrifying chasm. Again Boito has reshuffled Shakespeare, taking Desdemona's words from earlier in the scene:

> Upon my knees, what doth your speech import?
> I understand a fury in your words
> But not the words.*

Never has a low, held oboe note sounded more menacing; nor the significance of the 'death figure' been more unequivocal than in these savage brass tritones.† (Ex. 211)

Having reached a cadence by far from orthodox means, Desdemona now leads the music through six bars of more tranquil A minor to a new, expansive idea which forms the still centre of the duet ('io prego il cielo per te con questo pianto'). This time the words are not Shakespeare's at all. Desdemona is weeping the first tears she

---

* *Ibid.*, IV, ii, 33–4.

† The basses' pizzicato notes are enjoined only on those basses which possess a fourth string.

211

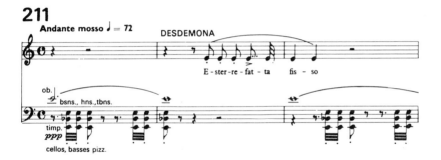

has shed since their marriage, to a heart-easing melody whose rich progressions would sound intolerably cloying with any other composer.*

212

Once again the three-limbed structure gives the effect of a miniature aria within the duet. As at the end of 'Figlia, a tal nome' in the revised *Simon Boccanegra* the orchestra epitomizes the theme in a similar access of warmth while Otello denounces his wife between clenched teeth and Desdemona protests her innocence. A free agitato episode finds Otello at breaking-point ('Ah, Desdemona — away! away! away!'). The old device of agitated syncopations is called into play as in many a previous opera, but with richer harmonies and lighter scoring. Desdemona's 'Am I the motive of these tears, my lord?' rounds off the period with a derivative of Ex. 212; after which the music again dissolves into syncopations as Otello breaks down. During the next transition the music gathers strength for a final blow. 'Alas, what ignorant sin have I committed?' 'Was this fair paper, this most goodly book made to write whore upon?' The first exchanges of Boito's paraphrase are set to music that is strangely muted. At Otello's words 'Il più nero delitto' the three trombones give out a sustained intermittent low E while fragments of Ex. 209 are heard on cellos beneath tremolando violas and violins. Then as Otello becomes more direct in his accusations there are sudden tutti outbursts. Desdemona repudiates the charge of strumpet in a magnificently emphatic descending arpeggio phrase ('O, non son ciò che esprime quella parola orrenda'). Otello, suddenly changing from anger to the most terrible

* A continuity sketch for this passage can be found in Gatti's *Verdi nelle Immagini*, p. 187, where it is wrongly labelled as a sketch for *Falstaff*. The melody is identical with that of the definitive score except for two E's in the second half of bar 21 ('Vede l'eterno') where the score has F's.

ironical calm, takes Desdemona by the hand and leads her to the door by which she entered.

> I cry you mercy, then.
> I took you for that cunning whore of Venice
> That married with Othello.*

This is Othello sane again, as Aldous Huxley puts it, but sane with the base ignoble sanity of Iago, cynically knowing only the worst, believing in the possibility only of what is basest. The brutal effectiveness of Shakespeare's thrust depends on its verbal economy; by comparison Boito's equivalent with its otiose parenthesis, 'Perdonate se il mio pensiero è fello', seems comically wordy; yet only by drawing out the sense of Shakespeare's lines could he enable Verdi as music dramatist to match the effect of the original play, if not to supersede it, by an ironical partial reprise of Ex. 208b twisted towards a hysterical minor cadence and followed by a fearsome outburst from the orchestra during which 'Otello with a movement of his arm but without loss of composure forces Desdemona away'. Not only is the dramatic impact overwhelming at the moment; there is the additional sense of a large-scale structure rounded off in the most logical way possible. The return to the original E major through a chromatic chord of E flat minor emphasizes the sense of false courtesy; likewise the fidgeting second violin part that starts after the words 'vo' fare ammenda' hints at the explosion to come as well as providing one of those elaborations of detail with which Verdi always liked to embellish his reprises. Even the inept parenthesis is effective as a 'reculer pour mieux sauter' being marked *a voce bassa parlando* and followed by 'quella vil cortigiana', which Otello is required to deliver at the top of his voice.

As the music winds down after Desdemona's exit Otello returns to the centre of the stage to deliver his longest solo in the opera, his nearest approach to a conventional aria ('Dio! mi potevi scagliar').

> Had it pleas'd heaven
> To try me with affliction; had they rain'd
> All kind of sores and shames on my bare head . . .
> I should have found in some place of my soul
> A drop of patience: but, alas! to make me
> The fixed figure for the time of scorn
> To point his slow unmoving finger at!
> Yet could I bear that too; well, very well;
> But there where I have garnered up my heart,
> . . . to be discarded thence!
> Or keep it as a cistern for foul toads
> To knot and gender in! – Turn thy complexion there,
> Patience, thou young and rose-lipp'd cherubim
> Ay, here, look grim as hell.†

* *Otello*, IV, ii, 89–91.

† *Ibid.*, IV, ii, 48 ff. Here again we have a piece of music for which any kind of description in theatrical terms would be pointless, not to say harmful. This monologue of Otello's can be regarded as divided into four parts, through which a single thought is developed and expressed in four different sentiments. *After the extremes of violent emotion aroused in the previous scene with Desdemona, Otello is in a state of general prostration. In this first period his voice is stifled, his words broken by pain and sobbing; complete immobility is*

Otello's speech, treated as a soliloquy, transforms the minor–major romanza to such an extent that the listener is no longer consciously aware of the design itself but only of the expressive use to which it is put. Otello, having spent himself in his encounter with Desdemona, is now in a state of numb misery. He can only murmur brokenly on a single note. His desolation is reflected in the orchestra which sinks wearily down a chromatic scale on to the tonic pedal; while the musical thought evolves through repetitions and developments of a forlorn triplet figure on the first violins (Ex. 213a).

213a

After the rich harmonic texture of the duet the hollowness of Otello's solo is especially telling – a unique expression of spiritual exhaustion, with even the triplet figure fettered by the unrelenting A flat of the basses and horns and producing unusual harmonic combinations in its effort to escape. The three statements of the downward scale of Ex. 213a at five-bar intervals act as a framework giving a tripartite division which matches the three-limbed structure of the major section to come; four bars after the second pedal note is dropped, the triplet figure wanders more freely and the voice begins to recover some of its energy. The cadence preparing the major-key section 'Ma, o pianto, o duol' (Ex. 213b) is especially original: a dominant ninth so unexpected as to give the effect of a thrill of pain. The relation of this new section to the first (E flat major–A flat minor) effectively deprives it of

---

necessary apart from some slight movement of the head: only at the words: 'È rassegnato al volere del ciel' Otello should raise his right arm towards heaven, and his voice should become firmer and more definite; at the same time he should rise to his feet and take two or three paces downstage. (See diagram.)

So to the second period, which needs to be sung more expressively as he remembers past joys: then Otello should come forward another couple of paces for the third period which begins with the words 'Tu alfin, Clemenza' and his mind should aspire to loftier thoughts; but then he should move rapidly and without any transition to the fourth period. Here he should break out in savage, fearful inexorable fury like a thunderbolt. Otello cries: 'Ah, dannazione . . . Pria confessi il delitto . . . e poscia muoia!' and his words should increase in power and violence. Disp. scen., pp. 62–3.

213b

any traditional sense of relief. Otello's lyricism is tense and coloured by minor and chromatic inflections (note the echo of Macbeth's dagger soliloquy at the cadence 'dov' io, giulivo, l'anima acqueto'). The orchestral epilogue against which Otello declaims the final lines of the monologue ('Tu alfin, Clemenza') strikes a note of almost Mozartian consolation for grief.

214

But the rising sequences break off as Otello, now resolved that Desdemona must die, becomes incoherent and hysterical ('Dannazione. . . . Pria confessi il delitto e poscia muoia!'). At this point Iago enters to announce that Cassio has arrived. 'O joy!' exclaims Otello and immediately afterwards, 'Horror, obscene torture!', the two reflected in a major 6/4 followed by a minor interrupted cadence in the minor; and in the orchestral busyness that follows, all of it built round an implied full close in E flat minor, Iago directs Otello to a hiding-place behind a pillar while he will trap Cassio into betraying himself.

Once again a closed form has been welded seamlessly into its context. The expected E flat minor cadence never arrives; instead the musical discourse runs aground on a diminished seventh extended over fourteen bars by varied figuration. Particularly striking are the last four with sustained horn notes in unison over hushed trombone triads.

With the 'handkerchief trio' Boito's libretto reverts to Shakespeare's ordering of events. After the powerful slow movement of Otello's transplanted monologue this terzettino takes on the quality of a light-fingered scherzo; it also allows Otello himself something approaching a respite since his interventions are few and not particularly taxing to his voice. The first two ideas show Iago at his most falsely suave and playful.

Iago begins by addressing Cassio as 'Captain', so leading him in due course to bring up the name of Desdemona through whom he hopes to have his rank restored. Otello duly takes note ('Ei la nomò'). Then, to Ex. 215b, Iago leads Cassio near the column where Otello is concealed and quizzes him about the persistent attentions of his inamorata, taking care to murmur the name 'Monna Bianca' too softly for Otello to overhear. Cassio falls in with Iago's jesting tone, and Otello naturally assumes that their badinage refers to Desdemona. For reasons of economy Bianca's entrance is eliminated; and it is Cassio himself who produces the handkerchief which Iago planted in his lodgings. He is naturally curious to know how it came to be there. Iago takes it from him and distracts Cassio's attention while he passes it behind his back, bringing it close enough to Otello for him to be able to recognize it – a piece of stage business that comes dangerously near to farce. Otello reacts appropriately; and the chatter continues until the sound of trumpets and the boom of the harbour cannon cause Cassio to retire precipitately. He has no wish to meet the ambassador in his present disgrace.

If we did not know from a letter to Ricordi of 1864 that Verdi admired the sonatas of Domenico Scarlatti* the main theme of this terzetto would be sufficient witness of the fact.†

216

The discourse is lightly scored and exquisitely agile, the displaced accents giving a piquant touch of rhythmic ambiguity. The form, classically balanced, is very much Verdi's own, a kind of scherzo and trio with a faint suggestion of the 'bar'. The first twenty-four bars are repeated identically in the orchestra as the dialogue proceeds, Otello's anguished comments ('L'empio trionfa . . .' and 'L'empio m'irride') forming a contrasted subject in the dominant minor. Then as Iago leads Cassio out of earshot a six-bar transition takes the music through A flat minor to C flat where it assumes an air of mystery, with piccolo tremolando and the strings reduced to four first violins, four second, two violas, two cellos and one bass. This is the trio within the scherzo: and is there not something here of the moment when Leporello finally brings himself to transmit Don Giovanni's invitation to the statue? (Ex. 217)

Much of the dialogue between Cassio and Iago is carried on in dumb show but with the occasional phrase audible so that we shall understand that Cassio is talking about

---

* Letter to Giulio Ricordi, 2.11.1864. *Carteggi Verdiani*, IV, p. 241.

† Part of a sketch for this terzetto has recently found its way into the Mary Flagler collection of the Pierpont Morgan Library, New York. Beginning at Cassio's words 'Son già di baci sazio' the orchestral part, set out on two staves, is no different to that of the finished result, though in places otherwise notated. The divergences are all in the voice parts, showing Verdi's preoccupation – unremitting since the days of *I Due Foscari* – for truthfulness of declamation and in this case rhythmic efficacy, since in its definitive form the dialogue trips more sharply off the tongue than in the sketch. The changes would seem to have been made at quite a late stage in the composition, for the original voice-parts can be seen erased or cancelled in the autograph.

217

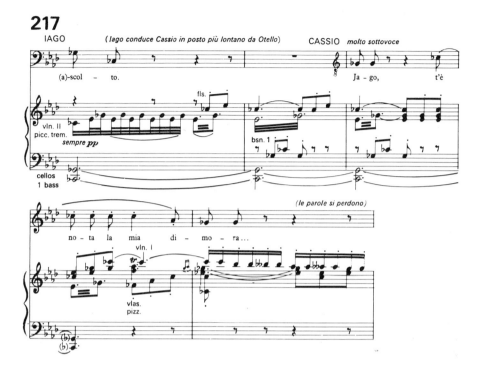

the handkerchief. Just as Iago asks him to produce it a reprise is reached, with the orchestra now at full strength and Ex. 216 fused with part of Ex. 217 in a continuous line, the first played on strings and bassoon beneath wind pulsations, the second overlapping it on flutes, oboes and clarinets. This is the kind of jewelled workmanship that will characterize *Falstaff*; and how unbelievably remote it seems from the world of the early Risorgimento operas!

Violas and cellos are again momentarily reduced to two as the music moves into a hushed C major transitional passage for Iago's pantomime with the handkerchief. Otello's outburst ('È quello . . . è quello') is set to an orchestral pattern suitably deriving from Ex. 216 but loaded with every negative device available – cross rhythms, unison writing which implies diminished seventh harmony, savage trilling figures such as marked Iago's 'Credo'. Now Otello believes he has the ultimate proof of his wife's infidelity. The scene is wound up with an allegro brillante ('Questa è una ragna dove il tuo cuor') whose purpose is musical rather than dramatic; a pattering 6/8 cabaletta (1880s style) with no Shakespearian counterpart, in which Iago continues to tease Cassio about the handkerchief (Ex. 218a); but it allows Cassio himself, lost as he is in admiration over the embroidery, to enjoy a brief moment of lyrical glory. His answer to Iago ('Miracolo vago') is set to a fine-spun sensitive melody with a luminous texture of widely spaced strings and horns (Ex. 218b). Already halfway to Fenton, Cassio reveals that 'daily beauty' that causes Otello to envy and Iago to hate him.

Ex. 218a is resumed and followed by twelve bars of coda which are brought to an abrupt end as the trumpet signal is heard in the distance. For the last time, and more

218a

218b

excitingly than ever, Verdi experiments with multi-directional fanfares.* The six
stage trumpets are divided into pairs, one sounding from the harbour, the other two
from the two wings of the castle. Distant cries of 'Evviva!' are heard. It is all straightforward C major against which the trumpets' sudden switch to B flat makes a very
striking effect, one possibly recalled unconsciously from the end of the second act of
Meyerbeer's *L'Etoile du Nord*. During the build-up of sonority Iago and Otello carry
on a grim conversation. Desdemona is clearly guilty and must be killed. But how?
Otello is for smothering her; meanwhile she must be brought into the presence of the
Venetian ambassador. Iago goes to fetch her, having in the meantime been named by
Otello as Cassio's successor (another touch which has nothing to do with
Shakespeare).†

At the entrance of Lodovico after a huge outburst of chorus and orchestra the stage
fanfares are transferred to the cornets, trumpets and trombones in the pit; and the
scene proceeds to conversational music in suave, dignified crotchet motion, as if to

* Twelve trumpets are specified by the production book. See *Disp. scen.*, p. 72.

† *Otello comes forward and takes up a position by a column. At the same time enter immediately the Chorus L.:
(Ladies, Gentlemen, Knights, Captains, etc., etc.); the tenors should range themselves on the right, the women and
the basses on the left; note that as there are only a few bars of orchestra the Chorus should be ready to execute this
movement so as to be already in position at the start of the ff 'Viva!' While the Chorus enter the 10 guards of honour
should mount the raised parapet backstage, together with the ensign, who should carry the banner.*

indicate that the dominant personality is that of Lodovico. Otello manages to be gracious and correct, kissing the seal that encloses the Senate's dispatch.* As he reads it Lodovico asks Iago, who has returned with Desdemona, why Cassio is not present. Iago replies that there has been an 'unkind breach' between him and Otello. 'But,' puts in Desdemona, 'he will perhaps soon be restored to favour.' This in a simple descending crotchet scale from mi to mi. 'Are you sure of that?' Otello mutters, still apparently reading the dispatch; and cellos and bassoon give out a distorted version of that same scale beneath tense harmonies on tremolando strings. So far so obvious; but when Iago repeats Desdemona's words to the same caressing downward scale we can at once understand the effect on Otello without his having to utter a word. As Desdemona continues to plead for Cassio, Otello first mutters ('Frenate dunque le labbra loquaci') then yells at her ('Demonio, taci!') to the consternation of all present. He has now finished reading the dispatch and orders the herald to send for Cassio. Lodovico meanwhile expresses his amazement and distress at Otello's behaviour ('Is this the noble Moor whom our full Senate/Call'd all in all sufficient? Is this the nature/ Whom passion could not shake?') Iago's reply, 'He is that he is; I may not breathe my censure' ('È quel ch'egli è) answers Lodovico's thematic fragment with the kind of dry, deliberate understatement used in the scene of Cassio's disgrace. The music rises in a crescendo as Cassio appears in answer to the summons and a sequence of five tutti chords preludes Otello's public reading of the dispatch. The Senate has recalled him to Venice and appointed Cassio to govern the island in his stead. His speech, delivered as one would expect over tremolando violins and violas,

From the left enter the 16 guards; they should range themselves backstage by the steps leading from the parapet; behind them 4 trumpeters who should take up a position on the steps themselves, on either side; they should pretend to play to the end of the fortissimo of the offstage trumpets, thereafter holding their instruments by their right sides; behind the trumpeters enter 4 Councillors, 2 Captains, 4 Venetian nobles, 4 Knights, 2 young Venetians, 2 gentlemen . . . behind them the Herald accompanying Lodovico who holds a parchment; behind Lodovico enter Roderigo; at the same time from the door R. enter Desdemona escorted by Iago; behind them Emilia; they cross the stage and take up a position L. These last three characters should be in position before the entry of Lodovico.

From the same door (R) enter 4 Knights of the Garter — 4 pages-in-waiting on Desdemona, 4 pages-in-waiting on Otello. . . . The Herald should come to a halt in the centre of the stage after having bowed to Lodovico. Disp. scen., pp. 72–3.

* Maurel credits Otello with 'une soumission presque enfantine envers les chefs de la République de Venise' (op. cit., p. 43).

is punctuated by savage asides to Desdemona. Roderigo signalizes his presence with a fine operatic cliché ('Infida sorte!'), Iago has a moment of blind fury ('Inferno e morte!'). Cassio kneels and expresses his thanks. ('Do you see, the villain exults?' says Otello, turning swiftly to Iago.) Lodovico begs Otello to comfort the sobbing Desdemona in one of those passages that seem to arise from youthful memories of *Don Giovanni*; and here the acciaccatura figure reverts to its original connotations (Ex. 219). Otello merely announces that they will set sail the next day. Then as the orchestra breaks into a wild fury of semiquavers he grasps Desdemona by the arm and hurls her to the ground ('A terra, e piangi!'). The orchestral passage that follows is especially impressive by reason of the Wagnerian spacing of the chords and the Wagnerian scoring in which the flute and piccolo are absent and the weight of sonority is concentrated in the middle range:

220

So begins the most elaborate finale concertato that Verdi ever wrote and to which he gave something of the character of an action piece.* For the moment, however, all must remain frozen in horror while Desdemona pours out her grief in a long solo comprising three quite separate melodic ideas each in a different key.

221a

* There is no need to weary the reader with Giulio Ricordi's extremely wordy directions for the acting of this concertato since they are mostly concerned with obviating that sense of stasis to which Verdi himself so strongly objected but which is to some extent inevitable in any piece of music in which time is suspended. *A stage director who has sufficient authority and who can explain the dramatic situation and the passions which well out from it can work miracles . . .' Disp. scen.*, p. 81. Essentially this is no more than a pious hope.

221b

221c

The first ('A terra! . . . sì . . . nel livido fango') contains a clear reminiscence of Ex. 185a – an ironical comment on her present plight.* Ex. 221b and c both belong to the tradition of lyrical transfiguration into which wronged Verdian heroines often escape (compare Giovanna and Violetta). The transition between them, however, is so heavily chromatic as to wipe from the listener's consciousness any sense of the relationship of the respective keys; he is aware only that the second idea lies higher than the first. Not until Ex. 221c moves into A flat does he have the feeling of having arrived home. As so often Verdi appears more interested in schemes of pitch rather than in the inter-relation of tonalities in the Schenkerian sense.

* That it also recalls the main theme of the finale of Mozart's 'Jupiter' symphony is equally true, and is a further instance of Verdi's drawing upon classical melodic figuration in his last two operas.

Desdemona's statement concluded, Emilia, Cassio, Roderigo and Lodovico all comment in unaccompanied four-part harmony:

222

In this kind of piece it hardly matters if all four are singing different words or that whereas Emilia and Lodovico are absorbed in Desdemona's plight, Cassio and Roderigo are entirely taken up with themselves. All four together with the chorus are mere onlookers and their function is to contribute their several strands to the musical fabric; and for this purpose each needs a characteristic strophe to play with. Ex. 221b returns with fuller scoring and a harmonic backing of soloists. Then with the arrival of a new motif (Ex. 223) the attention becomes focused on Iago, who has kept silent for so long, having been momentarily stunned by the substance of the dispatch. Now he moves swiftly into action, whispering to Otello to bestir himself, not to waste time in futile anger but to kill his wife at the earliest opportunity; he himself will take care of Cassio. This new idea with its triplets has a model in the third-act finale of *Don Carlos*; but the developing character is something new. All melodic parts are marked *cupo*, as befits a theme that moves through progressions that are at times almost Tristanesque. The first violins and cellos are required to play on their G strings.

This leads to a considerably varied reprise of Ex. 222 starting in B flat and modulating widely, with the divided chorus supplying a background of continuous semiquavers in the manner of *Stiffelio/Aroldo* (Act I finale). At the third phrase Desdemona takes over the melodic line, which wilts into a curious sequence of dying falls. Meanwhile Iago has turned his attention to Roderigo, his intended cat's-paw for the murder of Cassio. His opening taunt ('I sogni tuoi saranno in mar domani') stands out in high relief from the prevailing lyrical context, in which the choral semiquavers have now ceased. 'If anything were to happen to Cassio,' he hints, 'Otello and his wife would be forced to remain in Cyprus. A street brawl in the darkness would be sufficient . . .'.

By this time Ex. 223 has been resumed 'come un lamento' and is now being tossed between wind and strings in steeper sequences and with greater elaboration in the vocal lines. This in turn leads to a full-scale reprise of all three ideas of Ex. 221, each in its original key but with typical modifications. Taking its cue from the reprise of Elisabeth's 'Toi qui sus le néant', Ex. 221a starts with a rapping of cornet and, later, trumpet semiquavers. The melody, in faster time than before, is confined to chorus at first but with soloists reinforcing the second, dominant cadence. With that sure instinct for the just scale of a reprise, Verdi has saved half a bar by making the second

223

limb of the melody overlap with the first. This involves giving the second choral sopranos an important lead such as he would never have risked in earlier years.* At Ex. 221b the string texture takes on a new sheen with a pattern of demisemiquavers from the first violins arco combined with semiquavers on second violins and violas pizzicato. At the second phrase the demisemiquavers are extended to all the strings except basses. Then for the third and last time Ex. 223 appears, now as a sequential transition to the final culminating return of Ex. 221c sung by Desdemona, Emilia and Cassio in unison with thunderous triplets on trombones, bassoons and lower strings reinforcing the lines of Lodovico and Iago. It is at this point that Otello rouses himself, and the ensemble breaks off into a free 'scena'. Otello orders everyone to leave. As they prepare to obey, cries of 'Viva Otello!' are heard behind the scenes together with a 'fanfare théâtrale' of four trumpets and four trombones. To Desdemona's 'Mio sposo' Otello returns a terrifying 'Anima mia, ti maledico!' over a grotesque splash of orchestral colour – with trilling trumpets and cornets, a roll on the cymbal and a squeal from the flutes and piccolo. All leave in consternation except for Iago. As the long E minor tutti spends itself Otello exclaims, Stiffelio-like, in a

* For the first time in any Verdi opera the chorus is set out on four staves instead of the usual three.

downward arpeggio that he cannot escape himself. Scraps of remembered conversation pass before him in a montage of horror that begins softly, rises to a climax and then dies away into incoherent cries as Otello faints. Over a low villainous sustained note on trombones and bassoon Iago gloats over his handiwork ('Il mio velen lavora') while the fanfares continue and the crowds shout 'Evviva Otello!' and 'Gloria al Leon di Venezia!' 'Who shall prevent me spurning his forehead with my heel?' Iago asks rhetorically as he surveys the recumbent Moor. His question, 'Chi può vietar che questa fronte prema col mio tallone!', seems a little verbose for the occasion; but it enables him to repeat almost identically the phrase in Act I in which he prayed that Otello might be drowned. The fanfares and shouts mount towards a triumphant C major cadence with something of the same dramatic irony as the acclamations of Escamillo in the final bars of *Carmen*. 'Here is the lion!' cries Iago, and the curtain falls to a succession of brutal, hammered chords and a Tchaikovskian cadence – F flat major to C.

The curtain to Act III, which had caused both composer and librettist so much heart-searchings, is magnificent and a fitting crown to an act which has the architectonic power and thematic variety of a symphony. In fact it might be asked whether in the concertato the music does not overweight the action, and whether the intention of combining movement with lyrical contemplation was realized better in theory than in practice. Does Iago stand out in sufficient relief as he spurs Otello and Roderigo to further activity? Many productions at this point make a cut of seventy-six bars from the second statement of Ex. 221b to the final reprise of Ex. 223, which tells its own story. That Verdi himself may not have been entirely convinced will appear in due course.

ACT IV

Scene: Desdemona's bedroom. A bed, prie-Dieu, table, looking-glass, chairs.
A lighted lamp hangs in front of the image of the Madonna, which is above the
*prie-Dieu. Door to the left. A lighted candle on the table. Night.**

The last act of *Otello* begins with a prolonged moment of repose. The prelude and first scene (that is, up to Emilia's exit) is one of the most remarkable feats of harmonic and instrumental colouring in all opera. It is as though Verdi were determined to outdo Rossini's 'Nessun maggior dolore' in creating that atmosphere of indefinable sadness on which the scene depends. The harmonic palette with its prevailing minor tonality and piquant modal inflexions stems from a French rather than Italian tradition. As always the scoring is inseparable from the harmonic idea. The opening prelude is for woodwind and horns. Replacing second oboe, the cor anglais, at its

---

* The only two props of any significance added by the production book are a chest of drawers from which Emilia will take Desdemona's wedding dress and on which Otello will lay his scimitar, and a fine chandelier of wrought iron in Moorish style with coloured glass; it hangs from the ceiling by a chain of ornaments, also of wrought iron and with a cord of darkish colour; it is lighted. Great importance, however, is attached to the colour scheme of the bedroom. *Although the room should be richly appointed and elegant in its general effect, it should have an air of tranquillity and almost of sadness; the furniture should be of seasoned oak, carved and with panelling cut in squares; some of the decorations should be of gold. The pillows, the chairs, the couch, the coverlet and the curtains of the bed should be of blue-green plush. On the bed there should be a pillow with a pillow-case of white cloth with lace embroidery. Disp. scen.*, pp. 86–7.

most mournful and desolate, dominates the picture. Three important motifs appear at the outset, starkly juxtaposed.

224

The first (*x*) anticipates the opening line of Desdemona's 'Willow Song'. But why in C sharp minor when the song itself is rooted in F sharp minor? Because the cor anglais could not play it effectively in Desdemona's key. Tonal consistency is therefore sacrificed to considerations of emotional colour, though without any detriment to the music as a whole. One can only repeat that conventional rules about key weighed little with Verdi. The second motif (*y*) is the main vehicle for such development as takes place during the scene. The third (*z*) merely establishes an atmosphere of gloom and foreboding. The musical discourse, winding on in strands of two, three and four parts, never coalescing into a definite theme, has an eerie quality, far more telling than the self-consciously ghostly gallows-prelude in *Un Ballo in maschera*. Three bars of lower strings in unison raise the curtain on Desdemona and Emilia. As usual the recitative is interspersed with fragments from the prelude, but Desdemona can never keep to mere declamation for long; and her lyrical nature asserts itself with the phrase in which she asks for her wedding dress to be laid out – an arpeggio climb in C sharp minor followed by a chromatic descent, taken from bars 23–4 of the prelude ('Distendi sul mio letto la mia candida veste nuziale'); then with an independent arioso ('Se pria di te morir dovessi'), whose syncopations and offbeat accents suggest a flood of suppressed tears.

> If I do die before thee, prithee shroud me
> In one of those same sheets.*

Then 'sitting down mechanically before the looking-glass' she returns to recitative, spoken in a weary monotone:

> My mother had a maid call'd Barbary.
> She was in love, and he she lov'd prov'd mad,
> And did forsake her . . .†

Her introduction to the 'Willow Song' brings in two more significant motifs: the first a mere swaying of two chords, as it might be the poor maid rocking herself to and fro in listless grief, the second a ritornello suitable to a song, which, however, it may apply to Desdemona's condition, is none the less in inverted commas. The major tonality serves only to enhance its pathos. (Ex. 225a, b)

Herein lies the explanation of the very individual design of Verdi's 'Willow Song'. It is not, like Rossini's, or like Verdi's own 'Non so le tetre immagini' from *Il Corsaro*, a straightforward interpolated number, any more than is Iago's drinking song. It

---

* *Othello*, IV, iii, 23–4.
† *Ibid.*, 25–7.

225a

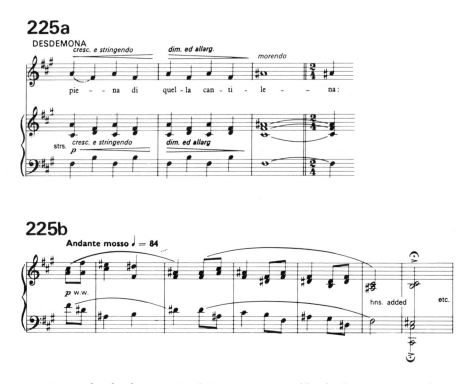

225b

contains two levels of perspective.* One is represented by the first two verses of Barbary's song, quoted without comment, apart from the recitative aside corresponding to Shakespeare's 'Prithee hie thee; he'll come anon'. In the third verse, however, Boito, taking his cue from Shakespeare's 'Nay, that's not next', makes Desdemona increasingly inconsequent as she broods on Barbary's case, half applying it to her own. So what begins as a musical episode dissolves into an association of motifs from the main melody, interspersed with fragments of Ex. 225a and b, and with one

---

* The production book prescribes the following moves for Desdemona and Emilia throughout the 'Willow Song':

'Mi disciogli le chiome'

Desdemona turns slightly towards Emilia, who passes behind her and, removing a kind of brooch which binds her mistress's hair, allows it to cascade upon her shoulders; she puts the brooch away in a jewel box.

At the ritornello of the 'Willow Song' Desdemona clasps her hands, rests her elbows on the little table and so supports her head; she moves from this position as she says, 'Salce.' Emilia passes R. behind the table and takes up a listening attitude.

'Cantiamo'

Desdemona rises to her feet but without moving away from the chair; and as she finishes the first part, 'Sarà la mia ghirlanda', she resumes her seat almost mechanically.

'Scendean l'augelli a vol'

She raises her left arm as though indicating the flight of the birds, gradually lowers it, keeping it outstretched.

'E gli occhi suoi'

She remains motionless with an expression of extreme sorrow: then suddenly her gaze alights upon a ring which she wears on her finger; she removes it, and turning R., hands it to Emilia saying, 'Riponi quest'anello.' Emilia puts it away in the casket.

graphic interruption ('Ascolta . . . odo un lamento') where Desdemona mistakes a gust of wind for the sound of somebody knocking at the door. (In the opera, as distinct from the play, she seems to hear a groan as well – one of the many details of this act taken over from Rossini's tragedy.) This third section is neither a development nor a return to free scena music; despite the pauses, the fragmentation of phrase and the apparent breakings-off, the lyrical continuity is perfect. The 'Willow Song', then, presents a variety of bar-form with *a1* and *a2* – the song itself – balanced by a larger and more complex *b* in which the musical content of the song is broken up and diversified by the expression of Desdemona's personal feelings.

In an article already mentioned Edward Dannreuther, staunch champion of Wagner but not unsympathetic to the best of the Italian tradition, expresses a preference for Rossini's 'Willow Song' over Verdi's, which he finds by comparison bizarre and rather contrived.* Such a judgement only shows how far the mature Verdi was capable of outstripping the conservative tastes of his time. The most salient feature of the song ('Piangea cantando nell'erma landa') is its total liberation from all the conventional trammels in which Verdian melody had been born and reared. The background of symmetry seems as remote as in Berlioz; passages of harmony and unison alternate according to no traditional scheme but with complete sureness of touch. Within the first melodic sentence *a* the faintly exotic F sharp–E sharp–C

'*Povera Barbara*'

She rises to her feet with an air of grief; then she comes downstage two or three paces, saying with great simplicity, '*Solea la storia*' . . . *Emilia moves slightly L.*

Just as she is about to finish the song she seems to hear a groan, and suddenly stops short; turning towards Emilia she makes a sign of listening.

'*Odo un lamento*'

Alarmed, she takes a couple of paces backstage, while Emilia also moves in the same direction, then she suddenly turns to speak. Desdemona says to her, '*Be silent,*' *then, troubled once more, points to the door L. and cries out:* '*Chi batte a quella porta?*'

Emilia goes hurriedly to the door, then turns and reassures Desdemona as she replies, '*È il vento.*'

Desdemona recovers her calm; and turning towards the audience comes forward slowly for a couple of paces, then she resumes her former position to finish the song: Emilia should have moved a little nearer to her.

'*Salce! Salce! Salce!*'

This last lament should be sung with a strange, mournful voice that seems to come from a distance; then Desdemona should remain motionless for a moment; then as though to dispel such gloomy thoughts she pulls herself together, turns to Emilia and says to her affectionately: '*Emilia, addio.*'

'*Come m'ardon le ciglia!*'

She covers her eyes with one hand; she remains thoughtful, adding with great sadness: '*È presagio di pianto.*' '*Buona notte.*'

She speaks with decision, making a gesture of salutation to Emilia; Emilia returns the salutation and moves slowly and sadly towards the door L.

Seeing Emilia go, Desdemona recalls her with the passionate cry: '*Ah! Emilia!*' *and takes two steps towards her. Emilia halts, turns and runs to Desdemona, who enfolds her in an affectionate embrace, then dismisses her with a kiss on the forehead. These movements should be calculated so that the embrace takes place exactly on the second* '*Emilia, addio.*' *Disp. scen., pp. 89–91. See also U. Pesci, 'Le prove dell' Otello', in Interviste e Incontri con Verdi,* ed. M. Conati (Milan, 1980), pp. 178–9.

A manuscript arrangement for voice and piano of the 'Willow Song' made by Michele Saladino prior to the publication of his vocal score shows interesting melodic variants and corrections clearly representing an earlier stage in its composition. The score is in the Ricordi archives and contains annotations by Verdi himself.

* *Oxford History of Music*, VI (London, 1932), 2nd edition, pp. 64–5.

sharp is followed after three bars by the modally inflected F sharp–E natural–C sharp at the lower octave. The refrain 'O salce, salce, salce' is not only unharmonized but impossible to harmonize without making musical nonsense. At the repetition of Ex. 224 ('Sedea chinando sul sen la testa') the final C sharp is shortened by a bar, and joined by a portamento to the 'Salce' refrain, which by way of compensation is extended by a final echo on the cor anglais. The greatest emphasis – again unobtrusive – is reserved for the third limb ('Cantiamo, cantiamo'), a mere phrase of four bars beginning with a 6/4 chord and ending with an interrupted cadence. It will be balanced by a somewhat similar phrase at the climax of *b* ('Povera Barbara!'). The conclusion of the verse ('Il salce funebre sarà la mia ghirlanda') is prolonged by a 3/4 bar whose extra beat seems to arise from the implications of the melody itself. You could not finish it in any other way.

A busier accompaniment is carried by *a2* with light scales in the lower strings, trills and quasi-tremolandos on flutes, sustained notes on piccolo and cor anglais – all somewhat in the manner of Aida's 'O patria mia'. The resemblance between the two pieces is partly explained by their common parent: Inés's romance ('Adieu, mon doux rivage') from Meyerbeer's *L'Africaine*. The kinship is particularly marked in the present piece as a comparison of Ex 224 (*x*) with the first phrase of Meyerbeer's romance will show.

226

Meyerbeer : L'AFRICAINE

Similar filigree writing on flutes and piccolo makes possible an illustrative point at the start of *b* ('Scendean l'augelli a vol dai rami cupi') where the birds can be heard twittering as they fly down. Much of this episode is sited rather unexpectedly in G sharp minor, two keys removed from the tonic; how much more desolating as a result is the final return to F sharp minor with 'Egli era nato per la sua gloria, io per amar' – Boito's happy if somewhat Puccinian substitution for Shakespeare's brutally cynical 'If I court more women, you'll couch with more men', which his chaste Desdemona quotes without a hint of embarrassment.

The most astonishing stroke of all is reserved for the coda, set in F sharp major and based on the ritornello, Ex. 225b. 'Mine eyes do itch. Doth that bode weeping?' This to subdued recitative against fragments of the orchestra melody. The clarinet recalls the 'Salce' refrain with a mere sustained D natural, after which Desdemona bids Emilia goodnight (see Ex. 229).

This tremendous outburst, as moving as it is unexpected, is the last transfigured remnant of the cabaletta, purged of all show and mechanical repetition, reduced to a moment of emotional truth. Paradoxically it justifies the cabaletta in retrospect by revealing one of its reasons for existing: the need to release pent-up emotion. But more remarkable still is the preparation: four F sharp major common chords in root

227

position, seemingly final yet 'voiced' in such a way as to suggest a subtle sense of propulsion. The divided cello minims reach down to C sharp below the bass stave; only the double basses playing pizzicato give out the fundamental note. By slightly underweighting the low F sharp and stressing the dominant above it Verdi gives to the chord a subliminal hint of a 6/4. It is the end and at the same time not the end; as a result Desdemona's 'Ah Emilia, addio', though unexpected, is entirely logical.

Emilia leaves, and a sixteen-bar transition based on Ex. 224 (γ) above a chromatic bass leads into A flat major and an 'Ave Maria', another feature borrowed from Rossini's opera and for a good reason. The entrance of Otello cannot follow the 'Willow Song', nor does it in Shakespeare's play; the two scenes are separated by one in which Cassio is wounded and Roderigo killed. A prayer for Desdemona has an obvious advantage in that it disperses the clouds of the previous scene, so enabling Otello to make his sinister appearance against a clear sky. The orchestral palette is accordingly changed to one of muted strings alone, undisturbed by the harsh cor anglais; and the haunted atmosphere of the 'Willow Song' gives way to an ethereal tranquillity with echoes of Liszt in his religioso mood:

228

Desdemona murmurs a vernacular version of the Latin prayer in a low monotone against a soft cushion of sustaining strings. Then as she adds her personal prayer for the weak, the afflicted and the innocent she moves into a periodic melody – bipartite like any cantabile of Donizetti's day (*a*1–*a*2–*b*–*a*3); but the variety of stress within the mainly three-bar phrases takes away any suggestion of formality. The melody too, with its abundance of conjunct motion, has a hint of plainsong about it.

229

A small but memorable idea occurs where the three-bar pattern finally gives way to two-bar regularity. Here the acciaccatura figure on violas is a sob transfigured into a tranquil memory.

230

A cadential phrase of elliptical progressions brings the melody to an end. Desdemona remains 'kneeling with forehead pressed against the prie-Dieu, as mentally she repeats the prayer of which only the first and the last words are audible'. The orchestral postlude, consisting of Ex. 228 and Ex. 230 juxtaposed forms a thumbnail resumé of her thoughts. At the end it rises like incense to the upper ether of sound. Desdemona rises and retires to bed.

Hardly have the last notes died away when Otello makes his presence felt with a famous passage on muted double basses, so remarkable in its effect that Richard Strauss thought fit to incorporate it into his edition of Berlioz's treatise on orchestration. As three-string double basses were still in use in many Italian theatres Verdi specified that only those instruments with the additional string were to play at this point; there were to be no unwanted higher octaves. Again credit must be given where it is due. Rossini also marked Otello's entrance with an ominous string figure; it is only Verdi's infinitely more powerful realization of a similar idea that makes Rossini's sound like a gesture from one of Haydn's more humorous symphonies. (Ex. 231a, b)

231a

Rossini : OTELLO

231b

The stage directions at this point are very detailed even in the score. Otello appears on the threshold of a secret door . . . he comes forward . . . he lays a scimitar on the table (this at *x* in Ex. 231b)* and stops in front of the torch undecided whether or not to put it out. . . . He looks at Desdemona . . . he extinguishes the light.' This is as near as Boito and Verdi felt able to come to Shakespeare's:

> Put out the light, and then put out the light.
> If I quench thee, thou flaming minister
> I can again thy former light restore
> Should I repent me; but once put out thine
> Thou cunning pattern of excelling nature,
> I know not where is that Promethean heat
> That can thy light relume.†

To read all this into the double bass line is to run the risk of emulating Sheridan's Puff in the significance that he attributed to Lord Burghley's nod. Yet the expression here is intense if not articulate. As the melodic line tumbles into semiquavers‡ Otello 'makes a movement of rage . . . he approaches the bed . . . he stops [*here a tutti full close*]. He raises the curtain and contemplates for a long while the sleeping Desdemona'. A motif derived from the opening bars of Ex. 231b, its last three notes twice repeated with an affect of infinite longing, steals in on cor anglais and bassoon against tremolando strings – a minor variant on the Grail motif from *Parsifal*. (Ex. 232)

This turns out to be a preparation for the most important melody in the opera, the motif of the Kiss (Ex. 191); and indeed Otello kisses the sleeping Desdemona at the

* *On the chest of drawers. Disp. scen.*, p. 94.

† *Othello*, V, ii, 8–14.

‡ See *Disp. scen.*, pp. 94–6, for detailed instructions for Otello's movements with relevant musical quotations.

232

points where in the love duet from Act I he had sung the words: 'Un bacio . . . un bacio ancora . . . un'altro bacio.' But Desdemona wakes up before the last tender phrase can be completed; so the C major which should have been the springboard for a return to E turns into an ominous dominant of F minor. From here on the opera proceeds rapidly towards the catastrophe, carried mostly on repetitions and developments of (*x*) in Ex. 231b. First it is worked into a broad but rapid 3/2 with offbeat sustaining notes from the brass – an effect so unusual in Verdi as to deserve quotation.

233

After nine bars, including a passage of recitative 'senza misura' ('have you pray'd tonight, Desdemona?'), the time reverts to 4/4 as Otello questions his wife about any sin she may have committed. Desdemona has a moment of panic conveyed in chattering semiquaver bi-chords on strings and woodwind when she realizes that Otello means to kill her. She asks for Cassio, who will vindicate her. 'Dead,' Otello replies; the music freezes to a solitary low clarinet note.* 'Then I am lost and he betray'd!' 'O strumpet, weep'st thou for him to my face?' ('E pianger l'osi?' is Boito's more decorous paraphrase.) A swift crescendo in two stages with the savage gesture (*x*) from Ex. 231b worked into continuous patterns leads to the murder. Desdemona screams over a diminished seventh outburst 'con tutta forza', in which the sense of shock is immeasurably increased by the sudden switch into triplet motion.

What follows is inevitably recitative and scena music designed to pass over the various revelations as quickly as possible and so arrive at the denouement. Emilia knocks and is admitted; she tells how Cassio has killed Roderigo in a brawl, he himself escaping unhurt (not as in Shakespeare, where it is Iago who kills Roderigo and wounds Cassio, though not mortally). Desdemona returning for a moment to consciousness is allowed a few broken lyrical phrases to melting string harmonies;

* Winton Dean associates this effect with Bizet's *Carmen*, though it is not uncommon in Verdi. See 'Verdi's *Otello* a Shakespearean masterpiece', in *Shakespeare Survey* (London, 1964), p. 96.

after which the music returns to the baldest, most summary declamation in another exchange between Otello and Emilia. Though it is not marked as recitative Verdi must have thought of it as such, since he marks the passage *Più presto possibile senza appoggiature*, even though by the 1880s recitatives were no longer modified by singers at will. Lodovico, Cassio and Iago enter, and after them Montano with armed followers. As one revelation follows another – musically a matter of sweeping scales, hammered chords and arpeggios – Iago remains cool and offhand. Unlike his Shakespearian counterpart he does not murder his wife; nor is he arrested; he merely slips away with the soldiers in pursuit.* Likewise no incriminating letter is found on Roderigo's body; instead he has made a dying confession. Such divergencies from the original are unimportant (the disappearance of Iago is even an advantage). True, Otello appears at one point to lapse into a fine old librettist's cliché ('E il ciel non ha più fulmini?'), but for this Boito cannot be blamed; the sentiments are Shakespeare's ('Are there no stones in heaven but what serve for the thunder?'). Montano, Cassio and Lodovico try to disarm him; but he replies with the noble speech 'Be not afraid though you do see me weapon'd' ('Niun mi tema'); once again note a magical use of the full orchestra pianissimo, with breath-pauses that make each chord sound like the tolling of a bell.

234

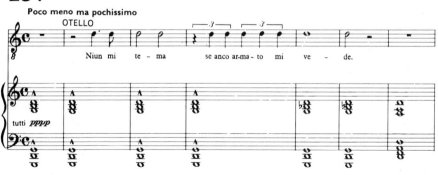

Though occasionally performed as an excerpt, Otello's death speech is in no sense an aria, but a highly charged arioso-recitative in the tradition of *Macbeth* and *Rigoletto*. Otello's sense of annihilation is summed up in the phrase 'Gloria . . . Otello fu' – a blaze of woodwind and brass followed by a void, then the faint thud of double bass and bass drum, and a hollow unison on low clarinet, bassoon and horn. To a drooping Tristanesque phrase on the oboe with wind harmonies Otello turns his attention to Desdemona. For Shakespeare's magnificent, ranting poetry Verdi gives us a restrained utterance that is unbearably moving. 'In this single line of music,' Toye writes, 'half sung, half sobbed, without accompaniment of any kind, lies the kernel of the whole tragedy.'† (Ex. 235‡)

---

* *Iago cries, 'No!' draws his sword and brandishes it wildly to prevent anyone from approaching him; at the same time he takes a leap, darts between the two guards and escapes through the door. Disp. scen., pp. 105–6.*

† Toye, p. 426.

‡ This cadence is a notable example of the type which up to 1840 or thereabouts would automatically have carried an appoggiatura. Since the earlier instruction *Più presto possibile senza appoggiature* could be taken to imply that this ornament was still in vogue for contemporary music, ought we to consider the

235

At the words 'Cold . . . even like thy chastity' ('Fredda come la casta tua vita') the timpani begin a pattern of five-note death figures; while the mention of heaven ('in cielo assorta') prompts a gesture of high triplets on the three flutes — both well-worn devices from which even after so many years Verdi can derive something new. 'Desdemona, Desdemona; Ah morta, morta, morta' is again unaccompanied — an inconclusive phrase of 'sounds almost without key', as Verdi put it.* The low trombones sound a warning. Otello furtively draws a dagger from his clothing ('Ho un'arma ancor') and stabs himself before anyone can restrain him.

> I kissed thee ere I kill'd thee; no way but this —
> Killing myself, to die upon a kiss.†

Ex. 232 sounds once more, the melody reinforced by a clarinet; and as before it leads to Ex. 191 with slightly altered scoring. Now Otello repeats the words of the love duet 'Un bacio . . . un bacio ancora . . . un altro bacio', but the final syllable fails in a gasp. A short orchestral decrescendo with the bass sonorities heavily accentuated brings down the curtain. That the last cadence of all should have something striking in reserve might have been taken for granted; over a tonic pedal of E a sequence of descending chords (C major–A minor–F major) produces a variety of plagal cadence wholly Lisztian in its boldness.

---

possibility of inserting it here? Happily this is one of the rare musicological problems that can be solved outright. In his last years Tamagno made a recording of Otello's death scene (G.DS 100) in which he sings the cadence precisely as written. It would be interesting to know whether the gruesome gasps and groans with which he embroiders the last cadence of all also carry the composer's authority. . . .

* Letter to Giulio Ricordi, 21.1.1888. Abbiati, IV, p. 356.   † *Othello*, V, ii; 359–60.

236

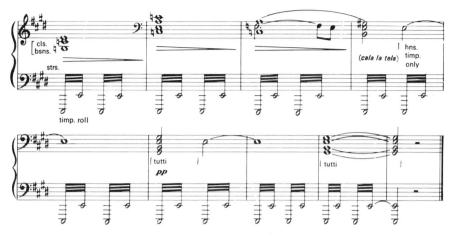

Théâtre de l'Opéra, Paris, 1894

Despite Verdi's repeated declaration that the Opéra was no place for *Otello* a production there was already in view in the last months of 1886, and Boito was preparing the French translation with du Locle. 'A good idea to have the ballet in the second act,' Verdi wrote to Boito, 'and it will make them happy. But of course the ballet must serve only for the Opéra: everywhere else *Otello* must remain as it is now.'* And when Giulio Ricordi, who intended for the first time to print a full score as well as the usual reduction for piano, asked to be sent the ballet that Verdi was composing for Paris, so that it could be included with the rest of the music, he received a very irritable reply. 'As for the ballet, or rather divertissement, why print it at all? It's a weak concession (*lâcheté*) which authors make to the Opéra and wrongly; but artistically speaking it's a monstrosity. In the heat of the action to interrupt with a ballet?!!! The opera should stand as it is; pointless therefore to print the ballet.' What was still more pertinent was that he had not yet written it, though Ricordi had been assiduous in providing him with period models. 'Those wretched dances from the seventeenth century are not the slightest use to me,' he went on. 'However, there should be something a little nearer our own time. What were the sarabandes, the gavottes, the gigues like? Could you find me some? They could be found in Corelli but they're too workmanlike and sophisticated. . . . They've never been any use for ballet.'† Ricordi enlisted the help of the musicologist Oscar Chilesotti, who sent Verdi two galliards each by an obscure Renaissance composer. But in the meantime the failure, or unwillingness, of the Directors of the Opéra to find an adequate Desdemona caused Verdi to break off negotiations with them; and nothing further was done until the beginning of 1894 when Verdi was approached with an especially attractive proposition: *Otello* at the Opéra followed by *Falstaff* at the Opéra Comique. There were still some difficulties to be overcome, especially as regards the translation, which Gailhard, the Director, had criticized in certain respects. He had

---

* Letter to Boito, 29.10.1886. *Carteggio Verdi–Boito*, I, pp. 116–17.
† Letter to Giulio Ricordi, 25.3.1887. Abbiati, IV, p. 329.

gone so far as to commission someone else to rewrite the offending passages. Boito, however, smoothed out the difficulty with his usual tact, and persuaded Verdi, who had wished to defer the performance until the following year, to consent to its being given in October 1894, provided that he had the opportunity of hearing Mme Caron, the proposed Desdemona, beforehand.*

So in July and August of that year the hunt for ballet music was resumed. To judge from the type of music required we may assume that poet and composer had given up their idea of making the ballet a pendant to the choruses in honour of Desdemona and had decided on its present position. Ricordi's own practical suggestion that Verdi should search for it in the library of his own head was not well received. 'If nothing can be found I shall do nothing,' he wrote. 'Meanwhile one can look and see if there's anything in the *Thesaurus Harmonicus* of Besardo. . . . And then where's that book *Lutenists of the Sixteenth Century* by Chilesotti? Anyway if no one helps me I shall do nothing. P.S. And where can I find Venetian songs and dances?'†

Accordingly the net was cast wide. Verdi himself made inquiries of Riccardo Gandolfi, librarian of the Florence Conservatoire, concerning the *Canto del Conte Ugolino*, an early instance of the 'stile rappresentativo' by Vincenzo Galilei, father of the astronomer, but was informed that the piece was lost – to musicologists it was no more than a name. Meanwhile Ricordi sent, and induced others to send, various specimens of folk music to Verdi, now staying at Montecatini as he usually did during the height of the summer. All to no avail. 'I've received the Greek melodies. There is nothing there that will do for me, though they're interesting even if one doesn't realize they're from Greece or the Orient. . . . Now I want something Venetian as well as the furlana. There's something of Bizet's but it isn't enough. . . .'‡ Next day: 'What wretched stuff, that music that Tebaldini has sent! Even in those days there must have been something better. We should need something from a later age. Go on looking! But all these savants don't seem to know any more of the matter than I do. Well then what's the point of being a savant? It's not worth the trouble. Meanwhile send me a nice furlana; there should also be a farandole by Bizet. Coraggio, coraggio!'§

Two days later:

Alas, alas, I'm half in despair. I've received the furlana and the farandole. There's nothing for me and I just don't understand it. Are there really no Venetian folk songs even from nearer the present day? Anyway, what I need is:
    Something Turkish
    Something Greek-Cypriot
    Something Venetian
If it can't be found, rather than write something of no consequence it's better to do nothing. Add to this the trouble it's going to cost me, the heat of the season and, let me admit it, the small inclination I have for work, and I think that really the best thing to do would be to write to Gailhard that he should think of something else and give up the ballet, or . . . I was going to say let him get

* See letter from Boito, 11.5.1894. *Carteggi Verdiani*, IV, p. 136.
† Letter to Giulio Ricordi, 12.6.1894. Abbiati, IV, p. 547.
‡ Letter to Giulio Ricordi, 9.7.1894. *Ibid.*, p. 549.
§ Letter to Giulio Ricordi, 10.7.1894. *Ibid.*

somebody else to write it. . . . No, not that! Well then let's think about it a bit more. You must help me to find something; search out, make inquiries, and if nothing comes of it we shall write to Gailhard as I have suggested.*

Ricordi next plied the composer with national anthems from all over the world. 'I've gone ahead and examined all the anthems,' Verdi wrote back. 'They're all modern; the oldest is Haydn's and it's also the most beautiful. So nothing at all there for me. Now that I remember it, Félicien David in Le Désert must have written something of the sort that I'm looking for – either a Hymn to Allah or Song of the Muezzin. Get someone to hunt it out and if it exists send it to me even on a single sheet.'† Ricordi did so and the ice was miraculously broken. In asking for music by Bizet (the farandole is presumably that from L'Arlésienne) it is hard to believe that Verdi meant to plagiarize it or quote it literally; but that is in effect what he did with the prayer to Allah from David's symphonic ode which had made such an impression on him just half a century earlier. The six bars of the ballet marked 'Invocation à Allah' are a direct orchestral transcription of a melody given by David to his tenor soloist.‡ Did he imagine it to be traditional and therefore common property? And was he perhaps right?§

Verdi sent off the ballet to Ricordi on 21 August with instructions that it be dispatched immediately to Gailhard to be studied by the Maître de Ballet in good time so that he should not devise mass-movements during the soft passages or have only a few people dancing during the loud ones. In his accompanying note he allowed himself a dig at all the musicologists who had failed to help him. 'Your doctors of music have not been able to find me anything . . . but I've found a Greek song dating from 5000 years before Christ. If the world didn't exist yet, so much the worse for the world. Then I found a Muranese that was composed 2000 years ago for a war that took place between Venice and Murano, and the Muranese won. It doesn't matter if Venice didn't yet exist. . . .'¶ The parcel also contained a detailed scenario:

(5 minutes and 59 seconds)
Having in mind the splendid scene with columns in the third act I've thought fit to compose the music as follows: straightaway at the start of the fanfares a group of Turkish slaves should appear, who dance reluctantly and with bad grace because they are slaves.

However, at the end of this first movement on hearing the Canzone Araba they liven up gradually and end by dancing wildly.

At the Invocation to Allah all prostrate themselves on the ground. . . . At this

---

* Letter to Giulio Ricordi, 12.7.1894. Ibid., pp. 549–50.

† Letter to Giulio Ricordi, 26.7.1894. Ibid., p. 550.

‡ Attention was first drawn to this fact by A. Porter in his 'Verdi's ballet music and La Peregrina', in Atti del IIº Congresso del I.S.V., p. 366.

§ There are many cases in the nineteenth century to say nothing of the eighteenth in which a greater composer has helped himself without scruple to a folk-melody, real or imitation, that has been published by a lesser one. The so called 'Thème slave variée' in Delibes's Coppélia was taken from Moniuzsko's Echos de Pologne. The Habanera from Carmen is an improved version of Yradier's 'El Arreglito, ou la promesse de mariage'. Richard Strauss nearer our own time quoted Luigi Denza's 'Funiculì, funicolà' in his Aus Italien under the impression that it was a genuine folk-tune.

¶ Letter to Giulio Ricordi, 21.8.1894. Abbiati, IV, pp. 551–2.

moment there appears among the columns a group of beautiful young Greek girls
and four bars later another group; they come forward and at the thirteenth bar
join in a dance that is tranquil, aristocratic, classical. . . .

There follows at once the Muranese, allegro vivace 6/8; here a group of
Venetian men and girls should come forward through the columns . . . after eight
bars another group. At the fortissimo (bar 18) they should arrive downstage and
begin dancing.

After the fortissimo there is a passage in F sharp of very lightly scored music
which should be danced by only two people. The melody is repeated with
heavier scoring and then all the Venetians should join in. The first 6/8 melody is
resumed and there I should like to see another group of Venetians appear
backstage.

The dance of the Canto Guerriero should be performed by men only. The first
tune is taken up again and here all the Venetians can join the dance; then at the più
mosso Venetians, Turks, Greeks and the whole lot can dance. . . . Amen.*

Verdi went to Paris in mid-September to direct some of the rehearsals. The première
took place on 12 October and was as successful as he could have wished. No company,
however, has performed the Paris version in recent times,† though the ballet music has
been recorded separately more than once. Certainly the dances contribute nothing to
the dramatic impact; and there is surely something naïf about the view that the
arrival of ambassadors from Venice should require a display of this kind from the
city's island colony. None the less the ballet is inventive, well constructed, colourful
and above all brief. Verdi's timing is not far short of the mark. The ballet does not
begin at the first fanfare, as Verdi had originally indicated, but at the moment when
Iago leaves to fetch Desdemona. In the French version Otello follows him. Then as
trumpets again sound outside, pages appear, draw back the curtains which up to this
point have formed the backcloth and reveal a vast hall. 'Lords and Ladies, drawn
by the fanfares, cross the galleries to see the Ambassador disembark.' As before the
fourth trumpet adds a B flat to the root of the C major chord, which abruptly changes

237

* See Gatti, II, p. 479.
† See, however, p. 412.

to A major 2/4. So begins the Danse Turque, an ingenious little piece of pseudo-Orientalism in the manner of the Bacchanale from *Samson et Dalila* with augmented intervals between the second and third, and the sixth and seventh degrees of the minor scale. Oboe and piccolo trace the melody over a percussion accompaniment similar to that of Grieg's Arabian Dance. (Ex. 237)

The so-called 'Danse arabe' (Ex. 238a) forms the major complement to the above; it is in the form of a continuous crescendo and allows little time for the dancers to pass from listlessness to wild abandon: nor indeed do the directions in the score specify where the change of mood takes place. The crescendo culminates in the Invocation (Ex. 238b):

238a

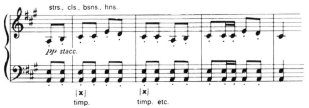

238b

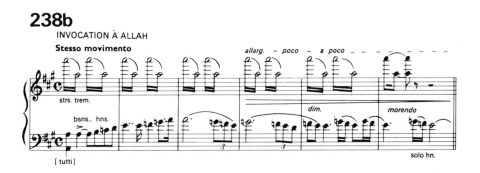

The 'Danse grecque' might have found a place in Boito's *Classical Sabbath*, so pure and limpid is the scoring, so graceful the melodic line. The first twelve bars carry the instruction: 'Two groups of young Greek girls interlace their poses, harmonious and calm.' Verdi too had used the word 'intrecciare' ('to weave'). Both metaphors are reflected in the intertwining of melodic threads which characterizes the music. The opening presents two ideas closely dovetailed:

239a

239b

At the beginning of the dance proper at bar 13 Ex. 239b, originally an answering phrase, becomes the main subject, while flutes, oboe, cor anglais and clarinets spin a counter-theme full of Grecian curves, marked *dolcissimo e senza accenti*, whose sustained legato line makes an effective contrast to the tripping motion of the strings. Wide intervals characterize both melodies. Finally Ex. 239a is made to yield a codetta of the utmost sweetness over twelve bars of implied tonic pedal.

240

An astonishing harmonic epigram in bars 11 and 12 reveals the aged Verdi as one of those who like Mozart tend to make their boldest strokes unobtrusively.

241

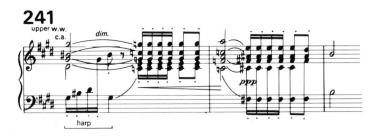

The final panel in the triptych is robustly Italianate, with alternation of major and minor in the opening phrase – folk-like, perhaps, but far from primitive (Ex. 242a). Whether or not the 'Muranese' ever existed as a special dance with steps and rhythms of its own, the passage which Verdi insisted should be danced by a couple only is indistinguishable from a Neapolitan tarantella, though more graceful than any traditional product of the South (Ex. 242b).

The 'Danse des guerriers' forms an episode within the 'Muranese' with the same 6/8 rhythm but turned into a species of march. It is mainly an affair of cornets and

242a

trumpets, the first playing the melody in thirds, the second being used to rap out a triplet rhythm between the phrases. Not only is it free of vulgarity; it even contains one of those subtle melodic touches that only reveal themselves on close acquaintance. As at the start of the 'Chanson grecque' the answering idea of the first section (Ex. 243a) becomes the main idea of the second (Ex. 243b) but with an important modification. The second half phrase is no longer a straight repetition of the first but is lowered to form a pattern of descending sequences. A simple change but supremely right.

The reprise of the 'Muranese' ends with a bustling 2/4 coda. Then the B flat sounds from behind the scene, the fanfare chord builds up, and the music proceeds as before up till the concertato. This, however, is considerably shortened and tightened, with much of the monumental polyphony removed. Writers differ in accounting for the change. According to Toye it was because Verdi had his doubts about the ability of

243a

243b

the Paris ensemble to play the concertato as originally written.* Gatti believes that the composer wanted to save the time that had been taken up by the ballet and so restore the original proportions of the act.† His view is shared by Hughes.‡

But there was a much more cogent reason than either of these. It is clear from his correspondence with Ricordi after the première that Verdi was not happy about the theatrical effect of the concertato. In connection with a revival at La Scala in 1889, 'I would suggest bringing the orchestra down in the concertato of the finale terzo at bar 38 in E flat minor. . . . At the same time I would group the chorus close together on stage in an isolated group and very distant, so that Iago can dominate and hold the attention with his movements, his actions, his infamous words to Otello and Roderigo, without being disturbed by the muffled din of the orchestra. It is the sort of place in which you really need a void in the orchestra – a void that is dramatic.'§ Later: 'I come back to the third-act finale. Here too there can be no dramatic truth or dramatic effect if you don't manage to isolate Iago completely; to ensure that the eyes of the audience are directed to him alone, that his words – not his voice – dominate everything and beneath them you hear an indistinct murmur – imprecise, if you like. Imprecise! This word will make a musician's hair stand on end, but no matter. I say once more, try, try and try again.'¶

The truth is that while Iago is speaking so much of interest is happening elsewhere that it is not easy to fix one's attention on what he is saying. For the Paris version Verdi decided, not for the first time, to sacrifice musical elaboration to dramatic clarity; hence the drastic simplification of his most imposing operatic ensemble. To begin with, Ex. 221c is eliminated from the first part of the movement, so that Desdemona's opening solo becomes a two-tiered instead of a three-tiered structure with Ex. 221b extended by the kind of cadential phrase which had originally belonged to the melody that has been removed. The intervention of Lodovico, Cassio, Emilia and Roderigo is no longer a self-contained theme as in the original but merely a simple phrase variously extended. If this means one melody the less, at least it removes those unwelcome associations of Joseph Barnby and John Bacchus Dykes which chromatically inflected themes like Ex. 222 usually evoke for English

* Toye, p. 425.
† Gatti, II, p. 459.
‡ Hughes, p. 464.
§ Letter to Giulio Ricordi, 3.2.1889. Abbiati, IV, p. 371.
¶ Letter to Giulio Ricordi, 9.2.1889. *Ibid.*, p. 372.

244

DESDEMONA: tout sombre, hélas ___ tout sombre tout est fi - ni!... tout est fi -

EMILIA: - ge. Ne soit pas le pré - - sa - ge de plus cru - els, cru-els mal -

CASSIO: un vent d'o-ra-ge qui me por-te au som - met, au ___ som -

LODOVICO: el-le pa-rait l'i - ma-ge, l'i-ma-ge morne du dé - ses -

IAGO: Lâche! Es-pè-re encor. Il faut vaincre ton étoi - le.

CHORUS: Dieu. Dieu! ge! cle!

[w.w.]   strs. *dolcissimo*

listeners. Iago, recovering from his stunned amazement sooner than in the Italian version, begins to mutter in Otello's ear during the solo quartet. The reprise of Ex. 221b is delayed four bars while to a faint adumbration of the triplet figure (Ex. 223) Iago tells of his plan to kill Cassio. Chorus and soloists meanwhile have hushed sustaining chords which allow Iago's words to come across with no difficulty. Ex. 221b is then resumed in the same E flat as in the original, with Desdemona once more on the top line; but it is far more quietly and simply set out. Then in place of the dark E flat minor motif in triplets (Ex. 223), which underwent so many transformations in the original concertato, a milder, gentler idea carries us across six bars while Iago incites Roderigo to the murder of the newly appointed governor; Desdemona still makes her scenic presence felt with a characteristic droop; the sympathy of the onlookers is also conveyed; but there is no towering musical structure to distract attention from Iago's words. (See Ex. 244)

At last Ex. 223, much lightened in texture, begins the long gradient of its development at the point where in the Italian version it had been marked 'come un lamento', and the concertato proceeds to its climax with Ex. 221c, which now has the force of a new theme. The reprise of Ex. 221a with the rapping trumpets is no longer choral but has become a solo for Iago.

Does all this amount to an improvement on the original? And if Verdi himself thought that it did why did he not insist that it should be carried in all future Italian editions of the score, as he had done with the extended ballet music in *Aida* written for Paris? Did he perhaps think that only the inclusion of the ballet music could justify such a noticeable reduction in architectural scale? In order to judge the matter, without any considerations of false reverence, it is, of course, necessary to see the new version performed on stage. Significantly, experiments in that direction by Riccardo Muti in Florence in 1980 and Mark Elder in London in 1981 have not been repeated.

That *Otello*, given the composer's age and eminence, should be hailed by the majority as the greatest Italian opera of its day as well as the composer's crowning achievement could be taken for granted. Has time upheld these judgements? The first of them, most certainly. Indeed no opera of the 1880s comes within leagues of it except for *Parsifal*. While the 'veristic' melodramas, *Tosca* and *Madama Butterfly* included, which shocked and thrilled the Europe of the fin du siècle, are still very much of their period, *Otello* remains as fresh, as challenging, as essentially modern as the day it was written. To detractors of Italian opera it remains, together with *Falstaff* and the *Requiem*, the composer's passport to immortality. Indeed many have come to a full understanding of Verdi's genius by starting from *Otello* and working back to *Ernani* and *Nabucco*.

As to whether it is his tragic masterpiece, again the verdict of the majority is 'yes'. A residue of doubt remains, partly among certain Verdians who believe that in writing a work of this complexity their hero was renouncing his national birthright and losing contact with the public whom he had both led and served over the years, partly for those who consider that Italian composers should be like the lilies of the field, taking no thought for the morrow. Obviously there is no arguing with personal tastes, or for that matter musical appetites; nor is it easy to convince someone for whom Verdi ends with *Aida* that the fault of *Otello* may simply be that it contains tougher music than he is prepared to chew. It can, however, be shown that the so-called abstrusities of Verdi's last tragedy are the logical outcome of procedures which he had adopted over the years and that the opera as a whole represents a goal of music drama to which he had been striving since the start of his career. And surely it is not surprising that as a creative artist reaches ever wider and deeper his art should become in certain respects caviare to the general.

As for Baldini's view that in *Otello* Verdi had sold out to the intellectualism of Boito, a glance at other operas for which Boito supplied the libretti will suffice to show that his influence on composers was an entirely liberating one. With his vast resources of vocabulary and metrical ingenuity he was able to provide composers with the kind of poetry their musical thought required; it is the Cammaranos and Ghislanzonis who restrict the musician's terms of reference. At the same time it must be said that though Baldini occasionally misses the mark he never aims at non-existent targets; and his objection to *Otello* has this much of substance to it – that here Verdi does not operate on the same level of musico-verbal immediacy as in his earlier operas and for the very reason that Baldini gives, namely the recherché artificiality of Boito's language. While it is impossible to recall the melody of 'Cortigiani, vil razza' without the words, the most memorable tunes of *Otello* often recur to the mind independently simply because such phrases as 'S'inaffia l'ugola' and 'Chi all'esca ha morso' are too self-consciously coined to have any directness; they lack even the emotional charge of Cammarano's agglomeration of adjectives. One wonders how long it took an audience to realize that the metaphor 'Edera orribile' ('horrible ivy') refers to an army storming ramparts or battlements. If the expression were not a contradiction in terms one could say that *Otello* is a more symphonic opera than its predecessors; but the dramatic voltage is there just the same.

The shadow of the great Tamagno has always hung over the title role; and we often hear that this or that international tenor has declared that he is not ready for Otello yet, meaning that he has not yet developed the ear-splitting resources of a 'tenore di squillo'? Maurel has some wise observations here:

L'idéal de la puissance vocale que nécessite le personnage a été fourni par le créateur du rôle, M. Francesco Tamagno, avec une intensité étonnante; mais il nous paraît dangéreux de laisser pénétrer dans l'idée de la généralité des futurs interprètes d'Otello que cette puissance vocal extraordinaire soit une condition *sine qua non* d'une bonne interprétation. . . .

Que ceux des ténors qui ambitionnent de chanter Otello ne se laissent pas intimider par les récits, réels d'ailleurs, faits à propos de l'organe unique que possède le créateur du rôle. Ils doivent se pénétrer de cette importante remarque: *au bout de dix minutes un public est habitué à une tonalité sonore quelque grande qu'elle puisse être. Ce qui l'étonne et le captive toujours, c'est la justice, l'énergie et la variété des accents.**

To which it might be added that no tenor lead in all Verdi is so encrusted with nuances which a heavy performance will always tend to obliterate. A singer of the weight of a Placido Domingo or a Carlo Bergonzi has much to recommend him in this role over those massively built tenors who bellow and stagger about the stage like gored bulls.

In common with all the greatest tragedies *Otello* harrows but at the same time uplifts. Despite the horrifying course of events a sense of idealism, of man's dignity under suffering, is what remains at the end. At the final curtain of *La Bohème* the spectator whose cheek remains unbedew'd is indeed hard of heart. Of the conclusion of *Otello* it could be said as in the epilogue of *Samson Agonistes*:

> Nothing is here for tears, nothing to wail
> Or knock the breast.

Verdi's music has all the strength, nobility and compassion of Shakespeare's poetry to turn a sordid intrigue into one of the finest testaments to the worth of the human spirit.

---

* Maurel, *op. cit.*, pp. 50–1.

5 FALSTAFF

FALSTAFF

Comic opera in three acts
by
ARRIGO BOITO
(after the comedy, *The Merry Wives of Windsor* by William Shakespeare and parts of
the same author's historical drama *King Henry IV*)

first performed at the
Teatro alla Scala, Milan
9 February 1893

SIR JOHN FALSTAFF	BARITONO	Victor Maurel
FORD, husband of Alice	BARITONO	Antonio Pini-Corsi
FENTON	TENORE	Edoardo Garbin
DR CAIUS	TENORE	Giovanni Paroli
BARDOLFO } followers of Falstaff	TENORE	Paolo Pelagelli-Rossetti
PISTOLA }	BASSO	Vittorio Arimondi
MRS ALICE FORD	SOPRANO	Emma Zilli
NANNETTA, her daughter	SOPRANO	Adelina Stehle
MRS QUICKLY	MEZZO-SOPRANO	Giuseppina Pasqua
MRS MEG PAGE	MEZZO-SOPRANO	Virginia Guerrini
Mine Host of the Garter	MIMA	Attilio Pulcini
ROBIN, page to Falstaff	MIMA	N.N.
Page to Ford	MIMA	N.N.

Burgesses and populace – servants of Ford – Masquerade of will-o'-the-
wisps, fairies, witches, etc.

The action takes place in Windsor

Epoch: the reign of King Henry IV of England

At the end of 1890 the seventy-seven-year-old Verdi wrote to that indefatigable scribbler on matters theatrical Gino Monaldi, 'What can I tell you? I've wanted to write a comic opera for forty years, and I've known *The Merry Wives of Windsor* for fifty; . . . however, the usual "buts" which are everywhere always prevented me from satisfying this wish of mine. Now Boito has resolved all the "buts" and has written me a lyric comedy quite unlike any other. I'm enjoying myself writing the music; without plans of any sort and I don't even know whether I'll finish it . . . I repeat . . . I'm enjoying myself. Falstaff is a rogue who gets up to every kind of mischief . . . but in an amusing way. He's a *type*. Types are so various! The opera is entirely comic! Amen.'*

Here in a nutshell is the history of Verdi's last opera, the fulfilment of a long-cherished ambition. Forty years takes us back to the composition of *Rigoletto*, whose opening scene up to the entrance of Monterone is pure comedy. Yet among the 'buts' must have been the consideration that *opera buffa* still remained a genre apart, constrained by that formalism which in the late eighteenth century had seemed so fruit-ful. True, it continued to throw up an occasional well turned novelty capable not only of outlasting the season in which it was produced but even of travelling abroad: *Crispino e la Comare* by the brothers Ricci (1850), *Una Follia a Roma* (1869) by Ricci the younger, *Papà Martin* (1872) by Cagnoni. All are permeated by the stock gestures, the rhythms and types of melodic period that had obtained since Donizetti's day. Only the superficial properties show any variation – the Riccis' predilection for the 2/4 jogtrot, Cagnoni's preference for angular melodic contours (his first popular success, *Don Bucefalo*, written in 1847 when he was still a student, is, needless to say, pure Donizetti). The basic tradition remained hard and fast. If Verdi found difficulty in coming to terms with it creatively in 1840, how much less could he do so ten, twenty, fifty years later? Here then is the force of the phrase 'a lyric comedy quite unlike any other'. That Verdi could enliven tragedy with comic elements he had demonstrated not only in *Rigoletto* but in *Un Ballo in maschera* and *La Forza del destino*, but to write an opera that was to be 'entirely comic' Verdi needed new rules, such as only a Boito could help him to devise. As a comic opera *Falstaff* inherits no tradition; but it could be said to start one. The Venetian comedies of Wolf-Ferrari and of his later epigones Lualdi and Mortari, the first acts of Cilea's *Adriana Lecouvreur* and – allowing for a characteristic thickening of texture – of Puccini's *La Bohème*, and the whole of his *Gianni Schicchi*, each pay it homage. For an artist to blaze a new trail in his eightieth year is no mean achievement.

Verdi may have known Shakespeare's comedy since 1840 or thereabouts, but when his thoughts turned to comic opera in 1850 there is nothing to indicate that he aspired to *The Merry Wives of Windsor*. But if he did so there would have been a certain appropriateness in his choice. In 1849 Otto Nicolai had died after producing his masterpiece *Die lustige Weiber von Windsor*, so winning, it might be thought, the tournament which had been forced on both composers. It had begun with the

* Letter to G. Monaldi, 3.12.1890. *Copialettere*, p. 712.

triumph of Nicolai's *Il Templario* coupled with the downfall of *Un Giorno di regno*; two years later it was Verdi's turn to triumph with a libretto that Nicolai had turned down; while Nicolai himself suffered a total fiasco with a libretto that had been ceded to him by his rival. If Verdi's subsequent career compared to his own seemed to tilt the balance in favour of the Italian, it was partly redressed by the one work through which Nicolai is remembered today. The delightful overture made its way round the concert halls of Europe very quickly; and if it turned Verdi's thoughts in the direction of Shakespearian comic opera as early as 1850 this would not have been surprising.

The earliest mention of *Falstaff* as an operatic subject occurs in a letter to Arrivabene during the years after *Don Carlos* when Verdi was looking for a plot that might be suitable for the Opéra Comique. True, his statement is an explicit denial: 'I am not writing *Falstaff* nor any other operas.'* At the same time Ghislanzoni published in Ricordi's *Gazzetta Musicale* a paragraph to the effect that the journal which had given out the news that Verdi was at work on a *Falstaff* to a libretto by himself was a 'journal of the future and fabricates news for a future generation – no matter if the present one makes fun of it'. † It was the stock gibe against the Wagnerians and their *Zukunftmusik*. This time, however, it was not so far from the literal truth.

Falstaff, as a character, turns up again in the letter to Clarina Maffei of 1876 quoted in the preceding chapter in which he proclaims the necessity of inventing truth.‡ As his is the first name mentioned, the fat knight was clearly not far from the surface of Verdi's mind.

In 1879, with the idea of an *Otello* precariously launched, Giulio Ricordi was dismayed to receive a brusque letter from S. Agata complaining of an article in the *Gazzetta Musicale di Milano* which quoted Rossini as having declared that Verdi was incapable of treating a comic subject. 'But look here,' the letter continued, 'for twenty years now I have been searching for a libretto for an *opera buffa* and now that I have so to speak found one all ready to hand, you, by that article, put in the public's head a crazy desire to hiss the opera even before it is written, thus prejudicing your interests and mine. But have no fear! If by chance, by misfortune, by fatality, in spite of the Great Sentence, my evil genius leads me to write this *opera buffa*, have no fear, I say: I'll ruin another publisher.'§ Ricordi hastened to explain that he had unfortunately not, as usual, supervised the production of that particular issue. 'But if I had seen it,' he added in a postscript, 'I would have added a note something like this: "Just how erroneous this judgement is Verdi has shown in his *Forza del destino*, where he created in Fra Melitone an entirely new type, comic and not comic, characterizing him with the most original music which has no parallel in any other opera and which shows the author of so many masterpieces in an entirely new light."'¶ Half placated, Verdi replied, 'That passage, it seemed to me, could have no other purpose in your *Gazzetta* except to say to me, "Take care, Signor Maestro, never to write comic operas"; and I felt in duty bound to say to you, "I'll ruin another publisher." If,

---

* Letter to Arrivabene, 28.7.1868. Alberti, pp. 93–4.
† Abbiati, IV, p. 381.
‡ Letter to Clarina Maffei, 20.10.1876. *Copialettere*, p. 624.
§ Letter to Giulio Ricordi, 26.8.1879. *Copialettere*, pp. 308–9.
¶ Letter from Giulio Ricordi, 28.8.1879. *Copialettere*, pp. 309–10.

however, I do write this *opera buffa* and you want to ruin yourself, so much the worse for you.'* What the subject was must for the present remain a mystery. Nor is it impossible that its existence had been invented for the purposes of belabouring Ricordi, whom Verdi always held personally responsible for any reservations expressed about him in the firm's house magazine.

Falstaff, prototype of all likeable fat scoundrels, is surely a natural subject for comic opera; and it may well seem surprising that so few composers have exploited him, until we remember that the Falstaff whom we know and love is a creation of the chronicle plays, which do not lend themselves to operatic treatment. In *The Merry Wives of Windsor*, which does, he is a pale reflection of his former self. The traditional explanation already current in the eighteenth century is probably the true one. Queen Elizabeth had expressed a desire to see the 'fat knight in love', and commanded a performance of the new play at some inconveniently early date. The outcome was the untidy, ill focused comedy about Sir John's attempts on the virtue of two rich tradesmen's wives with a view to helping himself to their husbands' money. Throughout the eighteenth and nineteenth centuries, operas were distilled from whole plays, and it would have taken an unusually inventive librettist to have anticipated the example of Gustav Holst in *At the Boar's Head* and made a one-act opera out of the tavern scenes in *King Henry IV*, Part 2. A Falstaff opera would have to be based on *The Merry Wives of Windsor*; with the result that in none of them does Sir John emerge in all his ripe, rich magnificence. Salieri's *Falstaff ossia Le tre Burle* of 1799 was written for a Viennese public who would have known their Shakespeare. But of the six numbers which make up Artaria's abbreviated vocal score, only one includes a part for Falstaff – a mock-amorous duet of no distinctive character for himself and Mistress Ford. She it is who would seem to dominate the opera. She is her own emissary to Falstaff, disguised as a German woman – a device which gives her an excuse for singing an aria in macaronic Italian. Another favourite number was her duet with Mistress Page (here, strangely, called Mistress Slender), 'La stessa, la stessissima', which served Beethoven as the basis for a set of piano variations. The subject is of course the identical letter that both neighbours have received.

Balfe's *Falstaff*, produced very successfully in Her Majesty's Theatre in 1838, is a fully professional Italian opera capable of holding its own against the average product of its day; moreover, it was written for the great Luigi Lablache, to whose artistic gifts was added a truly Falstaffian physique. But, alas, Balfe's notions of characterization were conservative to say the least. The entire opera remains within the normal straitjacket of the 1830s, with cantabiles and cabalettas, Rossini-style duets, lyrical concertati and noisy strettas. Falstaff, returned from his ducking in the Thames, chatters away to the guests of the Garter Inn like Don Gherardo to the Duke's retainers in Donizetti's *Torquato Tasso* or Tom Radcliffe to his fellow warders in Ricci's *La prigione di Edimburgo*. He is the 'solito pagliaccio' which Verdi had been so anxious to avoid when he created Fra Melitone. The one scene which might have been expected to hold possibilities for an Irish romantic – namely that of Windsor Forest – turns out to be wholly commonplace despite some experimental scoring which includes a trombone solo. The composer of 'Killarney' could produce some charming and individual music for Fenton and Nannetta in Irish-inflected Bellinian style; but for the rest his imagination remained tethered to the Italian conven-

* Letter to Giulio Ricordi, Aug. 1879. *Copialettere*, p. 311.

tions to which his profession as conductor at Her Majesty's had accustomed him.

The same certainly cannot be said about Nicolai, whose *Lustige Weiber von Windsor* is by far the best operatic setting of Shakespeare's play before Verdi's. The Windsor Forest scene is both delicate and evocative in Weber's manner; the comedy bubbles and sparkles, carried along by a swift current of invention. Yet we can never quite forget that Nicolai had his operatic apprenticeship in Italy. Not only does Mistress Ford remind us from time to time that she is a prima donna (her 'Verführer! Warum stellt ihr der tugendsamen Gattin nach?' presents a variant of the Rossinian 'open' melody at its most brilliant, while 'Frohsinn und Laune' is a cabaletta in all but name); but once again Falstaff fails to stand out in proper relief. He is still a chattering buffo. In the duet 'In einem Wäschkorb' he and Ford ('Herr Bach') are Teutonic Pasquale and Malatesta respectively.*

Verdi and Boito, then, in attempting a genuinely Shakespearian comedy on the subject of Falstaff, had the field clear. Only a composer with the experience of Fra Melitone behind him and with Verdi's technique of expressive declamation could have done justice to the protagonist in all his aspects, while it took a librettist of Boito's intellectual range to understand that he would have to go beyond the *Merry Wives of Windsor* and into the chronicle plays to furnish the composer with the necessary material.

For the rest he carried out the necessary economies on Shakespeare's plot with his usual skill. He followed Salieri and Balfe in giving chief prominence among the women to Mistress Ford; eliminated the genial Master Page, the affected Nym with his incessant misuse of the word 'humour', and the delightfully fatuous Slender (not an easy character to treat operatically though Smetana's Vashek is a near-equivalent). Ann therefore becomes Ford's daughter. The humour of Parson Evans and Dr Caius consists mainly in their crimes against the English language; only the latter is retained therefore as Ann's unsuccessful suitor, deprived of his French nationality. He also takes the place of Slender and Justice Shallow in the first scene, so saving yet another character. Mistress Quickly, no longer Caius's landlady, is a mere neighbour and considerably more sympathetic than her counterpart in the *Merry Wives* (neither, it seems, bears any relation to the hostess of the Boar's Head). Mine Host of the Garter is reduced to a walking-on part. The most ruthless excision of all is the episode of the fat woman of Brainford, which both Balfe and Nicolai had included. Falstaff's discomfiture is concentrated at two points only – the basket scene and the masquerade in Windsor Forest; so we are spared the tautology of two rough-and-tumbles in Ford's house.

Since the première of *Otello* the distance between poet and composer had narrowed considerably. Gone was the necessity of tact and delicacy in their mutual dealings. For Verdi Boito was now one of the family – not so much a son, which might have been expected given the difference in their ages, as an honorary brother. Despite their formal mode of address (Boito always uses 'Lei' to Verdi, and Verdi 'Voi' to Boito) their letters to each other read like those of coevals. To Boito falls much of the credit for rejuvenating Verdi in his old age, even to the extent of infecting him with his own passion for conundrums and brain-teasers. So it was that when in August 1888 a certain Crescentini of Bologna published a 'scala rebus' or 'puzzle

* For a general survey of these and other operatic settings of *The Merry Wives*, see W. Dean, 'Shakespeare and Opera', in *Shakespeare in Music* (Essays), ed. P. Hartnoll (London, 1964), pp. 120–7.

scale' in the *Gazzetta Musicale di Milano*, inviting composers to try their hand at a logical harmonization, Verdi began to show an interest. It is almost the story of the Diabelli Variations. Numerous solutions were offered; all simple four-part chords keeping the scale in the bass, except for one by a certain Ottorino Varsi who treated it as a cantus firmus, placing it in the tenor voice and weaving three 'real' parts around it. It is a laboured, uninteresting piece of work; but to Verdi it must have suggested possibilities. That he discussed these with Boito during the winter of 1888–9 is clear from a letter in which he asks Boito to send him part of the setting of the scale, having accidentally thrown away his own copy. At the same time he proposed setting the piece as an Ave Maria ('Another Ave Maria! It would be my fourth! So I might hope to be beatified after my death.');* and Boito, enclosing the missing pages, 'I did well to copy out those two pages of fractured scale round which you've circled up and down with so much ease. . . . In polyphonic pieces which are sung there is a sad beauty which brings to mind the evening prayer. So let's have this fourth Ave Maria. . . . Plenty of Ave Marias will be needed for the Holy See to forgive you Iago's "Credo".'† To which Verdi: 'It's you; you're the main culprit who needs to be granted a pardon for Iago's "Credo".'‡ So was born the first of the *Quattro Pezzi Sacri*, with Boito in the role of midwife. §

From a piece of polyphony based on the solution of a conundrum to a sparkling comedy abounding in cunning verbo-musical interplay and cross-reference the step was not so large. Correspondence on the subject of *Falstaff* begins suddenly in the summer of 1889 when Verdi was staying in the Tuscan spa of Montecatini.

'Excellent! Excellent!' was his comment on having read Boito's synopsis:

> Before reading your sketch I wanted to re-read *The Merry Wives*, the two parts of *Henry IV*, and *Henry V*, and I can only repeat: excellent, for no one could have done it better than you have done.
>
> A pity that the interest (it's not your fault) doesn't go on mounting until the end. The culminating point is the finale of the second act; and the appearance of Falstaff's face amid the linen, etc., etc., is a truly comic invention. I'm afraid too that the last act, in spite of its touch of fantasy, will be trivial, with all those little pieces, songs, ariettas, etc., etc. You bring back Bardolph – and why not Pistol too, both of them, to get up to some prank or other?
>
> You reduce the weddings to two! All the better, since they're only loosely con-nected to the main plot.
>
> The two trials by fire and water are enough to punish Falstaff; all the same I should like to have seen him soundly thrashed as well! I'm talking off the top of my head – take no notice. We now have very different matters to discuss if this *Falstaff* or *Merry Wives* that was in the realm of dreams two days ago is now to take on flesh and to become a reality. When? How? . . . Who can tell? . . .¶

* Letter to Boito, 6.3.1889. Abbiati, IV, pp. 375–6. The other three are of course the two prayers from *I Lombardi* and *Otello* and the setting for soprano and strings in 1880 of the 'Ave Maria' in the vernacular of Dante.

† Letter from Boito, 7.3.1889. *Ibid.*, IV, p. 376.

‡ Letter to Boito, 11.3.1889. *Ibid.*, IV, p. 376.

§ For a detailed account of the genesis of the 'Ave Maria' and the two versions in which it exists, see M. Conati, 'Le *Ave Maria* su scala enigmatica dalla prima alla seconda stesura (1889–97)', in *Rivista Italiana di Musicologia*, XIII, No. 2 (Florence, 1978), pp. 280–311.

¶ Letter to Boito, 6.7.1889, Walker, p. 495.

Boito replied by return of post:

> No doubt about it, the third act is the dullest. This is always the trouble in the theatre. Unfortunately it's a basic law of comedy. In tragedy the opposite rule obtains. The approach of the catastrophe – whether foreseen as in *Othello* or unforeseen as in *Hamlet* – increases the excitement prodigiously because the end is terrible. Therefore the last acts of a tragedy are the finest. In a comedy as soon as the knot is about to be untied the interest lessens because the ending is happy. You have read Goldoni recently and you will recall how in the final scenes, though the marvellous interweaving of the dialogue and the characters remains admirable, the action always weakens and with it the dramatic interest. In *The Merry Wives* even Shakespeare, with that extra bit of energy that he had, could not escape this basic law. Neither could Molière, nor Beaumarchais nor Rossini. The last scene of *The Barber* has always seemed to me less wonderful than the rest. If I'm wrong, correct me. In comedy there comes a point at which the stalls say, 'It's finished,' whereas on the stage it's not yet finished.

An important point, this; and it explains among other things why in eighteenth-century *opera buffa* the third act becomes progressively shorter until it eventually becomes absorbed into the second. There was no other way of preventing the public from leaving after the second interval. Boito went on to suggest possible remedies.

> Above all we must make as much as we can of the last scene, which offers certain advantages. The fantastic ambience which has not been touched upon in the rest of the opera can help here; it strikes a note which is fresh and light and new. Then we have three very good moments of comedy; first, Falstaff's monologue with the horns; second, the inquisition (we'll have it done by Bardolph or Pistol to the sound of thwacks on Falstaff's stomach, as he lies on the ground, and with each thwack he'll confess one of his sins); third, the blessing of the two weddings in disguise. We could put back the duettino for Nannetta and Fenton to the beginning of the same act. This love between Nannetta and Fenton must come in frequent bouts; in all the scenes in which they take part they will keep on kissing by stealth and in corners, astutely, boldly, without letting themselves be discovered, with fresh little phrases and brief, very rapid little dialogues, from the beginning to the end of the comedy; it will be a most lively, merry love, always disturbed and interrupted and always ready to begin again.
>
> Certainly Fenton's song is put in to give the tenor a solo, and that's a bad thing. Shall we take it out?*

In the meantime, his letter had crossed with one of Verdi's, coyly drawing back with an apprehension which was perhaps more apparent than real:

> As long as one wanders in the realm of ideas every prospect pleases, but when one comes down to earth, to practical matters, doubts and discouragements arise.
>   In outlining *Falstaff* did you never think of the enormous number of my years? I know you will reply exaggerating the state of my health, which is good, ex-

---

* Letter from Boito, 7.7.1889. *Carteggi Verdiani*, II, pp. 144–5.

cellent, robust . . . so be it, but in spite of that you must agree I could be accused of great foolhardiness in taking on so much! Supposing I couldn't stand the strain? And failed to finish it? You would then have wasted your time and trouble to no purpose! And I wouldn't wish that for all the gold in the world. The idea is intolerable to me, and all the more so if by writing *Falstaff* you had to, I won't say abandon, but distract your attention from *Nerone* or delay its production. I should be blamed for this delay and thunderbolts of ill-will would fall about my head!

How are we to overcome these obstacles? Have you a sound argument to oppose to mine? I hope so, but I don't believe it. . . . Still, let's think it over (and take care to do nothing that would harm your career), and if you can find me one, and I can find some way of casting off ten years or so . . . then what joy to be able to say to the public: 'Here we are again! Roll up!' . . .*

Boito's reply was both frank and subtle.

The fact is that I never think of your age either when I'm talking to you or when I'm writing to you or when I'm working for you.

The fault is yours.

I know that *Otello* is little more than two years old, and that even as I am writing to you it is being appreciated as it should by Shakespeare's compatriots. But there is a stronger argument than that of age, and it's this: it's been said of you after *Otello*: 'It's impossible to finish better.' This is a great truth and it enshrines a great and very rare tribute. It is the only weighty argument.

Weighty for the present generation, but not for history, which aims first and foremost to judge men by their essential merits. Nevertheless it is indeed rare to see a lifetime of artistic endeavour conclude with a world triumph. *Otello* is such a triumph. All the other arguments – age, strength, hard work for me, hard work for you, etc., etc. – are not valid and place no obstacle in the way of a new work. Since you oblige me to talk about myself I shall say that notwithstanding the commitment I should be taking on with *Falstaff* I shall be able to finish my work within the term promised. I'm sure of it.

I don't think that writing a comedy should tire you out. A tragedy causes its author *genuinely to suffer*; one's thoughts undergo a suggestion of sadness which renders the nerves morbidly sensitive. The jokes and laughter of comedy exhilarate mind and body.

'A smile adds a thread to life's tapestry.'

I don't know whether these are Foscolo's exact words but they express a truth.†

You have a great desire to work, and this is an indubitable proof of health and strength. 'Ave Marias' are not enough. Something else is needed.

---

* Letter to Boito, 7.7.1889. Walker, pp. 495–6.

† Foscolo's words are 'Che un sorriso possa aggiungere un filo alla trama brevissima della vita,' and they provide a thread of another sort, stretching from Laurence Sterne to Puccini. The adage in question comes from *Tristram Shandy* and is quoted in the preface to Foscolo's translation of the same author's *A Sentimental Journey*. The thread was subsequently picked up by Boito's friend and literary protégé Giuseppe Giacosa, co-author with Illica of the libretto of *Madama Butterfly*, in the first scene of which Suzuki says to Pinkerton: 'Il riso è frutto e fiore, / Disse il savio Ocunama; / Dei crucci la trama smaglia il sorriso.' There is thus considerable aptness in Pinkerton's reply: 'A chiacchiere costei mi pare cosmopolita.'

All your life you've wanted a good subject for a comic opera, and that is a sign that the vein of an art that is both joyous and noble is virtually in existence in your brain; instinct is a wise counsellor. There's only one way to finish better than with *Otello* and that's to finish triumphantly with *Falstaff*.

After having sounded all the shrieks and groans of the human heart, to finish with a mighty burst of laughter – that is to astonish the world.

So you see, dear Maestro, it's worth thinking about the subject I've sketched; see whether you can feel in it the germ of the new masterpiece. If the germ is there, the miracle is accomplished. Meanwhile let us promise to maintain the most scrupulous secrecy. I've told nobody about it. If we can work in secret we can work in peace. . . .*

And Verdi:

Amen, so be it!

We'll write this *Falstaff* then! We won't think for the moment of obstacles or age or illness!

I too wish to preserve the profoundest Secrecy – a word that I too underline three times, to tell you that no one must know anything about it! But wait . . . Peppina knew it before we did, I believe! Be sure, however, she will keep the secret; when women have this quality they have it in greater measure than we [*a heartwarming tribute, this, to one whom he had not always treated too kindly in middle age*].

Meanwhile, if you feel in the mood, make a start at once. In the first two acts there's nothing to alter, apart, perhaps, from the monologue of the jealous husband, which would be better at the end of the first part than at the beginning of the second. It would be more gripping and effective.†

Boito's reply was joyous and brief. He would start work on the libretto at the beginning of August; meantime he sent his best wishes to 'Signora Giuseppina, Prophetess'. Verdi then returned to the problem of the conclusion. The double wedding, he felt, had the effect of slackening the interest and at the same time distracting the attention from the central character. 'At this point,' he continued, 'there's a piece all ready made in Shakespeare'; and he added his own digest of the *Merry Wives*, V, v, 105–65, which could be rendered roughly as follows:

MIS. FORD *(orig. Mistress Page)* I pray you, come, hold up the jest no higher.
FALSTAFF And these are not fairies?
MIS. FORD Why, Sir John, do you think, though we would have thrust virtue out of our hearts by the head and shoulders we would have chosen a man like you for our delight?
FORD A whale.
FALSTAFF 'Tis well.
ANOTHER A puffed man.
FALSTAFF 'Tis well.

* Letter from Boito, 9.7.1889. *Carteggio Verdi–Boito*, I, pp. 145–7.
† Letter to Boito, 10.7.1889. *Ibid.*, p. 147.

ANOTHER	Old, cold and withered.
FALSTAFF	Very well.
ANOTHER	And one that is slanderous as Satan.
FALSTAFF	Again, well.
OTHERS	And as poor as Job.
FALSTAFF	Very well.
ALL	And given to fornications, and to taverns and wine and metheglins and drinkings and swearings and to blaspheming God.
FALSTAFF	Amen: . . . and so be it.
MIS. FORD	And now, good Sir John, how like you Windsor wives?
FALSTAFF	I do begin to see that I am made an ass.
TUTTI	Good! Well said! Well said! Long live Falstaff!
	(*All clap their hands and the curtain falls.*)*

As with the finale of Act III of *Otello*, if Verdi's first thoughts had been allowed to prevail the opera would have lost much. Fortunately Boito was gentle but firm.

All your ideas are good. . . . The fragment of dialogue that you mention was already marked by me to be included. But marriages are necessary; without marriage there can be no happiness (don't say that to Signora Giuseppina or she'll start talking to me again about marriage),† and Fenton and Nannetta must get married. I like that love of theirs; it serves to make the whole comedy fresher and to hold it together. This love should enliven everything so much and so continually that I'm almost inclined to cut out a duet for the two lovers altogether. In every ensemble scene that love is present in its own fashion . . . in the second part of the first act, in the second part of the second, and in the first and second parts of the third. It's therefore pointless to make them sing by themselves in a real duet. Even without the duet, their part will be very effective; more so in fact than with it. I can't quite explain it; I would like as one sprinkles sugar on a cake to sprinkle the whole comedy with that happy love without concentrating it at any one point.‡

On 1 August he was ready to set to work and asked for his sketch back. Verdi obliged, and about the middle of the month wrote again: 'You are working, I hope? The strangest thing of all is that I'm working too! I'm amusing myself by writing fugues. Yes, sir; a fugue . . . and a *comic fugue* which would be in place in *Falstaff*! You will say: "But how do you mean, a comic fugue? Why comic?" I don't know how or why but it's a comic fugue!'§

By way of reply Boito seems to have sent him an amplified sketch, doubtless incorporating Verdi's own suggestions. He added: 'A comic fugue is just what's needed; we shan't lack a place to put it in. Artistic games are made for a playful art.' (It is impossible to translate Boito's pun: 'I giuochi dell' arte son fatti per l'arte giocosa'.) He himself had not found the libretto an easy matter.

In the first few days I was in despair. To sketch the characters in a few strokes, to weave the plot, to extract the juice from the enormous Shakespearian orange without letting the useless pips slip into the little glass, to write with colour, with clarity, with brevity, to delineate the musical plan of the scene so that there results an organic unity which is a piece of music and yet is not, to make the joyous comedy live from beginning to end, to make it live with a natural and infectious gaiety, is very, very difficult; and it must appear very, very easy. Courage and forward march. I'm still on the first act. September, the second; October, the third. That's my programme.*

Like most programmes it evidently fell behind schedule; and when Boito came to S. Agata in early November he brought only the first two acts with him. He had already altered the second part of Act II, so that Alice no longer explained the details of the joke to be played on Falstaff, since this would lead to a slackening of the interest in an act which is 'red-hot to the touch'.† The third act was not completed till March of the following year. 'It has turned out longer than I had hoped,' Boito wrote, 'but it is the most varied of all.'‡ On 8 March Verdi sent him the sum of money agreed between them. Nine days later Verdi was able to announce: 'The first act is finished without any alterations at all to the poetry – just as you gave it to me. I believe that the same thing will happen with the second act, apart from a few cuts in the pezzo concertato, such as you yourself suggested. We won't talk of the third, but I don't suppose there will be much to do in that either.'§ Boito replied encouragingly, authorizing any cuts in the text of the concertato that might be thought necessary. 'I spread myself on purpose,' he wrote, 'so that amidst all that wealth of material you could tailor the piece in your own way and with more ease. In the developments of an ensemble it is impossible to foresee the needs of the music, therefore it is better for the lines to be generously supplied.'¶

Again, Boito has neatly formulated a truth of Italian opera. What is interesting is that from the start the scene with the basket should have been referred to by both composer and librettist as 'the pezzo concertato'. The opera is full of ensembles; but only this one preserves the faint lineaments of the old largo–stretta formula, yet so altered, refined and subtilized, and so lacking in the usual stasis, that the listener is hardly aware of its ancestry. To Verdi's question as to how the title should be stressed Boito replied, 'Falstaff, like all English disyllables, carries the accent on the first. Ask Signora Giuseppina whether I am right or wrong. As far as I can remember I have never come across an English name of more than one syllable that is accented on the last. Only the French, who are incorrigible in garbling foreign names, pronounce the word Falstaff.' ‖ Presumably Boito's English amounted to what is usually described as a 'smattering'; Giuseppina at least wrote it fluently if not always very idiomatically.

After such a lively start the composition slowed down to a halt, due partly to Verdi's reluctance in later years to work during the summer months but also no doubt affected by the sad news of Faccio's decline. Signs of mental disturbance had

---

* Letter from Boito, undated – evidently towards the end of August. *Ibid.*, pp. 153–5.

† Letter from Boito, 30.10.1889. *Ibid.*, pp. 155–6.

‡ Letter from Boito, 1.3.1890. *Ibid.*, p. 158.

§ Letter to Boito, 17.3.1890. *Ibid.*, p. 163.

¶ Letter from Boito, 20.3.1890. *Ibid.*, pp. 163–4.

‖ *Ibid.*

been apparent the previous year to those who had accompanied him to Bayreuth for the first performance there of *Die Meistersinger*, which Faccio himself was to present at La Scala in an Italian version during the carnival season of 1889–90. The event duly took place and, as we shall see later, was in all probability witnessed by Verdi; but it needed all his colleagues' powers of persuasion to convince Faccio that the opera was not over with the second act. For some weeks it was hoped that his condition was merely due to overwork and consequent nervous strain; but soon a more sinister possibility suggested itself. ('One of the causes of his illness,' Boito wrote, 'is an infection of the blood which is cured by injections of mercury.')* In April he was taken to Kraft-Ebbing's clinic for mental diseases in Graz; but all the doctor could advise was that he should return to Milan and be placed in a suitable asylum, a victim of that same disease that had claimed Donizetti, Luigi Ricci, and, it is now thought, Schumann. He died in a home in Monza in July.

By late May Verdi was no longer in the mood for work; and he wrote to his collaborator: 'As for old Paunchy . . . alas! alas! I've done nothing more . . . except for a few full stops or commas added or altered in what was already written,' and taking up a reference to the text of the final fugue for which Boito had just supplied a new variant, he finished, 'L'uomo è nato poltrone' ('Man is born lazy' for 'Man is a joker'.)† With the approach of autumn the opera began to move again. 'I haven't worked much,' Verdi wrote, 'but I have done something. The sonnet in the third act has been tormenting me and to get it out of my head I put aside the second act and beginning with that sonnet I went on and on, one note after another, and got right to the end. . . . It's only a sketch! And who knows how much of it will have to be rewritten?'‡ The sonnet is of course Fenton's solo 'Dal labbro il canto estasiato vola', over which Boito had expressed grave reservations, quite unjustly since it is an eminently Shakespearian conceit – a discourse on the metaphysical paradoxes of a kiss; and Verdi would rise to its challenge magnificently.

Meantime after more than a year word had inevitably got about concerning the new project. On 26 November the *Corriere della Sera* 'leaked' the news that *Falstaff* was on the stocks, to be confirmed four days later by Ricordi's *Gazzetta*. At once a certain Lily Wolffsohn, enterprising correspondent of the English *Daily News*, wrote to Verdi offering to print the libretto in her newspaper prior to a stage performance – greatly to the amusement and exasperation of poet and composer. By the end of the year Verdi was fighting off inquiries about the date of production. To one person he would insist that he had hardly written a note; to another that he had merely sketched the music (which, from a knowledge of his methods of working, was probably not far from the truth). Who could say when it would be finished or even whether it would be finished? To Giulio Ricordi he wrote patiently:

> Let me explain myself. I began writing *Falstaff* simply to pass the time, without preconceived ideas, without plans; I repeat, *to pass the time*. . . . I told you that only half the music has been composed, but let's be quite clear on this; what I meant was 'half sketched' and within that half the greater amount of hard work remains to be done; the co-ordination of the parts, the revisions, the alterations, quite apart from the scoring which will be extremely fatiguing. In fact, to put it

---

* Letter from Boito, 16.3.1890. *Ibid.*, pp. 164–6.
† Letter to Boito, 23.5.1890. *Ibid.*, pp. 173–4.
‡ Letter to Boito, 6.10.1890. *Ibid.*, pp. 176–7.

in a word, the whole of 1891 will not be sufficient for me to get to the end. . . . When I was young, even if I was under the weather, I could stay at my desk for up to ten hours at a stretch . . . and more than once I would begin work at four o'clock in the morning and go on till four o'clock in the afternoon with only a cup of coffee to keep me going . . . and working continually without stopping to take breath. Now I can't.*

For Verdi's name-day, however, Ricordi repeated the ploy of the chocolate figurine; and a joint letter of greetings contained a cheerful, swag-bellied figure in Elizabethan costume sketched by Boito in the left-hand corner. Verdi replied good-humouredly enough: '. . . What a surprise! Old Paunchy! I've had no news of him for four months. He meanwhile, dead drunk, has probably gone to sleep for ever! Let him sleep on! Why wake him up? He might commit some piece of villainy that would shock the world. Well, what of it? . . . Meantime my compliments to the painter-musician-poet. . . .'† And to Boito, who had sent him a watercolour of the fat knight by Hohenstein asking for his comments: 'I confess I have not been able to warm up the engine';‡ but he asked once more for clarification on certain points of metre and accent in the second act; and Boito, taking this as a good omen, hastened to reply. 'Gaie comari di Windsor, è l'ora, etc. It's exactly as you say, an eleven-syllable metre with the accent on the seventh syllable . . .' and he repeated what he had said the previous year about English accentuation; then added:

I must confess that once in this libretto I have broken the rule . . . but only once and in a line a long way off from the one I've just quoted. . . . It's where Falstaff says:

> Quand' ero paggio del Duca di Norfolk
> Ero sottile, etc.

The character of the line would imply an accent on the sixth syllable whereas the word 'Norfolk' should be accented on the first syllable like 'Falstaff', 'Windsor', etc. I have tried several times to correct that line but if I put the accent right I spoiled the line and of the two I preferred to falsify the verbal accent. . . . Meanwhile I note that you have arrived at the line 'Gaie comari di Windsor, è l'ora' and that comforts me with the thought that the engine is already beginning to warm up; after a few pages you will find that the engine is already boiling and then: full steam ahead! . . . The four lost months will be regained in a week.§

'After his four months' illness,' Verdi replied, 'Falstaff is skinny, very skinny. Let's hope we can find some fat capon to fill up his belly. Everything depends on the doctor. Who knows? Who knows?'¶ By June the engine was certainly working at full pressure. 'Old Paunchy is in a fair way to going mad. There are days when he won't budge but sleeps and is bad-tempered. At other times he shouts, jumps, causes a

* Letter to Giulio Ricordi, 1.1.1891. *Copialettere*, pp. 712–13.
† Letter to Giulio Ricordi, 19.3.1891. Abbiati, IV, p. 418.
‡ Letter to Boito, 21.3.1891. *Carteggio Verdi–Boito*, I, pp. 180–1.
§ Letter from Boito, 22.3.1891. *Ibid.*, pp. 181–2.
¶ Letter to Boito, 1.5.1891. *Ibid.*, p. 186.

devil of a rumpus. I let him indulge his whims a bit; if he goes on like this I'll put him in a muzzle and a straitjacket.'*

Boito was delighted. 'Three cheers! Let him go, let him run; he will break all the windows and all the furniture in your room – no matter, you can buy some more. He will smash your piano – no matter, you will buy another. Let everything be turned upside down so long as the great scene is finished. Three cheers! Go on! Go on! What pandemonium! But pandemonium as clear as sunlight and as dizzy as a madhouse.'†

There was still a long way to go. In September it seems that Verdi had again decided to break his usual rule and begin scoring what he had already sketched before even starting on the first scene of Act III, '. . . because I'm afraid of forgetting certain blends and colours of instrumentation. Afterwards I'll do the first part of the third act and then – Amen! That part is shorter and less difficult than the rest. However, I must take trouble with Falstaff's first recitative and the bit where the wives leave. Here we need, I should say, a *tune* which gets gradually softer until it vanishes, perhaps on a solo violin up in the ceiling. Why not? If nowadays they put the orchestra in the cellar, why couldn't we put a violin in the attic?'‡ In fact the ending of that scene was to give Verdi more trouble than he had bargained for.

But for the moment all was plain sailing. Delayed by a few seasonal ailments in the winter the first act was in score by April 1892, and by August ready for the publisher. Acts II and III followed within two months.

During the long process of composition the alterations made to Boito's text were remarkably few.§ Mostly they consist of omissions; twelve lines for Quickly and two apiece for Alice and Falstaff in the finale to the second act; two for Ford in the duet with Falstaff in the first part of Act II and a strophe for Nannetta as Queen of the fairies in Act III, Scene ii. It would seem to have been Verdi's notion that Falstaff should be made to share Ford's mock-sentimental madrigal 'Amor, l'amor che non ci dà mai tregua', alternating words and phrases with exquisitely humorous effect. Quickly's narration in Act II, Scene ii was a late addition 'to be sung as fast as possible mezza voce, in a single breath, making the syllables clear and precise'.¶ So too Falstaff's short monologue after the discovery of Fenton's marriage to Nannetta. During 1892 Boito himself offered a number of minor improvements which need not detain us, especially since they were not made at Verdi's instance; indeed, a variant for the final fugue proposed in September was not in fact adopted.‖

Even before the composition was finished the long process of casting the first performance had begun. That it would be given at La Scala had been taken for granted by all concerned. Nor can it be doubted that Faccio, had he lived, should have been the conductor. His death had deprived La Scala of its artistic director as well as Italy of her finest conductor; and attempts were made to involve Verdi in the choice of his successor. The composer gave his views to Boito at some length. He was not in favour of a competition since these were usually won by mediocrities; a good conductor could only be judged at work. His own preference would be for Luigi Man-

* Letter to Boito, 12.6.1891. *Ibid.*, p. 190.
† Letter from Boito, 14.6.1891. *Ibid.*, p. 191.
‡ Letter to Boito, 10.9.1891. *Ibid.*, p. 196.
§ All are charted in *Carteggi Verdiani*, II, pp. 151–4.
¶ Letter to Giulio Ricordi, 5.11.1892. Abbiati, IV, p. 465.
‖ See letter from Boito, 27.9.1892. *Carteggio Verdi–Boito*, I, pp. 214–15.

cinelli, whose annual schedule was at present divided between London and Madrid, and whose wife had already told Giuseppina that he was looking for a more settled post; but if, as seemed more than likely, Luisa Cora Mancinelli was voicing her own rather than her husband's view, Verdi would favour Edoardo Mascheroni, '. . . above all because I'm told that he is a hard worker (and at La Scala hard work is what's needed) and a conscientious person without likes or, better still, antipathies.' His advice did not end there:

> But it's not enough to choose the conductor. He must be independent of the management; he must assume the total musical responsibility before the commission, the management and the public.
>
> More: choose a good chorus master, who is subordinate to the conductor and whose job it is not only to teach the notes but also to assist the production as directed by the producer; and at the performance the chorus master or his assistant should dress up and sing with the chorus. Then choose a head producer who is again subordinate to the conductor.
>
> And finally they should plan a clear. precise programme and not choose the operas at random as has been done over the last few years. And the same should go for the singers who are engaged. Either choose the singers for the opera, or the opera for the singers.*

A familiar theme; but the notion of a chorus master taking part in a performance in costume as a chorister is certainly an unusual one.

Mascheroni was duly appointed; but the news that a certain Piontelli had been made impresario was not well received; a disaster for the theatre, Verdi considered, but for himself perhaps a blessing in disguise, since he could now safely give up all thoughts of mounting *Falstaff* at La Scala, which would be too vast to allow the words to come over clearly, and put on the opera at the Teatro Carcano instead. Boito and Giulio Ricordi were appalled; and the publisher exerted all his diplomacy to convince Verdi that at La Scala he would have complete freedom to organize the performance he wanted with all the singers he wanted. Verdi then returned to another well-worn theme. 'In writing *Falstaff* I haven't been thinking of theatres or of singers. I have written it for my own pleasure and on my own account and I think that rather than give it at La Scala it should be given at S. Agata'.† Whatever his objections to Piontelli they cannot have been insuperable; there was no further question of giving the new opera elsewhere than at La Scala – just so long as Verdi was not expected to deal directly with the management.

From the summer of 1891 poet and composer kept their eyes open for likely interpreters. A letter of Verdi's written the following year to Giulio Ricordi is of extreme interest since it sets out at length his views about the special nature of the opera. First of all the designers. 'To paint theatrical scenes you want theatrical painters – painters whose dearest wish is not to make a parade of their own virtuosity but to serve the drama. . . . At the most, send to London for figurines of the *Merry Wives* as performed there.' (Boito too had expressed himself forcibly in the matter of avoiding the picturesque, and even suggested clothing Bardolph and Pistol in rags like Murillo

---

* Letter to Boito, 29.4.1891. *Copialettere*, pp. 368–9.
† Letter to Giulio Ricordi, 6.6.1891. *Copialettere*, p. 713.

beggars.)* Neither of them trusted Hohenstein, the Scala's resident scene-painter, not to excel himself in romantic fantasy. 'As for machinery,' Verdi continued, 'there's a little to do apart from the basket scene, which in any case presents no difficulty because there are no pointless complications. As for effects of illumination all that's needed is a little bit of darkness in the Park scene, but let's be clear about this: the kind of darkness that allows you to see the faces of the artists. No special lighting effects as in the last scene of *La Wally*: very beautiful if you like but they ruined the dramatic effect completely and the opera fell flat at the end.' Clearly Verdi's ideas had changed since the distant days in which he had suggested to Piave a sunset for the third act of *I Due Foscari* merely because 'sunsets are always so beautiful'. 'As for the orchestra, *something is rotten in the state of Denmark*.' So to a tirade about the slackness of La Scala's players such as could have been directed against all opera orchestras of the time except possibly that of Bayreuth: passengers among the violins, poor tuning in the winds, trombones unable to play softly, and so on. Would Mascheroni please take note and do something about it.

'Now we come to the most serious aspect. Alas, the difficulties grow greater and greater and are choking us. La Fabbri with her fine voice could be successful with melodies based on agility, as in *Cenerentola*, etc.† But the part of Quickly is something quite different. You need to sing and to act, to move with complete assurance on stage, and to put the right stress on the main syllable. She hasn't these qualities; and so we run the risk of sacrificing a part which is the most original and colourful of the four.' Indeed, the colouring of Dame Quickly's character – so slippery and deceitful in *The Merry Wives* that Meg and Alice refer to her as 'this carrion' – is one of Verdi's most delightful transformations. However, all praise to Boito for not having followed Shakespeare in making her play the Fairy Queen in the last act.

> The part of Alice [*Verdi continues*] needs the same qualities, together with a greater vivacity. She must have a bit of a devil about her. It's she who *stirs the porridge*. Guerrini will be fine in the part of Meg; I'm only sorry the part isn't more important. Nannetta must be very young and sing very beautifully; she must sparkle on stage, above all in the two little duets with the tenor, and especially in one of them which is very lively and very funny. You see, it won't be easy to find what's needed! . . . .
>
> For the juvenile lead, no one better than Masini, but I'm afraid of his sulks when he finds out at rehearsals that the parts of Falstaff, Alice, Quickly, Ford, etc., are more important than his, and whether or not he means to be, he's too lachrymose. . . .
>
> Pescina is a good artist but he's more of a singer than an actor and a bit too heavy for the part of Ford, who when he's mad with jealousy yells and shouts and jumps about, etc., and unless he can do this the second act finale will fall flat. All the attention is concentrated on him and switched to Falstaff whenever he sticks his nose out of the basket.

* Letter from Boito, 9.5.1892. *Carteggio Verdi–Boito*, I, p. 206.

†Guerrina Fabbri had already been indicated as an excellent choice for Quickly on the basis of a recent performance of *Cenerentola* at the Teatro Dal Verme – with the reservation that she had no feeling for Rossinian style whatever! Letter from Boito, 9.6.1891. *Ibid.*, pp. 189–90.

Caius needs clear diction.

Cesari is too much for the part of Pistol. But if he's happy with it we could enlarge the part, giving him several of Bardolph's phrases; and we'll have a word with Boito about this.

Even for Bardolph we need a self-assured actor and one who can carry his nose in the air. . . .

I should add that the piano and production rehearsals will be lengthy, because it won't be easy to perform the work as I should like, and I shall be very demanding and not as I was in *Otello* when out of deference to this person or that and in order to pose as someone serious and grave and venerable I put up with everything. No, no; I shall go back to being a bear as I used to be and we shall all gain by it.

The music isn't difficult but it must be sung differently from modern comic operas and the old *opera buffa*. I wouldn't want it sung like for instance *Carmen*, nor even like *Don Pasquale* or *Crispino*. It's a study all on its own and needs time. Generally speaking our singers can only sing with full voice; they haven't vocal elasticity or clear and easy syllabation, and they lack verbal and musical attack [*accento*] and breath control . . .*

Yet he had to admit that the advantage of having Masini, one of the stars of the Requiem, for the Sonetto would be considerable. 'If the music succeeds Masini could make a great deal of it.' Apart from that Fenton's was 'a charming, sparkling role that takes part in many of the scenes without being in the least tiring'.†

But *Falstaff*, it will be gathered, was to be above all an opera of teamwork. So Verdi was not unduly discouraged when Masini hesitated to throw up a profitable contract for St Petersburg which would have prevented him attending the early rehearsals. ('Too many celebrities, too many Divi; too much of a good thing can do harm.')‡ He was replaced by Edoardo Garbin, a tenor in whom the old habits of poor diction and over-vocalization were unfortunately ingrained.

He's had no experience [*Verdi complained*] and he knows nothing about music. I don't know how he'll fare in the final fugue. . . . Almost all the operas written up to now are scored so that violins, trumpets and horns double the vocal line, and there he's all right; and with his magnificent high notes he can drag applause from an over-indulgent public. But *Falstaff* is another matter. Each note and syllable has to be given its proper due. Then too he has the confounded habit of opening out his voice on the final vowel of a word. Thus in 'Allor la nota che non è più sola' he doesn't put the accent on the 'o', he puts it on the 'a', so that it comes out distorted and changes the vocal timbre.§

And later:

He's only too happy to be able to miss a rehearsal . . . and so I beg you to get Pini to make him work hard at his part so that at least he's sure of his notes. A good

* Letter to Giulio Ricordi, 17.6.1892. Abbiati, IV, pp. 442–4.
† Letter to Giulio Ricordi. *Ibid.*, pp. 445–6.
‡ Letter to Giulio Ricordi, 5.8.1892. *Ibid.*, p. 451.
§ Letter to Giulio Ricordi, 16.11.1892. *Ibid.*, p. 466.

deal more is needed besides. I'm worried about the Sonetto in Act III; not because I regard it as important in itself – as far as the drama goes we could do without it; but because the whole piece provides me with a new colour for the musical palette; and it rounds off Fenton's character.*

The ideal Quickly was found in Giuseppina Pasqua, a thoroughly intelligent artist who was soon to become a member of the Verdi circle at Montecatini. True, Verdi had been alarmed by a highly coloured account of her dramatic qualities given to Ricordi by Puccini (she had sung Tigrana for him in Madrid in February); he therefore suggested to the publisher that he write to her personally and tell her outright that there would be no place for tantrums and high emotional drama in *Falstaff*. 'This is comedy – music, notes and words; no *cantabili*; mobility on stage and plenty of dash.'† A visit to S. Agata confirmed Verdi's favourable opinion of her. He wrote to Ricordi.

> In her heart of hearts perhaps she would have liked a part which would stand out on its own; but she's intelligent and she understands what it's all about; she will be happy to do this part and should do it well. Only I myself have noticed that at certain points in the third act Quickly is on stage too long without having anything to say, and I think that we could take the odd word or sentence here and there from Alice and Meg and give them to Quickly without spoiling the comedy; and the performance would lose nothing. I'll write to Boito about it when I've been over the third act.‡

So it seems that even in an opera written uncompromisingly to please no one but himself, Verdi was not above making concessions to the qualities of a great executive artist; and we may be sure that it was to Pasqua's prowess as a comédienne that we owe Quickly's substantial solo at the start of Act II, Scene ii.§

The search for a suitable Alice was rewarded about the same time. Gemma Bellincioni had been rejected as 'very intelligent but too sentimental'.¶ Likewise Emma Calvé, a specialist in heavy dramatic and 'veristic' roles and a prima donna in the worst sense of the word. The conductor Usiglio had recommended a certain Tetrazzini, 'not the one who does Desdemona so well, but the other who they say has run away to America with the bass Cesari'.‖ But in the end he settled, on Ricordi's advice, for Emma Zilli, not without certain misgivings. 'I too realized that there was something good about her voice, but I felt let down when I heard the pieces from *Aida* which are her warhorses. However, if we managed to find all the rest we could make a fresh experiment with Zilli. I would like her to be sent a couple of passages; then I'd work on them with her myself a few times and after that we can decide. What do you say?'** Ricordi was agreeable, and La Zilli even more so; and in due course Verdi was

---

* Letter to Giulio Ricordi, 21.12.1892. *Ibid.*, pp. 468–9.

† Letter to Giulio Ricordi, 17.6.1892. *Ibid.*, pp. 444–5.

‡ Letter to Giulio Ricordi, 12.7.1892. *Ibid.*, pp. 446–7.

§ See J. Hepokoski, 'Verdi, Giuseppina Pasqua and the Composition of *Falstaff*' in *Nineteenth Century Music*, III (March 1980), pp. 239–56.

¶ Letter to Giulio Ricordi, 17.6.1892. *Ibid.*, pp. 444–5.

‖ Letter to Giulio Ricordi, 12.7.1892. Information is tantalizingly lacking; but, at a guess, the one who 'does Desdemona so well' was Eva, and the other, whom Verdi wanted, was Luisa.

** Letter to Giulio Ricordi, 14.7.1892. Abbiati, IV, p. 447.

talking with pleasure of her 'feroce voluntà' in learning the part, in marked contrast to Garbin's laziness.*

The part of Nannetta was given to Adelina Stehle, a singularly happy choice since this meant that the young lovers of the opera were lovers in fact and would marry later in the year of *Falstaff*'s première. She and Garbin would soon be delighting audiences up and down the peninsula as Mimi and Rodolfo in Puccini's *Bohème*. Originally Stehle had been considered for Alice but 'her voice is too thin', Verdi said; 'she would be all right for the part of Nannetta, however, provided she has a bit of sentiment as well as dash. In the third act there's an ethereal, fantastic, pathetic song which must be beautifully sung.'†

About the same time Verdi specified certain instrumental requirements – an oboe with good low notes for Quickly's scene in Act II ('and no harm if they say that I don't know the range of the instrument'); a flute in D flat with an E flat for the Honour speech; a bass clarinet in A for the 'Litanies' in Windsor Forest; and in the prelude to the same scene a genuine *corno da caccia* without valves in A flat basso ('the instrument will have to be rather bulky').‡

Ford was satisfactorily entrusted to Antonio Pini-Corsi, a lusty baritone with a penchant for comedy (he had made his debut in *La Cenerentola*, was a noted exponent of Ponchielli's fatiguing satire *Il parlatore eterno* and would be Puccini's first Schaunard). For Falstaff himself, as for Iago, only one name had suggested itself from the start, Victor Maurel. Yet curiously enough it was he who came nearest to upsetting the applecart through his exorbitant claims: the right to the first performance in several of the major cities of Europe, including London and Madrid, 4,000 lire for each performance, 10,000 lire for attending rehearsals (in those days the rehearsals were included in the artist's global fee). After a visit to S. Agata by Mme Maurel, intent on smoothing the path, Verdi wrote to Giulio Ricordi in a fury: 'Never has such a thing happened to me in fifty years of theatrical hard labour' (he used the old phrase 'anni di galera'). 'There are no words to describe such a claim and there can be no arguing about it. You mustn't hesitate, you must publish Maurel's claim straightaway together with my telegram and add that *for this reason we can't put on Falstaff*.'§ After two more thunderbolts from Busseto the Maurels gave way on all three counts, Mme Maurel covering her retreat with as much dignity as she could muster by means of a letter to the publisher in which she admitted the unwisdom of troubling impractical musicians with business matters when they are floating 'in the empyrean of their artistic dreams'. This letter Ricordi was unable to resist passing on to Verdi himself. 'Dear good soul,' was the composer's comment. 'I would have thought she'd have had a bit more sense.'¶ Finally Maurel himself came to see the composer and all was set fair once more.

Piano rehearsals under Verdi's direction began in November. Ricordi had already supplied him with a proof copy of the piano reduction on which as rehearsals proceeded he marked a number of corrections and alterations. This copy was presented by Verdi to the conductor Mascheroni, who in turn left it to the Library of

---

* See letter to Giulio Ricordi, 21.12.1892. *Ibid.*, pp. 468–9.
† Letter to Giulio Ricordi, 17.6.1892. *Ibid.*, pp. 444–5.
‡ Letter to Giulio Ricordi. *Ibid.*, p. 445.
§ Letter to Giulio Ricordi, 30.8.1892. *Ibid.*, p. 454.
¶ Letter to Giulio Ricordi, 7.9.1892. *Ibid.*, p. 457.

the Milan Conservatory. It has recently been the object of a close study by the late Guglielmo Barblan.* Corrections of misprints abound; here and there a fragment of dialogue will be more effectively paced, as for instance 'Che c'è dentro quel cesto?' 'Il bucato' in the hectic finale to Act II. Again, a line of declamation will be changed to give greater clarity and a more appropriate verbal inflection, as in Nannetta's 'Col Dottor Cajo non mi sposerò' in Act II or Ford's penitent 'Riconosco i miei demeriti' in Act III, Scene i – a procedure familiar from the sketch for *I Due Foscari* in the Busseto museum.

More interesting are the points where both melody and harmony are modified, as in the phrase from Act I, 'Rubar con garbo e a tempo', giving an effect of irresistible ironic effrontery to the original idea:

Likewise the conclusion of the Honour speech receives a new dismissive emphasis through the addition of an extra bar (Ex. 246b), a greater harmonic movement and the insertion of a Neapolitan sixth into what had originally been a mere plain V–I cadence (Ex. 246a). A further correction in the autograph (Ex. 246c) itself involving two repetitions of the word 'No!' in the course of the inserted chord was never carried over into the published score but is obviously available to any baritone who wishes to make use of it.

* G. Barblan, 'Un prezioso spartito del *Falstaff*', Edizione della Scala (Milan, 1957). The author was wrong, however, in attributing to this rehearsal period the two very substantial alterations in the Act II concertato and the end of Act III, Scene i, for a discussion of which see below.

246c

As usual there are plenty of surprises. The evocative motif for four horns that occurs during Ford's monologue before the words 'L'ora è fissata' and which raises an appropriate echo of King Philip's loneliness and jealousy, originally consisted of mere syncopated thirds:

247a

247b

Fenton's Sonetto was tortured into its final form like any symphonic melody of Beethoven's in his various sketchbooks. It will be sufficient to quote the opening phrase as it existed up till the winter of 1892.

248

A change in the distribution of the finale ultimo is explained by Verdi himself in a letter to Giulio Ricordi. 'A huge, stupid, unforgivable slip. A composer who perpetrates this kind of thing should be shot. In the penultimate scene of the third act after Falstaff has said, "I begin to perceive that I am made an ass," I've made everyone cry out, "And a stag, a bull and a rare monster," without realizing that Nannetta, Fenton, Ford and Caius are no longer on stage. . . . I'm sorry about the plates that you'll have to remake. . . . Shoot me!'* Presumably Ricordi noticed that in sending this correction the composer had made another, minor slip. He meant Bardolph, not Ford.

Throughout the proof copy there are notes and observations regarding the production. At the end of the second-act finale there is the cryptic direction: 'Pay great attention to the falling of the basket and the entrance of the men – *Patatrac.*' Evidently in this most carefully written of all his operas Verdi was prepared to leave nothing to chance. Finally we may note two timings at the end of Scenes i and ii of Act I jotted down with obvious satisfaction: '14 minutes!!' and '14½ minutes!!' To have struck this kind of internal balance without having consciously striven for it was clearly a source of delight.

Needless to say, the first night was a national occasion with correspondents present from all over Europe and telegrams from the King and Queen of Italy. The audience included the Princess Letizia Bonaparte, the Minister of Education, the poet Carducci, the playwright Giacosa, the painter Boldini, not to mention two young composers who had recently made their mark in opera of a very different stamp – Puccini and Mascagni. The quartet of women in Act I, Scene ii, was encored; so too Falstaff's solo 'Quand' ero paggio del Duca di Norfolk'. The press was enthusiastic – it could hardly have been otherwise – and some of the reactions will be noted later. What concerns us at the moment is that the opera had still not reached its definitive form. The weak spot, Verdi felt, not for the first time, to be the final concertato of Act II. Reading his correspondence with Giulio Ricordi on the subject one seems to be watching the same critical process at work that operated on the Act III finale of *Otello*. Less than a month after the first night the composer confessed his doubts:

> I don't know whether you know that at one of the orchestral rehearsals at which I went and listened to the opera in the stalls I was so dissatisfied with the concertato finale that I got all the artists together and said to them, 'The piece won't do like this; either you must perform it more quietly and entirely *sotto voce* and standing in isolated groups or else it must be cut or changed.' No one breathed a word, but what I said did not produce a good impression, as they will be able to tell you.
>
> Next evening they performed it better and no more was said. But at the performances I noticed that on stage the piece is long and is too obviously a pezzo concertato.
>
> I wanted to change it at Milan but I never had an hour of complete leisure. I say 'change it' because I am totally opposed to cuts. To cut a section is like cutting off an arm, a stomach, two legs, etc., etc. In pieces which are conceived on too big a scale cuts have to be made sooner or later but it always results in a monstrosity; a body without a head or without legs.
>
> In the concertato of *Falstaff* it would be easy to make a cut and jump straightaway to 'dolci richiami d'amor', but the piece of music wouldn't remain

* Letter to Giulio Ricordi, 27.11.1892. *Ibid.*, p. 467.

intact; it would lack a belly. I've rewritten six bars and the piece is now shortened by ten bars. I'll send it you tomorrow. I'd like it to be performed before the run at La Scala finishes.*

The following day he dispatched the piece, again expressing satisfaction at having saved ten long bars.

As theatre it's better, as music I don't know . . . except that it's good to bring back the wives, and at any rate the piece lacks neither stomach nor legs.

Do what you like with it. Look at it with Mascheroni and Boito; in fact Boito will have to adjust a few lines. The singers know that I wasn't happy with that piece; and so they won't mind coming for half an hour to the rehearsal room. I'll be there myself; indeed give me half an hour's warning and I'll come with the speed of a telegraph horse. . . .

It was hardly the best time to insist on such a change, especially in a score so finely wrought, and it placed Ricordi, Mascheroni, Boito and the artists in a quandary. Through Ricordi, Boito transmitted his impression that the revised passage somehow seemed a bar short. Verdi was surprised but admitted that the passage might perhaps be improved by shortening a phrase of the cantilena of Fenton and Nannetta. 'Try it out with the singers; and once you've rehearsed it thoroughly, if you still have the impression that a bar is missing don't let's speak of it any further and let matters continue as they have done up to now.' Not unnaturally neither Boito, Ricordi nor Mascheroni were willing to take upon themselves such a responsibility. Verdi must do as he had originally suggested and pay a flying visit to Milan and so decide for himself whether the new version was better than the old. But now it was Verdi who was unwilling to come all the way from Genoa to Milan for the sake of six bars; and eventually he realized the folly of making any changes to the score during the present run of performances. ('Later, who knows . . . possibly for a revival.')

For in the meantime he had become convinced of the need to make an even more substantial alteration to the end of the first scene of Act III. On 18 March he wrote to Ricordi '. . . I've never liked that kind of mazurka which ends the first part of Act III . . . and the fact is that I had all ready to hand a tune ('avrò con me dei putti') – which would have been far more effective if I'd developed and worked it out properly. It was the continuation of the plan for the masquerade 'che fingeran folletti . . . spiritelli . . . farfarelli', etc., etc. It would have been so easy to do! What wretched heads we have! Better to dash them against a wall!' However, he did not write out this second revision till the first of April, when he sent it to Ricordi with instructions to copy out all the voice parts so that he could rehearse it in Genoa with the artists 'not to have it performed in the theatre either here or anywhere else, at least for the moment, but for my own artistic satisfaction'.

The two variants were finally performed on stage at the revival at the Teatro Costanzi, Rome, of 15 April, which a reluctant Verdi had been persuaded by poet and publisher to attend. They were duly incorporated in all future vocal scores as being definitive. Of the original versions no trace remains in the autograph since in

* Letter to Giulio Ricordi, 7.3.1893. For the correspondence on this subject see Abbiati, IV, pp. 499–503, and *Carteggio Verdi–Boito*, II, pp. 433–5.

accordance with his usual practice Verdi had torn out the superseded pages and replaced them with new ones. But a number of the earliest vocal scores are in circulation containing Verdi's first thoughts on both passages; and these will briefly be discussed in their context.

No further revisions of any substance follow. In May Verdi authorized Mascheroni to add oboes and clarinets to the a cappella female quartet in Act I at the Venice revival so long as he avoided a low B in the oboe 'which always produces an unpleasant effect'.* In successive editions of the vocal score (always with the same plate number) tiny variants will be found. The last of any importance was made for the first Parisian performance in French in May 1894 and required extra lines from Boito which had then to be translated into Italian. (As with *Otello* Boito shared in the French translation, taking as his partner on this occasion Paul Solanges, translator of his own *Mefistofele*, not to mention *La Gioconda, Cavalleria Rusticana* and a host of Italian romanze.) After Falstaff's 'Sono le fate. Chi le guarda è morto' and before Nannetta's song 'Sul fil d'un soffio etesio' the original score carried a passage of twelve bars for orchestra alone. Over these Verdi now thought fit to insert a number of brief comments from Alice, Nannetta herself and the fairies ('Come this way', 'He is there', 'On the ground', etc.) all of which were included in the latest editions. Whether the other minute divergences come before or afterwards, and how much weight should be given to them as expressing the composer's definitive ideas, it is difficult to be certain. However, with the Paris performance the opera for all practical purposes attains its final form.

It was never to become a popular favourite. Even at the triumphal first night it was possible to discern through 'the roaring and the wreaths' a certain puzzled disappointment among the public. According to Monaldi: 'After the fairy music and the exquisite romance for tenor, the music, though graceful and elegant, no longer pleased. Even the final fugue, a splendid piece of music, seemed too long and in no wise beautiful. The success of the opera, so unmistakable in the first act, reaching its climax in the second, definitely waned in the third.'† For this he followed the usual habit, when a great composer's opera falls short of expectation, of blaming the libretto; but he also admits that the musical style of the times with its emphasis on harmonic and contrapuntal 'dottrina', not to mention Verdi's advanced age, militated against the belly laugh that *Il Barbiere* had taught audiences to expect from *opera buffa*. Indeed it was the craftsmanship and above all the orchestral brilliance rather than the substance that seems to have impressed most of the Italian critics, though they duly paid tribute to its 'classical purity'. Alfred Bruneau, standard-bearer of 'verismo' in France, probed a little deeper. 'The score of *Falstaff*,' he wrote in *Gil Blas*, 'not so much in its form as in its musical essence, derives directly from Rossini and the Italian composers who preceded him, with here and there some exquisite recollections of Mozart and Haydn. I heard people around me say that the influence of *Meistersinger* was apparent, but frankly I cannot see it. Neither on this nor on any other occasion does Verdi seem to have wished to assimilate the polyphonic style of Richard Wagner, and his lyrical comedy remains in the key of *bouffonnerie*

* Letter to Mascheroni, 7.5.1893. *Copialettere*, pp. 717–18. This was not an afterthought so much as a reversion to first thoughts, since these instruments are scored out in the autograph.

† G. Monaldi, *Le Opere di Giuseppe Verdi al Teatro alla Scala* (Milan, 1914), p. 138; see also the same author's *Verdi* (4th edition, Milan, 1951), pp. 301 ff.

with snatches of poetry whose grace, though it is delicious, has no true analogy with the luxuriant grandeur of the German work.'* For Charles Villiers Stanford, reporting for the *Daily Graphic*, the dominant influence on the score was Beethoven. 'The close student of the quartets and the piano sonatas was evident everywhere; the composer of the "Waldstein" is the ancestor of this great creation. Other influences there are. Occasionally there are traces of Meyerbeer but cleansed of his banalities and tricks; more often there is a twinkle of *Meistersinger*. Over all is the unmistakable stamp of Verdi, master of vocal writing, of an orchestration and of a pure Italian method of expression. His very memories of Beethoven are tinged by his affection for Scarlatti.' He had only two reservations; the scene in which Falstaff is tortured in Act III seemed to him unduly long; and he felt the lack of one really broad, central melody 'which without being too intrusive would give a rest-point to the ear and clamp together the rest of the score'; and he cited the 'Preislied' in *Meistersinger* as an instance of what he meant. For the rest he found the opera 'clear as crystal in construction, tender and explosive by turns, humorous and witty without a touch of extravagance or a note of vulgarity'.†

As so often, the most perceptive comments came from fellow-composers rather than professional reviewers. The Wagnerian critic John Runciman, while duly noting the advance shown in sheer craftsmanship over *Aida* and *La Traviata*, questioned the opera's lasting vitality (indeed, had not Cosima Wagner professed herself unable to see any real difference between *Falstaff* and *Il Trovatore*?). Richard Strauss, no less than Runciman a worshipper at the Bayreuth shrine, declared it to be one of the masterpieces of all time.

Before proceeding to the commentary we may briefly consider *Falstaff*'s relation both to the composer's previous works and to the operatic music of its period.

From the moment that the project became public knowledge Verdi made it clear that his latest opera would be quite different in kind from anything he had written to date. First it was a comedy such as he had wanted to compose all his life but had been prevented from doing for lack of the right libretto; and second he was writing it to please himself rather than the public. 'Certain passages,' he told another correspondent of the *Daily Graphic* in January 1893, 'are so droll that the music has often made me laugh while writing it.'‡ The correspondent was rather shocked, and even regretted that the composer of *La Traviata* had 'lived to employ his magnificent genius for the purpose of making himself and others laugh'. *Falstaff*, then, was to be a private joke which the public was welcome to share if they liked. But it was possible that neither the right singers nor the right theatre existed for it. It belonged to the realm of the ideal.

This theme, which recurs constantly in Verdi's letters and communications, needs to be interpreted in the light of his personal, and by now deeply ingrained, attitude towards his art. He was not an artist like Wagner who wished to mould the public in his own image and whose whole life could be seen as a sacrifice to that end crowned by the magnificent edifice of Bayreuth. He did not plough his own furrow regardless of obstacles and without stooping to compromise, as some of the rugged in-

---

* Quoted in Toye, p. 205.

† C. V. Stanford, *Studies and Memories* (London, 1908), p. 175.

‡ 'Verdi's *Falstaff*: a visit to the composer' was published in the *Daily Graphic* of 14.1.1893.

dividualists of our own century have done. As one who frequented the theatre constantly, despite his professed lack of interest in what his younger contemporaries were doing, he was always ready to put himself in the position of the most unprejudiced spectator. If a special effect failed to please the fault might lie with the performers rather than himself, but something would have to be done about it. Like Mozart he wrote for the present; he was even ready to make concessions to the taste of a foreign public, as his French versions of *Il Trovatore* and *La Forza del destino* demonstrate, though he would only carry the resulting alterations into the definitive scores if they satisfied his artistic conscience. In other words Verdi's creations are the outcome of a dialogue between composer and public.

On the face of it, *Falstaff* should be an exception to the rule; the public's pleasure had been specifically excluded as a factor in the opera's creation. But the habits of a lifetime are not so easily put aside. The two substantial alterations to the finale of Act II and the first scene of Act III were the consequence of Verdi's having seen the opera as a member of the audience. Apart from its subject matter the difference between *Falstaff* and the operas that preceded it is less great than Verdi himself would have us believe; and in stating that the work showed not a trace of his earlier manner the critic of *The Times* was making a purely superficial observation. In fact *Falstaff* represents the culmination of all those tendencies observed from the composer's earliest days: from progress by sharp contrasts to progress by transition; from blunt, rugged fragments to a seamless continuity. The almost total lack of vocal melisma is anticipated in the first *Boccanegra* (a lack which, Verdi had said, should not cause the singers to clutch their hair and throw a mad fit).* Ever since *Rigoletto*, comedy had been making incursions into Verdi's operas. Not even *Otello* is free from it – witness the scenes involving Iago and Cassio in Acts I and III. With comedy comes a lighter, more delicate style of scoring with plentiful use of piccolo. Finally we have noted an increasing use in late Verdi of classical figuration, beginning with the revised version of *Simon Boccanegra*. This style of writing will come to predominate in *Falstaff*, giving to the score something of the character of a Beethoven quartet. It is not precisely contrapuntal, yet every fibre of the texture has life and interest even where the material amounts to little more than academic commonplace. An instance from the letter-reading scene in Act I, Scene ii, will suffice to illustrate this. (Ex. 249)

This method of deploying orchestra and voices, especially as it appeared in the buck-basket scene, inspired Bernard Shaw, who loved Verdi as he loved Dickens, to one of his most delightful if perverse 'I-told-you-so' sallies.

> ... If I had said ten years ago that *Ernani* was a much greater work than Mendelssohn's Scotch Symphony or any of his concertos, words could not have conveyed the scorn with which so gross an opinion would have been received. But here, today, is the scorned one, whom even Browning thought it safe to represent as an empty blusterer shrinking amid a torrent of vulgar applause from the grave eye of – of – well- of ROSSINI! (poor Browning!), falling back in his old age on the Mendelssohnian method, and employing it with ease and

---

* See Vol. 2, p. 254.

249

brilliance. Perhaps when Verdi turns a hundred and feels too old for opera composition he will take to concerto writing and cut out Mendelssohn and Schumann and the pretty pattern work which the pundits love them for.*

It will be noticed that although few reviews of *Falstaff* failed to mention such names as Cimarosa, Scarlatti, Rossini and other composers of the past in connection with it, not one suggested that the opera was in any way behind the times. Indeed if anything *Falstaff* is ahead of them, but not with an obvious modernity. Verdi's distaste for chains of what seemed to him discords has been observed on more than one occasion; † nor did he have much sympathy for what were regarded as advanced methods of operatic construction. Returning to his critique of Bruneau's *Le Rêve* we find:

> There are many good intentions in it but, as they say, the way to Hell is paved with good intentions. The opera contains neither recitativo parlato nor verbal repetitions nor *couplets* nor thematic reminiscences nor so many of those formulae that are so much in vogue, especially at the Opéra Comique. All this is good; what's not so good is that all the action is confined and stifled within a circle of three or four, I won't say tunes, but orchestral phrases which go round and round throughout the opera without a single extended passage for the voice.

He pointed to various moments in the libretto where it would have been possible to

---

* *Shaw's Music*, II, pp. 855–6. The reference to Browning concerns a passage in his poem 'Bishop Blougram's Apology'.
† See Vol. 2, p. 46.

write 'expressive, dramatic and simple music without so many orchestral frills, which are not only not beautiful but quite pointless. As well as that there is a continuous legato throughout the opera, the effect of which can only be highly monotonous.'[*] So the slow, Wagnerian swirl, verismo's most notable legacy from the Master of Bayreuth, was no more for Verdi than the chromaticisms, the piling up of suspensions and appoggiature that were to lead through Mahler and Reger to the world of German expressionism.

Yet *Falstaff* shares one common ancestor with verismo – namely *Carmen*. If Mascagni and his followers took from Bizet's masterpiece its low-life ambience, and its moments of brutal passion, it is the elegance, the light-fingered, brilliant scoring and the clear, sometimes astringent harmonic palette that left its mark on Verdi. Despite their different metres, Fenton's Sonetto has a certain kinship with the Flower Song: and indeed the final cadence of Don José's romance with its striking use of non-functional harmony prefigures the kind of novelty that will stamp Verdi's boldest strokes elsewhere in the opera. Where the situation demands it, Verdi can show the most sophisticated harmonic resources. The passage depicting the enchantment that descends on Windsor Forest before Nannetta's song is as richly evocative as any piece of late nineteenth-century tone-painting. The series of chords that underpin the chimes of midnight are as 'pioneering' as anything written at the time and for many years afterwards. And if Verdi refused to tread in the path of those with whose aesthetic ideals he was out of sympathy, this did not prevent him from learning from and even imitating certain features of them. Not only is the orchestra of *Falstaff* identical with that of *Meistersinger*, with a piccolo in addition to two flutes and a third trumpet; the first acts of both operas end with an ensemble laid out on very similar lines, as will be shown.

But the essential modernity of *Falstaff* is the modernity of Rossini's 'Péchés de Vieillesse'. It anticipates a later aesthetic in which the heavy romantic gesture gives way to a light irony. Born at the end of a romantic century *Falstaff* reaches above and beyond romanticism.

ACT I

Part 1: Inside the Garter Inn. A table. A large armchair. A bench. On the table the remains of a meal, several bottles and a mug. A pen, quills, paper, a lighted candle. A broom propped up against the wall. Entrance backstage; a door on the left. When the curtain rises Falstaff is discovered in the act of heating some sealing-wax in the flame of the candle; he then seals two letters with a signet ring, blows out the candle and begins to drink at his ease, stretched out in his chair. Enter a furious Dr Caius.[†]

As in *Otello* the music plunges *in medias res* without prelude or overture – or so it appears. But in fact the opening scene reveals itself to the attentive listener as its own overture, constructed thematically while at the same time giving point to the stage

---

[*] Letter to Boito, 5.7.1891. *Carteggio Verdi–Boito*, I, p. 191–2.
[†] Curiously, no production book for *Falstaff* has yet come to light.

action at each moment.* The first theme, with its imperious up-beat gesture, is associated with the futile expostulations of Dr Caius; the motif (*x*) being broken down as the music proceeds into sequences suggesting a mounting sense of grievance:

250

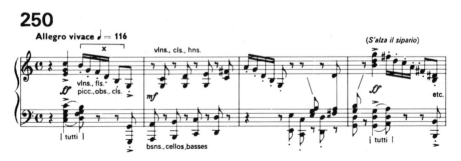

In fact Caius has more to complain of than either Shallow or Slender in the play. Falstaff had poached the lands of the first and beaten the keepers who tried to prevent him; while his own followers had made Slender drunk and picked his pocket. Caius, however, owns no deer park. Verdi's Falstaff had broken into his house, beaten his servants and exhausted his bay mare, while Caius himself has suffered Slender's misfortune. Falstaff, fully at his ease in the armchair, merely calls for another bottle of sherry. Here a short transition in quavers contains a muted echo of the semiquaver figure (*x*), from Ex. 250 on the violas, showing Falstaff making light of the whole matter. Caius returns to the charge. 'You have forced my house.' 'But not your housekeeper.' 'Too kind. A blear-eyed old hag.' This exchange is Boito's and only distantly related to Shakespeare's quip '. . . But not kissed your keeper's daughter,' but it provides Verdi with the opportunity for an ironic cadence ('Troppa grazia') which forms a bridge to an abbreviated Ex. 250 which now begins to move away from the tonic area. '. . . if you were twenty times John Falstaff, Knight I would

251

* For this account of the *modus operandi* of the first scene I am indebted to a talk given by Pierluigi Petrobelli on B.B.C. Radio 3 in 1974. A tiny sketch for this scene is printed in facsimile by Gatti in his *Verdi nelle Immagini*, p. 87, where, like the sketch for *Otello* already mentioned, it is wrongly labelled. Not only is the pitch of the declamation different from that of the definitive score; it is also shorter by eight bars than the corresponding passage of the finished product.

force you to answer me!' 'Here is my answer. I have done all you say; I did it on purpose.' Falstaff's phlegmatic reply provides the contrasted theme, or, in textbook language, second subject, its huge three-octave span suggesting the immensity of the speaker. (Ex. 251)

No one familiar with Verdi's penchant for the *Terzverwandschaft* will be surprised at the tonality – E major instead of G – for which in any case there is a perfect classical precedent in the 'Waldstein' Sonata. 'The Council shall know this.' ' 'Twere better for you if it were known in counsel [i.e., *in secret*]! You'll be laughed at.' Shakespeare's pun is neatly rendered by Boito's 'M'appellerò al Consiglio Real.' 'Sta zitto o avrai le beffe; quest'è il consiglio mio.' During all this Ex. 251 pursues a majestic course through C sharp minor, amplified by a descant in contrary motion. Ex. 250 is recalled as Caius launches the development section with the appropriate words 'Non è finito'. He switches the attack to Bardolph, who turns it aside with mock-pathos. He asks the doctor to feel his pulse and curses all innkeepers who put 'lime in the wine' (he is of course quoting Falstaff's complaint in *King Henry IV*, Part I, about 'lime in the sack'). Does Caius see his red nose? – the result of drinking bad wine. Here the musical basis is Ex. 251 deployed in repetitions and sequences on lower strings and bassoon and decorated by a triplet figure (*y*) shared between first violins and piccolo which will become more insistent as the scene proceeds (Ex. 252). At first it seems no more than an insignificant fidget designed to tone up the rhythm; but in *Falstaff* everything works to a purpose; and this figure tossed from one instrument to another will in due course generate a primitive melodic pattern (Ex. 253).

252

253

As Caius's accusations become more coherent ('M'hai fatto ber, furfante, con lui, narrando frasche; poi, quando fui ben ciùschero, m'hai vuotate le tasche' . . .) so his line takes melodic shape with one of those near-themes that abound in this most subtle of scores (Ex. 254) – a neat developmental ploy which catches perfectly the singer's aggrieved tone. Here too the triplets of Ex. 252 have a part to play.

Bardolph denies having picked Caius's pocket. 'Who was it then?' – and angry tutti chords give vent to the doctor's frustration. Once again Falstaff takes charge of the situation with a recollection of Ex. 251, now in B major. 'Pistol, did you pick this gentleman's purse?' But Caius gives him no time to reply, breaking in with a paraphrase of Slender's speech about 'seven groats in mill-sixpences and two Edward shovel-boards'. Here the development tightens with elements of Ex. 250 and 251, the latter in diminution and with Ex. 253 as its vertical complement, dissolving into six bars of indignant quaver chatter. Pistol seizes the broom and challenges Caius to a fight; and here the recapitulation begins as Ex. 250 bursts upon us unexpectedly in the home key, the second bar of the melody embellished by semiquaver figuration.

So to a comic slanging match – 'Gonzo!' 'Pezzente!' 'Bestia!' 'Can!' 'Vil!' 'Spauracchio!' The growing excitement is again quelled by Falstaff, this time with another quotation from the Histories where his follower is about to cause an affray in the Boar's Head: 'No more, Pistol; I would not have you go off here.' This is of course a reprise in C major of the second subject (Ex. 251) but with a new continuation which points up the musical structure as well as the dramatic situation. For as Bardolph protests that 'the gentleman had drunk himself out of his five senses' Ex. 251 is restated in its original key of E major, spelt out in notes of double value with glinting embellishments from piccolo, violin and flute. Here then is a confrontation of C major, the key of the prosecution, and E major, the key of the defence, which may be said to form the axis on which the 'overture' turns. Falstaff then abandons his attitude as inquisitor to conclude in this same E major ('You hear all these matters denied') with seven bars to suave declamation and an ironic cadence ('Go in peace!'). Naturally Caius is far from satisfied and returns via A minor to C major, trombones shaking an angry fist ('I'll never be drunk again whilst I live but in honest, civil, godly company!'). For the words 'Civile e pia' he opens out his voice into a fine heroic cadence while the orchestra throws off a few reminiscences of Ex. 250. Caius's sentiments prompt Pistol and Bardolph to a pious 'Amen' sung in rough schoolroom two-part counterpoint as they show him the door, clapping their hands in time to the rhythm. Falstaff cuts them short with a reproof which Boito has ingeniously quarried from Act I, scene iii of The Merry Wives. In the play Falstaff takes advantage of the Host's offer to employ Bardolph as a tapster, remarking, 'His thefts were too open; his filching was like an unskilled singer, he kept not time.' Nym: 'The good humour is to steal at a moment's rest.' In the opera this becomes:

FALSTAFF Stop this antiphony. You yell it out of time.
The art lies in this maxim: 'steal with charm and at the right time.'
You are unskilful artists.

Here the sudden turn into A flat major at the words 'rubar con garbo' (Ex. 245b) is like the dropping of the mask and the raising of a curtain. At once we are made aware of the extent to which Falstaff and his followers have been play-acting for Caius's benefit. At the same time the tonal spectrum is opened up in preparation for the next episode. However, there is no clean break with what has gone before. Pistol and Bardolph are allowed a brief return to their antiphony before Falstaff imposes silence with a gesture, and a derivative of Ex. 253 on unison strings provides a transition to what follows. At the end of his autograph of the overture to Alzira Verdi had written, 'AMEN!' At the end of his Falstaff 'overture' he allows himself the same comment, but this time publicly.

In a short bout of 'parlando' recitative over an open chord of sustaining horns Falstaff examines his bill: 'Six chickens – six shillings; thirty flagons of sherry – two pounds; three turkeys . . .'. He asks Bardolph to search, as he continues to read out the items. The harvest is meagre – 'Un mark, un mark, un penny'. An insignificant pattern of arpeggiated semiquavers starts up in the violas and develops polyphonically through the strings, culminating in Falstaff's outburst, 'Sei la mia distruzione!' – one of those rare excursions into high romantic harmony, whose effect is always humorous and ironical.

255

Boito is indebted once more to *King Henry IV*, Part I, for Falstaff's next sally, directed against Bardolph's red nose, which 'has saved me a thousand marks in links and torches with thee in the night betwixt tavern and tavern'. The melody begins periodically but soon strays from the path of symmetry under the presssure of the fat knight's mounting irritation; unremarkable in itself it takes on charm from the smooth delicacy of the scoring and a certain piquancy from the tiny rhythmic motif (*x*) that accompanies it, which has seemingly wandered in from Beethoven's 'Pastoral' Symphony, and not only enlivens the texture but serves as a principle of rhythmic continuity, lightly touched in at points where the freedom of declamation threatens to weaken the rhythmic structure.

256

Both Bardolph and Pistol cost him too much. He calls for another bottle of wine, adding after the music has pounded to another pseudo-romantic climax, 'Mi struggete le carni.' Ex. 256(*x*), unobtrusively present in the preceding passage, now develops into continuous semiquavers on second violins, forming the background to Falstaff's solemn pronouncement: if he becomes slimmer he will be no longer Falstaff; no one will love him. 'In this belly there are a thousand tongues which speak my name. This is my kingdom [*and here he points to his stomach*]; I shall increase it.' Piccolo and cello, four octaves apart, spell out the grotesque possibility of a slender, disembodied Falstaff.

257

A rolling pentatonic idea twice repeated and rising to a powerful climax portrays his actual rotundity and hoped-for increase.

258

At the word 'regno' note how even at this date Verdi liked to reinforce his climaxes with a 6/4 chord in a remote key (F major in relation to D flat). His followers meanwhile acclaim 'immense Falstaff' with all the solemnity of the Egyptian priesthood invoking Vulcan, as Ex. 258 blazes away in the brass. Next the fat knight unfolds his plan to make love to the wives of two Windsor burghers. The burden of this episode is carried by two themes: the first conversational and cheerfully insouciant (Ex. 259a); the second characteristically growing out of the final cadence of the first, amorous and increasingly seductive (Ex. 259b).

259a

259b

Verdi's Falstaff, unlike Shakespeare's, discourses on the beauties of Alice Ford ('Sguardo di stella! Collo di cigno! e il labbro?') before proceeding to his own attractions for her, so building up a mood of voluptuous anticipation which music can express so much more vividly than a mere lust for gold. At 'Alice è il nome' Ex. 259b is decorated with a counterpoint of violin semiquavers. As he tells how 'love's inspiration flamed up in my heart' Ex. 258 once more imposes its triplet swagger for five bars. Next elements of Ex. 259b, extended in a series of expansive gestures, accompany the mention of Alice's concupiscent glances ('Sometimes the beam of her view gilded my foot, sometimes my portly belly . . .' – lines which in the play refer to Meg Page). The sense of his own massiveness is enhanced by a tramping bass reminiscent of Iago's drinking song.

260

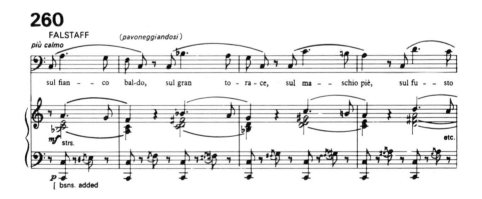

A tonal scheme that progresses by minor thirds (F–D–B) with caressing restatements of Ex. 259b marks Falstaff's growing self-confidence. Where Alice is imagined as saying, 'Io son di Sir John Falstaff,' Verdi makes use of the time-honoured buffo device of male falsetto. The subject of Meg is briefly touched upon with derivatives of Ex. 259a, enlivened by a divisi string scoring of combined pizzicato quavers and bowed, repeated semiquavers and ending in a great upward sweep for 'They shall be my East and West Indies' (in the opera Golconda and Gold Coast) together with a caricatured melisma at the cadence. At the reference to 'a fine St Martin's Summer' the music momentarily subsides into G major *pour mieux sauter* into the final restatement of Ex. 259b which rounds off the narration neatly and logically.

Falstaff then gives his two letters to Pistol and Bardolph respectively to deliver to the two wives (again the triplets of Ex. 254). Both men refuse, Pistol because the sword he wears will not allow him to play 'Sir Pandarus' (and here trombones growl a muted approval), Bardolph simply because 'honour forbids'. The next seventeen bars in which Falstaff sends for his page and hands him the two letters make up one of those musical gems that are scattered with apparent prodigality throughout the score yet are always relevant to the developing drama. In the light-fingered melody (Ex. 261) that proliferates in fine-spun counterpoint we hear the scurrying page and at the same time Falstaff's fury with his recalcitrant followers rising to boiling-point.

The basic structure here is regular, as is clear from the first eight bars; but then Ex. 261 plunges into the minor key, breaks down into repetitious fragments as Falstaff loses his temper, and finally works up to a fierce unison reinforced by woodwind, horn and trumpets, which in turn serves to detonate the superbly contemptuous 'Onore! Ladri!' Here the declamation, as in so much of late Verdi, is faithful to the natural inflexion of human speech; and how much more effectively do the trombones intervene in their echo of 'Ladri' for not having taken part in the preparatory gesture.

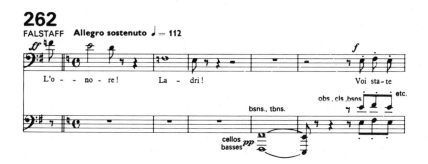

Boito had skilfully stitched the text of Falstaff's famous outburst from three sources: successively, his speech to the repentant Pistol in the *Merry Wives*, Act II, scene ii; his self-catechism in *King Henry IV*, Part I, Act V, scene i; and finally the *Merry Wives*, Act I, scene iii, the equivalent of its present context, where Nym and Pistol are ordered out of the Garter Inn. Each of these passages forms a separate section of a piece in which declamation and motif are fused in a wholly original manner. Stanford aptly described it as the smiling sister of Iago's Credo.*

The first section, despite its strict pulse, retains something of the character of recitativo accompagnato. 'You stand upon your honour? Why, thou unconfinable baseness, it is as much as I can do to keep the terms of my honour precise: I, I, I myself sometimes, leaving the fear of heaven on the left hand and hiding mine honour in my necessity am fain to shuffle, to hedge and to lurch; and yet you, you rogue, will ensconce your rags, your cat-a-mountain looks . . . under the shelter of your honour?' So much is magnificent ranting. Note the madrigalism at 'usare stratagemmi ed equivoci' where the vocal line twists and turns with suitable evasiveness; also the fine orchestral gesture of contempt after 'che baja' – savage unison trills leaping across a tritone. Yet the total effect would be amorphous were it not for the tiny melodic germ ('Devo talor da un lato') which yields a clear eight bars of periodicity of the kind that has held together many a Verdian declamatory scene, like chainmail in a slab of reinforced concrete. A delightful detail of texture is the combination of held low C on basses and horns doubled at the octave above by viola semiquavers.

263

Can honour set to a leg? no: or an arm? no: or take away the grief of a wound? no. Honour hath no skill in surgery, then? no. What is honour? a word. What is in that word? Honour. What is that honour? air. A trim reckoning! Who hath it? he that died o' Wednesday. Doth he feel it? no. Doth he hear it? no. Is it insensible, then? yea, to the dead. But will it not live with the living? no. Why? detraction will not suffer it: – therefore I'll none of it . . .

With 'Può l'onore riempirvi la pancia?' (Boito's anatomical variant on Shakespeare's original was evidently felt to be justified by the new context) the 'aria' section of the monologue could be said to begin. Note, however, that the main theme (Ex. 264a) is entirely born of verbal inflexion; nor does it take on harmonic flesh and blood until it has been 'planted' by the voice alone. Thereafter it will be worked and developed as an orchestral motif (Ex. 264b), finally appearing in full lyrical flower in the coda, where it rounds off Falstaff's comprehensive dismissal of honour and everything associated with it (Ex. 264c).

* *loc. cit.*

264a

264b

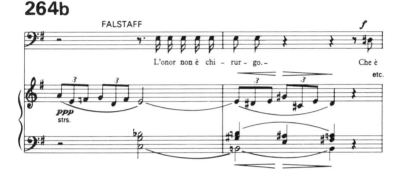

264c

The scoring throughout is very light so that the verbal accent emerges in all its clarity. At 'Può l'onor rimettervi uno stinco?' the double basses are reduced to two, the first being required to lower his fourth string so as to reach the low D – a reminder that though by 1893 the three-string bass was a thing of the past, the five-stringed instrument of today was not yet in general use. For 'Che c'è in questa parola? . . . dell'aria che vola' flutes and piccolo, with solo cello doubling the voice, blow a cloud of thistledown, to be brutally mocked by the rest of the orchestra at 'Bel costrutto!' At first this section may sound capricious and rhapsodic, with music reduced to mere verbal illustration. Closer acquaintance will reveal an organizing principle in the form of an ever-tighter motivic working of Ex. 264. It was surely for this reason that Boito provided some rather otiose lines to the effect that 'flattery swells it [i.e., *honour*], pride corrupts it, calumnies infect it' (Ex. 265). Here the acciaccatura figure which has accompanied the 'no's' rises into the upper woodwinds to become indistinguishable from a traditional lament. Never can its connotations have been less mournful than in the present context.

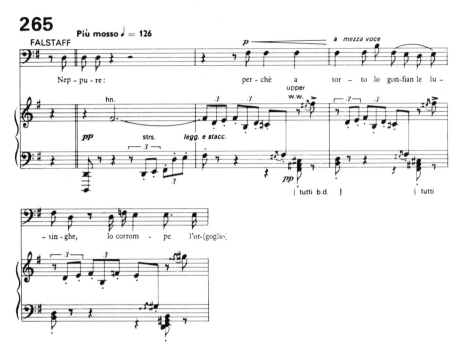

By the time we reach 'e per me non ne voglio, no' (see Ex. 246), Ex. 264 has become a line of continuous quaver triplets. In the final tutti (Ex. 264c) it is able to form a sequential transition to the third section.

> Rogues, hence, avaunt, vanish like hailstones, go;
> Trudge; plod away i' th' hoof; seek shelter, pack!

To call this a cabaletta would be very wide of the mark even if it fulfils some of a cabaletta's functions. 'Stretta substitute' would be more appropriate; for in the orchestral theme which forms its basis (Ex. 266) with its rushing violin semiquavers and punctuating wind and lower strings there is a distinct echo of the Act I finales of *I Lombardi* and *Macbeth*, but with no sense of impending fate.

Verdi again reverts to old habits when for the final appearance of Ex. 264 superimposed on Ex. 266 he doubles solo trumpet with woodwind on the melody. Coupled with the flamboyant trill in the second bar the effect is delightfully parodistic. Blatancy and vulgarity have long since vanished from Verdi's musical language. Indeed the only danger of vulgarity lurks in the stage directions, according to which Falstaff first takes up the broom and chases Bardolph and Pistol furiously; twelve bars later we read *Bardolph and Pistol escape through the door on the left; Falstaff pursues them*. Without disrespect one may wonder whether Verdi and Boito were not imposing too much speed and vigour on a man of Falstaff's supposed age and girth. Stage performances are liable to fall into elementary slapstick at this point, Falstaff moving with an energy of which he would be completely incapable were not the actor a man of normal proportions padded out. But given the dynamism of the music it is difficult to envisage a remedy.

> *Part 2: A garden. On the left Ford's house. Groups of trees in the centre of the stage.*

The scene is set with a tripping melody on upper wind and horns which seems faintly to anticipate Reznicek's overture to *Donna Diana* of the following year – not perhaps surprisingly since the Leipzig-trained Reznicek, like our own Sullivan, represented the Mendelssohnian aspect of the German academic tradition that Verdi admired in Ferdinand Hiller:

267

Verdi's version of this scene is the only one which brings all the women on stage at the same time – an impudent reversal, no doubt, of the age-old convention whereby every principal soprano or mezzo-soprano should have an entrance to herself. *Meg and Mistress Quickly enter right; they go towards Ford's house and on the threshold run into*

Alice and Nannetta who are on the point of coming out – so run the stage directions. Their greetings spring like a fountain from the last cadence of Ex. 267: 'Alice . . . Meg . . . Nannetta . . . Escivo appunto per ridere con te. . . . Buon dì, comare. . . . Dio vi doni allegria. . . . Botton di rosa.'

In this lyrical mosaic, a species of musical blank verse whose basic regularity stems from the sixteen-bar structure of Ex. 267, it is noticeable at once how much more elegant and aristocratic in manner are the Italian Merry Wives than their English equivalents. What is more they show a correspondingly different moral attitude. Shakespeare's Meg Page is genuinely upset and indignant at Falstaff's letter as a good burgher's wife should be ('What a Herod of Jewry is this? O wicked, wicked world,' etc.). Throughout it is implied that Falstaff's social rank compounds the offence: our betters ought to set us an example. Likewise Page objects to Fenton as a son-in-law not because he is poor but because he is an aristocratic scapegrace ('He kept company with the wild prince and Poins; he is of too high a region . . .'). None of these social considerations weigh with Verdi's 'comari'; they find the fat knight's proposals merely very funny – though highly impertinent too and deserving of punishment; and Mistress Quickly, no longer 'that carrion', is musically speaking as high-born as any of them – witness the ineffable grace of the cadence which underpins her greeting to Nannetta. This preparatory scene in which the women break their startling news to one another is managed by Boito with neat dispatch. The main motivic stiffening is provided by the upward scale of Ex. 267, which comes into special prominence where Alice declares, 'If I would go to hell for an eternal moment or so I could be knighted'; while the phrase which follows serves to round off the entire first paragraph. (Ex. 268)

268

- mos - - sa al gra - - do   di Ca - val - le - res - - - sa!

Meg picks up the thread in the dominant key and leads the music through fourteen brief bars of transition to the reading aloud of the identical letters. This will form a huge lyrical period of forty-four bars rivalling the letter duet in *Figaro* in its combination of naturalism with artifice. To begin with the orchestra carries the melodic burden as Alice and Meg, sometimes in unison, sometimes in alternation, declaim the contents of the letter, breaking off from time to time to comment in amazement; then as the language becomes warmer and the women enter into the spirit of the comedy the melody becomes more continuous and mock-passionate. The casual opening is traced by a cor anglais, the clarinet supplying the low D which it is unable to reach:

269

Ful - gi-da A - li - ce!   a -mor t'offro...   Ma

come?! Che co-sa dice?   Sal- vo che il nome   la frase è u - guale.

The women have exchanged letters. Meg and Alice each read a line then stop as they recognize the identical wording. 'Ask me no reason why I love you, for though love use Reason for his physician he admits him not for his counsellor,' writes Shakespeare's Falstaff. Boito's expresses himself more bluntly ('. . . non domandar perchè, ma dimmi: t'amo . . .'). Alice anticipates Meg's 'T'amo', so prompting a more substantial declamatory diversion than the last three bars of Ex. 269. The women now return each other's letters and continue in unison with a counter-theme to Ex. 269 ('. . . sei la gaia comare, il compar gaio son io, e fra noi due . . . facciamo il paio'). This double reference to a pair sparks off more ribald comment from Quickly and Nannetta; whereupon Alice establishes herself as the strongest personality present by taking over the rest of the melody ('Facciamo il paio in un amor ridente di donna bella e d'uom appariscente'), though she cannot prevent the others looking over her shoulder and joining in on the word 'appariscente'. So to the melodic climax ('e il viso tuo su me risplenderà', Ex. 270) which is musical irony of the most pointed kind with romantic ninths and suspensions caricatured almost to the point of ugliness:

270

The pun on the word 'immensity' — i.e. of space and of Falstaff himself — is Boito's, not Shakespeare's, but singularly happy; and it sets off a peal of merry E major laughter from the women. Alice reads out the signature ('Rispondi al tuo scudiere, John Falstaff Cavaliere') in a monotone; whereat the general mood changes to one of not very serious indignation, as the women decide that Falstaff must be paid out. In the discussion which follows — musically a free development based on such formal devices as sequence and threefold repetition — observe how each phrase implies a gesture or an attitude, so harking back to those qualities in Pergolesi which so impressed Rousseau and his contemporaries. In 'Mostro! Mostro!' the brass chords are the musical ideogram of a clenched fist. In 'Dobbiam gabbarlo' and 'E farne chiasso' we see (or hear) heads nodded vigorously in agreement. Most obvious of all, Alice's 'Quell'otre! quel tino!' must prompt the singer to a gesture descriptive of Falstaff's rotundity. (Ex. 271)

In fact so clear is the verbal sense from the musical image that Verdi has felt it safe to set different lines simultaneously before each has been heard by itself. Thus Nannetta's 'Se ordisci una burla vo anch'io la mia parte' never emerges distinctly from the vocal mêlée — a lack, however, which any singer of moderate acting ability should be able to make good.

The women's scene is wound up with a self-contained, homophonic melody of

sixteen bars extended to eighteen in the same dancing 6/8 as Ex. 271 but slightly broadened. Despite the supportive oboes and clarinets (a mere safety device like the old *fisarmonica*) the effect is of an *a cappella* ensemble such as might be performed by that ideal vocal quartet which in Verdi's view the Milan Società del Quartetto *ought* to have instituted, to sing music by Palestrina and his contemporaries.* Even without instrumental support it was one of the pieces which were encored on the first night.†

* See draft letter to an unknown correspondent, April 1878 (*Copialettere*, pp. 626–7); and letter to Arrivabene, 30.3.1879 (Alberti, pp. 226–33).

† For a piece identically constructed, also in 6/8 time and in E major but of a very different mood, see the 'Shepherds' Farewell' from Berlioz's *L'Enfance du Christ*. It is unthinkable that this can be anything more than coincidence; yet it shows once again how far Verdi's style had now reached into the general European tradition.

The women now retire to work out their plan of revenge. From time to time one or other of them may be seen among the trees, unnoticed by anyone on stage.

Meanwhile enter Ford, Dr Caius, Fenton, Bardolph and Pistol conversing eagerly. Theirs too is a formed melody, but of a far more elusive cast since each singer gives it his own variation. Announced by Caius it is taken up a bar later at the minor third below by Bardolph with a different continuation; next Fenton alters the opening; and Pistol makes still further changes. The general effect is of a chaotic canon, a highly ingenious variation on the device used by Rossini in *Il Barbiere di Siviglia* where each character is giving his or her own version of events to the officer of the guard but always to the same theme. Here the theme itself is diversified to suit individual attitudes of the singers.

All Ford can make of this is 'a buzzing of wasps and a humming of angry hornets

273

and a rumbling of storm-bellied clouds', and if these words too are unintelligible their meaning is brought out by onomatopaeia: a chromatic motif on voices and wind rising and falling twice in pitch and volume and backed by buzzing strings. Meanwhile the women repeat their objurgations in the distance to which a death figure on the bass trombone and timpani gives out a note of underlying menace.

274

The music continues as a free development of motifs from Exs. 273 and 274. Sometimes the voices join in a succession of repeated quaver chords, sometimes a single voice will stand out on its own;* the texture thins and thickens sometimes with

* At the second bar of the *a cappella* chatter at figure 27 in the full score, Ford sings on his own 'Se parlaste uno alla volta' in what had originally been four crotchets of silence, as a comparison with the first printed edition will show. This revision brings benefits both musical and dramatic: it clarifies the situation and strikes a neat balance with Pistol's mock military, trumpet-and-drum-backed 'State all'erta, all'erta, all'erta, all'erta', two bars earlier. See L. Dallapiccola, 'Su un passo del *Falstaff*', in *Appunti, incontri, meditazioni* (Milan, 1970), pp. 29–32.

the aid of further intervention from the women offstage. Fenton, to whom the whole affair is a joke, develops his own variant of Ex. 273, fresh and lilting, as befits one who in the words of Mine Host of the Garter 'capers, dances . . . speaks holiday, smells April and May.'

275

The lucid complexity of the music makes for a witty contrast with the verbal confusion, which Caius confounds still further by accusing Pistol and Bardolph as well as their master. In vain the exasperated Ford asks them to speak one at a time ('Se parlaste uno alla volta . . .'). The others continue with an energy which gathers itself up in a climbing figure of broken thirds like a comic parody of Handel's 'And the government shall be upon his shoulders', yet arising quite naturally from Ex. 273 and its derivatives. Obviously analysis is reaching its limits when it deals in units of two notes; yet this is the scale on which so much of *Falstaff* operates. So it is that when the men have broken off as though out of breath the orchestra gives out a twice-repeated gesture of two notes (Ex. 276a), which will be unobtrusively recalled twenty-nine bars later (Ex. 276b), when Falstaff's catholic taste in women is referred to ('He loves the gallimaufry').

276a

276b

Meanwhile Ford has taken advantage of the general pause for breath to ask Pistol for his version of the story. Over a variant of Ex. 273 on cellos, basses and bassoons Pistol expeditiously sums up Falstaff's intentions ('In due parole. L'enorme Falstaff vuole'). A decent hesitation before the final outrage (E . . . e . . . sconquassarvi il letto') prompts some violent orchestral bumps and Verdi's last use of a gesture that he usually reserved for menacing ghosts. 'Caspita!' cries Caius at this revelation (remember that he knows nothing of Falstaff the seducer), and Ford has to exclaim his 'Quanti guai!' through nearly two bars of orchestral tutti on a chord of D flat major. With this outburst the harmonic rhythm slows down and the key of D flat is confirmed by a new orchestral theme over which Pistol and Bardolph in turn relate their virtuous refusal to carry Falstaff's letters. It is very much in the vein of Ex. 259b from Scene i, and indeed could be said to derive from it. In both cases the subject is Falstaff's amorous designs; and here the mood of cunning suavity is further underlined by the first violins' use of the G string.

277

The two men earnestly urge Ford to beware: Falstaff ogles every woman, ugly or beautiful, young damsel or matron – all, all (Ex. 276b). Then, to another idea which has grown directly from the rhythm of Ex. 277, Bardolph warns him with the crafty emphasis of Iago to see to it that he does not wear the crown that girt the shaggy locks of Actaeon. 'By that you mean?' says the puzzled Ford. '*The horns*' whispers Bardolph. Here the music temporarily sinks into a morass of gloom and suspicion with a suitably dark orchestral palette of lower strings and wind. (Ex. 278)

Ford duly promises to keep a careful watch on his wife and on Falstaff himself. The music regains its energy in a series of upward scales as the women reappear; then fades out on a flurry of recognitions in whispered asides ('È lei . . . è lui . . . etc.). 'Ford is jealous,' Alice murmurs to her companions as she and they retire left while the men move away to the right. Fenton and Nannetta, left alone on the stage, now emerge in their true guise as Verdi's most poetic pair of young lovers. This is in itself a departure from Shakespeare whose Fenton honestly admits that his first reason for wooing Ann Page was her father's wealth.

278

Yet wooing thee I found thee of more value
Than stamps in gold or sums in sealed bags.*

The Fenton of the opera would be incapable of such pragmatism. He and Nannetta are far closer to Ferdinand and Miranda. Their love is bathed in the pure radiance of a youth transfigured by the imagination of age. Their brief duettino ('Labbra di foco!') is marked *allegretto* but the metronome indication ($\downarrow$ = 126) is that of an allegro. The music is borne along on a fast rhythmic current continuing the previous movement, as though the movers' moments of happiness had to be snatched from the jaws of time – so much more voracious in the eyes of the elderly than of the young themselves. Boito's words, which compare the exchange of kisses with the cut and thrust of a duel (a typical Elizabethan conceit), would permit a full-blooded setting. Verdi prefers a diaphanous texture with a basis of muted strings. (Ex. 279)

The duet is cast as an irregular dialogue over a basically symmetrical melody, a three-limbed organism in Verdi's late manner with most of the incident in the final limb. The tonal scheme has all the freedom that we have come to expect. The first period ('Labbra di foco!') passes from A flat major to the 'incompatible' key of G flat, using the Italian identity of E flat major and minor to effect the transition. The second period ('Labbra leggiadre!') proceeds to an orthodox half-close in the dominant (E flat major again). The third ('T'amo!' . . . 'Imprudente . . .') is interrupted at its most expressive moment which is also its furthest point from the original tonality – the dominant ninth in C flat major beneath Fenton's words 'Mi piaci tanto'. 'Vien

* *The Merry Wives of Windsor*, III, iv, 15–16.

279

gente,' exclaims Nannetta; four bars of triplet flurries on solo wind instruments carry the music still further away to F flat. Fenton hides amongst the trees. As a solitary oboe sustains high A flat (a mediant turned pivotal dominant) his unseen voice launches the magical concluding lines of the duet, to be answered by Nannetta, so restoring the original key by an unexpected, plagal route.*

280

* In the autograph these two lines are underscored, since they are in fact a fourteenth-century proverb which Boito lifted directly from Boccaccio (*Decameron*, 7th *novella* of the 2nd day). See in this connec-

Although unrhymed, these two lines have the function of the rhyming couplet that concludes the Shakespearian sonnet and indeed will be used precisely in that way in Act III. A nine-bar coda based on Ex. 279 rounds off the duet, correcting any residual subdominant bias by maintaining a dominant pedal throughout the first seven.

From lyrical paragraph to motivic development as the women return. The principal motif is one of those chips of academic commonplace that play so vital a part in the opera's organization. Again Beethoven's 'Pastoral' Symphony is not far away.

There are two episodic themes both associated with Alice herself – the one who in Verdi's words 'stirs the *polenta*'. To the first (Ex. 282) she tells Mistress Quickly to carry letters of acceptance from Meg and herself to Falstaff at the Garter Inn. The dancing, coquettish rhythm of the first violins suggests a legacy from French ballet such as found its way into many Italian operas of the time – witness the Colombina/Taddeo scene in *Pagliacci*. (Ex. 282)

To the second theme (Ex. 283) Alice declares that Falstaff must be led on with a show of flattery and then taught a lesson. In the acciaccature in the second bar Mistress Ford for all her good humour unmistakably shows her claws (as Verdi had said, she has 'il diavolo addosso').

The other women are suitably delighted and allow their enthusiasm to work up through developments of Ex. 281b to a triplet climax ('Che gioia, che gioia!'). Then Quickly, about to set off on her errand, notices someone lurking in the trees (it is of course Fenton). She and her companions disperse, all but Nannetta. The lovers

---

tion his letter to Camille Bellaigue inviting him to the première of *Falstaff*: 'L'éclatante farce de Shakespeare est reconduite par le miracle des sons à sa claire source toscane de Ser Giovanni Fiorentino.' C. Bellaigue, 'Arrigo Boito, Lettres et Souvenirs', in *Revue des deux mondes*, LXXXVIII (sixième période, Vol. 46, 1918), p. 9061. In fact Giovanni Fiorentino's *Pecorone* is one of the sources for Shakespeare's *The Merry Wives of Windsor*.

282

Poco più lento ♩ = 88

ALICE (a Quickly)

Da quel bri-gan-te tu an-

vln. I

pp strs.
pizz.

- drai...

etc.

283

Come prima
con brio
ALICE

Pri – ma, per at-ti-rar-lo a noi lo lu-singhia – – mo, e poi glie-le cantiamo in

NANNETTA

bur-la! e poi...

fl., cl.
added

[ob. added]

cl.

etc.

p strs.

[bsns. added] [w.w. added]

resume their amorous contest ('Torno all'assalto') to a fuller and more elaborately accompanied restatement of the duet. Here, the busy semiquavers and the excited pizzicato quavers (one of Verdi's earliest personal mannerisms) emphasize the swiftness of the musical pulse. This time the central E flat cadence ('Il labbro è l'arco') is followed by an episode in which the simile is stretched to its limit. Fenton's kiss misses its mark and lands on Nannetta's tresses. She is then the victor. Fenton begs for mercy; they agree to make peace, then they will start all over again. Note here the use of frequent pedals, actual or implied, to create a sense of calm and serenity within the brisk tempo. Whether the persistent 'paradiddle' on trumpets (*ppp*) first occurring after the word 'dardo' carries the time-honoured connotation of death is one of those points on which it is unwise to be dogmatic; but as a fresh element in the tapestry of sound it is enchanting. Another orchestral variation on Ex. 279 (woodwind triplets against pizzicato string quavers) begins, to be broken off at the sixth bar as Nannetta again senses the presence of intruders. She and Fenton leave in opposite directions but their final couplet sounds from the distance beneath the same sustained oboe note, prolonged as before into the coda, with its echoes of Ex. 279.

Now it is the men who return with a plan of action. Ford will visit Falstaff at the Garter Inn under an assumed name and so find out how the land lies. As always, Ford's utterances have a greater lyrical weight than those of any of the other men, except for Fenton. But the structural motif of this short exchange is provided by a figure which irresistibly recalls the curtain rise of the original prologue to *Simon Boccanegra*.

284

During the men's reprise of Ex. 273 to new, ingenious, but alas indistinguishable words, re-enter the women backstage to provide a brilliant concertato, both groups not crudely superimposed, but woven alternately into a musical continuum of thirty-five bars. Throughout, the women and upper woodwind keep in 6/8 time, the men and the remaining instruments in 4/4, producing the kind of rhythmic conflict of which the earliest well-known example occurs in the second act finale of *Die Entführung*. Between the two, distinct from either yet binding them both together as contrasting elements within a single design, Fenton springs into relief with a firm lyrical line not unlike that of Don Carlos in the terzetto from Act III of that opera, except that he must dominate eight singers, not merely two – a good reason why for this part Verdi never considered a tenorino. Then too the passage goes beyond mere lyrical transfiguration. Every detail of Boito's text has its musical reflection. So long as Fenton is merely observing one group of chattering men and another of women ('Qua barbotta un crocchio d'uomini . . . Là cinguetta un stuol di femine') his rhythm is indistinguishable from that of his companions; but when he mentions 'her who bears my name in her heart' ('Ma colei che in cor mi nomini') it broadens out into soaring flights of minims and crotchets. A highly original design, one might say, and what a novel way to end an act! But there was a model for it in an opera which there is every reason to believe that Verdi had seen performed in Milan in 1889 – *Die Meistersinger*. Here too the first act ends with an ensemble consisting of the apprentices singing in compound duple time, the Mastersingers in chattering 4/4 and Walther rising above the tumult. Verdi's vocal mass is of course lighter, and the fact that his upper group consists of sopranos, a mezzo-soprano and a contralto, Wagner's of altos and tenors, reflects the lower 'mean sonority' of the German. Then too, while the merry wives' music is set out in 6/8 that of the apprentices is noted in 6/4 – a difference of convention only, where as usual the German is more mathematically accurate. This passage is surely Verdi's most substantial debt to his great contemporary.

At the final cadence the men retire, leaving the women and the 6/8 rhythm in possession of the field. In a modulating passage (*Più presto*) Alice and Meg settle the final details of their plan, without, however, telling us precisely what it is (that, Boito thought, would lessen the interest of the Act which follows). All we know is that it will make Falstaff swell up until he bursts – an event, needless to say, that the orchestra graphically illustrates with a slow-building climax which shatters in a downward chromatic scale for all four trombones and bassoons. Then as though in mockery Alice recalls to the same melting E major harmonies as before Ex. 270 ('Ma il viso mio su lui risplenderà'). First Nannetta, then Meg and Quickly join in; and again the cadence is followed by a burst of laughter which is taken up orchestrally with a noisy reprise of Ex. 267. Curtain and applause.

ACT II

Part 1: Inside the Garter Inn.

The act begins with an Italianate 'call to action' theme: rapid 6/8 quavers, peremptory crashes from full orchestra and sudden silences: Rossini de-conventionalized. Note the weighting of sound towards the middle and bass registers obviously designed to conjure up the massive figure of the protagonist, seated once more in his armchair and drinking his favourite sherry. A fortissimo trill on high woodwind at the eleventh bar redresses the balance of sonority and prepares the way for the gesture of authority at the thirteenth.

285

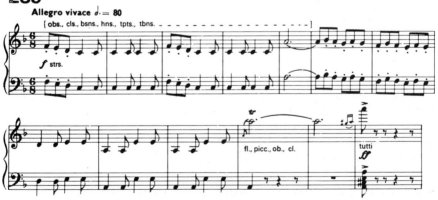

Convention would require here a symmetrical answer beginning in the subdominant and ending in the tonic. Something of the kind occurs, but it is far from symmetrical. Ex. 285 is resumed in B flat, its first four bars shortened to two, and its continuation not only different but harmonized and prolonged in a succession of tiny sequences to end naturally and inevitably in the expected parallel cadence. It is one of those subtle variations on an ordinary idea in which *Falstaff* abounds, and as usual it yields plenty of thematic material for the scena that develops.

Bardolph and Pistol enter in suitable attitudes of contrition ('Siam pentiti e contriti'), beating their breasts in time to the music. Falstaff receives them with indifference. He knew they would return anyway ('L'uomo ritorna al vizio, la gatta al lardo'). Immediately Bardolph announces the arrival of a 'lady who begs to be admitted'. 'Let her come forward,' Falstaff replies and settles himself to wait. For all this Ex. 285 variously extended has furnished the musical basis. Mistress Quickly, however, enters to a stately minuet-like theme with a deep curtsey built into it.

286

She begs for a word with Sir John alone. Falstaff accordingly dismisses Bardolph and Pistol who retire making grimaces. Then Quickly closes the brief minuet movement with another 'Reverenza!' and proceeds with her story, during which she continues to show a penchant for the verbo-musical gesture. 'Poor woman!', she keeps exclaiming as she describes Alice's supposed turmoil of spirits on receiving Falstaff's letter; a deep contralto cadence underlines her sympathy:

287

Also cadential is the jaunty motif, prepared by flying triplet figures in the inner texture, indicating the hour when Alice will be free of the surveillance of her jealous husband; 'from two till three'. (Ex. 288)

Mistress Quickly's becoming diffidence is conveyed not only by rests and prolongations but in the kind of total ambivalence to be found in Rigoletto's 'Pari siamo'. The music has an F major orientation as the key signature attests; yet the cadences are invariably in C, as though Quickly could never allow herself the frankness of a full close. For Falstaff this is enough: he will not fail, he says, in his duty, whereat violins then cellos round off the paragraph with mental notes of

288

Ex. 288. This established, Quickly can be more explicitly tantalizing over Meg Page, no longer avoiding a cadence in the home key. She is 'an angel who fires with love all who look upon her'. Sensual chromaticisms are combined with an instrumentation that recalls poignant moments in *La Traviata* – all height and depth.

289

'She too greets you' ('Anch'essa vi saluta') returns to 4/4 in unequivocal F major; but again the cadence ('Povera donna!') is in C. Ex. 289 is repeated with different scoring ('un giglio di candore e di fè') and now leads to an A major 6/4 of delicious temptation, with violin harmonics, oscillating piccolo and a single double bass sustaining the lowest note. 'You bewitch them all,' Quickly simpers. 'No witchcraft,' Falstaff replies, 'only a certain personal charm.' But, he wants to know, does each of his conquests know about the other? Here Quickly pulls the music back to C major with an enigmatic 'Women are born cunning, never fear!' ('La donna nasce scaltra; non temete.'). Unlike Strauss's Baron Ochs, Falstaff is more than willing to remunerate his 'She-Mercury', who retires to a brief reprise of the minuet and, in the *bozza di stampa*, a repetition of 'Reverenza'. In the definitive score Verdi as so often decided that the reminiscence could be more effectively left to orchestra alone, Quickly supplying a counterpoint ('M'inchino') which implies an even deeper curtsey than before. 'Alice is mine!' Falstaff exclaims in parentheses (i.e., to the audience). Four noisy bars of tutti convey his delight: a gargantuan peal of laughter (Ex. 290a) which frames the miniature aria 'Va, vecchio John' (Ex. 290b). 'Say'st thou so, old Jack? Go thy ways; I'll make more of my old body than I have done.'

There is no melodic charm, only an immense – not to say gross – self-satisfaction. Note the heavy tramp of strings, trumpets, trombones, bassoons and timpani, the demisemiquaver figures at the word 'ancora' suggesting slaps on a quivering mountain of flesh, the two bars of crowing brass and woodwind where Falstaff talks of the number of women prepared to risk damnation for his sake ('Tutte le donne ammutinate insieme Si dannano per me!') and the fact that both third and fourth phrases of the melody end with a perfect cadence. Ex. 290a is about to lead to a second verse when Bardolph interrupts to announce the arrival of a certain Maestro Fontana (Fountain, i.e. 'Mr Brook') with a demijohn of Cyprus wine. 'The Brook is welcome to me that o'erflows such liquor,' Falstaff cries; and the operatic medium allows the pun to be illustrated onomatopoeically with a patter of semiquavers in the strings. He has time for one conclusive 'Va, vecchio John, per la tua via' (a typical instance of late Verdian dove-tailing) before: *Enter left Ford in disguise preceded by Bardolph who halts at the threshold and bows him in; he is followed by Pistol holding the demijohn. Bardolph and Pistol remain in the background; Ford carries a bag in his hand.*

So to the last of Verdi's great duets, which like so many of its predecessors occupies a central point in the action, to be followed by that other great pivot in Verdian opera, the baritone aria. For once there is no trace of vocal polarity; both participants are baritones. If Ford appears marginally the more lyrical of the two that is because he has more to say; yet when Falstaff goes beyond mere complacent acknowledgement he invariably adapts his tone to Ford's. Unlike most previous examples of the genre, where the characters lay bare their feelings more and more with each stage of the dialectic, this duet is permeated by a note of comic dissimulation. Only when Falstaff has momentarily left the scene can Ford, like Ortrud, give himself up to an all-consuming rage. Even so Verdi does not entirely abandon his technique of progression through contrasting ideas; he merely pares it down so as to produce a smooth continuity that all but defies analysis. There are no sudden switches of tempo. Themes are stated, broken down into sequences, then transformed into new ideas; an episode will develop into a principal subject; the end of one period will change into the beginning of another. A seemingly inconsequent transition whose purpose appears to be to give an appropriate outline to a verbal phrase will be riveted to what has gone before by some tiny linking figure that develops through it, often in an inner part; for here as always the texture in *Falstaff* is never inert. The ghosts of cantabile and cabaletta still haunt the design but never as self-sufficient movements; rather they crystallize imperceptibly out of preceding material. Tchaikovsky's *Eugene Onegin*, another masterpiece of lyrical continuity, seems schematic by comparison.

Ford's entrance is marked by a series of musical bows that gradually develop first in sequences then more freely into a discourse of twenty-four bars to reach a dominant half-close. The 3/4 rhythm and the pattern ♪ |♩. ♫ |♩ will recur at an important point later on. More immediately relevant is the contour of the violin melody at the sixteenth bar (*x*).

291

Ford introduces himself with many apologies for intruding without ceremony, though his manner could hardly be more ceremonious. Even after his host's courteous 'Voi siete il benvenuto' he can scarcely bring himself to come to the point. 'In me you see one who has an abundance of life's amenities' ('In me vedete un uom ch'ha un'abbondanza grande degli agi della vita'). The crotchet remains constant but the tempo is now 2/4, the pace allegro moderato and the writing a spare unison relaxed only at the words 'abbondanza grande' to allow a suitably expansive gesture. But the figure (*x*) in flute, clarinet, violins and violas links it formally to Ex. 291, just as (*y*) will give the patent of relevance to what comes next. (Ex. 292)

292

The period proceeds normally through two parallel eight-bar phrases, until Ford announces his assumed name, whereupon Falstaff bursts in with an effusive 'Caro Signor Fontana' in C major as he grasps the other's hand and so reciprocates with suitably false bonhomie. But the strangeness of the new key is lessened by the triplet figure on 'Voglio fare con voi', corresponding to (γ) in the previous example.

293

There is a brief interlude as Bardolph and Pistol chuckle in the background ('Atten-to' 'Zitto') until overheard by Falstaff who sends them out with a gesture. 'For they say, "If money go before, all doors lie open,"' Ford continues, giving more weight to the proverb by preceding it with a phrase of recitative *senza misura*. The phrase 'Si suol dire che l'oro apre ogni porta,' beginning as an answer to the recitative phrase becomes the start of a new eight-bar period in which the rhythmic motif (*x*) recurs transformed on the words 'talismano' and 'tutto'.

294

The full cadence ('l'oro è un buon capitano che marcia avanti') contains some remarkably delicate writing for the three trumpets and trombone. Ford then holds up the bag of gold – a passage half episode, half transition, in which the chink of coins is conveyed by pairs of staccato quavers with acciaccature alternating between wind groups combined with strings arco and pizzicato and garnished with that time-honoured symbol of gold, the triangle. High woodwind chatter as he sets the bag on the table. Now at last Ford begins his story. 'In Windsor there lives a lady, fair and charming, Alice by name, the wife of a certain Ford.'

295

From this bland, conversational opening the central cantabile develops in the subtlest way imaginable. The figure at 'Si chiama Alice' (*x*) is rhythmically derived from that in Ex. 291. As Ford builds up the story of his frustrations 'Io l'amo e lei non m'ama . . . le scrivo, non risponde') the figure reappears in a modified guise but within the original 3/4 rhythm, finally blossoming out into its original form at 'Per lei sprecai tesori', though with an entirely different melodic contour.

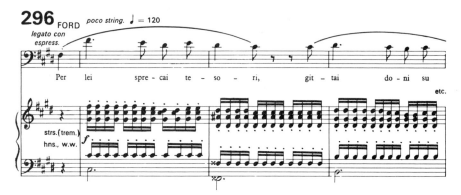

As in Ex. 291 its evolution is loosely sequential, reaching a half-close at 'madrigale' – a musical pun where the word itself is illustrated by a 'madrigalism' in the form of a long melisma.

> 'Love like a shadow flies when substance love pursues,
> Pursuing that that flies, and flying what pursues.'*

quotes Shakespeare's Ford; but in the opera it is Falstaff who sings its equivalent ('L'amor, l'amor che non ci dà mai tregue') with Ford alternating certain phrases and half-phrases.† The duet has reached a moment of stasis, both characters indulging in that type of reflection which marks the central slow movement of a Rossinian duet:

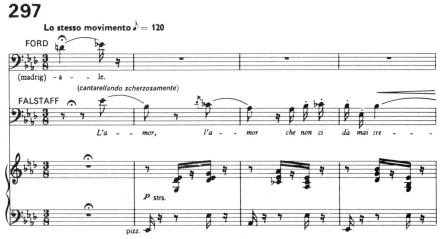

* *The Merry Wives of Windsor*, II, ii, 208–9.

† An arrangement which apparently occurred to the composer during rehearsals since it does not appear in the proof copy of the score.

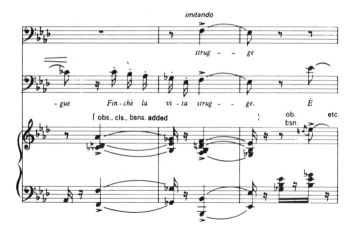

and indeed without any change of pace the music does in fact form itself into a miniature cantabile. (Ex. 297)

But, as befits the text, the melody just avoids settling into a definite mould; six bars are followed by ten in which it dwindles away into repetitions of 'l'amor', while Falstaff's 'fugge', a Tchaikovsky-like flourish of demisemiquavers, flits from one string group to another like an emblem of love's shadow. Then Ex. 296 is woven back into the fabric of the cantabile as an episode ('E questo madrigale', etc.) and at the same time its climax in sound. The return of Ex. 297 sung now by Ford is accompanied by a delicate and ingenious filigree pattern for flutes and piccolo. There is of course no full-close; the music moves through the dominant into a B major transition. 'To what purpose have you unfolded this to me?' Falstaff asks. 'You are a gentleman of excellent breeding, admirable discourse, of great admittance, authentic in your place and person, generally allowed for your many war-like, court-like and learned preparations.' The fulsome reply of Shakespeare's Ford is condensed by Boito into neat, pithy lines which allow the music an aptly military flavour. Ford and the music then revert to the theme of money ('Spendetele! spendetele!'), extending it into a full G major 8-bar period. 'Strange request!' Falstaff murmurs. Then Ford expounds on the subject of Alice's great reputation for virtue which Falstaff alone would be able to assail. This, the nub of the argument, is marked by just such a sinuous theme as introduced King Philip's confession to Rodrigue of apparently very different thoughts. But there is no essential contradiction since Ford genuinely does suspect his wife and is hoping in this way to find his suspicions confirmed or denied. But if the procedure is similar in both operas note the economy of the later Verdi, who finds it unnecessary to add a single note of harmony until the sixth bar. (Ex. 298)

After his falsetto mimicking of Alice ('Guai se mi tocchi!') the melody takes on a lyrical warmth, its harmonies all the more telling for the austere unison writing that has gone before. If Falstaff will induce her to yield, then there may be hope for Ford also, since one slip always leads to another. Ford does not complete this outrageous proposition either verbally or musically but breaks off with a 'What do you think?' ('Che ve ne par?'). Falstaff, delighted, completes and rounds off the musical paragraph in fifteen bars of lyrical E flat declamation ('Prima di tutto, senza complimenti,' etc.); he accepts Ford's commission; he shakes him by the hand and assures

298

him that he will possess Ford's wife with all the confidence of Mozart's Bartolo prophesying Figaro's downfall.

299

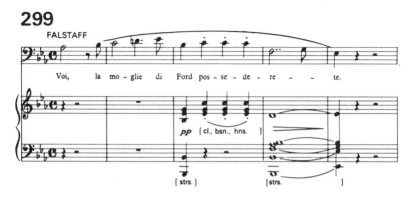

In what follows Verdi has surely improved on Shakespeare. So far Ford has achieved his purpose and has got the answer that he wanted; he has if not proof at least a strong indication that Falstaff is pursuing his wife. It should be the end of the matter for the moment as the musical cadence implies; but it is not. Calmly Falstaff continues: 'I am already well advanced (there is no reason why I should be silent about it); in half an hour she will be in my arms.' The first words and the parenthesis are examples of the kind of inert verbiage which for musical reasons Boito was required to put into the text so as to enable the conclusion to detonate effectively. (Ex. 300)

Ford, in the opera, certainly did not bargain on this piece of news; just for a moment he drops the mask with a shout, that Falstaff, serenely vain, interprets merely as a tribute of amazement to his own powers of fascination. The cadence at 'possederete' (Ex. 299) could afford to appear conclusive because it represents a false conclusion; the more offhand 'nelle mie braccia' marks the real final phrase of the duet, from which something very like a cabaletta emerges. Not only does the key, F major, contradict E flat in the most emphatic way possible; it is also the key toward which the music has been tending ever since the entrance of Mistress Quickly, and to which she has been tempting Falstaff with her continual C major half-closes, as we are reminded almost immediately when he specifies the time of his meeting with Alice – 'Dalle due alle tre' (Ex. 288). The same C major cadence is reached; but despite the presence here and there of F sharps the sense of F major as the ultimate goal persists.

300

After echoing mechanically Falstaff's 'Dalle due alle tre' without pitch Ford asks whether he knows the jealous husband; here Ex. 288 generates a rapid triplet rhythm that recalls another 'cabaletta-substitute' – that which concludes Eboli's 'O don fatal'. Falstaff meanwhile launches into a diatribe corresponding to Shakespeare's 'Hang him, hang him, poor cuckoldly knave', returning twice to a musical punchline 'Te lo cornifico netto, netto!' ('I will cuckold him for you neatly, neatly') that will echo round Ford's mind when he is left alone.

301

So strong is the sense of having reached a 'home' key that within the next few bars Verdi can modulate almost as far afield as Beethoven in the coda of the finale to his Eighth Symphony while always keeping F major in view. Equally strong is the sense of having launched a new, final movement even though the new tempo, allegro agitato, was established as early as Ex. 299. However, it is not strictly speaking a duet movement but rather a solo for Falstaff while Ford looks on aghast. 'If he thwarts me I'll rain a shower of blows over his horns.' Doubtless it was the unexpected technical prowess of Maurel that led Verdi to turn what had been simple crotchets into a flurry of triplets. It is a neat madrigalism, which sorely taxes the average baritone of today. At the end of the movement Falstaff breaks off to remark that it is late; Ford must wait while he goes and attends to his appearance ('Vado a farmi bello'). The fatuously expansive cadential phrase is concluded by the full orchestra ending with a reminiscence of Ex. 301. After Falstaff has left taking the bag of money with him Ford at length finds speech. 'Is this a dream . . . or reality' ('È sogno? o realtà'). His monologue is a conflation of Shakespeare's II, ii, 300–30 and III, v, 140–55, and it is the only passage to recall the world of tragedy that was once Verdi's domain. Ford's sufferings are genuine enough; and as with all who tend to jealousy his suspicions have a twisted logic of their own, which Shakespeare, if not Boito, exposes very cogently (see Act III, scene ii, 236–44). His sense of total unreality Verdi limns like Liszt before him and Debussy after him with combinations of the whole-tone scale.

302

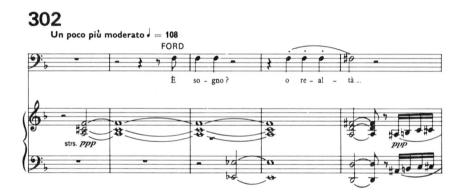

'I feel two mighty branches growing upon my head.' The climbing crotchets (Ex. 303) are not only descriptive; they also recall the bitter gloom of Renato's 'Nell' ombra e nel silenzio' from *Un Ballo in maschera*.

303

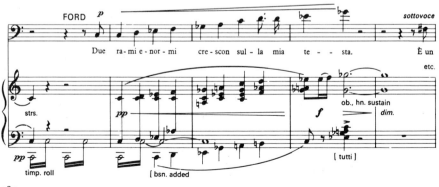

Renato is heard again in the sudden switch to allegro agitato with a pattern of violin semiquavers at 'Mastro Ford! Mastro Ford!' (Master Ford, awake!'). Syncopated brass chords, brutal gestures in lower strings and bassoons, tremolando violins – all the traditional devices of violent emotion are brought back in a new context. 'The hour is fix'd; the match is made' ('L'ora è fissata . . . tramata l'inganno'); the haunting sinister motif of the horns is linked to Falstaff's previous allegro by a triplet figure (see Ex. 247b). A three-fold varied repetition leads to a surprisingly lyrical outcome 'And they say that a jealous husband is a fool' ('E poi diranno che un marito geloso è un insensato').

304

The last cadence is bitten off as Ford imagines the finger of scorn pointed at him in the streets. 'Te lo cornifico' (Ex. 301) is now developed through different keys, culminating in another wild outburst of cascading strings and rapping brass in A flat ('Inferno! Donna: demonio!'). A new brusque gesture forms the basis of Ford's next flight of rhetoric: 'I will rather trust a Fleming with my butter, Parson Hugh the Welshman with my cheese, an Irishman with my aqua-vitae bottle, or a thief with my ambling gelding than my wife with herself.' The comparisons are all altered in the Italian, as would have been necessary anyhow since Parson Hugh does not appear in the opera and the proverbial predilections of the Welsh and the Irish would mean little to an Italian audience of Verdi's time. Ford would therefore sooner trust a German with his beer, a Dutchman with all his victuals and a Turk with his brandy bottle; the comparisons thus reduced to three permit the building up of a characteristic triple pattern. More developments of Ex. 301 follow, woven ever more tightly together, as Ford broods on his horns, and his thirst for revenge. He will catch Falstaff and his wife in the act ('Prima li accoppio e poi li colgo'). As he pauses, out of breath, six bars of transition prepare the solemn lyrical fervour of his final phrase ('Laudata sempre sia nel fondo del mio cor la gelosia') recalling both in key and contour Otello at the close of his Act III solo ('Dio, mi potevi scagliar'). (Ex. 305)

To this Ex. 304 blazing forth on full orchestra forms a complement; so giving the necessary element of reprise to a somewhat rhapsodic structure. Once again its final cadence is interrupted, this time by Falstaff's return with a new doublet, hat and stick. After the intensity of Ford's monologue the gently tripping theme that accompanies him is irresistibly funny. (Ex. 306)

But it is in no way incongruous; fat men often show an unexpected grace of movement; here Falstaff is displaying the poise of the late Oliver Hardy. For the

305

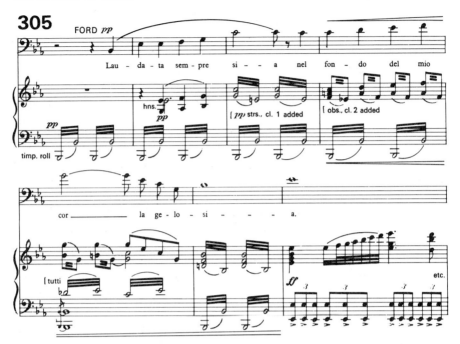

306

fatuous exchange of courtesies as each tries to bow the other out of the room Boito had recourse to a dialogue between Anne and Slender in the first scene of Act I of *The Merry Wives* (lines 15–21).

SLENDER Mistress Anne, yourself shall go first.

ANNE Not I, I pray you, keep on.

SLENDER Truly, I will not go first; truly, la! I will not do you that wrong.

ANNE I pray you, sir.

SLENDER I'll rather be unmannerly than troublesome.

You do yourself wrong indeed, la! (*Exeunt*)

In its original context this exchange helped to delineate the tiresome personality of Slender. In the opera it is little more than drama's tribute to the musical stage, where it is quite unthinkable that a duet should end without a movement that gives both singers equal prominence. The repeated courtesies are the equivalents of those automatically repeated sentiments that normally close a duet cabaletta; and if they add nothing to Ford's or Falstaff's characters they make for a delightful ending to a scene without any concessions to operatic routine. In the final bars we find Verdi and Boito imitating – unwittingly, no doubt – the wit of another famous pair of collaborators, Gilbert and Sullivan, who delighted in making naturalistic sense out of operatic conventions. Having failed to agree over precedence Ford and Falstaff decide simultaneously to go out arm in arm; a perfect excuse for a joint cadence such as too often in Italian opera will end a duet in which the characters are talking to themselves rather than each other and voicing totally opposite sentiments. A noisy reprise of Falstaff's triumphant guffaw (Ex. 290a) brings down the curtain.

> *Part 2: A room in Ford's house. A large window at the back. A door on the right and one on the left, and another door towards the right-hand corner leading to the staircase; another staircase in the left-hand corner at the back. From the open French windows there is a view of the garden. A closed screen is propped up against the left-hand wall next to a large fireplace. A wardrobe is attached to the right-hand wall. There is a small table and a chair. Ranged along the walls a sofa and some high chairs. On the armchair there is a lute. Flowers on the table.*

Beethoven's gifts, according to Wagner, included the ability to spin whole worlds out of nothing. Something very similar happens at the start of the present scene. The violins begin by tracing a pattern too indefinite to be called a theme though it grows and develops like one. (Ex. 307)

Two parts grow to three with the entry of the violas in the ninth bar, and to four with that of the cellos in contrary motion in the fourteenth. Once more the lines are not sufficiently independent of one another to form classical polyphony; yet each makes horizontal sense. Alice entering with Meg shapes the quavers into a melody ('Presenteremo un *bill* per una tassa al parlamento') (Ex. 308a); at the fifth bar the melody passes Beethoven-fashion to the accompanying strings, though whether the primacy should be accorded to cellos or to the second violins could be disputed. But it is the violas and cellos that furnish the melodic cell (x) on which the four transitional bars following Alice's prolonged cadence are based. These lead to what is essentially the third limb of the melody (Ex. 308b); but there will be no fourth. Not only does this new idea wander off sequentially, it will return later in the scene as a theme in its own right. The entire scene up to Quickly's narrative solo exemplifies a structural style and method unique to Verdi's last opera – neither purely lyrical nor

307

purely declamatory, neither basically vocal nor basically instrumental, neither strictly periodic nor freely developmental, but an individual compound of each.

308a

None of it has any parallel in Shakespeare, though Boito has as usual quarried his material from elsewhere in the play, Alice's words being based on Meg's first, solitary outburst on receiving Falstaff's letter: 'Why, I'll exhibit a bill in the parliament for the putting down of [fat] men.'* Before she can say more Quickly hurries in, followed by a despondent Nannetta. Falstaff, Quickly announces, has fallen into the trap completely – and by way of illustration Verdi gives her the option of descending to an E, a note generally regarded nowadays as being available only to 'freak' voices such as are required for Gaia in Strauss's *Daphne*. 'Tell us,' cry the other two in pairs of quavers which are in themselves a breaking down of Ex. 308b. Quickly begins her narration – dramatically quite superfluous, but Verdi was not loath to take advantage of an excellent stage artist to increase the musical incident, round still further the role itself and forge thematic links with the previous act. Her opening lines ('Giunta all'albergo della Giarrettiera') with their suave progressions and the incursion of triplets into the second phrase suggest a more sophisticated Ferrando beginning his narrative at the start of *Il Trovatore*. But the third phrase sketches Falstaff's majestic rotundity as it was presented to us in the first part of Act I.

309

Having described how Falstaff received her 'pompously, in a rascally attitude', she relives the scene with a quotation at pitch and supported by four growling horns of Falstaff's 'Buon giorno, buona donna' followed by her own 'Reverenza', now sounding almost high by contrast. The quotation continues over the next five bars after which Quickly breaks off in an eager six-bar preparation ('poi passo alle notizie ghiotte') in the same 3/4 rhythm but faster and in F minor. The concluding sentence returns to the 4/4 in quaver motion with which the scene started. It is the kind of idea one would expect to find in Nicolai's *Lustige Weiber*, but with Ex. 308b embedded in it at a salient point. Note once more the tonal ambivalence. Mistress Quickly has begun in C major and despite the clear F major orientation of the previous example with its apparent conclusiveness she will in fact end in C major with 'dalle due alle tre' (Ex. 288). Much play is made with this last motif as Alice looks at the clock and finds that it is already two. She calls for Ned and Will to bring in the laundry basket – Ex. 308b once more – then for the first time she notices her daughter's expression of misery: a snatch of oboe, an acciaccatura sob, poignant chromatics leading to one of

* Clearly the Italian translation consulted by Boito must have been based on the now discredited quarto text. The first folio, on which most modern editions are based, omits 'fat'.

those passages that owe their inspiration to eighteenth-century keyboard music in general, and in particular to Clementi's pathetic Sonata in F sharp minor.

310

Her father wants to marry her to Dr Caius. Alice, Meg and Quickly, to whom this is news, break into suitable exclamations of dismay ('A quel gonzo!' . . . 'A quel grullo!'). This is of course librettist's licence due to the economics of the musical stage. Shakespeare's Anne is Meg's daughter, not Alice's, and it is Meg herself who wants her married to Dr Caius. Nannetta would sooner suffer death by lapidation; 'With a volley of cabbage-stalks,' Alice cries, underlining the quip with a change into triplet motion; the woodwind chuckle appreciatively, and, 'Well said!' Quickly comments. The sad little episode concluded, Ex. 308b now resumes with its carefree bustle. Nannetta, her spirits quite restored, declares that she will never wed Dr Caius; and it is appropriate that her final cadence should echo the rhythm of Ex. 251, the opera's opening theme associated with the doctor's impotent rage.

Meanwhile the two servants, Ned and Will, have entered with the basket. Alice tells them in recitative that when she gives the sign they must tip it into the river. Nannetta imagines the bump ('Che bombardamento!') which the orchestra at once illustrates. 'Let us set the scene,' Alice says; she hurriedly takes a chair and sets it by the table; Nannetta picks up her lute and puts it on the table; Meg and Quickly move the screen to a point between the fireplace and the laundry basket, then open it out. All this takes place to Ex. 307, extended and at the same time dismembered by inter-jections from the women ('Qua una sedia.' . . . 'Qua il mio liuto') and the ensemble that now follows ('Gaie comari di Windsor', Ex. 311a) parallels the conclusion of the terzetto in Act III of *Otello* ('Quest'è un ragno'). Neither has any direct parallel in the play; both are there in obedience to the Verdian law that requires a musical crystallization of a dramatic moment in terms of a regular, near-finite structure. But whereas the conclusion of the handkerchief trio had been an episode of light relief, though essential to Shakespeare's plot, Alice's solo with pendant quartet is the nub of the drama – its statement of intent. 'Merry Wives of Windsor, the hour is near to raise the great resounding laugh! . . .' Indeed the piece itself is shot through with musical laughter, its 6/8 allegro rhythm associated throughout the opera with the women's mischievous mockery; and if they themselves are too well bred to laugh like Wagner's Valkyries, oboes, clarinets, horns and strings are ready to do so for them (Ex. 311b).

311a

311b

The implicit symmetry of Verdi's punctuating statements is usually masked by natural phrase extensions or contractions. 'Gaie comari di Windsor' works on the converse principle, the melody losing itself in irregular phrases which ultimately balance themselves in a perfectly fashioned double period of thirty-two bars ending at 'Di gioia nel cor'. The rest is comment and coda as the women rehearse once more their parts in the trick. Embedded in the text is the Shakespearian quatrain from which the ensemble has taken its cue:

We'll leave a proof, by that which we will do,
Wives may be merry and yet honest too.
We do not act that often jest and laugh;
'Tis old but true: 'Still swine eats all the draff'.*

Once again Alice has taken what originally belonged to Meg; while the 'still swine' becomes the woman who plays the 'dead cat' (i.e., the cat that shams dead). For these sentiments the music broadens out into moderato crotchets, the 'gatta morta' being given weight and emphasis by violins playing on the G string as well as by Alice's 'ingrossando la voce'. Temporarily dammed, the 6/8 bursts out again, shorter phrase-lengths more frequently repeated giving an impression of greater speed. The vocal harmony here is three-part since while the others are singing Quickly is looking out for Falstaff's approach. She sees him ('Eccolo! . . . È lui!'); all take up their agreed positions while the orchestra traces a pattern of cadential arpeggios which would bring the music to a full stop but for a switch into A major during the last few bars. Falstaff enters to find Alice lazily thrumming her lute (for the generation that knew not Dolmetsch, this meant in practical terms a guitar; and hence no doubt the slightly Spanish-sounding triplet that decorates the emerging melody):†

312

Falstaff's 'Have I caught thee, my heavenly jewel?' is lightly sung to the guitar melody (Ex. 312) as he 'takes her by the bosom'. Hastily she gets up and puts the lute on the table, so forcing him to proceed more conversationally. After a few caressing phrases, corresponding to 'Why, now let me die, for I have lived long enough: this is the period of my ambition. O, this blessed hour!' we hear the heavy tramp of Ex. 290b as Falstaff apologizes for his lack of fashionable graces. But one thing he will say outright. 'That is . . .' Alice prompts. 'That is,' he echoes, 'I wish that Master Ford might pass on to a better world.'‡ Verdi's Falstaff expresses himself more euphemistically here than Shakespeare's, but the bland effrontery of his wish is pointed up by an unexpected modulation to G. 'You would be my Lady . . .' 'A pitiful Lady . . .'. A typically agogic 6/4/3 underlines Alice's teasing disclaimer. Falstaff's wooing, pursued in Shakespeare with that richly colourful yet absurd vocabulary that never deserts him, is matched in the opera with an equally fantastic musical design. For 'I imagine thee graced by my lineage' Verdi draws on what Donald Tovey called the Great Bassoon Joke, alluding to the instrument's propensity for clowning when played staccato (Ex. 313a). The effect is akin to that of the Rossinian open melody with free declamatory phrases which coalesce into a periodic melody. Here the process is accompanied by a change of tempo into 3/4 as Falstaff compares Alice to the diamond. Falstaff's line is now smooth and suave, but bassoons,

* *The Merry Wives of Windsor*, IV, ii, 96–9.

† In the autograph, however, this is written as a quaver C sharp with a pair of grace notes. Here the guitar chords are fuller than in the printed score, being spread over all six strings.

‡ A lamentable tradition among interpreters of Falstaff ordains that he should mimic Alice's tone of voice and sing 'Cioè' in near falsetto. Of all the recorded Falstaffs only Giuseppe Valdengo holds aloof from it, doubtless at the insistence of the conductor, Toscanini.

still active in the bass, keep up the air of fatuity (Ex. 313b). Alice's 'dissimilar' answer employs all the subtlest resources of Verdi's harmonic palette (Ex. 313c), as she declares herself suited only to the plainest apparel.

313a

313b

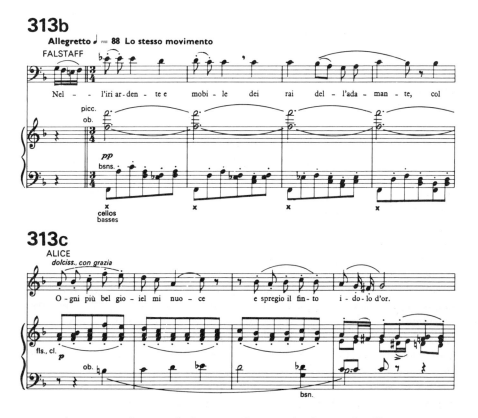

313c

Suiting the action to her words she puts a flower in her hair. Falstaff becomes more pressing, Alice more temptingly evasive; the music quickens and makes towards E major as the dominant of A for a reason that is not quite clear until the solution is sprung on us with a suddenness which never loses its impact through familiarity. A reference to Falstaff's bulk prompts him to a reminiscence that has nothing to do with the *Merry Wives* but is taken straight from *King Henry IV*, Part 1 ('When I was thy

years, Hal, I was not an eagle's talon in the waist. I could have crept into any alder-
man's thumb-ring').*

314

How better could Falstaff have illustrated his own past slightness than by one of the
smallest arias ever written — so small in fact that its perfectly finite shape of twenty-
four bars can slot into the scene without causing any sense of stasis? It is easy here to
detect a recollection, perhaps unconscious, of 'Fin ch'han dal vino' from *Don Giovanni*
in the tripping 2/4 rhythm; but not even Mozart, with his unrivalled ability to pack
volumes of meaning into a narrow compass, ever wrote a self-sufficient number that
lasts exactly half a minute.

The dialogue resumes with material derived freely from Ex. 311a and its consequent. Alice playfully accuses Falstaff of deceiving her. Is he not in love with Meg
Page? Falstaff insists that Meg disgusts him. What happens next is partly Boito's own
invention, partly the result of having conflated two episodes of Shakespeare's play.
Quickly's voice is heard calling to Alice that Meg is on her way to the house in great
agitation. Falstaff at once conceals himself behind the screen. The dialogue is culled
partly from Shakespeare's Act III, scene iii, partly from Act IV, scene ii; in both Meg
is warning Alice of Ford's imminent entry to search the house. Shakespeare's Alice is
aware that her husband suspects her; he has already spoken rudely to her in Act II,
scene i; nor is there anything to show that she does not take Meg's warning at its face
value, being confident that she can get the better of both Falstaff and Ford. In the
opera her exchanges with Meg amount to no more than play-acting, with the object
of frightening Falstaff into the buck-basket. For this, two action themes (Ex. 315a, b)
are made to serve, the second faintly recalling the disarray of the Israelites in *Nabucco*:

* Act II, scene ii.

315a

315b

But when Quickly enters for the second time it is to warn of real danger: Ford is on his way with a crowd at his heels to search the house for the fat knight. The tempo quickens, and a more significant theme takes shape in the second violins: a sophisticated variant of the principal melody of the Act I finale from Delibes's *Coppélia*, all sixteen bars of it given out unaccompanied, like a fugue subject. 'The devil bestrides a violin bow,' Falstaff comments by way of a typically Boitian operatic pun. (Ex. 316)

If any part of the opera more than justifies Tovey's description 'Chinese in its workmanship' it is this finale. Indeed so delicate are its details that many of them will be lost on the unprimed spectator. Like a fugue subject Ex. 316 is answered in the dominant, but Verdi does not develop it as a fugue. Rather he subjects it to every possible vertical combination, like the *sommossa* theme in Act I of the revised *Simon Boccanegra*, later breaking it down into tiny sequences based on the two elements (*x*) and (*y*). The busy eventfulness of the music is matched by the activity on stage. As

316

Ford's voice is heard outside ('Malandrino!'). Falstaff, on the point of escaping, hurriedly steps back behind the screen which Alice now closes round him. Ford bursts in, followed first by Caius and Fenton, then by Bardolph and Pistol, whom he sends off to search the adjoining rooms. He himself makes straight for the buck-basket and gives it a kick.

What follows belongs in the play to the episode of the fat woman of Brainford, by which time Shakespeare's Ford had good reason to begin his search in that quarter, having, as Brook, heard from Falstaff's own lips the story of his ducking in the Thames. Unable to translate Shakespeare's pun on 'buck' Boito matches it with another, where Ford twice snarls at his wife, 'Mi lavi, rea moglie!' He sends Dr Caius out by another door with a bunch of keys, then proceeds to scatter the contents of the basket over the floor, while Ex. 316 is put through its inexhaustible variety of paces, at one point ('Ti sguscio . . . lenzuola . . . berretti da notte') supplying the bass to a lyrical melody played by oboes and clarinets. His search having yielded nothing, exit Ford, shouting, by the door on the left. As Falstaff emerges from behind the screen there is a new toccata-like theme, soon to be combined with fragments of Ex. 315a. His only hope of concealment is now the buck-basket, and he steps gingerly into it. Alice meanwhile goes to call the servants – a departure, this, from Shakespeare's scheme in which Alice has only to clap her hands and the two servants convey the loaded basket out at once. In the opera, however, Alice's absence from the scene will be a determining factor in Ford's behaviour. If as in the *Macbeth* of 1865 a vital exit is masked by too much musical activity, at least Falstaff can now plausibly tell Meg that he loves her alone as she and Quickly begin covering him with the foul linen. Neither notice the furtive entry of Fenton and Nannetta. Without any change of pulse the music moves into the familiar lyrical 3/4; the accompaniment is mostly horn and woodwind with smooth clarinet quavers and a sporadic pattern of Ex. 316 (*x*) to form a link with what has gone before and at the same time to maintain the rhythmic momentum which is to some extent counteracted by harmonic stasis; for of all the thirty-three bars only four are not underpinned by a dominant pedal, real or implied. This too is appropriate. The hustle of the household has become enveloped in the serenity of the young lovers' personal paradise. (Ex. 317)

'They are mad with anger,' says Nannetta, 'And we with love,' Fenton replies. He takes her by the hand and leads her behind the screen, where they remain in an embrace, unseen by the others. The calm is once more shattered by Ex. 316 thundered out with full orchestra as the four men come running in from different directions, having failed to find their quarry. The hunt is continued with an accompaniment of increasing complexity and closer sequential workings of the ubiquitous Ex. 316, not to mention an Elizabethan wealth of vocabulary, especially on the part

317

of Ford and Dr Caius, the two most interested parties. Bardolph and Pistol are again sent out to search the rest of the house. Ford at first tries the cupboard, then the chest, even in an excess of paranoia the table drawer. To match his obsession Ex. 316 (*x*) is transformed into a cadential figure repeated eight times in an ascending sequence by keys a fifth apart, the cadences themselves being partly masked by cross-phrasing in the bass. The effect is of a kitten chasing its tail.

318

Suddenly Ford and the music stop in their tracks, an orchestral tutti fading away in a flourish of high woodwind. In the silence a loud kiss is heard behind the screen. 'There he is' – in Italian the monosyllable 'C'è' – murmurs first Ford then Caius under their breaths. Without any help from Shakespeare Boito and Verdi have found the perfect situation for a concertato. The two men's muttered threats as they advance stealthily toward the screen provide its first rhythmic element.

If Caius's 'T'arronciglio' traces its pedigree to similar moments in both *Un Giorno di regno* and *Ernani*, the concertato as a whole is quite unlike any that Verdi had written previously. There is no lyrical groundswell building up to the kind of climax we find even as late as *Otello*. From first to last the texture remains transparent. The next theme is couched in those mischievous triplets associated with the inward chuckling of the women (Ex. 320), as Quickly and Meg decide to make a pretence of being busy with the washing and at the same time to stand between the men and the basket so as to conceal it from their view. Both alternate double senario lines. The scoring is of the lightest, flute and piccolo picking out Quickly, oboe Meg, and four horns *piano* the exclamations of Caius and Ford; but note also how delicately the tradition of sustaining at the point of modulation is applied first by horns and bassoons then by pianissimo strings.

By the end of Meg's second line the string texture has become more continuous, as Bardolph and Pistol have now returned together with various neighbours, all male. While the G major cadence is gently reiterated by woodwind groups Ford announces to them in a whisper that the hunt is over. He points to the screen: 'There is Falstaff with my wife.' The cadences are now taken up in E major by strings. 'Filthy despicable hound!' Bardolph cries out in a sudden volley of semiquavers; Caius, Ford and Pistol tell him to be quiet; Falstaff putting his nose out of the basket cries out that he is suffocating; Quickly pushes him down again – all this in tiny fragments within a

320

QUICKLY

Fac - cia - mo le vi - ste d'atten - de - re ai pan - ni; pur ch'ei non c'in - gan - ni con mos - se im - pre - (viste)

CAIUS *(sottovoce)*

Guai a te! Guai!

fl., picc.

p e staccato

hns.   hns.

steady pulse marked by alternating strings and wind, where the effect of Bardolph's outburst and its quick dampening is curiously like that of a slipped wheel in the world of steam traction. The vocal texture is kept light through a variety of internal rhythms. Meg and Quickly continue to admonish Falstaff in triplets; Bardolph's next intervention, urging them to catch the mouse while he's at the cheese ('Noi dobbiam pigliare il topo mentre sta rodendo cacio'), moves by double-dotted quavers and demisemiquavers. With Ford's 'Ragioniam' ('Let's consider') the music returns once more to the E major cadence now given extra weight through sustaining horns, bassoons and strings as well as threatening 'death-figures' from a solo trumpet. Then to a gently patterned accompaniment Fenton springs into lyrical relief ('Bella! ridente!') as in the finale to the first act. Nannetta's line assumes at first a 'merry wives' character; but soon it will intertwine with Fenton's in notes of similar value. Ford, as he works out his plan of action ('Colpo non vibro senz'un piano di bat- taglia') to the approval of his supporters, moves in quavers and semiquavers, cun- ningly disposed so as nowhere to duplicate the rhythm of the accompaniment (Ex. 321). The trend towards an old-fashioned concertato is once more corrected as Nan- netta and Fenton break off their poetic nothings at the second phrase, leaving Ford to give his orders in chattering semiquavers and with a marked change of key. Pistol and two of his companions are to advance from the right; he, Bardolph and Caius will complete the pincer movement from the left; all the others will protect their rear. When Nannetta and Fenton resume it is to a new accompaniment and in the key of G minor ('Già un sogno bello d'Imene'). Again they finish on a dominant; and there is something richly comic about the way their lyrical line now in G major is transformed into pathos when taken over by Falstaff, calling for just one vent-hole ('Un breve spiraglio, non chiedo di più'). Meg and Quickly push him down again with brusque finality to a C major cadence. Here the concertato reaches its highest point of complexity, the sustained element being provided by Nannetta and Fenton, now in unison supported by murmuring male chorus, Meg and Quickly in triplets, the rest of the men in semiquavers (Ex. 322).

Elaborate as this is, it represents a compression of something very much more so. Originally Fenton's and Nannetta's melody had run to sixteen bars instead of six, fetching a wide circle of tonalities and wandering as far afield as G flat major – and all to an unremitting chatter of semiquavers in the bass (see Ex. 323).

321

322

323

As Verdi pointed out, it would have been possible to cut it out entirely without damage to the musical continuity. Structurally, however, it was, in his words, the 'belly' of the ensemble and its removal would have been a monstrous piece of butchery. By rewriting it in more compendious form not only did he preserve the integrity of the structure while avoiding that hypertrophy of the concertato which had bothered him in *Otello*; he was also able to work in a useful recall of Ex. 320 by way of a counter-theme – all ample compensation for the loss of forty-two lines of text including a learned reference by Pistol to the legend of Alpheus and Arethusa.

As the melody sinks to rest in melting triplet exchanges between the lovers ('Dolci richiami d'amor,' etc.) Alice returns unobserved to take her part in keeping Falstaff in order; not that there is any real danger since all attention is now fixed on the screen, and his cries for help pass unnoticed as Ford whispers a count of three. The men charge, the screen is overturned and Nannetta and Fenton discovered in each other's arms. The concertato mood is thus effectively broken. Ford storms first at Nannetta ('Ancor nuove rivolte!') then at Fenton ('Tu va pe' fatti tuoi!'); he has told him a thousand times that Nannetta is not for him. Doubtless he would say more but at that point Bardolph suddenly cries out that he has spotted Falstaff on the stairs. To another noisy reprise of Ex. 316 Ford and his followers rush out of the room. This gives Alice her chance. She rings a handbell: 'Ned, Will, Tom, Isaac!' Re-enter Nannetta with four servants and a small page. The servants are ordered to empty the basket through the window into the Thames, warning them that it contains a large item – 'un pezzo grosso', which is also slang for an important person. Ex. 316 which has formed the basis of this transition reappears pianissimo as Alice tells the page to fetch her husband; the sight of Falstaff floundering in the water, she tells Meg, should cure him of his jealousy. Fierce orchestral unisons depict the efforts of the servants to hoist the basket onto their shoulders; Nannetta hearing a creak fears that the bottom will give way; but all is well and Alice is able to take her husband by the arm to witness the defenestration. Quicker on the uptake than his Shakespearian counterpart, Ford joins in the general laughter and cry of 'Patatrac!' while the orchestra concludes the scene with a suitably merry coda, the three trumpets cavorting in C major fanfares.

ACT III

Part 1: A square. On the right the exterior of the Garter Inn, with a sign and the motto 'Honi soit qui mal y pense'. A bench by the doorway. It is about sunset.

The tradition of a third act prelude founded on previous material, universal in Italian opera by 1880, is observed, like everything else in *Falstaff*, in the briefest and most concentrated form imaginable. Its basis is Ex. 315a, starting on the basses alone, building up harmonically at first through repetition, then developing by fragmentation into sequences; the reprise is hammered out fortissimo in chords by three trumpets and three trombones while the rest of the orchestra reiterate the note E over five octaves (a characteristically original twist, this, to the opaque Rossinian tutti that Verdi had inherited). The theme is again repeated with a more orthodox distribution and accompanied by a soft roll on the cymbals. The climax is a sequence of discordant hammer blows that subside ruefully in the direction of B minor.

Despite the dangers of reminiscence-hunting the temptation to hear an echo of Beckmesser is irresistible – and all the more in that his situation in the third act of *Die Meistersinger* is similar to Falstaff's. He too has been 'roughed up', and when he comes to visit Sachs his mind is full of the previous night's turmoil. If only for the briefest of moments the two baritone rogues join hands.

324a

Sehr mässig

Wagner : DIE MEISTERSINGER

324b

Allegro agitato

The curtain has risen to disclose a miserable Falstaff seated on a large chair. All at once he leaps to his feet, bangs the table and calls for the innkeeper, his gesture matched by a sweeping staccato scale-passage for the violins (this too a device often encountered in Wagner, but always legato). It is the Falstaff of *King Henry IV*, Part 1, who settles back gloomily in his chair; the Falstaff to whom Prince Hal's apparent betrayal (not to be compared to his real betrayal at the end of the next play) and the presence of lime in his cup of sack are evidence of depraved humanity and a world headed for destruction. 'There is nothing but roguery to be found in villainous man . . . a bad world, I say.' The orchestra takes up his thoughts in rhythmically disjointed mutterings like a voice from Respighi's Roman catacombs:

325

The text returns to *The Merry Wives of Windsor* for the recollection of his ducking in the Thames, with one minor departure. Shakespeare's Falstaff attributes his salvation to the fact that the water was shallow ('. . . you may know from my size that I have a kind of alacrity in sinking'). Boito, more scientific, knew that the fatter the man the more easily he floats. In the opera therefore it is Falstaff's mighty paunch that keeps him from drowning ('Che se non galleggiava per me quest'epa tronfia'). But as in Shakespeare he abhors a watery death which 'swells a man' – an observation that gives rise to some effective word painting in the orchestra with horns slithering about in legato semiquavers. Falstaff returns to his refrain 'mondo ladro' and Ex. 325 whose black colour is now reinforced by bass trombone. 'Go thy ways, old Jack, die when thou wilt; if manhood, good manhood, be not forgot upon the face of the earth then I am a shotten herring.' Falstaff used a similar turn of phrase in *The Merry Wives* after Quickly's visit ('Say'st thou so, old Jack? Go thy ways . . .'). Thus a fortuitous connection between the two plays provides the pretext for a most effective musical reminiscence. To the words, 'Va, vecchio John', Ex. 290b reappears in the minor key, all its swagger gone. After four bars it takes a new, slightly freer turning; and in the reflection that when Falstaff himself has died all true manhood will have left the earth sustaining trombones and a timpani roll add just a touch of complacency to the

D flat major cadence. But then gloom returns with a brief recall of Ex. 315a ending with what commentators have claimed to be a thinly disguised quotation of Klingsor's motif from *Parsifal*.*

326

Certainly Verdi possessed a score of that opera, though he could never have seen it performed. But surely if the quotation were deliberate in this of all operas, the point would have been underlined by some punning reference in the text, such as can hardly be found in the words 'Che giornataccia nera'. More likely, as in *Otello*, Act III, we are dealing with an unconscious reminiscence, if not mere coincidence. Like so much in *Falstaff* it makes its immediate effect as the musical stylization of a natural vocal reaction – in this case a resentful growl. The black mood does not last long. To a return of the flourish of first violins the innkeeper re-enters with a huge beaker of mulled wine. 'Let us pour a little wine into the Thames water,' he cries, thereby disposing of the much debated question as to whether or not a day or more has elapsed since his ducking.† The snatch of melody to which he sings the words sounds intriguingly like the first line of an English glee; and indeed the marking, *cantarellando*, denotes singing outside the operatic convention.

327

Two bars of string semiquavers depict the act of pouring; then, as Falstaff sips appreciatively, a delicious warmth steals over him. Not even Simon Boccanegra cooling his brow in the sea breezes of Genoa felt such consolation. If the musical expression seems too poetic for the subject we should remember that Falstaff's ideals of bliss reach no higher than the satisfaction of the stomach. (Ex. 328)

In more prosaic vein he goes on to describe the little cricket ('grillo') that gets into a man's veins when he is drunk ('brillo') and his body alive with a huge trill ('trillo').

* See Hughes, p. 510.

† For a pertinent discussion of Boito's treatment of the single-day convention as followed in *Le Nozze di Figaro* and *Così fan tutte*, etc., see Hughes, pp. 508–9.

328

The conceit with its recurrent jingle is, of course Boito's,* while the musical illustration of the trill is one of Verdi's most famous orchestral tours de force. Starting on the second flute, while first and third give out cricket-like twitters, it spreads to the strings, desk by desk, through the wind and finally as the 'trill invades the world' to the full orchestra in a wide harmonic arc that finishes in E major, thus rounding off with the most satisfying finality Falstaff's loosely knit and highly entertaining monologue. It is a variant of the device used in *Attila* to paint the rising of the sun; but put to far more effective purpose. The very schematicism that had seemed obvious and two-dimensional in the earlier opera contributes to the wit of the later one.

But nothing is truly final in *Falstaff* until the last chord. Barely has E major been touched upon when the music veers sharply away with a unison G natural and Falstaff is startled by Mistress Quickly's 'Reverenza. La bella Alice' (Ex. 286).† Its effect on Falstaff is electric. He rounds on Quickly in a tirade of chattering quavers ('Al diavolo te con Alice bella!'). His recital of misfortune, graphically illustrated in the music, ends with a downward rush of strings for his ducking in the Thames. Meanwhile not only Alice, Meg and Nannetta but also Ford, Caius and Fenton have crept onto the scene and are eavesdropping at a distance. They observe Quickly

* Boito's text seems to have taken as its point of departure Falstaff's speech in *King Henry IV*, Part 2, IV, iii when he ascribes Prince John's priggish manner and behaviour to the fact that he drinks no wine. He then describes the action of 'sherris-sack': 'it ascends me into the brain; dries me there all the foolish and dull and crudy vapours that environ it: makes it apprehensive, quick, forgetive, full of nimble, fiery and delectable shapes . . .', etc.

† The autograph contains two bars of transition here that do not appear in the printed score; presumably the advantages of suddenness occurred to Verdi after the manuscript had been sent to the publisher.

bowing before the storm of words, hear her making excuses in phrases as soothing as the fast tempo will allow. It was not Alice's fault; merely the stupidity of her household that was to blame. Alice meanwhile is in despair, weeping, calling upon the saints to help her – 'Poor lady!' Here Quickly returns to her other refrain of Act II (Ex. 287), whose rhythm furnishes the basis of a brief transition during which she takes from her pocket a letter and hands it to the partly mollified Falstaff. Meanwhile the onlookers note gleefully that the fat knight has once more swallowed the bait. First, it would seem, he reads the letter in silence; then re-reads it aloud in a free parlando monotone *senza misura*: 'I will await you in the Royal Park at midnight. You will come disguised as the Black Huntsman to the oak of Herne.' 'Love delights in mystery,' Quickly puts in helpfully. She then begins to tell him about the legend of Herne the Hunter. Beginning cheerfully ('Per riveder Alice') the music takes on an increasingly dark mysterious tone, more appropriate to Shakespeare's horrifying imagery than to Boito's more prosaic version:

> There is an old tale goes, that Herne the Hunter,
> Sometime a keeper here in Windsor Forest,
> Doth all the winter-time, at still midnight,
> Walk round about an oak, with great ragg'd horns;
> And there he blasts the tree, and takes the cattle,
> And makes milch-kine yield blood, and shakes a chain
> In a most hideous and dreadful manner.*

'Quella quercia è un luogo da tregenda' forms the first phrase of that comic litany that will occur in the next scene. Soft trumpets and a trombone touch in the end of the otherwise unison phrase in which Quickly describes how the black huntsman hanged himself from one of its branches. There are those, she adds impressively, who believe they have seen him reappear. Horns begin to sustain and triplets stir in the bass in a manner faintly recalling Wolf's Glen. Falstaff asks her to continue her story as he leads her into the inn.

So begins a transition of the utmost ingenuity from the world of everyday bustle to one of enchantment. Gothic horror, we have seen, came no more easily to Verdi than to most Italians. His early essays in Schauerromantik in *Giovanna d'Arco* suggest no more than the attempts of Dickens's fat boy 'ter make yer flesh creep'. In *Stiffelio* and *Un Ballo in maschera* he evokes terror more convincingly, having by then assimilated the stock vocabulary of the romantic age for situations of this kind. Yet he never surpassed the opening of the storm scene in *Rigoletto* for spine-chilling eeriness, especially since the means are his own and nobody else's. The high oboes above the open fifth in the basses† are an effect to be sought in vain in the works of any other composer; and it is worth many bars of routine pounding on diminished sevenths – 'that rock and refuge of all those of us who can't compose four bars without half a dozen of those sevenths', as Verdi put it.‡ For the story of Herne the Hunter Verdi reverts to the methods of *Rigoletto*; a sustaining horn in D, then a piccolo on A. Quickly's narration keeps to the major key with chromatic inflexions and occasional hints of the minor in the accompaniment. 'When the chimes of midnight spread their

---

* *The Merry Wives of Windsor*, IV, iv, 27–33.
† Vol. I, Ex. 356.
‡ Letter to Florimo, 4.1.1871. *Copialettere*, pp. 232–3.

hollow sound . . .'. Falstaff's presence during this would be fatal to the creation of the right atmosphere. Therefore, while he goes into the Garter Inn with Quickly, Alice takes over the story and tells it to her companions with an imitation of Quickly's portentous manner. Pedal notes from the other three horns now suggest the chimes, while the first horn supplies an ambiguous counter-melody to the vocal line, the sinister whistle of the piccolo persisting above. The Black Huntsman 'walks slowly, slowly, lethargic from his long burial'. By now bassoons, horns and second violins have launched a chromatic *marche funèbre* with rapidly oscillating clarinet and low strings and punctuated by timpani and bass and low, held brass chords. Gradually the harmonies thicken; yet the sound never rises above a pianissimo. Meg and Nannetta begin to be genuinely frightened; so Alice feels it necessary to dispel their fears with a gay, mazurka-like theme which assumes great importance later in the scene (Ex. 329a). All nonsense, she declares; the kind of stories one tells to children to send them to sleep; but 'women's vengeance must not fail' – this to what can only be called a stylized laugh which is not only appropriate dramatically but also the perfect conclusion to the musical period. (Ex. 329b)

Alice completes her story with a reprise of the opening, now accompanied by four horns, a punning illustration of the 'long, long' horns that grow out of Herne's head as he advances towards the oak tree. 'Well done!' Ford cries. 'Those horns shall be my joy.' But Alice is not prepared to let him off without a word of reproof; and in the short F major episode he is made to apologize.* Evidently Alice has not forgotten Ford's opening of the table drawer: 'That savage mania – looking for your wife's lover in a nutshell,' she says, to a delightful finger-wagging phrase.

* His phrase 'Riconosco i miei demeriti' was sufficiently important for Verdi to have had second thoughts about its setting, as the proof copy shows.

330

But time, she adds, is getting short; and she proceeds to give instructions. Nannetta is to be the Fairy Queen, wearing a white robe and veil and a crown of roses ('And I shall sing harmonious songs,' Nannetta murmurs). Meg is to be the nymph Silvana; and Quickly will be a befana.* This is undoubtedly a better arrangement than Shakespeare's, which makes Quickly into the Fairy Queen, though in an earlier scene Meg Page had claimed that right for her own daughter. Here the score is at its most tenuous. No other nineteenth-century composer (and only Britten in our own time) would have dared to reduce it to single threads of arpeggiating wind instruments as Verdi has done here. The most solid element in the entire fifteen bars is provided by a short triplet pattern on the flute with clarinet and oboe supporting at the point where Nannetta mentions her 'harmonious songs', and this in turn finds its place in Alice's peroration which now follows. She will bring with her a crowd of children (*putti*) who will dress up as sprites and fairies and together they will fall upon Falstaff in his ridiculous disguise. In the gathering dusk we seem to see the dancing fireflies as voice, violins and piccolo trace a glinting theme, not unlike the kind of melody one finds in Nicolai's opera but with a delicacy and brilliance all its own.

331

* 'La Befana', her name contracted from Epifania, is a kindly witch who is supposed to appear on Twelfth Night and bring presents to children, like a female Santa Claus.

A brief episode brings in a new musical idea, which looks backward to the prancing cabalettas of Verdi's youth and forward to *Gianni Schicchi*, also at a point at which 'dressing-up' is in question.

332

From this point until the end of the scene a wide divergence opens up between the original and revised versions. To say that the definitive one is shorter by some twenty-eight bars is true but misleading, since most of the 'new' bars are in 4/4 against the original 3/4. In fact the scene as it stands now is more spacious and varied than formerly, containing as it does an additional theme and an entirely different deployment of existing thematic resources. In both cases there is a reprise of Ex. 331. But in the first version this occurs beneath Alice's words 'L'appuntamento è alla quercia di Herne'. This is logical enough, if somewhat pleonastic, since it gives too much importance to Alice's brief reminder, as well as suggesting the automatic repetitions of a cabaletta. Then as she, Fenton and the other two women retire, leaving Ford and Caius together, the mazurka theme (Ex. 329a) originally provided an instrumental transition, and from then on dominated the scene with sundry developments and variants. In the revision Verdi postponed the reprise of Ex. 331 for eight bars, so allowing Alice's peroration and the subsequent farewells to fade away in unimportant derivations from the triplet pattern in Ex. 332. So now it is Ex. 331, not 329a, that provides the instrumental transition, and such is the character of the theme itself as well as its new positioning that it takes on the additional aspect of a postlude. For the moment in which Ford, overheard by Quickly, plots to marry Nannetta to Caius during the midnight revels, Verdi introduced a new theme in common time clearly derived from the mazurka but offering the supreme advantage of possible combination with fragments of Ex. 332 – as happens within the first five bars. (Ex. 333)

Caius is asked to remember Nannetta's disguise – a white robe and veil and a wreath of roses; Caius will be disguised as a monk and 'I will bless you as bride and bridegroom,' says Ford. And how infinitely better he says it in the revised (Ex. 334a) than in the original version (b) where he is bedevilled by the insistent mazurka fidget.

333

334a

334b

(original version)

After Quickly's aside ('Stai fresco') the scene empties to a magical sequence based on Verdi's favourite consecutive 6/4/3's which loses nothing on its transformation from 3/4 into 4/4:

335

The scene ends with the voices of Quickly, Meg and Nannetta heard calling to one another; and to a final reprise of Ex. 331 and a rising pattern derived from Ex. 335 floating into the upper ether the curtain falls.

> *Part 2: Windsor Park. In the centre the great oak of Herne. At the back the edge of a ditch. Very thick foliage. Shrubs in flower. It is night.*

'J'aime le son du cor, le soir, au fond des bois' – Vigny's celebrated line had already found its way into a Verdian literary text, but as a cruel, ironical parody; for the horn whose distant sound delighted Ernani's bride was the signal for his own death. But in the distant horn calls that open the final scene in *Falstaff*, played on natural instruments crooked in A flat *basso*, there is no menace, only enchantment (they are the horns of the royal gamekeepers on their nightly patrols of the forest). After each phrase woodwind recall Ex. 279 from the lovers' first-act duettino. As the last call fades in the distance, enter Fenton to sing his Sonetto, 'Dal labbro il canto estasiato vola', his only extended solo in the opera. Boito, even more than Verdi, was concerned to avoid anything in the nature of a detachable number designed to allow the tenor to show his paces at the expense of the dramatic continuity; he therefore planned the sestet so that the fourth and fifth lines should consist of the exchange 'Bocca baciata non perde ventura'/'Anzi rinnova come fa la luna' (Ex. 280) – a triumph of ingenuity given the complex rhyming scheme of the Italian sonnet, and one which enabled Verdi not only to conclude with a musical reminiscence but also to break up the solo itself with an intervention from Nannetta which would make the Sonetto seem in retrospect like a delayed episode within the duettino.*

* For the literary ancestry of Boito's text, its relation to Shakespeare's Sonnets Nos. 8 and 128, and the place of the sonnet in general in sixteenth- and seventeenth-century drama, see Wolfgang Osthoff's excellent 'Il Sonetto nel *Falstaff* di Verdi', in *Il Melodramma italiano dell'Ottocento – studi e ricerche per Massimo Mila* (Turin, 1977), pp. 157–83.

In choosing to set to music a sonnet with its fourteen lines of eleven-syllable verse, its caesura between octet and sextet and lesser breaks within each Verdi was accepting a formidable challenge for an opera composer. Generally speaking the sonnet finds no place in traditional music theatre, except by way of parody, as in Galuppi's *Le Virtuose ridicole* and Strauss's *Capriccio*.* (Indeed, who apart from Britten and Wolf has ever set a sonnet successfully even in a non-theatrical context?) In his later years Verdi had shown a certain fondness for experimenting with eleven-syllable verse in a lyrical context – witness the final duet in *Aida* and the love-duet in *Otello*. The two solutions are quite different. In *Otello* the verse is treated in the grand manner with a faintly march-like articulation that brings to mind French grand opera and the earlier works of Wagner. In *Aida* on the other hand each line begins with a three-note anacrusis, analogous to the two-note anacrusis to be found in most slow settings of octosyllabic metre, and leading to a special stress on the eighth syllable. This is the method followed here, with the difference that where in 'O terra addio' the stress was essentially a harmonic one here it is enhanced by the leap of a fifth.

This perfect spanning of the long line in a manner both ardent and gently poetic and without a trace of over-emphasis was, as we have seen, not achieved

336

* See Osthoff, *ibid.* A possible exception is the setting of 'Devouring Time, blunt thou the lion's paws' in Holst's one-act opera *At the Boar's Head*, which, however, is too experimental to furnish a rule.

straightaway. The jump of a seventh and the conclusion of the first line on a high A flat in Ex. 248 shows that tendency to anticipate the salient features of a melody that marks so many of Verdi's first thoughts. No doubt, too, the downward motion of the first three notes he quickly felt to be inconsistent with the character of a melody whose every phrase has a tendency to levitate. (Ex. 336)

The traditional divisions of the sonnet are scrupulously observed. The first quatrain forms a self-contained period of eight bars extended at the cadence to nine. At the second ('Allor la nota che non è più sola') the pace slightly quickens, the anacrusis becomes one of three repeated notes sung semi-staccato, and for the first time in the opera the texture is coloured by the harp. This quatrain too forms a period but with a longer extension; and its full close is reached not in A flat but in E. For the

337a

337b

first half of the sextet ('Quivi ripiglia suon, ma la sua cura') Verdi was originally content to let Fenton pursue his metaphysical speculations in a freer, more conversational tone by way of a contrasting episode (Ex. 337a). It was not until the proof stage that he conceived the idea of making it a species of reprise with the melody of Ex. 336 carried on cor anglais with no other instrumental support; and what better illustration could be found for the words 'ripiglia suon'? (Ex. 337b)

The setting of the final tercet is of course predetermined ('Bocca baciata', etc.); it is the point where the musical organism of the Sonetto must submerge its identity into that of the duettino, a transformation symbolic of the two-in-one image that underlies the sense of Boito's text. The transition to Ex. 280 is effected with rippling arpeggios on the harp, whose intermittent presence in this piece is all the more telling for the delicate transparency of the scoring throughout – a legacy, it would seem, from those panels of selective instrumentation that occur in some of the earliest operas. There, too, the cor anglais was always prominent and the double basses reduced to a single instrument; here it is one of four strings, the lowest of which the player is twice required to retune. Needless to say the scoring of the Sonetto is far more varied, its colours softer and the instruments made to yield a far greater diversity of sound than formerly. Note the rapidly oscillating flutes and piccolo – that favourite device of late Verdi – to illustrate the 'aer antelucano' ('the air of morning twilight').

But in this opera not even a love duettino is allowed a normal full close; so Verdi does not bother to correct the subdominant bias of Ex. 280 and the last line of the sonnet, sung by both voices in unison, points unambiguously at D flat. It is the practical Alice and her friends who restore the main key, by which time the mood has changed completely. She has brought Fenton a black monk's cloak and hood and a mask which he must put on at once. This is of course to foil Ford's plan for marrying Nannetta to Dr Caius. And whom meanwhile will they dress up to act as decoy for the good doctor? That 'robber with the nose', whom he so detests, says Quickly, already robed as the good witch of Epiphany. While Alice and Nannetta help Fenton on with his disguise, enter Meg in a green dress to say that the troop of urchins is already stationed along the ditch. Alice catches sight of the 'pezzo grosso' approaching. All scatter and hide.

The twenty-nine bars of action music that accompany these movements are, like so many of the transitions in *Falstaff*, not precisely athematic but spun from threads so

338a

fine as to elude the clumsy fingers of the analyst. The germinating motif is compounded of a semiquaver triplet and two quavers (Ex. 338a). The first period is rounded off by Meg's compliment to Fenton on his 'trappist' appearance ('È un fraticel sgusciato dalla Trappa', Ex. 338b); and it is from the first four notes of this that the following bars are generated in mock fugato fashion.

At Quickly's 'Un gaio ladron nasuto' the quavers form themselves into a reprise of

338b

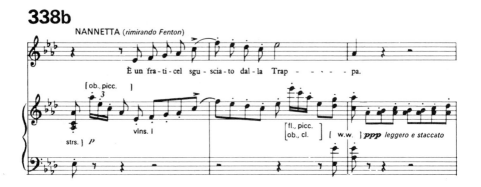

Ex. 308b, only to dissolve once more into the scales and arpeggios of schoolroom exercises, miraculously illumined by an indefinable melodic spark.

As the women hide the motion is suddenly arrested; and although the stage remains empty for the next eight bars the imminence of Falstaff, fantastically arrayed in a pair of antlers, is indicated by a portentous orchestral theme (Ex. 339). Here Verdi's skill at harmonic epigram can be seen at its most striking; for the theme itself is as near to an eight-fold repetition of a single idea as a theme can be while at the same time forming a complete musical sentence. It is first prodded into motion at the fourth bar by a variation of the bass. At bar 6 it is given a heavy jolt into a new key with a displacement of all but the highest note; and it is precisely this persistence of D flat that returns the melody to its original point of departure but with a change of mode and a cadence cushioned by soft trombones. A remarkable instance, this, of how to move from one place to another by apparently stepping once to the side and back again.

339

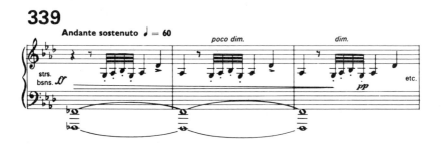

As the first strike of midnight chimes, Falstaff appears. Here Verdi extends the

idea of Ex. 339, repeating a single note ad infinitum with changes of harmony beneath – just the kind of game likely to appeal to the author of the 'Ave Maria' based on the scala enigmatica. The result must have sounded strange to contemporary ears. (Ex. 340)

Ex. 339 returns elaborated by Falstaff's comments ('Quest' è la quercia. . . . Numi, proteggetemi!'). A sense of his own ridiculousness is touched with a faint apprehension. He tries to dispel both by recalling classical precedents for his disguise. 'Jove, thou wast a bull for thy Europa.' The musical setting appropriately mixes the solemn with the grotesque, with the suggestion of a bellow on the word 'bove'. (Ex. 341)

Falstaff's musings are interrupted by the sound of a 'sweet footfall'. There follows a passage of rapid conversational music, akin to Ford's 'Spendetele! spendetele!' from Act II, with an accompaniment of alternating two-note figures but without the chink of gold. Falstaff welcomes Alice with a great show of excitement; nor is he disconcerted by the news that Meg will soon join them. 'Divide me like a bribe-buck, each a haunch . . .'. His final burst of 'Io t'amo' several times repeated has a perfunctory ring about it as though he were anxious to finish the uncomfortable business as soon as possible. But suddenly Meg's voice offstage sounds the alarm; Alice hurries away; the orchestra makes a few panic noises and Falstaff crouches down against the oak tree's trunk, muttering that the devil does not want him damned. ('Il diavolo non vuol ch'io sia dannato' – a pointless remark without Shakespeare's concluding clause: 'lest the oil that is in me should set Hell on fire.')

Enchantment fills the air once more. Beneath tremolando violins and violas, oboe, cor anglais and clarinet give out a series of delicate 'View-halloos' (Ex. 342a); while

342a

342b

Nannetta's voice can be heard summoning her attendant fairies ('Ninfe! Elfi! Silfi! Doridi! Sirene!'). Her words are echoed in a faint chorus floating in from the distance while Falstaff murmurs, 'they are the fairies; whoever looks at them shall die,' and crouches still lower. The fairies gather in the darkness with a sense of hopping, twittering and fluttering like some unearthly *rappel des oiseaux* (Ex. 342b). As a stroke of orchestral imagination it is unsurpassed by the 'faerie' evocations of Berlioz or Mendelssohn. The bass line reveals a natural derivation from Ex. 342a; and in the acciaccature figures for piccolo we hear a device from the world of *I Lombardi* ('O Signore dal tetto natio') etherealized by its content.

Here the stage directions become very detailed. The first to enter is Alice, with various little girls dressed as white and blue fairies. She points out to them Falstaff lying motionless on the ground, and they all approach him stealthily. Meanwhile Nannetta, dressed as the Fairy Queen, has also come in with attendants, who do likewise. Alice then disposes her girls according to plan and leaves. The smaller fairies form a ring round Nannetta; the others make up a separate group on the left. All this takes place to a long preparation based on Ex. 342b not unlike that which sets the scene for the first movement of Ponchielli's 'Dance of the Hours' but with real gold for tinsel. All the magic is in the music; for the comments of the 'fairies' are distinctly earth-bound ('He is hiding. . . . Let us not laugh. . . . All gather round me. . . . It's up to you. . . . Let's begin'). This last is the cue for Nannetta's song 'Sul fil d'un soffio etesio'. It is the equivalent of Quickly's

> Fairies, black, grey, green and white,
> You moonshine revellers and shades of night.*

in the *Merry Wives*. But apart from the one line, 'Fairies use flow'rs for their charactery', Shakespeare has contributed little to Boito's text; for of course Boito and Verdi had no Queen Elizabeth whose favour they could court with sly flattery. Nannetta's song with chorus remains on the level of imaginative poetry: the thread of the night breeze, the moonbeams like a pale dawn, the sleeping wood whose green

---

* *The Merry Wives of Windsor*, V, v, 38–9.

343

leaves are like a cool haven at the bottom of the sea. Nowhere is the scoring more diaphanous, the melodic writing more delicately seductive. The song is in a modified couplet form with refrain, its first idea formed from the dovetailing of two motifs, one orchestral, the other vocal, and each apparently in common time. This is of course an illusion, but the triple metre does not become unequivocal until the third phrase ('Fra i rami un baglior cesio'). Note the final experiment with the diversified sonority of upper strings of the kind that began with Lina's aria in *Stiffelio* forty-three years earlier. (Ex. 343)

The second quatrain ('Danzate! e il passo blando') begins with a new idea containing a hidden reference to Ex. 342b in the accompaniment; but its last two lines return to the third phrase of Ex. 343 – this tiny reprise being enhanced by varied scoring. The voice part is accompanied not by a flute in thirds but by a combination of bass clarinet and harp harmonics in tenths, giving the sound of some soft celestial harmonium. During the refrain the little fairies perform a solemn 'gentle' dance:

For the first 'couplet' this forms a normal eight-bar period moving to the relative minor for the third phrase, and ending in the tonic with a discreet harmonic epigram involving a touch of C major.

Nannetta's second couplet, 'Erriam sotto la luna', has a slight melodic variation at the start of the second quatrain; then, far more strikingly, a ten-bar extension of the last line to which sustaining wind and a more continuous pattern of harp arpeggios bring a new warmth. The refrain by compensation is not shortened but simplified so as to incorporate the effect of the coda, the first two bars of Ex. 344 being repeated four times with harmonic or melodic variations: on violins, on wind, on harp, and finally on cellos and basses, while Nannetta delivers a ravishing counter-melody similar to that of Desdemona in the quartet in Act II of *Otello*.

The song dies away on repeated tonics and dominants in the lower strings; and enchantment gives place to comedy. Alice appears (*back L.*) in a mask; with her are Meg as a fairy in green and Quickly in her 'befana' costume, both masked. They are preceded (so run the directions) by Bardolph in a red cloak, without a mask but with a hood drawn down over his face, and by Pistol dressed as a satyr. Dr Caius follows in a grey cloak without a mask, and after him Fenton, masked and in a black cloak, and Ford wearing neither cloak nor mask. Several 'burghers' wind up the cortège, dressed in fantastic costumes; these form themselves into a group on the right. At the back of the stage are other masked men carrying lanterns of various shapes and styles.

It is Bardolph who first stumbles over Falstaff's body. He halts the fairies 'with a grand gesture' and a cry of 'Alto là', echoed by Pistol's 'Chi va là?' Touching the recumbent knight with her stick, Quickly cries out, 'A man!'; during the controlled pandemonium that follows, full of anathematic and 'scongiuro' gestures, Alice observes that Caius appears to be searching for someone, and warns her daughter accordingly ('Evita il tuo periglio. Già il dottor Cajo ti cerca'). Fenton and Quickly shield Nannetta from the Doctor; then Quickly hurries the two lovers away, and they therefore take no part in the proceedings which follow. With Bardolph's summoning of infernal spirits ('Spiritelli! Folletti! Farfarelli! Vampiri!') the movement tightens into a 6/8 sommossa with gently thudding brass. A group of boys dressed as 'Folletti' appear from nowhere; some throw themselves on Falstaff and begin rolling him towards the front of the stage ('Ruzzola! Ruzzola!'); others dance around waving lanterns and brandishing rattles. Then the torture begins in earnest. He is whipped on the stomach with osiers, stung with nettles and jumped upon. So far the orchestra has borne the main musical burden of the proceedings. But the central, regular theme to which all such busy transitions inevitably tend is a vocal one: a delicate trio sung by Alice, Meg and Quickly accompanied by divisi strings playing pizzicato (what else, since Falstaff is being punched to cries of 'pizzica, pizzica'?). No passage in *Falstaff* is quite so vulnerable in a stage performance where the inevitable amount of 'business' combines with the natural heaviness of the operatic voice to turn it into a tuneless jingle. The corresponding melodies in Nicolai's *Lustige Weiber* and Vaughan Williams's *Sir John in Love* may be less finely imagined; but their coarser fibre stands up better to the rough and tumble of the dramatic action.

345

(*I Folletti più vicini gli pizzicano le braccia, le guancie, lo fustigano coi vimini sulla pancia, lo pungono con ortiche*)

There follows an episode for unison chorus backed by vigorous orchestral counterpoint, its sonority enhanced by the crackling assonances of Boito's recherché wordplay ('Meniam scorribandole, danziamo la tresca, treschiam le farandole sull'ampia ventresca'). It halts abruptly in a diminished seventh shriek; then after a pause Ex. 345

resumes with high woodwind joining in the accompaniment, moving on to another episode, less noisy than the first but with more elaborate vocal participation. This too breaks off as Bardolph, Pistol, Ford and Caius haul Falstaff to his knees and call him a variety of names. A change of rhythm from 6/8 to 2/4 brings two new ideas both of which will play an important part in the development of the scene, the first making powerful play with bunched horns.

Words are followed by deeds; Bardolph and Pistol take it in turns to thrash their master, each blow being marked by a fierce orchestral outburst in Verdi's old melodramatic style with rapping trumpets and sweeping string scales. An eight-bar transition based on Ex. 346a with the rhythm of Ex. 346b on violas and bassoons concludes with one of those verbal jokes that only the most intimate of stage performances can make plain. Bardolph, approaching his face closely to Falstaff's, cries out, Commendatore-like, 'Riforma la tua vita!', to which Falstaff replies 'Tu puti d'acquavita!' ('You stink of brandy'); and in fact it is Bardolph's weakness that will be responsible for betraying his disguise. For the present it seems that Falstaff is prepared to believe that nocturnal spirits may have spirits on the breath. But of course his last word is swallowed up in the mock-litany begun by the three merry wives – a new idea that incorporates elements of Exs. 345 and 346b. Once again Boito resorts to word-play: '*Domine* fallo casto.' . . . 'Ma salvagli l'ad*domine*,' Falstaff replies, as to an antiphon, sacrificing sense to verbal wit.*

347

His trials culminate in a typical three-fold judgement ceremony, the end of a line that includes the degradation of Gaston in *Jérusalem*, the condemnation of Radames in *Aida* and the 'inquisition' that originally preceded the apparition of the Emperor at the end of *Don Carlos*. 'Globo d'impurità! Rispondi.'. . . 'Ben mi sta.' It is the last of these that comes especially to mind in the present passage (doubtless the fact that it had been superseded in the revised *Don Carlos* emboldened Verdi to risk the comparison). Once again note the semitone rise after each statement. Note too the extra touch of savagery obtained by making the trumpet and trombone attack anticipate that of the voices. (Ex. 348)

In the discharge of energy that follows Bardolph as usual gets carried away. At his words 'Ed or che il diavolo ti porti via' the hood falls back and Falstaff, already half

---

* As both Hughes (p. 521) and Osborne (p. 448) point out, the two phrases of this parody derive respectively from the 'Hostias' and 'Ingemisco' from Verdi's own Requiem.

348

overcome by the fumes of his breath, suddenly recognizes the famous red nose. Now it is he who takes the initiative, leaping up with a volley of insults, many of Shakespearian provenance, mounting to a climax with 'If I tell a lie, may my belt burst apart!' ('Se mentisco, voglio che mi si spacchi il cinturone!'). The machinery of the joke has gone into reverse; the hectic momentum has exhausted itself; everyone is out of breath; and the result is a long musical subsidence on an F major tonic pedal such as followed the brawl in Act I of *Otello*, but with the rhythm of Ex. 346b continuing for a while to pulsate in the texture. However, the laugh is still on Falstaff, as Ford reminds him with a phrase which, while full of charm, is a musical stylization of a jeer worthy of Mozart. (Ex. 349).

He would be less confident if he had seen Quickly hurrying Bardolph away nine bars earlier ('Vieni. Ti coprirò col velo bianco') and known the reason. However, Falstaff takes his defeat with a kind of good-humoured exasperation. 'Caro Signor Fontana . . .' he exclaims, the dominant tonality giving a note of delighted surprise to Ex. 293. 'No,' Alice puts in, returning him firmly to F major, 'this man is my husband.' General laughter, expressed in a three-bar leaping figure on strings and woodwind.

Then Quickly steps forward with a 'Cavaliero' sung to Ex. 286 and at once taken up by Falstaff as in a flash of recognition. She follows it with a characteristic strophe in which the minuet rhythm quickens to a little dance of triumph. The words mostly paraphrase Meg Page's: 'Why, Sir John, do you think, though we would have thrust virtue out of our hearts by the head and shoulders and have given ourselves without scruple to Hell, that ever the devil could have made you our delight?' The third line – equivalent to Page's cruel 'Old, cold, wither'd and of intolerable entrails' – indulges in the vocal gesturings already encountered in the first part of Act II.

'I do begin to perceive that I am made an ass,' Falstaff replies, with a suitably 'hee-hawing' madrigalism on the word 'somaro'. 'A bull, a rare monster, a stag,' the others rejoin, finally dissolving into peals of laughter.

At this point, possibly because the play was a royal commission, Shakespeare decided to throw his weight on the side of official morality and reform his most likeable ruffian. ('I was three or four times in the thought they were not fairies; and yet the guiltiness of my mind, the sudden surprise of my powers, drove the grossness of the foppery into a received belief, in despite of the teeth of all rhyme and reason, that they were fairies. See now how wit may be made a Jack-a-Lent when it is upon ill-employment.')* Boito, however, opted for the Falstaff of the chronicle plays who brazens out his roguery. 'What says the doctor to my water?' Falstaff asks his page in *King Henry IV*, Part 2.† 'He said, Sir, the water itself was a good healthy water, but for the party that owned it, he might have more diseases than he knew for.' 'Men of all sorts take a pride to gird at me,' Falstaff grumbles: 'the brain of this foolish compounded clay, man, is not able to invent anything that tends to laughter more than I invent or is invented on me: I am not only witty in myself but the cause that wit is in other men.' This rejoinder forms the substance of Falstaff's strophe 'Ogni sorta di gente dozzinale', set in the free half-lyrical, half-declamatory manner, full of personal inflexions, that Verdi had first used to such good effect in the part of Melitone. Everything is in the vocal line and the 'accento', the orchestral part being reduced to the merest punctuation.

351

All present are delighted with this effrontery. Only Ford, remembering what he has been made to suffer, remarks, 'If I were not laughing I would break your neck.' But now, he continues in free recitative, let us conclude the masquerade with the wedding of the Fairy Queen. The double wedding was, as we know, included at Boito's insistence; Verdi had been afraid of an anti-climax: and in the event he insured against it by releasing a melody which is not only breathtakingly beautiful in itself but quite unlike anything that has yet occurred in the score. The listener is beguiled into attention in a way that he never imagined possible; violins and violas playing on their lowest string in unison with three flutes enhance the lyrical sweetness. (Ex. 352)

This raises for the last time the question of local colour in Verdi's scores. Generally speaking it was of no interest to him, and if he was tempted occasionally to ask his friends to send him a folk-song for operatic use he usually ended by sending it back unused. But is it mere coincidence that the English soldiery in *Giovanna d'Arco* sing a melody which brings to mind 'Heart of Oak'? Likewise this minuet (Ex. 352) has a

---

* *The Merry Wives of Windsor*, V, v.
† Act I, ii, 24–31.

352

perfectly respectable ancestry in *Un Giorno di regno* and *Rigoletto*; behind all three instances stands the minuet from Act I of Mozart's *Don Giovanni*. But the fact remains that the 'musette' bass for the first three bars and a frequent recourse to pentatonic intervals combine to suggest not so much Mozart or Boccherini as Arne or Boyce in their 'Scotch' vein. In particular the second half-phrase (*x*) is a well-known commonplace amongst Lowland eighteenth-century songs. It appears in 'The Yellow-haired Laddie', on which J. C. Bach wrote a set of variations as the finale of one of his piano concertos, to which Nancy Storace sang her 'Farewell to Vienna' in 1787 and which was sufficiently well known to be quoted in Boïeldieu's *La Dame blanche*. Little known as it is today, apart from its overture, that opera remained in the repertory of the Opéra Comique long enough for Verdi himself to have heard it during any of his visits to Paris (indeed its notorious popularity is the subject of an operetta by Delibes, called *L'Ecossais de Chatou*, first given in 1869). There is no evidence to show that this reminiscence was deliberate; and it must be faint indeed to have escaped most of the English commentators. Yet to anyone versed in the folk-songs of Scotland it remains amazingly difficult to eradicate from the mind.

The melody unfolds as a classical ternary design – *aba* (shortened) – though the melting harmonies created by the cellos in the theme's final line belong strictly to Verdi's private world of the 1890s. Dr Caius advances with Bardolph dressed as a bride to receive Ford's blessing. During the C major episode Alice presents to her husband another couple – Fenton and Nannetta, both masked. The opening of this episode, derived from the final cadence of the main theme, will have a brief but important part to play before the opera is over. (Ex. 353)

353
(Bardolfo e il Dr. Caius si portano nel mezzo: le Fate li circondano)

(presenta Nannetta e Fenton che saranno entrati: Nannetta è tutta coperta da un gran velo celeste: Fenton ha la maschera e la cappa)

FORD

Cir-con-da-te-la o Nin - fe!

ALICE

Un'al - tra coppia d'a-manti de-si - o - si

fls., strs.

hns., bsns. sustain

And so to the return of Ex. 352 embellished by a rhythmic 'tic' in the cellos (relic of the old busy accompaniments of Verdi's youth). The final cadence reached, Ford commands the couples to unmask. Consternation and laughter! 'Fenton with my daughter!' cries Ford; 'I have married Bardolph!' cries Caius; 'Evviva!' cries everyone else. Ford is too stunned to say more; but Alice remarks in a phrase of mischievous charm that men often fall victim to their own intrigues. Now at last it is Falstaff's turn to laugh as he repeats to altered words the music of his 'Caro Signor Fontana', adding a personal variant of Ford's sly taunt 'Lo scornato chi è?'. Never were tables so beautifully turned. . . . The passage is worth quoting in its entirety for the masterly use Verdi makes of tonal relationships in conveying both situations and the tone of voice of each character. (Ex. 354)

Who has been made to look the greater fool? Caius, says Ford; Ford, says Caius; both of them, says Falstaff. 'No', Alice puts in, 'all three of you!', so clinching the matter. By tradition outwitted fathers in comic opera lose no time in admitting that what cannot be cured must be endured. But Ford cannot so plausibly be invested with the original Page's equability. Not only that; in *The Merry Wives* both Page and his wife were thwarted in their designs; but in the opera Alice has in fact deceived her husband, though not in the way he had imagined. So Ford is given twelve bars based on Ex. 353 during which to reconcile himself to events – a passage which modulates away from and back to A flat major with an almost Brahmsian autumnal sadness. He then rouses himself and gives the young couple his blessing; while his fellow-baritone suggests a final chorus to end the scene. 'And then,' Ford cries, 'with Sir John Falstaff, let us go in to supper!'

Most analyses of the opera stop short at the start of the fugue 'Tutto nel mondo è burla', merely pointing to its gaiety combined with perfect mastery of contrapuntal technique – the supreme snub to those pedants who refused Verdi admission to the Milan Conservatory. Certainly it contains all the ingredients of a school fugue: subject, answer, countersubject, stretto and so on, treated with a boldness and freedom that lifts them as far above the schoolroom and the conservatoire as the contrapuntal moments of the Requiem. But Verdi had called it a 'comic' fugue; and that is precisely what it is. The thematic material is quarried from the heart of the opera. The first three notes of the fugue subject (Ex. 355a) mirror the bass of the opening bar of Act I (Ex. 250); the counter-subject contains an important motif (Ex. 355b) that later forms the basis of an episode, and whose antecedents can be found in the counter-melody to 'Gaie comari di Windsor' (see Ex. 311a).

354

355a

355b

What is more, the fugue itself holds a delightful academic joke in store. Between figures 59 and 60 a dominant pedal is set up in C major. In all the fugues of Mendelssohn and his followers this betokens the approach to the final cadence which in turn will be spun out with varieties of plagal harmony. But after four bars we are without warning whirled off into E flat major and a succession of fresh developments. Eventually the fugue breaks off in mid-air; in slower tempo Falstaff's voice is heard with 'Tutti gabbati' ('all gulled') echoed by the rest in unison; and so without more ado to the brilliant conclusion. Falstaff has spoken for all of us, listeners as well as fellow actors. As we know Verdi wrote much if not all of the fugue before he received the words; and Boito supplied at least one variant of the text that was never used; we might conclude that Verdi was not entirely happy with the original solution, which he set none the less. Certainly 'Tutto nel mondo è burla' ('All the world is a prank') with its Shakespearian echo of 'All the world's a stage' could hardly be improved upon; but 'L'uomo è nato burlone' ('Man is born a joker') is misleading. The message of the fugue and indeed of the whole opera is: 'Man is born to be made a fool of.'

A noted exponent of the title role has been heard to ask whether Falstaff for all his buffoonery has a tragic dimension. In Shakespeare's chronicle plays most certainly he has; and a great actor can indicate the heartbreak that lies behind the bravado ('I shall be sent for in private to him; he must seem thus to the world') following the King's devastating rebuff. But the pathetic old man that lies mortally sick, his heart 'fracted and corroborate', as Pistol puts it in the second act of *King Henry V*, has no place in the opera. Falstaff himself is all comedy and nothing else. Ford brings a darker colour to the drama; his monologue in Act II is Verdi's nearest approach to the melodramatic manner of his previous works. But even here Ford's passion of jealousy falls a long way short of Otello's, never for one instant overcoming his self-importance. Stanford may have expressed surprise that the audience should have found the monologue funny; but surely the repeated 'li colgo, li accoppio' provide opportunities for comic business that a baritone of Pini-Corsi's talents must have found irresistible. It is rather in the music of the two lovers that we find that countermeasure of seriousness that no complete portrayal of the human condition, however merry the context, can do without. The duettino, the sonetto, the second act concertato melody, the final minuet – all are instinct with the 'lacrimae rerum', that underlying melancholy that Keats associated with

> . . . beauty that must die
> And joy whose hand is ever at his lips
> Bidding adieu.

It is here above all that Verdi's art joins hands with Mozart's, and *Falstaff* reveals itself the heir of *Le Nozze di Figaro*.

'How far a man goes depends on where he starts from.' Like 'The greater the infant prodigy, the lesser the mature composer', this is the kind of platitude that is either meaningless or wrong. Verdi disproved the first, just as Mozart disproved the second. Starting with a technique cruder and more primitive than that of any young composer of comparative stature the provincial from Busseto achieved a refinement of musical craftsmanship and thought that has never been surpassed and rarely equalled. The upward path can be traced in detail from opera to opera, but no amount of foresight could have deduced the end from the beginning. Looking backwards from the vantage point of 1893 we can discern the seeds of *Falstaff* even in the most unpromising moments of, say, *Il Corsaro*. That the mechanical commonplaces of 1848 should have been fanned into such magnificent life forty-five years later is a miracle of regeneration difficult to parallel in the history of music. As to why after a lifetime as Italy's leading composer of tragic melodrama Verdi should have chosen to close his career with a comedy, let us remember that his huge life-span covered an era of rapid change. He had grown up in the days of the stagecoach and candlelight; he died in the age of steam and electricity. He had seen empires rise and fall, ideals overturned, age-old beliefs blown away by events. He had seen the Risorgimento and the cause of Italian unity gathering force through the heroism of its leaders only to collapse in petty squabbles. He could have observed with Oscar Wilde that there is only one tragedy greater than being baulked of one's heart's desire, and that is attaining it. By his eightieth year he knew that nothing in this world can be taken for granted and that 'Man is born to be made a fool of'. That he was no mere destructive cynic; that, if no orthodox Christian, he thought seriously on first and last things and was capable of religious experience we know from the Requiem and the *Quattro Pezzi Sacri* that were his last compositions; but the final message of the secular Verdi is one of tolerance, comprehension and humour. If we cannot all agree we can at least laugh with each other and at ourselves. It is a message of hope.

BIBLIOGRAPHY

F. ABBIATI. *Giuseppe Verdi*. 4 vols. (Milan 1959)

S. ABDOUN. See *Quaderno 4*

G. ADAMI. *Giulio Ricordi, l'amico dei musicisti italiani* (Milan 1945)

AIVS NEWSLETTER (see VERDI NEWSLETTER)

A. ALBERTI. *Verdi intimo. Carteggio di Giuseppe Verdi con il conte Opprandino Arrivabene, 1861–86* (Verona 1931)

L. ALBERTI. 'I progressi attuali (1872) del dramma musicale. Note sulla disposizione scenica per il opera *Aida* compilata e regolata secondo la messa in scena del Teatro alla Scala da Giulio Ricordi' in *Il melodramma italiano dell'Ottocènto: studi e ricerche per Massimo Mila* (Turin 1977)

L. ARDITI. *My Reminiscences* (London 1896)

ATTI DEI CONGRESSI INTERNAZIONALI DI STUDI VERDIANI. 3 vols. (Parma 1969, 1972, 1974)

L. BALDACCI. *Libretti d'opera e altri saggi* (Florence 1974)
'I libretti di Verdi' in *Il melodramma italiano dell'Ottocènto* (Turin 1977)

G. BALDINI. *Abitare la battaglia: la storia di Giuseppe Verdi* (Milan 1970). English translation by R. Parker *The Story of Giuseppe Verdi* (Cambridge 1980)

G. BARBLAN. 'Un prezioso spartito del *Falstaff*' in *Edizioni della Scala* (Milan 1957)
See also *Atti* 1, 2, 3; *Bollettino* II 2

A. BASEVI. *Studio sulle opere di Giuseppe Verdi* (Florence 1859)

H. BEARD. See *Atti* 2

I. BERLIN. See *Atti* 1

BOLLETTINI DELL'ISTITUTO DI STUDI VERDIANI. I nos. 1–3 (Parma 1960); II nos. 4–6 (1961–6); III nos. 7–9 (1969, 1973)

G. BONGIOVANNI. *Dal Carteggio inedito Verdi–Vigna* (Rome 1941)

P. BONNEFON. 'Les métamorphoses d'un opéra: lettres inédites de Eugène Scribe' in *Revue des deux mondes* (Paris, September 1917)

M. BRUNI. See *Atti* 1

J. M. BUDDEN. 'The two *Traviatas*' in *Proceedings of the Royal Musical Association* 99 (London 1972–3)
'Varianti nei *Vespri Siciliani*' in *Nuova Rivista Musicale Italiana* VI no. 2 (Rome, April–June 1972)
See also *Atti* 2, 3; *Verdi companion*

H. BUSCH. *Verdi's 'Aida': the history of an opera in letters and documents* (Minnesota 1978)
See also *Atti* 3

B. CAGLI. See *Verdi companion*

L. CAMBI (ed.) *Bellini: Epistolario* (Verona 1943)

A. CAMETTI. *La musica teatrale a Roma 100 anni fa: 'Il Corsaro' di Pacini* (Rome 1931)

F. CARENA. See *Atti* 3

A. CAVICCHI. See *Atti* 1, 2, 3

R. CELLETTI. See *Atti* 2; *Quaderno* 3; *Bollettino* III 1; *Verdi companion*

G. CENZATO. *Itinerari verdiani* (Milan 1955)

G. CESARI and A. LUZIO. *I copialettere di Giuseppe Verdi* (Milan 1913)

E. CHECCHI. *Verdi*. 3rd ed. (Florence 1926)

H. F. CHORLEY. *Thirty years' musical recollections* (London 1862)

M. CHUSID. *A catalog of Verdi's operas* (Hackensack, New Jersey 1974)

See also *Atti* 1, 2, 3; *Verdi companion*

'CINQUE LETTERE VERDIANE'. *Rassegna Musicale* XXI, no. 3 (Rome, July 1951)

M. CLÉMEUR. 'Eine neu entdeckte Quelle für das Libretto von Verdis *Don Carlos*' in *Melos/Neue Zeitschrift für Musik* 6 (1977)

M. CONATI. *Interviste e incontri con Verdi* (Milan 1980)

'Formazione e affermazione di Gomes nel panorama dell'opera italiana. Appunti e considerazioni' in *Antonio Carlos Gomes* (ed. Vetro) (Milan 1977)

'Saggio di critiche e cronache verdiane dalla *Allgemeine Musikalische Zeitung* di Lipsia (1840–48)' in *Il melodramma italiano dell'Ottocènto* (Turin 1977)

'Le *Ave Maria* su scala enigmatica della prima alla seconda stesura (1889–97)' in *Rivista Italiana di Musicologia* XIII no. 2 (Florence 1978)

See also *Atti* 1, 2, 3; MEDICI and CONATI

L. DALLAPICCOLA. 'Parole e musica nel melodramma' in *Quaderni della Rassegna Musicale* 2 (Turin 1965)

'Su un passo del *Falstaff*' in *Appunti, incontri, meditazioni* (Milan 1970)

F. D'AMICO. See *Bollettino* I 3

W. DEAN. 'Shakespeare and Opera' in *Shakespeare in Music*. Ed. P. Hartnoll (London 1964)

'Otello: a Shakespearean masterpiece' in *Shakespeare Survey* 21 (London 1968)

See also *Atti* 3

F. V. DE BELLIS and F. GHISI. See *Atti* 2

G. DE NAPOLI. *La Triade melodrammatica altamurana* (Milan 1931)

Amilcare Ponchielli (1834–1886). La vita, le opere, l'epistolario, le onoranze (Cremona 1936)

G. DEPANIS. *I Concerti Popolari ed il Teatro Regio di Torino*. 2 vols. (Turin 1914–15)

R. DE RENSIS. *Franco Faccio e Verdi* (Milan 1934)

DISPOSIZIONI SCENICHE. *Les Vêpres siciliennes*, opéra à cinq actes, paroles de MM. E. Scribe et Ch. Duveyrier, musique de G. Verdi, représenté pour la première fois à Paris sur le Théâtre Impérial de l'Opéra le 13 juin 1855 (collection de mises-en-scène rédigés et publiés par M. L. Palianti) (Paris 1855)

Disposizione scenica per l'opera *Giovanna de Guzman* del maestro cavaliere Giuseppe Verdi ufficiale della Legion d'Onore compilata e regolata sulla mise-en-scène nel Teatro Imperiale dell'Opera di Parigi (Milan ?1855)

Disposizione scenica per l'opera *Un Ballo in Maschera* di G. Verdi sulla messa in scena del Teatro Apollo in Roma il carnevale del 1859, del direttore di scena del medesimo, Giuseppe Cencetti (Milan 1859)

La Forza del Destino, opera del maestro Giuseppe Verdi, libretto di Francesco Maria Piave, ordinazioni e disposizione scenica (Milan ?1863)

Disposizione scenica per l'opera *Don Carlo* di Giuseppe Verdi compilata e regolata secondo la messa in scena del Teatro Imperiale dell'Opera di Parigi (1st ed. Milan 1867, 3rd ed. 1884)

Disposizione scenica per l'opera *Aida* versi di Antonio Ghislanzoni, musica di Giuseppe Verdi, compilata e regolata secondo la messa in scena del Teatro alla Scala da Giulio Ricordi (Milan 1872)

Disposizione scenica per l'opera *Simon Boccanegra* di Giuseppe Verdi compilata e regolata secondo la messa del Teatro alla Scala da Giulio Ricordi (Milan 1881)

Disposizione scenica per l'opera *Otello*, dramma lirico in quattro atti, versi di Arrigo Boito, musica di Giuseppe Verdi, compilata e regolata secondo la messa in scena del Teatro alla Scala da Giulio Ricordi (Milan 1887)

L. EÖSZE. See *Atti* 1, 2, 3

L. ESCUDIER. *Mes souvenirs* (Paris 1863)

F. FLORA. See *Bollettino* I 1

C. GALLICO. See *Atti* 1, 2, 3

L. A. GARIBALDI. *Giuseppe Verdi nelle lettere di Emmanuele Muzio ad Antonio Barezzi* (Milan 1931)

C. GATTI. *Verdi.* 2 vols. (Milan 1931); 2nd ed. in 1 vol. (1951); abridged English translation by E. Abbott, *Verdi: The Man and his Music* (London 1955)

    Verdi nelle immagini (Milan 1941)

    Catalani: lettere a Giuseppe Depanis (Milan 1946)

    Revisioni e rivalutazioni verdiane (Turin 1952)

G. GATTI-CASAZZA. *Memories of the opera* (London 1977)

L. K. GERHARTZ. *Die Auseinandersetzungen des jungen Giuseppe Verdi mit dem literärischen Drama* (Berlin 1968)

    See also *Atti* 1, 2; *Bollettino* II 3

H. GERIGK. *Giuseppe Verdi* (Potsdam 1932)

A. GHISLANZONI. *Libro serio* (Milan 1879)

V. GODEFROY. *The dramatic genius of Verdi: studies of selected operas.* 2 vols. (London 1975, 1978)

P. GOSSETT. 'The candeur virginale of *Tancredi*' in *Musical Times* vol. 112 no. 1538 (London, April 1971)

    'Verdi, Ghislanzoni and *Aida*: the uses of convention' in *Critical Enquiry* I no. 2 (Chicago, December 1974)

T. GOTTI. See *Quaderno* 3

K. D. GRÄWE. See *Atti* 1, 2, 3

G. GUALERZI. See *Atti* 2; *Bollettini* passim

U. GÜNTHER. 'La genèse de *Don Carlos*, opéra en 5 Actes de Giuseppe Verdi, représenté pour la première fois à Paris le 11 mars 1867' in *Revue de Musicologie* LVIII (Paris 1972), LX (1974)

    'Problèmes de création musicale au XIXme siècle' in *Acta Musicologica* XLIII (Basle 1971)

    'Zur Entstehung von Verdis *Aida*' in *Studi Musicali* II no. 1 (Florence 1973)

    Preface to *L'edizione integrale del Don Carlos di Giuseppe Verdi* (Milan 1974)

    'Der Briefwechsel Verdi–Nuitter–du Locle zur Revision des *Don Carlos*' in *Analecta Musicologica* XIV (Cologne 1974) and XV (1975)

    See also *Atti* 2, 3

E. HANSLICK. *Die moderne Oper.* 4 vols. (Berlin 1875–88)

J. A. HEPOKOSKI. 'Verdi, Giuseppina Pasqua and the composition of *Falstaff*' in *19th Century Music* III (University of California, March 1980)

F. HILLER. *Erinnerungsblätter* (Cologne 1884)

S. HOLLAND and W. S. ROCKSTRO. *Jenny Lind, the artist.* 2 vols. (London 1892)

C. HOPKINSON. *A bibliography of the works of Giuseppe Verdi.* 2 vols. (New York 1973, 1978)

S. HUGHES. *Famous Verdi operas* (London 1968)

J. HUMBERT. '*L'Aida* entre l'Egyptologie et Egyptomanie' in *L'Avant-Scène Opéra* 4 (Paris 1976)

    'Le scénario original de A. Mariette pour *Aida*' in *Revue de Musicologie* LXII (Paris 1976)

D. HUSSEY. *Verdi* (London 1940). 5th ed. (revised C. Osborne), 1973.

U. JUNG. *Die Rezeption der Kunst Richard Wagners in Italien* (Regensburg 1974)

J. KERMAN. 'Notes on an early Verdi opera' in *Soundings* 3 (University College, Cardiff 1973)

D. R. B. KIMBELL. 'Poi . . . diventò l'*Oberto*' in *Music and Letters* LII no. 1 (London, January 1971)

'The young Verdi and Shakespeare' in *Proceedings of the Royal Musical Association* 101 (London 1974–5)

'Verdi's first Rifacimento: *I Lombardi* and *Jérusalem*' in *Music and Letters* LX no. 1 (London, January 1979)

    See also *Atti* 3

M. LAVAGETTO. *Un caso di censura: 'il Rigoletto'* (Milan 1979)

    See also *Atti* 3

D. LAWTON. See *Atti* 1, 3; *Bollettino* II 3

R. LEIBOWITZ. See *Atti* 1, 3; *Bollettino* III 2

S. LEVARIE. 'Key relations in Verdi's *Un ballo in maschera*' in *19th Century Music* II no. 2 (University of California 1978)

F. LIPPMANN. *Vincenzo Bellini und die italienische Opera Seria seiner Zeit: Analecta Musicologica* VI (Cologne 1969)

'Der italienische Vers und der musikalische Rhythmus' in *Analecta Musicologica* XII (1973), XIV (1974), XV (1975)

    See also *Atti* 1

A. LUALDI. *Viaggio musicale in Italia* (Milan 1927)

H. LUDWIG. See *Atti* 2; *Quaderno* 3

B. LUMLEY. *Reminiscences of the opera* (London 1864)

A. LUZIO. *Profili biografici e bozzetti storici.* 2 vols. (Milan 1927)

Carteggi verdiani. 4 vols. (Rome 1935, 1947)

L. MAGNANI. See *Atti* 3

G. MARCHESI. *Giuseppe Verdi* (Turin 1970)

Giuseppe Verdi e il Conservatorio di Parma 1836–1901 (Parma 1976)

    See also *Atti* 1, 3; *Quaderno* 3; *Bollettino* II, III

E. MARIETTE. *Mariette Pacha. Lettres et souvenirs personnels* (Paris 1904)

G. MARTIN. *Verdi, his music, life and times* (New York 1963)

    See also *Atti* 2, *Bollettino* II 2

A. MARTINELLI. *Verdi. Raggi e penombre. Le ultime lettere* (Genoa 1926)

M. J. MATZ. See *Atti* 1, 2, 3; *Bollettino* III 1; *Verdi Newsletters* passim

V. MAUREL. *Dix ans de carrière*, including 'A propos de la mise-en-scène du drame lyrique d'*Otello*' (Paris 1897)

M. MEDICI and M. CONATI. *Carteggio Verdi/Boito.* 2 vols. (Parma 1978)

M. MILA. *Il melodramma di Verdi* (Bari 1933, revised and enlarged as *Verdi* 1958)

Les Vêpres Siciliennes (Turin 1973)

La giovinezza di Verdi (Turin 1974)

L'arte di Giuseppe Verdi (Turin 1980)

'Verdi e Hanslick' in *Rassegna Musicale* XXI, 3 (Rome, July 1951)

'Lettura del *Corsaro*' in *Nuova Rivista Musicale Italiana* (Turin, January–February 1971)

    See also *Atti* 1, 3; *Bollettino* I 1

F. MOMPELLIO. See *Bollettino* II 3

G. MONALDI. *Verdi, la vita, le opere.* 4th ed. (Milan 1951). Title changed from *Verdi 1839–98*

Le opere di Verdi al Teatro alla Scala (Milan 1914)

G. MORAZZONI and G. M. CIAMPELLI. *Lettere inedite: le opere verdiane al Teatro alla Scala, 1839–1929* (Milan 1929)

M. T. MURARO. See *Atti* 1

P. NARDI. *Arrigo Boito. Tutti gli scritti* (Verona 1942)

Vita di Arrigo Boito (Verona 1944)

O. NICOLAI. *Tagebücher nebst biographischen Ergänzungen von B. Schröder* (Leipzig 1892)

J. NICOLAISEN. *Italian opera in transition 1871–1893* (Ann Arbor 1980)

M. NOIRAY and R. PARKER. 'La composition d'*Attila*: étude de quelques variantes' in *Revue de Musicologie* 62 (1976)

M. NORDIO (ed.). *Verdi e la Fenice* (Venice 1951)
See also *Atti* 1

F. NOSKE. *The signifier and the signified. Studies in the operas of Mozart and Verdi* (The Hague 1977)

A. OBERDORFER. *Giuseppe Verdi, autobiografia dalle lettere* (Milan 1951)

C. OSBORNE. *The complete operas of Verdi* (London 1969)
See also *Atti* 2

W. OSTHOFF. 'Die beiden *Boccanegra*-Fassungen und der Beginn von Verdis Spätwerk' in *Analecta Musicologica* I (Cologne 1963)
'Il sonetto nel *Falstaff* di Verdi' in *Il melodramma italiano dell'Ottocènto* (Turin 1977)
See also *Bollettino* III 2

G. PACINI. *Le mie memorie artistiche* (Florence 1875)

A. PASCOLATO. *'Rè Lear' e 'Ballo in Maschera'. Lettere di Giuseppe Verdi ad Antonio Somma* (Città di Castello 1902)

F. PASTURA. *Bellini secondo la storia* (Parma 1959)

G. PESTELLI. 'Le riduzioni del tardo stile verdiano. Osservazioni su alcune varianti del *Don Carlos*' in *Nuova Rivista Musicale Italiana* VI no. 3 (1972)
See also *Atti* 2

P. PETROBELLI. 'Nabucco' in *Conferenze dell'Associazione Amici della Scala* (Milan 1966–7)
'Osservazioni sul processo compositivo in Verdi' in *Acta Musicologica* XLIII (Basle 1971)
See also *Atti* 1, 3

I. PIZZETTI. 'Contrappunto e armonia nell'opera di G. Verdi' in *Rassegna Musicale* XXI, no. 3 (Rome, July 1951)

I. PIZZI. *Ricordi verdiani inediti* (Turin 1901)
Per il primo centenario della nascita di Giuseppe Verdi (Turin 1913)

A. PORTER. 'A sketch for *Don Carlos*' in *Musical Times* vol. 111 no. 1531 (September 1970)
'A note on Princess Eboli' in *Musical Times* vol. 113 no. 1554 (August 1972)
'The making of *Don Carlos*' in *Proceedings of the Royal Musical Association* 98 (1971–2)
'Don't blame Scribe!' in *Opera News* vol. 39, no. 20 (New York 1975)
'*Les Vêpres Siciliennes*: New letters from Verdi to Scribe' in *19th Century Music* 2 (1978)
See also *Atti* 2, *Verdi companion*

A. POUGIN. *Giuseppe Verdi: vita aneddotica con note ed aggiunte di 'Folchetto'* (Milan 1881)

J. G. PROD'HOMME. 'Unpublished letters from Verdi to Camille du Locle' translated T. Baker in *Musical Quarterly* VII no. 4 (New York 1921). See also *Revue Musicale* nos. 10 and 11 (Paris 1929)
'Lettres inédites de G. Verdi à Léon Escudier' in *Rivista Musicale Italiana* XXXV (Rome 1928)

G. PUGLIESE. *Quaderno* 2; *Bollettino* I 1, II 1

QUADERNI DELL'ISTITUTO DI STUDI VERDIANI. nos. I–II (Parma 1963); III (1968); IV (1971)

G. RADICIOTTI. *Gioacchino Rossini. Vita documentata, opere ed influenza su l'arte*. 3 vols. (Tivoli 1927–9)

L. ROGNONI. *Rossini* (Modena 1956)

U. ROLANDI. *Libretti e librettisti verdiani dal punto di vista storico-bibliografico* (Rome 1941)

G. RONCAGLIA. *L'ascensione creatrice di Giuseppe Verdi* (Florence 1940)
Galleria verdiana (Milan 1959)

D. ROSEN. 'La "Messa" a Rossini e il "Requiem" per Manzoni' in *Rivista Italiana di Musicologica* IV (Florence 1969)

'Le Trouvère' in *Opera News* vol. 41 (April 1977)

'Virtue Restored' in *Opera News* vol. 42, no. 9 (December 1977)

See also *Atti* 2, 3

D. SABBETH. See *Atti* 3

G. SALVETTI. 'La Scapigliatura milanese e il teatro d'opera' in *Il melodramma italiano dell'Ottocènto* (Turin 1977)

C. SANTLEY. *Student and Singer: Reminiscences* (London 1892)

C. SARTORI. 'Rocester, la prima opera di Verdi' in *Rivista Musicale Italiana* XLIII no. 1 (January–February 1939)

F. SCHLITZER. *Mondo teatrale dell'ottocènto* (Naples 1954)

G. B. SHAW. *Music in London (1890–4).* 3 vols. (London 1932)

London Music in 1888–9 as heard by Corno di Bassetto (London 1937)

C. SIMONE. 'Lettere al tenore Mario De Candia sulla cabaletta de *I due Foscari*' in *Nuova Antologia* LXIX (Florence, October 1934)

A. SOFFREDINI. *Le opere di Giuseppe Verdi* (Milan 1901)

P. SOUTHWELL-SANDER. *Verdi: his life and times* (Tunbridge Wells 1978)

F. TOYE. *Giuseppe Verdi, his life and works* (London 1931)

G. UGOLINI. See *Atti* 1, 2; *Bollettino* II 3

G. C. VARESI. 'L'interpretazione di *Macbeth*' in *Nuova Antologia* LXVII (Florence, November–December 1932)

A. VARGIÙ. 'Il libretto dell' *Aida*' in *Rassegna Musicale Curci* XXI no. 3 (Milan 1968)

P. P. VARNAI. See *Atti* 1, 2, 3; *Bollettino* II 2, 3; III 2

G. VECCHI. See *Quaderno* 1; *Bollettino* III 2

VERDI NEWSLETTER. Journal of the American Institute for Verdi Studies (New York 1976–)

G. N. VETRO (ed.). *Antonio Carlos Gomes: Carteggi italiani* (Milan 1977)

R. VLAD. 'Anticipazioni nel linguaggio armonistico verdiano' in *Rassegna Musicale* XXI 3 (Rome, July 1951)

'Unità strutturale dei *Vespri Siciliani*' in *Il melodramma italiano dell'Ottocènto* (Turin 1977)

See also *Atti* 3

F. WALKER. *The Man Verdi* (London 1962)

'Mercadante and Verdi' in *Music and Letters* XXXIII 4, and XXXIV 1 (London, October 1952, January 1953)

'Verdi and Francesco Florimo: some unpublished letters' in *Music and Letters* XXVI (London, October 1945)

'Verdian Forgeries' in *The Music Review* XIX (London, November 1958) and XX (February 1959)

'Verdi and Vienna: some unpublished letters' in *Musical Times* vol. 92 nos. 1303, 1304 (London, September, October 1951)

See also *Bollettino* I 1, 2, 3; II 1

W. WEAVER. *Verdi. A documentary study* (London 1977)

See also *Atti* 3

—— and M. CHUSID. *The Verdi companion* (London 1980)

G. ZAVADINI. *Donizetti: Vita – Musiche – Epistolario* (Bergamo 1948)

U. ZOPPI. *Angelo Mariani, Giuseppe Verdi e Teresa Stolz* (Milan 1947)

INDEX